THE ROUTLEDGE HANDBOOK OF ACCOUNTING ETHICS

The perspective of this book is to present "ethics" as a conversation about how we decide what is good or bad, right or wrong. It is a collection of conversations employed by educators to assist accounting students in developing their understanding of accounting's ethical aspects and to help them develop into critical thinkers who consider the ethical complexities of the function of accounting in human society.

Because we are social beings, ethics is a central human concern, since it involves determining the ethicality of human actions and their effect on other individuals, as well as determining the collective societal acceptance or rejection of an action. Thus, the book's primary goal is to call attention to the intersectionality of accounting and ethics and to encourage students and researchers to consider the ethical implications of accounting decisions. The book contains a diversity of perspectives within which discussions of accountants' and accounting's ethical responsibilities may occur. The contributing authors were deliberately chosen for their diverse perspectives on whence moral guidance for accounting may come. Each chapter stands on its own and represents the thinking of its authors. The book is not a primer on correct behavior for accountants but a place where educators may spur the conversation along.

Eileen Z. Taylor, PhD, CPA, CFE, is a professor of accounting in the Poole College of Management at North Carolina State University. Her teaching and research focus on whistleblowing, ethics, and data security.

Paul F. Williams, PhD, is a professor of accounting in the Poole College of Management at North Carolina State University. His scholarly interests include accounting ethics, theory, and critical perspectives in accounting.

"Trading upon their professional accounting status, four massive firms (the Big Four) audit and advise the world's most powerful institutions (corporations and governments). However, they have not always acted in the public interest, so this work, which is directly concerned with accounting ethics, is of extreme contemporary importance."

— *Professor Christine Cooper, University of Edinburgh, Scotland.*

THE ROUTLEDGE HANDBOOK OF ACCOUNTING ETHICS

Edited by Eileen Z. Taylor and Paul F. Williams

Routledge
Taylor & Francis Group

LONDON AND NEW YORK

First published 2021
by Routledge
2 Park Square, Milton Park, Abingdon, Oxon OX14 4RN

and by Routledge
52 Vanderbilt Avenue, New York, NY 10017

Routledge is an imprint of the Taylor & Francis Group, an informa business

British Library Cataloguing-in-Publication Data
A catalogue record for this book is available from the British Library

Library of Congress Cataloging-in-Publication Data
Names: Taylor, Eileen Z., editor.
Title: The Routledge handbook of accounting ethics / edited by Eileen Z.
Taylor and Paul F. Williams.
Description: Abingdon, Oxon ; New York, NY : Routledge, 2021. |
Series: Routledge international handbooks | Includes bibliographical
references and index.
Identifiers: LCCN 2020038148 (print) | LCCN 2020038149 (ebook) |
ISBN 9781138591967 (hbk) | ISBN 9780429490224 (ebk)
Subjects: LCSH: Accounting—Moral and ethical aspects. |
Accountants—Professional ethics.
Classification: LCC HF5625.15 .R68 2021 (print) |
LCC HF5625.15 (ebook) | DDC 174/.4—dc23
LC record available at https://lccn.loc.gov/2020038148
LC ebook record available at https://lccn.loc.gov/2020038149

ISBN: 978-1-138-59196-7 (hbk)
ISBN: 978-0-429-49022-4 (ebk)

Typeset in Bembo
by Apex CoVantage, LLC

This volume is dedicated to our spouses, Glenn M. Taylor and Katherine Williams, who have supported us through this journey.

CONTENTS

FIGURES

TABLES

CONTRIBUTORS

Khalid R. Al-Adeem, PhD, is an associate professor of accounting in the College of Business at King Saud University, Saudi Arabia. He has taught 24 different courses at the bachelor's, master's, and doctoral levels, was the director of the PhD program, and served on editorial boards of international journals. Dr. Al-Adeem earned his PhD from Case Western Reserve University.

Michael Alles, PhD, is an associate professor at the Department of Accounting and Information Systems at Rutgers Business School, The State University of New Jersey. His specialties are the design of strategic control systems, continuous auditing, management accounting, and corporate governance. He is widely published in all these areas. Dr. Alles holds a PhD from Stanford Business School and a First Class Honors in Economics from the Australian National University.

Charles Richard Baker, PhD, CPA, is a professor of accounting at the Willumstad School of Business, Adelphi University, New York. His main research interests are focused on public accounting, in particular the history of the profession, comparative systems of regulation, ethical issues, independence, and legal liability. Professor Baker has published over 120 academic and professional articles. He earned his PhD from the University of California, Los Angeles.

Michalis Bekiaris, PhD, is an associate professor of accounting at the University of the Aegean in Greece. He has supervised numerous dissertations and researches financial reporting and auditing. Dr. Bekiaris earned his PhD at Panteion University of Social and Political Sciences.

Robert Bloom, PhD, is Professor and Andersen Fellow in the Kramer School of Accountancy and Information Sciences at John Carroll University, University Heights, Ohio. He has taught at several other universities in the US, UK, Canada, and China. His articles appear in both academic and professional journals. Dr. Bloom earned his PhD at New York University's Stern School of Business.

Christine Cheng, PhD, is an assistant professor of accountancy at the Patterson School of Accountancy at the University of Mississippi. Her research interests include data analytics, tax, fraud, and how incentives drive behavior. Dr. Cheng has published in the *Journal of Accounting and Finance*, among others. She earned her PhD from The Pennsylvania State University.

Mary B. Curtis, PhD, CPA, CISA, is the Horace Brock Centennial Professor of Accounting at the University of North Texas. Her teaching and research interests span audit, accounting information systems and ethics. Dr. Curtis has served as senior editor of the *Journal of Information Systems* (*JIS*) and associate editor for *Behavioral Research in Accounting*. Her publications have appeared in such journals as *Journal of Business Ethics*, *JIS*, *The Accounting Review*, and *Accounting, Organizations and Society*.

Phebian Davis, PhD, is a clinical assistant professor of accounting at Clemson University. Professor Davis has over 14 years of corporate experience in the field of accounting as well as six years of teaching experience. She earned her PhD from Florida Atlantic University.

Amy M. Donnelly, PhD, is an assistant professor of accounting at Clemson University. Professor Donnelly's research focuses on auditor judgment and decision making utilizing behavioral research methods. She is interested in examining how various factors in an auditor's work environment influence their judgments and decisions. She earned her PhD from the University of Central Florida.

Richard B. Dull, PhD, CPA, CFE. CISA, CFF, is the GoMart Professor in Accounting Information Systems at West Virginia University's John Chambers College of Business and Economics. His teaching includes accounting information systems, analytics, and forensic accounting. His research focus includes continuous auditing/monitoring, accounting education, and non-profit organizations. Dr. Dull earned his PhD from Virginia Tech University.

Jonathan Farrar, PhD, is an associate professor of accounting at the Lazaridis School of Business and Economics at Wilfrid Laurier University, where he teaches courses in personal and corporate taxation. He conducts behavioral tax research exploring individual taxpayers' decision-making related to ethical decisions. Dr. Farrar earned his PhD from York University.

Dov Fischer, PhD, is an associate professor of accounting at Brooklyn College's Murray Koppelman School of Business. His research focuses on accounting ethics. He has recently published in *Journal of Business Ethics*, *Humanistic Management Journal*, and *Journal of Corporate Accounting and Finance*. Dr. Fischer received his PhD from the University of Colorado at Boulder.

Renee Flasher, PhD, is an assistant professor in accounting at The Pennsylvania State University – Harrisburg. Her research interests include fraud cases involving standards violations, where individuals or corporations have been held responsible, and how standards are developed in society, specifically within business and accounting arenas. Dr. Flasher earned her PhD at The Pennsylvania State University.

Timothy J. Fogarty, PhD, CPA, JD, is a professor in the Department of Accounting at the Weatherhead School of Management at Case Western Reserve University. He is also the Thomas Dickerson Faculty Fellow at that institution. Dr. Fogarty has over 200 publications in peer-reviewed journals and has served as the editor for *Accounting and the Public Interest*. Dr. Fogarty earned his PhD from The Pennsylvania State University.

Hershey H. Friedman, PhD, is a professor of business at Brooklyn College's Murray Koppelman School of Business. He has held both the Bernard H. Stern Chair of Humor and the Murray Koppelman Professorship. He has published in *Decision Sciences*, *Journal of Business Ethics*, and the *Journal of Leadership Studies*, among others. His research interests include biblical leadership, business ethics, and humor. Dr. Friedman earned his PhD from CUNY.

Nathan C. Goldman, PhD, is an assistant professor of accounting in the Poole College of Management at North Carolina State University. His research focuses on corporate tax issues and he teaches taxation at the graduate level. He has published in *The Accounting Review*. Dr. Goldman earned his PhD at the University of Arizona.

Patrick T. Kelly, PhD, is a professor of accountancy and the Director of the Ethics in Business Education Program at Providence College in Providence, Rhode Island. He has published in *Accounting and the Public Interest* and *Research on Accounting Ethics*. Dr. Kelly earned his PhD at the University of Connecticut.

Larita J. Killian, EdD, CPA, CGFM, is a professor of accounting at Indiana University-Purdue University Columbus, a visiting professor at Universidad Privada Boliviana, and a Fulbright Specialist in business. Previously, she served in the US Department of Defense. Her research interests include accountability and special district governments. Dr. Killian earned her EdD at Stanford University.

Michael Kraten, PhD, is a professor of accounting and the Chair of Accounting, Economics, and Finance programs at Houston Baptist University. He is Publisher, Editor-In-Chief, and Contributing Columnist for AAAPublicInterest.org. Dr. Kraten earned his PhD at the University of Connecticut.

Cheryl R. Lehman, PhD, is a professor of accounting, taxation, and legal studies in business at Hofstra University, New York. As Associate Editor of *Critical Perspectives on Accounting* and Editor of *Advances in Public Interest Accounting*, Dr. Lehman is regarded as a trailblazer and innovator in research and teaching interdisciplinary and critical accounting for over four decades. Dr. Lehman earned her PhD at New York University.

Margarita Maria Lenk, PhD, CMA, is an associate professor at Colorado State University. She has mentored diverse accountants and academics for three decades. Her research areas of expertise include business intelligence analytics, strategic risk management, critical thinking skill development, and university-community partnerships. Dr. Lenk earned the Michael J. and Mary Ann Cook Award for the international best undergraduate accounting professor in 2019.

Christina M. Lewellen, PhD, is an assistant professor of accounting in the Poole College of Management at North Carolina State University. Her research focuses on corporate tax issues, and she teaches taxation at the undergraduate level. She has published in *Contemporary Accounting Research* and won two outstanding dissertation awards. Dr. Lewellen earned her PhD at Florida State University.

Timothy J. Louwers, PhD, is an emeritus professor of accounting at James Madison University and was the Director of their School of Accounting. He authored or coauthored 13 books and over 50 articles on accounting, auditing, and technology-related topics. He is the Co-Founder of MonthsToYears.org, a not-for-profit dedicated to improving the quality of life for those facing end-of-life situations and their caregivers. Dr. Louwers earned his PhD at Florida State University.

Dawn W. Massey, PhD, CPA, CMGA, is a professor of accounting in the Charles F. Dolan School of Business, Fairfield University, Connecticut, where she teaches undergraduate and graduate courses in financial accounting practice and theory. She received the 2001 AAA Innovation in Accounting Education award. She has published numerous articles in the areas of accounting ethics and pedagogy. Dr. Massey earned her PhD at the University of Connecticut.

Francine McKenna is an adjunct professor of International Business at American University's Kogod School of Business in Washington, DC. An independent journalist, she authors the newsletter *The Dig*. McKenna spent more than 20 years in public accounting and consulting and 15 years as an investigative reporter for leading financial publications such as MarketWatch.com, *Forbes*, *American Banker*, and her own blog, *re*TheAuditors.com.

William F. Miller, EdD, CPA, CGMA, is a professor of accounting at University of Wisconsin, Eau Claire. He teaches in the areas of accounting ethics and advanced financial accounting and researches in accounting ethics and international accounting. Dr. Miller earned his EdD in leadership, policy, and administration at the University of St. Thomas.

Steven M. Mintz, DBA, CPA, is a professor emeritus of accounting at California Polytechnic State University, San Luis Obispo. Dr. Mintz has published two textbooks on accounting ethics and dozens of research papers in the areas of accounting and business ethics. He earned his DBA at George Washington University. Dr. Mintz is a recipient of the Accounting Exemplar Award given out by the Public Interest Section of the American Accounting Association.

Dr. Louella Moore, PhD, CPA, CGMA, is a professor of accounting at Washburn University. She is the Associate Editor for *Accounting Education* and teaches financial and managerial accounting at the undergraduate through master's level. Dr. Moore earned her PhD at the University of Arkansas.

Dr. Athar Murtuza, PhD, CMA (inactive), is an associate professor in the Department of Accounting and Taxation at Seton Hall University, where he teaches both undergraduate and graduate courses in the areas of cost accounting, managerial accounting, and accounting ethics. He researches accounting history and the nexus of accountability and religious beliefs and is published in *Accounting Perspectives* and the *Accounting, Auditing & Accountability Journal*. Dr. Murtaza earned his PhD at Washington State University.

Marc Peter Neri, PhD ACMA, is an assistant professor of Professional Practice at the Neeley School, Texas Christian University. Dr. Neri studied humanities at the University of Dallas, which fostered his interest in Aristotelian ethics. Marc continues to research and write on professional ethics. Dr. Neri earned his PhD at the University of North Texas.

Dr. Wioleta Olczak, PhD, is an assistant professor at Marquette University's Department of Accounting in Milwaukee, Wisconsin. Her current research interests include performance measurement, evaluation, and compensation. Dr. Olczak earned her PhD at the University of Central Florida.

Georgios Papachristou is a doctoral student of accounting at the University of the Aegean in Greece and a financial officer in the Hellenic Army. His research is focused on fraud.

Robin R. Pennington, PhD, is a retired associate professor of accounting from the Poole College of Management at North Carolina State University. She is a past president of the Accounting Information Systems Section of the American Accounting Association. During her career in academia, she focused on research and teaching in the area of accounting information systems. Dr. Pennington earned her PhD at the University of South Carolina.

Robin R. Radtke, PhD, is an associate professor of accounting at Clemson University. She has published 30 academic articles and book chapters, with the majority focusing on accounting ethics related issues. Dr. Radtke earned her PhD from the University of Florida.

Sara Reiter, PhD, is a professor of accounting at Binghamton University (SUNY). Her research focuses on ethics and public interest, and she has published in *Critical Perspectives on Accounting* and *Accounting, Organizations and Society*, and many others. Dr. Reiter earned her PhD at the University of Missouri-Columbia.

Diane H. Roberts, PhD, is a professor of accounting at the University of San Francisco. She has published frequently on accounting ethics and accounting history. She is a past chair of the Professionalism and Ethics Committee of the American Accounting Association (AAA) and past director of the AAA Research Symposium on Accounting Ethics. Dr. Roberts earned her PhD at the University of California–Irvine.

Dr. Robin W. Roberts, PhD, serves as the Al and Nancy Burnett Eminent Scholar and Pegasus Professor of Accounting in the Kenneth G. Dixon School of Accounting at the University of Central Florida in Orlando, Florida. His research focuses on ethics and regulation in the public accounting profession as well as corporate social responsibility disclosure. Dr. Roberts earned his PhD at the University of Arkansas.

Kristy Schenck, PhD, is a clinical associate professor in accounting in the Smeal College of Business at the Pennsylvania State University. Her research interests include financial reporting choices, financial misreporting, and pedagogical research, and she has published in *Accounting Horizons*. Dr. Schenck earned her PhD at the University of Pennsylvania.

Lydia F. Schleifer, PhD, is an associate professor of accounting at Clemson University, South Carolina. Her teaching interests include financial accounting, cost accounting, and auditing. Her research interests include ethics and approaches to learning. Dr. Schleifer earned her PhD at the University of Georgia.

Martin Stuebs, PhD, is the R. E. and Marilyn Reamer Associate Professor of Accounting at Baylor University in Waco, Texas. He has published research in the *Journal of Information Systems*, *Journal of Business Ethics*, and *Accounting and the Public Interest*.

Eileen Z. Taylor, PhD, CPA, CFE, is a professor of accounting in the Poole College of Management at North Carolina State University. Her teaching and research focus on whistleblowing, ethics, and data security. She has published in the *Journal of Business Ethics*, *Accounting Horizons*, *and Behavioral Research in Accounting*. She coedited a special issue of the *Journal of Information Systems* on AIS and Ethics. Dr. Taylor earned her PhD at the University of South Florida.

Linda Thorne, PhD, is a professor of accounting at the Schulich School of Business, York University, Toronto. She has been awarded numerous grants and published many articles on ethical decision making among professionals, especially professional accountants. Dr. Thorne earned her PhD at McGill University.

John M. Thornton, PhD, CPA, is the L.P. and Bobbi Leung Chair of Accounting Ethics and Professor of Accounting at Azusa Pacific University in Azusa, California. His popular press publications are examples of innovative ways he encourages people to handle wealth with integrity. Dr. Thornton earned his PhD at Washington State University.

Paul F. Williams, PhD, is a professor of accounting in the Poole College of Management at North Carolina State University. His scholarly interests include accounting ethics, theory, and critical perspectives in accounting. He has served as chairperson of the Public Interest Section of the American Accounting Association and editor of *Accounting and the Public Interest*. He received the Public Interest Section *Accounting Exemplar* award in 2013. Dr. Williams earned his PhD at the University of North Carolina at Chapel Hill.

INTRODUCTION

Eileen Z. Taylor and Paul F. Williams

"Ethics" and "morals" are two terms about which there is ambiguity. Some scholars consider the terms to be synonymous. Others make a distinction that ethics pertains to right conduct *vis-à-vis* others, while morals pertains to one's personal sense of right conduct; still others reverse that distinction. Philosophers tend to regard the distinction between "ethics" and "morals" to be that ethics pertains to a centuries-old conversation about how we decide what is good and bad, right and wrong, while morals is the content of good and bad, right and wrong. The perspective on "ethics" taken in this book is this latter sense; thus the title *Companion to Accounting Ethics*. The book's purpose is not to be a handbook of accounting rights and wrongs but rather a collection of conversations employed by educators to assist students of accounting to become more attuned to accounting's ethical aspects and to become more critical thinkers about the ethical complexities of the function of accounting in human society.

As a social science, accounting is the creation of people, for the purpose of accounting for transactions (generally monetary) between and among groups of people. Accounting does not exist without people, and its rules of the day are determined by people; it is mutable and wholly dependent on both the decisions made by people with economic power and acceptance of those decisions by those same people. Similarly, ethics are enacted by people, and the ethicality of an action is determined by the individual affected by the action, as well as by the collective societal acceptance or rejection of an action.

Accounting, because it is people driven, inherently has an ethical component. Every decision about how to account for a transaction at some point affects an individual, either directly or indirectly. For example, decisions about recording revenue affect those whose income is commission-based. Decisions about recording an expense affects taxes paid (and received by the government for the benefit of society). Our primary goal with this book is to call attention to the intersectionality of accounting and ethics and to encourage students and researchers to consider the ethical implications of accounting decisions.

The book contains a diversity of perspectives within which discussion of accountants' and accounting's ethical responsibilities may occur. We deliberately chose authors for their diverse perspectives on from where moral guidance for accounting may come. Each chapter stands on its own and represents the thinking of its authors. We divide the book into six sections representing various perspectives, for example, religious, practice area, etc. Within each section there are chapters that focus on specific elements within a perspective; for example, within the religious perspective we have chapters on Judaism, Islam, and Christianity.

We recognize that not all perspectives are included and not all that are included are complete. We view this book as a place to spur the conversation along and look forward to reading about advancements that come.

Part I: Historical perspectives on business and accounting ethics (Chapters 1, 2, and 3)

This section is devoted to providing a historical context for accounting ethics. In the first chapter, Professor Roberts provides a general history of the development of accounting ethics. As business became an academic discipline within universities, the ethical missteps of business and accounting became a subject of concern and a subject of study. She explains the course that history took to bring us to the current ethicality of accounting in the form of a **code.** Professor Baker follows up in Chapter 2 with the history of the accounting profession's code of conduct. Rather than a code of ethics, as many professions have, the accounting profession has evolved a lengthy code of conduct. Baker chronicles the historical development of the current code of conduct and provides an analysis of the shortcomings of a code of conduct in guiding genuinely ethical behavior on the part of professional accountants. Chapter 3, written by Professor Fogarty, is a provocative essay about the lack of progress accounting has made in improving the ethicality of the practice. He attributes this lack of progress to the zeitgeist of the historical era in which we find ourselves – the period of "modernity." Modernity has enticed accounting scholars to seek answers to ethical problems in accounting via practices of the social sciences to little avail. Fogarty argues that improving the ethicality of accounting practice requires discourses other than those provided by positive social science.

Part II: Alternative perspectives for thinking about accounting ethics (Chapters 4, 5, 6, and 7)

The basic accounting equations – Assets = Liabilities + Owners' Equity and Net Income = Revenues − Expenses − reflect the predominant mode of ethical reasoning in Western capitalistic societies, which is utilitarianism. Accounting is a technology that assists in making the utilitarian calculations that provide the net "good." Because accounting implicitly contains utilitarian ethical reasoning, accountants may remain desensitized to the fact that there are alternatives to a utilitarian calculus when thinking about accounting ethics. Part II of the book provides the reader with some prominent alternative perspectives on ethics. Professor Neri explains virtue ethics in Chapter 4. Accounting is a practice, and the primary aim of the practitioner is that of perfecting the practice. For any practice to strive toward more perfect practice necessitates that participants in that practice possess certain virtues, and through the continuous exercising of virtuous behaviors one can strive to perfect the practice. Neri explains how virtue ethics pertains to a practice like accounting. What are the virtues people who choose to practice accounting cultivate, in order to improve their practice? Neri addresses that question by suggesting what those virtues might be.

In Chapter 5, Professor Killian explains the ethical theory of the famous philosopher and sociologist Jurgen Habermas. Discourse ethics is based on Habermas's theory of communicative action. Killian presents Habermas's theory and then relates the theory to explain the capacity of people to reach ethical consensus. She then elaborates upon the relevance of discourse ethics for accounting, noting that stories are a central way for people to teach important lessons.

Story-telling is central to a peoples' understanding of their culture and their place in the world. In Chapter 6, Professor Reiter continues in this vein by explaining how important stories are for human understanding and particularly how the stories we tell as accountants affect our ethical understanding. Just as Aesop told stories with a moral, accountants tell stories about themselves, too, to help communicate what is good or not good behavior for an accountant. Professor Lehman, a prominent feminist scholar in accounting, writes the final chapter of Part II. Utilizing feminist theory and the research in accounting deploying feminist theory, Lehman illustrates how the seriousness of the problem of violence against women may be understated via the measures we use to "account" for it. Accounting has considerable power to shape society's perceptions of things based on how we account for them. Lehman gives us a profound appreciation for this fact through her feminist analysis of "measuring" the violence done to women in our society.

Part III: Religious perspectives on accounting ethics
(Chapters 8, 9, and 10)

Academic accounting literature written from a religious perspective is not often found in publications today. However, a consideration of religions, from which many people derive or attribute their ethics, is relevant to a compilation of accounting and ethics knowledge. In Part III, we focus on three major religious influences in the United States and Canada, recognizing that this is a very short list and provides a limited set of perspectives. In the Judaic tradition, Professors Fisher and Friedman present a value-driven approach to ethics rooted in the guiding principles of Judaism, as found in the Torah and Talmud. They provide examples of Talmudic stories that recount how individuals go beyond the law to act ethically, placing others' interest above their own. They also explain the concept of lovingkindness, at the intersection of form and substance. In the next chapter, Professors Stuebs and Thornton explore accounting ethics from a Christian perspective, which places God at the center of aspirational human behavior. Accountability for behavior rests within a person's heart, and people should be guided by service to God rather than fall to the temptations of human nature. Finally, Professors Al-Adeem, Curtis, and Murtaza present an Islamic understanding of accounting and ethics, providing examples from the Qur'an that relate to business ethics. They also explain the concepts of *Riba*, *Zakat*, and *Hisba* and link them to accounting-related ideas.

Part IV: Topical perspectives on accounting ethics
(Chapters 11–18)

This section takes a discipline-specific approach similar to the structure of an undergraduate curriculum. In these chapters, experts in their fields focus on a particular aspect of accounting and relate how ethics is evident in that area. We begin with ethics in auditing, since auditors are the regulated members of our profession and must abide by a code of professional conduct to maintain their government-issued licenses. Professors Papachristou and Bekiaris make the case that an auditor's obligation to the public welfare interest requires them to be transparent and objective. They provide a listing of auditor independence research that academics can rely on to gain an understanding of what we have learned about this concept.

In their discussion of management accounting, Professors Olczak and Roberts point out the shortcomings of management accounting ethics research, lamenting its narrow focus on economic outcomes rather than on ethical implications. They argue that management accounting holds much potential for enacting ethical practices and for examining how decisions made by management accountants affect individuals rather than the company alone. They apply a six-question framework to analyze existing research with respect to topics, research paradigms, theories, viewpoints, and ethical perspectives, concluding with an exploration of ways to increase the ethical focus on management research.

Professor Bloom's chapter examines efforts to measure and report on an organization's efforts toward sustainability, an area that continues to challenge conventional accounting standard setters. He evaluates and compares three models for sustainability reporting. The focus on measuring how an organization's actions affect humans, as well as the viability of the planet itself, is a critically important opportunity to apply an ethical lens to accounting.

Professor Kelly takes on the vast, varied, and often overlooked area of governmental accounting, emphasizing the underlying importance of integrity as a necessary trait for those entrusted with public resources. He provides a helpful summary of key US ethical principles and independence guidelines, and shares examples where government accountants have failed to meet those guidelines. The chapter concludes with a discussion of the COSO integrated framework for internal control and how it can be applied in a governmental setting.

Chapters 15 and 16 focus on accounting information systems and ethics. First, Dull and Schleifer trace the roots of ethics in accounting information systems; then they examine the relevance of ethics to specific accounting-related technologies, including big data, privacy, the Internet of Things, cloud computing, and blockchain. In Chapter 16, Professor Pennington provides a deeper examination of blockchain, noting that decisions made about blockchain design and implementation can result in unethical behavior. She describes the following areas of concern: confidentiality versus transparency, design choice issues, and governance. Blockchain is used for many traditional accounting transactions, and the ethical implications of its use are widespread.

The final two chapters in this part are tax-related. Professors Goldman and Lewellen explore corporate tax decisions from various corporate stakeholder perspectives, noting that the decision to avoid tax is a complex one, with corporations obligated to pay only what the law prescribes, leaving the ethicality of avoidance, a consideration of who may benefit. They conclude that avoidance benefits a wide variety of stakeholders. Professors Farrar, Massey, and Thorne examine individual taxation, which in the United States and many other nations is based on the honor system, bringing into sharp focus the importance of personal ethics. This chapter provides a review of the individual tax literature and focuses on three areas: tax return reporting compliance, tax amnesty declarations, and tax whistleblowing.

Part V: Education and accounting ethics (Chapters 19–22)

Chapters 19–22 examine accounting ethics and education, specifically higher education. In Chapter 19, Professors Mintz and Miller share their concept of how educators can help students develop practical wisdom, which will enable them to act ethically in the face of ethical dilemmas. They begin with a discussion of Rest's Model of Moral Development and then introduce experiential learning using Gentile's Giving Voice to Values. In Chapter 20, Professors Cheng, Schenck, and Flasher describe how the profession was instrumental in motivating universities to add ethics education to the accounting curriculum. They then provide an overview of the accounting ethics education literature, followed by a discussion of how more recent accounting frauds have renewed interest in ethics in accounting education. They conclude with an analysis of current education methods, student perspectives of ethics education in accounting, and a guide for publishing accounting ethics research.

Professor McKenna, in Chapter 21, takes on accounting ethics education from a critical perspective, addressing the question of whether advanced degrees have increased ethical professionalism for auditors and concludes – not necessarily. In Chapter 22, Professors Alles and Kraten provide an innovative method, based on Location Maps, to assist practitioners in resolving moral dilemmas.

Part VI: Ethical accountants and ethical accounting (Chapters 23–26)

In this final part, we include chapters that address specific challenges in promoting ethics in accounting. Chapter 23, written by Professors Kelly, Louwers, and Thornton, provides examples of role models in accounting. From these exemplars, readers can begin to learn how ethics can be accomplished in the field and better understand the challenges that must be overcome. Chapter 24, by Professors Davis, Donnelly, and Radtke, continues the practical discussion by focusing on whistleblowers, specifically those in accounting roles. They provide a comprehensive review of the literature and offer a snapshot of current policy and outcomes in the United States. They conclude by discussing ethical implications of whistleblowing, both for the whistleblower and for the organization.

In Chapter 25, Professor Moore undertakes a critical analysis of certain taken-for-granted premises in accounting. She particularly points out how truly problematic is the notion of a boundary that separates a business from the rest of society. We teach every novitiate to accounting about the entity assumption but provide little regard for how uncertain we can be about identifying what the boundaries of that entity are. She provides us with an excellent example of critical thinking by explaining how those misunderstood premises affect the way accounting does or does not contribute to the good of society. This issue is particularly critical now, as society moves deeper and deeper into a digital environment where data about the individual are more extensive and commodified.

Finally, no volume would be complete in this time without including a discussion of diversity. In Chapter 26, Professor Lenk makes the case for diversity and documents the actions being taken by the largest public accounting firms in the world to address systemic and persistent inequality and lack of fair representation by diverse groups in the profession. She makes clear that although large firms have implemented policies, programs, and strategies, the profession has much work to do to create a true environment of inclusion.

PART I

Historical perspectives on business and accounting ethics

1

HISTORY OF PROFESSIONAL ACCOUNTING ETHICS

Diane H. Roberts

Overview

The aim of this chapter is to examine the historical background to contemporary accounting ethics. The separation of management and ownership created a need for owners to have reliable, accurate and honest information about the performance of the entities they owned. This gave rise to a need for accountants to provide such data. Ethical development of the accounting profession (codes and regulations) tended to be reactive rather than proactive, with each new accounting fraud or scandal providing the impetus for a response to reassure stakeholders of accounting practitioners' bona fides and commitment to providing high quality services. Early in their professionalization, accountants held that the character of the individual accountant was the safeguard for investors. Character is an overtly moral or principles-based concept based on the individual's core internal traits and is a personal internally evaluated characteristic. However, the McKesson & Robbins fraud in December 1938 demonstrated the fallacy of that approach, and the ethics narrative of character was replaced with a scientific or technique ethics narrative. Technique is an objective scientific or rules-based concept in which specialized knowledge or expertise is used on behalf of the public. Both character and technique are necessary for accountants to serve the public interest; however, only science and technique are externally observable. Ethics codes are a technique-based listing of canons of behavior and a component of the quest for professional status. Public accountants were the first accountants to professionalize but were followed by management accountants and other emerging credential and status-seeking subsets of accounting personnel.[1]

Ethics in business

Early business noneconomic activities could be termed corporate social responsibility practices rather than business ethics (Husted 2015). Religious beliefs were the foundation of US business ethics (McMahon 1999). Professions in the United States from 1750 to 1900 were limited to clergy, medicine, and the law (Haber 1991) and did not include accounting. (For a review of historical studies on religion and accounting, see Cordery 2015.)

Medieval Catholic theology viewed trade as morally suspect; however, Protestantism regarded being both an ethical person and a financial success as possible to achieve (Vogel 1991a). In the 17th century, Protestant or Calvinist tenets commanded adherents to labor diligently and emphasized predestination (one's fate determined by God when born) and signs of electness (being selected by God for success). The common good was held to be more important than an individual's self-interest (Gerde, Goldsby, and Shepard 2007). In the 18th century, Protestant teachings minimized predestination and allowed fulfillment of economic self-interest. The Protestant ethic aided in legitimating capitalism by positing that being good is a requirement but not a guarantee for market success (Vogel 1991a).

The market is the mechanism by which capitalism allows an individual to achieve financial success by creating goods and services that improve the consumer's situation (Vogel 1991a). Wealth was considered divine favor, and business people/merchants were to be trustees for the public good. These two ideas combined to motivate merchants toward good deeds and led to the "divine right of businessmen" that appeared with the industrial revolution (McMahon 1999). Advocates of big business and social Darwinism (only the fittest should survive in business) considered progress was only the result of long work, self-discipline and savings, the "middle class virtues." (See McCloskey 2006 for a discussion of virtues and capitalism's success.)

Businesses in the 1800s had informal family ethics based on the religious beliefs of the founder (Knouse, Hill, and Hamilton 2007). Business ethics lost its connection to religion and property by 1890, and contracts became the underlying principles (McMahon 1999). The industrial revolution and the replacement of people with machinery in factories removed the personal and individualism characteristics of early business ethics (McMahon 1999). The robber barons of the late 1800s followed business precepts that emphasized self-glorification and obtained power for personal ends. Backlash toward their business practices led to establishment of the Interstate Commerce Commission in 1886 and the Sherman Antitrust Act in 1890.

Significant external events affect business codes of ethics immediately (Knouse, Hill, and Hamilton 2007). As the influence of the stakeholders changes the focus of company behavior, the financial reporting regarding that behavior changes (Morf et al. 2013). Disclosures of social responsibility topics in annual reports in the 1900s were for internal audiences of employees. Information added as the 20th century progressed was directed at external stakeholders such as shareholders, customers, and regulatory authorities (Morf et al. 2013).

The manager's role was redefined as business size increased and ownership dispersed across many stockholders. Managers were guardians or stewards of the company's resources (Knouse, Hill, and Hamilton 2007). Professionalization of management followed World War II and focus on profits moved business toward value-free procedures and methods. Companies developed rule-based ethics codes to implement compliance with government regulation.

When Harvard Business School wanted to educate students in 1924 about the moral impact of business and technology on society, the initial approach was a history course to place business into social culture (Ciulla 2011). Academic interest in business ethics as a discipline started in 1957 with publication of Herbert Johnston's comprehensive college textbook. The 1963 publication of *Business and Society* by J. W. McGuire was the beginning of formal business and society study. In the period between these two books, the reputation of US business was sullied by price fixing in the electrical industry. Illegal and unethical business practices were demonstrated to be pervasive, changing the positive reputation large business had achieved by supplying the war effort in World War II and rebuilding Europe and Japan under the Marshall Plan. Baumhart's (1961) seminal survey of business executives and managers found extensive unethical behavior. The article influenced government, trade associations, universities, and churches to attempt to improve business ethics. Practical concerns during this period were safe working conditions, expense accounts, trade secrets, conflicts of interest, and hiring practices (McMahon 1999).

Social issues in business were part of the broader 1960s era of rebellion against authority and a strong antibusiness attitude as young people opposed the military-industrial establishment (De George 1987). Business schools began to include social issues as course and research topics (see Abend 2013 for a survey of early business ethics topics in universities). The 1964 Civil Rights Act and the social legislation that followed altered the focus of business ethics from the individual businessperson to corporate activity as a whole.

In the 1970s and 1980s, the public perception of business was one of company excess and multiple disasters involving companies' behavior occurred, including the Three Mile Island nuclear reactor meltdown; the Union Carbide factory explosion in Bhopal, India; and Nestlé's Latin American marketing of breast milk substitutes. Morals and values were once again considered appropriate business attributes (Knouse, Hill, and Hamilton 2007). Companies attempted to develop a nonreligious culture of ethics to achieve coherence with the social values of the time. Business ethics became secularized, with less focus on individual character, as most activity takes place through organizations (Vogel 1991b).

Environmental issues became prominent when Rachel Carson (Carson 1962) wrote *Silent Spring* about the dangers of pesticides in the environment and testified before Congress. President Nixon's executive order transferred 15 units of four agencies to create the Environmental Protection Agency (EPA) in 1970. Companies were legally responsible for the environmental harm they caused.

The Foreign Corrupt Practices Act (FCPA) was passed in 1977 in response to bribes paid by corporations to foreign officials (Badua 2015). The FCPA both prohibited payment of bribes and required maintenance of sufficient accounting records and internal controls. The importance of internal audit increased as a business function with the passage of the FCPA (Burns, Greenspan, and Harwell 1994), and the professionalism of internal auditors improved.

Accounting ethics

Capital market development prompted the need for better accounting methodologies, more accomplished accounting practitioners, and ethical behavior by those practitioners. While the term "business ethics" was deemed a potential oxymoron prior to the start of the 1980s (De George 1987), accountants had been attempting to institute a code of professional ethics for accountants since 1905, because all professions have one. The first issue of the *Journal of Accountancy*, the house organ of the American Institute of Accountants, included an editorial that announced accounting parity with medicine and law as a learned profession as the publication's goal (Anon. 1905). Ethical responsibilities of professionals include technical competence in their field and a mindset that they perform their duties proficiently to warrant the public's trust (Abdolmohammadi and Nixon 1999).[2]

Medicine is the oldest profession in the United States, with its initial code of ethics established in 1846, prompted by the deregulation of medical practitioners by many states (Backof and Martin 1991). An influx of unqualified doctors produced by diploma mill medical schools created a need for the American Medical Association to enact a code of ethics. The medical profession's need to distinguish qualified practitioners from quacks paralleled the need for CPAs to distinguish themselves from bookkeepers and uncertified practitioners. As the newest of the professions, accounting was in the process of obtaining regulation through enacting state-by-state CPA legislation (see Edwards 1978 for dates of specific states' CPA legislation).

The American Bar Association (ABA) and the American Institute of Certified Public Accountants (AICPA) faced similar divisions among their members in response to changing economic and social conditions that created member segments with different attitudes toward professional ethics codes. Contemporaneous with public accounting's initial ethics code efforts, the ABA's first ethics code was enacted in 1908 during the US transformation from a rural-based to an urban and industrial society and the arrival of many immigrants to urban areas (Backof and Martin 1991). The emerging corporate wealth produced by this change caused a professional schism between lawyers with national prominence who could exploit these opportunities and small town lawyers. The code of ethics was promoted by established corporate lawyers and prohibited advertising, solicitation, and court supervision of contingent fee agreements. Small town and urban immigrant lawyers had their practice development difficulties increase from these rules. The public interest aspect of the code was a requirement that attorneys represent clients the attorney deemed guilty and let the court determine the verdict.

Accounting was affected by the same social conditions as the law, the transition from a rural to an urban industrial economy and small versus large practitioners. As business size increased and the providers of capital diverged from management (roles performed by different sets of people), there was an increased need for independent financial reporting. Unlike in law, no single national organization was recognized as representing the accounting profession. The development of professional ethics was intertwined with the development of professional accountancy organizations, and there were two schools of thought on the need for a code of professional ethics. The New York-based American Institute of Accountants (AIA) developed formal rules of conduct termed "professional conduct rules" (Carey 1969) and was viewed as East Coast elitist, restricting membership to those who passed the AIA uniform CPA exam regardless of whether the accountant held a CPA certificate (Previts and Merino 1998). The American Society of Certified Public Accountants (ASCPA) did not enact a code of ethics (Edwards 1978). Membership in the ASCPA was open to CPA certificate holders from any state (Previts and Merino 1998) and thus included rural and smaller practitioners as members.

The AICPA adopted its contemporary name in 1957 (Cook 1987) and is the successor to the merger of several prior accounting professional organizations. The organization began in 1887 under the name American Association of Public Accountants (AAPA) and primarily operated in New York City and other urbanized areas (Previts and Merino 1998). A rival national organization, the Federation of Societies of Public Accountants in the United States, was formed in Illinois in 1902 and merged with the AAPA in 1905 (Roberts 1987). In 1916 the name was changed to the Institute of Accountants in the United States of America and then to American Institute of Accountants (AIA) in 1917 (Roberts 1987). In a final successful merger with a rival national organization in 1936, the American Society of CPAs (ASCPA), the AIA consolidated its position as the national voice for US accountants (Montgomery 1936). Throughout this chapter, the name of the professional organization at the date discussed will be used.

Professionalism

Ethics is one part of the quest for professional status. An attributes approach to defining a profession considers these factors: Set of values, body of knowledge, formalized educational process, formal testing, formal recognition through licensing, code of ethics, symbols, professional associations, personal qualities, and unwritten rules of behavior (Montagna 1974). Ethical aspects are contained in the set of values, code of ethics, personal qualities, and unwritten rules of behavior. The ethics code functions as a legitimatizing device for the public accounting profession (Preston et al. 1995). Expertise used on the public's behalf validated the profession's legitimacy (Roberts 2010). Both character and technique are required to serve the public interest (Roberts 2010).

Table 1.1 Timeline of Accounting Professional Organizations

1887	American Association of Public Accountants (AAPA) created in New York.
1902	Federation of Societies of Public Accountants in the United States (FSPA), rival organization created in Illinois.
1905	FSPA merges with AAPA, and AAPA name is used for the merged entity.
1916	AAPA changes its name to Institute of Accountants in the United States of America (IAUSA).
1917	IAUSA changes its name to American Institute of Accountants (AIA).
1936	AIA merges with final rival national organization, the American Society of CPAs (ASCPA), and uses AIA name for the merged entity. One national professional\organization represents all CPAs for the first time.
1957	American Institute of Certified Public Accountants (AICPA) name adopted.

Ethics are value laden and complex to implement. Standardization implied by codification of ethics codes is useful but unlikely to cover every situation or motivation. The public interest aspect of the code of professional ethics focuses the orientation of the professional community toward social responsibility (Parker 1994). Public interest components comprise protection of client economic interests, protecting third parties' economic interests, delineating the client-profession relationship, and community orientation/social responsibility. Private interest is to protect the profession itself and includes minimization of interference by outsiders, maintaining professional authority and autonomy, exclusiveness, and socioeconomic status preservation (Parker 1994). The code also ensures exclusiveness of provision of audit services. Economic interests of the profession are also served by establishing criteria for professional membership, as these criteria also serve as barriers to entry (Lee 1995).

Ethical conduct before the US federal government was first regulated in 1884 with passage of the Deficiency Appropriation Act by the US Congress (Broden and Loeb 1983). Individuals had to be competent and of good moral character or the Secretary of the Treasury could disbar or suspend those individuals. Further departmental regulations (Treasury Circulars) in 1886 and 1890 expanded to cover attorneys and agents.[3]

Public accounting

Codes of ethics often stipulate a higher standard of conduct than required by law (Backof and Martin 1991; Carey 1956). The need for a code of professional ethics was far from a settled matter at the inception of public accounting in the United States. The accountant's character was viewed as an innate quality that rendered ethics rules unnecessary for the true professional. An internal, state-of-mind ethics approach justified a small number of written rules. Terms used to discuss ethics issues reflect the evolution of attitudes toward ethics. Historical terms that belong in the same era as character-based ethics include honest, reliable, virtue, moral, and character (Neu 2001). Traditional concepts of character lessened in importance in society in general and in professions over the course of the 20th century (Preston et al. 1995). Modern ethical terms evoke a competent technician/scientist and consist of independence, integrity, and objectivity (Neu 2001).

The degree to which science and social structures impact a profession influences the comparative movement from use of character to use of technique for legitimation (Abbott 1988). Regulation is the most impactful social structure; however, public accounting was initially self-regulated. Efforts to secure legislative recognition for CPAs occurred at the state level. Regulation was not enacted at the federal level until the Securities Acts of 1933 and 1934. The Federal

Trade Commission was designated the overseer of accountants in the 1933 act, but responsibility was transferred to the newly established Securities and Exchange Commission (SEC) in the 1934 act (Moran and Previts 1984).

The *Journal of Accountancy* was the AIA's publication during an era where print media was a primary communication channel and professional ethics was a frequent topic. An October, 1907, *Journal of Accountancy* article titled "Professional Ethics" claimed to be the initial focus of an accounting professional body on professional ethics (Sterrett 1907). The analysis of accountants' ethics (responsibilities) was considered in terms of three groups – clients, general public, and fellow accountants – and the bulk of the discussion was regarding treatment of "professional brethren."

The initial ethical rules were in the 1906 AAPA bylaws under "Miscellaneous" and consisted of two rules prohibiting (1) nonmembers practicing accounting in the name of the AAPA and (2) receipt or payment of commissions to brokers or other non-accountants (Bishop and Tondkar 1987). Seven years later, a follow-up *Journal of Accountancy* ethics article proclaimed accountancy had achieved professional status, and the main concern was relations with fellow accountants (Joplin 1914). Concerns included derogatory competition with other accountants, solicitation of business from strangers, client confidentiality, contingent fees, competitive bidding, and advertising (circular letters) related to the federal income tax law. The AAPA had a great deal of intra-profession education work to do, in addition to educating potential clients and the public about the benefits of certified statements.

The AAPA instituted a formal ethics committee to promulgate ethics rules in 1906, but enforcement issues were not added to the committee's agenda until 1916 (Lowe 1987). Following the 1929 stock market crash, enforcement of regulations increased, and in 1939 the Securities and Exchange Commission began to notify the AIA of the SEC's investigations into accountants.

AIA professional conduct rules adopted in 1917 comprised (1) use of the title "Member of American Institute of Accountants"; (2) certification of statements with misstatements of fact or omissions; (3) practice in the name of a member; (4) payment or receipt of commissions; (5) conduct of incompatible occupations; (6) lack of satisfactory supervision of an audit; (7) notification to AIA if lobbying for legislation; and (8) solicitation of another AIA member's clients (Carey 1969).

A ninth rule passed in 1919 prohibited employment offers to fellow members' employees, and contingent fees were banned by the tenth rule (Carey 1969). Advertisements were banned in the 11th rule, and the 12th rule barred participation in activities of schools whose promotional activities were discreditable to the profession. By 1931, 12 rules had been passed and numbered in the order they were adopted.

The code of professional ethics was a set of prohibitions that were not based on ethical theories. They were image-conscious, practical rules needed to develop public confidence and achieve recognition as professionals for accountants. Auditor independence was not covered by the professional conduct rules and the majority of the rules focused on proscribing accountants' intra-professional activities (Roberts 2015). Private interest elements served by the rules included exclusivity of services, just compensation, maintaining political power, self-regulation of the profession and maintenance of social status (Parker 1994). Only the prohibition on certification of statements which contained essential misstatements (rule 2) was primarily focused on serving the public interest.

The AIA published *The Ethics of a Profession* by long-time association secretary A. P. Richardson in 1931. This small volume propounded/presented the opinions of an AIA employee, initially hired in 1911, who interacted with the highest levels of AIA leadership. By this time the AIA's ethical code had 12 rules, listed in the order of adoption, and shown in the Appendix to Richardson (1931). These rules dealt with

1 use of the title "Member American Institute of Accountants"
2 certification of statements that contained essential misstatements
3 prohibition of a non-AIA member from practicing in the name of a member
4 commissions
5 incompatible occupations
6 certification of statements not verified under supervision of an AIA member
7 efforts to secure legislation without notification of the Institute
8 solicitation or encroachment on the practice of another member
9 offers of employment to employees of fellow members
10 contingent fees
11 advertisements
12 participation in activities of educational institutions whose promotional activities were discreditable to the profession.

SEC oversight was passive during the 1930s, and the SEC considered the independence of the auditor to assure fair disclosure in financial statements (Moran and Previts 1984). The McKesson & Robbins fraud was revealed in December 1938 and brought auditors and accounting practices to the public's attention in a significant way for the first time (Barr and Galpeer 1987). Salacious human-interest aspects of the case (false identities, suicide, arms dealing, bootlegging, and blackmail) kept the case and the audit procedures that were implemented in the public eye. Accountants testified before the SEC for the first time and focused on techniques, not moral or ethical attributes, of auditing (Roberts 2010). The negative publicity from this audit failure prompted increased regulatory oversight. In 1940 the SEC released regulation S-X that codified SEC rules on accounting content and financial statement format. In March 1942, the SEC issued its first rules regarding conduct of accountants who practiced before the SEC.

An evaluation of the ethics rules was conducted in 1956 by the AICPA's council, and extension of the rules to non-audit services such as tax and management advisory services were considered. The revised code of ethics was issued in 1962, with a single code for all types of services (Lowe 1987). The five conduct areas were member relationships with clients and the public; technical standards; promotional practices; operating practices; and relations with other AICPA members. The securities acts were amended in 1964; however, the SEC retained the existing relationship between the SEC and the accounting profession (Moran and Previts 1984).

The 1970s were a challenging decade for the accounting profession, with both congressional and SEC hearings and regulation (Moran and Previts 1984). Alleged cost overruns in defense contracts prompted Congress to establish the Cost Accounting Standards Board in 1970. No longer passive, the SEC solely originated and implemented changes to regulation S-X requiring a new statement, sources and uses of funds, and creating form 10-Q, quarterly reporting. The accounting profession responded by promoting establishment of the Financial Accounting Standards Board. By 1973, the AICPA revised the code of professional ethics. The code was codified into three parts: (1) concepts or goals members were to aspire to, (2) enforceable standards known as Rules of Conduct, and (3) ethics rulings and rule interpretations (Lowe 1987; AICPA 1977). Independence, integrity and objectivity were the most important issues faced by members (Carey 1970).

The AICPA appointed the Special Committee on Standards of Professional Conduct for Certified Public Accountants, known as the Anderson Committee, in 1983 (Shaub 1988). Unaltered rules included independence, acts discreditable to the profession, advertising and solicitation, and commissions. Substantial changes were recommended that especially affected potential conflicts of interest for CPAs who provided non-audit services. Contingent fees and a fictitious name that indicates a specialization were allowed for the first time. The code was to be more responsive to congressional and public concerns by giving broad positive standards, specific behavioral rules, and proactive monitoring.

Independence

Independence was not initially in the code of professional ethics. Independence in fact was the term applied to the concept of independence as a manifestation of character and the account-ant's mental attitude. Independence has a distinctive connotation/meaning in public accounting and audit opinions; however, a specific, complete definition was not developed by the AICPA (Carey and Doherty 1966). Independence *in fact* was the self-knowledge of the CPA regard-ing one's own mental state. This implemented the professional man metaphor that maintained the moral character of the accountant was such that ethics rules were unnecessary (Reiter and Williams 2004). Independence *in appearance* was the externally observable lack of conflicts of interest in the SEC regulations (Sutton 1997).

Auditors avoided much public anger following the US stock market crash of 1929, as audi-tors had a low profile (Carey 1979); however, the New York Stock Exchange (NYSE) required all new listings as of July 1, 1933, to have independent audits. To be truly valuable, the NYSE determined that audits had to be adequate in scope and the responsibility of the "independent" auditor defined (Barton 1933). Independence was not yet an ethics standard but was considered a manifestation of character and a mental attitude termed independence in fact.

Parker's (1994) private interest model of professional accounting ethics holds creation of a professional mystique that renders the profession immune to evaluation by outsiders to be a cru-cial private interest goal. Independence only the accountant can ascertain rendered individual members of the profession sole evaluators of a central facet of the profession. The profession's private interest of insulation from external monitoring was served.

AIA President Frederick Hurdman proposed a complete ban on dual relationships of audi-tor and corporate executive or director in 1931 that was voted down by AIA membership (Hurdman 1931). Under pressure from government regulators and the financial press, the AIA enacted a standard that prohibited certification of a publicly traded client's financial statements if the auditor was an actual, prospective, or beneficial owner of a substantial financial interest in the client (Carey 1937). The dual relationship of auditor and director was not banned in this standard, nor were incompatible services addressed.

There was a strong belief in the fitness of the individual accountant and much written in the *Journal of Accountancy* about the negative, long-term economic consequences for the unethical accountant. The lack of success that was deemed to result from unethical practice was consid-ered a sufficient deterrent to protect the public, and thus additional rules or legislation were deemed unnecessary.

SEC rule 650(b) on auditor independence was instituted in 1934 and prohibited an account-ant with a direct or indirect substantial ownership from being deemed independent. Banned incompatible relationships for auditors included officer, employee, promoter, underwriter, trustee, partner, director, or person performing similar functions (Carey 1937). So-called independence in fact, the internal knowledge of the individual CPA, was rejected in favor of independence in appearance, an externally observable characteristic (Sutton 1997). This change circumscribing the extent of the auditors' behavior made the rules around independence more consistent with the "thou shalt not" phrasing of other ethical rules. The previous lack of an independence principle rendered the auditor-client relationship open to individual auditor determination of what that relationship constituted and thus dependent upon the individual accountant's character. While this rule implemented constraints on the auditors' conduct, on a practical level the prior no-rule situation was vulnerable to abuse.

Accountants responded to SEC independence regulations by trying to regulate how clients appointed auditors, thus increasing auditor independence from clients. US auditors were primarily engaged and compensated by the elected board of management without shareholder oversight, the director method. England used the shareholder method that involved direct election of auditors by shareholders (Richardson 1932). This proposal did not place additional constraints on accountants but instead strengthened the auditor's position over the board of directors and management (Roberts 2010).

In the post-1933 and -1934 period, thinking on the issue of acceptability of ownership in clients was divided, as exemplified by the two-tier independence rules of SEC and non-SEC practicing accountants (Andrews 1934). Correspondence between the two requirements was not achieved until issuance of *Opinion No. 12: Independence* by the AICPA's Division of Professional Ethics in 1961 (AICPA 1970). English accountants evinced surprise that their American counterparts would allow this inference that integrity could be impaired by a financial interest in a client (Carey 1975).

Both practitioner-independence and profession-independence are essential for the public confidence necessary to accomplish the auditor's mission (Mautz and Sharaf 1961). Practitioner-independence is the individual accountant's approach and attitude toward professional work and the maintenance of that independence while under pressure during the audit. Profession-independence is the public's impression of auditors as a whole, the meaning they attribute to the terms "auditor" and "CPA." Public acceptance of auditor independence is essential to the profession's existence and ability to provide auditing services.

Management advisory services (MAS) became a contentious issue, as it had concerns about conflicts of interest and auditing one's own work (Abdolmohammadi and Nixon 1999). CPA firms have offered non-audit services since their inception. Arthur Andersen & Co.'s 1913 announcement of its founding advertised offerings of audits, designing and installing financial and cost accounting systems (Mednick 1990). The AICPA in 1947 concluded that providing audit, tax, and management advisory services to the same client would not impair independence for the audit if the CPA did not make management decisions (Carey and Doherty 1966). Carey and Doherty (1966) suggested that MAS engagements are nonrecurring but audits are an annual engagement; thus, no auditor would sacrifice the audit engagement. As MAS became increasingly lucrative, the profession had a serious image problem (Hartley and Ross 1972).

The decade of the 1930s was emblematic of an ethical decision- and rule-making process that is characteristic of American public accounting. The 1929 stock market crash was an economic crisis that featured some accounting scandal aspects, given the poor quality of accounting standards and the lack of mandatory audits. The profession introduced a rather weak independence standard that prohibited some dual auditor–corporate executive relationships but did not ban ownership in an audit client. The membership did not pass the weak standard, and the SEC enacted its own stronger independence standard that banned ownership in an audit client. The profession reluctantly ratified a weaker independence standard. The decade ended with another accounting scandal, the McKesson & Robbins fraud of 1938/39, which prompted the first congressional hearings on the accounting profession. The cycle of the profession's lagging responses began again.

Advertising

A ban on advertising was deemed a hallmark of a profession, and the professions whose status accountants aspired to attain, attorneys and doctors, regarded advertising as unethical. As early as 1894, the AAPA prohibited advertising except for publication of a "card" with name, profession, and address (Wood and Sylvestre 1985). The rule was widely ignored, and the *Journal of Accountancy* exposed egregious/offensive ads that in its opinion portrayed accounting as a trade (see Previts and Merino 1998 for examples of early advertisements).

Both law and medicine deemed advertising an inappropriate method of attracting clients (Sterrett 1907). Opposition to advertising was due to concern about unfair competition, as clients who already have an accountant may see the advertisements, and return on investment was deemed doubtful, since hiring an accountant not personally known to the client would not occur. Incredulity regarding hiring an accountant who was a stranger to perform confidential engagements persisted through the 1930s (Richardson 1931). Indirect advertising of an educational nature about accounting professional services, such as pamphlets or reprints of speeches, was acceptable and considered to increase the profession's reputation with the public (Sterrett 1907; Richardson 1931).

In 1920, a standing committee to censor AIA member advertising was established, and distribution of publicity items without the consent of the committee was prohibited. The AIA council frequently met as a trial board on advertising violations, and few public accountants were acquitted. A.C. Ernst and two of his partners were accused of violating the bans on advertising and solicitation and resigned from the AIA in protest in 1923 (Zeff 2003).

In 1931, Richardson devoted entire chapters of *The Ethics of a Profession* to the topics of soliciting, advertising, and contingent fees. These rules were the most contentious issues between the AIA and the ASPCA (Previts and Merino 1998). Solicitation involved oral appeals to specific prospective clients (often consisting of poaching another accountant's client), and advertising was written and impersonally delivered through the mail or press. Both were considered trade-like behavior that might enable the client to determine the engagement's results. Bookkeepers served at the pleasure of their employers and followed their directives; however, the public accountant determined the particulars of his or her work.

"Cards" were limited in 1947 to publication when the firm changed location or name. The rule specified card size, two columns wide and three inches deep. A full ban on advertising, including "cards," was enacted by the AICPA in 1958 (Wood and Sylvestre 1985).

As the profession's national organization aimed to achieve professionalism by banning advertising, federal regulators had concerns that the prohibition was anticompetitive. During the 1960s, the AICPA and state CPA societies received document requests from the U.S. Department of Justice that resulted in the 1966 AICPA Council proposal to eliminate the prohibition on competitive bidding (Mason 1994). The AICPA's status as a private organization meant the state boards of accountancy that granted CPA licenses were affected. State boards of accountancy were subject to disputes regarding their regulations.

In 1977 the U.S. Supreme Court held in *Bates v. State Bar of Arizona* that prohibitions on advertising violated attorneys' free speech rights (Clow et al. 2009). This ruling applied to other professions with advertising bans, and the AICPA altered its ethics rulings to ban only false, misleading, or deceptive promotional materials.

The ruling made advertising by professionals legal, but attitudes of the profession's members remained to be changed (Bullard and Snizek 1988). Some practitioners considered advertising to undermine the essence of professionalism. Some professions considered the ban on advertising to be protection of the public from fraudulent promoters (Darling 1977). Advertising costs are expenses that will be passed on to the client. Older accountants and those with larger corporate-focused practices were very opposed to the change (Clow et al. 2009).

Fees, contingent fees, bidding, and commissions

Contingent fees were the tenth rule enacted by the AIA and were part of a larger set of issues – commissions and bidding (Richardson 1931). Both giving and receiving commissions were prohibited. Accountants should not pay commissions to obtain an engagement, nor should they pay a commission to providers to clients. This was viewed as compromising the objectivity of the accountant. No independence rule banning dual auditor–owner relationships was adopted, but a ban on commissions for letterhead/stationary for a client was the AIA ethical code's fourth rule.

Richardson (1931) claimed work should have an appropriate monetary reward, and if the client was unsatisfied, the danger of no compensation was too high for contingent fees to be appropriate. Impartiality and not advocacy as the accountant's role was a less-cited reason for contingent fee bans. Most contingent fee situations were in tax practice.

The FTC proposed in 1988 that CPAs be permitted to receive commissions and contingent fees. Use of fictitious or trade names were also proposed. The ban on fictitious or trade names was considered a form of advertising ban (Allen and Ng 1997). The ethics code required CPA firms to feature past or current partners' names, but this was open to antitrust criticism. The AICPA further removed rules forbidding incompatible occupations (Mason 1994). The ethics change recommendations were voted on in a mail ballot that gave rise to a legal challenge by some members. The rule changes were adopted.

The FTC's consent decree issues were similar to the issues that were most contentious in Richardson (1931). In 1931, the profession was attempting to make itself into a profession in fact and in appearance; however, in the 1960s through 1994, some accounting professionals considered the FTC was attempting to transform the profession into an industry (Mason 1994).

The FTC charged the AICPA in its 1990 consent order with illegal restraint of trade (Allen and Ng 1997). The code of ethics provisions the FTC objected to were bans on (1) trade names that indicated specialization, (2) receipt of commissions for referring clients to non-CPA vendors, (3) payment or receipt of referral fees for client referrals between CPAs, and (4) contingent fees that depended on outcomes of work performed (Allen and Ng 1997). The AICPA settled out of court; thus, the FTC did not prove guilt and the AICPA did not admit guilt. The FTC alleged that these rules constituted restraint of trade. The trade name ban was an advertising ban; however, the other ethics rules were bans on receipt of particular types of fees by CPAs and not generally anticompetitive.

Tax practice

Initial accountant participation in tax practice occurred in 1909 with enactment of a corporate excise tax law (Broden and Loeb 1983). Passage of the 16th amendment to the US Constitution in 1913 accelerated interest in income tax as an accounting practice area. Although qualified practitioners had increased job security from this expansion of services, many unqualified individuals proclaimed themselves tax expert accountants (Previts and Merino 1998).

Self-regulation by the profession lagged in tax practice due to strong governmental regulation and the variety of competing occupational groups involved in tax preparation and planning. No unique tax practice ethical rules were developed by the AIA, but advertising, contingent fees, and confidentiality rules applied to tax practice.

The AIA focused its ethics rule development on the attest function, which is the exclusive jurisdiction of CPAs. The Treasury Department's rules applied to all tax practitioners, which included CPAs, accountants, lawyers, and enrolled agents. Treasury Circular No. 230 was issued in June 1922 to regulate advertising in tax practice. Advertising was strictly limited to name, address, and a brief description of services on offer. Prohibited advertising included the implication of ability to obtain consideration from the Treasury Department that is not available to the public at large. The AIA followed suit by adopting a rule that prohibited all non-business card advertising.

Contingent fees in tax grew after World War I, and the Bureau of Internal Revenue lost seasoned employees who left to work for taxpayers on a contingent fee basis. Treasury Circular No. 230 was amended to prohibit contingent fees in 1922. It was not until 1936 that the AIA amended its own ban on contingent fees to allow such fees in tax cases that are decided by the tax authorities and not by the accountant.

Accountant's work papers were objects of attempted Bureau of Internal Revenue examination in 1923, but CPAs primarily refused to disclose the papers without client consent. The agency agreed to not pursue work paper access without a subpoena (Broden and Loeb 1983). The Revenue Act of 1937 required CPAs to divulge work papers related to taxes of foreign corporations. The AIA enacted an ethics rule in 1941 formalizing the confidential client–CPA relationship. Extension of the Code of Professional Ethics to tax practice occurred with issuance of Opinion 13 of the AICPA Committee on Professional Ethics in 1962. CPAs were charged with observing the same standards of integrity and truthfulness as in any other professional engagements; however, CPAs were allowed to resolve a tax issue in the client's favor if there is reasonable support for the tax position.

The reorganization of the AICPA's Code of Professional Ethics in the 1970s brought changes to tax practice as well (AICPA 1977). Professional competence, exercise of due professional care, and conclusions based on relevant data were instituted as ethical requirements in tax practice. The new advertising rule in 1978 allowed tax practitioners to advertise but prohibited uninvited solicitation of specific businesses, yet this was removed in 1979. Solicitation was further modified in 1983 but prohibited coercive or harassing conduct.

Managerial accounting

Managerial accounting is conducted within an organization to achieve that organization's goals. There is no external requirement for any specific type of management accounting; thus, development of managerial accounting ethics occurred later than for public accounting.

One internal occupation that organized early was the salaried middle managers inside companies, including some banks, who made the credit extension decisions for their employers. Called credit men, these employees controlled access to credit for both retailers and consumers from their positions inside companies and organized the National Association of Credit Men (NACM) in 1896 (Smith 2010). The NACM still exists under the revised name of the National Association of Credit Management.

Institute of Management Accountants – code of ethics

The Institute of Management Accountants (IMA) was organized in 1919 and established a standing Committee on Ethics. Efforts to initiate a code of ethics began in 1981 with an IMA publication, "Towards a Code of Ethics for Management Accountants," and proposing an ethics section for the Certified Management Accountants (CMA) exam. The first US code for management accountants appeared in 1983 when the IMA issued SMA 1C "Standards of Ethical Conduct for Management Accountants." This standard was first revised in 1997 and again in 2005 in response to the Sarbanes-Oxley Act of 2002. The code was designed to be more direct and globally oriented.

This later development of an ethics code mirrors the stagnation in management accounting methods. Competitive conditions in the 1980s prompted development of new cost accounting methods. There had been little change in cost accounting methods since 1925 (Kaplan 1984). Short-run opportunistic behavior was brought about by a focus on current period profit center performance and a lesser concern with long-term health/performance of the organization.

Kaplan (1984) notes that there was less emphasis on short-term financial results in the 1920s and 1930s compared to the 1970s and 1980s. Managers remained in the same position/job longer in the 1920s and 1930s, so the long-term impact of their performance could be observed. Organizations in the 1980s were much larger than in the 1920s.

The Institute of Management Accountants' (IMA) initial set of 15 ethical standards were issued in June 1982 (Moyes and Park 1997) and comprised the following:

1 maintain appropriate level of professional competence
2 professional duties performed in accordance with laws, regulations, and technical standards
3 prepare complete and clear reports based on appropriate analysis of relevant and reliable information
4 refrain from disclosing confidential information
5 inform subordinates regarding confidentiality of information and monitor their activities to assure confidentiality is maintained
6 do not use confidential information for unethical or illegal advantage
7 avoid conflicts of interest and advise appropriate parties of any potential conflict
8 refrain from activities that would prejudice the ability to carry out duties ethically
9 refuse any gift or hospitality that would influence actions
10 refrain from subverting the attainment of the organization's legitimate and ethical objectives
11 recognize and communicate professional limitation that would preclude responsible judgment or successful performance
12 communicate unfavorable and favorable information with management
13 refrain from engaging in any activity that would discredit the profession
14 communicate information fairly and objectively
15 disclose fully all relevant information that could reasonably be expected to influence understanding of reports and recommendations.

Although promulgated in different eras (1931 and 1982), the different responsibilities of the public accountant and the managerial or corporate accountant create both differences and similarities in the groups' initial ethical standards. The public interest orientation of CPAs is reflected in rules to promote competence in audit opinions. Many initial public accounting ethics standards attempted to regulate behavior within the profession itself. Managerial accounting rules relate to activities conducted within one organization, so the competitive rules needed for public accounting were not needed. Confidentiality, competence in performing one's duties, and avoidance of conflicts of interest were stressed in the managerial standards.

Since managerial accountants do not have a state-granted license with a regulatory enforcement apparatus, the efficacy of the ethical standards implementation was an empirical question.

A survey of CFOs in 1992 found most agreement with No. 2, comply with laws, No. 4, do not disclose confidential information, and No. 6, do not use confidential information for illegal or unethical purposes (Moyes and Park 1997). There was less agreement with No. 11, people should recognize and communicate their professional limitations, No. 13, refrain from acts discrediting the profession, and No. 9, refusal of gifts or hospitality that might influence a decision.

Conclusion

Accountants' external responsibilities to an expanding variety of stakeholders created an environment in which an internally verified, "trust me" approach to accounting ethics was not tenable. Initially self-regulated and adhering to a character-based narrative of legitimacy, accounting professional organizations promulgated codes of professional conduct that were as sparse as possible. Rulemaking was in response to external negative occurrences such as audit failures or frauds. Additional ethics rules were adopted when further deleterious events transpired. No coherent or overarching ethics philosophy guided rule development, but instead rules were developed on an as-needed basis to defensively react to accountants' current problem.

Following the 1929 stock market crash, the Securities Acts of 1933 and 1934 were legislated and brought public accounting and auditors under federal regulatory authority. Created to wield that authority, the SEC was initially passive, leaving the accounting professional organization to develop professional ethics and accounting principles. Prominent negative publicity from the McKesson & Robbins audit failure of 1938 prompted the SEC to actively regulate auditors. The accountants' national professional organization responded by ratifying formal constraints in the code of professional ethics that delineated appropriate behavior for auditors. These external rules were capable of verification by external parties and were not dependent solely upon the personal assurance of the individual auditor.

The change from a character-based, private ethics to a technique-based set of canons of behavior in the 1930s set the tone for the further development of constraining, thou-shalt-not style rules to be added. A philosophical, aspirational professional ethics guide for auditors first appeared as an ethics code section in 1973. Independence is a key ethical precept for auditors that has been increasingly refined with expanded constraints. Each new ethics rule's behavior specification or constraint allowed increased external verification and more explicit means to evaluate and discipline auditors' actions.

Dailey (1984) modeled US accounting as a three part cycle: reactive, proactive, and synthesis. In the reactive phase a strong external environment creates a situation requiring the profession to respond. The proactive phase encompasses the accounting profession's processes to resolve the conflict. Synthesis is the resulting code change, guideline implementation, or other decision. A new cycle is begun as business, government, and other stakeholders react to the decision reached in the synthesis phase. The historical trend of an accounting scandal (reactive phase), the profession's reexamination of its code of ethics (proactive phase), and the change in profession's ethical standards (synthesis) still operates in contemporary times. Graeber's (2015) "iron law of liberalism" holds that government attempts to reduce regulations to promote markets will yield increased official procedures and create more government bureaucracy. Accounting's cyclical response, per Dailey's (1984) model combined with Graeber's (2015) inevitable government regulation proliferation, results in the continuing evolution of the originally self-determining accounting profession toward a bureaucratically controlled industry.

Notes

1   The modern period is deemed to begin around 1988 for purposes of this chapter. For information on current accounting ethics see Chapter 3, "In Our Time: Accountant Ethics and Historical Relativity," in this volume.
2   Academic interest in teaching accounting ethics was first evidenced by an article in *The Accounting Review* in 1931 (Myer 1931).
3   For an overview of accountancy's pursuit of professional status throughout the Anglo-American world, see Poullaos (2009), and in the United States, see Miranti (1990).

References

Abbott, A. 1988. *The System of Professions: An Essay on the Division of Expert Labor.* Chicago, IL: University of Chicago Press. doi:10.7208/chicago/9780226189666.001.0001.

Abdolmohammadi, M. J., and M. R. Nixon. 1999. "Ethics in the Public Accounting Profession." In *A Companion to Business Ethics*, edited by Robert E. Fredrick, 164–77. Oxford: Blackwell Publishers Ltd. doi:10.1002/9780470998397.ch14.

Abend, G. 2013. "The Origins of Business Ethics in American Universities, 1902–1936." *Business Ethics Quarterly* 23 (2): 171–205. doi:10.1017/S1052150X00005509.

Allen, P. W., and C. K. Ng. 1997. "Financial Stake and Support for Banning Trade Names, Commissions, Referral Fees and Contingent Fees." *Accounting Horizons* 11 (1): 1–6.

American Institute of Certified Public Accountants. 1970. Division of Professional Ethics. *Summaries of Ethics Rulings.* New York: AICPA.

American Institute of Certified Public Accountants. 1977. *Professional Standards.* Volume 2. Chicago, IL: Commerce Clearing House.

Andrews, F. B. 1934. "The Public Accountant and the Investing Public." *Journal of Accountancy* 57 (1): 55–65.

Anonymous. 1905. "Editorial, Purpose and scope of this journal." *Journal of Accountancy* 1 (1): 57–59.

Backof, J. F., and C. L. Martin Jr. 1991. "Historical Perspectives: Development of the Codes of Ethics in the Legal, Medical and Accounting Professions." *Journal of Business Ethics* 10 (2): 99–110. doi:10.1007/BF00383613.

Badua, F. 2015. "Laying Down the Law on Lockheed: How an Aviation and Defense Giant Inspired the Promulgation of the Foreign Corrupt Practices Act of 1977." *Accounting Historians Journal* 42 (1): 105–26. doi:10.2308/0148-4184.42.1.105.

Barr, A., and I. J. Galpeer. 1987. "McKesson & Robbins." *Journal of Accountancy* 163 (5): 159–61.

Barton, R. 1933. "Independent Audits for Investors." *Journal of Accountancy* 56 (2): 91–101.

Baumhart, R. C., S. J. 1961. "How Ethical are Businessmen?" *Harvard Business Review* 39 (July–August): 6–9.

Bishop, A. C., and R. H. Tondkar. 1987. "Development of a Professional Code of Ethics." *Journal of Accountancy* 163 (5): 97–100.

Broden, B. G., and S. E. Loeb. 1983. "Professional Ethics of CPAs in Tax Practice: An Historical Perspective." *Accounting Historians Journal* 10 (2): 81–97. doi:10.2308/0148-4184.10.2.81.

Bullard, J. H., and W. E. Snizek. 1988. "Factors Affecting the Acceptability of Advertisements Among Professionals." *Journal of the Academy of Marketing Science* 16 (2): 57–63. doi:10.1007/BF02723317.

Burns, D. C., J. W. Greenspan, and C. Harwell. 1994. "The State of Professionalism in Internal Auditing." *Accounting Historians Journal* 21 (2): 85–116.

Carey, J. L. 1937. "Editorial, 'Independence' of Accountants." *Journal of Accountancy* 63 (6): 407–8.

Carey, J. L. 1956. *Professional Ethics of Certified Public Accountants.* New York: American Institute of Certified Public Accountants.

Carey, J. L. 1969. *The Rise of the Accounting Profession From Technician to Professional 1896–1938.* New York: American Institute of Certified Public Accountants.

Carey, J. L. 1970. *The Rise of the Accounting Profession to Responsibility and Authority 1937–1969.* New York: American Institute of Certified Public Accountants.

Carey, J. L. 1975. "Old Style Independence." *Journal of Accountancy* 149 (5): 80.

Carey, J. L. 1979. "Early encounters between CPAs and the SEC." *Accounting Historians Journal* 6 (1): 29–37. doi:10.2308/0148-4184.6.1.29.

Carey, J. L., and W. O. Doherty. 1966. "The Concept of Independence – Review and Restatement." *Journal of Accountancy* 121 (1): 38–48.

Carson, R. 1962. *Silent Spring*. Greenwich, CT: Fawcett Publications Inc.

Ciulla, J. B. 2011. "Is Business Ethics Getting Better? A Historical Perspective." *Business Ethics Quarterly* 21 (2): 335–43. doi:10.5840/beq201121219.

Clow, K. E., R. E. Stevens, C. W. McConkey, and D. L. Loudon. 2009. "Accountants' Attitudes Toward Advertising: A Longitudinal Study." *Journal of Services Marketing* 23 (2): 124–31. doi:10.1108/08876040910946387.

Cook, J. M. 1987. "The AICPA at 100: Public Trust and Professional Pride." *Journal of Accountancy* 163 (5): 370–80.

Cordery, C. 2015. "Accounting History and Religion: A Review of Studies and a Research Agenda." *Accounting History* 20 (4): 430–63. doi:10.1108/08876040910946387.

Dailey M. J. 1984. "Cyclical Aspects of Twentieth Century American Accounting." *Accounting Historians Journal* 11 (2): 61–75. doi:10.2308/0148-4184.11.2.61.

Darling, J. R. 1977. "Attitudes Toward Advertising by Accountants." *Journal of Accountancy* 153 (February): 48–53.

De George, R. T. 1987. "The Status of Business Ethics: Past and Future." *Journal of Business Ethics* 6: 201–11. doi:10.1007/BF00382865.

Edwards, J. D. 1978. *History of Public Accounting in the United States*. Tuscaloosa, AL: The University of Alabama Press.

Gerde, V. W., M. G. Goldsby, and J. M. Shepard. 2007. "Moral Cover for Capitalism The Harmony-of-Interests Doctrine." *Journal of Management History* 13 (1): 7–20. doi:10.1108/17511340710715133.

Graeber, D. 2015. *The Utopia of Rules*. Brooklyn, New York and London: Melville House Publishing.

Haber, S. 1991. *The Quest for Authority and Honor in the American Professions, 1750–1900*. Chicago and London: The University of Chicago Press.

Hartley, R. V., and T. L. Ross. 1972. "MAS and Audit Independence: An Image Problem." *Journal of Accountancy* 134 (5): 42–51.

Hurdman, F. H. 1931. "Relation of Client and Accountant." *Journal of Accountancy* 52 (4): 297–304.

Husted, B. W. 2015. "Corporate Social Responsibility Practice from 1800–1914: Past Initiatives and Current Debates." *Business Ethics Quarterly* 25 (1): 125–41. doi:10.1017/beq.2014.1.

Joplin, J. P. 1914. "The Ethics of Accountancy." *Journal of Accountancy* 17 (3): 187–96.

Kaplan, R. S. 1984. "The Evolution of Management Accounting." *The Accounting Review* LIX (3): 390–418.

Knouse, S. B., V. D. Hill, and J. B. Hamilton III. 2007. "Curves in the High Road A Historical Analysis of American Business Codes of Ethics." *Journal of Management History* 13 (1): 94–107. doi:10.1108/17511340710715197.

Lee, T. 1995. "The Professionalization of Accountancy A History of Protecting the Public Interest in a Self-Interested Way." *Accounting, Auditing and Accountability Journal* 8 (4): 48–69.

Lowe, H. 1987. "Ethics in Our 100-Year History." *Journal of Accountancy* 163 (5): 78–87.

Mason, E. 1994. "Public Accounting – No Longer a Profession?" *The CPA Journal* 64 (7): 34–37.

Mautz, R. K., and H. A. Sharaf. 1961. *The Philosophy of Auditing*. American Accounting Association. Menasha, Wisconsin: George Banta Company, Inc.

McCloskey, D. N. 2006. *The Bourgeois Virtues Ethics for an Age of Commerce*. Chicago and London: University of Chicago Press. doi:10.7208/chicago/9780226556673.001.0001.

McMahon, T. F. 1999. "A brief history of American business ethics." In *A Companion to Business Ethics*. Edited by Robert E. Frederick, 342–52. Oxford: Blackwell Publishers Ltd. doi:10.1002/9780470998397.ch27

Mednick, R. 1990. "Independence: Let's Get Back to Basics." *Journal of Accountancy* 161 (5): 56–62.

Miranti, P. 1990. *Accountancy Comes of Age The Development of an American Profession 1886–1940*. Chapel Hill: The University of North Carolina Press.

Montagna, P. D. 1974. *Certified Public Accountants: A Sociological View of a Profession in Change*. Houston, TX: Scholars Book Co.

Montgomery, R. H. 1936. "Report of the President." *Journal of Accountancy* 62 (5): 322–33.

Moran, M., and G. J. Previts. 1984. "The SEC and the Profession, 1934–1984: The Realities of Self-Regulation." *Journal of Accountancy* 158 (1): 68–80.

Morf, D., D. L. Flesher, M. Hayek, S. Pane, and C. Hayek. 2013. "Shifts in Corporate Accountability Reflected in Socially Responsible Reporting: A Historical Review." *Journal of Management History* 19 (1): 87–113. doi:10.1108/17511341311286213.

Moyes, G. D., and K. Park. 1997. "Chief Financial Officers' Perceptions Concerning the IMA's Standards of Ethical Conduct." *Journal of Business Ethics* 16 (2): 189–94. doi:10.1023/A:1017948531122.

Myer, J. C. 1931. "Teaching the Accountant the History and Ethics of His Profession." *The Accounting Review* 6 (1): 47–50.

Neu, D. 2001. "Ethical Discourse and Canadian CA's, 1912–1997." *Journal of Business Ethics* 30 (3): 291–304. doi:10.1023/A:1006418809745.

Parker, L. D. 1994. "Professional Accounting Body Ethics: In Search of the Private Interest." *Accounting, Organizations, and Society* 19 (6): 507–25. doi:10.1016/0361-3682(94)90021-3.

Poullaos, C. 2009. "Professionalization." In *The Routledge Companion to Accounting History*, edited by J. R. Edwards and S. P. Walker, 247–73. Abingdon: Routledge.

Preston, A, M., D. J. Cooper, D. P. Scarbrough, and R. C. Chilton. 1995. "Changes in the Code of Ethics of the U.S. Accounting Profession, 1917 and 1988: The Continual Quest for Legitimation." *Accounting, Organizations, and Society* 20 (6): 507–46. doi:10.1016/0361-3682(94)00033-R.

Previts, G. J., and B. D. Merino. 1998. *A History of Accounting in America The Cultural Significance of Accounting.* Columbus: Ohio State University Press.

Reiter, S. A., and P. F. Williams. 2004. "The Philosophy and Rhetoric of Auditor Independence Concepts." *Business Ethics Quarterly* 14 (3): 355–76. doi:10.5840/beq200414329.

Richardson, A. P. 1931. *The Ethics of a Profession.* New York: The Century Co.

Richardson, A. P. 1932. "Selection of Auditors." *Journal of Accountancy* 62 (5): 321–26.

Roberts, A. R. 1987. "The 'Other' Public Accounting Organizations." *Journal of Accountancy* 5 (2): 41–42.

Roberts, D. H. 2010. "Changing Legitimacy Narratives About Professional Ethics and Independence in the 1930s Journal of Accountancy." *Accounting Historians Journal* 37 (2): 95–122. doi:10.2308/0148-4184.37.2.95.

Roberts, D. H. 2015 "Socialization of Novice Accounting Professionals Through Professional Discourse in 1931." *Accounting Historians Journal* 42 (2): 61–87. doi:10.2308/0148-4184.42.2.63.

Shaub, M. K. 1988. "Restructuring the Code of Professional Ethics: A Review of the Anderson Committee Report and its Implications." *Accounting Horizons* 2 (4): 89–97.

Smith, D. S. 2010. "The Elimination of the Unworthy: Credit Men and Small Retailers in the Progressive Era." *Journal of the Gilded Age and Progressive Era* 9 (2): 197–220. doi:10.1017/S1537781400003935.

Sterrett, J. E. 1907. "Professional Ethics." *Journal of Accountancy* 4 (6): 407–31.

Sutton, M. H. 1997. "Auditor Independence: The Challenge of Fact." *Accounting Horizons* 11 (1): 86–91.

Vogel, D. 1991a. "The Ethical Roots of Business Ethics." *Business Ethics Quarterly* 1 (1): 101–20. doi:10.2307/3857595.

Vogel, D. 1991b. "Business Ethics Past and Present." *The Public Interest* 102 (Winter): 49–64.

Wood, T. D., and A. J. Sylvestre. 1985. "The History of Advertising by Accountants." *Accounting Historians Journal* 12 (2): 59–72. doi:10.2308/0148-4184.12.2.59.

Zeff, S. A. 2003. "How the U.S. Accounting Profession Got Where it is Today: Part I." *Accounting Horizons* 7 (3): 189–205. doi:10.2308/acch.2003.17.3.189.

2

HISTORICAL DEVELOPMENT OF THE CODE OF ETHICS OF THE US PUBLIC ACCOUNTING PROFESSION

Charles Richard Baker

Introduction

This chapter discusses the historical development of the code of ethics of the US public accounting profession and argues that the primary purpose of such a code has been to regulate accounting practice rather than to enhance the ethical behavior of accounting professionals. The changes that have been made to the code of ethics over a period of many years have been prompted primarily by changes in the market for accounting services, to which professional accountants have responded out of economic interest. Extending Preston et al. (1995) and Beets (1999, 305), we contend that the changes to the code of ethics have been caused by market forces and the accounting profession's desire to expand its scope of its services. Agreeing with Parker (1994), we view these changes as accommodating the accounting profession's desire to enhance its socioeconomic status and professional autonomy and self-control rather than enhancing the ethical stature of the profession. The chapter also seeks to demonstrate that the ethical discourse of the US public accounting profession can be best located not in the pronouncements of the code of ethics but in certain self-forming practices that commence early in the career of a prospective accountant that shape the accountant into an idealized "ethical" being: not an ethical being who complies with a code of ethics but rather an ethical being who is self-regulated and self-formed into an idealized member of the profession. Thus, the informal ethical discourse of the accounting profession is concerned primarily with the kind of person a person aspires to be when he or she behaves in a "moral" manner as a public accountant. In the US public accounting profession, this is exemplified by the partner in a large international public accounting firm who is an "ethical being," not in the sense of one who conforms to a code of ethics but one who is able to satisfy clients, bring in new business, and be technically astute, while simultaneously exuding an impression of acting in the highest ethical manner (Covaleski et al. 1998; Baker 1993, 1999).

The remainder of the chapter is organized as follows. The second section provides an outline of key historical developments with respect to the code of ethics of the US public accounting profession. The third provides a theoretical discussion of codes of ethics based upon Foucault's concept of codified discourse. The final sections offer a critical examination of the changes to the code of ethics and link them back to the concept of codified discourse.

The historical development of the American code of ethics

Developments prior to the 1980s

The American Association of Public Accountants (AAPA) was the first body of professional public accountants to issue a code of ethics (Previts and Merino 1979; Preston et al. 1995). The 1905 code contained only two rules. One prohibited members of the AAPA from allowing nonmembers to practice using the member's name. The second rule prohibited the payment of referral fees (Carey 1965). This initial code clearly focused on regulating the practice of public accounting rather than serving the public interest.

When the American Institute of Accountants (AIA) was formed in 1917, its Rules of Professional Conduct contained eight rules. The first rule restricted the types of firms that could describe themselves as being members of the AIA (i.e., only sole practitioners or general partnerships could be members; all partners had to be CPAs). The second rule warned that willful misstatements of facts in any accounting work might result in the expulsion of the member from the AIA. The third rule was similar to the AAPA's 1905 rule that prohibited any person who was a not a member of from practicing in a member's name. The AIA's fourth rule proscribed the acceptance of commissions and brokerage fees. The fifth rule barred members from engaging in any business incompatible with public accounting. AIA's rule six required that members certify only accounting work prepared under their direct supervision. Rule seven mandated that a member inform the Secretary of the AIA before engaging in any lobbying activity. Finally, AIA rule eight prohibited encroachment on another member's business (Preston et al. 1995; Previts and Merino 1979). With the exception of the second rule, it can be seen that these rules regulated the practice of accounting rather than the ethical behavior of accountants. The 1917 AIA code involved "profession building" (Abbott 1988), which focuses on marking off exclusive domains in order to advance the commercial prospects of the profession's members. These early codes equated practice regulation with serving the public interest. However, it was not acknowledged that the primary purpose of the rules was to restrict competition.

Between 1917 and 1941, the number of rules in the code of ethics gradually increased. By 1941, there were 15 rules, including eight from the 1917 code. Among the new rules were ones that prohibited contingent fees, advertising, and competitive bidding. These rules were primarily directed toward regulating the practice of accountancy rather than enhancing ethical conduct. Interestingly, independence from clients was not part of the code at that time. The code's focus on regulating the practice of public accounting prevailed into the post-World War II period. Several codifications of the rules took place during the 1950s, '60s, and '70s, but the underlying principles remained virtually unchanged (Preston et al. 1995). In 1988, the AICPA adopted a revised code of ethics (now called a Code of Conduct) based on the recommendations of a special committee. The 1988 Code has served as the basis for subsequent revisions to the Code, including the most recent revision which took place in 2014 (see Section 2.5).

Developments in the 1990s and 2000s

In 1998, three events significantly affected the code of ethics of the US public accounting profession, and these events also had an impact on the codified discourse of the profession. The first event was the issuance of a new Uniform Accountancy Act (UAA).[1] The UAA addressed several regulatory and ethical issues, including acceptance of commissions, regulation of public accounting firms, public accountants working in non-accounting firms, and the experience requirements for entry into the profession (Kirtley and Brown 1998). The second event involved modifications and interpretations of the 1988 AICPA Code of Conduct. These modifications removed the remaining barriers to contingent fees and commissions and allowed alternative practice structures (APSs). The third event was the passage of the Sarbanes-Oxley Act in 2002.

Before discussing the UAA and the changes to the AICPA Code, the following section discusses changes in the market for accounting services. These changes had a significant impact on the ethical discourse of the US public accounting profession.

Changes in the market for accounting services

Since its inception, the US public accounting profession has been defined in terms of its provision of auditing and tax services. The designation certified public accountant conveyed the impression that public accountants provide a public service, primarily by through independent audits of company financial statements. While this continues to be the case, the market for accounting services has changed dramatically during the last three decades. These changes include the removal of prohibitions against advertising, competitive bidding and encroachment, competition and merger activity among accounting firms, growth in non-audit services, and the acquisition of public accounting firms by non-accounting firms. Many of these changes are related to efforts by public accounting firm to expand into alternative practice areas, including information technology and management consultancy that do not involve the traditional audit and tax services.

Two primary market segments distinguish the market for accounting services. The first segment is composed of large international accounting firms that perform audits for virtually all companies with publicly traded shares in the United States and who also provide a wide range of services for corporations and other entities. The second segment of the US public accounting profession is composed of many small and medium-sized practice units that provide accounting, tax, and other services to closely held businesses and individuals.

Non-auditing services began to constitute a significant portion of revenues for public accounting firms in the latter years of the 20th century. Even after the passage of the Sarbanes-Oxley Act of 2002, this continued to be the case. Many of the members of the US public accounting profession do not provide any type of audit service, nor are they even involved in the practice of public accounting (only 42% of the members of the AICPA are employed by public accounting firms) (AICPA 2012). The auditing revenues of all accounting firms declined during the 1990s, and it was only after the enactment of the Sarbanes-Oxley Act that audit revenues again began to increase (The Economist 2005). During the same time period, consulting revenues increased and revenues from "other services" also increased. These figures suggest that the nature of public accounting practice changed significantly in recent decades. In addition, there was a trend toward the acquisition of public accounting firms by non-accounting firms, such as American Express TBS (now part of RSM McGladry).

The business strategy of American Express TBS was illustrative of the changes in the market for accounting services. During the 1990s, TBS acquired small and medium-sized public accounting firms in 55 cities located in 18 states. Prior to a merger in 2005 with RSM McGladry, TBS employed more than 1,000 CPAs, making it one of the largest public accounting firms in the United States (Craig 1998). Previously, under the laws of most states, audits could be performed only by public accounting firms that were wholly owned by CPAs. To overcome this restriction, American Express TBS developed a business strategy that had the following features: TBS employed all of the personnel of the acquired public accounting firm, including the partners. The non-audit services previously performed by the public accounting firm were conducted under the TBS name. Even though it had no employees other than partners, the public accounting firm continued to be a licensed entity in the state of operation, and it performed audit services for clients. The public accounting firm leased the audit staff below the partner level from TBS and paid an administrative fee for the use of office space and equipment and other services. The partners supervised the audit work and issued reports in the public accounting firm's name (Craig 1998).

Although there was concern expressed about the TBS structure, various states approved the strategy after analyzing their public laws and discovering that the laws did not prevent such a structure. Since the law did not prevent it, certain ethical barriers that might have impeded the implementation of such structures needed to be changed as well. The business strategy of American Express TBS and other similar organizations (see Mancuso 1999 for a discussion of alternative forms of accounting practice) has therefore underscored the changes taking place in the market for accounting services. As a result, state regulatory boards of accountancy reexamined the manner in which the US public accounting profession was regulated (Huefner 1998). In response to these changes, the AICPA and the NASBA created the Uniform Accountancy Act (UAA) (D'Angelo 1998), and the AICPA modified its Code of Conduct. The following section describes the changes that were made to the UAA.

The Uniform Accountancy Act

In 1998, the AICPA and the NASBA issued a new UAA (Kirtley and Brown 1998). The UAA addresses a number of ethical and regulatory issues. Selected provisions of the UAA follow.

Substantial equivalency

Substantial equivalency means that the education, examination, and experience requirements of one state are comparable to the education, examination, and experience requirements in the UAA. If a state meets this test, its public accountants would be allowed to practice in other states without obtaining permission to do so. Substantial equivalency allows CPAs to practice in any state, but it also reduces the regulation of CPAs by individual states.

Experience requirement

A one-year experience would be requirement for licensure. Public accountants performing audit work may be required to meet additional experience requirements. Public accountants not doing audit work would be able to obtain the required one-year's experience in non-audit work. Non-audit experience could be performed while in industry or working for a non-CPA firm. Non-audit experience would be verified by a CPA, but such experience did not need to be under the supervision of a CPA.

CPAs practicing in non-CPA firms

CPAs could practice in non-accounting firms as long as they did not offer audit services. This provision was central to permitting companies like American Express TBS to employ CPAs and to offer accounting services traditionally performed by CPAs.

Non CPA-ownership of CPA firms

Most states specified that only CPAs could own public accounting firms. The UAA provided that CPAs only needed to own a majority of an accounting firm that performed audit services.

Commissions

The UAA ratified the agreement between the AICPA and the Federal Trade Commission, which allowed commissions to be paid.

CPA = CPA

All individuals who wanted to advertise their CPA credential would be allowed to do so, as long as they were subject to the same licensing requirements (Kirtley and Brown 1998).

Discussion

The UAA modified the concept of who and what a public accountant is. In the first place, CPAs would neither be trained nor engaged in auditing. The AICPA and the NASBA publicly acknowledged that ordinary CPAs would be educated in auditing only to a minor extent, if at all. The concept of a public accounting professional would then change. Most CPAs historically spent at least some time during their careers performing audits, and they often identified themselves as being a former member of a large public accounting firm. This is no longer the case.

Moreover, most professional accountants in the United States are employed by organizations that do not derive their primary revenues from auditing. The advent of business structures such as those of American Express TBS has exacerbated this trend. The notion that public accountants are professionals who practice in professional partnerships has all but disappeared. The UAA confirms the fact that the market for accounting services has moved beyond professionalism. The only increment in regulation under the UAA is related to mandatory continuing professional education. Other provisions have led to reductions in the regulation of accounting practice. These are market-driven changes that appeared at a point in time when the revenues from auditing declined in relation to other aspects of accounting practice. In effect, the public accounting profession decided that it no longer needed the market-restricting practices that the codes of ethics provided from 1917 through 1988. The changes enhanced the profession's ability to compete in alternative practice areas. The lesser degree of regulation provided ease of entry into alternative practice areas, allowing the profession to develop an entry into these areas.

Changes to the code of ethics as a result of the UAA and the changes in accounting services

Simultaneously with the issuance of the UAA, the AICPA Professionalism and Ethics Committee (PEEC) modified the AICPA's Code of Conduct. The changes to the code facilitated alternative practice structures such as those of American Express TBS. Essentially, this interpretation described the American Express TBS structure and indicated that the activities of American Express TBS and similar entities did not raise independence problems. Interpretation 101–14 purports to extend the provisions of the AICPA Code to the immediate supervisors of persons who are engaged in attest functions. This provision raises an interesting question, in that non-CPAs may supervise CPAs while they work for American Express TBS. Interpretation 101–14 related to the direct supervisors of CPAs even though the AICPA had no jurisdiction over such persons. The question of enforceability thus became paramount.

Other provisions of the AICPA Code changed the definition of who the client is when assessing whether a CPA can accept contingent fees, commissions, and referral fees. The changes stated that when a CPA provides professional services (such as investment advisory or other consulting services) for the owners or employees of an audit client or for an employee benefit plan sponsored by an audit client, the owners, employees, and benefit plan are considered separate from the audit client. Consequently, a CPA can request contingent fees and also sell products on commission to the owners and employees of an audit client (Spaulding 1998b). A ruling under Rule 302 of the code allowed the charging of contingent fees when providing investment advisory services for an audit client. These provisions raise questions about the independence of auditors, but they are consistent with the competition among professions discussed by Abbott (1988).

Criticisms of the changes

There have been a number of criticisms of the changes to the AICPA Code. Vincent Love, the former chairman of the New York State Society of CPA's Professional Ethics Committee, stated that he was "very concerned about the erosion of the appearance of independence" that appears in these changes. Love commented that "[t]he AICPA and the state society should think long and hard before allowing any service for a commission or contingent fee to be performed for owners of an attest client. You need to be very careful when separating the owner from the business in determining if you can accept contingent fees or commissions" (Spaulding 1998b).

The US Securities and Exchange Commission also criticized the changes. The SEC indicated that the changes which allowed alternative practice structures conflicted with SEC rules and would not be accepted for publicly traded companies (Spaulding 1998a). The changes to the code appeared to be primarily designed to accommodate the American Express TBS business structure. The change to ethics interpretation 505–2 states that if a CPA controls a non-accounting firm (i.e., TBS), then the non-accounting firm and its other owners and employees must comply with the AICPA Code. If the CPA does not control the non-accounting firm, the AICPA Code would not apply to the non-accounting firm, but it would apply to the CPA. Since more than 50% ownership defines control, it is unlikely that CPAs in the American Express TBS structure would be deemed to be in control; consequently, the AICPA Code does not apply to TBS or its non-CPA employees. Therefore, there is essentially no ethical structure for these new forms of accounting practice.

A question can also be raised whether a public accountant's independence, integrity, and objectivity is compromised if he or she is employed by two different firms while serving the same client (Mancuso 1999). The same persons are performing both audit and non-audit work, even though they are employed by two separate legal entities. The revenues of the public accounting firm flow to the non-accounting firm in exchange for the services provided to the public accounting firm (e.g., administrative fees and the salaries of accounting staff). Questions such as who is actually providing the services have not been answered (Mancuso 1999).

The Sarbanes-Oxley Act

The Sarbanes-Oxley Act of 2002 (SOX) has been described as "ground-breaking" legislation because of its creation of new institutional structures for the regulation of public accountancy but also for the breadth of its scope, which affects many different actors in the capital markets.

The law includes 11 titles comprising over 60 sections. The various provisions of SOX affect different parties in different ways. Among the sections, there are topics dealing with auditors and public accounting firms, corporations and their officers and directors, the Financial Accounting Standards Board (FASB), financial analysts, securities lawyers, financial analysts and investment banks. Perhaps the most important part of the law, from the perspective of the public accounting profession, is found in Title I, which created the Public Company Accounting Oversight Board (PCAOB).

The PCAOB is a quasi-governmental entity that operates under the aegis of the US Securities and Exchange Commission (SEC), but with independent funding provided through fees charged to corporations issuing securities pursuant to the US federal securities laws (SEC issuers). Section 102 of SOX requires all public accounting firms that audit SEC issuers to register with the PCAOB. The larger public accounting firms (those with more than 100 audit clients) must have their audit practices inspected annually by the PCAOB. The PCAOB has the authority to censure, fine, or suspend an accounting firm that violates its standards, rules, or regulations. The PCAOB also has the power to issue auditing standards, quality control standards, independence standards, and ethics standards for registered accounting firms. Essentially, SOX removed self-regulation from the US public accounting profession, thus causing a significant change in the ethical discourse of the profession.

Title II of SOX addresses auditor independence by prohibiting certain types of non-audit services if provided to audit clients (e.g., bookkeeping; information systems design and implementation; actuarial services; appraisal or valuation; internal audit; human resources; investment banking; and legal services)(section 201). Title II also requires mandatory audit partner rotation (section 203) and mandatory audit reports to audit committees (section 204), and it prohibits auditors from being hired as financial officers of the audit client for a period of one year (section 206). Rulings of the PCAOB under the SOX have prevented alternative practice structures for companies with publicly traded shares. Thus, the ethical discourse of the public accounting profession has had to adapt to the fact that the PCAOB has removed certain opportunities for the profession to exploit the market for non-audit services. However, due to the large increase in audit fees that resulted from the increased work required by SOX with respect to audits of internal control structures, the public accounting profession has not reacted strongly to the removal of self-regulation from the profession. In fact, the ethical discourse has been relatively silent with respect to many of the provisions of SOX.

The 2014 codification of the code of conduct

The AICPA Code of Professional Conduct was recodified on June 1, 2014, and became fully effective on December 15, 2015. Similar to the 1988 Code, the 2014 Code of Professional Conduct consists of principles and rules. Principles are ideals of ethical conduct and provide a broad conceptual framework for professional conduct. Rules provide more detailed guidance to help public accountants in carrying out their public responsibilities and are enforceable under AICPA bylaws.

One significant change in the revised 2014 code was the creation of a new section on "Ethical Conflicts" (1.000.020), which linked independence to the conflicts of interest provision. Conflicts may exist that create a potential impairment of integrity, objectivity, or professional skepticism, and the assessment of when a conflict of interest exists that impairs objectivity directly influences whether independence may be impaired.

Another change in the 2014 Code was the addition of a Conceptual Framework for Independence (1.210.010), which provides a structure to assess the importance of a conflict of interest with respect to independence in appearance. When a conflict exists, the public accountant is supposed to determine whether such influences, if present, create a threat to compliance with the rules. An example is a familiarity threat that exists because of a long or close relationship between senior personnel of the firm and the client or employee of the client with a key position. If a threat exists, the public accountant should determine whether the threat can be mitigated by safeguards (e.g., quality controls). If adequate safeguards exist, then the public accountant can provide the audit services; if the identified threats cannot be mitigated by any safeguards, then independence is impaired (Mintz 2018).

A question arises as to whether the public accounting profession is now relying too much on the threats and safeguards approach when conflicts of interest exist rather than prohibiting audit services when certain types of relationships exist. It seems questionable to leave assessments of threats and safeguards to the practitioner's judgment when conflicts exist, especially in light of the code provision that the effectiveness of safeguards will vary, depending on the circumstances. The problem with this situational ethics approach is that it leaves the question of whether independence is impaired open to interpretation (Mintz 2018).

Theoretical discussion of the purpose of a code of ethics

A review of prior literature reveals that practicing public accountants have produced a large amount of discourse pertaining to the code of ethics. This literature has generally maintained that the function of a code of ethics is to foster self-regulation in the public interest (see, for example, Higgins and Olson 1972; Olson 1979; Anderson 1985; Anderson and Ellyson 1986; Collins and McRae 1987; Larson 1987; Lowe 1987; Mason 1994).

In contrast, academic accountants have often taken a more critical view of the practicing profession's assertion that self-regulation through the code of ethics serves the public interest (e.g. Briloff 1990; Willmott, Cooper, and Puxty 1993; Mitchell et al. 1993; Parker 1994; Preston et al. 1995; Beets 1999). For example, Preston et al. (1995) examined certain changes in the code of ethics between 1917 and 1988. These authors argued that the changes during this period up to 1988 were the result of challenges to the profession's legitimacy and that the changes were attempts to fend off those challenges. Preston et al. also maintained that the changes to the code of ethics reflected wider transformations taking place in American society, such as a general reduction in religious beliefs.

Parker (1994) has argued that there are five functions for a code of ethics which largely focus on protection of the profession's self-interests.

1   *Professional insulation*: Ethical codes are constructed with a view to insulating the public accounting profession from observation and evaluation by outside parties.
2   *Interference minimization*: Avoiding or minimizing interference in what the accounting profession regards as its own domain, including the type and scope of work undertaken, style of organization adopted, position in the business community, and regulation of members and activities.
3   *Self-control*: Allowing the exercise of control over the profession's own activities and members.
4   *Professional authority*: Emphasizing the unique technical knowledge base of the profession, along with its resulting authority.
5   *Socioeconomic status preservation*: This function pertains to member competition, service pricing policies, transfer of clients among members, tendering practices, and so forth.

Beets (1999) has argued that the code of ethics "is an emaciated symbol of its former self." He maintained that even prior versions of the code of ethics "were not filled with ethical guidance but were corpulent with rules that mitigated practitioner competition." He also maintained that the changes to the code were the result of the accounting profession's acquiescing to agencies of the federal government. While I agree with Beets that the code of ethics has not restricted or reduced unethical behavior, I contend that market forces (rather than professional legitimacy and governmental influence) and the profession pecuniary desires have been the primary reasons for changes to the code. In support of this argument, I cite Abbott's (1988) argument that professions fight for established areas of jurisdiction. The "winning" profession has the privilege of dominating desirable work areas. Professions maintain dominance through competitive strategies (Abbott 1988, 216). For example, medical doctors drove out competitors (i.e., non-licensed medical practitioners) and subordinated the nursing profession (Abbott, 71–72). Likewise, lawyers and accountants have vigorously contested the area of tax practice and insolvency (Abbott 1988, 233). In recent years, the members of the US public accounting profession have been contesting the fields of information technology and management consultancy. This has caused a disruption in the codified discourse of the profession. As the US profession has sought to move into more lucrative practice areas, the code of ethics has needed to be modified to accommodate these efforts. The code can now be seen as serving primarily the interests of the profession by protecting and advancing its "turf" or domain. In this sense, the code of ethics has essentially become a public relations exercise to reassure the public that public accountants are maintaining high standards of integrity and ethical conduct.

A code of ethics as a codified discourse

A codified discourse comprises the totality of linguistic usages attached to a given social practice, which, in turn, constitutes a regularized way of acting that involves relationships between the semiotic sphere (to which texts belong), the sphere of mental representations, and the physical sphere (Marks 2006; Jary and Jary 1991). In social theory, a codified discourse is considered to be an institutionalized way of thinking or mental boundary, determining what can be validly said about a given topic and establishing "the limits of acceptable speech" – or acceptable truth (Butler 1997; Foucault 1970). Codified discourses construct our worldviews because they provide us with the means to communicate what we think about the world. Codified discourses are intimately linked with power. The allowable range of discourses at any given point in time is determined by an "episteme," which constitutes a total way of thinking about the world (Foucault 1970). Foucault's concept of codified discourse must be understood both in its particular form and in its more general form, as a framework that establishes the boundaries surrounding a particular discourse. In its more general sense, a discourse includes not only words but physical dispositifs, such as an organization chart. The dispositif comprises the network of relationships that connect and construct codified discourses (Foucault 1970).

According to Foucault, discourses emerge out of conflict. He argues that truth is not objective or absolute but rather emerges out of conflicts over goals and objectives. Because truth and power are inextricably linked, Foucault maintains that power relations are immanent to discourse. Furthermore, discourse has no essentialist meaning. The same discourse can change political sides, thereby being appropriated and modified; hence there is a "polymorphic tactics" of discourse. In addition, discourses are not created by subjects; rather, the subject is a social construction of discourse. An important aspect of Foucault's concept of codified discourse is that social phenomena are constructed from inside a discourse; there are no social phenomena outside of a discourse.

In *The History of Sexuality* (1986), Foucault examined "ethics" as a form of codified discourse. Foucault viewed morality as a meta-concept incorporating several sub-concepts, such as moral codes, moral behavior, and ethics. The moral code encompasses the set of rules (e.g., codes of ethics) established by dominant entities such as professional institutes, governments, religious institutions, schools and universities, etc. The moral code includes the rules and regulations that must be followed upon pain of sanction. These rules exist within a "complex interplay of elements that counterbalance and correct one another, and cancel each other out on certain points, thus providing for compromises and loopholes" (Foucault 1986). Because Foucault did not believe that the moral code is immutable, there is a significant difference between Foucault's concept of a moral code and a deontological view of ethics. In contrast, moral behavior describes the actual behavior of individuals with respect to their moral code. The questions to be addressed here are whether individuals comply more or less fully with their code; the manner in which they obey or resist an interdiction or a prescription; and the manner in which they respect or disregard a set of values. Finally, from Foucault's perspective, ethics is concerned with the kind of relationship a person has with himself or herself and the manner in which the individual constitutes himself or herself as a moral subject. Thus, ethics deals with the manner in which a person conducts himself or herself so as to become the "right kind" of person. Ethics deals with the self-forming practices that are directed toward creating an individual as an ethical subject (Foucault 1986).

From a public accounting perspective, the self-forming practices associated with ethical behavior are not to be found in codes of ethics. They are to be found instead in the practices that commence early in the career of a prospective accountant, ranging from difficult entry level examinations, to social rituals associated with joining accounting institutes, to the recruitment rituals of public accounting firms, to the long work hours devoted to tedious tasks. These ritualized practices are self-forming exercises that shape the prospective accountant into an idealized ethical being; not an ethical being who complies with a code of ethics but rather an ethical being who is self-regulated and self-formed into an idealized member of the public accounting profession. The disciplinary and self-forming practices of the public accounting profession are closely associated with the kind of person an individual aspires to be when he or she behaves in a moral manner (Covaleski et al. 1998; Baker 1993, 1999). Rather than the formal pronouncements of the code of ethics, it is instead the informal (yet codified) ethical discourse surrounding the "professional accountant" as an idealized being that constitutes the ethical discourse of US public accounting profession. We will return to this idea in a later section, but first we will examine the historical background of the code of ethics of the US public accounting profession in order to demonstrate its purpose in regulating the practice of public accounting.

Discussion

The changes in the market for accounting services that has occurred in the United States have had a significant impact on the ethical discourse of the US public accounting profession. A code of ethics created during a time when the public accounting profession sought recognition as a legitimate profession has been seen as an anachronism in a period of post-professionalism where market forces and expansion into alternate practice areas have been the primary determinants of public accounting practice. The historical evolution of the codes of ethics indicates that the code has reacted to market forces in order to accommodate new market opportunities. It is insufficient to focus on the formal discourse of the profession without recognizing the more informal ethical discourse (i.e., the codified discourse in a Foucaultian sense), both in the way that formal and informal ethical codes restrict the market for professional services and also the way that they open up such markets. As Beets has said, the AICPA Code became an emaciated version of its former self. This slimming effect allowed public accountants to pursue market opportunities wherever and whenever it seemed profitable to do so. The AICPA Code, "asked very little of practitioners beyond what is already required by court precedents, laws, and regulations" (Beets 1999, 313). Beets argued that there "should be a repeal of the rules, interpretations, and rulings of the AICPA Code while retaining the principles, thereby providing high ethical standards that would serve as guiding tenants in professional practice." This may be a meaningless gesture unless the idea of serving the public interest becomes a more important focus. Effectively, the formal code of ethics serves public relations functions. Through the code, the AICPA seeks to convince the public that CPAs adhere to high standards of ethical conduct and integrity. If this idea is accepted by the public, the perception will then allow CPAs to pursue economic opportunities with few limitations.

We return here to the subject of ethical discourse as envisioned by Foucault. In *The History of Sexuality* (1986), Foucault was intrigued by ethics as a form of discourse. Foucault considered the subject of morality to be meta-concept that incorporated sub-concepts like moral codes, moral behavior, and ethics. While the moral code includes rules like codes of ethics, moral behavior involves the actual behavior of individuals with respect to their moral code. From Foucault's perspective, ethics is concerned with the kind of relationship a person has with himself or herself and the manner in which the individual constitutes himself or herself as a moral subject. Ethics focuses on the self-forming practices that are intended to create an individual as an ethical subject (Foucault 1986).

In the US public accounting profession, the self-forming practices are not found in the code of ethics. Instead they are located in the practices that commence early in the career of a prospective accountant, ranging from difficult entry level examinations, to social rituals associated with accounting institutes, to the recruitment rituals of public accounting firms, to the long work hours devoted to tedious tasks expected of junior accountants. These ritualized practices are self-forming exercises that shape the prospective accountant into an idealized ethical being; not an ethical being who complies with a code of ethics but rather an ethical being who is self-disciplined and self-formed into the idealized member of the public accounting profession. The disciplinary and self-forming practices of the accounting profession are closely associated with the kind of person an individual aspires to be when he or she behaves in a moral manner. This is exemplified by the partner in a large international public accounting firm who is an ethical being, not in the sense of conforming closely to the code of ethics, but one who is able to satisfy clients, bring in new business, and be technically astute, while simultaneously exuding an image of activity in the highest ethical manner (Covaleski et al. 1998; Baker 1993, 1999). Regardless of the formal discourse found in the code of ethics, it is the informal (codified) discourse about the ideal professional that constitutes the true discourse of the public accounting profession. It is this informal discourse that has the greatest power over accounting professionals.

Conclusion

The purpose of this chapter has been to examine the evolution of the code of ethics of the US public accounting profession. Since the emergence of the profession in the late 19th century, there have been various changes to the code of ethics. In examining these changes, it is clear that the formal code has focused on the regulation and control of accounting practice rather than on the ethical behavior of accountants. As discussed by Preston et al. (1995), prior codes aspired to produce legitimacy for the profession. In contrast, Beets (1999) argued that governmental influences actually drove many of the changes. As discussed in this chapter, market forces have also affected the code in significant ways. This development raised questions about the ethical discourse of the public accounting profession that were addressed by the AICPA and NASBA through the Uniform Accountancy Act and making changes to the AICPA Code. These changes removed the few remaining rules that were formerly considered to be important features of professionalism (i.e., rules about encroachment, competitive bidding, advertising, commissions, contingency fees, and prohibited forms of business practice). The primary purpose of these changes was to facilitate the competitive ability of public accountants in alternate practice areas. While the remaining sections of the code focused on independence, integrity, and objectivity, the AICPA did not stress these areas. In fact, these principles should be elevated beyond their "goal-oriented, positively stated and inspirational" status. These principles should become the hallmarks of a rejuvenated public accounting profession. Without a renewed emphasis on ethical excellence, a question remains: Will public accountants be dedicated to the principles of independence, integrity, and objectivity, or will they concentrate instead on achieving success in a competitive environment?

Note

1 Pursuant to American law, a "Uniform" act is a model law. A "Uniform" act does not constitute law in any jurisdiction until it is adopted in that jurisdiction.

References

Abbott, A. 1988. *System of Professions: An Essay on the Division of Expert Labor.* Chicago, IL: University of Chicago Press.

AICPA. 2012. *Membership Figures*, American Institute of CPAs, New York. Accessed on March 11, 2012. www.aicpa.org/About/Pages/About.aspx.

Anderson, G. (1985), "A Fresh Look at Standards of Professional Conduct." *Journal of Accountancy* (September): 91–106.

Anderson, G., and R. Ellyson. 1986. "Restructuring Professional Standards: The Anderson Report." *Journal of Accountancy* (September): 92–104.

Baker, C. R. 1993. "Self-Regulation in the Public Accounting Profession: The Response of the Large, International Public Accounting Firms to a Changing Environment." *Accounting, Auditing, Accountability Journal* 6 (2): 68–80.

Baker, C. R. 1999. "Theoretical Approaches to Research on Accounting Ethics." *Research on Accounting Ethics* 5: 115–34.

Beets, S. 1999. "The Vanishing AICPA Code: Past, Present, and Future Significance." *Research on Accounting Ethics* 5: 289–326.

Briloff, A. 1990. "Accountancy and Society: A Covenant Desecrated." *Critical Perspectives on Accounting* 1: 5–30.

Butler, J. 1997. *Excitable Speech.* London: Routledge.

Carey, J. L. 1965. *The CPA Plans for the Future.* New York: American Institute of Certified Public Accountants.

Collins, S., and T. McRae. 1987. "Plan to Restructure Professional Standards." *Journal of Accountancy* (July): 71–75.

Covaleski, M. A., M. W. Dirsmith, J. B. Heian, and S. Samuel. 1998. "The Calculated and the Avowed: Techniques of Discipline and Struggles Over Identity in Big Six Public Accounting Firms." *Administrative Science Quarterly* 43 (2): 293–328.

Craig, J. 1998. "The Real American Express Tax and Business Services." *The CPA Journal* (February): 26–32.

D'Angelo, D. 1998. "American Express Enters NY Market with a Bang." *The Trusted Professional* 1 (1): 1.

Foucault, M. 1986. *The History of Sexuality, Volume 2.* New York: Vintage Books.

Foucault, M. 1970. *The Order of Things: An Archaeology of the Human Sciences.* Translated by A. Sheridan-Smith. New York: Random House.

Higgins, T., and W. Olson. 1972. "Restating the Ethics Code: A Decision for the Times." *Journal of Accountancy* (March): 33–39.

Huefner, R. 1998. "The Future of Non-CPA Ownership." *The CPA Journal* (February); 14–19.

Jary, D., and J. Jary. 1991. *Collins Dictionary of Sociology*. London: Harper Collins.

Kirtley, O., and M. Brown. 1998. "New Regulations for a New World." *Journal of Accountancy* (November): 65–67.

Larson, R. 1987. "For the Members, by the Members." *Journal of Accountancy* (October): 116–22.

Lowe, H. 1987. "Ethics in Our 100-Year History." *Journal of Accountancy* (May): 78–87.

Mancuso, A. 1999. "Alternative Forms of Practice: More than Just American Express." *The CPA Journal* (January): 14–21.

Marks, L. 2006. *A Little Glossary of Semantics*, Accessed April 22, 2011 from, www.revue-texto.net/Reperes/Glossaires/Glossaire_en.html#social%20practice.

Mason, E. 1994. "Public Accounting – No Longer a Profession?" *The CPA Journal* (July): 34–37.

Mintz, S. 2018. "Accounting in the Public Interest: An Historical Perspective on Professional Ethics." *The CPA Journal* (March): www.cpajournal.com/2018/03/19/accounting-public-interest/ accessed: August 23, 2018.

Mitchell, A., T. Puxty, P. Sikka, and H. Willmott. 1993. "Ethical Statements as Smokescreens for Sectional Interests: The Case of the UK Accounting Profession." *Journal of Business Ethics* 12: 161–73.

Olson, W. 1979. "The Eye of the Storm." *Journal of Accountancy* (March): 76–81.

Parker, L. D. 1994. "Professional Accounting Body Ethics: In Search of the Private Interest." *Accounting, Organizations and Society* 19 (6): 507–25.

Preston, A., D. Cooper, P. Scarbrough, and R. Chilton. 1995. "Changes in the Code of Ethics of the U.S. Accounting Profession, 1917 and 1988: The Continual Quest for Legitimation." *Accounting, Organizations and Society* 20 (6): 507–46.

Previts, G., and B. Merino. 1979. *A History of Accounting in America*. New York: Ronald Press Publication-John Wiley and Sons.

Spaulding, A. 1998a. "SEC Critiques Proposed AICPA Ethics Changes." *The Trusted Professional* (September): 14.

Spaulding, A. 1998b. "AICPA Proposal Redefines 'Client': Permits Commissions in Relation to Attest Clients." *The Trusted Professional* (December): 1.

The Economist. 2005. "Special Report: A Price Worth Paying? – Auditing Sarbanes-Oxley." *The Economist* 375 (8427): 82–84.

Willmott, H., D. Cooper, and A. Puxty. 1993. "Maintaining Self-Regulation: Making 'Interests' Coincide in Discourses on the Governance of the ICAEW." *Accounting, Auditing and Accountability Journal*: 68–93.

3

IN OUR TIME

Accountant ethics and historical relativity

Timothy J. Fogarty

Accounting scholars who focus their attention on the ethics of accounting practice do so in order to learn how it might be possible for the accounting profession to be better positioned in order to do good in the world. Each gathering of these scholars should pose the question why, after all the study of accountant ethics over many years that researchers have been at work in this area, good answers that would amount to progress have not emerged. The purpose of this chapter is to resuscitate the question and to offer an answer that is not really an answer but a provocation. Dialogue is important, and therefore the hope is to spur others into formulating their own positions.

Perhaps more than other forms of research, the study of ethics should remind us of the time in which we live. That which we consider correct, or even appropriate, is subject to change over time. Although transitions in the normative realm are gradual, and therefore imperceptible in the short run, they require recognition as a means of understanding the historical limitations of our scholarly efforts.

This chapter takes a much different approach to accountant ethics than is found in much of the literature. Rather than trying to isolate a single empirical regularity, an attempt is made to make the assumptions of our historical period more visible. This "30,000 foot" context is termed modernism and is contrasted to a previous period (premodernism) and a slowly emerging alternative (postmodernism). Since the transition from premodernism to modernism lies in the historical past, an intuitive appreciation of it exists. More attention is required for a future movement that is neither broadly accepted nor fully formed.

We live in a "modern age," so "modernism" is a convenient way to describe a host of attitudinal and institutional circumstances that most of us accept without question as essential or commonsensical. This includes a secular state that is accountable to the public, professions that serve the public interest, capitalism as a dominant economic system that provides useful incentives and resultant allocations of resources, and a belief in inevitable progress. Bolstered by the scientific method, modernism has prevailed over earlier world orders based on religion, kinship, and primitive technical knowledge. Even in such an enviable position, modernism may not be sustainable. Accordingly, the possibility of a new way of knowing and being should be entertained. This chapter makes the case that sufficient "cracks" in modernism have appeared such that we may require a new template. In other words, we cannot expect to make "progress" in the conventional sense because we are increasingly out of step with unrecognized or unacknowledged changes in our world.

This chapter is organized into two subsequent sections. The first identifies how the central notions of modernity shape the conventional knowledge about accountants' ethics. As modernism proves to offer an incomplete and increasingly unsatisfactory answer, ethics research becomes problematic. The second section shows that these are different pathways of approaching truth about this topic. To the extent that we can reset our research upon postmodern assumptions, there may be more promise for ethics research. In both sections, propositions attempt to summarize the salient aspects of the narrative. This will allow critics to focus on its specific elements.

Ethical inquiry as a modernistic enterprise

This section offers a number of propositions that collectively support the conclusion that the study of ethics is ill suited to the current era. The consequence of this section is to further the notion that research progress, as conventionally understood, should not be expected.

Accounting ethics attempts to establish itself as a field of investigation equivalent to any other. Accordingly, it seeks to deploy a grand theory from which to accumulate regularities about behavior. This approach assumes that a singular, measurable truth exists and that progress toward its revelation, albeit slow at times, is inevitable. At the same time, the process of inquiry is haunted by a yearning for a simpler time less marked by the arms-length spirit of the day whereby all human relations are transactional. This section discusses accounting ethics as a product of this increasingly weary age.

Debatable proposition 1: theory guides our work

Although a singular theory about the ethics of accountants has not emerged, strong presumptions about theory exist in the literature. These ideas limit the search of theory, as they simultaneously provide inadequate structure for its continuation.

As members of the business school, academic accountants are trained to adhere primarily to the insights developed in the mainstream economics discipline. For these purposes, we believe in a calculus of comparison between costs and benefits. We also maintain as a first-order premise that people will predictably respond if this balance is tipped. Our thinking is micro-marginalist, as we more or less are interested in prices, quantities, and steady state equilibriums.

Accounting researchers interested in ethics cross-fertilize their mooring to the economics mothership with an auxiliary tether to modern psychology. Since we are all interested in behavior, we subscribe to the psychological idea that people differ in their motivations, their information processing schemata, and their normative beliefs. Although psychology lacks the mainstream agreement present in economics, it provides a rich tableau of variables from which accounting ethics research can draw.

Together economics and psychology are the great theoretical contributions of modernism. Accounting ethics would seem well grounded at the intersection of these two traditions. After all, accounting practice generates profits in classic capitalistic ways, but accountants remain people whose interests are more diverse.

Grand as these theoretical sources appear from the perspective of the accounting discipline, they also leave much to be desired. First, one needs considerable faith to believe that either body of knowledge produces the predictions that we need. Both become less certain the more we examine them. Both psychological and economic knowledge are continually undermined by the empirical evidence collected in their names.[1] Second, only by having been very selective within these disciplines can we even extract the uniformities that we invoke. For example, we need analytically to separate the micro-perspective from wider macro contexts for economic analysis. In psychology, we choose when to stress the cognitive and when to focus on the motivational. Furthermore, to what extent we choose to believe that people are influenced by others is highly inconsistent from one application to another. We think we have the theory that we need, but we do not.

Should we be so concerned that there is such reasonable disagreement in the places from which we look to borrow our theories? Could it be that by not knowing that we have choices, we are choosing badly? More likely, our failure to appreciate that we have been selective has forced us to overreach our theories. When our results are mixed, it is likely that we had the wrong expectations or the wrong data. Theoretical uncertainty introduces all sorts of explanatory possibilities.

The answer to why we have tended to make the choices that we have starts with our academic training. Few among accounting scholars did dissertations in accounting ethics, and we have not had the luxury of a lengthy period wherein we could survey the extant theoretical choices. Most of us undertook topics fairly far from this area. Our appreciation of economics and psychology is predicated upon the needs of these other topics. What we have available to us is skewed systematically by virtue of our theoretical lacunae. Accounting's use of psychological and economic theories is for manipulating behavior in the pursuit of ends that have not undergone any serious ethical scrutiny. The consequences for the people whose behavior is manipulated is largely unexamined.

First and more importantly, our work strongly promotes the primacy of the individual practicing professional. Despite the fact that accountants tend to be employees of firms for greater portions of their careers, we scarcely choose to characterize the firm as the actor of consequence. The focus on the individual allows us to imagine the meaningfulness of ethical codes as statements of the accepted social contract. It also facilitates a psychological orientation that helps us characterize shortcomings in behavior or attitudes as merely demographic variation or the result of flawed training.

Thus, we are in a situation worse than not having theory. We believe we have good theory and therefore we do not wander from it. The phenomenon that we see by using our theory seems like the only game in town. Thus, we talk in circles.

Debatable proposition 2: "normal" science will lead gradually to the next paradigm

Graduate school usually includes an introduction to Thomas Kuhn's (1962) book about so-called scientific revolutions. For most, this analysis provides a convenient rationale for the importance of what we are doing in the accounting field. Our research contributions, according to this line of thought, make modest contributions to the revising of what we believe. In this way, the path for the next and better paradigm is paved. Our "normal" work enables a future tectonic shift toward the truth.

Kuhnian interpretations of the history of the natural sciences provide lofty aspirations that crash when imported to the social sciences and burn when applied to accounting. The best one can do is to suggest that Pacioli's (Geijsbeek 1914) double entry protocols created a paradigm of sorts. This launched the normative debate over concepts such as "asset," "income" and "expense" that preoccupied accounting academics for many decades and can still be seen in the discourse surrounding accounting standard setting. Academic work in this area succumbed to a new orientation traditionally attributed to Ball and Brown (1968) or the early work of William Beaver (1968), in which accounting was more generically conceived as information that could be used to price securities or to compensate executives. The later incursion of principal/agent theory (Watts and Zimmerman 1986) into accounting further diminished the consumers of accounting data to robots maximizing their narrow economic interests. This economic orientation made moot questions about how people *should* behave. This refocused accounting research away from what should be to the consequences of what was and the possibilities of what could be.

The field of ethical study in accounting is constructed on the same scientific basics as any other. With the assumption that knowledge about ethics is obtained through the application of the methods of natural science, researchers sought to build a set of factual statements that could serve as the field's foundation. The idea that the normative nature of ethics would not preclude the possibility of knowledge that was objective and independent of the actors allowed these efforts to proceed toward a set of reliable propositions about behavior. Although ethical knowledge was behavioral in nature and therefore would always be less deterministic than other fields of study, very little reason existed to doubt that ethical study could not develop as firm a footing as many other areas of study.

The lack of usable paradigm has also impaired the structure of development in accounting ethics. What study would the researchers of this field point to as consequential? The only contender proved to be Rest (1979), who applied the work of Kohlberg (1984), who, in turn, applied the work of Piaget (1932). The early work of Larry Ponemon (1990, 1992) and his associates showed us how this theory could be empirically rendered into bite-sized chunks. This nomination would soon devolve to the measure used, wherein ethicality came to be understood as one's position on a scale of stage progression. The traction created by this work was one of convenience and opportunism rather than of original ideas or unique perspective. Despite an accumulation of evidence that the central ideas and measures of this legacy are flawed, they continue to be our ongoing paradigm.

Our decision to believe and to persevere with the notion that accountants are arrayed on a set of stages enables countless applications. Usually, ethicality is an independent variable that contributes to the explanation of some other behavior of interest.

When our paradigm is no more than a measure or a measurement approach, we cannot afford to question it too closely. Instead, we use it as a means to an end rather than an end in itself. Without a truly unifying perspective, a thousand applications amount to little. Now that all the obvious studies have been done, where do we go?

Lacking real knowledge, we resort to metaphor and anecdote. This work is both entertaining and lively. Read the *Wall Street Journal*, paraphrase the atrocity, and tell us what it is just like. Enron launched hundreds of "ethics" papers, mostly written with an indifference to the ongoing progression of this literature. All the shenanigans revealed as part of the 2008 financial crisis brought on by the financial sector/housing market implosion kept up the effort. One should anticipate that our current pandemic will bring us more of the same. However, volume should not be confused with progress.

Debatable proposition 3: the study of ethics is a reflection of our times

More than any other field, ethical studies are grounded in a past that is becoming progressively more difficult to recapture. Ethical analysis, in holding out the existence of a correct behavior or a correct attitude, conjures a time gone by when people adhered to such standards. Without such a realistic historical benchmark, the belief that ethical behavior is possible and is at all reasonable as a yardstick for conduct is difficult to sustain.

In the Western world, the simpler era when the standard of ethicality was established is commonly associated with organized religion. When religious faith was closer to the center of social organization, ethical action had a power and consequence for people that was unparalleled (MacIntyre 1984). This era preceded the rise of the independent and secular state, the growing separation of religion and the polity as an established doctrine, and the emergence of science as the dominant engine of social change. Nonetheless, drawing upon the normative power of the first period offers leverage against the limitations of the second period.

The characterization of the world that we now find ourselves in as corrupt and morally challenged appears *de rigueur* for ethical research. We have indeed lost our way, as evidenced by the thousand stories of countless individuals who violated the trust bestowed upon them, usually to secure some ill-gotten gain. Motivating ethical research has never been a problem; it does not even require the rash of frauds that occurred shortly after the turn of the century. We will never come to a moment when we should not expect another installment of the apparent triumph of greed and opportunism over fairness and trust. At no time within memory has there been inadequate evidence to establish that people are not as good as they should be. Each new episode helps us forget those that have gone before and perhaps redraw the materiality line at a less ethical place.

Whether people are worse now than they ever have been before is doubtful. Once one controls for more systematic linkages through the economy that makes few acts localized, we cannot be sure if in fact we are just seeing better reportage. More advanced technology also facilitates more interlocking financial connections, which magnifies the potential dollar amount of any dishonesty.

A good deal of our adherence to the purity of the past resides in our continuing loyalty to the classic model of professionalism. The essence of this arrangement is the expectation that certain occupations are differentially obliged to pursue the public interest. Professionals are required to sacrifice some degree of personal advancement and wealth maximization in order to further benefits that can be more widely shared. Thus, our outrage over deficits in the behavior of external auditors exceeds our reaction to the many business leaders who prioritize the welfare of stockholders over all other legitimate stakeholders. The social contract stipulations of classic professionalism harken back the image of the priesthood in that special behavioral stipulations are seen as necessary and right for those whom we have chosen to trust the most.

The golden era of professionalism never existed. People have always used their titles and their social memberships to enhance personal gain. What may have changed is the cloak that disguised self-interest and the transparency with which avarice is tolerated. Let us remember that the so-called "golden era" was also marked by systematic refusals to compete and by blatant employment discriminations that injured many deserving parties.

In sum, the spirit of the age has allowed much that the ethics academy does to slip within that which is now taken-for-granted. By banging the drum of a present crisis, we get intellectually sloppy. We invent a mythology and a history that fits our purposes. By not seeing assumptions and constraints, the work is unable to transcend the boundaries that we are now increasingly recognizing.

Debatable proposition 4: we know moral truth

Ethics research may be unique in its straddle between normative prescription and empirical detachment. In science, the observed association between a certain condition and a resultant event holds, with a high degree of confidence, that the researchers' opinion about what association is preferable is not a major element. Unfortunately, the existence of a singular virtuous state that is established *a priori* pervades the accounting ethics literature. That the researcher has a preferred outcome is often very clear and unbalanced in its articulation. Although we appreciate the conflict that this creates with the norms of science, we excuse ourselves based on the obvious importance of improving our world with the correctness of our positions.

Accepting that moral indignation might produce the passion necessary to motivate the pursuit of our work, we still cannot conclude that it is more likely to produce good work. Believing to the contrary requires one to open the question about why any work is done. If one lacks the spirit rendered by evildoers that must get their comeuppance, will the work necessarily be inferior? The idea that one result is necessary and its opposite flawed is a dangerous precedent.

Confidence about what is right not only might be a source of bias but also essentially arbitrary. Many things are wrong, but we choose to react to only some of them. All organizations do some actions that may not be great offenses (perhaps strategic processes or being moderately inequitable), but they would not like them publicized beyond their boundaries. Every profession has similar "dirty little secrets" that enable corners to be cut and deviations from the letter of behavior to occur. Collectively we agree to "look the other way," essentially extending a belief that the efficiencies that are gained offset the harm that may be caused. Additionally, we argue that the extras earned by moderate forms of deviance are necessary additions to the incentives of key participants. Joining the club essentially entails a slight redrawing of the line between right and wrong, parsing perhaps in a technical sense when we want.

Over time, some environmental shift also occurs in our moral sense. That which once was considered wrong does not become right. However, that which used to be wrong gradually steps into a moral neutrality. Acts that used to be condemned, and therefore avoided by most, lose their strict and universal sanction. The reputational damage that used to be inevitable becomes less of a problem to endure or less certain to happen. The loss of stigma is an interesting conclusion in that it expresses the uncertainty that we feel about an act. Whereas before the circumstances were irrelevant as the reputational loss was automatic, we now enter a new place where we make consequences conditional on the specifics. The willingness to excuse tempts some to offset their behavior with exculpatory rhetoric that is occasionally successful. In fact, that which was once misbehavior of a grievous nature now becomes the basis for notoriety if not celebrity. Our sense of shame seems to have lost its power for self-accountability.

Our disgust about moral underpinnings extends to whom we nominate as heroes, as well as whom we choose to vilify. Whereas more that deserved vilification through moral approbation have escaped in the modern era, we have changed the nature of those that we celebrate. The rise of the CEO as modern cultural icon suggests a shift toward success as the ultimate exemption. We celebrate not those who deserved to do well, but those who did well even if it means overlooking some of the means used in the process. Business leaders who succeeded in capturing market share and bringing us products/services that enhanced our life as consumers we allow to immiserate workers and despoil communities. On the other hand, we can barely tolerate whistleblowers. Within professions, despite lip service to work–life balance, those held up for admiration are those who sacrificed the most for the client. Those who took principled stands against clients we admire only if doing so saved the firm additional costs and subsequently discovered embarrassments with the advantage of hindsight.

Our growing ambivalence about moral right has great consequence for ethics research. The need to demonstrate the value of ethics rather than establish that as a maintained hypothesis turns us away from concern over the nature of ethics. We move from dependent to independent variable when we feel compelled to associate certain levels of ethics with other outcomes for which there is more of an indigenous appetite.

Debatable proposition 5: we are in control

The major advantage of science is the increase in causal knowledge. In order to obtain desired results and avoid undesirable ones, we must appreciate their antecedents and have some understanding of the transformation process. Our lives have benefitted in countless ways from the accumulation of this knowledge. Each success of enhanced mastery calls for more to be sought and for more control over the previously unknown.

The greatest achievements made have occurred in those matters that are mostly reducible to their physical properties. The social realm has remained somewhat more resistant to strict causality. At best, here we have had to content ourselves with statistical associations that fall well short of causation. We suspect in many instances that a host of factors may be implicated in a certain result, but we cannot say how they combine. Nor can we rule out the relevance of other conditions that cannot be isolated or measured. Even that which we do know tends to be trumped by factors that might be called political correctness, allowing them to be disbelieved by many.

The business school is a classic example of how inadequate causal knowledge limits what we know. Observing the winners and losers in the market place, theories are developed that "explain" their differences. Strategy courses cheerlead the "obvious" superiority of the behaviors of the winners. "Monday morning quarterbacking" also renders that which had been plausible into the dustbin of history if it failed. However, in a dynamic environment, such prescriptions will prove unable to sustain an advantage. This method of anecdotal knowledge construction falls short when we try to predict the next set of winners.

Within the realm of business topics, those matters that transcend the individual are the most troublesome. When people get together, a dimension beyond psychology comes into play. This further reduces outcome certainty. When we transcend the small group or dyad, reaching the full organization, more complexity ensues. Our knowledge of how these associations constrain or encourage behavior is primitive at best and maybe nonexistent.

Whereas the maximization of profits has some degree of uncertainty, it seems very straightforward relative to ethicality. Ethicality is shared uncomfortably as an attribute dependent upon the agency of specific individuals but ascribable to the benefit of the organization or community. The extent to which ethical behavior is consistent with other objectives of the organization is uncertain unless one has a calculus that balances short- and long-term horizons. Thus, organizations lack control over how ethical their members should be and lack a specific target for how much good behavior is really desired. Research can pretend that these ambiguities do not exist by charging either individuals or organization with complete responsibility and by asserting that ethicality is never oversubscribed.

Debatable proposition 6: free will exists

The essence of ethicality is choice. The selection of an alternative more likely to injure others is typically condemned as unethical, especially if its selection results in personal gain. Here, complete knowledge of results may not be needed if an individual either acts with reckless indifference to the prospect of collateral damage or has sufficient reason to believe that adverse consequences to others are made more likely by the action chosen. Without choice, an individual can rarely be blamed.

In a literal sense, choice would seem always to exist. Tempted to perpetrate a known evil, members of organizations can always refuse. Consequences might be extreme, including marginalization and dismissal. When incentives of an extrinsic sort are heavily aligned in favor of one alternative, choice may not exist in a real sense. While it is true that an individual does not have to pursue tangible rewards, their alignment is neither accidental nor incidental.

Choice also entails some degree of mental freedom. How one weighs both the likelihood and the size of consequences stemming from one's actions cannot be *a priori* impressions. Instead, they are the product of a sustained socialization effort. Herein, one could highlight the values that a person could have developed early in life, as they might have been derived from parents, teachers, and religious authorities. More likely, due to its topical relevancy and its temporal recency, a person is swayed by the training he or she has received on a formal or an on-the-job basis. Whereas a person always has a choice to defy what they are urged repetitively toward, the odds do not favor its exercise.

When people believe they have choice but a sustained effort was made to ensure the predictability of how they will choose, we need to examine the power exerted. If power is important, parties are not equal and free will is a myth. Power comes in many forms and is likely to be resisted if it is exerted in an overt or heavy-handed way. Power is most effective when it operates through knowledge and with the approval of the experts.

Free will is likely to gain more expression when the power that opposes it, or at least strives to keep free will in check, is viewed as illegitimate. As members of society, we surrender some of our action choices to those institutions that we believe to be legitimate. Therefore, free will is a product of how we form impressions of righteous power over ourselves.

Summary

In sum, our modern world has many features, including ways to foster our continuing support. Upon closer examination, some central tenets of modernity are quite debatable. Research on accounting ethics is a representative of modernity and therefore should reflect its tenets. If this foundation is cracking, progress in understanding the phenomenon is highly conditional.

New ways of thinking about ethics

Admittedly, we can never see the time in which we live with sufficient clarity. Only with the advantage of hindsight can we take stock with any sort of certainty. Therefore, slapping labels on eras has to be done with caution and reservation. The end of modernism and the onset of postmodernism might be helpful to some in situating the nature of these ideas. All one needs to believe, however, is that we need to find a bit of a reset for the study of accounting ethics. Perhaps these ideas are connected to getting past the fallacies discussed earlier.

Study what is said

We need to attempt to go beyond good and evil with our ethics research. Much of the problem with ethics research is that this has not been recognized as an objective. This is not to say that you cannot possess predispositions and passions, but making it clear that you possess the moral high ground is problematic.

One way to do this is to recognize that ethics has been weaponized. Therefore, the lead is not turpitude but protestation of its absence. For example, while it might be tempting to declare professionalism either dead or neutered, one should not underestimate its ongoing rhetorical power. Professionalism is believed in and therefore will continue to be true, albeit in a postmodern sense. That occupational groups possess ethical codes and believe themselves special for ethical purposes will also be observed in the literature. Academics find the storyline of a social contract between professions and the larger society to be such a compelling narrative that they also will extend its life. We shall continue to see ethical research based on what can only be called romantic thinking about a mostly mythical past, but a better story is that their advantages accrue to those who can sell this, and selling it is easier when you believe it.

Expose that which is ersatz

A more pervasive cynicism is displayed by those who go further down this path. Rather than just question whether ethical action can be reduced to measurable variables, some problematize the possibility of ethical action by accountants. This follows the idea that the real has been effectively replaced by simulacra (Baudrillard 1988). Accounting ethics lacks substance because what accountants do exists only as signs, a secondhand derivative whose value depends upon convincingly substituting for the real. Work on accounting ethics therefore prioritizes the establishment and propagation of myth. Whatever theory we use should focus our attention on the symbols that are central to the semipermanent façades that allow unobserved self-interest in buffered cores to thrive. This works only because of a certain level of disengagement that can be documented throughout the professional socialization cycle, wherein the inferior currency displaces the real (see also Cory and Treviño 2017).

Assume it is all about the money

The success of capitalism at the end of modernity also needs to be recognized as the only template for ethical research. The bottom line on ethical research is the faith that capitalism can be reformed or at least tempered by the systematic ideation of sustainability. The pursuit of self-interest is both the engine of action and the ultimate condition of its probable downfall. We have overwhelming evidence of the thesis that advantage should be pursued ruthlessly by accounting professionals. That, or something close to it, is the premise of the business school, and accountants are not exempted. Ethical obligation and constraint are positioned at best in premodernity and will always be fighting a rearguard battle. The commodification of knowledge has mostly aligned against any meaningful ethical antithesis, since that would necessitate its own commodification. Ideas are now judged on their performativity (Lyotard 1984). Progressively, we see a hardening of an advocacy culture and the lessening of remorse for self-interest, with the former advanced in the name of democracy and the latter striking a blow for honesty. We are here to document how this is done, not to pointlessly bemoan its existence. That does not make us unindicted coconspirators.

Own your bias

Ethics research may have gone astray when it tried to copy the fake neutrality of mainstream accounting research. This desire mostly appears in what questions are asked and what questions are ignored. If one's commitment to empiricism is too rigid, one passes up the opportunity to ask important and pointed questions even if the measures are only suggestive and mostly unconventional. These selections let everyone know what you value and what you want the world to know about. The problem shared by mainstream accounting research and bad ethics work is the belief that the availability of "good" data delimits exploration.

The quality of passion should not be strained. Without it, we might as well be content producing automatons. At the same time, we are obligated to pursue the objects of our bias in a way capable of convincing others that we buy into the boundaries of reasonable conversation, if for no other reason than to persuade those on the fence.

Let go of the illusion of control

Academic research is the effort to exert control over a phenomenon in the effort to describe it and to study its effect on another phenomenon over which a similar degree of control is claimed or demanded. Since the journey through modernity could be described as the growing confidence of such control, to the questioning of such control in many circles, consequences for the study of accounting ethics are likely.

A possible fundamental tension exists between the dominant social sciences discipline of the age, economics, and ethical analysis. Economics presumes selfish behavior and has great difficulties explaining the existence of altruism. The prospect of behavior aligned with a moral compass exists only as "noise" in economic analysis. Accordingly, ethical behavior exists outside the tight world of reactions to incentives and to signals. For the most part, ethical research can be seen as the effort to find the set of regularities that would move the effort into that which can be explained or predicted. Ironically, economics works well only without a moral logic, but the study of ethics wants to be more like economics.

If we were to relax the assumption that control was possible, the effort to understand accounting ethics could be repositioned. Ethics could have more free-standing existence since it no longer had to serve the superior rationality of the organization, the belief of which may be unfounded (Reed 1993). Accounting itself presents boundaries that are difficult to defend (Cooper et al. 2000). If accounting ethics are no longer subservient to totalities with cross-purposes, a clearer view might be possible. At that point when the domination of a mostly illusionary causality is abandoned, we can at least see whose interests are being served.

Seek freedom

Just as auditing's existence depends upon making things auditable (Power 1996), ethics existence in modernity is largely dependent upon a reproduction process that has skewed the meaning of ethical behavior. Accounting ethics has been captured by the accounting establishment while simultaneously pretending to be the result of a scientific process (see Bjorkegren 1993). Dominant groups sustain their position by naturalizing the status quo and deflecting attention from the problematic. We must resist the study of accounting ethics that have been made all too consistent with organizational interests. We also must be emancipated from our own vocabularies.

Speaking of liberation, our progression with late modernity also should renew our appreciation for the role of choice in ethical action. Modernity built a proverbial iron cage for people in that it prioritized organizational dictates and scientific regularities. So, too, accounting ethics research was imprisoned in rigid ideas about how it should be conducted and what questions it should address. Choice always existed, but it was increasingly painted as a Hobson's one, tinged as it was by an industrial morality.

As accounting ethics scholarship realizes it is in late modernity, a renewed agency will be given to free will. The power of organizations and progressions to socialize individuals will be understood as much more contingent and circumstantial. Their diminishment as omnipotent actions will be partly attributable to the growing awareness of their purposeful efforts and their self-interest.

Summary

Left with the individual, what will research do? Perhaps explore the intuitive ideas about the contours of the good society. Here a fine line exists between that which is an unarticulated natural state and that which is a rationalization of consequences. Research must recast responsibility if we believe in free will lessening that which we now attribute to "systems" or to the vagaries of psychology. Perhaps all we can hope for is localized logic and individualized solutions. In a world where we should not presume that individuals cannot compute the natural thing to do, the expectation that universal laws exist to be discovered seems fanciful. When the literal is losing to the symbolic, ethical research needs to find and go with the flow.

Note

1 All of the social sciences are currently experiencing a crisis in confidence prompted by the "file drawer problem." Many major findings in psychology have failed to replicate when reexamined (Ferguson and Heene 2012). The failures of economics as a science are well known (Keen 2001).

References

Ball, R. J., and P. Brown. 1968. "An Empirical Examination of Accounting Income Numbers." *Journal of Accounting Research* 6 (Autumn): 159–68.

Baudrillard, J. 1988. *Jean Baudrillard: Selected Writings*. Edited by M. Poster. Stanford CA: Stanford University Press.

Beaver, W. H. 1968. "The Information Content of Annual Earnings Announcements." *Empirical Research in Accounting: Selected Studies*. Supplement to the *Journal of Accounting Research*: 67–92.

Bjorkegren, D. 1993. "What can Organization and Management Theory Learn from Art." In *Postmodernism and Organizations*, edited by J. Hassard and M. Parker, 101–13. London: Sage.

Cooper, D. J., T. Rose, R. Greenwood, and B. Hinings. 2000. "History and Contingency in International Accounting Firms." *Globalization of Services: Some Implications for Theory and Practice* 19: 93–124.

Cory, S. N., and M. R. Treviño. 2017. "An Exploratory Study: Moral Disengagement Levels in Accounting Majors." *Southern Journal of Business & Ethics* 9: 135–43.

Ferguson, C. J., and M. Heene. 2012. "A Vast Graveyard of Undead Theories: Publication Bias and Psychological Science's Aversion to the Null." *Perspectives on Psychological Science* 7 (6): 555–61.

Geijsbeek, J. B. 1914. *Ancient Double-Entry Bookkeeping*. Reprinted 1974 by Scholars Book Company. Houston, TX: Scholars Book Co.

Keen, S. 2001. *Debunking Economics: The Naked Emperor of the Social Sciences*. Annandale, NSW Australia: Pluto Press.

Kohlberg, L. 1984. *The Psychology of Moral Development: The Nature and Validity of Moral Stages (Essays on Moral Development Volume 2)*. New York: Harper and Row.

Kuhn, T. S. 1962. *The Structure of Scientific Revolutions*. Chicago, IL: The University of Chicago Press.

Lyotard, J. 1984. *The Postmodern Condition*. Minneapolis: University of Minnesota Press.

MacIntyre, A. 1984. *After Virtue*. Notre Dame, IN: University of Notre Dame Press.

Piaget, J. 1932. *The Moral Judgement of the Child*. London: Kegan Paul, Trench, Truber and Co.

Ponemon, L. 1990. "Ethical Judgements in Accounting: A Cognitive Developmental Perspective." *Critical Perspectives on Accounting* 1: 191–215.

Ponemon, L. 1992. "Ethical Reasoning and Selection-Socialization in Accounting." *Accounting, Organizations and Society* 7 (3/4): 239–58.

Power, M. 1996. "Making Things Auditable." *Accounting, Organizations and Society* 21 (2–3): 289–315.

Reed, M. 1993. "Organizations and Modernity: Continuity and Discontinuity in Organizational Theory." In *Postmodernism and Organizations*, edited by J. Hassard and M. Parker, 163–82. London: Sage.

Rest, J. 1979. *Development in Judging Moral Issues*. Minneapolis, MN: University of Minnesota Press.

Watts, R. L., and J. L. Zimmerman. 1986. *Positive Accounting Theory*. New York: Prentice Hall.

PART II

Alternative perspectives for thinking about accounting ethics

4

VIRTUE ETHICS AND THE ACCOUNTING PROFESSION

Marc Peter Neri

Introduction

High-profile ethical failures during the 1960s and 1970s resulted in increasing regulation and oversight of the accounting profession (Cowton 2017); yet scandals have continued to plague the profession in more recent decades. Accounting is an art (*techne*) requiring considerable professional judgment, and lists of rules cannot anticipate every situation (Melé 2005; West 2017). In fact, accounting rules often require significant professional judgment to interpret, and these rules require frequent amendments to accommodate new social trends and economic practices. Therefore, regulations that focus on specific actions may be an insufficient foundation upon which to build the profession (Cowton 2017; West 2017, 2018a). Virtue ethics represents an alternative perspective that focuses on the character of the professional rather than specific actions or outcomes. Virtue ethics starts by asking what it means to be a good accountant. Then it asks which intellectual and moral virtues an accountant must develop in order to act in the best way. Virtues should make it easier, or even instinctive, for professionals to serve their clients' needs and the public interest even in unique or novel situations. However, we need to establish which virtues accountants need and how they may develop them. This requires research by subject matter experts who understand the accounting profession as well as virtue ethics.

Virtue ethics is one of the three leading schools of ethics, along with deontology and consequentialism (Besser-Jones and Slote 2015). Systems of ethics based upon virtue were the norm in ancient and medieval Western philosophy (Frede 2015) and have remained in favor in non-Western ethics.[1] However, virtue ethics is essentially a contemporary movement that began as a critique of both deontology and consequentialism (Anscombe 1958; Hursthouse and Pettigrove 2017; Snow 2017).[2] Therefore, perhaps the simplest way to understand where contemporary virtue ethics stands is by contrasting its position with those of deontology and consequentialism.

Whereas deontology asks what a person should *do*, virtue ethics asks what a person should *be* (MacKinnon and Fiala 2014). So virtue ethics places primacy on the goodness of a person's character rather than the rightness of a person's actions (Oakley and Cocking 2001).[3] Virtue ethics is certainly concerned with the consequences of actions; however, virtue ethics does not require the common good to be maximized by an act for that act to be considered "good"

(Nussbaum 1988). Rather, virtue ethics places primacy on the development of a person's character, because only a person of good character can live in a state of human flourishing (Kraut 2018).

Accounting ethics research happens to have been dominated by deontology and consequentialism. The Defining Issues Test (DIT) has had an overwhelming influence on behavioral research in accounting ethics (Bailey, Scott, and Thoma 2010). The DIT proposes a six-stage hierarchy of morality wherein the highest levels of moral development are exemplified by utilitarian consequentialism (stage 5) and deontology (stage 6), the highest level of moral development (Rest 1994). The DIT questions also happen to focus on actions and outcomes. Consequently, there has been relatively little attention paid to virtue ethics within accounting research.

Virtue ethics can certainly be applied to business, and there are several notable contributions from management scholars (Alzola 2015; Audi 2012; Moore 2005a, 2005b; Murphy 1999; Whetstone 2001). There have also been a few notable exceptions within accounting literature. These papers have considered virtue ethics as it relates to the profession as a whole (Francis 1990; Melé 2005), accounting education (Melé 2005; Mintz 1995, 2006), and tax practice (West 2018b). In addition, at least one accounting ethics textbook emphasizes the virtue ethics approach (Cheffers and Pakaluk 2007).

More recently, some accounting scholars have begun to address how virtue ethics might inform codes of professional conduct (Cowton 2017; West 2017, 2018a). They argue that scandals continue to occur despite increased regulation and oversight of the profession (Cowton 2017; West 2017, 2018a). Since accounting is an art, requiring considerable judgment, lists of rules focusing on outcomes may be insufficient to anticipate every situation (Melé 2005; West 2017). While it may be unwise to dispense entirely with lists of rules, virtue ethics may provide a more nuanced philosophical underpinning for a code of ethics through its focus on professional excellence and character (West 2018).

Contemporary virtue ethics does not present a unified theory (Sanford 2015). While many draw from Aristotelean ethics (Snow 2017)[4], others draw on diverse traditions, such as Confucianism (Loy 2014; Luo 2015; Sim 2015), Buddhism (Goodman 2015; Adams 2017) and Hinduism (Bilimoria 2014; Perrett and Pettigrove 2015). In an increasingly multicultural world, one of the benefits of adopting a virtue ethics approach may be the fact that theories of virtue already exist in so many different cultures around the world. Reading these different accounts, it is apparent that the lists of virtues share more similarities than differences.

The review of existing accounting literature in this chapter suggests that accounting scholars have focused primarily on two works to date: Aristotle's *Nicomachean Ethics* (*NE*) and Alasdair MacIntyre's *After Virtue* (*AV*). Since Aristotle was the first thinker to provide a systematic, comprehensive study of virtue (Frede 2015), *NE* provides a useful starting point for a discussion of virtue. MacIntyre aims to extend Aristotelean ethics. So *AV* provides an interesting insight into how contemporary virtue ethics has revived the study of virtue and contributed its own ideas. Therefore, I shall start my discussion with Aristotle's concept of virtue and, drawing on the work of other accounting researchers, attempt to formulate a list of essential virtues for accountants. Then I shall discuss some of the important concepts introduced by MacIntyre, including the concepts of a practice and internal goods. This frames the discussion of accounting as a practice that can help develop the essential virtues. As I do this, I shall point to some opportunities for future research, accounting education, and professional development.

Aristotle's concept of virtue

Aristotle seems to provide the accounting researcher a pragmatic and applicable concept of virtue, since the stated outcomes of virtue are that a person will be good and will do their own work well:

> The virtue (*arete*) of a human being would be the active condition (*hexis*) from which one becomes a good human being and from which one will yield up one's own work well.
>
> *(NE, II 6, 1106a23–25)*

Aristotle's word for virtue, *arete*, means excellence. But excellence does not imply some kind of exclusive ability that only a few can achieve (Frede 2015). Rather, *arete* simply means that something is fit for its purpose. To illustrate excellence, Aristotle uses the example of a knife that is sufficiently sharp to cut well. For this reason, Aristotle's virtue ethics is teleological; it is based upon the notion that humans have an ultimate purpose (*telos*), namely a life of excellence.

The passage cited refers to virtue as an active condition (*hexis*). The word *hexis* has been translated variously as "state of character" and as "disposition of character," and virtue has been identified as both a character trait (Audi 2015; Miller 2018) and a state (Alzola 2018) in the literature. However, the term *hexis* suggests an "active condition" of being ready to act in a certain way, like an Olympic athlete coiled, ready to throw a discus (Sachs 2002). Virtue is similar to a disposition in the sense that it makes one ready to choose the right course of action when a situation to exercise virtue arises (*NE* II 6, 1107a).[5]

The suggestion that a person has one ultimate purpose does not mean that there is only one important virtue to consider. The virtues are irreducibly plural (Oakley and Cocking 2001). And human excellence does not imply only moral virtues; Aristotle makes a distinction between moral virtues (*ethike*) and intellectual virtues (*dianotike*). Each sphere, moral and intellectual, is further divided into numerous virtues. The intellectual virtues include demonstrative knowledge, craftsmanship, practical wisdom, good intuition, and philosophical wisdom. The moral virtues include courage, moderation, generosity, magnificence, magnanimity, and justice (Pakaluk 2005).

The intellectual virtues are developed through teaching and practice. Aristotle is very careful to point out that practical wisdom (*phronesis*) is developed only through practical experience. The moral virtues are developed through habit (*NE* II 1, 1103a11–25). Therefore, we are not virtuous by nature, but we become virtuous by actively pursuing virtue, just as a craftsman becomes expert by practicing their craft. For instance, we become courageous by acting courageously (*NE* II 1, 1103b2–3). And when we practice all the moral (*ethike*) virtues, we develop excellent character (*ethos*). Because the virtues are acquired through practice, virtue has also been described as a skill (Haidt and Joseph 2007; Stichter 2018).

Intellectual virtues and practical wisdom

Intellectual virtues are "active conditions of the soul (*hexis*) which can disclose the truth" (Sachs 2002). This definition suggests their importance to the accounting profession. Some of the intellectual virtues that Aristotle names clearly relate to accounting, such as domain knowledge (*episteme*), and technical knowledge (*techne*). Some of the intellectual virtues appear to parallel *Bloom's Taxonomy* of critical thinking skills, which has influenced accounting education and the professional examinations in the United States. And some help a professional govern their moral actions, specifically the intellectual virtue of practical wisdom (*phronesis*). The intellectual virtues Aristotle mentions in his *Nicomachean Ethics* are listed in Table 4.1. Table 4.1 also offers examples from the accounting profession that exemplify each of the intellectual virtues.

Art (techne) includes the ability to use processes, tools, and judgment. This is important to accountants when selecting and analyzing financial data, pulling together financial reports, auditing, or tax planning (West 2017). The virtues of intellect (*nous*) and knowledge (*episteme*) involve the processes of induction and deduction, respectively. Intellect grasps how an example represents a universal rule (Sachs 2002, 108). Knowledge is not just comprehension but the virtue of active, deductive thinking in order to achieve understanding of a situation starting from universal rules. Theoretical wisdom draws on both intellect and knowledge. Aristotle refers to wisdom as "knowledge with its head on" (*NE VI* 7, 1141a 20), while the other intellectual virtues support theoretical wisdom's contemplative process by helping a person think things through issues (*eubolia*), evaluate the actions of others (*sunesis*), and develop opinions (*gnome*).

The Aristotelean understanding of the intellectual virtues is not synonymous with Bloom's taxonomy of critical thinking skills. However, some apparent parallels would be worth investigating further given the attention that Bloom's taxonomy has received in the profession. Intellect (*nous*) involves induction, so one could liken it to comprehension in Bloom's taxonomy. Since knowledge (*episteme*) involves deduction, it resembles analysis in Bloom's taxonomy rather than what is referred to as knowledge in the taxonomy. Theoretical wisdom resembles the higher levels of critical thinking that bring ideas together, such as synthesis and evaluation. However, these conjectures should be examined further.

Practical wisdom (*phronesis*) is different from other intellectual virtues. While it is concerned with figuring out the truth, it is also concerned with action (Sachs 2002, 106). Since it is concerned with good actions, it helps direct the moral virtues:

> Virtue is an active condition that makes one apt at choosing, consisting of a mean condition in relation to us, which is determined by a proportion and by the means by which a person with practical wisdom would determine it.
>
> *(NE II 6, 1107a1–2).*

In other words, virtue is a mean condition that lies between deficiency and excess. For instance, courage is the mean between cowardice and rashness (*NE* II 2, 1104a11–25). And practical wisdom (*phronesis*) plays the critical role of helping the virtuous person figure out the best course of action in a given situation: what action does courage require in this situation? Therefore, practical wisdom is also referred to as a governing or administrative ability (Pakaluk 2005).

As indicated in Table 4.1, one example of practical wisdom in auditing may be professional skepticism.[6] Cowton specifically lists skepticism as a virtue in his analysis, relating this virtue to the principle of objectivity in the code of professional conduct (Cowton 2017). According to AU 230.07, professional skepticism is as "an attitude that includes a questioning mind and a critical assessment of audit evidence" (AICPA 2013). One way that professional skepticism has been operationalized in research is by looking at how much evidence an auditor gathers (Hurtt et al. 2013). Professional skepticism helps the auditor to determine the mean between the excess of gathering too much evidence (inefficient auditing) and the deficiency of gathering too little evidence (ineffective auditing). Therefore, professional skepticism may be an application of practical wisdom in the auditing profession.

One important observation is that the intellectual virtues need to be taught (West 2017). Therefore, practical wisdom is central to Doménec Melé's (2005) discussion of ethical education

Table 4.1 List of Intellectual Virtues from Book VI of the Nicomachean Virtues

Major Intellectual Virtues		Description	Examples in accounting
Greek	English		
τέχνη	techne	art	art*; craft expertise**; craftsmanship***; "an active condition involving a true rational understanding that governs **making**" (p105)	technical knowledge of the revenue recognition rules, the necessary journals to record transactions in the books, and the analytical and substantive testing that are used in auditing
φρόνησῖς	phronesis	practical wisdom	practical judgment*; practical wisdom**; administrative skill***; "a truth-disclosing active condition involving reason that governs **action**, concerned with what is good and bad for a human being" (S.106)	professional skepticism; knowing when it is necessary to act, to gather more audit evidence, but also governing the courage to act upon that knowledge
νοῦς	nous	intellect	intellect*; intuitive understanding**; good intuition***; inductive; "that which grasps the universal when a particular [example] is perceived" (S.108)	comprehending the terms in a client's sales contract and recognizing that the contract has multiple performance obligations with different performance dates
ἐπιστήμη	epistêmê	knowledge	knowledge*; science**; demonstrative knowledge***; deductive; "an active condition of the soul that governs demonstration" (S.105)	being able to apply the revenue recognition rules to the contract to determine how much revenue should be recorded on what dates and being able to defend a recommendation
σοφία	sophia	theoretical wisdom	wisdom*; theoretical wisdom**; philosophical wisdom***; a combination of intellect and knowledge; "knowledge with its head on" (S.108)	being able to contemplate the truth and fairness of a set of financial statements as a whole

Minor Intellectual Virtues		Description	Examples in accounting
Greek	English		
εὐβουλία	eubolia	deliberation	deliberating well* (B.196); thinking properly about the right end; giving good counsel	advising a client on the best way to present a transaction in the financial statements

(Continued)

Table 4.1 (Continued)

Major Intellectual Virtues		Description	Examples in accounting
Greek	English		
σύνεσις *synesis*	astuteness	astuteness*; literally, "putting together" . . . and appreciating when someone else displays practical judgment (S.113); "the ability to judge particular matters well according to common rules of thumb" (B.196)	recognizing when management assumptions are reasonable
γνώμη *gnome*	opinion	thoughtfulness*; which Aristotle links to compassion (*sun-gnome*) and being a considerate person (*eugnome*) (S.108); opinion; "the ability to judge when common rules of thumb are insufficient" (B.196)	appreciating the relational issues that might increase risk of fraud or earnings management, but also in arriving at an audit opinion

Notes: Explanations given by Budziszewski (2017) referenced as (B. page no.) in the Table 4.1.
* translations used by Sachs (2002); explanations referenced as (S. page no.) in the Table 4.1.
** translations used by Kraut (2018)
*** translation used by Pakaluk (2005)

in accounting. And while the focus of contemporary virtue ethics concerns the moral virtues, it is important to understand that the intellectual virtues complement those moral virtues by helping the accountant choose an appropriate action in the course of their practice (West 2017). Therefore, it is important to understand the role of the intellectual virtues in accounting.

Professional virtues

One criticism is that virtues do not tell you what to do in a given situation, so we need to develop rules and principles (West 2017). However, virtue ethics does not exclude a code of conduct. On the contrary, Aristotle claims that good laws help to make good citizens by habituating them in the virtues (*NE* II 1, 1103b4–7). In terms of the profession, a code of conduct should help accountants habituate good accounting virtues by requiring them to act in certain ways. For instance, the professional code in the United States requires accountants to exercise professional skepticism. This requirement should help auditors hone the virtue of practical wisdom by having them repeatedly determine when to gather more evidence. The requirement to remain objective and avoid subordination of judgment to others should encourage accountants to practice the intellectual virtue of thinking things through for themselves (*eubolia*).

However, rules cannot anticipate every situation. In fact, virtues are necessary for a practitioner to appreciate when and which rules apply in a situation. For instance, practical wisdom should help an accountant recognize when they lack objectivity, when they have exercised due care, or in what situations they may face impaired independence. Therefore, the intellectual and moral virtues and the professional rules form an interdependent relationship (Melé 2005).

Finally, a focus on outputs (actions) rather than inputs (virtues) may give professionals a false impression that they are "good accountants" if they simply check the list of requirements (West 2017). A focus on virtues rather than rules implies a focus on continuing professional development. Therefore, any professional codes of conduct in accounting should be constructed with virtue ethics in mind.

Christopher Cowton's "first approximation" at a virtue ethics approach to the IESBA code of ethics is quite detailed (Cowton 2017). He lists the fundamental principles in the current code of ethics and associates each principle with one or more virtues that he deems necessary for the accountant (see earlier reference to skepticism). Some of the other virtues noted include honesty, diligence, discretion, and competence. Some of these virtues appear to be moral virtues, such as honesty, and some appear to be intellectual virtues, such as competence.

An issue noted by Andrew West (2017) is that the list of virtues that accounting researchers often provide are not identified as virtues by Aristotle. Cowton's own list (a first approximation by his own admission) is not grounded in the rich tradition Aristotelean thinking provides on the subject.[7] Rather than invent a list of virtues, West attempts to ground the same code of ethics in terms of an Aristotelian perspective.

West points out that the ultimate purpose of an accountant is the same as for any other human person, namely a life of happiness (*eudaimonia*) through pursuit of the virtues (West 2017). However, the professional environment necessitates, as well as offering the accountant the opportunity to develop, certain virtues. West lists the intellectual virtues of scientific knowledge and practical wisdom, as well as the moral virtues of courage, justice (West 2017), and honesty (West 2018a).

While I would agree with West's list of intellectual virtues, I would add art (*techne*), which deals with the use of tools, methods, and technical issues of the profession, and the ability to think through and give good counsel regarding those technical issues (*euboulia*). Inasmuch as professionals engage in the management of others, interact with clients, and need to analyze the motivations of others to misreport, I would also add sympathetic understanding (*gnome*).

With regard to the moral virtues, courage seems out of place, since the Aristotelean virtue of courage is concerned with risking one's life (Pakaluk 2005). And possessing virtue implies action. For instance, a professional only possesses the virtue of justice if they are ready to act in a just way. However, opinion is divided among virtue ethicists on this issue, some arguing that courage can also apply in the face of loss of reputation, livelihood, etc. (Sanford 2010). Moral courage is also an important mediator between moral judgment and moral behavior in the literature (Hurtt et al. 2013; Jones, Massey, and Thorne 2003). And focusing on moral courage has been shown to increase resolve to behave ethically (Barnes 2007).

I would suggest the moral virtues an accountant should focus on developing first are justice, self-mastery, and magnanimity:

1   Justice (*dikaiosyne*) is of two kinds; the first involves ensuring each person receives their due, the second "sets things straight in transactions" (*NE* V 2, 1130b30–35). Though both forms of justice are important to an accountant, it is perhaps the second kind of justice with which an accountant should be particularly concerned. Accounting involves ensuring that each transaction is properly recorded, that it is reported in a true and fair way to investors and other stakeholders, and that controls are established to ensure no person involved in the transaction is defrauded. This is the epitome of setting things straight in transactions. However, it is also the responsibility of accountants to ensure that all parties receive the information they are due: that investors receive accurate financial reports, that corporations receive the correct audit opinion, and that governments receive the tax the law demands.

2   Self-mastery (*sophrosyne*), sometimes translated as temperance, concerns being able to enjoy a reasonable amount of the good things in life without being overcome by acquisitiveness. It seems important that an accountant should avoid seeking inordinate gain from their work, as it might induce them to misappropriate the financial assets entrusted to their care, subordinate their judgment to the client they are supposed to be auditing, or assist a client in engaging in tax evasion.

3   Magnanimity (*megalopsychia*) is the virtue of high-mindedness that concerns doing honorable actions. This virtue appears to be more appropriate than courage for the kinds of issues an accountant faces. Magnanimity involves good actions with regard to big issues, such as deciding when to issue a going concern opinion or deciding when to report a client's actions to a regulatory body. High-mindedness with regard to accounting suggests holding professional standards in high esteem, even seeking out opportunities to practice objectivity and professional skepticism, and to serve the public interest.

I have not included "honesty" in my list. This is not because honesty is not important. Aristotle mentions "truthfulness" as one of the moral virtues associated with sociability (Pakaluk 2005). However, truthfulness between friends is not consistent with the kind of duty an accountant has to the public interest. MacIntyre does include the virtue of honesty in his discussion. However, honesty appears to be a component of justice. In fact, Hume uses the term "honesty" interchangeably with justice (LeBar and Slote 2016). Insofar as the intellectual virtues involve a disposition toward discovering the truth, as has been said, honesty would seem to be an essential component of all the intellectual virtues.

The work of attributing virtues to the accounting profession needs considerable work. It may be wrong-headed to attempt short lists of virtues, as all the virtues may be necessary to some degree when all aspects of accounting practice are considered. Before we can continue, therefore, it is critical to better define what we mean by accounting practice and the goods that are internal to its practice.

MacIntyre's concepts of practice and inner goods

Perhaps the most influential concepts MacIntyre introduces to virtue ethics, at least from the standpoint of accounting research, are practice and internal goods:

> By a practice, I am going to mean any coherent and complex form of socially established cooperative human activity through which goods internal to that form of activity are realized in the course of trying to achieve those standards of excellence which are appropriate to, and partially definitive of, that form of activity, with the result that human powers to achieve excellence, and human conceptions of the ends and goods involved, are systematically extended.
>
> *(MacIntyre 1984, 187)*

A practice is not a simple activity; rather, it is a complex set of interrelated activities. Therefore, "bricklaying is not a practice; architecture is . . . planting turnips is not a practice; farming is" (MacIntyre 1984, 187). Geoff Moore gives one of the most extensive analyses of MacIntyre's concept of practice within the context of business management (Moore 2002). Moore refers to accounting as an "activity" within the practice of selling goods to customers. However, Moore points out that he is only discussing the activity of booking a transaction. The work of a professional accountant involves far more than booking transactions.

A practice has some set of goods internal to the practice, which can be extended and perfected by the practice. The internal goods are contrasted with external goods. External goods include prestige, status, money (*AV*, 188); they arise from a practice but are not internal to the practice. In accounting, such external goods might include being promoted, receiving a bonus, becoming certified, or being invited to join the partnership. These goods arise from doing accounting well, but they are external to the practice of accounting.

Internal goods are of two kinds: the first relates to the product or performance of the practice (AV, 189), and the second relates to the good a practitioner discovers in living the life of continual improvement (*AV*, 190). In the case of accounting, examples of the first kind of internal good would be high-quality managerial or financial reports (West 2018a), a tax return that avoids tax without evading it, or an accurate audit opinion. So the pursuit of the first kind of internal good will also benefit external parties, such as capital markets, governments, clients, and organizations. The second kind of internal good is achieved when an accountant devotes her life to continuing professional development.

In this light, "a virtue is an acquired human quality the possession of which tends to enable us to achieve those goods which are internal to practices and the lack of which effectively prevents us from achieving such goods" (AV, 191). Therefore, the virtues are not the internal goods that we achieve, but they are that by which we achieve the goods internal to a practice. And without the virtues, practices might still result in external goods, but we will never achieve the internal goods proper to that practice.

For practices to be maintained, they require institutions that provide the material resources necessary to practice (*AV*, 194). However, institutions also focus on external goods, such as remuneration, prestige, and power. As a result, practices are vulnerable to the acquisitiveness of institutions, and virtues such as justice, courage, and truthfulness are required to resist the corrupting power of institutions (ibid).

Accountants are organized into professional associations, and they work for corporations, firms, and governments. These institutions promulgate processes, systems, finance, and other material resources that support the practice of accounting. However, in doing so, they also offer the external goods of remuneration, status, and power that could come into conflict with the internal goods of the practice of accounting. Arguably, these external goods attract new professionals to the practice of accounting (West 2018a); however, they have also contributed to the greed and deception that devolve into accounting scandals. Therefore, accountants need to develop the moral virtues, particularly the virtues of justice and magnanimity, to keep the corrupting power of institutions and external goods in check.

Many practices in one profession

Accounting virtue ethics research seems to struggle with the definition of accounting practice. This may be because accounting is made up of several distinct practices, each with different goals (Cowton 2017).

West attempts to define the function of accounting as broadly as possible to cover financial and managerial accounting, audit, and tax work: "to collect and summarize quantitative information in order that the position and/or performance of an organization may be reported to particular stakeholders" (West 2017, 8). It is possible for one practice to be associated with multiple internal goods, as suggested in the previous discussion.

However, professionals tend to contrast the practice of public accounting with managerial accounting and auditing with tax accounting as if it is far more than the products of these practices that are different. It is as if the kinds of professionals that pursue each of these different paths are very different.

Returning to the code of conduct, we see that auditors must be independent of their clients, while tax accountants are not held to the same standard so long as a tax position is reasonable. Therefore, it is reasonable to suppose that the practice of auditing is fundamentally different to the practice of tax accounting and that the internal goods proper to each practice may be different as a result. Being a good auditor may be slightly different to being a good tax practitioner. Rather than trying to define one practice, it may be valuable for future research to define several distinct practices.

Teaching and developing moral virtues

As has been said earlier, Aristotle held that moral virtues are habituated rather than taught. Therefore, there is some doubt whether it is possible to "teach" the moral virtues at all. One possible solution may be reflective learning (Mintz 2006), where accounting students and professionals reflect upon their classroom and professional experiences. Since moral virtues must be habituated, the opportunity to practice is important. Research in moral psychology suggests that reflection is a more realistic was of involving the reason in developing the moral virtues (Haidt and Joseph 2007).

Another, complementary, method of "teaching" moral virtue is storytelling. Stories are a part of moral education in every culture (Haidt and Joseph 2007). Stories appeal to the poetic imagination and offer a vision of the consequences of those choices upon which the learner can reflect. Stories could be particularly important within college education, where they offer vicarious experiences to students who lack direct personal experience. Research finds that accounting students who reflect upon their own ethical decision-making within situational ethics develop moral and intellectual virtues (Mintz 2006). This research integrates reflective learning, virtue ethics, and situational ethics.

Reflective learning and storytelling may already be important parts of the mentoring process that exists in accounting firms. New associates in accounting firms usually have a mentor. Some have proposed that restoring a sense of professional virtues through mentoring is essential (Lail, Macgregor, Marcum, and Stuebs 2017). And mentoring has been found to increase professional commitment (Allen, Eby, O'Brien, and Lentz 2008; Herda and Martin 2016; McManus and Subramaniam 2014), develop leadership (Sosik and Lee 2002), and encourage moral behavior (Taylor and Curtis 2018) in accountants.

With regard to virtue, it is important to note that reflection upon the actions of others, "social persuasion," is a stronger predictor of moral behavior than is instruction, "rational persuasion" (Haidt 2001). A mentor's behavior may be more persuasive than instructions. Through their ability to offer vicarious experience, stories may be more persuasive in communicating virtue than discussion of norms. To this point, it is interesting to note that trust mediates the relationship between mentoring and moral behavior (Taylor and Curtis 2018), implying consistency between the message and the actions of the mentor is important. Certainly, storytelling and reflection in the mentoring process are worthwhile avenues for further research.

Conclusion and summary of future research opportunities

Virtue ethics has not provided a unified theory, but the most influential thinking has been based upon combining Aristotle's understanding of virtue with MacIntyre's concept of a practice.

There are two kinds of virtue: intellectual virtues and moral virtues. The intellectual virtues support the moral virtues, particularly the intellectual virtue of practical wisdom, which helps a person choose the best course of action in a given situation.

Accounting researchers have discussed how to educate accounting students and professionals in the virtues, though very little experimental work has been done in this area. Research has also tried to establish a list of virtues that are important to the accounting profession, though most lists to date seem either incomplete or lack the benefit of being grounded upon the time-tested list of virtues that Aristotle identified. Therefore, there is much more work that can be done to ground our understanding of the practical virtues in the theory.

If we can establish a list of virtues, experimental work demonstrating the utility of the virtue ethics approach in drafting codes of conduct, in accounting education, and in regulation would be desirable. To this end, moral psychologists have developed experimental models that incorporate virtue ethics. Virtue ethics is discussed at some length in relation to the social intuitionists model (Haidt and Joseph 2007), while others have worked to fit the concepts of the rationalist model to virtue ethics (Melé 2005). Finally, Robert Audi lists six dimensions to virtue that may further help behavioral researchers to operationalize the concept of virtue (Audi 2012, 2015).

Since virtue is teleological – each virtue must aim at some end – we must endeavor to better define the purpose of accounting. According to the MacIntyrean definition, there appear to be several separate though related practices in accounting. Therefore, there needs to be further research into what we mean by a "good" accountant, or perhaps what we mean by a "good" auditor, a "good" tax professional, a "good" management accountant, etc. Only with good working definitions of accounting practice is it possible to establish a list of virtues that an accountant ought to possess in order to resist the corrupting power of institutions.

Notes

1 Ancient and medieval Western philosophy encompasses the Classical Roman and Hellenic periods, as well as traditional Christian, Jewish, and Islamic philosophy. Most non-Western traditions also emphasize virtue, such as Confucianism (Loy 2014; Luo 2015; Sim 2015), Buddhism (Goodman 2015; MacKenzie 2017), and Hinduism (Bilimoria 2014; Perrett and Pettigrove 2015).

2 This is not to say that premodern approaches to ethics are not also virtue ethics; rather, the term virtue ethics is a modern invention and is now applied to ancient and traditional philosophies when discussing their focus on virtue (for examples, see the list of essays in the note 1).

3 We are discussing the emphasis of each school of thought. Action is important to virtue ethics. For instance, actions can be a sign of good character (Pakaluk 2005). And deontology is not devoid of the concept of virtue. Kant is clearly interested in virtue, and he writes a treatise on virtue. However, Kant places priority on the imperative to act in the right way rather than the character or virtue that empowers the action or develops as a result of the action (Schroth 2008).

4 It is worth noting that many of the foremost philosophers in Judaism (e.g., Maimonides), Christianity (e.g., Augustine and Aquinas), and Islam (e.g., Avicenna and Averroes) were influenced by Plato and Aristotle. As a result, each of the cultures that have been touched by these three major religions have been imbued with a tradition of virtue theory inherited from Plato and Aristotle.

5 Behavioral researchers interested in further discussion of the nature of virtues may be interested in reading Robert Audi's research (Audi 2012, 2015). He delineates six dimensions of virtue, which have yet to be incorporated in accounting ethics research: the field, the target, the beneficiaries, the agent's understanding of the practice, the agent's motivation, and grounding.

6 The precise nature of professional skepticism has been debated. At various times it has been claimed as a trait, a state, and an attitude (Hurtt 2010; Hurtt et al. 2013; Nolder and Kadous 2014). Could it be a virtue?

7 Note that West (2017) is writing at the same time as Cowton (2017) and, to my knowledge, working independently on the same problem. Therefore, West is not directly critiquing Cowton's list of virtues; rather, West is discussing a trend in earlier accounting research, notably the work of Steve Mintz (1995).

References

Allen, Tammy D., Lillian T. Eby, Kimberly E. O'Brien, and Elizabeth Lentz. 2008. "The State of Mentoring Research: A Qualitative Review of Current Research Methods and Future Research Implications." *Journal of Vocational Behavior* 73 (3): 343–57. https://doi.org/10.1016/j.jvb.2007.08.004.

Alzola, Miguel. 2015. "Corporate Roles and Virtues." *Handbook of Virtue Ethics in Business and Management*, 1–10. https://doi.org/10.1007/978-94-007-6729-4_110-1.

Alzola, Miguel. 2018. "Character-Based Business Ethics." In *The Oxford Handbook of Virtue*, 591–620. New York: Oxford University Press.

American Institute of Certified Public Accountants. 2013. *Code of Professional Conduct and Bylaws*. New York: AICPA.

Anscombe, Gertrude Elizabeth Margaret. 1958. "Modern moral philosophy." *Philosophy* 33 (124): 1–19.

Audi, Robert. 2012. "Virtue Ethics as a Resource in Business." *Business Ethics Quarterly* 22 (2): 273–91.

Audi, Robert. 2015. "Business Ethics from a Virtue-Theoretic Perspective." In *The Routledge Companion to Virtue Ethics*, 553–566. New York: Routledge.

Bailey, Charles D., Irana Scott, and Stephen J. Thoma. 2010. "Revitalizing Accounting Ethics Research in the Neo-Kohlbergian Framework: Putting the DIT into Perspective." *Behavioral Research in Accounting* 22 (2): 1–26.

Barnes, Jeffrey N. 2007. "Developing Resolve to have Moral Courage: A Field Comparison of Teaching Methods." *Journal of Business Ethics Education* 4: 79–96. https://doi.org/10.5840/jbee200745.

Besser-Jones, Lorraine, and Michael Slote. 2015. "Introduction." Introduction in *The Routledge Companion to Virtue Ethics*, xxi–xxiii. New York: Routledge.

Bilimoria, Purushottama. 2014. "Ethics and Virtue in Classical Indian Thinking." In *The Handbook of Virtue Ethics*, edited by S. van Hooft, 294–305. New York: Routledge.

Budziszewski, J. 2017. *Commentary on Thomas Aquinas's Virtue Ethics*. Cambridge University Press.

Cheffers, Mark, and Michael Pakaluk. 2007. *Understanding Accounting Ethics*. Sutton, MA: Allen David Press.

Cowton, Christopher J. 2017 *Virtue Theory and Accounting*. Springer.

Francis, Jere R. 1990. "After Virtue? Accounting as a Moral and Discursive Practice." *Accounting, Auditing & Accountability Journal* 3. https://doi.org/10.1108/09513579010142436.

Frede, Dorothea. 2015. "Aristotle's Virtue Ethics." In *The Routledge Companion to Virtue Ethics*, edited by L. Besser-Jones and M. Slote, 17–29. New York: Routledge.

Goodman, Charles. 2015. "Virtue in Buddhist Ethical Traditions." In *The Routledge Companion to Virtue Ethics*, edited by L. Besser-Jones and M. Slote, 89–98. New York: Routledge.

Haidt, Jonathan. 2001. "The Emotional Dog and its Rational Tail: A Social Intuitionist Approach to Moral Judgment." *Psychological Review* 108 (4): 814.

Haidt, Jonathan, and Craig Joseph. 2007. "The Moral Mind: How Five Sets of Innate Intuitions Guide the Development of Many Culture-Specific Virtues, and Perhaps Even Modules." *The Innate Mind* 3: 367–91.

Herda, David N., and Kasey A. Martin. 2016. "The Effects of Auditor Experience and Professional Commitment on Acceptance of Underreporting Time: A Moderated Mediation Analysis." *Current Issues in Auditing* 10 (2): A14-A27.

Hursthouse, R., and G. Pettigrove. 2017. "Virtue Ethics." In *Stanford Encyclopedia of Philosophy*, 1–22. Stanford, CA: Stanford University.

Hurtt, R. Kathy. 2010. "Development of a Scale to Measure Professional Skepticism." *Auditing: A Journal of Practice and Theory* 29 (1): 149–71.

Hurtt, R. Kathy, Helen Brown-Liburd, Christine E. Earley, and Ganesh Krishnamoorthy. 2013. "Research on Auditor Professional Skepticism: Literature Synthesis and Opportunities for Future Research." *Auditing: A Journal of Practice and Theory* 32 (sp1): 45–97.

Jones, Joanne, Dawn W. Massey, and Linda Thorne. 2003. "Auditors' Ethical Reasoning: Insights from Past Research and Implications for the Future." *Journal of Accounting Literature* 22: 45.

Kraut, Richard. 2018. "Aristotle's Ethics." In *The Stanford Encyclopedia of Philosophy*. Stanford University. https://plato.stanford.edu/archives/sum2018/entries/aristotle-ethics/.

Lail, Bradley, Jason MacGregor, James Marcum, and Martin Stuebs. 2017. "Virtuous Professionalism in Accountants to Avoid Fraud and to Restore Financial Reporting." *Journal of Business Ethics* 140 (4): 687–704.

LeBar, Mark, and Michael Slote. 2016. "Justice as a Virtue." *Stanford Encyclopedia of Philosophy*. Stanford University, https://plato.stanford.edu/entries/justice-virtue/.

Loy, Hui-chieh. 2014. "Classical Confucianism as Virtue Ethics." *The Handbook of Virtue Ethics*. New York: Acumen Publishing.

Luo, Shirong. 2015. "Mencius' Virtue Ethics Meets the Moral Foundations Theory: A Comparison." In *The Routledge Companion to Virtue Ethics*, 101–12. New York: Routledge.

MacIntyre, Alasdair, and After Virtue. 1984. "A Study in Moral Theory." *Notre Dame, IN*.

MacKinnon, Barbara, and Andrew Fiala. 2014. *Ethics: Theory and Contemporary Issues*. Nelson Education.

McManus, Lisa, and Nava Subramaniam. 2014. "Organisational and Professional Commitment of Early Career Accountants: Do Mentoring and Organisational Ethical Climate Matter?." *Accounting and Finance* 54 (4): 1231–61.

Melé, Domènec. 2005. "Ethical Education in Accounting: Integrating Rules, Values and Virtues." *Journal of Business Ethics* 57 (1): 97–109.

Miller, Christian, B. 2018. "Virtue as a Trait." In *The Oxford Handbook of Virtue*, edited by Nancy. E. Snow, 9–34. New York: Oxford University Press.

Mintz, Steven M. 1995. "Virtue Ethics and Accounting Education." *Issues in Accounting Education* 10: 247–68.

Mintz, Steven M. 2006. "Accounting Ethics Education: Integrating Reflective Learning and Virtue Ethics." *Journal of Accounting Education* 24 (2–3): 97–117.

Moore, Geoff. 2002. "On the Implications of the Practice – Institution Distinction: MacIntyre and the Application of Modern Virtue Ethics to Business." *Business Ethics Quarterly* 12 (1): 19–32.

Moore, Geoff. 2005a. "Corporate Character: Modern Virtue Ethics and the Virtuous Corporation." *Business Ethics Quarterly* 15 (4): 659–85.

Moore, Geoff. 2005b. "Humanizing Business: A Modern Virtue Ethics Approach." *Business Ethics Quarterly* 15 (2): 237–55.

Murphy, Patrick E. 1999. "Character and Virtue Ethics in International Marketing: An Agenda for Managers, Researchers and Educators." *Journal of Business Ethics* 18 (1): 107–24.

Nolder, C., and K. Kadous. 2014. "The Way Forward on Professional Skepticism: Conceptualizing Professional Skepticism as an Attitude." *Suffolk University and Goizueta Business School at Emory University*.

Nussbaum, Martha C. 1988. "Non-Relative Virtues: An Aristotelian Approach." *Midwest Studies in Philosophy* 13: 32–53.

Oakley, Justin, and Dean Cocking. 2001. *Virtue Ethics and Professional Roles*. Cambridge University Press.

Pakaluk, Michael. 2005. *Aristotle's Nicomachean Ethics: An Introduction*. Cambridge University Press.

Perrett, Roy, and Glen Pettigrove. 2015. "Hindu Virtue Ethics.".

Rest, James R. 1994. "Background: Theory and Research James R. Rest." In *Moral Development in the Professions*, 13–38. Psychology Press.

Sachs, J., 2002. *Aristotle Nicomachean Ethics: Translation, Glossary, and Introductory Essay*. Indianapolis, IN: Focus Publishing.

Sanford, Jonathan J. 2010. "Are you Man Enough? Aristotle and Courage." *International Philosophical Quarterly* 50 (4): 431–45.

Sanford, Jonathan J. 2015. *Before Virtue*. CUA Press.

Schroth, Jörg. 2008. "The Priority of the Right in Kant's Ethics." *Kant's Ethics of Virtue*. Berlin, and New York: Walter de Gruyter.

Sim, May. 2015. "Why Confucius' Ethics is a Virtue Ethics." *Besser-Jones and Slote (2015)*: 63–76.

Snow, Nancy E., ed. 2017. *The Oxford Handbook of Virtue*. Oxford University Press.

Sosik, John J., and David L. Lee. 2002. "Mentoring in Organizations: A Social Judgment Perspective for Developing Tomorrow's Leaders." *Journal of Leadership Studies* 8 (4): 17–32.

Stichter, Matt. 2018. *Virtue as a Skill*. New York, USA: Oxford University Press.

Taylor, Eileen Z., and Mary B. Curtis. 2018. "Mentoring: A Path to Prosocial Behavior." *Journal of Business Ethics* 152 (4): 1133–48.

West, Andrew. 2017. "The Ethics of Professional Accountants: An Aristotelian Perspective." *Accounting, Auditing and Accountability Journal* 30 (2): 328–51.

West, Andrew. 2018a. "After Virtue and Accounting Ethics." *Journal of Business Ethics* 148 (1): 21–36.

West, Andrew. 2018b. "Multinational Tax Avoidance: Virtue Ethics and the Role of Accountants." *Journal of Business Ethics* 153 (4): 1143–56.

Whetstone, J. Thomas. 2001. "How Virtue Fits within Business Ethics." *Journal of Business Ethics* 33 (2): 101–14.

5

HABERMAS AND DISCOURSE ETHICS

Larita J. Killian

Introduction: Habermas in perspective

Since his first major publication in 1962,[1] Jurgen Habermas's work has influenced our understanding of philosophy, sociology, religion, democracy, accountability, global capitalism, and the fate of the European Union. His early work was a continuation of the Frankfurt School of critical theory (Finlayson 2005). Numerous scholars have critiqued and extended his work. The theory of ethical discourse that occupies a central place in Habermas's *oeuvre* highlights the primacy of speech in establishing accountability and binding communities.

Habermas speaks to the modern "post metaphysical" world (1993, 94). Premodern societies are based on kinship and shared religious traditions. In contrast, individuals in modern, complex societies face competing interpretations of the world and competing ethical claims. Pluralistic societies can no longer draw from a central moral authority to settle questions of ethical value and "the good life" (Gilbert and Rasche 2007, 188). This forces us to relinquish either the principle of tolerance or the belief that we can privilege one way of life over another, thus shattering the "naiveté of dogmatic modes of belief founded on absolute truth claims" (Habermas 1993, 94).

Skeptics might conclude that modern society is ruled by systems (e.g., commercial or technical interests) and instrumental, self-serving behavior, but this is not the complete story. Habermas insists that society is comprised of both system and lifeworld,[2] and they meet in the public sphere. The lifeworld embodies the values, experiences, and "life projects" of individuals. The lifeworld's "cultural patterns of interpretation, evaluation, and expression serve as resources for the achievement of mutual understanding" by participants (Lodh and Graffikin 1997, 448). Through discourse, individuals are capable of learning from each other and forming new understandings of what is "good" (ethical) for themselves and others. This communicative action alters the horizons and contours of the lifeworld of participants. Further, communicative action results in public will-formation that can (potentially) influence and limit the behavior of systems (Habermas 1994). "[I]t is through the idea of 'communicative power' that the lifeworld is institutionally effective" (Power and Laughlin 1996, 453). System and lifeworld coexist in a "fragile equilibrium" (Finlayson 2005, 56). There is always the danger that subsystems will colonize the public sphere to such a degree that the lifeworld withers and communicative action is stymied. To Habermas, whether this occurs is an empirical question, not preordained by theory (1993).

Habermas's ethical discourse theory is a reaction to excessive individualism. Habermas seeks to counter excessive individualism that, among other ills, corrupts modern capitalism with "an atomistic concept of the person" and a "contractualist concept of society" (Habermas 1993, 121). The self is not a primary phenomenon; rather, it is the "product of a process of socialization" that presupposes reciprocal recognition (Habermas 1993, 46). A person can be "individuated" only through socialization and reciprocal recognition (Habermas 1993, 67). Individual intentions, interests, and desires are not essentially individual because they are constructed through language and culture (Lodh and Graffikin 1997, 450).

By the same token, individuals cannot "step out" from their lifeworld (Lodh and Graffikin 1997, 450). Self and community are constructed and renewed simultaneously. In the "communication community," networks of "reciprocal recognition" reproduce themselves; without these networks, self-identity as well as social bonds would disintegrate (Habermas 1993, 154). Through the process of ethical development and learning, individuals may modify their own interests based on an understanding and recognition of the interests of others (Finlayson 2005). Thus, political and social participation are required for human development and well-being; to be prevented from participation in the political life of the community is a major deprivation (Sen 1999).

Habermas is often contrasted to Kant, and indeed makes this comparison himself (Habermas 1988, 1993, 1990).[3] For Kant, ethical guidelines transcend experience: "[T]he categorical ought, has its roots in pure reason alone" (2008, 13). Through reasoning and reflection, an individual can determine the proper ethical path. Kant's test for an ethical norm is whether it is suitable to become a universal maxim applicable to all.

Habermas believes, however, that the validity of a norm cannot be justified in the mind of an isolated individual. Individuals cannot discover ethical truths through autonomous reasoning because we are not autonomous beings. "In discourse ethics, the idea of autonomy is intersubjective. It takes into account the fact that the free actualization of the personality of one individual depends on the actualization of freedom for all" (Habermas 1988, 49). He eschews ethical absolutism: "This *relativistic ethics of responsibility* [emphasis original] deals with real moral dilemmas, not merely hypothetical ones, it takes the complexity of lived situations into account" (Habermas 1990, 176). Like Kant, Habermas has a universal test, but the test applies to the *process* of identifying ethical norms, not the content: "*Only those norms may claim to be valid that could meet with the consent of all concerned, in their role as participants in a practical discourse*" (Habermas 1988, 40; emphasis original).

Frequently, Habermas is contrasted to Marx (Lehman 2001; Lodh and Graffikin 1997; Finlayson 2005). Habermas and Marx share a critical perspective and a concern for the impact of capitalism on society, especially the impact on social solidarity (Lodh and Graffikin 1997). They would agree that system, in the guise of capitalism, is colonizing the public sphere and expanding its instrumental (profit-seeking) behavior (Power and Laughlin 1996). Habermas, however, finds that Marx's work is limited because it "under-theorizes communication" and the role of the lifeworld in the public sphere (Lehman 2001, 725). Habermas places more emphasis on the ability of communicative action and "democratic will-formation" to influence and constrain systems (1996, 336), so triumph of a subsystem (e.g., corporate capitalism) over the lifeworld is not inevitable.

Habermas's far-ranging work has evolved over six decades. No single chapter or article can fully capture the "twists and turns of Habermas's theoretical apparatus" (Power 2013, 226). This chapter is meant to introduce scholars, especially accountants, to his work and to ethical discourse theory in general.

Principles of discourse ethics

Primacy of speech

The core of discourse ethics is the primacy of speech. We cannot separate discourse from language (Habermas 1993). Society develops and progresses through increased linguistic skills. Through speech, meanings are "discovered and defined" (Laughlin 1987, 481). Through language, participants "articulate their ethical feelings and judgments" and competing visions of the good (Habermas 1993, 73). Human rationality and mutual understanding are outcomes of the successful use of language (Gilbert and Rasche 2007). Speech acts inherently involve claims about the nature of the world or what is "good," and speakers tacitly commit themselves to justifying their claims.

The critical aspect of language is what it *does*. Speech coordinates actions of multiple individuals and provides "invisible tracks along which interactions can unfold in an orderly and conflict-free manner" (Finlayson 2005, 34). The purpose of language is to promote understanding and thus consensus. Habermas opposes the view that humans are, essentially, instrumental and self-serving creatures.[4] If this were true, why is there not constant and universal conflict? According to discourse ethics, cooperative behavior is pervasive because humans are capable of reaching understanding and consensus through discourse.

To Habermas, a speech act is an utterance that contains the speaker's intention as well as content. The intention is a claim to some form of validity, such as effectiveness, goodness, rightness, or truth (Gilbert and Rasche 2007). The hearer may accept or reject the (often implied) claim. The speech act is socially binding. Social integration depends on "the illocutionary binding energies of a use of language oriented to reaching understanding" (Habermas 1996, 8). "Sociality" is created through the process of discourse, and this function of speech has priority over its function of "denoting the way the world is" (Finlayson 2005, 33). The speech act contributes to both "individuation" and to strengthening social bonds:

> [T]he lifeworld of a language community is reproduced in turn through the communicative actions of its members. This explains why the identity of the individual and that of the collective are interdependent; they form and maintain themselves together. Built into the consensus-oriented language use of social interaction, there is an inconspicuous necessity for participants to become more and more individuated. Conversely, everyday language is also the medium by which the intersubjectivity of a shared world is maintained.
>
> *(Habermas 1988, 42)*

During discourse, individuals assume alternating roles of speaker, addressee, or bystander, and each role assumes a different perspective. As participants assume different roles, their individual perspectives become "intertwined with a system of *world perspectives*" (Habermas 1990, 135; emphasis original). As language skills develop, individuals progress from a position of "primitive egocentrism" toward a capacity for coping with the external, social world in a "differentiated but integrated manner" (Laughlin 1987, 487). Today, efforts to promote communal discourse often involve virtual tools and online platforms. For instance, a city may use an online forum to seek public input on budget priorities. Such virtual techniques have value but are no substitute for face-to-face discourse (Van Peursem 2005).[5] In written dialogue, for instance, the "speaking subject disappears" and is replaced by symbolic marks: "The discursive transaction becomes one between the text and the reader, not the author and the reader" (Arrington and Francis 1993, 116).

During ethical discourse, participants seek understanding and consensus. Individuals make validity claims about what is "right" or "good" and offer reasons for those claims. "Argumentation is not a decision procedure resulting in *collective decisions*, but a problem-solving procedure that generates *convictions*" (Habermas 1993, 158; emphasis original). Discourse is a cooperative process of interpretation aimed at "intersubjectively recognized definitions of situations" (White 1988, 39). Discourse seeks to answer *What should we do?* Participants justify or refute validity claims before an audience; this presupposes membership in a community and that other members of the community are capable of understanding and judgment (Habermas 1996). In fact, it presupposes learning. During discourse, participants learn from each other and adjust attitudes along with meanings. Of course, consensus is not always achieved: participants "agree on the validity claimed for their speech acts or identify points of disagreement, which they conjointly take into consideration in the course of further interaction" (Habermas 1996, 18).

Ideal speech

Ethical discourse theory is criticized for being overoptimistic. One vulnerable target is the concept of "ideal speech," the "notoriously demanding procedural conditions for a discourse capable of legitimating its outcomes" (Froomkin 2003, 752). The goal of ideal speech is that individuals may enter into discourse, learn from one another, and reach consensus on what is "good" for themselves and others. This cannot attain unless all relevant voices are heard, the best available arguments are expressed given the current state of knowledge, and only the "unforced force of the better argument" determines the outcome (Habermas 1993, 145). Absent these conditions, we cannot convince anyone, least of all ourselves, of the rightness of the outcome. Habermas provides a framework for ideal speech (1990, 87–89). Core requirements include the following:

- Every subject with the competence to speak and act is allowed to take part in a discourse.
- Everyone is allowed to question any assertion whatever.
- Everyone is allowed to introduce any assertion whatever into the discourse.
- Everyone is allowed to express his attitudes, desires, and needs.
- No speaker may be prevented, by internal or external coercion, from exercising his rights.[6]

Further, no topic or theme is "off limits," for "Only participants themselves can decide what is and what is not of common concern to them" (Habermas 1996, 312). Ideal speech is designed to achieve rational consensus by avoiding "deception, coercion, or manipulation" (Rasche and Esser 2006, 258) and by ensuring a just and neutral process where no individual's "particular interests or good" are favored over that of any other (Rehg 1994, 7). The interacting participants become "mutually accountable" in presenting, challenging, and defending validity claims (Power and Laughlin 1996, 450).

Critics cite numerous impediments to ideal speech. For instance, threat, force, coercion, or trickery may taint the outcome (Froomkin 2003). The "privileged or powerful" may dominate discourse and deny others equal opportunity to participate (Van Peursem 2005, 61). Habermas recognizes these impediments, noting that successful discourse requires a capacity for learning, both at the cultural and personal level, and such capacity may not always be present. "[D]ogmatic worldviews and rigid patterns of socialization can block a discursive mode of sociation"

(Habermas 1996, 325). Attempts to achieve ideal speech, however, will facilitate equity among stakeholders and diminish the sway of economically powerful stakeholders (Gilbert and Rasche 2007). As discussants approach ideal speech conditions, discourse improves and outcomes become more valid (Habermas 1993). Ideal speech cannot be fully realized because we cannot foresee all possible arguments and may be unaware of some individuals who will be affected by the outcome and who should, therefore, participate in the discourse. Ideal speech can be approximated but never attained (Habermas 1993).

Communicative action

Communicative action[7] is a broad concept that encompasses ethical discourse and its consequences. One consequence is mutual conviction regarding norms.

> I shall speak of *communicative* action whenever the actions of the agents involved are coordinated not through egocentric calculations of success but through acts of reaching understanding. In communicative action participants are not primarily oriented to their own individual successes; they pursue their individual goals under the condition that they can harmonize their plans of action on the basis of common situation definitions.
>
> *(Habermas 1984, 285–86)*

Mutual understanding is a "mechanism for action coordination" (Habermas 1996, 17). Once tested and accepted, "consensual" norms coordinate actions and provide the basis for social order (Finlayson 2005). Through communicative action, participants conceptualize and change their world for the better. Communicative action allows nonviolent change to happen and "leads to changes in both the social and technical reality" (Laughlin 1987, 496). It can expand and alter the contours of the lifeworld and exert pressure to constrain the instrumental behavior of systems.

Communicative action creates and repairs social integration. Through language, "interactions are woven together and forms of life are structured" (Habermas 1996, 3–4). The most critical part of the speech act is the "performative aspect," not the content. Speaker and hearer "encounter each other" and turn toward each other "in authentic togetherness" (Habermas 2015, 125–27). By engaging in discourse and exchanging reasons for validity claims, participants acknowledge their mutual accountability. When basing their actions on consensual norms, "each agent's own critical capacities are increasingly integrated into the on-going reproduction of the lifeworld" (Lodh and Graffikin 1997, 449). The binding power of communicative action is especially important in modern societies where religious traditions and antecedent moral values are less effective in creating social order (Finlayson 2005).

Communicative action is egalitarian in nature. To engage in discourse is to open oneself to being "answerable" and "*called to account*" (emphasis original) by another (Habermas 2015, 128). Because the direction of dialogue can be reversed and each can be speaker or hearer, the process "lends the dialogical relation an egalitarian character" (Habermas 2015, 128). Even intercultural clashes of "us" versus "them" necessitate a "*symmetrical relation*" (emphasis original), like two boxers in a ring (Habermas 1993, 104–5). Ideals of justice and solidarity are implicit in the reciprocal recognition of communicative action. Through reciprocal recognition, both the integrity of the individual person and the social fabric are safeguarded (Habermas 1993). When communicative action is successful and consensus is reached, this shared understanding feeds back into the lifeworld. The shared understandings of the lifeworld support communicative action, and in turn communicative action nourishes the lifeworld (Finlayson 2005).

No discourse or communicative action is final, because circumstances and participants change (Habermas 1996). Ideal speech conditions require that proposed norms be assessed from the perspective of all who will be affected, but we cannot truly identify all those individuals and bring them into the discourse: some are still making their way toward a specific language community, and some are not yet born. Consensual norms have been tested and found acceptable for a particular community in a particular place and time, and they can be quite powerful. For instance, the accounting profession in the United States was norm-based prior to the establishment of the Securities and Exchange Commission (SEC).[8] As circumstances and actors change, all norms are open to challenge. The only universal constant is the process of testing and legitimizing norms.

The broader context: systems and institutions

Systems and strategic action

Ethical discourse theory explains how norms are identified and how communicative action nurtures social cohesion, but of course there are countervailing forces. The lifeworld shares the public sphere with systems, "sedimented structures and established patterns of instrumental action" characterized by money, technology, or administrative power (Finlayson 2005, 53). Systems[9] arise from linguistic development and *specialization* within the lifeworld; they are tangible expressions of the lifeworld but distinct from the lifeworld (Laughlin 1987). Finlayson characterizes systems as "parasitic" to the lifeworld (2005, 47). Lifeworld and systems exist in a state of tension. Ideally, the lifeworld will continue to influence and "steer" systems so that systems serve the purposes of the lifeworld. There is growing distance, however, between the common, shared "linguistic resources" of the lifeworld and the diverse, specialized language of subsystems (Power and Laughlin 1996, 444). As systems become more specialized, they no longer possess the common language necessary to receive and articulate "the relevant issues and standards of evaluation that apply to society as a whole" (Habermas 1996, 352).

Lifeworld and systems both have the capacity to integrate and coordinate the actions of individuals through speech, but there is a crucial difference. Communicative speech is concerned with understanding, while strategic speech is concerned with success. In communicative action, integration emanates from the intentions of the participants and their shared "intuitive background understanding of the lifeworld" (Habermas 1993, 166). In contrast, systems coordinate behavior strategically, "over the heads of the participants," through interlocking consequences of action, such as rewards and sanctions (Habermas 1993, 166). Strategic speech is concerned with getting other people to do things as means to realizing one's own ends (Finlayson 2005). This contrasts to ethical discourse, which seeks understanding and consensus on what the proper end should be.

> [A]n actor who acts strategically primarily seeks to manipulate and influence the behavior of another by threatening sanctions or by the prospect of gratification, and does not rely on the power of communicative understanding.
>
> *(Gilbert and Rasche 2007, 191)*

In practice, individuals may switch from an orientation of reaching understanding to that of a "strategically acting subject concerned with his own success" (Habermas 1993, 78).

Systems perform vital functions in complex societies. For instance, they coordinate actions to ensure the production and circulation of goods and services (Finlayson 2005). In doing so, however, they cut deep channels into social life and induce individuals into strategic behavior that may not correlate with aims of the lifeworld. "Oppressive social systems survive, not because individuals mistake their own interests, but because their actions fall into pre-established, bewilderingly complex patterns of instrumental reasoning" (Finlayson 2005, 58).

Systems arise from and remain dependent on the lifeworld. While systems have a legitimate role, the lifeworld should remain dominant. Problems arise when systems become so specialized and autonomous they decouple from the lifeworld. "[T]hey develop their own codes and own semantics, which no longer admit of mutual translation"(Habermas 1996, 335). Rather than being steered by shared meanings and norms of the lifeworld, systems may become self-referential and driven by instrumental goals that do not serve the broader society. Eventually, this leads to internal colonization, "a reversal of the order of dependency between system and lifeworld" (Power and Laughlin 1996, 444) in which systems absorb the functions of the lifeworld and impose instrumental goals upon it. The domain of the lifeworld shrinks, along with its ability to renew social cohesion through communicative action (Finlayson 2005).

As colonization advances, important decisions are left to markets or placed in the hands of technical experts. "The transparency of the lifeworld is gradually obscured and the bases of action and decision are withdrawn from public scrutiny and from possible democratic control" (Finlayson 2005, 56). This results in "distorted outcomes" that support the interests of a few powerful players rather than society as a whole (Healy 2004, 94). Social pathologies arise, including "the negative effects of markets on the non-market domains they colonize" (Finlayson 2005, 56).

Institutions and mediation

Institutions, when properly functioning, mediate between system and lifeworld. Habermas places particular importance on the institutions of law and the administrative state (government) as steering mechanisms. Even in a democracy, the communicative power generated through ethical discourse cannot "rule" by itself but can only "point the use of administrative power in specific directions" (Habermas 1994, 9). During discourse, participants engage in "public opinion-formation" that is transferred into "communicative power" through political elections, and again transferred into "administrative power" through legislation (Habermas 1994, 8). Institutions absorb communicative power and use that power to steer systems; they allow the "normative priorities" of the lifeworld to flow into systems (Power and Laughlin 1996, 444). To be perceived as legitimate, institutions must act in ways that align with "communicatively *produced* power" (emphasis original), a scarce resource that organizations compete for and officials manage but that none of them can produce (Power and Laughlin 1996, 453). Communicative power affects the administrative system by "cultivating the pool of reasons" on which administrative decisions must draw; not everything that could be done may be done by administrative systems (Habermas 1993, 170).

The highest purpose of the administrative state is not to protect equal private rights but to assure an "inclusive opinion- and will-formation in which free and equal citizens reach understanding on what goals and norms are in the interest of all" (Habermas 1994, 2). Institutions enforce ground rules for the deliberative process; as the process approaches ideal speech conditions, citizens can be confident that policy outcomes are impartial, transparent, and accountable (Healy 2004). Even where consensus is not achieved, an open and inclusive process will ensure that any political compromise is reasonable. Once communicative power is encoded in law, the law bolsters confidence that as individuals fulfill their obligations, others will "behave recipro-cally in the future if need be" (Habermas 2015, 23).

This discussion presupposes a healthy public sphere in which lifeworld and systems exist in beneficial equilibrium. When society is "structurally coupled," the lifeworld guides and legiti-mates the institutional steering mechanisms, and systems accept and comply with the regulatory steering (Broadbent and Laughlin 2003, 29). It is possible, however, that regulatory institutions intended to mediate between lifeworld and systems will impose the systems' interests against the popular will: "Steering media expand to constitute the lifeworld rather than mediate on its behalf" (Power and Laughlin 1996, 445).

It is reasonable to ask whether ethical discourse theory is overoptimistic and whether it is sufficient to address current social ills. For instance, Lehman writes, "[W]e must recognize that 'information' and 'discussion' are not enough to transform the social fabric and the inter- and intra-class relationships which limit reform proposals in modern communities" (2001, 727). Gilbert and Rasche (2007, 210) note that the conditions of "real-world communication," such as unequal power distribution, weaken the applicability of discourse ethics. Rasche and Esser (2006, 262) observe that "Habermas works with rather idealized assumptions. Conditions of real-world discourses differ substantially from this framework." Despite these criticisms, Haber-mas perseveres and takes the long view:

> To be sure, this estimate [criticism] pertains only to a *public sphere at rest*. In periods of mobilization, the structures that actually support the authority of a critically engaged public begin to vibrate. The balance of power between civil society and the political system then shifts.
>
> *(1996, 379; emphasis original)*

Ethical discourse and professional accounting practice: selected studies

Habermas delves deeply into intersubjective accountability but does not specifically address accounting practice. Multiple scholars, however, have applied his theory in analyzing account-ing practice and its impact on society. Like Power and Laughlin (1996, 441) they seek to "build analytical bridges between his grand social-theoretical orientation, with all its philosophical underpinnings, and relatively concrete forms of practice."

Conceptual studies

Laughlin (1987) was among the first to apply Habermas's discourse theory to the study of accounting systems. His treatment is complex and has been characterized as "a sustained effort at theorizing," so deep and involved that "the labour and difficulty are there to see" (Power 2013, 226–27). Laughlin stresses that accounting has both social-cultural and technical elements. The accounting system, a specialized language, helps shape the organization; as instrumental speech, it also influences the behavior of individuals. Laughlin (1987) emphasizes that broad social interests (lifeworld) should steer changes in the technical design of accounting systems rather than technology imposing its objectives on (colonizing) the lifeworld. For instance, (writing in 1987) he advises it may be necessary to defer plans to computerize accounting information and to refuse to implement technical procedures advanced by standard setting bodies if they are "out of line with cultural expectations and desires" (Laughlin 1987, 494). He calls for inclusive discourse ("speech acts") to generate alternative designs for accounting systems rather than having design imposed by technical experts.

Lodh and Graffikin (1997) address the relationship between the methodological framework of critical accounting research and the goal of applying the results of critical research. In a multilayered discussion, they stress that critical researchers will not truly have applied Habermas's framework unless they adopt an "emancipatory" perspective, an approach that blends the technical and nontechnical (or practical) and that results in a "critical ethnography" concerned with the impact of accounting practice in specific contexts (Lodh and Graffikin 1997, 466). It is not enough that the research methodology incorporates discourse between the researchers and the researched, as described by Laughlin (1987). Research is incomplete if it lacks an emancipatory aspect.

Roberts (1991) analyzes the dual nature of accounting as both ethical (communicative) and strategic (instrumental) discourse, and concludes the split between the ethical and the strategic is detrimental to both. "The search for the possibilities of accountability should be oriented to the reconciliation of this divide" (Roberts 1991, 356). He explores the nature of accountability within an organization. Hierarchical accountability exerts strategic, instrumental force on individuals and "isolates" them as solitary beings who must produce certain strategic results for the organization or face expulsion. "Hierarchical accountability, in which accounting information typically plays a central role, serves to individualize" (Roberts 1991, 363). This concept is echoed by Williams (2002), who finds modern accounting to be a "technology of control" in which the interests of property are translated into "outcome measures imposed on persons who are monitored" (2002, 15). Individuals in an organization, however, also experience socializing (integrating) forms of accountability:

> It is these conditions – a relative absence of asymmetries of power, and a context for the face-to-face negotiation of the significance of organizational events – that are the basis for what will be characterized here as socializing forms of accountability. At the heart of these is a form of talk which whilst confirming of self, at the same time openly acknowledges the interdependence of self and other.
>
> *(Roberts 1991, 362)*

Like Habermas, Roberts recognizes there are legitimate roles for both strategic and ethical discourse. His aim is not to eliminate strategic accountability but to reconcile "individualizing and socializing forms of accountability" so that socializing forms are not subordinate to hierarchical, individualizing forms and to ensure that strategic discourse remains within the "normative regulation" of ethical discourse (Roberts 1991, 365). Business organizations are more likely to be successful if individualizing forces do not "stand in the way of freeing up and pooling of collective energies in pursuit of common goals" (Roberts 1991, 366).

Schweiker (1993), a theologian, adopts Habermas's perspective as well as religious perspectives (Judaic and Christian) to explore the role of accounting as both moral and economic discourse. Moral identity and membership in a community are enacted through giving and receiving of accounts. The fact that corporations render accounts (through accountants) "evokes some awareness of pre-given relations to others, relations subject to claims about what is good and evil (Schweiker 1993, 241). He admonishes accountants to remember their role as guardians of the "fiduciary relation through the scope of time and community" between corporations and society (Schweiker 1993, 249).

Law and the administrative state derived from law are subsystems, but Habermas (1994) assigns them special status as mediators between the lifeworld and system. Power and Laughlin (1996) build on this concept and posit that accounting now occupies a mediating role similar to law:

> Critical accounting is interesting precisely because accounting, rather than public law, has become the language of system mediation itself. It is accounting that operates at the interface between markets and hierarchies and it is accounting which *may or may not* mediate system and lifeworld.
>
> *(1996, 457; emphasis added)*

Per Power and Laughlin (1996), the question of whether accounting practice is beneficial or harmful to the lifeworld in any specific situation is empirical. They caution against foregone conclusions that the impact is always negative. In practice, accountants must constantly navigate the tension between using their expertise to interpret the lifeworld to the financial system or allowing the financial system to steer the lifeworld: "[I]t is experts who are now entrusted as mediators and interpreters between lifeworld and sub-systems" (Power and Laughlin 1996, 452).

Lehman (2001) respects Habermas's theory but maintains it is insufficient to bring the changes desired by critical accountants, especially with regard to social and environmental accounting. Like other critical scholars, he wants to transform institutions that perpetuate injustice in the name of "economic growth and progress-unfettered capitalism" (Lehman 2001, 717). He warns, however, that those who look to ethical discourse for a remedy underestimate the capacity of capitalism to avoid reform.

> [P]rocedural reform models are caught within the essence of capitalism from which they cannot escape. Capitalism creates a social system which contains within it systemic barriers that deflect attempts to reform the system *(wesenlogik)*. That is, capitalism avoids reforms and has the ability to absorb and deflect critique.
>
> *(Lehman 2001, 726)*

Lehman points to Tinker, Lehman, and Niemark (1991), who, adopting a Marxist perspective, view social accounting as a "rationalization of the capitalist process" (Lehman 2001, 718). From a Marxist perspective, "improvements" such as social and environmental accounting are mere modifications within a fundamentally flawed system. To achieve true reform, we must reconsider "Hegelian dialectics and Marx's critical appropriation" and combine them with ethical discourse (Lehman 2001, 724). To this end, he proposes a "placement ethic" as a device to create a "discourse arena" to consider different perspectives on accounting reform and to move beyond the "usual deadlock between procedure and critique" and "think about whether insights from different traditions can be combined in constructing new social and environmental accounting pathways" (Lehman 2001, 724).

Williams (2002) employs Habermas's framework, *inter alia*, to explore the incoherence in much accounting discourse. Accounting is often presented as a technical measurement system that provides objective information for economic decisions, yet those who violate accounting standards are considered unethical. Thus, accounting standards are moral directives as well as measurement techniques. Recent discourse emphasizes the technical role of accounting, which "masks the inherently ethical nature of accounting practice that is explicit in accountability" (Williams 2002, 5). When the ethical role is concealed, it "immunizes" practitioners and standard-setters from contemplating the ends and interests they serve with accounting technology.

As illustration, Williams explores the impact of FASB SFAS No. 106, which requires companies to report liabilities for post-retirement health benefits. This FASB directive may motivate companies to reduce or eliminate post-retirement benefits to avoid recognizing large liabilities. Per Habermas's theory, norms are valid only if arrived at through open discourse in which all affected parties may participate, yet FASB standards are developed via a process that privileges "residents of a closed, technicist discursive community" (Williams 2002, 14). In the case of FASB SFAS No. 106, the retirees who risk losing their benefits were not equal participants in the discourse. As Habermas observes, "If the discourse of experts is not coupled with democratic opinion- and will-formation, then the experts' perception of problems will prevail at the citizens' expense" (Habermas 1996, 351). Williams concludes that since accounting standards are treated as moral norms, "accountants should be concerned about justifying their moral authority, which can come only from the habit of providing persuasive reasons (and doing a bit more diverse research) as to why everyone benefits from accounting procedures" (Williams 2002, 19).

Dillard and Bricker (1992) assess the potential impact of expert (computer) systems on audit practice from three perspectives: technical-empirical, historical-hermeneutical, and critical. The technical-empirical perspective is concerned with efficiency and productivity. The historical-hermeneutical perspective "recognizes the central position of the social as manifest in language, conversation and context in audit judgement and decision making," thus setting the stage for the critical perspective (Dillard and Bricker 1992, 206). The critical perspective draws primarily from Habermas and focuses on systemic forces motivating and motivated by technological innovation.[10]

Dillard and Bricker do not explicitly oppose expert systems but rather seek to minimize negative effects of such technology. From a critical perspective, they analyze the forces behind technological innovation and the corresponding effects. Expert systems manifest the technological colonization of the auditor's lifeworld, and "such colonization obscures the repressive forces which restrict human social intercourse, impede social development and lead to crisis" (Dillard and Bricker 1992, 216–17). In surrendering to expert systems, the auditor forfeits a portion of personal "sovereignty," a loss of meaning and relevance in professional life:

> The auditor becomes alienated from his or her work, no longer able to make the requisite professional commitments because of the absence of ethical or value considerations.
>
> *(Dillard and Bricker 1992, 217)*

Expert technology provides the "judgments" that the auditor might previously have made in consultation with others. As the process continues, decisions become more "instrumentalized (automated)," mutual discourse withers, and the possibility of ethical, value, and political considerations becomes more remote (Dillard and Bricker 1992, 219). As the auditor's lifeworld is colonized, the common ground for professional discourse and transformation is diminished, and appeal to technical, instrumental authority rises. System-driven, instrumental action takes hold, and "the normative and subjective dimensions are lost, leading to distorted understandings and ultimately to distorted actions" (Dillard and Bricker 1992, 221).

Applied studies

Broadbent and Laughlin (2003) apply Habermas's concept of institutional steering mechanisms to the United Kingdom's private finance initiative (PFI) of 1992 and efforts to legitimize this initiative. They start from the premise that electoral control over a government is less direct and more reactive than managerial control over corporate agents. Voters can eventually remove officials from office if not satisfied with their performance, but voters have little direct control on the programs and daily activities of government. This contrasts, per Broadbent and Laughlin (2003), with managerial controls in a business, where the principal delegates responsibility to an agent but has more direct, forward-looking control over actual performance.

The PFI initiative is highly controversial; critics are concerned that it eliminates public sector jobs and may not actually save money. To address these concerns, the National Audit Office (NAO) began conducting "value for money" analyses of PFI projects. Drawing lessons from the PFI experience, Broadbent and Laughlin (2003, 44) conclude that pressure for more accountability over government programs will result in increased managerial-type control mechanisms, but electoral control over government operations will not increase. The NAO audits do not strengthen "structural coupling" between the lifeworld and system, nor do they increase the electorate's ability to control government operations. Rather, the audits serve to legitimize the PFI projects and provide the government with more managerial control over the projects.

Rasche and Esser (2006) address the issue of stakeholder accountability from the perspective of social and ethical accounting, auditing, and reporting (SEAAR), comparable to corporate social accountability (CSR) reporting. For corporations and individuals alike, to be accountable is to be willing to give justifications for claims and actions (Rasche and Esser 2006). A corporation desiring to engage in SEAAR has a choice of several reporting standards; some standards focus on the societal dimension, whereas others are mainly concerned with environmental impact. If corporate management chooses the SEAAR standard, the result is "managerial capture." The process of social accounting is controlled by management "and therefore lacks an accountable determination of scope" (Rasche and Esser 2006, 252). At best, this means the SEAAR process is limited to management's perspective; at worst, it means that only information that advances the corporate image is reported, at the cost of true accountability. To remedy "managerial capture," Rasche and Esser propose "to view stakeholder engagement not as an outcome of standard selection, but rather as a precondition" (2006, 252). They recommend Habermas's discourse ethics as a framework for ensuring that all affected stakeholders are involved in the standard selection process. Further, they address practical problems associated with trying to identify and involve all legitimate stakeholders.

Gilbert and Rasche (2007) apply Habermas's ethical discourse theory to SA 8000, "the first social accountability standard for retailers, brand companies, suppliers, and other organizations to maintain decent working conditions throughout the supply chain on a global basis" (2007, 197). SA 8000 defines minimum requirements for workplace conditions for corporations *and their suppliers*. SA 8000 is worthy of attention due to its global reach and because it is "one of the most developed and widely used social accounting standards" for multinational corporations (Gilbert and Rasche 2007, 200). There are three problems with SA 8000, however: the norms contained in SA 8000 are based on an insufficient justification; the standard provides no guidance on how to design dialogues with affected stakeholders; and commitment to the standard often seems to result from strategic action (coercion) rather than voluntary, communicative action.

To remedy these problems, Gilbert and Rasche recommend a *"discourse-ethically extended version of SA 8000"* (2007, 203; emphasis original). The Social Accountability International (SAI) Advisory Board should "initiate a practical discourse to critically evaluate" the normative basis of the standard; the discourse should involve "fringe stakeholders like suppliers, workers, and customers" (Gilbert and Rasche 2007, 205). Further, SAI should foster multiple discourses at the micro level to "deal with cultural diversity and the local adaptation of the macro-level norms" (Gilbert and Rasche 2007, 205). Ultimately, ethical norms must be validated within a specific linguistic community.

Van Peursem (2005) attempts to apply Habermas's framework to policy development within a New Zealand hospital. Motivated by the concepts of ideal speech and communicative action, Van Peursem designs and executes a process for engaging varied members of the hospital community in policy development. The goals are to deploy the "emancipatory precepts of ideal speech" to encourage participants to undergo their own personal and political transformation and to achieve "stakeholder-considerate accounting policy" for the hospital (Van Peursem 2005, 57). Habermas-inspired field research should involve a "democratically inspired range of participants, all of whom are favored with linguistic skills and a willingness to apply them using logical argumentation," and "equal and unfettered opportunities for expression" (Van Peursem 2005, 62–63).

This project resulted in a proposed reporting framework for New Zealand public health. Per ethical discourse theory, however, the success of this "values-directed approach" must be gauged by "whether and how conditions conducive to ideal speech have been fulfilled" (Van Peursem 2005, 59). In this regard, the author reports that participants may have experienced improved listening skills, expanded horizons, and a growing understanding of others' views, commensurate with the developmental expectations of ethical discourse.

Van Peursem's project appears beneficial to the participants and the broader hospital community. It illustrates limitations, however, that future researchers must strive to overcome if the goal is to apply Habermas's framework. For instance, all communication among participants was anonymous and occurred via the researcher. In an ideal speech situation, participants confront others, acknowledge the essential equality of others, and are subject to immediate demands from others to justify their claims. It is difficult to see how these criteria can be achieved, even approximated, when communications are anonymous and mediated by the researcher. Van Peursem's research seems more representative of the "Delphi technique" than ethical discourse (see Hsu and Sandford, 2007). This critique must be tempered, however, with appreciation for Van Peursem's effort to foster ideal speech and promote communicative action in a specific organization.

Conclusion

This chapter presents an introduction to Habermas's ethical discourse theory and to literature that extends, critiques, and applies this theory. The primary criticism of the theory relates to the "ideal speech" conditions necessary for communicative action. Further, Marxist scholars assert that however powerful communicative action may be, it is insufficient for tackling the capacity of modern capitalism to co-opt and deflect reform (Lehman 2001).

Habermas (1993, 164) acknowledges that his theory contains "an ideal content to which we can only approximate in reality," yet maintains that efforts to approach ideal speech conditions can result in communicative action that nourishes the lifeworld and steers systems. Ultimately, such efforts can help restore the proper balance between lifeworld and system in the public sphere. Ethical discourse theory inspires accounting reform efforts, per the studies summarized in the previous section. These scholars believe that ethical discourse can help improve (reform) accounting practice so that it serves the lifeworld rather than being a device by which systems force instrumental values upon the lifeworld. Without explicit intent, yet unsurprising given the reach of his scholarship, Habermas has a significant impact on critical accounting.

Habermas has been developing his framework for six decades, and the work continues. This introductory chapter does not attempt to explore the finer details that have evolved over time, such as the distinction between ethical discourse and moral discourse (both are validated through speech acts), or the dynamic relationship between institutions and steering mechanisms. Readers who want to explore further might start with the References, especially Habermas's own work and Finlayson (2005).

Notes

1 *The Structural Transformation of the Public Sphere: An Inquiry into a Category of Bourgeois Society.* First published in German in 1962. English translation, 1989, by Thomas Burger with Frederick Lawrence.

2 In the writings of Habermas and other scholars, these terms appear alternately as single or plural, i.e., "lifeworld" or "lifeworlds." Because individuals are bound together through speech and develop their identity through interaction with others (Habermas 1988), and because lifeworlds have permeable boundaries, the distinction between single or plural lifeworlds is nebulous.

3 See also Laughlin 1987; Froomkin 2003; Healy 2004; Finlayson 2005; Rasche and Esser 2006; Gilbert and Rasche 2007.

4 Michael Shermer (2004) summarizes research that supports Habermas's view of human nature. Drawing from the field of evolutionary ethics, Shermer concludes there is an evolutionary basis for moral and ethical behavior. "[H]umans evolved powerful neurological mechanisms to reinforce cooperation, accentuate pro-social behavior, and bond non-related people through the process of social exchange" (Shermer 2004, 257). For instance, "cooperation leads to stimulation of the pleasure centers of the brain" (Shermer 2004, 256). (The author thanks Paul Williams for this reference.)

5 The power of face-to-face communication is illustrated, *inter alia*, by the meeting of the heads of state from the United States and North Korea in 2018. This face-to-face meeting was broadly seen to put the officials on "equal" footing. A face-to-face context is perceived to absolve "asymmetries of power" (Messner 2009, 922).

6 While Habermas takes a "process" rather than "content" approach to validating ethical norms, the ideal speech requirements for ethical discourse constitute an *a priori* maxim. Later (1994, 5–6), he refers to these conditions as "communicative presuppositions."

7 Habermas develops the concept of communicative action in a two-volume work: *The Theory of Communicative Action: Reason and the Rationalisation of Society* (1981, English translation by T. McCarthy 1984) and *The Theory of Communicative Action: Lifeworld and System (1981,* English translation by T. McCarthy 1987).

8 Even today, the establishment of accounting standards involves a due-process procedure characterized by, *inter alia*, face-to-face and written discourse among affected parties. While the FASB and IASB due-process procedures may fall short of perfection, they are more analogous to Habermas's description of how norms are developed than to an empirical search for the "right answer." (The author is indebted to the Paul Williams for this insight.)

9 In the literature, both "systems" and "subsystems" are used. For instance, in his 1996 work, Habermas uses "systems" where others might use "subsystems."

10 At writing, the technology in question was "Lotus 123 and other spreadsheet packages," but the authors' critique applies in general to the tension between technology-driven decisions and decisions based on intersubjective human discourse.

References

Arrington, C. E., and J. Francis. 1993. "Giving Economic Accounts: Accounting as Cultural Practice." *Accounting, Organizations and Society* 18 (213): 107–24.

Broadbent, J., and R. Laughlin. 2003. "Control and Legitimation in Government Accountability Processes: The Private Finance Initiative in The U.K." *Critical Perspectives on Accounting* 14: 23–48.

Dillard, J., and R. Bricker. 1992. "A Critique of Knowledge-Based Systems in Auditing: The Systemic Encroachment of Technical Consciousness." *Critical Perspectives on Accounting* 3: 205–24.

Finlayson, J. 2005. *Habermas: A Very Short Introduction.* Oxford: Oxford University Press.

Froomkin, A. M. 2003. "Habermas@discourse.net: Toward a Critical Theory of Cyberspace." *Harvard Law Review* 116 (3): 749–873.

Gilbert, D., and A. Rasche. 2007. "Discourse Ethics and Social Accountability: The Ethics of SA 8000." *Business Ethics Quarterly* 17 (2): 187–216.

Habermas, J.1984. *The Theory of Communicative Action: Reason and the Rationalization of Society, Volume I.* Translated by T. McCarthy. Originally published in German in 19622. Cambridge, UK: Polity Press.

Habermas, J. 1988. "Morality and Ethical Life: Does Hegel's Critique of Kant Apply to Discourse Ethics?" *Northwestern University Law Review* 83 (1&2): 38–53.

Habermas, J. 1990. *Moral Consciousness and Communicative Action.* Translated by C. Lenhardt and S. Nicholson. Originally published in 1983. Cambridge, MA: MIT Press.

Habermas, J. 1993. *Justification and Application.* Translated by C. Cronin. Originally published in German in 1991. Cambridge, MA: MIT Press.

Habermas, J. 1994. "Three Normative Models of Democracy." *Democratic and Constitutional Theory Today* 1 (1): 1–10.

Habermas, J. 1996. *Between Facts and Norms: Contributions to a Discourse Theory of Law and Democracy.* Translated by W. Rehg. Originally published in German in 1992. Cambridge, MA: MIT Press.

Habermas, J. 2015. *The Lure of Technocracy.* Translated by C. Cronin. Originally published in German in 2013. Cambridge, UK: Polity Press.

Healy, P. 2004. "Making Policy Debate Matter: Practical Reason, Political Dialogue, and Transformative Learning." *History of the Human Sciences* 17 (1): 77–106.

Hsu, C. C., and B. Sandford. 2007. "The Delphi Technique: Making Sense of Consensus." *Practical Assessment, Research & Evaluation* 12 (10): 1–8.

Kant, I. 2008. *The Mete physical Elements of Ethics.* Translation by T. Abbott. Originally published in German in 1780. Auckland, New Zealand: The Floating Press.

Laughlin, R. 1987. "Accounting Systems in Organisational Contexts: A Case for Critical Theory." *Accounting, Organizations and Society* 12 (5): 479–502.

Lehman, G. 2001. "Reclaiming the Public Sphere: Problems and Prospects for Corporate Social and Environmental Accounting." *Critical Perspectives on Accounting* 12 (6): 713–33.

Lodh, S., and M. Graffikin. 1997. "Critical Studies in Accounting Research, Rationality and Habermas: A Methodological Reflection." *Critical Perspectives on Accounting* 8: 433–74.

Messner, M. 2009. "The Limits of Accountability." *Accounting, Organizations and Society* 34 (8): 918–38.

Power, M. 2013. "Theory and Theorization: A Comment on Laughlin and Habermas." *Critical Perspectives on Accounting* 24 (3): 225–27.

Power, M., and R. Laughlin. 1996. "Habermas, Law and Accounting." *Accounting, Organizations, and Society* 21 (5): 441–65.

Rasche, A., and D. Esser. 2006. "From Stakeholder Management to Stakeholder Accountability: Applying Habermasian Discourse Ethics to Accountability Research." *Journal of Business Ethics* 65: 251–67.

Rehg, W. 1994. *Insight and Solidarity: A Study in the Discourse Ethics of Jurgen Habermas.* Berkeley: University of California Press. (Reprinted 1997. Citations in this article from 1994 edition.)

Roberts, J. 1991. "The Possibilities of Accountability." *Accounting, Organizations and Society* 16 (4): 355–68.

Schweiker, W. 1993. "Accounting for Ourselves: Accounting Practice and the Discourse of Ethics." *Accounting, Organizations and Society* 18 (203): 231–52.

Sen, A. 1999. "Democracy as a Universal Value." *Journal of Democracy* 10 (3): 3–17.

Shermer, M. 2004. *The Science of Good and Evil: Why People Cheat, Gossip, Care, Share, and Follow the Golden Rule.* New York: Times Books/Henry Holt and Company.

Tinker, T., C. Lehman, and M. Niemark. 1991. "Falling Down the Hole in the Middle of the Road: Political Quietism in Corporate Social Accounting." *Accounting, Auditing and Accountability* 4 (2): 28–54.

Van Peursem, K. 2005. "Public Dialogue Toward Social Policy: A Methodology for Accounting Research." *Accounting and the Public Interest* 5 (1): 56–87.

White, S. 1988. *The Recent Work of Jürgen Habermas: Reason, Justice and Modernity.* Cambridge: Cambridge University Press.

Williams, P. 2002. "Accounting and the Moral Order: Justice, Accounting, and Legitimate Moral Authority." *Accounting and the Public Interest* 2 (1): S1–S21.

6

STORIES AND ACCOUNTING ETHICS

Sara Reiter

Introduction

Story-telling is essentially intertwined with ethics. As MacIntyre (1984, 121) notes, the telling of stories has been the "chief means of moral education" in classical societies. We are all familiar with the use of biblical stories in religious education and of parables in classical education and understand the role of genesis myths and stories in explaining, preserving, and maintaining the culture of native societies. Stories serve a similar role in our organizations, professions, and society, although we may be less aware of it. In all these cases, stories are used to connect people, make sense of lived experience, and communicate common values and beliefs (Da Costa 2017). Stories have unique features that engage listeners, connect to emotions, and lead to action (McGee 2017). Stories are inextricably connected to ethics – we are all familiar with conclusions about "the moral of the story" and the assumption that most all stories contain some lesson for the listener.

This chapter reviews the unique qualities of stories and their potential for use in ethics education and in improving the ethical climate in organizations, as in the use of admirable examples (Watson 2003) and humanizing narratives (Shapiro 2016). However, the same qualities that make stories potential instruments for positive change can be used for manipulation, as in stories used to sell products (Da Costa 2017) or to justify corporate actions (Driscoll and McKee 2007). When evaluating truth claims, we tend to equate "telling stories" with lying. What distinguishes between ethical and nonethical and true and untrue stories? And while stories may be used for enlightenment, they also promote hidden and unexamined ideologies and can block consideration of the ethicality of organizational and professional behavior (Poulton 2005).

How stories work

Stories organize experience. The basic structure of narrative is that, starting from some place in time, there are a series of events that are ordered in time and lead to some conclusion or resolution. In this way stories connect the past, present, and future. Stories engage the listener (reader) who identifies at some level with the protagonist of the story (empathy). The power of stories goes beyond the intellectual realm because stories also engage other, nonrational, areas of the brain (McGee 2017). I am sure we have all experienced physiological changes when reading stories with exciting plots that put the protagonist in danger. This may result in enhanced retention of information, and the emotional engagement may be connected with a greater likelihood of action – whether the story is being used to sell a product (Da Costa 2017) or prepare students to take action in their professional lives. In addition, stories are how we process stressful situations and come to accept the potentially disturbing nature of professional conflicts (they would not be conflicts if they had easy answers). It may be helpful to consider the different roles of semantic memory, which records knowledge, abstract ideas, and concepts, as opposed to episodic memory, which captures experiences and emotions (Notre Dame 2019b). When people encounter conflicts and issues in their work lives, they are more likely to look to their episodic memory for help, and stories are more concerned with creating episodic memories.

How stories can be used to promote ethical understanding and behavior

Preus and Dawson (2009) explain that stories can fulfill four different roles. They help people make sense of phenomena they encounter in their lives. They aid in problem solving. They illustrate ethical judgments by either disciplining or legitimating actions. And they empower actors to act in ways implicitly sanctioned by the stories and narratives of the organization. Before providing examples of the use of stories in accounting ethics, I need to consider the question of who the storyteller is. In this discussion, the storyteller is an academic – using stories in classroom ethics education (whether aimed at students or professionals), consulting with firms and other organizations about enhancing ethics, and/or analyzing stories told in organizations and professional societies to uncover hidden ideologies and assumptions.

Also, while stories are inherently moral (about how we act or should act), when are stories also ethical? While the terms "ethics" and "morals" are often used interchangeably, a distinction can be drawn between them. As Poulton (2005) explains, ethics is a

> societal discussion of what ought to be considered for overall human well-being, including the broader concepts of fairness, justice and injustice, what rights and responsibilities are operable under certain situations, and what virtues a society admires and wants to emphasize.
>
> *(4)*

Morality is not as conceptual and refers more to our everyday experience. Poulton explains that

> (m)orality is the sum total of a particular society's or organization's current perceived traditions, beliefs, values, attitudes and norms that have been cultivated over time, institutionalized in religious doctrine, laws, regulations and codes of conduct with explicitly or implicitly suggest how an individual should behave in situations which they encounter daily.
>
> *(5)*

Stories are inherently moral, having always to do with action in the context of societal or institutional expectations. As Taylor (1995) explains, "at the heart of all stories is choice, the necessity of choosing coupled with the uncertainty of consequences." Actions that are normalized in stories may or may not be deemed ethical.

To promote ethical behavior, stories need to be framed in the context of examining the narrative events through some ethical lens, or the stories need to be carefully chosen to exemplify some predetermined ethical virtue. Accounting ethics education is more likely to be concerned with the morality of accountants' actions in relation to professional moral expectations than with questions about whether the professional codes of conduct satisfy philosophical societal expectations.

Stories in classroom ethics education

The use of stories and narratives are closely associated with moral imagination approaches to accounting ethics education. As Johnson (1993) points out, moral understandings are fundamentally imaginative. The advantages of using stories for moral instruction include making abstract ideas concrete, improving retention of concepts, passing on collective wisdom, setting standards of behavior and patterns to emulate, and inspiring and creating an emotional attachment to goodness (Watson 2003). As Reiter and Flynn (1998, 1999) explain, the moral imagination model emphasizes moral action "through strengthening character and self-awareness, developing ethical sensibility, cultivating ethical reasoning and critical thinking skills, engendering qualities of emotional empathy, and understanding the effects of organizational policies and economic incentives on ethical behavior" (1999, 218). The moral imagination model emphasizes the concept that "life is a journey," is based on understanding of past experience and the environment, and uses the process of moral imagination (development of moral character, mental models and ideals, and personal narrative) to guide reaction to ethical situations and promote ethical conduct (Johnson 1993). While a number of pedagogical techniques may be associated with moral imagination approaches to accounting ethics education, the use of stories is a natural fit.

Several examples include using stories to help students generate positive and innovative solutions to problems. The ethics of rights and the ethics of care are differing ethical points of view (Reiter 1996). In brief, rights approaches use abstract or formal thinking, focus on rules and legalities, and focus on the individual (40). The ethics of care, on the other hand, focuses on connections and consideration of relationships. Johnson (1988) uses a fable to illustrate the ethics of care approach:

> It was growing cold, and a porcupine was looking for a home. He found a most desirable cave but saw it was occupied by a family of moles.
>
> "Would you mind if I shared your home for the winter?" the porcupine asked the moles.
>
> The generous moles consented and the porcupine move in. But the cave was small and every time the moles moved around they were scratched by the porcupine's sharp quills. The moles endured this discomfort as long as they could. Then at last they gathered their courage to approach their visitor. "Pray leave," they said "and let us have our cave to ourselves once again."
>
> "Oh no!" said the porcupine. "This place suits me very well."
>
> (71)

Responses from the rights perspective focus on issues such as rights of ownership (of the moles) and who was first in the cave (moles). Responses from the care viewpoint respond to the needs of both groups and include solutions such as taking turns and trying to make the hole bigger (Reiter 1996, 42). The story provides an engaging way to explore the differences between ethical frameworks. Another example of a pedagogical example is the use of positive exemplars in ethics education and training. Negative examples can "have the unintended effect of making unethical behavior seem normal and acceptable" (Notre Dame 2019a). When dealing with employees, a valuable exercise is to ask them to recall and analyze stories about "a person at their company who exemplifies the 'organization at its best.'" When instructing students who do not have experience in organizations or in dealing with real world problems, stories about "people who have exemplified leadership, values or integrity" show students examples of behaviors that can be emulated and demonstrate that values are upheld within organizations.

Stories can act as a sort of "moral gymnasium"(Fairbairn 2002) for the consideration of possible actions and outcomes. For example, Fairbairn follows discussion of somewhat artificial ethical dilemmas (should a person kill one person to save 19 others, for example) with more realistic stories of difficult situations that arise in the medical profession. The illustrative stories are about babies with different types of problems and prognoses, with parents and doctors asked to make critical decisions. Shifting through different scenarios helps nursing professionals consider and cope with difficult situations that come up in their work lives. Similar stories and scenarios could be used in accounting professional education.

Stories to promote ethics in organizations

Another potential use of stories to promote ethical behavior is to use storytelling in organizations – whether consciously or subconsciously. Poulton (2005) explains the role of "genesis" narratives in organizations. These powerful origin stories provide firms with "a definition of how they see themselves and provide their employees with an organizational gestalt" (8). For example, the Apple Computer genesis story about Steve Jobs and Steve Wozniak and the family garage that served as the birthplace of Apple computers is familiar to many inside and outside of the organization. PwC's video about founder Sam and his horse (PwC 2019) provides a similar unifying story with brand identification. In addition to genesis stories, Driscoll and McKee (2007) suggest that "leader storytelling that integrates a moral and spiritual component can transform an organizational culture so members of the organization begin to feel connected to a larger community and a higher purpose" (209). Stories about organizational leaders are told to influence and create a social reality, engage employees, provide meaning for a vision, and legitimize a leader's role and ideas (Auvinen et al. 2013). Driscoll and McKee (2007) provide an example of a leader story that exemplifies an organization's ethical and spiritual values:

> (a)n often told story about Malden Mills is that of Aaron Feuerstein, the President, who kept his staff of 3200 on payroll while the factories were being rebuilt after a fire . . . during a time when many other textile owners were increasingly moving toward offshore labor.
>
> *(213)*

Watson (2003) provides another example of a leader story:

> Over thirty years ago the managing director of Caterpillar's European operations in Grenoble, France was desperately looking for a suitable apartment. The housing there for Americans was very hard to come by. The city was bulging. Decent accommodations were not to be found. He persisted to look for an apartment to buy. One was finally located – A brand new, seven room suite on the sixth floor of the Park Hotel. When they finally got down to negotiating for the final price, which had previously

been agreed to and determined, the negotiator for the seller said, "Well, of course there's the accommodating payment to give you priority to get this apartment." It was the first time anything like that got into the issue. At that Wally, the managing director, simply got up and said, "The meeting's adjourned. I don't want your damned apartment." And he walked out. That particular example permeated the whole community. Every one knew from then on that whenever they dealt with Caterpillar in general or Wally in particular everything was on the top of the table.

(103)

The genesis and leader stories are embedded in organizational culture and experience.

In the accounting profession, a number of firms and organizations use stories to convey their view of organizational culture through genesis stories and stories about exemplars. The EY website features stories of winners of a global award program and how they are helping the world. For example, there is the story of Faith Moyo from Zimbabwe, who has organized a free business accelerator program to support entrepreneurs launching small business ventures, as a way of providing the help her family venture needed but could not access (EY 2019). The Deloitte website (Deloitte 2019) has stories of employees overcoming odds to be successful. In addition to written stories, websites also feature video stories, such as the PwC video "our purpose" which explains the corporate values of PwC with humorous cartoon appearances of the founder Sam and his horse (PwC 2019).

A related tactic is the use of stories to change or promote corporate culture. Wines and Hamilton (2009) explain that "new" stories told to increase ethical awareness need to be compatible with "the dominant national and regional myths" and "not clash with the accepted larger stories, legends, and myths of the industry and society as a whole" (443). This might be a challenge when the dominant myths and ideologies promote one-sided neoclassical economic ideals, but the "new" stories can introduce counterbalancing ideological assumptions and promote examination of "hidden" assumptions. For example, William Reeb, incoming chair of the AICPA, tells stories in this inaugural address that are meant to disrupt conventional ways of professional thinking and open the minds of CPAs to new ways of thinking.

> Just a few months ago, every single senior black belt in our school, each with at least 30 years of practice, spent more than an hour relearning how to do a back-stance – something you are taught as a white belt the first day of training. Think of the humility you experience unlearning and relearning something that you are so confident you know well and that you have been teaching others for decades.
>
> We are big on humility. If there is one lesson I get to learn over and over, it is "with each new level of understanding, I gain the ability to relearn how to do something better given that I have a broad base of knowledge to build on this time around." This mindset requires you to put your ego aside, shut down your defenses and listen all of the time, no matter what you have achieved or who you are. I know that everyone has something to teach me. When you take this approach to learning, it is far easier to not just make an incremental improvement, but to jump instantly to whole new levels of performance.
>
> *(Reeb 2019)*

Statler and Oliver (2016) explain how reframing business ethical codes as narrative processes can be effective in disseminating ethical conduct expectations throughout organizations. West

(2018) explains how virtue ethics is inextricably embedded in a concept of narrative unity. Stories are at the center of this process by providing the context for actions and appreciation of the intersection of the narratives of an actor with the narratives and roles of other actors – an appreciation which is essential to thoughtful decision-making. Statler and Oliver (2016) suggest that organizations should carefully consider integrating narrative aspects in the implementation of codes of ethics by, for example, basing discussion and formulation of code provisions on stories from employees about conflict situations. Illustrating key principles through stories may be more effective than delivering code expectations as a series of rules.

Ethical storytelling

While telling stories to portray ideal organizational values and effect organizational change appears to be a worthy endeavor, the question of the ethics of storytelling comes up. What kind of stories are ethical for management or leaders to use to portray or attempt to change their organizations? What kind of stories are ethical for professional organizations to tell in their public relations and marketing efforts? Is storytelling always ethical?

Determination of whether a story is ethical by examining if it is "true" is probably not a very helpful approach. Even if a person is recounting events that happened to themselves, they are not going to provide a completely detailed chronological account of everything that happened. That would not make a good story (McGee 2017). Shawn Callahan (2016), a business consultant, explains how to test whether a story meant to influence has crossed an ethical line. If you tell the story recipient about your motives for telling the story, and their reaction is that the story was helpful in understanding the situation, the attempt to influence was OK. In other words, the test of the ethics of an attempt to manipulate is whether the subjects feel manipulated or aided. Another perspective is that the motive of the storytelling is important. Was it meant to do good for the individual and the company? Of course the individual and the company could have conflicting objectives, as in the Rhodes, Pullen, and Clegg (2010) study of stories in a firm engaged in downsizing – the survival of the firm and the continuation of an individual's employment may conflict. A couple of suggested good practices in constructing stories are to tell stories as you believe they happened, to tell people when a story is made up, and not to tell other people's stories as if they are your own (Callahan 2016).

Two deliberate approaches to ethical storytelling are "authentic storytelling" (Driscoll and McKee 2007) and "humanizing narratives" (Shapiro 2016). Authentic storytelling is "inherently connected to ethical leadership and the creation of a more ethical culture (Driscoll and McKee 2007, 211). Some of the characteristics of authentic stories are that they "embrace compassion, forgiveness, vulnerability, tolerance and respect," they "encourage a 'mind of reflection,'" and they "incorporate individual and personal development in a time of uncertainty and ambiguity." In other words, they are imbued with character and virtue. It would presumably be unethical and manipulative for leaders of firms and organizations to emulate a concern with these values if they are not indeed the ethical and spiritual values of the organization. Shapiro (2016) explains "how organizations may embed humanizing narrative devices and related activities in their management control systems to enact humanizing business practices." Humanizing narratives "respect a person's dignity and capacity for personal growth, respect human rights, promote care and service for others, and improve an organization's ability to serve the common good rather than only narrow special interests (Shapiro 2016, 1).Shapiro (2016) explains how narratives can be integrated into the management control systems of the organization, such as belief systems like corporate histories and mission statements, boundary systems such as codes of conduct and strategic plans, control systems such as budgeting and control systems, and interactive venues such as meetings, surveys, and awards.

The dark side of stories

Auvinen et al. (2013) study leadership manipulation through storytelling. While many stories are told to influence others, "manipulation is about influencing someone so that he or she does not know the intention of the manipulator" (417). Various forms of deceptive behavior, such as lying or providing misleading information, come under the category of manipulation. Since stories have a powerful subconscious influence, it may be hard to determine when subjects do or do not know the intention of the manipulator. In the context of using stories in accounting ethics education, the students undoubtedly realize the intention of the stories to illustrate and instruct. However, the use of stories about unethical behavior and its consequences may actual help normalize unethical behavior. In any case, manipulation is not necessarily unethical, depending on the motives and the consequences. While it is questionable that any story tells the whole truth, presumably leaders and others are aware when a story deliberately falsifies or misleads or suppresses important information.

Takala and Auvinen (2014) explain that stories in organizations are often connected to leadership power and authority and may indicate a softer and less direct form of leadership intervention. The narrator of a story assumes a position of power to influence others through the constructions of the story. "The narrator may pursue good as well as bad outcomes with his/her story" (Takala and Auvinen 2014). For example, Takala and Auvinen (2014) explain how the image of Hitler as a heroic leader was developed through "collective and public storytelling, which took advantage of existing national salvation legends and semi-religious expectations . . . produced and maintained largely by the force of stories" (4).

Auvinen et al. (2013) conducted a field study to identify and study manipulative stories told by managers in an organization. About half of the manager subjects had engaged in manipulative storytelling practices such as humorous stories, meant to diffuse tensions and reconcile employees to poor working conditions, pseudo-participative stories giving personnel a false impression of free choice and participation in decision making, seductive manipulation by telling overly positive stories, and pseudo-empathetic stories where managers pretend to empathize with employee concerns to reduce conflict. The manipulative stories relied on outright lying as well as misinformation and disinformation, which is the sharing of truthful but purposefully misleading information. For example, a manager explains the use of a deceptive story:

> The Oldsmobile car manufacturer has been experimenting with all kinds of alternative engines in its time. In those days there were steam engines and combustion engines of numerous different kinds. He had all the potential engine technologies under development at the factory, but then luck had it that his factory burned down. And the fire destroyed everything except for a car that was driven by a petrol engine. And he no longer had any money to develop the others, so the one and only thing he had left was the petrol engine, which was the technology that ultimately made the breakthrough. The point of my story is: what fire do we need to identify that single, clear focus. I've sought to ask them what would be the one thing they wished would survive.
>
> *(425)*

The stories within organizations are a part of the process of creating myth – "a set of interlocking stories, rituals, rites, and customs that inform and give the pivotal sense of meaning and direction to a community of culture" (Wines and Hamilton 2009, 440). These mythic systems provide a framework for the sense-making activities of employees and others, but they also reflect a certain set of ideological assumptions and frame discourse in ways that potentially hide a number of potential concerns from consideration. For example, Rhodes et al. (2010) examine the role of stories in normalizing layoff practices in a struggling organization and removing them from ethical examination. A typical example from an employee says, "And see I wouldn't fight it because I just look at it thinking, it's not a big, huge profitable company that is trying to make money. It's a company struggling to succeed so I see what they're doing is for the benefit of the staff plus the stockholders, so I don't see what they're doing is wrong" (543). While this fatalistic acceptance was common in the struggling firm, very different stories could have been told to explain the events and their meaning. The downsizing and layoffs in an organization were understood by a plot that Rhodes et al. (2010) call "the inevitable fall from grace," and the layoffs were therefore only examined within a procedural framework. In this way, the stories served to "shelter organizations from moral responsibility for their actions" (547). Another example of the use of stories to create myths that frame events is the Horatio Alger stories told a hundred years ago about a "fantasy world of rags to riches" (Wines and Hamilton 2009). While the young heroes of the Horatio Alger stories were advised to work hard, their massive elevations in fortune generally resulted from some implausible opportunity offered by a successful businessman – not something that happened frequently or at all outside of this myth.

What stories tell us about organizations

Stories can also be analyzed to discover the underlying ideologies of the storytellers. This a form of ethical analysis through analysis of narratives. For example, Reiter and Williams (2016) undertake a narrative analysis of speeches by leaders of various accounting professional bodies. Narrative is a basic way of conveying understandings of the world, managing/manipulating the perceptions and actions of others, and providing a template for analyzing phenomena. Part of this process is the ideology represented by the story, and the ideology of stories can be analyzed to see what basic hidden assumptions are part of the worldview being expressed. Analysis of speeches from three different professional representatives highlights differences in views of the ethics of the profession. A speech by a PCAOB representative (Harris 2016) reviews the recent regulatory history of the accounting profession with a narrow focus on auditors of publicly traded firms with the basic plot of how government intervention in the regulation of auditing (PCAOB) saved the profession but that further threats (consulting and technology) need to be overcome. In this view, the ethics of the profession are completely defined by the role of the core auditing profession in the capital markets. This is the classical view of professional ethics as a bargain between the profession being given exclusive rights to perform essential work in return for the expectation that professionals will put the public interest first (Freidson 1986).

The inaugural speech by a new leader of the AICPA (Ellison-Taylor 2016) relates several personal stories to illustrate that taking on new initiatives, such as the professionalization of management accounting and advocacy on behalf of the profession, will work against forces threatening loss of professional status. In this view of the profession, ethics are not a matter of playing a key role in the capital markets but rather a matter of accountants continuing to provide good service to clients. Instead of a professional potentially making sacrifices to serve the public interest, the professional should be prepared to make sacrifices to better serve clients. In contrast, a speech by the outgoing leader of the IFAC (Cohn 2016) emphasizes the social service roles of the profession – apparently an aspect important to Europe constituencies.

Conclusion and recommendations

In conclusion, stories are powerful and we need to be aware of the potential for stories to engage and influence students but also to potentially mislead and hide conflicts from view. Stories can be used in ethics education, to engage participants at more than an intellectual level, in hopes of promoting commitment to ethical action and rehearsing responses to ethical problems likely to arise in professional careers. Stories are also widely used in portraying the identity and values of organizations such as accounting firms and the accounting profession. Finally, stories may also be used to stimulate ethical awareness and discussion in organizations.

However, given the ubiquitous and increasing use of stories to portray the accounting profession, more attention needs to be paid to the ethics of storytelling. As Meretoja and Davis (2018) explain:

> Storytelling practices may help define who we are, refine our moral sensibilities and open new possibilities of experience, action and self-invention, but, at the same time, they may be the vehicle of simplifications, obfuscations or plain lies that corrupt our moral standing. . . . Storytelling is bound up with power, sometimes repressive, sometimes emancipatory.
>
> *(1–2)*

Beyond a concern with the accuracy of stories and the consent of the subject to the way their story is being told, we need to be concerned that stories are broadly representative of lived experience and that they are not obscuring ethical issues and concerns.

References

Auvinen, T., A. Lamsa, T. Sintonen, and T. Takala. 2013. "Leadership Manipulation and Ethics in Storytelling." *Journal of Business Ethics* 116: 415–31. doi:10.1007/s10551-012-1454-8.

Callahan, S. 2016. "The Ethics of Storytelling in Business." www.anecdote.com/2016/07/ethics-storytelling-in-business.

Cohn, M. 2016. "IFAC Reaches Out to Pope Francis on Role of Accountants." *Accounting Today*, November 17, 2016. www.accountingtoday.com/news/ifac-reaches-out-to-pope-francis-on-role-of-accountants.

Da Costa, C. 2017. "Why Every Business Needs Powerful Storytelling to Grow." www.forbes.com/sites/celinnedacosta/2017/12/19/why-every-business-needs-powerful-storytelling-to-grow/#254301b143b0.

Deloitte. 2019. https://www2.deloitte.com/us/en/pages/careers/topics/career-journeys.html.

Driscoll, C., and M. McKee. 2007. "Restorying a Culture of Ethical and Spiritual Values: A Role or Leader Storytelling." *Journal of Business Ethics* 73: 205–17. doi:10.1007/s10551-006-9191-5.

Ellison-Taylor, K. 2016. "Bringing Our 'A' Game: Bold Steps for a Vibrant Future." Inaugural Speech, October 25, 2016. Accessed January 15, 2017. www.aicpa.org.

EY. 2019. "How One Woman is Inspiring Sustainable Business Growth." ey.com.en_gl/better-begins-with-you/how-one-woman-is-inspiring-sustainable-business-growth

Fairbairn, G. 2002. "Ethics, Empathy and Storytelling in Professional Development." *Learning in Health and Social Care* 1: 1–11. doi:10.1046/j.1473-6861.2002.00004.x.

Freidson, E. 1986. *Professional Powers: A Study of the Institutionalization of Formal Knowledge.* Chicago, IL: University of Chicago Press.

Harris, S. 2016. "Current Priorities of the PCAOB. Speech to the NYSSCPA SEC Conference." New York. https://pcaobus.org/News/Speech/Pages/Harris-speech-NYSSCPA-10-25-16.aspx.

Johnson, D. 1988. "Adolescent's Solutions to Dilemmas in Fables: Two Moral Orientations –Two Problem Solving Strategies." In *Mapping the Moral Domain*, edited by C. Gilligan, J. Ward, and J McLean Taylor, 49–71. Harvard University Press.

Johnson, M. 1993. *Moral Imagination: Implications of Cognitive Science for Ethics.* Chicago: University of Chicago Press.

MacIntyre, A. 1984. *After Virtue: A Study in Moral Theory*. London: Gerald Duckworth.

McGee, P. 2017. "The Power of Telling Stories." 31–33. Accessed August 15, 2019. www.trainingjournal.com

Meretoja, H., and C. Davis. 2018. "Introduction: Intersections of Storytelling and Ethics." In *Storytelling and Ethics*, edited by H. Meretoja, H. and C. Davis, 1–20. New York: Routledge.

Notre Dame Deloitte Center for Ethical Leadership. 2019a. "Ethics Training is Broken. Can Storytelling Fix It?." https://ethicalleadership.nd.edu/news/the-power-of-storytelling.

Notre Dame Deloitte Center for Ethical Leadership. 2019b. "The Power of Storytelling." https://ethical leadership.nd.edu/.news/the-power-of-storytelling.

Poulton, M. 2005. "Organizational Storytelling, Ethics and Morality: How Stories Frame Limits of Behavior in Organizations." *Electronic Journal of Business Ethics and Organization Studies* 10 (2): 4–9. http://ejbo.jyu.fi/pdf/ejbo_vol10_no2_pages_4-9.pdf.

Preuss, L., and D. Dawson. 2009. "On the Quality and Legitimacy of Green Narratives in Business: A Framework for Evaluation." *Journal of Business Ethics* 84: 135–49. doi:10.1007/s10551-008-9693-4.

PwC. 2019. "Our Purpose." pwc.com/us/en/careers/videos.html.

Reeb, W. 2019. "AICPA 2019 Spring Council Inauguration Speech," aicpa.org/about/leadership/2019-spring-council-inauguration-speech.html.

Reiter, S. 1996. "The Kohlberg-Gilligan Controversy: Lessons for Accounting Ethics Education." *Critical Perspectives on Accounting* 7: 33–54.

Reiter, S., and L. Flynn. 1998. "Developing Ethical Conduct and Ethical Leadership in Accounting Ethics Education." *Advances in Accounting Education* 1: 251–66. JAI Press Inc.

Reiter, S., and L. Flynn 1999. "Moral Imagination and Accounting Ethics." *Research on Accounting Ethics* 5: 217–40. JAI Press Inc.

Reiter, S., and P. Williams. 2016. "Making Sense of Public Interest Narratives." Working Paper, Binghamton University.

Rhodes, C., A. Pullen, and S. Clegg. 2010. "'If I Should Fall from Grace . . .': Stories of Change and Organizational Ethics." *Journal of Business Ethics* 91: 535–51. doi:10.1007/s10551-009-0116-y.

Shapiro, B. 2016. "Using Traditional Narratives and Other Narrative Devices to Enact Humanizing Business Practices." *Journal of Business Ethics* 139: 1–19. doi:10.1007/s10551-015-2645-x.

Statler, M., and D. Oliver. 2016. "The Moral of the Story: Re-framing Ethical Codes of Conduct as Narrative Processes." *Journal of Business Ethics* 136: 89–100. doi:10.1007/s10551-014-2505-0.

Takala, T., and T. Auvinen. 2014. "Storytelling and Ethics." *Electronic Journal of Business Ethics and Organization Studies* 19 (1): 4–5. http://ejbo.jyu.fi/archives/vol19_no1.html.

Taylor, D. 1995. "The Ethical Implications of Storytelling." *Mars Hill Review* 3: 58–70. www.marshill review.com/issues/toc3.shtm.

Watson, C. 2003. "Using Stories to Teach Business Ethics – Developing Character Through Examples of Admirable Actions." *Teaching Business Ethics* 7 (2): 93–105. doi:10.1023/A:1022660405619

West, A. 2018. "*After Virtue* and Accounting Ethics." *Journal of Business Ethics* 148: 21–36. doi:10.1007/s10551-016-3018-9.

Wines, W., and J. Hamilton. 2009. "On Changing Organizational Cultures by Injecting New Ideologies: The Power of Stories." *Journal of Business Ethics* 89: 433–47. doi:10.1007/s10551-008-0009-5.

7

FEMINISM AND ETHICS IN ACCOUNTING

Emancipatory perspectives

Cheryl R. Lehman

Introduction

None of us are free, [if] one of us are chained *(Solomon Burke 2002)*

What greater challenge can there be than to consider, if we are free to shape our world, "how do we want that world to be?" (Bakewell 2016, 9). Freedom in creating our world, so fundamental to feminism, resonates with morality, ethics, and philosophy as well. Humans create their world, and it matters for us to design "choices as though you were choosing on behalf of the whole of humanity" (Bakewell 2016, 10). Here, too, accounting is implicated, given that accounting makes things governable and thinkable, configuring "persons, domains and actions as objective and comparable" (Mennicken and Miller 2014, 25). As stated by Bay (2017), accounting's ability to affect "people's minds and behaviour, has been widely acknowledged in accounting literature" (Bay 2017, 44). Accounting often legitimates knowledge, and given accounting's role in social creation, this chapter recognizes the significance of creating our world and considers accounting's emancipatory possibilities.

Critical accounting acknowledges alternative ways of knowing the world, and this chapter explores this knowledge production. One would hope a "feminist ethics" would be rendered as a relic and that feminist ideals of social justice and well-being were ubiquitous. Acknowledging many differences in terms, here feminism and ethical behavior encompass human will and social justice as essential, equalitarian, and fundamental to being human. We also recognize that given cultural, religious and economic differences, the issues are vexing. Instabilities of classism, sexism, and racism are explored[1] in the chapter while briefly introducing familiar debates and feminisms' overlaps with ethics and philosophies. Given the voluminous nature of the topic the focus here is on a particular immorality: violence against women. Such violence communicates fundamental injustices, connecting to accounting, since "taking account" is central to the discipline where visibilities or silences endure. An essential element of human existence on which ethics and morality rest is safety. Without elimination of violence against women[2] – in other words, without security as an essential element of well-being – ethics and morality are nonexistent. This emphasis speaks to central debates regarding female bodies: who controls and speaks for women's bodies? What are women's bodies "about" – reproduction? Sexuality? Commodification? Are women excluded in [numerous] arenas under the façade that their bodies are detractors? This chapter recognizes the prevalence of these controversies and addresses the creation of knowledge by silencing and distorting issues of violence regarding women. As we shall see, these issues parallel feminist ethics both in redefining the terrain of struggle (that which is silenced) and in emancipatory aims (redefining how to take account).

The chapter's two main aims are (1) engaging with a specific area of a moral dilemma: women and violence, illustrating with critical accounting literature, and (2) examining on a global scale how measuring is selective and distorting regarding women and violence. The chapter proceeds in the second section with a brief overview of feminist ethics literature and corroborating research in accounting. The third section examines accounting research on symbolic violence and other arenas of violence in accounting, including engaging in issues of women and violence. The fourth explores controversies of measuring social phenomena: potentially distorting and potentially enhancing. The case of measuring violence against women on a global scale is considered using Gender Gap Reports compiled by the World Economic Forum, linking taking account and accounting's role. The fifth section concludes.

Feminist ethics and accounting and ethics

Exploring oppressive social structures, psychological marginalization, material impairment, and societal configurations all comprise feminist ethics issues. Social relationships of power, privilege, inequality, and critiquing concepts of gender as binary (given it maintains oppressive social structures) are among reflections in feminist ethics, and philosophy and researchers have redefined an array of ideas (e.g., Ehrenreich and English 1976; Fraser 2010; Haraway 1989; Hartmann 1979; Held 1993; Kessler-Harris 1981; Snitow 2010; Waring 1988). Their work critiques conventional philosophical theories for failing to examine gender as a variable in social orders where men's privileges are naturalized and unchallenged.

Significant among these writers, de Beauvoir in *The Second Sex* (1949) provided formative insights that individuals are shaped by forces of oppression and experiences so crucial that philosophy is inadequate if these dynamics are disregarded. Beauvoir notably observed "one is not born, but rather becomes, woman . . . the figure that the human female takes on in society . . . [results from] the mediation of another [that] can constitute an individual as an Other" (Beauvoir 1949, 329). The social creation of women – their expectations and rights – are founded on discriminatory and powerful structures. Beauvoir advocated an ethical theory tackling women's oppression, influencing feminist ethics as a field of philosophy (and was particularly significant during a period when women's rational and moral abilities were being questioned).

Ideas and idealization regarding "female characteristics" continues to be a controversy, regarding innate and social constructions of moralities or separate realities. This problematic centers upon whether biology is destiny or whether social norms (nurturing) are crucial in differences? What does it mean to be female or male – is it encoded in us? Burkett proposes, "That's the kind of nonsense that was used to repress women for centuries" (Burkett 2015) or, as de Beauvoir (1949) wrote, was among the socialized thinking of women as "other." New measurement techniques renew this conversation that brains are shaped by experience (e.g., culture) and thus expectations and society impact differences, inequities, and hierarchies. Of course biological differences exist. The idea is that both nature and nurture are relevant and that biology is not destiny in creating *hierarchical* inequalities. Feminists suggest in early life status and roles regarding work and life were equally shared and there was no particular status between male labor and female labor upon which to establish differences of morality (Coontz and Henderson 1986; Cott 1987; French 1986; Held 1993; Irigaray 1985; Lerner 1986; Pollitt 2005).

As such, philosophers such as Jaggar dispute separatism as producing a morally better world. A society valuing personal relationships, efficiency, emotions, and rationality "cannot be achieved through sexual separation" (Jaggar 1974, 288). Approaches to ethics continued emerging and overlapping including androgyny, gender bending and gender-blending in the 1990s (Butler 1990; Held 1993) and humanist approaches to feminist ethics and social philosophy in the 21st century (Dill 2010; Lorde 1984; Pateman 1988; Snitow 2010). A critique of gender binarism emerged, recognizing its impact on marginalizing nonconforming individuals with intersectionality, providing some resolve to the controversies.

> Philosophers of Black Feminism, intersectionality, queer theory, critical race theory, disability studies, and transfeminism, among others, contribute to a view that there is no universal definition of femininity or of the category of woman that neatly applies to all women.
>
> *(Norlock 2019)*

Intersectionality attends to those unjustly ignored or denied by a conception of women or femininity that turns out to be white, ableist, and cisgender (Collins 1990; Giddings 2007; Holvino 2010; hooks 1984).

Spivak also critiques myopias and the tendency to collapse struggles in north and south capitalism and postcolonialism in urban and rural flows, integrating the notion of "subaltern" in the dialogue (a complex term of persons completely outside access to social structures) (Spivak 1995, 1996). By virtue of what Randeria (2002) calls "entangled histories," it is impossible to reduce postcolonial analysis to national boundaries, boundaries themselves an invention of colonial discourses.

> Subalternity is the name I borrow for the space out of any serious touch with the logic of capitalism or socialism. Please do not confuse it with unorganized labour, women as such, the proletarian, the colonized, migrant labour, political refugees etc. Nothing useful comes out of this confusion.
>
> *(Spivak 1995, 115)*

Those among the subaltern spaces are increasingly the targets of new globalization, forming the basis of exploitation in the arenas of bio piracy, pharmaceutical dumping in the name of population control, and micro loans to women.

Rather than comprising theories beholden to abstract and universal principles, feminists supporting virtue ethics acknowledge "moral reasoning might be an extraordinarily complex phenomenon . . . what the ethical life requires of us cannot be codified or reduced to a single principle or set of principles" (Moody-Adams 1991, 209–10). Resistance itself may be a "burdened virtue," a term allowing for moral agents, including those who are oppressed, to operate not as victims but to resist extending virtues to applications in nonideal circumstances (Nussbaum 2000; Tessman 2005).

Barad (2007) integrates philosophy, feminism, and other social theories, redefining concepts of space, matter, and objectivity in what is referred to as new materialism. Matter is subject and subjected to analysis, pointing at processes of meaning-making ("to matter"). The innovativeness of new materialist approaches lies in that they provide ways for signification to be simultaneously material and semiotic (Haraway 1989; Barad 2007), asking not only how discourses come to matter but also how matter comes to matter (Barad 2007; Orlikowski 2010). Corresponding to feminist reflections, meaning-making is an affair of the mind that happens after the fact of an event in the ecological, sociocultural or politico-economic sphere, dramatizing "the fragility of things today and helps to explain why many constituencies refuse to acknowledge and address it" (Connolly 2013). Resonating with feminist ethics, new materialism rejects artifices between the physical world and the social constructs of human thoughts but rather explores "how each affects the other, and the agency of things other than humans (for instance, a tool, a technology or a building)" (Fox 2017).

As is evident from the preceding, feminist ethics is not monolithic with divergence among feminists regarding purpose, activism, essentialism, and strategy. Recent manifestations of gender mainstreaming illustrate the tensions that while "there may be synergy and greater power; on the other there may be loss of visibility and vitality . . . these dilemmas need to be faced rather than avoided" (McRobie 2012). Nussbaum concurs, suggesting we need to "think through our own intuitive ideas . . . [particularly] when we consider the interests of the powerless, who rarely get the chance to bring their own ideas about such matters to the table" (Nussbaum 2000, 300). Humans need to reflect on their world views and assumptions whether studying ethics, philosophy, or accounting (Lehman 1992, 2012), as we shall examine next.

Accounting and ethics

In her work on environmental accounting, Andrew (2000) describes an ethical perspective encouraging "a re-imagination of nature as a site of multiplicity and multi-vocality . . . perspectives that have been excluded or erased from the main texts" (Andrew 2000, 199). Traditionally, ethics was considered a guide between right and wrong, good and bad, praise and blame, virtue and vice. Resonating with Andrew, we view ethics not as a statement of fact but "fluid, contextual, dynamic, and often times contradictory" (Andrew 2000, 201). Ethics informs and guides action, forming assumptions we use for aspirations and goals (Andrew 2000). Cooper (1992) similarly describes feminist aims[3] in a "philosophy of praxis . . . as a way of seeing the world and a guide to action . . . it empowers women . . . [and] also liberates men . . . it allows for difference; it opens new possibilities" (Cooper 1992, 16).

In adopting reflective perspectives in accounting and recognizing quantifications are "physically violent removal of things and people from their embeddedness in social relations" (Joseph 2014, xviii), there is also potential for human emancipation in them. "No doubt, quantification and abstraction are powerful . . . [we] explore the extent to which their very potencies – the productivity of accounting, accountability, and abstraction . . . are subject to engagement, transformation and appropriation" (Joseph 2014, xix–xx). Research in this expanded realm examines accounting's role in rationalizing war (Chwastiak 2013), in labor deliberations (Cooper and Coulson 2014), and in setting immigration policy (Agyemang 2016; Agyemang and Lehman 2013), to name a few. We further this inquiry by examining an issue not always visible in accounting literature in the next section.

Ethical lapses: symbolic violence and "generalized" violence in accounting literature

"Why do we experience such difficulty even imagining a different society. . . . Our disability is discursive: we simply do not know how to talk about these things any more."

(Judt 2010, 34)

Research on accounting's symbolic violence exposes the discipline's role in power asymmetries. Its policies appear as objective in a subtle maneuver "through language and the construction and use of knowledge" (Farjaudon and Morales 2013, 157). Reproduction of relations of domination seem legitimate (Malsch, Gendron, and Grazzini 2011), while the silencing of alternative voices appear natural (Cooper and Coulson 2014). By privileging powerful and dominant interests, making them yet more powerful in contemporary struggles, those not in power are further marginalized. Accounting's symbolic violence is hidden and "not recognised as such when . . . enclosed and institutionalised within symbolic systems" (Bourdieu 1977).[4] Practices appear rational but remain mysterious, "a kind of hidden dark art which is too difficult for 'ordinary people' to understand" (Cooper and Coulson 2014, 240). Although appearing fair and natural, the task is a contested terrain, since the "giving of accounts is a complex social, hermeneutical, and moral task" (Perkiss 2014, v).

Denouncing how accounting neutralizes physical violence and symbolic violence is diverse in the literature.[5] Chwastiak (2013) illustrates war financing and social upheavals in Iraq implicating accounting as information is "rendered invisible" (Chwastiak 2013, 38). Accounting's hold on power in Dillard (2003) links IBM and the Holocaust, as does Funnell's (1998) research on Nazism: accounting disguises violence by making human consequences bureaucratic. Participating in eugenics (Graham et al. 2018) and normalizing violence regarding Indigenous populations (Neu, 2000; Neu and Graham 2006) reveal symbolic and physical integration with violence as well. Studying incarceration, researchers describe the dynamics of power, profits, and violence (Andrew 2007, 2011; Lehman, Hammond, and Agyemang 2018; Mennicken 2013; Scott 2015; Taylor and Cooper 2008). As such, "Accounting becomes an eminently suitable technology to manage and enact violence on racialized populations because of its capacity to de-humanize them or render them invisible as people" (Annisette and Prasad 2017, 9).

Women and violence in accounting literature

The manifestations of violence and women is less extensive in accounting literature, but the issues parallel those in feminist ethics. Tremblay, Gendron, and Malsch (2016) consider unconsciousness and discriminatory consequences related to gender in promoting applicants for corporate boards. While seeming to support women's role in the boardroom, "from a deeper perspective these discourses may also be viewed as channels for symbolic power to operate discreetly, promoting certain forms of misrecognition that continue to marginalize certain individuals or groups of people" (168). Symbolic violence is a "subtle, gentle and quite imperceptible domination" (Tremblay, Gendron, and Malsch 2016, 170), and in this sense, it is "invisible even to its victims, exerted for the most part through the purely symbolic channels of communication and cognition (more precisely misrecognition), recognition, or even feeling" (Bourdieu 2001, 2). Resonating with feminist ethics theories described earlier, Tremblay et al reveal how domination occurs daily, consciously and unconsciously, alongside structures sustaining these forms.

Isolation and exploitation is revealed in Killian's (2015) work of young women in what were known as the Magdalen Laundries. Accounting is implicated in its silencing, enabling women's labor to be exploited invisibly "where the women were 'accounted for' in ways that rendered 'accounting to' them unthinkable" (17). Killian observes how ideological mechanisms prevented women from seeing their own oppression where "the occluded nature of the Magdalen system facilitated . . . a separate, Catholic identity, untainted by ideas of prostitution, single motherhood or sexual violence" (18). Haynes also notes "Sexual violence can be understood as a social and cultural phenomenon . . . [and as] accounting is both a tool and political construct . . . [o]

ne might rightly ask therefore: what is the role of accounting in perpetuating sexual violence?" (Haynes 2017, 121).

Silva, Nova, and Carter (2016) reveal accounting and the confluence of race, gender, and segregation in Brazil forming destructive violence and repression while communities are excluded from "education, political and economic structures associated with competence, independence, power and social autonomy" (49). Describing an Afrodescendent accounting professor holding elected office, merging with views of minorities and women as inferior and sexually threatening, is "illustrative of the enormous potential to be paralytic, that is a 'violence' to their identity and is effective in establishing barriers to access" (2016, 51).

Violence in prison materializes in shackling during childbirth and forced sterilizations. These forms of violence control women's bodies, given that incarceration already "takes away your ability to voluntarily consent" (Barolone 2013). Control and efficiency is described in accounting literature as a major 20th-century momentum by Puxty (1993) as a totalizing apparatus. "The answer was eugenics: to sterilize those who were unfit. . . . This control over the body, far from being the concern of a few, was not just widely advocated but was also practised" (Puxty 1993, 120). The normalized dehumanization in the criminal justice system becomes so ingrained that questions of oppression are made invisible (Lehman 2016). For incarcerated women, physical violence and symbolic violence overlap replicating power and abuse experienced in the outside world. The loss of empowerment makes the person, "that is the body, more amenable to being managed and controlled" (Puxty 1993, 120).[6]

Violence takes on ubiquity and impact as it

> reconfigures its victims. . . . It isn't a passing phenomenon. . . . Violence becomes a determining fact in shaping reality as people will know it, in the future. So while a study of violence may begin with direct and immediate carnage, it shouldn't end there.
> *(Nordstrom 2004, 59–60 as quoted*
> *in Chwastiak 2008)*

We take up this call by examining how accounting privileges what is accounted for in contemporary life, maintaining immoralities for women when accountability regarding violence is invisible (Lehman 2012). The next section examines how reporting captures differing views of representing, measuring, and exploring violence and women.

The ethics of quantifying and taking account

What are the ethics of measuring? Quantifying social phenomenon is problematic, because they are "always invested with meaning, potentially disguising as much" as is revealed (Hansen and Muhlen-Schulte 2012, 1). The current preoccupation with "big data" exemplifies this, given "data is used to leverage and exercise authority . . . reaffirm[ing] the immediate power . . . to a machine" (Di Russo 2016). O'Neil, in *Weapons of Math Destruction: How Big Data Increases Inequality and Threatens Democracy* (2016), describes discriminatory models. Because of strong correlations (not cause and effect) between poverty and reported crime, big data, "even with the best of intentions . . . [adds] precision and 'science' to the process. . . . The result is that we criminalize poverty" (O'Neil 2016, 91). Measuring restricts what is viewed and erases that which is not "identified" (Spivak 1996, 2010). Gessen asks, how do you tell a story that is hidden, "How do you bring up a topic that has never before been discussed . . . for which there is no language?" (2017, 62).

Chwastiak and Young (2003) question the ethics of annual reports that

> rely upon the silencing of injustices in order to make profit appear to be an unproblematic measure of success . . . reproduc[ing] the dominant discourses . . . that sustain an unequal distribution of wealth and power and make such arrangements seem natural and therefore, unchangeable.
>
> *(548)*

They suggest that "Only by breaking silence and counter-posing corporate values with alternatives can we hope to free humankind from the limitations of profit maximization" (535). Such research adds to critical accounting's work on counter-accounts, intending to shed light on those aspects rendered invisible by traditional accounting (Gallhofer, et al. 2006; Lehman, Annisette, and Agyemang 2016; Paisey and Paisey 2006; Sikka 2006). They are alternative societal responses, expressing the "standpoints of the oppressed and underrepresented voices" (Apostol 2015, 213).

Why and how we choose to privilege ideas and data is problematic in a society dominated by an ideology of the bottom line. Global policies could not be enacted without support of economic theories, accounting numbers, and a claim that pure markets go hand in hand with democracy. Generally acknowledged is that neoliberalism has benefited a minority of the world's people, further bifurcating rich and poor and burdening women further (Cooper 2015; Jaggar 2002; Lehman, Annisette, and Agyemang 2016, 2018), and how this representation appears in quantifying the issue of violence and women is presented next.

A manifestation integrating accounting, feminism, and ethics: Gender Global Gap Reports

The World Economic Forum (WEF) compiles data, impacts policies, and is particularly known for its Davos meetings of CEOs, politicians, economists, and celebrities. As such it is significant on the world stage and has been the subject of criticism for elitism and negative impact on the world's most vulnerable populations.[7] The WEF has published the Global Gender Gap Report (GGGR) since 2006, with its most recent publication in 2018. Computing indices they are aimed at measuring the "relative gap between women and men" (GGGR 2018, v) with four key areas (four thematic dimensions): Economic Participation and Opportunity, Educational Attainment, Health and Survival, and Political Empowerment. As an overview, the initial 2006 report covered 115 countries (152 pages), the 2010 report covered 134 countries (334) pages, and the 2018 report was expanded to 149 countries (355 pages).[8] As we are told in the Preface of the 2010 Global Gender Gap Report, "Measuring the size of the problem is a prerequisite for identifying the best solutions" (GGGR 2010, v). And thus the question arise: How is measurement constructed? What are the assumptions? What is measured specifically in relation to violence against women? We address this next.

How do Global Gender Gap Reports (GGGR) measure violence?

It is stated the aim is for "consistent and comprehensive measures. The forum *does not seek to determine priorities* for countries, acknowledging different economic, political and cultural contexts" (GGGR 2017, 36). Implying advocacy is not an aim, an accounting-language orientation of comparability is proposed, and the following statement provides this view in the introduction to the GGGR of 2010.

> Never before has there been such momentum around the issue of gender parity on the global stage. Numerous *multinational companies have aligned core elements of their businesses and products* to support and provide opportunities for women. . . . There is a strong movement around greater *investment* in girls' education in the developing world. *Businesses around the world are starting to take into account the increasing power of women consumers* . . . there is an increased consciousness that [this] talent must be given the opportunity to lead. . . . *The World Economic Forum has been among the institutions at the forefront of driving this change in mindset and practice, primarily by emphasizing the message that gender gaps have an impact on competitiveness and by engaging the business community. . . . Every moment that we wait entails colossal losses to the global society and economy.*
> *(GGGR 2010, vi; emphasis added)*

The quote at the beginning of the paragraph uses italics to differentiate the statement "does not seek to determine priorities" to suggest the GGGR advocacy of multinational company profit orientation. The language includes investment in girls and women as consumers and impacts on competitiveness. Claiming an objective measure in using ratios while claiming the WEF drives change for betterment is an example of symbolic violence under which impacts on women are naturalized into the language of business objectives that claim dominant and normalized conviction. Through a particular business language, a mindset is molded and developed toward privileging competitiveness, consumerism, and profits. A movement is lauded not for social justice aims per se but for "deliverables" to the business community and economy. Measures are needed to prevent loss articulated with gentle advocacy, as if natural.[9]

In the most recent 2018 report an update to the preface harbingers big data and technology:

> To take full advantage of *new technologies*, we need to place emphasis on *what makes us human*: the capacity to learn *new skills* as well as our creativity, empathy and ingenuity . . . fast *technological change* and ensure broad-based progress for all. . . . More than ever, societies cannot afford to lose out on the *skills, ideas and perspectives of half of humanity to realize the promise of a more prosperous* and human-centric future *that well-governed innovation and technology* can bring . . . emerging gender gaps in Artificial Intelligence-related skills. In an era when human skills are increasingly important and complementary to technology, the world cannot afford to deprive itself of women's talent in sectors in which talent is already scarce.
> *(GGGR 2018, v; emphasis added)*

What emerges in the 2018 preface is a naturalization of technology skills for raising society toward prosperity and a better world. It is an interesting assertion and juxtaposition that "what makes us human" is first "the capacity to learn new skills" and secondly "our creativity, empathy and ingenuity." This directs society toward more technology, big data, skill sets with the hope that these will be the areas in which women direct their energies, where "talent is already scarce." Embedded in objective terms of metrics and technological processes is a privileging of technique into spheres that are unambiguously social and in line with neoliberal ideals.[10] It is notable that the measures regarding violence are neither highlighted or noted compared to the emphasis on "gender gaps in Artificial Intelligence (AI), a critical in-demand skillset of the future" (GGGR 2018, viii).

GGGR category "health and survival" as a measure of violence

Assessing the GGGR for its treatment of violence toward women presents a number of challenges. First, as noted earlier, the mindset of neoliberal ideals are inherent in the perspective and resulting categories. Second, violence was most often associated with and included in a particular category of "Health and Survival." There were 11 sub-categories[11] in this GGGR thematic, including mortality from birth, disease, accidents, and intentional injuries. These categories are rich for an analysis of differences between women and men regarding workplace treatment, medical hazards, and differentials in suicides. The category of sex ratio at birth states the report "aims specifically to capture the phenomenon of 'missing women', prevalent in many countries with a strong son preference" (GGGR 2018, 4). We note this category is also a category for exploring in the future and it is sometimes called a "genocide of females," although the GGGR description is a language sanitized, offering a cultural origin. We chose to describe (and challenge) one category representing violence toward women well understood in contemporary research, literature, and debates: Prevalence of gender violence in lifetime, described as the "Percentage of women who have experienced physical and/or sexual violence from an intimate partner at some time in their lives."[12]

In order to not overwhelm the reader, a random sample of the 149 countries from 2016 and 2018 is provided as a summary of the measure: Albania 31%; Bangladesh 53%; Brazil: 31%; Canada 6%; China 15%; New Zealand 33%; Poland 13%; Pakistan 13%; Turkey 42%; Ukraine 13; US 36%.[13] With this data, a pervasive violence is evidenced in the category "prevalence of gender violence in lifetime." Most frequently, one-third to one-half of women attest to this form of violence.

Along with questions regarding how the data is compiled and researched, we note an incongruous statement summarizing the results in the GGGR. Despite the previous statistics, the GGGR (2018) concludes an achievement. It states:

> the Health and Survival subindex is where the global gender gap is the smallest: 4% on average. While no country has yet achieved full parity, 74 countries have already closed 98% of their gap, and all 149 countries have closed at least 90% of their gap. Looking at the components of this subindex, parity has been essentially achieved in all countries in terms of life expectancy. . . . Gender parity on sex ratio at birth is also very advanced.
>
> *(GGGR 2018, 12)*

In the summary results and analysis there is no mention – a silencing – of the high prevalence of gender violence. It is a conspicuous creation of an invisibility, given approximately 33% of all women "experienced physical and/or sexual violence from an intimate partner at some time in their lives," which does not include violence from non-intimate partners which would surely increase the percentage substantively. How might we provide a different account and accountability?

Alternative numbers

Spivak (2010) remarks one might not disavow reports such as the GGGR as unimportant, because they may lead to the passing of important laws protecting women from violence, yet she likens these as gestures with "missionary impulses" and imperfect interventions. They may be considered a form of symbolic violence: "tremendously well-organized and broad repressive ideological apparatuses" (Spivak 1996, 22). While challenging measures, we also consider that quantification holds potential for furthering emancipation by infusing them with reflections of social values and making visible that which is otherwise silenced. We recognize the concern among feminists that quantification reduces or erases particularity and context "in the processes of categorization [that] often depends on categories that reconstitute . . . social hierarchies; and produces an illusion of objectivity" (Joseph 2014, xviii). Yet agreeing with Joseph, we can also stake out how we might want to form knowledge production with our values (Joseph 2014). Thus, data from outside the Global Gap Reports is considered here,[14] suggesting that violent practices are voluminous.

The International Labour Organization (ILO) reports:

> At any given time in 2016, an estimated 40.3 million people are in modern slavery, including 24.9 million in forced labour and 15.4 million in forced marriage, 4.8 million persons in forced sexual exploitation. . . . Women and girls are disproportionately affected by forced labour, accounting for 99% of victims in the commercial sex industry, and 58% in other sectors.
>
> *(International Labour Organization 2017)*

The World Health Organization estimates that globally, one woman in five will be the subject of rape or attempted rape: 700 million women have been raped during their lifetime (Kristoff and WuDunn 2009). More broadly, the number of women who die due to gender-related violence, deprivation, and discrimination "is larger than the casualty toll in all the wars of the 20th century combined" (Winkler in Lederer 2005).

> Violence against women is one of the four key reasons why women die on this planet, the other ones being war, hunger and disease. . . . Globally, women aged between 15 and 44 are more likely to be injured or die as a result of male violence than through cancer, traffic accidents, malaria and war combined.
>
> *(Winkler, in Lederer 2005)*

Challenging the inevitability of violence, refuting natural causations and advocating for accountability all provide opportunities for transformation. As Gayatri Spivak affirms, these can only be partial transformations until the economic and social systems and structures perpetuating the violence are revealed and no longer under the radar (Spivak 2010). What can be seen from the alternative numbers provided is the power to see differently, reflecting and expanding upon ways of knowing. Feminism is based upon notions of change and continually questioning our beliefs and their impacts. Dambrin and Lambert (2012) point out that any scholar, activist, or person runs the risk of limited reflexivity. Yet exposure to visionary ideas creates new theories, activism, and emancipatory potential to ensure there is no single story.

Concluding remarks

This chapter asks what connects ethics, violence, women, and accounting? How does one "account" for such violence and unpack accounting's role while acknowledging that taking account is contextual and there are always shifts in ways of knowing? Exploring accounting's role regarding women and symbolic violence, physical violence, quantification, and qualification have inevitable overlaps, and this chapter recognizes these complexities while beginning an exploration. The desire to illustrate accounting's ethical and discourse-creating position on the subject is based on an activist curiosity[15] and to enhance thinking, not as merely filling in a box. Encouraged by Gendron, "Box-breaking research should not be viewed as imbued with irrationality and foolishness; instead, this intellectual journey needs to be considered a political act against the threat of relentless gap spotting and intellectual stagnation" (Gendron 2018, 9).

What makes accounting powerful is the discipline's promotion of privileged positions, and in this chapter we take account of a complex moral issue. We make visible how, under contemporary processes of globalization, progressive feminist dialogues have taken place while the immorality of violence continues. It is impossible to provide a complete narrative of multiplicities of feminism and ethics, and as stated in our introduction, morality entails freedom to choose how to create our world. We have highlighted and made visible the circumstance around the globe rendering women without freedom: violence toward them.

While recognizing the complexity of the issues, morality includes, for women and men, the right to work, choose, and celebrate and to be free of violence: "To not only have a piece of the pie, but to choose the flavor and know how to make it" (Nussbaum 2000, x). We have precedent in accounting literature to consider the art of the possible and to research dialogue into nuances and explorations of impacts and perceptions. Accounting is a part of the social construction of society making things thinkable, and given accounting's role in social creation, this chapter recognizes the significance of creating our world and revealing a story that is hidden. Critical accounting research acknowledges accounting's capacity to erase, restrain, and reduce social phenomenon to abstractions of rules, procedures, and reports, and here we uncover injustices and accounting's participation. Accounting neither delivers the truth or is neutral in public arenas. Instability surrounds the nature of accounting such that Khalifa and Kirkham (2009) advocate scrutinizing what "is understood and accepted as an accounting task and why such understandings emerge" (439), as we have sought to do here. This chapter asks us to examine, given accounting is meaning-making, how we might reinvent it for a discourse fulfilling a crucial area of social justice.

Appendix
EXAMPLES OF SELECTED COUNTRIES FOR GGGR 2018, AS PER FOOTNOTE 8

Brazil GGGR 2018

Health	female	male	value
Mortality, children under age 5	23.4	29.0	[1] 0.81
Mortality, non-communicable diseases	436.1	480.9	[1] 0.91
Mortality, infectious and parasitic diseases	22.5	30.9	[1] 0.73
Mortality, accidental injuries	22.0	63.6	[1] 0.35
Mortality, intentional injuries, self-harm	8.8	67.9	[1] 0.13
Mortality, childbirth			[1] 44
Legislation on domestic violence			yes
Prevalence of gender violence in lifetime			31.0
Law permits abortion to preserve a woman's physical health			no
Births attended by skilled health personnel			99.10
Antenatal care, at least four visits			88.90

Norway GGGR 2018

Health	female	male	value
Mortality, children under age 5	0.1	0.1	[1] 0.75
Mortality, non-communicable diseases	18.0	16.6	[1] 1.09
Mortality, infectious and parasitic diseases	0.4	0.3	[1] 1.30
Mortality, accidental injuries	0.8	0.9	[1] 0.95
Mortality, intentional injuries, self-harm	0.2	0.4	[1] 0.47
Mortality, childbirth			[1] 5
Legislation on domestic violence			yes
Prevalence of gender violence in lifetime			27.0
Law permits abortion to preserve a woman's physical health			yes
Births attended by skilled health personnel			99.10
Antenatal care, at least four visits			–

USA GGGR 2018

Health	female	male	value
Mortality, children under age 5	11.0	13.9	[1] 0.79
Mortality, non-communicable diseases	1,169.2	1,129.5	[1] 1.04
Mortality, infectious and parasitic diseases	21.5	21.8	[1] 0.99
Mortality, accidental injuries	40.7	61.2	[1] 0.66
Mortality, intentional injuries, self-harm	14.2	48.8	[1] 0.29
Mortality, childbirth			[1] –
Legislation on domestic violence			yes
Prevalence of gender violence in lifetime			36.0
Law permits abortion to preserve a woman's physical health			yes
Births attended by skilled health personnel			–
Antenatal care, at least four visits			–

Acknowledgments

The author is grateful to the two editors for their invitation, scholarship, and camaraderie and to Hofstra University.

Notes

1 In this chapter we interchangeably use multiracial, feminist, gender, and intersectionality to denote research fostering the simultaneity of race, gender, and class in altering social relations (see Holvino 2010). Gender is a form of power relations enmeshed within societal hierarchies. Integral for transforming inequalities is the study of intersections of gender, class, ethnicity, race, colonial history, sexual orientation, and religious beliefs (Tanima 2015).

2 We recognize the fluidity defining women/female, men/male. The use of LGBTQQIP2SAA (lesbian, gay, bisexual, transgender, questioning, queer, intersex, pansexual, two-spirit (2S), androgynous, and asexual) demonstrates this idea, and the list is not exhaustive. The term "women" is used here for illustrative purpose, as one who may be identified in society, or by oneself, as such. Exploring violence and women does not prioritize it; violence on any member in society is violence upon all.

3 Research in the accounting literature on feminism with ethical dimensions includes Ciancanelli 1992; Dambrin and Lambert 2012; Gallhofer 1998, Haynes 2017; Komori 2008; Kyriakidou et al. 2016; Lehman 1992, 2012; Young 2015. Research on accounting and ethics appears in the chapters of this volume, providing extensive references for the reader.

4 Bourdieu's work is extensive (e.g., Bourdieu 1977, 2001, 2008), and we are presenting here a very limited discussion. His concepts include doxa, field, capital, habitus, misrecognition, and other significant contributions that have been extensively researched in the literature; see Cooper and Coulson 2014; Malsch, Gendron, and Grazzini 2011.

5 Finding a way to differentiate forms of violence is challenging given that symbolic, cultural, mental, physical, and all forms of violence overlap. A distinction is being made here between symbolic violence and what is being called "generalized" violence of a more physical nature. Recognizing these overlaps, our intention is to provide some delineation of how it has appeared in the literature.

6 This reviews only some of the substantive critical research undertaken regarding the accounting-violence nexus such as labor relations and violence, colonialism, the slave trade, economic violence in neoliberal policies, environmental violence, immigration and violence, etc.

7 The Transnational Institute (TNI) remarks, "Davos, perhaps more than any other gathering, epitomises the way political power and global governance have in recent decades been entrenched into a small corporate elite. This elite have succeeded not only in capturing our economy, but also our politics, and increasingly our culture and society too" (TNI 2014). As part of this critique is the evidence that

under neoliberalism the gap between rich and poor has increased, such that 47.9 percent of the world's wealth is held by the richest 1% (Vara 2015).

8 Examples in the appendix offer details of some aspects of the GGGR not included in the text to follow. It is noted that this paper covers only some of the significant issues raised by the 12 years of GGGR publications, hoping further research will follow.

9 Details of the measures: "There are three basic concepts underlying the Global Gender Gap Index. . . . First, the Index focuses on measuring gaps rather than levels. Second, it captures gaps in outcome variables rather than gaps in input variables. Third, it ranks countries according to gender equality rather than women's empowerment" (GGGR 2018, 3). A gap rather than level index is used "in order to make the Global Gender Gap Index independent from countries' levels of development" (GGGR 2018, 4).

10 The façade of separating economic and social issues is continually amplified with market techniques assessing social life, one feature of neoliberalism resonating in this preface. Neoliberalism is an over-arching doctrine and "a 'strong discourse' . . . [having] on its side all of the forces of a world of relations of forces" (Chiapello 2017, 52). The importance of neoliberalism and accounting has been well researched (e.g., Agyemang and Lehman 2013; Chiapello 2017; Cooper 2015; Lehman, Annisette, and Agyemang 2016, 2018; Merino, Mayper, and Tolleson 2010).

11 "Health and Survival: (1) Health Mortality of children under age 5, all causes, age-standardized deaths per 100,000 (female, male); (2) Mortality due to non-communicable diseases, age-standardized deaths per 100,000 (female, male); (3) Mortality due to infectious and parasitic diseases, age-standardized deaths per 100,000 (female, male); (4) Mortality due to accidental injuries, age-standardized deaths per 100,000 (female, male); (5) Mortality due to intentional injuries and self-harm, age-standardized deaths per 100,000 (female, male); (6) Maternal mortality in childbirth (per 100,000 live births); (7) Existence of legislation on domestic violence; (8) Prevalence of gender violence in lifetime; (9) Law permits abortion to preserve a woman's physical health; (10) Births attended by skilled health personnel (%) and (11) Antenatal care coverage, at least four visits (%)" (GGGR 2018, 51–52).

12 The measure is computed in GGG Reports using an OECD data base, described as "prevalence of gender violence in lifetime. Percentage of women who have experienced physical and/or sexual violence from an intimate partner at some time in their lives" Source: OECD, Gender, Institutions and Development Database 2015 (GID-DB) (accessed September 2017).

13 The author will provide additional information upon request, or it is available online for each year. For example: www.weforum.org/reports/the-global-gender-gap-report-2018.

14 What follows is a very brief summary of some key statistics available from the ILO, and we note the research and data on women in violence outside of the field of accounting is extensive (e.g. Davis 2011; Herman 2015; Jaggar 2002, Joseph 2014; Nussbaum 2000).

15 Activist in the desire to engage in different ways of knowing and thus produce and support practices and activities to impede violence against marginalized persons.

References

Adams, Mackenzie. 2017. "Big Data and Individual Privacy in the Age of the Internet of Things." *Technology Innovation Management Review* 7 (4): 12–24.

Agyemang, G. 2016. "Perilous Journeys Across the Seas: The Accounting Logic in Europe's Agenda for Migration." *Advances in Public Interest Accounting* 19: 1–28.

Agyemang, G., and C. Lehman. 2013. "Adding Critical Accounting Voices to Migration Studies." *Critical Perspectives on Accounting* 24 (4/5): 261–72.

Andrew, J. 2000. "The Environmental Crisis and the Accounting Craft." *Accounting Forum* 242: 197–223.

Andrew, J. 2007. "Prisons, the Profit Motive and Other Challenges to Accountability." *Critical Perspectives on Accounting* 188: 877–904.

Andrew, J. 2011. "Accounting and the Construction of the 'Cost Effective' Prison." *Journal of Australian Political Economy* 68: 194–210.

Annisette, M., and A. Prasad. 2017. "Critical Accounting Research in Hyper-Racial Times." *Critical Perspectives on Accounting* 43: 5–19.

Apostol, O. 2015. "A Project for Romania? The Role of the Civil Society's Counter-Accounts in Facilitating Democratic Change in Society." *Accounting, Auditing and Accountability Journal* 28 (2): 210–41.

Bakewell, S. 2016. *At the Existentialist Café: Freedom, Being, and Apricot Cocktails.* New York: Other Press.

Barad, K. 2007. *Meeting the Universe Halfway: Quantum Physics and the Entanglement of Matter and Meaning.* Durham: Duke University Press.

Barolone, P. 2013. "California Seeks Answers on Questionable Prison Sterilization." *National Public Radio.* Accessed September 20, 2013. https://www.npr.org/2013/09/20/219366146.

Bay, C. 2017. "Makeover Accounting: Investigating the Meaning-Making Practices of Financial Accounts." *Accounting, Organizations and Society* 64: 44–54.

Bourdieu, P. 1977. *Outline of a Theory of Practice.* Translated by Richard Nice. London: Cambridge University Press.

Bourdieu, P. 2001. *Masculine Domination.* Cambridge: Polity Press.

Bourdieu P. 2008. *Sketch for a Self-Analysis.* Chicago: Chicago University Press.

Burke, S. 2002 [1993]. *Song Recorded in Album* "Don't Give Up On Me." Song written by Barry Mann, Cynthia Weil and Brenda Russell.

Burkett, E. 2015. "What Makes a Woman?" *New York Times,* June 6.

Butler, J. 1990. *Gender Trouble: Feminism and the Subversion of Identity.* London: Routledge.

Chiapello, E. 2017. "Critical Accounting Research and Neoliberalism." *Critical Perspectives on Accounting* 43: 47–64.

Chwastiak, M. 2008. "Counting the Costs of War." *Critical Perspectives on Accounting* 19 (5): 573–90.

Chwastiak, M. 2013. "Profiting from Destruction: The Iraq Reconstruction, Auditing and the Management of Fraud." *Critical Perspectives on Accounting* 241: 32–43.

Chwastiak, M., and J. Young. 2003. "Silences in Annual Reports." *Critical Perspectives on Accounting* 14: 533–52.

Ciancanelli, P. 1992. "M[othering] View on: The Construction of Gender: Some Insights from Feminist Psychology." *Accounting, Auditing, and Accountability Journal* 53: 133–36.

Collins, P. 1990. *Black Feminist Thought.* Boston: Unwin Hyman.

Connolly W. 2013. "The 'New Materialism' and the Fragility of Things." *Millennium: Journal of International Studies* 413. Accessed January 2018. https://doi.org/10.1177/0305829813486849.

Coontz, S., and P. Henderson. eds. 1986. *Women's Work, Men's Property.* London: Verso.

Cooper, C. 1992. "The Non and Nom of Accounting for Mother Nature." *Accounting, Auditing, and Accountability Journal* 5 (3): 16–39.

Cooper, C. 2015. "Accounting for the Fictitious: A Marxist Contribution to Understanding Accounting's Roles in the Financial Crisis." *Critical Perspectives on Accounting* 30: 63–82.

Cooper, C., and A. B. Coulson. 2014. "Accounting Activism and Bourdieu's 'Collective Intellectual'–Reflections on the ICL Case." *Critical Perspectives on Accounting* 25: 237–54.

Cott, N. 1987. *The Grounding of Modern Feminism.* New Haven: Yale University Press.

Dambrin, C., and C. Lambert. 2012. "Who is She and Who Are We? A Reflexive Journey in Research into the Rarity of Women Executives in Accountancy." *Critical Perspectives on Accounting* 231: 1–16.

Davis, A. 2011. *Women, Race, and Class.* New York: Knopf Doubleday.

de Beauvoir, S. 1949 [2011]. *The Second Sex.* Translation by C. Borde and S. Molvany-Chevallier. New York: Vintage Books.

Di Russo, S. 2016. "The Power Struggle Behind Big Data: Forfeiting Emotional Autonomy to the Machine." Accessed November 2016. https://ithinkidesign.wordpress.com/2016/08/07/the-power-struggle-behind-big-data-forfeiting-emotional-autonomy-to-the-machine/.

Dill, B. 2010. "Intersectionality: Growth and Diffusion, Conference: 'No Longer in Exile: The Legacy and Future of Gender Studies'." The New School, New York, March 26, 2010.

Dillard, J. 2003. "Professional Services, IBM, and the Holocaust." *Journal of Information Systems* 17 (2): 1–16.

Ehrenreich, B., and D. English. 1976. *Witches, Midwives and Nurses: A History of Women Healers.* New York: The Feminist Press.

Farjaudon, A., and J. Morales. 2013. "In Search of Consensus: The Role of Accounting in the Definition and Reproduction of Dominant Interests." *Critical Perspectives on Accounting* 24: 154–71.

Fox, N. 2017. "New Materialism." Accessed January 2018. https://globalsocialtheory.org/topics/new-materialism/.

Fraser, N. 2010. "Feminist Thinking, Theory and Feminist Action, Conference: 'No Longer in Exile: The Legacy and Future of Gender Studies'." The New School, New York, March 26, 2010.

French, M. 1986. *Beyond Power: On Women, Men and Morals.* London: Abacus.

Funnell, W. 1998. "Accounting in the Service of the Holocaust." *Critical Perspectives on Accounting* 9 (4): 435–64.

Gallhofer, S. 1998. "The Silences of Mainstream Feminist Accounting Research." *Critical Perspectives on Accounting* 93: 355–75.

Gallhofer, S., J. Haslam, E. Monk, and C. Roberts. 2006. "The Emancipatory Potential of Online Reporting: The Case of Counter Accounting." *Accounting, Auditing and Accountability Journal* 195: 681–718.

Gendron, Y. 2018. "Beyond Conventional Boundaries: Corporate Governance as Inspiration for Critical Accounting Research." *Critical Perspectives on Accounting* 55: 1–11.

Gessen, M. 2017. *The Future is History: How Totalitarianism Reclaimed Russia.* New York: Riverhead Books.

Giddings, P. 2007. *When and Where I Enter: The Impact of Black Women on Race and Sex in America.* New York: HarperCollins.

Global Gender Gap Report (GGGR). 2010. *World Economic Forum.* Geneva, Switzerland.

Global Gender Gap Report (GGGR). 2017. *World Economic Forum.* Geneva, Switzerland.

Global Gender Gap Report (GGGR). 2018. *World Economic Forum.* Geneva, Switzerland.

Graham, C., V. Radcliffe, M. Persson, and M. Stein. 2018. "The State of Ohio's Auditors, the Enumeration of Population and the Project of Eugenics," Alternative Accounts Conference, Montreal May 2018.

Hansen H., and A. Muhlen-Schulte. 2012. "The Power of Numbers in Global Governance." *Journal of International Relations and Development*: 1–11.

Haraway, D. 1989. *Primate Visions: Gender, Race, and Nature in the World of Modern Science.* New York: Routledge.

Hartmann, H. 1979. "The Unhappy Marriage of Marxism and Feminism: Towards a More Progressive Union." *Capital and Class* 32: 1–33.

Haynes, K. 2017. "Accounting as Gendering and Gendered: A Review of 25 Years of Critical Accounting Research on Gender." *Critical Perspectives on Accounting* 43: 110–24.

Held, V. 1993. *Feminist Morality: Transforming Culture, Society, and Politics.* Chicago: University of Chicago Press

Herman, J. 2015. *Trauma and Recovery: The Aftermath of Violence – from Domestic Abuse to Political Terror.* New York: Basic Books.

Holvino, E. 2010. "Intersections: The Simultaneity of Race, Gender and Class in Organizational Studies." *Gender, Work and Organization* 17 (3): 248–77.

hooks, b. 1984. *Feminist Theory: From Margin to Center.* New York: Routledge.

International Labour Organization ILO. 2017. Accessed June 2019. www.ilo.org/global/lang – en/index. htm.

Irigaray, L. 1985. *This Sex Which Is Not One.* Ithaca: Cornell University Press.

Jaggar, A. 1974. "On Sexual Equality." *Ethics.* Chicago: The University of Chicago Press, 84 (4): 275–91.

Jaggar, A. 2002. "Vulnerable Women and Neo-Liberal Globalization: Debt Burdens Undermine Women's Health in the Global South." *Theoretical Medicine and Bioethics* 23 (6) 425–40.

Joseph, M. 2014. *Debt to Society: Accounting for Life Under Capitalism.* Minnesota: University of Minnesota Press.

Judt, T. 2010. *Ill Fares the Land.* New York: Penguin Press.

Kessler-Harris, A. 1981. *Women Have Always Worked: An Historical Overview.* New York: McGraw Hill.

Khalifa, R., and L. Kirkham. 2009. "Gender." In *The Routledge Companion to Accounting History*, edited by J. R. Edwards and S. P. Walker, 433–50. London: Routledge.

Killian, S. 2015. "'For lack of Accountability': The Logic of the Price in Ireland's Magdalen Laundries." *Accounting, Organizations and Society* 43: 17–32.

Komori, N. 2008. "Toward the Feminization of Accounting Practice: Lessons from the Experiences of Japanese Women in the Accounting Profession." *Accounting, Auditing and Accountability Journal* 214: 507–38.

Kristoff, N., and S. WuDunn. 2009. "'Why Women's Rights Are the Cause of our Time', Special Issue 'Saving the World's Women'." *New York Times Magazine*, 28–39.

Kyriakidou, O., O. Kyriacou, M. Özbilgin, and E. Dedoulis. 2016. "Editorial: Equality, Diversity and Inclusion in Accounting." *Critical Perspectives on Accounting* 35: 1–12.

Lederer, E. 2005. "Violence and Discrimination Against Women is a Major Cause of Death." Associated Press, November 18, 2005. Accessed June 2009. www.sacredchoices.org.

Lehman, C. 1992. "Herstory in Accounting: The First Eighty Years." *Accounting, Organizations and Society* 17 (3/4): 261–85.

Lehman, C. 2012. "We've Come a Long Way! Maybe! Re-Imagining Gender and Accounting." *Accounting, Auditing and Accountability Journal* 252: 256–94.

Lehman, C. 2016. "Unshackling Accounting in Prisons: Race, Gender and Class." *Advances in Public Interest Accounting* 19: 89–110.

Lehman, C., M. Annisette, and G. Agyemang. 2016. "Immigration and Neoliberalism: Three Cases and Counter Accounts." *Accounting, Auditing and Accountability Journal* 29 (1): 43–79.

Lehman, C., T. Hammond, and G. Agyemang. 2018. "Accounting for Crime in the US: Race, Class and the Spectacle of Fear." *Critical Perspectives on Accounting* 56: 63–75.

Lerner, G. 1986. *The Creation of Patriarchy*. Oxford: Oxford University Press.

Lorde, A. 1984. "Age, Race, Class, and Sex: Women Redefining Difference." In *Sister Outsider: Essays and Speeches*. Berkeley: Crossing Press.

Malsch, B., Y. Gendron, and F. Grazzini. 2011. "Investigating Interdisciplinary Translations: The Influence of Pierre Bourdieu on Accounting Literature." *Accounting, Auditing and Accountability Journal* 242: 194–228.

McRobie, H. 2012. "Gender Mainstreaming: The Future of Feminism? Or Feminism's Disappearing Act?" Accessed March 2018. www.opendemocracy.net/5050/heather-mcrobie/gender-mainstreaming-future-of-feminism-or-feminism's-disappearing-act.

Mennicken, A. 2013. "'Too Big to Fail and Too Big to Succeed': Accounting and Privatisation in the Prison Service of England and Wales." *Financial Accountability and Management* 292: 206–26.

Mennicken, A., and P. Miller. 2014. "Michel Foucault and the Administering of Lives." In *Oxford Handbook of Sociology, Social Theory and Organization Studies: Contemporary Currents*, edited by P. S. Adler, P. Du Gay, G. Morgan, and M. Reed, 11–38. Oxford: Oxford University Press.

Merino, B., A. Mayper, and T. Tolleson. 2010. "Neoliberalism, Deregulation and Sarbanes-Oxley: The Legitimation of a Failed Corporate Governance Model." *Accounting, Auditing and Accountability Journal* 23 (6): 774–92.

Moody-Adams, M. 1991. "Gender and the Complexity of Moral Voices." In *Feminist Ethics*, edited by C. Card. Lawrence: University Press of Kansas.

Neu, D. 2000. "Presents for the 'Indians': Land, Colonialism and Accounting in Canada." *Accounting, Organizations and Society* 25: 163–84.

Neu, D., and C. Graham. 2006. "Birth of a Nation: Accounting and Canada's First Nations." *Accounting, Organizations and Society* 31 (1): 47–76.

Nordstrom C. 2004. *Shadows of War: Violence, Power, and International Profiteering in the Twenty-First Century*. Berkeley: University of California Press.

Norlock, K. 2019. "Feminist Ethics." In *The Stanford Encyclopedia of Philosophy*, edited by Edward N. Zalta. Accessed June 2019. https://plato.stanford.edu/archives/sum2019/entries/feminism-ethics/.

Nussbaum, M. 2000, *Women and Human Development: The Capabilities Approach*. Cambridge: Cambridge University Press.

O'Neil, C. 2016. *Weapons of Math Destruction: How Big Data Increases Inequality and Threatens Democracy*. New York: Crown Publishing Group.

Orlikowski, W. J. 2010. "The Sociomateriality of Organisational Life: Considering Technology in Management Research." *Cambridge Journal of Economics* 341: 125–41.

Paisey, C., and Paisey, N. 2006. "The Internet and Possibilities for Counter Accounts: Some Reflections: A Reply." *Accounting, Auditing and Accountability Journal* 19 (5): 774–78.

Pateman, C. 1988. *The Sexual Contract*. Stanford: Stanford University Press.

Perkiss, S. 2014. "Intelligible Accounting for the Future: A Critical Study of Worth and Displacement." Ph.D. Thesis, School of Accounting, University of Wollongong, Australia.

Pollitt, K. 2005. "Marooned on Gilligan Island: Are Women Morally Superior to Men?" *Good News of the Twentieth Century*. Accessed 2010. www.academic.evergreen.edu/curricular/hhd2005

Puxty, A. 1993. *The Social and Organizational Context of Management Accounting*. London: Academic Press.

Randeria S. 2002. *Civil Societies, Caste Solidarities and Legal Pluralism in Post-Colonial India Civil Society Network*. Berlin. Accessed January 2011. http://wwwscribdcom/doc/37791593/Entangled-Histories

Scott, W. 2015. "Investigating the Need for Transparent Disclosures of Political Campaign Contributions and Lobbying Expenditures by US Private Prison Corporations." *Accounting and the Public Interest* 15 (1) (December): 27–52.

Sikka, P. 2006. "The Internet and Possibilities for Counter Accounts: Some Reflections." *Accounting, Auditing and Accountability Journal* 195: 759–69.

Silva, S., S. Nova, and D. Carter. 2016. "Brazil, Racial Democracy? The Plight of Afro-Descendent Women in Political Spaces." *Advances in Public Interest Accounting* 19: 29–55.

Snitow, A. 2010. "The State of the Art: Gender Studies, Conference: No Longer in Exile: The Legacy and Future of Gender Studies." The New School, New York, March 26, 2010.

Spivak, G. 1995. "Supplementing Marxism." In *Wither Marxism? Global Crises in International Perspectives*, edited by B. Magnus and S. Cullenberg. London: Routledge.

Spivak, G. 1996. *The Spivak Reader*. New York and London: Routledge.

Spivak, G. 2010 "Situating Feminism, Beatrice Bain Research Group Annual Keynote Talk." Accessed June 2011. https://berkeleyenglishblog.wordpress.com/2010/04/25/gayatri-spivak-on-situating-feminism.

Tanima, F. 2015 "Microfinance and Women's Empowerment in Bangladesh: A Study of 'Competing Logics' and their Implications for Accounting and Accountability Systems." Ph.D. Dissertation, Victoria University of Wellington, New Zealand.

Taylor, P., and C. Cooper. 2008. "'It Was Absolute Hell': Inside the Private Prison." *Capital and Class* 323, 3–30.

Tessman, L. 2005. *Burdened Virtues: Virtue Ethics for Liberatory Struggles* Oxford: Oxford University Press.

Tremblay, M., Y. Gendron, and B. Malsch. 2016 "Gender on Board: Deconstructing the 'Legitimate' Female Director." *Accounting, Auditing and Accountability Journal* 29 1 165–190.

Vara, V. 2015. "Critics of Oxfam's Poverty Statistics Are Missing the Point." *The New Yorker*. Accessed July 18, 2019.

Waring, M. 1988. *If Women Counted: A New Feminist Economics*, London: Macmillan.

Young, J. 2015. "Engendering Sustainability." *Critical Perspectives on Accounting* 26: 67–75.

PART III

Religious perspectives on accounting ethics

8

USE OF STORIES IN THE JEWISH TALMUD TO EMPHASIZE SUBSTANCE OVER FORM

Dov Fischer and Hershey H. Friedman

Introduction

The accounting profession and Judaism share an important insight into how rules can help society function. Both the profession and Judaism have traditionally recognized the primacy of substance over form. Judaism is a religion of both substance and form, but the two sometimes come into tension. This tension or dialectic is present in all religions, but especially so in Judaism. This is because the formalistic practice of Judaism has evolved into a highly technical code of rules. In this chapter, we show that while form is important, it is worthless without substance, ethics, and morality. Perhaps the most eloquent expression of the worthlessness of form without substance comes from the Prophet Isaiah (eighth century BC, Jerusalem):

> Stop bringing meaningless offerings! Your incense is detestable to me. New Moons, Sabbaths and convocations – I cannot bear your worthless assemblies. Your New Moon feasts and your appointed festivals I hate with all my being. They have become a burden to me; I am weary of bearing them. When you spread out your hands in prayer, I hide my eyes from you; even when you offer many prayers, I am not listening. Your hands are full of blood! Wash and make yourselves clean. Take your evil deeds out of my sight; stop doing wrong. Learn to do right; seek justice. Defend the oppressed. Take up the cause of the fatherless; plead the case of the widow.
>
> *(Isaiah 1:13–17)*

The lesson from Judaism is that both substance and form are necessary for a functioning society, whether it is a religious society or an economic society. Substance without form soon devolves into chaos and anarchy, even if all members of society are well meaning. The Mishnah in Avot expresses this: "Pray for the well-being of the temporal government, for without such government each man would swallow his friend whole." This saying recognizes that society requires rules backed by potential force. Otherwise, even relations between friends would soon devolve to economic cannibalism.

On the other hand, form without substance results in tyranny and oligarchy. In the Bible, Sodom represents such a society. According to Rabbinic homiletics, Sodom had a highly evolved legal system that actually prohibited hospitality to strangers. Such institutionalized evil was the defining feature of Nazi Germany, which actually maintained the functioning legal system and used it to its diabolical ends (Stolleis 1998).

Is it somewhat surprising that the term substance over form originated in the accounting profession? Equally surprising is that the concept has been deemphasized by the profession in recent years. Recently, though, the accounting academy has witnessed a lively debate on just this question (DeFond, Lennox, and Zhang 2018; Palmrose and Kinney 2018). Our study therefore draws on inspiration from Jewish ethics to inform the profession on potential ethical principles, legal techniques, and practical storytelling aids to transform the ethics of the profession from a compliance-based proscriptive code to a creative, visionary, and positive force for societal change (*tikkun olam*, discussed later).

The rest of the study is organized as follows. The second section shows why the topic is (still) relevant to the accounting profession. The middle sections draw on the Jewish ethical traditions as follows: The third provides examples of how Talmudic *stories* of positive ethical exemplars can raise the level of ethics dialogue; the fourth discusses the *biblical* basis for Jewish ethics, the difference between law and ethics and the qualities of justice, righteousness, and lovingkindness; and the fifth discusses Talmudic *fixes* to the law to ensure the primacy of ethics over the letter of the law. The last section concludes with recommendations on how *positive* stories can raise the level of ethical discourse in the accounting profession.

Relevance to accounting profession

The accounting profession has contributed the concept of "substance over form" to our social discourse (AICPA 1973, 57). This insight, which is applied to a range of accounting transactions, seeks to account for the underlying economic substance rather than its superficial legal form:

> The guidelines for reporting information should be expressed so that substance, not form, governs. The Study Group, in framing definitions and objectives, has attempted to follow this principle. For example, earnings cycles are defined in terms of highly probable cash receipts and disbursements, rather than actual cash receipts and disbursements. This definition emphasizes substantive information concerning the probabilities of cash flows rather than the actual receipt or disbursement. Similarly, the test for realization of sacrifices and benefits stresses probabilities rather than a formal event such as a sale. The definition of assets also highlights the substantive question of the presence of future benefits, regardless of the formality of ownership rights. The substantive economic characteristics, not the legal or technical form, should establish the accounting for transactions and other events. For example, this subordination of legal formality may affect the accounting for transactions between affiliated or related parties.

Yet tension between form and function is very present in the accounting profession. In fact, the rules-based versus principles-based controversy is this very tension expressed in different words (Fischer 2018). A recent issue of *Accounting Horizons* saw the dueling commentaries of Palmrose and Kinney (2018) versus DeFond, Lennox, and Zhang (2018) over the question of auditor responsibility beyond technical compliance with GAAP. Palmrose and Kinney are of the position that US standards do *not* require of the auditor anything beyond compliance with the GAAP code, while DeFond, Lennox, and Zhang (2018) view the auditor's responsibility to ensure faithful representation beyond mere compliance with the GAAP code.

Too often, however, the solution for ethics breakdown in accounting has been the call for more rules. The numerous accounting scandals during the 1990s and early 2000s (e.g., Enron, WorldCom, Global Crossing, Arthur Andersen, and Tyco) resulted in a loss of confidence in the profession and prompted the enactment of the Sarbanes-Oxley (SOX) Act in July 2002 (Chaney and Philipich 2002; Crutchley et al. 2007). The purpose of SOX was to protect the public and shareholders from deceitful practices and accounting fraud. SOX required companies to disclose whether or not they have adopted a code of ethics for their principal financial officers. If they did not, they had to explain the reason for not complying. Companies were also required to promptly report any waivers from the code of ethics (Myers 2003).

Friedman and Gerstein (2016) and Soltani (2014) demonstrate that corruption, dishonesty, and dubious accounting are still major issues, SOX notwithstanding. Friedman and Gerstein (2016) provide numerous examples from the financial, automobile, retailing, and accounting industries (e.g., Wells Fargo, Libor, Takata Airbag, Volkswagen emissions rigging, General Motors ignition switch scandal, Toyota sticky pedal, and Toshiba) to show that corporate leaders have no qualms about selling dangerous products or using deceitful accounting to enrich themselves. Apparently, little has changed: organizational leaders and boards may be paying lip service to the importance of integrity and ethics but are not practicing what they preach. It seems that the lessons learned from Enron and the Great Recession of 2008 are still not part of the corporate culture. Everyone is talking about the importance of ethical leadership, but little is being done to change the ways of conducting business. Having a code of ethics does not ensure that the organizational culture will change. Bazerman and Tenbrusel (2014) state that a huge amount of money is being spent to ensure compliance – about $1 million for every $1 billion in sales. Despite all this, unethical behavior has not been declining but rather increasing. In many organizations, leaders pay lip service to ethics but make it obvious that form matters more than substance (Friedman and Kass 2018). This is why codes of ethics are inadequate. Ethics must be value-driven, not rule-driven.

Beginning in the 1980s, the SEC (2012) implemented a process in which every proposed rule is supposed to be guided by rigorous economic analysis. In practice, this meant that the SEC now devotes a substantial budget to academic research, including accounting research. In theory, this seems to be in the interest of the profession and the general public. However, in practice, it often impedes the SEC from quickly implementing rules dictated by common sense. The National Securities Market Improvement Act of 1996 required the SEC to consider efficiency, competition, and capital formation whenever it engaged in rulemaking. It also required the SEC to consider or determine whether an action is necessary or appropriate in the public interest. In spirit, the act intended to simplify securities regulation. In practice, by emphasizing rigorous economic research, the result was the opposite. The lesson from the Talmud is that rules are sometimes not enough to ensure an ethical society. In fact, rules can sometimes cause the exact opposite of the original intent behind them. It is therefore critical that the accounting profession develop an infrastructure to revisit professional and ethical rules to ensure that they are still serving the original purpose.

Substance over form is a creative expression of the accounting profession's priorities. It is therefore unfortunate that FASB (2010, BC3.26) decided to deemphasize (emphasis added) this concept:

> Substance over form is *not* considered a separate component of faithful representation because it would be redundant. Faithful representation means that financial information represents the substance of an economic phenomenon rather than merely

representing its legal form. Representing a legal form that differs from the economic substance of the underlying economic phenomenon could not result in a faithful representation.

While the change may seem trivial, from the standpoint of accounting education, it is not. Only concepts that are in the FASB's codification and concepts are included on the CPA exam and therefore taught to students.

Throughout the rest of the chapter, we will be drawing upon the Jewish ethical tradition for guidance about ideas and techniques that can elevate the ethical discourse in the accounting profession. In the end, the actionable recommendation is to change the narrative of accounting ethics education from proscribing unethical behavior toward providing inspiring examples of positive ethical behavior. The traditional view of accounting ethics included integrity, objectivity, diligence, loyalty, and professionalism (Spalding and Oddo 2011). In a 2014 speech to an accounting conference in Rome, Pope Francis called upon the profession to adopt creativity and vision as professional virtues (Fischer 2017). Positive stories can provide the impetus toward our profession adopting a more creative and visionary mindset.

Talmudic device: use of stories

Rabbi Safra (c. 280–338, Babylonia) is described in the Babylonian Talmud (Makoth 24a) as an individual who abided by the verse (Psalms 15:2) "who speaks truth in the heart." One day, while Rabbi Safra was praying, a man offered to buy some merchandise from him. He made an offer, but Rabbi Safra did not want to respond in the middle of a prayer. The prospective buyer assumed that Rabbi Safra was holding out for more and kept increasing the bid. After Rabbi Safra concluded his prayer, he informed the buyer that he would sell the merchandise at the first price because he had "agreed in his heart" to this price. Legally, one is not required to do as Rabbi Safra; this is the "way of the pious." Rabbi Safra held himself to a very high level of ethics and went far beyond the requirements of the law. The purpose of this story is to demonstrate to people that, although for most people, abiding by the terms of an oral agreement may be sufficient, there is a standard higher than following the strict letter of the law to which one should aspire.

In his popular book *Skin in the Game*, Taleb (2020, 57) recounts the story of Rav Safra and gives it a utilitarian explanation. Rav Safra was practicing extreme transparency, which extends to transparency of thought. Taleb therefore speculates that these ethical rules would be relaxed or possibly lifted for what he terms "Swiss" outgroup members whom Rav Safra would be unlikely to encounter again.

While the Talmud does not tell us who the counter-party of Rav Safra was, various similar stories in the Talmud make it a point to indicate that the counter-party to the ethical behavior was indeed an outgroup member. Rabbi Simeon ben Shetah (Judea, second and first century BC) purchased a donkey from an Arab. Rabbi Simeon's disciples discovered that a valuable jewel was hung on the donkey's neck, hidden from view. When they happily informed their teacher of this discovery, Rabbi Simeon ran back to the marketplace, found the Arab, and returned the jewel to him (Jerusalem Talmud, Baba Metzia 2:5). The Babylonian Talmud (Baba Metzia 24b) explicitly states that individuals who go beyond the requirements of the law will return found objects even if the object was lost in a place where it is clear that the owner gave up any hope of recovery (e.g., if it fell into the sea), despite the fact that there is no legal obligation to return it.

Abba (c. 300, Babylonia) was a bloodletter/surgeon who was held in great esteem by the Talmud for his exemplary business practices. His patients paid as much of his fee as they could afford, leaving the money in a box in an outside room so that he could not see who had paid and who had not, so as not to embarrass the poor. In addition to this, when it was clear that a patient was impoverished, not only would Abba refuse payment, but he would give the patient money for food. He did this because he felt that it was important to eat a very substantial meal after a bloodletting (Babylonian Talmud, Taanis 21b). According to the Talmud, he was at such a high level of piety for the way he conducted business that he would miraculously receive heavenly greetings every day (Babylonian Talmud, Taanit 21b). Recording that Abba received daily heavenly greetings as a reward for his outstanding practices is another device that encourages people to act more ethically than the law requires.

The Talmud praised the "father of Samuel" (second and third century, Babylonia), an eminent and wealthy Talmudic sage, who insisted on selling his produce at low prices (the prices prevailing immediately after the harvest) and thereby keeping the market price stable all year long (Babylonian Talmud, Baba Batra 90b). This is clearly the way a highly pious individual does business.

Abba Chilkiyahu (early first century, Judea) was a day laborer who would not greet people while working since he did not want to waste time – even a few moments – that was not his (Babylonian Talmud, Makoth 24a). The Talmud uses him as an exemplar of the virtue "deals righteously" that is mentioned in Psalms 15.

The following story discussed in the Babylonian Talmud (Baba Metzia 83a) demonstrates how Rabbah bar Bar-Chana (Palestine and Mesopotamia, second and third century) was asked to follow "the way of the pious," probably because he was one of the Talmudic sages and therefore a role model for the other members of society. He was told to practice the highest form of ethics.

> Some porters negligently broke a barrel of wine belonging to Rabbah bar Bar-Chana who then confiscated the porters' garments as restitution. Rav, the judge, advised Rabbah to return the property belonging to the porters. Rabbah asked Rav whether this was indeed the law and was quoted the following verse from Proverbs (2:20): "In order that you may walk in the way of the good. . . ." The porters then complained to Rav that they were poor, had worked all day without earning anything, and were in need. Rav told Rabbah to pay them. Rabbah again asked whether this was the law. Rav responded with the conclusion of the verse from Proverbs: ". . . and keep the paths of the righteous."
>
> *(Babylonian Talmud, Baba Metzia, 83a)*

These stories are only a small sample of stories in the Talmud describing individuals who went well beyond the letter of the law. Gifter (2000) uses the case dealing with the negligent porters to prove that the purpose of the Torah and Talmud is not solely to provide precise answers to legal questions but to develop the morals and ethics of individuals. Because the Talmud is concerned with improving the ethics of the individual, cases are discussed in which the courts cannot legally prosecute the defendant. This is not surprising given that, in Jewish law, the legal content of the law is totally conjoined with ethics, religion, and morality (Silberg 1973, 83). Stories of individuals who followed the "way of the pious" are one way to make individuals aware that one must strive to be more ethical than the law requires.

In the next two sections we discuss the biblical foundation for Jewish ethics and specific Talmudic legal devices to ensure the primacy of ethical substance over legal form.

Righteousness: the biblical intersection of form and substance

It is important to recognize that the fact that something is unethical does not make it illegal, and the fact that something is illegal does not make unethical. Thus, people are not always truthful; this may be unethical but is not necessarily illegal. Indeed, if politicians went to prison for lying, there would be no one left to run the government. Ideally, ethics should be an integral part of every legal system. The reality is that it is quite possible to have a legal system that is completely unethical (e.g., at one time it was legal to own slaves in the United States). Nazi Germany had a legal system that was influenced by the political system and all kinds of crimes against humanity, including the murder of innocents, were permissible under the law. Stolleis (1998) makes the point that one can learn a great deal from examining Nazi law and studying how it evolved from the legal system prevalent during the Weimar Republic. Understanding this connection sheds light on ethical problems we see today in the legal profession.

Both justice and ethics are core values of the Torah, that is, the Five Books of Moses (the Pentateuch), so this chapter will first examine the Bible to see how it dealt with questions regarding these subjects and then see what the Talmud has to say. As we shall see, the ancient Talmudic scholars living approximately two millennia ago were concerned about issues concerning law and morality that are important today. The sages of the Talmud clearly believed that morality and ethics had to be part of any economic, political, and/or legal system.

Kirschenbaum (1991, xxi) observes:

> Similar to all other legal systems, ancient and modern, religious and secular, Jewish law had to – and still must – negotiate the tension between its static rules and the dynamic flow of events. The rules are characterized by an encompassing generality, whereas each event – the specific circumstances, the individuals involved, the conditions of the times – is informed of individuality, sometimes even uniqueness. Thus, the glory of the law – its sublime generality – is its very undoing. For its passion for uniformity and stability, the law enlists the aid of formalism. Its indifference to persons may produce heartlessness; its impartiality – injustice; its rigid consistency – absurdity.

Justice, righteousness, and lovingkindness

The Hebrew Bible speaks of *mishpat*, *tzedek*, and *chesed*. These three concepts represent a continuum of justice and ethics, from form to substance (Fischer and Friedman 2019). Figure 8.1 illustrates that the extreme of form is *mishpat* (justice) and the extreme of substance is *chesed* (lovingkindness), while *tzedek* (righteousness) occupies the intersection between form and substance. According to Sacks (2005, 51), *chesed* "exists only in virtue of emotion, empathy, and sympathy." It requires "not detached rationality but emotional intelligence." Justice, on the other hand, is "best administered without emotion." The correct way to administer justice is by being detached, disinterested, disengaged, and impartial. Sacks (2005, 33) observes that *mishpat* means retributive justice; *tzedek* means distributive justice. Thus, "A law-governed society is a place of *mishpat*." A decent, caring society requires more than that; it must incorporate *tzedek* as well. The prophet Hosea described an ideal society in the following terms (Hosea 2:19–20): "I will betroth you to Me in *tzedek u'mishpat* (righteousness and justice), in *chesed ve'rachamim* (lovingkindness and compassion). I will betroth you in faithfulness, and you will know the Lord."

The concept that justice must be "blind" and not confused with charity is important. One may feel sorry for an indigent mother who lost her child because of, say, a harmful side effect of

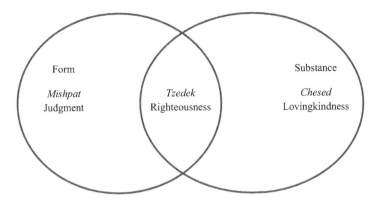

Figure 8.1 Righteousness as the Intersection of Form and Substance

a drug of which she had been warned prior to its administration. The pharmaceutical company may make billions in profits, but justice may not be served if the family wins a lawsuit solely because the jury feels sorry for the victim and the company can afford to pay.

Tzedek is similar to Aristotle's idea of equity. Aristotle says the following about equity:

> This is the essential nature of the equitable: it is a rectification of law where law is defective because of its generality. . . . Equity does not nullify the law. It upholds the law; it "corrects" it; it refines it; it brings it closer to perfection. It does not contradict the law. Rather, it claims to fulfill the true intention of the legislator.
>
> *(Kirschenbaum 1991, xxiv, xxxv)*

The Hebrew word *tzedaka* is translated as righteousness but also means charity, and actually hints at both (see Figure 8.2). The Talmud questions how King David did both when acting as a judge. In the words of the Babylonian Talmud (Sanhedrin 6b): "Where there is strict justice there is no charity, and where there is charity, there is no strict justice." One answer provided by the Talmud was that David was indeed impartial in his role as judge. If, however, he decided a case against a poor person, he would pay the claimant with his own money. In this manner, David was able to practice both *mishpat* and *tzedaka*.

Nonfinancial charity (e.g., visiting the sick) is performed directly with one's body, whereas financial charity is performed indirectly using one's money. The rabbis therefore considered nonfinancial charity (*Gemilut Chesed*) of even greater merit than financial charity (*Tzedaka*) (Babylonian Talmud, Succah 49b).

The Talmudic sages understood that obeying the letter of the law was not sufficient and devised numerous ways to incorporate ethics and *chesed* into the law. This chapter will examine some examples of devices used by the Talmud to make the law more moral.

Takanot – Talmudic "fixes" to the biblical law

The Babylonian Talmud represents the foundation of Jewish religious life, even more so than the Bible itself. For example, the Bible instructs Sabbath rest but is short on specifics. The Talmud, which was composed several centuries after the destruction of the Second Jerusalem Temple in 69 CE, developed the basic rituals of everyday religious life in the diaspora. In the

Tzedaka	Chesed
Financial charity	**Nonfinancial** charity

Figure 8.2 Rabbinic Derivations of *Tzedek* and *Chesed*

case of Sabbath, the rabbis formulated rituals such as candle-lighting on the eve of the Sabbath, prayer, *kiddush* (evening and morning benediction over wine), and *havdalah* (closing ceremony with wine, fire, and incense).

Jewish law is based on the Hebrew Bible. To understand the Hebrew Bible, it is also important to examine the Talmud, the compilation of Jewish oral law, which expounds on the written law contained mainly in the Pentateuch (the Five Books of Moses, i.e., the Torah), and consists of the *Mishna* and *Gemara*. The *Mishna*, originally an oral tradition, was compiled and redacted by Rabbi Yehuda the *Nasi* (President of the Sanhedrin), known as Rebbi, about the year 189 CE. The *Gemara*, mainly commentaries and discussions on the *Mishna*, was put into written form about 1,500 years ago in academies in Israel and Babylon. The Babylonian Talmud is considerably larger than the Jerusalem Talmud and it is more authoritative. The Midrash records the views of the Talmudic sages and is mainly devoted to the exposition of biblical verses. The Talmud, mainly concerned with *halacha* (Jewish law), also provides a detailed record of the beliefs of the Jewish people, their philosophy, traditions, culture, and folklore, that is, the *aggadah* (homiletics), and is replete with legal, ethical, and moral teachings. Solomon (2009, xi) maintains: "The Talmud, frequently censored and occasionally banned and burned by the Catholic Church, is one of the most influential, though seldom acknowledged or properly understood, writings of Late Antiquity."

The rabbis of the Talmud also greatly expanded on the moral, ethical, and commercial law of the Bible. For example, the Bible instructs the finder of an object to return it to its rightful owner but provides scant instructions on specifics and exceptions. The Talmud devotes an entire tractate to the moral and legal issues surrounding lost-and-found objects. For example, the Bible instructs the finder to gather the object to his home and watch over it if the finder does not know the identity of the rightful owner. The Talmud describes how long the finder must maintain the object, in what manner, at whose expense, how to advertise the find, and how to interrogate those who claim to be the true owner and what evidence they need to present to prove ownership.

The Talmud's constitution and *raison d'etre* was to expound upon the teaching of the Torah. However, this section discusses situations where the rabbis of the Talmud chose to *negate* the Torah law. As heretical as it may sound, in certain situations the rabbis took it upon themselves to "fix" (*tikkun*) dysfunctional Torah law. The Talmudic sages enacted numerous *takanot* (enactments/ordinances) as legal remedies when they saw that the technical Torah law was in conflict with a core value of the Torah, particularly as it relates to public welfare. The rabbis of the Talmud took the liberty to violate the letter of the Torah in order to protect its spirit. They expressed this liberty as "when service to God calls for it, undo the Torah" (cf. Psalm 119:126; the literal meaning of the verse is different, but the rabbis read it in a creative, homiletic manner to suit their moral purposes). Thus, for example, the sages instituted that one should greet another person using the name of God (Babylonian Talmud, Berachos 54a).

This section describes two categories of fixes implemented by the Talmud: fixes to ensure the proper functioning of markets and fixes to ensure human dignity.

Market fixes – Takanot Hashuk

The Talmud advocates an effective, functioning marketplace; society cannot be productive without markets that allow people to buy and sell goods. Berkovits (1983, 16–17) describes how the Talmudic sages used *takanot hashuk* (enactment for the marketplace) as a legal device to ensure the proper functioning of the marketplace. For example, the rabbis discuss the case of someone who recognizes his property (something movable) in someone else's possession and it is known that the first party was indeed robbed. The person who currently possesses the stolen property purchased it innocently, not realizing that it was stolen. According to Torah law, the true owner would simply take back his property after producing witnesses that it belonged to him. However, this would mean that everyone would be afraid to purchase goods in the marketplace. How can any buyer know whether or not the seller truly owns the merchandise on sale? In order to ensure that the marketplace would function, the rabbis used the principle of *takanot hashuk* and ruled that the true owner swears to the court how much he paid for the merchandise and buys it back. He then takes the thief to court to get reimbursed. This way the person who innocently purchased the stolen goods does not have to take a loss (Babylonian Talmud, Baba Kama 114b-115a).

Another example of a market fix is the rabbinic reversal of the Torah law on Sabbatical remissions of debt. According to Torah law (Deuteronomy 15), all debts are cancelled on the Sabbatical year, which falls every seven years. In principle, the cancellation of debts can be a boon for economic justice. In practice, however, creditors adjusted their behavior in accordance with the Torah Law. Hillel the Elder (first century BCE; Babylonia and Jerusalem) observed that creditors refused to extend credit as the Sabbatical year approached. In effect, the Torah Law was hurting, rather than helping, those most in need of credit. In response, Hillel instituted a legal technicality to circumvent the Torah law on canceling debt in the Sabbatical year. Technically, once a collection judgment has been entered by the court, the Sabbatical laws do not apply. Hillel therefore instituted the *Prosbul*, a document that immediately transfers the loan to the court, thus deeming it exempt from cancellation (Babylonian Talmud, Gittin 36a).

An anti-Jewish critic may very well construe Hillel's legal technicality as a legal gimmick to circumvent the spirit of the law. However, its true purpose was just the opposite. It invalidated the law because Hillel observed that the law itself was no longer a boon to social justice but had become its bane.

Fixes to promote human dignity, peace, and pleasantness

Tikkun olam (in Hebrew, *tikkun* means repair and *olam* means world) is the notion that one is obligated to repair and perfect the world by using the legal system to enact laws that help perfect society. The sages of the Talmud used the principle of *tikkun olam* to enact various laws to help society (e.g., Babylonian Talmud, Gittin 32a, 34b, 40b, 41b, 45a, b); it is also an important part of the cabala of Rabbi Isaac Luria (1534–1572). In the Talmud, however, *tikkun olam* is a legal tool for improving the law.

Using the principle of *tikkun olam*, testimony rules were relaxed to ensure that a woman whose husband disappeared would be able to remarry. The rabbis of the Talmud did not want a woman to be an *agunah* (anchored or chained), so they enacted various *takanot* so that a woman would not be "chained" to a marriage without a husband and thus have to remain alone for the rest of her life. For example, the testimony of one witness that the husband had died was deemed sufficient to allow a woman to remarry despite the fact that Torah law generally requires the testimony of two witnesses (Babylonian Talmud, Eduyyoth 8a). The principle of *tikkun olam* was also used to make it difficult for men to make trouble for their ex-wives (Babylonian Talmud, Gittin 32a, 34b).

Peace is a core Torah value that must be enhanced by rabbinic law; therefore, the Talmud instituted many laws, some of which are not consistent with biblical law, in order to prevent strife. The Talmud refers to this principle as *darkei shalom* (the ways of peace). Thus, the Talmud condemns one who removes a fish caught in a net in public waters as a thief (Babylonian Talmud, Gittin 59a-b). According to Torah law, one would not legally acquire the fish by placing a net in the ocean or sea, which is public property. In order to preserve peace, the rabbis enacted legislation to prevent people from taking fish from nets (or animals or birds from traps and snares set in forests). The Talmud discusses other laws that were enacted because of the principle of *darkei shalom* (e.g., allowing minors and the mentally ill to acquire a found object whose owners cannot be located). The Talmud also enacted various laws because of the principle of preventing ill feeling (*ayvah*) between husband and wife (Babylonian Talmud, Kethubos 58b).

The following example cited by Berkovits (1983, 38) demonstrates the importance of peace. According to Rabbi Yehuda HaNasi, if a man approaches a married woman and betroths her on the condition that the marriage would take effect after the death of her husband, this would technically be valid under Torah law (if the woman accepts). However, Rabbi Yehuda said that the reason the conditional marriage is not valid is because it would cause enmity between the husband and wife. One can imagine how angry the husband would be after finding out that his wife has chosen a replacement while he is still alive (Babylonian Talmud, Kiddushin 63a)!

Earlier, we showed how the Talmud uses stories to impart the importance of certain ethical traits. According to ancient tradition, Elijah the Prophet would visit pious people, and a visit by Elijah would confer evidence of piety. According to legend, Elijah is descended from Aaron, the brother of Moses. Like Aaron, Elijah is associated with peacemaking. Elijah once pointed out two passersby to Rabbi Beroka Hozaah and indicated that the two were destined for paradise:

> Rabbi Beroka approached them and asked them what they did. They replied: We are joyous people, and we cheer up people who are depressed. Also, when we see two people who are quarreling, we work hard to make peace between them.
> *(Babylonian Talmud, Taanit 22a)*

The principle of "Its [the Torah] ways are the ways of pleasantness and all of her paths are peace (Proverbs 3:17)" is used by the Talmud to establish laws that will preclude any kind of unpleasant situation that could be injurious to a marriage or disagreeable to a person (Babylonian Talmud Yebamoth 15a; Sukkah 32b). The Talmud mentions the principle of *chiena* (for the sake of pleasantness). They wanted pleasantness between husband and wife and also to make marriage attractive to those who were unmarried (Babylonian Talmud, Kethubos 84a, 97b; Gittin 49b).

The Talmud states that "The value of human dignity is so great that it supersedes a negative commandment of the Torah" (Babylonian Talmud, Berachos 19b-20a). The Talmud concludes that human dignity overrides rabbinic law and precepts of the Torah where the person is not actively engaged in a violation but is refraining from performing a mandated commandment. The Jerusalem Talmud has a somewhat different version of this: "The dignity of the public [the term used is *kvod harrabim*, which means the dignity of the many] is so great that it supersedes a negative commandment of the Torah temporarily" (Jerusalem Talmud, Berachos 3:1).

The Talmud discusses numerous cases where human dignity trumps biblical law. For example, the Torah (Deuteronomy 22:1) requires the finder of a lost object to return it to its owner: "You shall not see the ox of your brother or his sheep wandering and hide yourself from them."

The Talmud (Babylonian Talmud, Berachos 19b), however, makes the observation that there are exceptions to this law, for instance, when an elderly person finds it beneath his dignity to deal with the lost object (it has very little value and he would not bother with it even if it were his own); he is permitted to ignore it. This is clearly a case where human dignity overrides a Torah law.

There is a special law regarding a *meth mitzvah*, the burial of an unattended corpse (e.g., if a body is found in a forsaken place and there is no one to take care of it). A monk (*nazir*, see Numbers 6:1–21) is an individual who consecrates himself by taking a special vow; he is not permitted to drink wine, cut his/her hair, or come into contact with a corpse. However, if a priest or *nazir* is traveling and sees an unattended corpse on the side of the road and there is no one else to take care of it, he is obligated to bury it. Of course, this makes the priest impure and disqualified from priestly functions until he becomes purified (Babylonian Talmud, Berachos 19b, 20a). *Meth mitzvah* is so important that even the High Priest (*kohen gadol*) must bury the unattended corpse. This is a case where human dignity (leaving a corpse unattended is an embarrassment for the deceased) overrides Torah law. In order to preserve the dignity of the poor, the Talmud (Babylonian Talmud, Moed Katan 27a-27b) instituted numerous changes in the funeral ceremony. Friedman (2008) provides a thorough discussion of human dignity and Jewish law and cites Talmudic, post-Talmudic, and modern cases where Jewish law uses the importance of human dignity as a reason for setting aside various laws.

Accountants as advocates for human dignity

In November 2014, Pope Francis (2014) addressed thousands of delegates at the World Congress of Accountants in Rome:

> [E]veryone, especially those who practice a profession which deals with the proper functioning of a country's economic life, is asked to play a positive, constructive role in performing their daily work, knowing that behind every file, there is a story, there are faces. This task which, as we have said, requires everyone's cooperation . . . to do his duty well, with competence and wisdom; and then to "go beyond", which means to go to meet the person in difficulty; to exercise that creativity which enables one to find solutions to an impasse; to invoke reasons of human dignity in facing the rigidity of bureaucracy.

Francis called upon accountants to act as "advocates" for people in difficulty. However, the AICPA Code of Professional Conduct (2016, see Table 8.1) sees advocacy as a threat to professional ethics. The profession should therefore seriously consider Francis's implied suggestion that accountants and their professional standard setters need to be able to make exceptions to general principles when they require "fixes" to promote a greater good. Francis specifically called on accountants to embrace not just competence but also wisdom, creativity, and courage to make the right choices (see Figure 8.3, adopted from Fischer 2016). While accountants should not normally advocate for one set of interests over another, exceptions arise in situations that require "fixes."

Fischer (2017) provides an example of a situation in which the accountant is called upon to "advocate" for a particular position. In the real-world example, an activist investor used aggressive accounting assumptions to pressure a company to restructure and redirect free cash flow from pension contributions to share repurchases. In this situation, an imaginary

Table 8.1 AICPA Code of Professional Conduct (2016) – Threats to and Safeguards From Noncompliance

	Substance or Form?	
10 Adverse interest threat. The threat that a member will not act with objectivity because the member's interests are opposed to the client's interests.	Substance	
11 Advocacy threat. The threat that a member will promote a client's interests or position to the point that his or her objectivity or independence is compromised.		Form
12 Familiarity threat. The threat that, due to a long or close relationship with a client, a member will become too sympathetic to the client's interests or too accepting of the client's work or product.		Form
13 Management participation threat. The threat that a member in public practice will take on the role of client management or otherwise assume management responsibilities, may occur during an engagement to provide non-attest services.		Form
14 Self-interest threat. The threat that a member could benefit, financially or otherwise, from an interest in or relationship with a client or persons associated with the client.		Form
15 Self-review threat. The threat that a member will not appropriately evaluate the results of a previous judgment made or service performed or supervised by the member or an individual in the member's firm and that the member will rely on that service in forming a judgment as part of another service.	Substance	
16 Undue influence threat. The threat that a member will subordinate his or her judgment to an individual associated with a client or any relevant third party due to that individual's reputation or expertise, aggressive or dominant personality, or attempts to coerce or exercise excessive influence over the member.	Substance	

Source: Summary definitions from Spalding and Lawrie (2019). Numbers relate to paragraphs in AICPA (2016) Section 1.000.010 (Conceptual Framework for Members in Public Practice). Substance/Form is our subjective classification.

- Values of justice, legality, and solidarity
- Solidarity is awareness of the other, respect for their dignity and needs, and to help them develop as individuals
- Business professionals must play a positive role, not merely a neutral role
- Competence, wisdom, creativity, and courage to make the right choices

Figure 8.3 Themes of Pope Francis's Speech to the World Congress of Accountants in Rome, November 2014

accountant working for the firm should have rallied not just his/her competence but also his/her wisdom, creativity, and courage to present a counterargument to that presented by the activist investor. No one like the accountant could appreciate and convey the tenuous nature of the supposedly funded pension plan and how it relied on shaky assumptions. In our hypercompetitive, late-capitalistic business environment, there are motivated parties who creatively spin accounting data to suit their own narrow interests. Unfortunately, as a profession, accountants themselves have de-emphasized creativity, even when it is greatly needed (Bryant, Stone, and Wier 2011).

The accounting profession has focused more on ethical threats than on ethical opportunities. This is reflected in both the academic literature and in professional standards. Reinstein and Taylor (2017) highlight the value of "fences" as safeguards against fraud. Interestingly, they base their framework on the Jewish Talmud, as we do. In the professional standards literature, the AICPA (2016) has specifically identified seven threats to noncompliance by auditors to the code of professional conduct. Spalding and Lawrie summarize these threats, which we present in Table 8.1. The threats include adverse interest, advocacy, familiarity, management participation, self-interest, self-review, and undue influence.

The primacy of substance over form suggests that some threats are more serious than others. Table 8.1 relates three of the seven threats with substance, and four with form. In the example given earlier about the activist investor, the advocacy threat is one of form, not substance. In certain circumstances, accountants should have the flexibility to disregard a "form" threat for the greater "substantive" social good.

We illustrate our proposition in Figure 8.4, where we present a hierarchy of the seven AICPA (2016) threats. The adverse interest threat is the primary substantive threat to accounting ethics. On the other hand, advocacy, familiarity, self-interest, and management participation are "form" threats that can actually sometimes be opportunities and incentives for virtue! The intermediate threats of self-review and undue influence can guide the profession on when the "form" threats are truly threats and should be treated as such.

Reinstein and Taylor (2017) apply the notion of "fences" from the Jewish Talmud to reduce accountants' rationalization of fraud. This notion tends to add rules and safeguards, and we admit that it serves an important purpose in creating a culture of ethical awareness. We highlight a countervailing tendency in the Jewish Talmud. When safeguards and rules become too

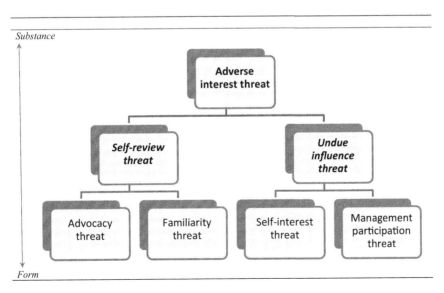

Figure 8.4 AICPA (2016) Threats to and Safeguards from Noncompliance, A Preliminary Hierarchy of Substance and Form.

focused on preserving a society's ethical form, it is imperative for leaders to allow professional judgment to promote the substance of ethical values.

Conclusion

The Great Recession of 2008 and the #MeToo revolution of 2018 demonstrated what happens when bankers, auditors, lawyers, CEOs, hedge fund managers, and many other leaders in various fields commit highly unethical behavior that falls short of breaking the law. In the Great Recession, trillions of dollars of investors' funds were lost and many people lost their jobs and homes, but most of the perpetrators of these immoral acts did not technically break the law (Morgenson and Rosner 2011). Accountants focus more on following GAAP than on being ethical (DeFond, Lennox, and Zhang 2018). In fact, it is quite possible for an accountant to behave in an unethical manner, for example, to use inventory valuation methods to make financial statements look better and not be in violation of GAAP (Palmrose and Kinney 2018).

The current #MeToo scrutiny shines the spotlight on the long-term quiet suffering of victims and survivors of sexual misconduct. Behavior that was tolerated for decades has come to light for the sinister and paralyzing effect it had on victims. In the case of #MeToo, companies and their lawyers focused more on protecting the company and its executives than on promoting a truly safe working environment that is free of sexual pressures. When Google fired a top executive for an alleged incident of sexual coercion in 2013, the news was kept quiet and the company gave the executive a $90 million severance (Wakabayashi and Benner 2018).

The opioid epidemic is a major health crisis in America. This crisis, too, was fueled by companies that followed the letter rather than the spirit of the law. It now appears that top executives at Purdue Pharmacy, manufacturer of Oxycontin, were aware of the wide abuse of their opioids in the late 1990s. They purposely hid this information from the government. The responsible executives ended up pleading guilty to misdemeanors, paid fines, and had to perform community service. Clearly, the misdemeanor plea sent the wrong message to other firms, and the United States is still suffering from an opioid epidemic. Over the last two decades, more than 200,000 people died from opioid overdoses (Meier 2018).

This chapter demonstrates that the ancient sages of the Talmud used legal devices and storytelling aids to improve the law. They saw the law as the floor to ethics and understood the limitations of focusing exclusively on rules rather than values. There is an ethics hierarchy, and individuals are encouraged to strive to reach the highest level of morality they are capable of reaching (Friedman 1985). The ultimate goal was to ensure that the law is adhered to, while at the same time people are taught to go beyond the requirements of the letter of the law. The sages understood how easy it was to be a vile person within the permissible realm of the law (this expression is used by Nachmanides in his commentary on Leviticus 19:2). This chapter showed how stories can raise the moral bar. In the words of A.J. Heschel:

> *Aggadah* (stories) deals with man's ineffable relations to God, to other men, and to the world. *Halakhah* (the Law) deals with details, with each commandment separately; *aggadah* with the whole of life, with the totality of religious life. *Halakhah* deals with the law; *aggadah* with the meaning of the law. *Halakhah* deals with subjects that can be expressed literally; *aggadah* introduces us to a realm that lies beyond the range of expression. *Halakhah* teaches us how to perform common acts; *aggadah* tells us how to participate in the eternal drama. *Halakhah* gives us knowledge; *aggadah* gives us aspiration.
>
> *(Heschel 1976, 336–37)*

The Talmudic sages used *aggadah* as a tool to stretch the law. Without *aggadah*, the *halacha* simply consists of rules. The spirit of the law is contained in the *aggadah*. This chapter will examine various devices used by the sages to enhance the law and make sure that ethics would be the foundation of the law.

Admittedly, it is much easier to convince people who believe in a final judgment and an afterlife to go beyond the simple requirements of the law than to convince those who do not subscribe to such belief. Nevertheless, it is the job of educators in a secular society to point out the dangers of living in a society where all that matters is following the letter of the law. A responsible person or organization must strive to do considerably more than just obey the law and adhere to a code of ethics. Ethics must be value-driven, not rule-driven.

An actionable recommendation from this study is to make use of positive stories; see Udani and Lorenzo-Molo (2013) for an example. The profession has distilled its ethics education in the form of negative rules. When we use stories, they are almost always of the "business sucks" narrative (Freeman 2018). The profession should formulate a program of positive ethical education through the use of positive narratives.

Foster (2018) provides inspiring stories of family-run firms motivated by Christian, Buddhist, Jewish, and Muslim ethics. He tells a particularly poignant story of a firm founded by Jewish-German refugees in Wales. In a time of lingering economic depression in Wales, the Jewish owners and the non-Jewish employees viewed themselves as an extended family. The Jewish owners were grateful for the refuge they found in the United Kingdom, while the non-Jewish workers were grateful for the steady work and pay. Particularly interesting is the following anecdote, "which is symbolic of the Sterns' approach to their staff:" (214)

> It was decided that there should be a "do" for the staff as a kind of thank you. It was decided to have a Christmas lunch, which perhaps axiomatically served non-kosher food: it was after all a Christmas lunch! The family however, being practicing Jews, felt that they couldn't eat this non-kosher food but they felt that they should attend the event to demonstrate their togetherness with the workforce. What to do? They attended the lunch and took along their own sandwiches to eat, while the staff enjoyed their festive fare! Thus, honor was satisfied on all fronts and team spirit was enhanced.

This anecdote is remarkable. For practicing Orthodox Jews, it is prohibited not just to eat pork but it is taboo to have any dealings with pork. It is even considered taboo to raise live hogs. However, the Jewish owners were savvy enough to understand the significance of the gesture to their employees. As we saw earlier, the Talmud itself sometimes abrogates the letter of the law to maintain its spirit.

References

American Institute of Certified Public Accountants. 1973. "Study Group on the Objectives of Financial Statements." In *Objectives of Financial Statements*. Vol. 1. New York City: American Institute of Certified Public Accountants.

American Institute of Certified Public Accountants (AICPA). 2016. *Code of Professional Conduct*. New York: AICPA.

Bazerman, Max H., and Ann E. Tenbrusel. 2014. "Ethical Breakdowns." *Harvard Business Review*. https://hbr.org/2011/04/ethical-breakdowns.

Berkovits, Eliezer. 1983. *Not in Heaven: The Nature and Function of Halakha*. New York: Ktav Pub. House.

Bryant, Stephanie M., Dan Stone, and Benson Wier. 2011. "An Exploration of Accountants, Accounting Work, and Creativity." *Behavioral Research in Accounting* 23 (1): 45.

Chaney, Paul K., and Kirk L. Philipich. 2002. "Shredded Reputation: The Cost of Audit Failure." *Journal of Accounting Research* 40 (4): 1221–245.

Crutchley, Claire E., Marlin R. H Jensen, and Beverly B. Marshall. 2007. "Climate for Scandal: Corporate Environments That Contribute to Accounting Fraud." *Financial Review* 42 (1): 53–73.

DeFond, Mark L., Clive S. Lennox, and Jieying Zhang. 2018. "The Primacy of Fair Presentation: Evidence from PCAOB Standards, Federal Legislation, and the Courts." *Accounting Horizons* 32 (3): 91–100.

Financial Accounting Standards Board (FASB). 2010. "Conceptual Framework for Financial Reporting." Statement of Financial Accounting Concepts No. 8.

Fischer, Dov. 2016. "My Spiritual Odyssey as an Accounting Professor." *Journal of Ethics & Entrepreneurship* 6 (1): 5.

Fischer, Dov. 2017. "Pope Francis Tells Accountants to Become Creative." *Ramon Llull Journal of Applied Ethics* 8: 98–120.

Fischer, Dov. 2018. "Substance and Form of the Palmrose/Kinney versus DeFond/Lennox/Zhang Debate." *Kinney Versus DeFond/Lennox/Zhang Debate*, November 21.

Fischer, Dov, and Hershey H. Friedman. 2019. "Tone-at-the-Top Lessons from Abrahamic Justice." *Journal of Business Ethics* 156 (1): 209–25.

Foster, M. John. 2018. "Socially Responsible Management as a Basis for Sound Business in the Family Firm." *Philosophy of Management* 17 (2): 203–18.

Francis, Pope. 2014. *Address of Pope Francis to Participants in the Plenary Session of the Congregation for Catholic Education (for Educational Institutions)*. Vatican City: Libreria Editrice Vaticana.

Freeman, R. Edward. 2018. "The 'Business Sucks' Story." *Humanistic Management Journal* 3 (1): 9–16.

Friedman, Hershey H. 1985. "Ethical Behavior in Business: A Hierarchical Approach from the Talmud." *Journal of Business Ethics* 4 (2): 117–29.

Friedman, Hershey H. 2008. "Human Dignity and the Jewish Tradition." SSRN 2295178.

Friedman, Hershey H., and Miriam GerStein. 2016. "Are We Wasting Our Time Teaching Business Ethics? Ethical Lapses Since Enron and the Great Recession." *Ethical Lapses Since Enron and the Great Recession*. Accessed September 14. https://ssrn.com/abstract=2839069 or http://dx.doi.org/10.2139/ssrn.2839069.

Friedman, Hershey H., and Frimette Kass. 2018." 'Substance Over Form': Meaningful Ways to Measure Organizational Performance." SSRN 3128595.

Gifter, M. 2000. "Human Law and Torah Law." In *The Ethical Imperative: Torah Perspectives on Ethics and Values*, edited by Nisson Wolpin, 243–51. Brooklyn, NY: Mesorah Publications.

Heschel, Abraham Joshua. 1976. *God in Search of Man: A Philosophy of Judaism*. New York City: Farrar, Straus and Giroux.

Kirschenbaum, Aaron. 1991. *Equity in Jewish Law*. Hoboken, NJ: Ktav Publishing House.

Meier, B. 2018. "Opioid's Maker Hid Knowledge of Wide Abuse." *New York Times A* 1: A18.

Morgenson, Gretchen, and Joshua Rosner. 2011. *Reckless Endangerment: How Outsized Ambition, Greed, and Corruption Led to Economic Armageddon*. New York City: Times Books.

Myers, Randy. 2003. "Ensuring Ethical Effectiveness." *Journal of Accountancy-New York* 195 (2): 28–34.

Palmrose, Zoe-Vonna, and William R. Kinney Jr. 2018. "Auditor and FASB Responsibilities for Representing Underlying Economics – What US Standards Actually Say." *Accounting Horizons* 32 (3): 83–90.

Reinstein, Alan, and Eileen Z. Taylor. 2017. "Fences as Controls to Reduce Accountants' Rationalization." *Journal of Business Ethics* 141 (3): 477–88.

RSFI and OGC to Staff of Rulewriting Divisions and Offices. 2012. Current Guidance on Economic Analysis in SEC Rulemakings, SEC, March 16. www.sec.gov/divisions/riskfin/rsfi_guidance_econ_analy_secrulemaking.pdf.

Sacks, J. 2005. *To Heal a Fractured World: The Ethics of Responsibility*. New York City: Schocken Books.

Silberg, M. 1973. *Talmudic Law and the Modern State*. New York: The Burning Bush Press.

Solomon, Norman, and Penguin Classics London. 2014. "2009, 822 pp., ISBN 978-0-141-44178-8, Soft Cover a Certain Academic Once Responded to a Paper I Had Given on Talmudic Texts, Saying How Much He Had Enjoyed the Sources and That He Would Now Definitely 'Read the Talmud'. I Could Only Chuckle at the Scope of Such an Endeavour.": 154–63.

Soltani, Bahram. 2014. "The Anatomy of Corporate Fraud: A Comparative Analysis of High Profile American and European Corporate Scandals." *Journal of Business Ethics* 120 (2): 251–274.

Spalding, Albert D., and Gretchen R. Lawrie. 2019. "A Critical Examination of the AICPA's New 'Conceptual Framework' Ethics Protocol." *Journal of Business Ethics* 155 (4): 1135–152.

Spalding, Albert D., and Alfonso Oddo. 2011. "It's Time for Principles-Based Accounting Ethics." *Journal of Business Ethics* 99 (1): 49–59.

Stolleis, Michael. 1998. *The Law Under the Swastika: Studies on Legal History in Nazi Germany*. Chicago: University of Chicago Press.

Taleb, Nassim Nicholas. 2020. *Skin in the Game: Hidden Asymmetries in Daily Life*. New York City: Random House Trade Paperbacks.

Udani, Zenon Arthur S., and Caterina F. Lorenzo-Molo. 2013. "When Servant Becomes Leader: The Corazon C. Aquino Success Story as a Beacon for Business Leaders." *Journal of business ethics* 116 (2): 373–91.

Wakabayashi, Daisuke, and Katie Benner. 2018. "How Google Protected Andy Rubin, the 'Father of Android'." *The New York Times* 25.

9

A CHRISTIAN ACCOUNTING ETHIC

God's image and work transform our image and work

Martin Stuebs and John M. Thornton

"I believe in Christianity as I believe that the Sun has risen, not only because I see it, but because by it I see everything else."

– *C.S. Lewis, The Weight of Glory*

Introduction

What can Christianity uniquely contribute to the accounting profession's ethics? Exploring that question is this chapter's purpose and can be of interest to both Christian and non-Christian accounting professionals. Presenting a Christian perspective's contributions to accounting ethics speaks directly and beneficially to Christian accounting professionals while also informing those unfamiliar with Christianity who wish to consider how Christian concepts can contribute to accounting ethics. Although the contributions of faith-based perspectives to accounting ethics have not received significant attention[1], exploring the contributions of Christianity importantly is warranted since Christianity, and more generally religion, is recognized to be "one of the strongest influences in individual's behaviour" (Espinosa-Pike and Barrainkua-Aroztegi 2014, 1127).

A Christian perspective on accounting ethics recognizes that God's image and work transform the Christian's image and work. God's Word revealed in the Bible[2] informs the Christian what God does for the Christian through His character and work. While we consider other important aspects of God's character like His righteousness and His sovereignty, it is God's love in Jesus Christ that is centrally important to a Christian ethic. The outpouring of God's undeserved love in Jesus[3] and His free gift of salvation distinguishes Christian identity and forms the basis for a uniquely Christian ethic. Christians call this outpouring of God's unmerited love "grace."[4]

The Christian ethic acknowledges two realities: (1) an accurate *diagnosis* identifying the severity and depth of the *problem* that everyone is born with a flawed sinful human nature (Psalm 51:5),[5] as an enemy of God (Romans 5:10),[6] and enslaved to and dead in sin[7] (Ephesians 2:1; John 8:34),[8] and (2) an adequate *prescriptive solution* that recognizes the necessity of God's love in the character and work of Jesus Christ to bring transformative rescue that restores God-glorifying motives, desires, and intuitions in the Christian's heart and mind. Since this Christian perspective to ethics begins with God's restorative unconditional love through Jesus, it is, in this sense, a radically backwards approach: Instead of our good performance leading to God's love for us, God's unconditional love for us leads to our good performance. We *perform* acts of love for God and others because God *first loved* us (1 John 4:19).[9] This Christian approach sees transformation as a relational process that begins with the conversion of the human spirit by God's love and ends in performance of accounting activity and social change for God's glory (Niebuhr 1951; Siker 1989).

With a focus that begins with the need for God's love to restore the motives of the heart, a Christian perspective can serve as a bridge to bring Haidt's (2001) recognition of the ethical significance of desires, intuitions and motives into accounting ethics. Haidt (2013) finds that morality is shaped more by emotions, intuitions, desires, and motives than reason and that we use reason to justify *post hoc* our motives and desired actions. This focus on desires and motives challenges earlier moral reasoning philosophies, which argue we use reason to determine the best course of action. In this chapter, we develop the implications and contributions of a Christian ethics perspective to enhance extant accounting ethics research. First, in the second section of this chapter, we review common attributes in familiar codes of accounting ethics and connect them to familiar approaches to accounting ethics (Kohlberg 1969; Mintz 1995, 1996a, 1996b). This sets the stage for placing a Christian ethics perspective in accounting ethics and identifying its useful contributions, which we do in our third section. In the fourth section, we discuss implications of this Christian perspective for the accounting profession (May 2001) and practice in the presence of opportunities and incentives to rationalize fraud (Cressey 1953). The fifth section concludes the chapter.

Codes and perspectives on accounting ethics

We begin by reviewing common attributes in accounting codes of conduct and connecting them to familiar perspectives in accounting ethics in preparation for identifying unique opportunities for Christianity's contribution to ethics in the next section.

Accounting practitioners are familiar with professional accounting codes of conduct.[10] A profession's members agree to be bound to higher standards and adopt a code's set of principles and rules to educate members and the public about their roles and responsibilities. Although unique in specifics, many codes of conduct share the common attributes of: (1) professional competence, (2) professional character and (3) professional public service. A succinct example of a professional code that embodies these attributes is that of the United States Air Force Academy: "Integrity first. Service before self. Excellence in all we do" – character, public service, and competence.

These familiar code-of-conduct attributes are informed and supported by the logic of ethical perspectives commonly used in traditional approaches to accounting ethics, including consequentialist, non-consequentialist, and virtue ethics theories (Cheffers and Pakaluk 2011; Crane and Matten 2007). Consequentialism considers consequences of conduct where moral reasoning results in "good" consequences. Non-consequentialism considers the "goodness" of the action itself independent of consequences. Virtue ethics focuses on the role of "good" character traits in self-regulating action.

Each of these perspectives views unethical accounting differently. For example, a general ethical challenge accountants face involves how to balance the reporting of financial information and management of economic resources with the welfare and safety of public stakeholders like investors, employees, customers, and other constituents. Consequentialism views reporting activities as wrong when they lead to ineffective and inefficient risks and outcomes.

Non-consequentialism's legalistic perspective views reporting activities as wrong when they violate just accounting standards, rules, and laws. From a virtue ethics perspective, reporting activities are wrong when they fail to comply with developed professional virtues. The next section explores how a Christian view adds the spiritual perspective that reporting activities are wrong when they fail to love, honor, and glorify God by using His resources to extend His love to others by following His righteous standards and sovereign laws.

In preparation for presenting this Christian perspective in the next section, this section reviews and compares how these traditional approaches to accounting ethics inform familiar attributes of codes of conduct in accounting practice.

Moral reasoning competence perspectives

Accounting ethics education's traditional focus on moral reasoning competence (Mintz 1995; 1996a, 1996b) supports the professional competence attribute found in codes of conduct and has its roots in Kohlberg's (1969) moral development theory, which measures moral reasoning development at pre-conventional, conventional, and post-conventional levels (Kohlberg and Hersh 2001). Both consequentialism and non-consequentialism inform approaches to moral reasoning competence. Two common forms of consequentialism are utilitarianism and egoism (Crane and Matten 2007). Under utilitarianism, actions are morally good if they result in the "greatest amount of good for the greatest amount of people affected" (Crane and Matten 2007, 100). Egoism as reflected in the work of Adam Smith (1976) considers self-interested pursuits morally acceptable if they produce morally desirable societal consequences through the marketplace's invisible hand (Samsonova-Taddei and Siddiqui 2016). Egoism narrows considered consequences from utilitarianism's societal outcomes to only individual self-satisfying outcomes consistent with Kohlberg's (1969) pre-conventional levels of moral reasoning. Consequentialist moral reasoning underlies the motives for opportunistic reporting choices that maximize economic consequences (Zeff 1978) in agency theory (Eisenhardt 1989; Jensen and Meckling 1976) and positive accounting theory (Watts and Zimmerman 1986). These ideas are summarized in the first column of Table 9.1.

Non-consequentialist moral reasoning competence entails applying general imperatives or rules regardless of consequence (Campbell 2005). Kant's categorical imperative is a form of non-consequentialism that states, in its simplest form, that a decision is moral only if the decision and the reasons for it (i.e., its "maxim") can be willed a universal law (Godar 2005). Kant's categorical imperative demonstrates that a code's formal rules and standards play the determinative role in guiding non-consequentialist moral reasoning consistent with Kohlberg's (1969) conventional levels of moral reasoning (Larry and Moore 2008). The second column in Table 9.1 summarizes these non-consequentialist ideas.

Virtue ethics character perspectives

Reflecting an Aristotelian ethical perspective, virtue ethics (Mintz 1995, 1996a, 1996b) guides and informs the professional character attribute found in codes of conduct by focusing on the *actor's* character traits instead of the *action's* underlying moral reasoning (Solomon 1992; Crane and Matten 2007; Cheffers and Pakaluk 2011). These virtues, or character traits, are defined as normative qualities that reflect an individual's ability to act ethically (Libby and Thorne 2004; MacIntyre 2013). Virtue ethics draws attention to the actor one should *be* instead of the actions one should *do*. The third, right-hand column in Table 9.1 summarizes these ideas from the virtue ethics perspective.

Table 9.1 Approaches to Improving Accounting Ethics

	Inform Moral Reasoning Competence: *Improve Awareness and Analysis*		*Reform Character:* *Improve Action*
	Pre-Conventional *Economic Perspective*	*Conventional* *Regulatory Perspective*	*Post-Conventional* *Self-Regulatory Perspective*
Means	Consequentialist logic guides moral accounting decisions by considering an action's consequences.	Non-consequentialist logic guides moral accounting decisions by considering the action itself.	Virtue ethics (or Aristotelian) logic guides moral accounting decisions by considering the needed professional virtues of the decision maker.
Motive/ Mission	Moral accounting decisions choose actions that maximize net outcomes (i.e., maximize benefits; minimize costs). Manage reported information, resources, expenses, and profits with welfare and safety considerations to maximize net outcomes.	Moral accounting decisions choose actions that comply with business rules and regulations (i.e., regulatory compliance). Manage reported information, resources, expenses, and profits with welfare and safety considerations that comply with regulatory standards.	Moral accounting decisions choose actions that comply with developed virtues (i.e., self-regulatory compliance). Manage reported information, resources, expenses, and profits with welfare and safety considerations to achieve societal flourishing.
Management	Management and control come from economic systems, markets, and price mechanisms that ensure actions lead to the best societal outcome (i.e., maximize the wealth creation of net outcomes).	Management and control come from regulatory system rules and regulations that guide behavior to the best societal outcome.	Management and control come from a self-regulatory system of trained professional virtues that guide behavior to the best societal outcome.

The virtue ethics perspective to accounting ethics has gained momentum (e.g., Cheffers and Pakaluk 2011; Mintz 1995, 2006, 2010) and usually starts by focusing on classical ethical theory's four cardinal virtues (i.e., justice, wisdom, courage, and self-control). Thorne (1998) integrated virtue ethics theory and the cardinal virtues with Rest's (1983, 1994) four component model of ethical action. Rest (1983, 1994) extended moral development beyond moral reasoning by describing moral action as a multifaceted phenomenon (Guthrie 1997) of (1) moral motivation, (2) moral awareness, (3) moral judgment, and (4) moral character. Table 9.2 incorporates this prior research to connect Rest's (1983, 1994) four components of ethical action (the first column in Table 9.2) with virtue ethics' four cardinal virtues (the second column in Table 9.2) and the common attributes of codes of conduct in accounting practice (the third column in Table 9.2).

Table 9.2 Framework for Virtue Development

Rest (1984) Model	Cardinal Virtue	Code of Conduct Attribute
Moral Will: Provides the underlying motives for an individual's actions (Schwartz and Sharpe 2010). 1 *Moral Motivation*: An individual's willingness to place the interests of others ahead of his or her own (Rest 1994).	1 *Justice*: Formulating and embracing ideals of fairness, equality, and lawfulness that provide the motives for action (Melé 2009).	Professional Public Service
2 *Moral Awareness*: The cognitive recognition that a dilemma's resolution may affect others' welfare (Rest 1994). 2 *Moral Judgment*: deciding what ought to be done (Navarez and Rest 1995).	2 *Wisdom*: An intellectual virtue by which important goods and principles are identified and ranked (Cheffers and Pakaluk 2011).	Professional Competence
Moral Skill: Provides the ability to implement judgment (Schwartz and Sharpe 2010). 3, 4 *Moral Character*: The virtues needed to carry out a chosen action.	3 *Courage*: The ability to act appropriately when faced with challenges or threats.	Professional Character
	4 *Self-control* (moderation): The ability to act appropriately as regards physical pleasures, desires, cravings and comforts.	

Table 9.2 explicitly recognizes the importance of developing virtues to support the: (1) *moral will* to handle incentives (the first row in Table 9.2) and (2) *moral skill* to appropriately respond to opportunities (the third row in Table 9.2) (Schwartz and Sharpe 2010). Moral will and moral skill guide and protect moral judgment (the second row in Table 9.2). This section has reviewed common and familiar perspectives on ethics and their contributions to moral reasoning competence (Kohlberg 1969) and moral character (Rest 1983; 1994) in accounting ethics and how they contribute support to code-of-conduct attributes in practice. This sets the stage for exploring a Christian perspective and how it can uniquely contribute to this accounting ethics landscape.

Christian perspective on accounting ethics

Comparing the code of conduct attributes (i.e., professional competence, professional character, and professional public service) with the traditional ethics perspectives (i.e., the moral reasoning perspective and the virtue ethics perspective) and Rest's (1983, 1994) moral action elements (i.e., moral awareness, moral judgment, moral character, and moral motivation) reveals opportunities for a Christian perspective's unique contribution to accounting ethics. While the moral reasoning perspective draws attention to a code of conduct's professional competence attribute and the virtue ethics perspective focuses on a code of conduct's professional character attribute, neither brings central attention to the moral motivation of the professional public service attribute. While Kohlberg's (1969) moral reasoning competence approach focuses attention on Rest's (1983, 1994) moral awareness and moral judgment factors and a virtue ethics approach centers attention on Rest's (1983, 1994) moral character factor, neither approach gives central attention to moral motivation.

A Christian perspective can contribute to these accounting ethics perspectives, then, by drawing attention to the foundational importance of Rest's (1983, 1994) moral motivation factor. Haidt (2001, 2013) finds that emotions, intuitions, desires, and motives shape morality more than reason, drawing attention to the significance of desires and motives, and a Christian approach can serve as a bridge to bring attention to these ideas in accounting ethics. Beneath the needs for moral virtue to change behavioral action and moral reasoning to improve judgment and decision making, a Christian perspective first recognizes the foundational need for Jesus and His love to transform the motives and desires of the human heart. The Bible recognizes the spiritual importance of the heart. When the Bible uses the term "heart," it refers to a person's causal core. The heart is the center of our loves and what we serve, commit to, worship, hope in, and trust. A Christian approach identifies first and foremost the importance of a love-based spiritual solution to transform the underlying spiritual condition, desires, and moral motives of the heart.

Presenting and articulating this Christian perspective begins by identifying what it means to be Christian. In the simplest sense, Christianity is "the religion based on the *person* and *teaching* of Jesus" (emphasis added).[11] Answers to two foundational questions about Jesus, also called the Christ (or Messiah), identify Christianity: (1) *Christ's person or image*: Who is Jesus? and (2) *Christ's work and teaching*: What did Jesus do and teach? Christians recognize that the *person* of Jesus is the Son of God and is fully God, Creator of all things.[12] They believe that God's Word in the Bible[13] shares what God has performed for us by His love, in that God's Word became human[14] in the *person* of Jesus to fulfill His *work* as our Savior and Redeemer through His perfect life, innocent death, and resurrection, to reconcile us to God and restore humans' relationship with God.

Jesus *taught* that through faith in Him and His redemptive work, Christians have the forgiveness of sins and eternal life in heaven.[15] Jesus' performance restored and secured God's acceptance, making believers members in God's family. But Christ's image and work does more than transform our *future, eternal* identity and existence. This section explores how Christ's image and work transform the ethics of our *present* image and work, redeeming the present moments of our daily living here and now. We begin by identifying God's intended plan and diagnosing the problem. We then consider God's provided prescription and the process through which God's image and work transform the ethics of our present image and work.

The plan and the problem: Why God's image and work are needed

Christians believe that God, our Sovereign[16] Creator, spoke everything in creation into existence.[17] All things were created through Him and for Him and His glory.[18] Importantly, God distinguished humans by creating them in His image: "God said, 'Let us make humankind in our image, in our likeness, so that they may rule . . . over all the creatures.' . . . So, God created mankind in His own image" (Genesis 1:26–27). The image of God was God's created ideal for humans, with notable implications. First, each human *structurally* is a unique creation having unique dignity imbued from God, our Creator. Second, humans *functionally* are God's representative managers (i.e., the image of God on earth), given the managing responsibility of "ruling over" God's creation for God's glory. In this sense, *relationally*, the image of God established an important principal-agent relationship between God and man, and this spiritual relationship with our Creator guides our physical and societal relationships with creation.

As a result, accounting and accountability were an important part of God's created functional and relational ideal. We give an account to a righteous God of our right stewardship and management of His creation, including the time, talents, and treasures with which He blesses us. As stewards and managers, have we managed His creation rightly for Him and His glory?[19] From creation, God instilled work with this sacred spiritual purpose of stewardship, service, worship, and accountability. Our English vocabulary uses the term *vocation*, or calling by God, to recognize work's spiritual underpinnings.[20] This is God's created ideal and intended well-lived life for human well-being and flourishing[21] from a Christian perspective.

However, instead of obeying and serving God, Adam and Eve, the first humans, *desired* to be like God (Genesis 3:4–6)[22] and mismanaged the fruits of creation by disobeying God's righteous words and commands. Consistent with Haidt's (2013) finding that morality is shaped more by motives and desires, the sinful motives of their hearts foundationally and problematically led them astray – desiring to use God's creation to serve, promote, and glorify themselves instead of serving and glorifying God – which then led to sinful reasoning and sinful actions. In this way, sin and death entered the world and came to all people (Romans 5:12; Romans 3:23).[23] As a result, humans became enemies of God (Romans 5:10),[24] born with a sinful human nature (Psalm 51:5),[25] and enslaved to and dead in sin (Ephesians 2:1, John 8:34).[26] Solzhenitsyn (1974) recognized the depth of human nature's brokenness: "The line separating good and evil passes not through states, nor between classes, nor between political parties either – but right through every human heart – and through all human hearts."

According to Solzhenitsyn (1974), our empirical human experience confirms the reality the Bible confronts us with: The change most needed within us is not in our reasoning or intellect or even in our actions, but in our hearts. Our "desires for change are not wrong; they are just not deep enough" (Lane and Tripp 2005, 16). The Bible recognizes the spiritual importance of the heart as a person's causal core. For example, the following passages underscore the importance of the heart:

- Above all else, guard your heart, for everything you do flows from it (Proverbs 4:23).
- As a person thinks in his heart, so is he (Proverbs 23:7).
- People look at the outward appearance, but the Lord looks at the heart (1 Samuel 16:7).
- All a man's ways are pure in his own eyes, but the Lord weighs the motives of the heart (Proverbs 16:2).

In diagnosing the problem of sinful human nature, the Bible also communicates the depth of the heart's spiritual brokenness:

- The heart is deceitful above all things and beyond cure. Who can understand it? (Jeremiah 17:9).
- For it is from within, out of a person's heart, that evil thoughts come – sexual immorality, theft, murder, adultery, greed, malice, deceit, lewdness, envy, slander, arrogance and folly (Mark 7:21–22).
- What causes fights and quarrels among you? Don't they come from your desires that battle within your hearts? You desire but do not have, so you kill. You covet but you cannot get what you want, so you quarrel and fight. You do not have because you do not ask God. When you ask, you do not receive, because you ask with wrong motives [in your hearts], that you may spend what you get on your pleasures (James 4:1–3).

The prescription and process: What God's image and work provide to produce transformation

The love of God

Given the recognized importance of motives and desires and broken spiritual condition of the heart, a Christian approach to ethics relies first on God's love in Jesus to transform foundationally the human heart (e.g., Ezekiel 11:19; Ezekiel 36:26),[27] consistent with Haidt's (2001, 2013) work drawing attention to the importance of the desires and motives of the heart in shaping morality. The right-hand column of Table 9.3 appends Table 9.1 by adding this Christian perspective.

Jesus viewed "the primary source of evil in the world as the evil in the individual's heart" (Cahill 1987, 153) and taught that the reign of the kingdom of God brings about a transformed heart capable of doing good in human community (Hengel 1973). The kingdom of God refers to God's spiritual rule and reign in a Christian's heart and life as a gift of God's grace in Jesus (Hagner 1997). Jesus details how the kingdom of God facilitates a process of Christian ethical change in the Sermon on the Mount (i.e., Matthew 5–7) – the most concentrated portion of Jesus' recorded ethical teaching (Sturz 1963, 3). It portrays a new relationship with God made possible by Jesus (Cahill 1987, 148).

Recognizing the foundational need to first restore our status, our identity, and the motives of our hearts, Jesus begins the Sermon on the Mount with the Beatitudes (Matthew 5:3–12), or blessings Christians receive in Jesus. God, in His love, sent Jesus to rescue us from sin and restore community and relationship with Him.[28] Jesus communicates that the Christian transformation process begins when Christians receive the blessings of pure hearts (Matthew 5:8; Psalm 51:10)[29] and new identities as children of God (Matthew 5:9)[30] as a result of His gracious work and sacrifice. The Beatitudes are not telling us to do anything but rather what Jesus and His coming have done for us.[31] They describe our human state and situation in general and how the coming of Christ and his kingdom in our hearts blessedly changes our relationship, status, and identity with God. Given the importance of the Beatitudes – or blessings in Jesus – to a Christian approach to ethical change, the Appendix provides the interested reader with an expanded analysis of them. The blessings of Christ's love transform our inner spiritual natures and redeem our identities from powerless sinners (Romans 5:6, 8)[32] and enemies of God (Romans 5:10)[33] to adopted and accepted children of God (Ephesians 1:5; Galatians 4:4–5, 7).[34]

Blessed with a new relationship and identity in Christ, Jesus next tells Christians in the Sermon on the Mount that they have a new outward-focused calling and purpose to live for God and His glory (2 Corinthians 5:15)[35] by serving others (John 13:34–35; Philippians 2:3–5)[36] as salt and light in the world (Matthew 5:13, 14, 16).[37] Later, Jesus encourages us to embrace the purpose of serving God and not money or creation (Matthew 7:19–21, 24).[38] Ramsey (2008, 179) concludes that identifying a clear purpose and maintaining "purity in heart" are important business ethics lessons from the Sermon on the Mount. These connections between God's love and a Christian's restored relationships, redeemed identity, and transformed motives and purpose are presented in the first row of Table 9.4. Table 9.4 appends Table 9.2 by connecting concepts from traditional accounting ethics perspectives in the two left-hand columns to corresponding concepts from the Christian perspective in the two right-hand columns, which summarize how aspects of God's character transform our Christian character and work.

In the Sermon on the Mount, Jesus is presenting a radically backwards approach to change. Instead of our good performance leading to God's love for us, God's unconditional love for us inspires our good performance. A Christian heart genuinely transformed by God's love responds

Table 9.3 Christian Approach to Improving Accounting Ethics

	Inform Moral Reasoning Competence: Improve Awareness and Analysis		Reform Character: Improve Action	Transform Spirit: New Motives of the Heart
	Pre-Conventional Economic Perspective	Conventional Regulatory Perspective	Post-Conventional Self-Regulatory Perspective	Post-Conventional Spiritual System Perspective
Means	Consequentialist logic guides moral accounting decisions by considering an action's consequences.	Non-consequentialist logic guides moral accounting decisions by considering the action itself.	Virtue ethics (or Aristotelian) logic guides moral accounting decisions by considering the needed professional virtues of the decision maker.	Christian (or theological) teachings guide moral accounting decisions by a God-enabled transformation of the spiritual condition, desires and motives of a person's heart.
Motive/ Mission	Moral accounting decisions choose actions that maximize net outcomes (i.e., maximize benefits; minimize costs). Manage reported information, resources, expenses, and profits with welfare and safety considerations to maximize net outcomes.	Moral accounting decisions choose actions that comply with business rules and regulations (i.e., regulatory compliance). Manage reported information, resources, expenses, and profits with welfare and safety considerations that comply with regulatory standards	Moral accounting decisions choose actions that comply with developed virtues (i.e., self-regulatory compliance). Manage reported information, resources, expenses, and profits with welfare and safety considerations to achieve societal flourishing.	Moral accounting decisions choose actions that love God by extending Christ's redemptive and restorative love to others and glorify God (i.e., love restores the motive to love God and others). Manage reported information, resources, expenses, and profits with welfare and safety considerations to extend Christ's love to others and glorify God (i.e., God-glorifying mission).
Management	Management and control come from economic systems, markets, and price mechanisms that ensure actions lead to the best societal outcome (i.e., maximize the wealth creation of net outcomes).	Management and control come from regulatory system rules and regulations that guide behavior to the best societal outcome.	Management and control come from a self-regulatory system of trained professional virtues that guide behavior to the best societal outcome.	Management and control come from a righteous and sovereign God. We manage business practices by His love and for His glory.

Table 9.4 Christian Approach to Ethics Development

Rest (1984) Model	Code of Conduct Attribute and Cardinal Virtue	Image and Character of God	Transform and Change Our Character
Moral Will: 1 *Moral Motivation*: An individual's willingness to place the interests of others ahead of his or her own (Rest 1994).	**Professional Public Service** 1 *Justice*: Formulating and embracing ideals of fairness, equality, and lawfulness that provide the motives for action (Melé 2009).	**The Love of God**	**Restores Community** Redeem Identity **Transforms Calling** Identify Purpose
2 *Moral Awareness*: The cognitive recognition that a dilemma's resolution may affect others' welfare (Rest 1994). 2 *Moral Judgment*: Deciding what ought to be done (Navarez and Rest 1995).	**Professional Competence** 2 *Wisdom*: An intellectual virtue by which important goods and principles are identified and ranked (Cheffers and Pakaluk 2011).	**The Righteousness of God**	**Guides Competence** Recognize responsibilities Judgment and Reasoning
Moral Skill: 3, 4 *Moral Character*: The virtues needed to carry out a chosen action.	**Professional Character** 3 *Courage*: The ability to act appropriately when faced with challenges or threats. 4 *Self-control* (moderation): The ability to act appropriately as regards physical pleasures, desires, cravings, and comforts.	**The Sovereignty of God**	**Develops Character**

to God and His character in new ways.[39] We now explore how the heart transformed by God's love leads the Christian to respond to God's righteousness and sovereignty in changed ways (the second and third rows in Table 9.4).

The righteousness of God

Jesus continues the Sermon on the Mount with examples illustrating God's righteousness and extending God's righteousness beyond right behaviors or right thoughts to right motives and "attitudes of the heart" foundationally (Hagner 1997, 50). Beneath right actions and right thoughts, Jesus communicates the importance of right motives and desires consistent with Haidt (2001, 2013). Murderous actions are a symptom of the sinful murderous motives from an angry heart (Matthew 5:21–22).[40] Adulterous activity is a symptom of sinful desires from a lustful heart (Matthew 5:27–28)[41] Jesus is leading Christians to recognize that the motive and principle of "love is the fulfillment of the law" (Romans 13:10)[42] and instructs Christians to use God's laws to guide expressions of responsive love for God to others in practice (e.g., Matthew 7:12).[43]

Jesus continues with several examples to underscore the important point that righteous thoughts and actions require righteous motives of genuine love for God and others. His examples illustrate that righteous actions performed with unrighteous motives of self-love and self-promotion become forms of false righteousness (Matthew 6:1).[44] Righteous practices like giving to the needy (Matthew 6:2),[45] praying (Matthew 6:5),[46] fasting (Matthew 6:16),[47] and providing counsel and judgment (Matthew 7:1–2)[48] become unrighteous if performed with motives of self-love and self-promotion.

Jesus continues by teaching that a Christian's responsibility to fulfill the motive and principle of love may extend beyond fair laws. While certain behaviors may be permissible and fair under the law, like retaliatory fairness (i.e., "eye for eye, and tooth for tooth") and hating your enemies who hate you, Jesus teaches that right love for others in these situations extends beyond the law – repaying bad with good (Matthew 5:38–39)[49] and loving your enemies (Matthew 5:43–44).[50] Instead of playing fair and trading good for good and bad for bad, Jesus encourages playing right, since the retaliatory standard of playing fair destroys relationships (Cloud 2006). Following the principle of love for God and love for others creates moral responsibilities that extend beyond compliance with laws of fairness, and Jesus is encouraging love-motivated, principles-based, post-conventional Kohlbergian (1969) moral reasoning when applying laws to practice in these situations.

Jesus' instructions in applying regulatory laws have implications for Christian accounting practice. In general, Christian motives of love for God and others complement accounting principles and standards in practice. Like Jesus' examples given earlier, the motive to glorify God by loving others should guide accounting judgments and inform application of accounting principles and standards in practice to fulfill the public service attribute in codes of conduct for the Christian accountant. Similarly, accounting principles and standards can serve as helpful aids for Christian accountants' practical expressions of love for God and others in the accounting domain. However, Christian accountants' moral motive to glorify God by loving others implies a moral responsibility to report accurate and useful information that extends beyond technical compliance with accounting standards (even if man-made accounting rules permit technical accounting treatments, judgments, or estimates that obscure users' reported information). We provide examples in our discussion of a Christian perspective on accounting ethics in the next section.

The principle and motive of love for God and others inform a Christian's moral responsibilities and guide a Christian's moral reasoning and application of the law. These connections between God's righteousness and a Christian's restored responsibilities and reasoning are presented in the second row of Table 9.4.

The sovereignty of God

The Christian with a heart transformed by God's love *reacts* to and trusts the sovereignty of a loving God and becomes more trustworthy and credible in character to God and others. In the Sermon on the Mount, Jesus instructs Christians to "not worry about your life . . . for . . . your heavenly Father knows [what] you need" (Matthew 6:25, 32). Instead, Jesus encourages Christians to "seek first His kingdom and His righteousness" (Matthew 6:33) in practice. The Christian can confidently and credibly *want to* follow God's guides and commands in practice knowing that God's love sovereignly controls situations, circumstances, and outcomes. Christians "know that in all things God works for the good of those who love Him, who have been called according to His purpose" (Romans 8:28). God, in His love for us, uses His sovereign control for our good. Trusting the sovereignty of God's love in any situation and circumstance, the Christian can react in credible and trustworthy ways. In this way, "the grace of God . . . teaches us . . . to . . . live self-controlled, upright and godly lives in this present age" (Titus 2:11–12), generating the Christian's character of credibility and trustworthiness in situations and circumstances regardless of outcome. These connections between God's sovereignty and Christian character are presented in the third row of Table 9.4.

The Christian approach recognizes that moral motives underly moral reasoning and moral practice and that God's love transforms how the Christian responds to God's characteristics, moving the Christian from moral motives to credible motions.[51] This Christian process shares similarities with Stoic philosophy. Pigliucci (2017) divides Stoicism into the three disciplines of desire, assent, and action. The discipline of desire deals with feelings and knowing what is proper to want or desire. The discipline of assent manages thought by applying reason to evaluate judgments. The discipline of action is about behavior balancing virtuous action for activities within our control with acceptance of outcomes beyond our control.[52] God's characteristics of love, righteousness, and sovereignty in Table 9.4 correspond to these Stoic disciplines of desire, assent, and action, respectively. Christianity provides a spiritual foundation for the philosophical Stoic disciplines. While Christianity and Stoicism share similarities, there are differences (Evans 2013). One primary difference of note is that love is the supreme ethic in Christianity focusing on the desires and motives of the heart (Haidt 2001, 2013), while rationality or reason is the supreme Stoic ethic.

Discussion of the Christian perspective on accounting ethics

The profession and practice: how God's image and work inform the accounting profession and protect accounting practice

According to May (2001, 7), a professional is someone who professes something (an intellectual characteristic) on behalf of someone (a moral characteristic) in the setting of colleagues (an organizational characteristic). All three professional characteristics are part of the accounting profession's identity and responsibilities. Table 9.5 incorporates these professional characteristics into Table 9.4's presentation of a Christian perspective to ethics.

So, how can the Christian accountant protect these professional characteristics in the midst of the opportunities and incentives of professional challenges? The contributions of the Christian perspective to limiting the fraud triangle's elements of trust violations (Cressey 1953) are presented in the right-hand column of Table 9.5. The Christian recognizes that God uses opportunities and incentives in situations and circumstances to test and train the heart (Proverbs 17:3; 1 Corinthians 4:5).[53] Managing blessings and burdens, treasures and trials reveals the spiritual condition of the heart and provides opportunities for training, development, and growth (James 1:2–4).[54] For the Christian, the process of growth embraces God's love in the middle of challenges. A heart attached to the love of Christ is better able to resist the attachments of economic and social *incentives*. A Christian secure in the sovereign provision, protection, and control of a loving God is able to exercise credibly self-control when presented with *opportunities*. A mind yielding to a loving God's righteousness is guided to avoid *rationalization*. As a result, the Christian is prepared to respond appropriately to situations and circumstances.

Jesus' encounter with Zacchaeus, a wealthy tax accountant, provides an example of how Jesus' acceptance limits fraud and leads to performance of professional activities motivated by Jesus' love (Luke 19:1–10). Although society considered Zacchaeus a sinner (Luke 19:7),[55] Jesus accepted Zacchaeus and wanted to enter his house and heart (Luke 19:5).[56] Jesus' love and acceptance transformed Zacchaeus' performance. With a new heart motivated by the love of Jesus, instead of *incentives* to accumulate wealth and cheat others, Zacchaeus wanted to follow Jesus and His righteous commands, avoiding *rationalization* and instead using the *opportunity* of his sovereignly God-given professional position and wealth to help the poor and compensate any person he had cheated (Luke 19:8).[57] The first row of Table 9.6 summarizes how Jesus' love

Table 9.5 Christian Approach to Ethics Development and Accounting Professionalism

Rest (1984) Model	Code of Conduct Attribute and Cardinal Virtue	Image and Character of God	Transform and Change Our Character	Professional Characteristics (May 2001)	Fraud Triangle Threat
Moral will: 1 *Moral Motivation:* An individual's willingness to place the interests of others ahead of his or her own (Rest 1994).	**Professional Public Service** 1 *Justice:* Formulating and embracing ideals of fairness, equality, and lawfulness that provide the motives for action (Melé 2009).	**The Love of God**	**Restores Community** Instill Identity **Transforms Calling** Identify Purpose	**Organizational Characteristic**	**Motive/Mission** Incentives
2 *Moral Awareness:* The cognitive recognition that a dilemma's resolution may affect others' welfare (Rest 1994). 2 *Moral Judgment:* Deciding what ought to be done (Navarez and Rest 1995).	**Professional Competence** 2 *Wisdom:* An intellectual virtue by which important goods and principles are identified and ranked (Cheffers and Pakaluk 2011).	**The Righteousness of God**	**Guides Competence** Recognize responsibilities Judgment and Reasoning	**Intellectual Characteristic**	**Management:** Rationalization
Moral skill: 3, 4 *Moral Character:* The virtues needed to carry out a chosen action.	**Professional Character** 3 *Courage:* The ability to act appropriately when faced with challenges or threats. 4 *Self-control* (moderation): The ability to act appropriately as regards physical pleasures, desires, cravings, and comforts.	**The Sovereignty of God**	**Develops Character**	**Moral Characteristic**	**Means:** Opportunity

Table 9.6 Christian Approach to Ethics Development and Accounting Practice

Activity in Accounting Practice	Limit Incentives	Limit Rationalizations	Limit Opportunities
Biblical Example			
Zacchaeus, the tax accountant	Jesus' love motivated a heart of love for God and others.	Motivated by Jesus' love, Zacchaeus decided to follow God's righteous guide to love others by helping the poor and compensating any person he cheated.	Zacchaeus used the opportunity of his position to glorify God by serving others with honesty, trusting God's sovereign provision.
Tax Accounting Example			
Use of tax strategies and structures like tax shelters	Jesus' love intrinsically motivates a heart of love for God and others that protects the tax accountant from extrinsic economic and social incentives and pressures.	Motivated by a love for God and others, the tax accountant applies the spirit of the tax law in developing tax strategies and performing compliance activities to serve others – the public, the tax system, and the client.	The tax accountant uses the opportunity of his/her position to glorify God by managing tax information that serves others by fulfilling responsibilities to the tax system (i.e., tax system administrative responsibilities) and responsibilities to the client (client advocate responsibilities)
Financial Accounting Example			
Managing reported financial results and information	Jesus' love intrinsically motivates a heart of love for God and others that protects the financial accountant from extrinsic economic and social incentives and pressures.	Motivated by a love for God and others, the financial accountant applies the spirit of accounting standards and uses professional judgment to produce relevant, reliable, and useful financial reports to serve others – financial statement users and the investing public.	The financial accountant uses the opportunity of his/her position to glorify God by managing reported financial information that serves others by fulfilling responsibilities to financial statement users, the company, and others
Auditing Example			
Providing auditing and assurance services to the investing public	Jesus' love intrinsically motivates a heart of love for God and others that protects the auditor from extrinsic economic and social incentives and pressures.	Motivated by a love for God and others, the auditor applies the spirit of accounting standards and uses professional judgment to carry out auditing and assurance services that serve others – the investing public, clients, and others in the financial system.	The auditor uses the opportunity of his/her position to glorify God by providing auditing and assurance services that serve others by fulfilling responsibilities to the investing public, clients, and others

(Continued)

Table 9.6 (Continued)

Activity in Accounting Practice	Limit Incentives	Limit Rationalizations	Limit Opportunities
Managerial Accounting Example			
Presentation and use of information for management, performance measurement, and control	Jesus' love intrinsically motivates a heart of love for God and others that protects the management accountant from extrinsic economic and social incentives and pressures.	Motivated by a love for God and others, the managerial accountant uses professional judgment to produce relevant, reliable, and useful managerial accounting information for planning, management, and control to serve others – management.	The managerial accountant uses the opportunity of his/her position to glorify God by managing reported managerial accounting information that serves others by fulfilling responsibilities to managers, the company, and others

and the Christian approach transformed and protected Zacchaeus's accounting activity from incentives, rationalizations, and opportunities for fraud.

In a similar way, Christian accounting professionals motivated by God's love to resist *incentives* for ill-gotten gains and led by God's righteous guides to avoid *rationalization* can use the *opportunities* of professional accounting positions sovereignly provided by a loving God to manage reported information resources to help others for His glory. For example, the Christian tax accountant motivated by God's love to glorify Him by loving others resists *incentives* to minimize tax liabilities and avoids *rationalizing* aggressive tax strategies like tax shelters. Instead, the Christian tax accountant uses the *opportunity* of his/her position to glorify God by managing tax strategies and information that serve others by fulfilling responsibilities to the tax system and clients. The Christian financial accountant motivated by God's love to love others resists *incentives* for gain by *rationalizing* obscuring and manipulating reported results through accounting treatments (e.g., off-balance sheet financing) or earnings management practices (e.g., adjusting accounting estimates and methods, channel stuffing). Instead, the Christian financial accountant uses the *opportunity* of his/her position to provide useful reported information that meets responsibilities to serve the investing public, financial statement users, the company, and others. The Christian auditor motivated intrinsically by the *incentive* of God's love to love others uses the *opportunity* of his/her position to glorify God by providing auditing and assurance services that serve others with *rational* judgments that fulfill responsibilities to the investing public, clients and others. The motive and *incentive* of God's love to love others guides the Christian managerial accountant to use the *opportunity* of his/her position to glorify God by using *rational* judgment to produce relevant, reliable, and useful accounting information serving and fulfilling responsibilities to managers, the company, and others.

Conclusion

The contributions of a Christian perspective to accounting ethics considered in this chapter are useful to Christians and non-Christians alike. Christian accounting professionals are better informed as to how to integrate their God-given professional work into their Christian faith. Moreover, this chapter informs those who come from different perspectives how to better understand a Christian perspective and its contributions to accounting ethics, bolstering communication and dialogue between various groups. Including faith-based perspectives offers new avenues to enhance accounting ethics and curb fraud.

Given flawed human character and sinful human nature, the Christian perspective recognizes the need for God's unconditional love to transform the heart's right motives and desires. This solution is consistent with Haidt (2001, 2013), who draws attention to the importance of desires and intuitions in ethics. The heart transformed by God's love is enabled to respond to God's righteous commands in new ways and is able to manage credibly and accountably professional situations and circumstances a loving God sovereignly provides as Christian professionals seek to serve the public interest with character and competence for the glory of God.

Appendix
ANALYSIS OF THE BEATITUDES

In the Beatitudes, Jesus describes our human state and situation in general and the Gospel (i.e., the "good news")[58] of the blessings of new relationship, status, and identity with God as a result of His coming and work. Consistent with Hagner (1997), we consider the whole Gospel of the New Testament when studying the Beatitudes. Christians who are poor in spirit are now blessed with a new, converted relationship with God and have a share in the kingdom of heaven because Jesus has come (Matthew 5:3)[59] (Cahill 1987). Christians who mourn in life with sorrow and shame receive the blessing and comfort of new status and identity because Jesus has come (Matthew 5:4).[60] Meek Christians with few worldly resources and wealth receive a spiritual inheritance and status as children of God because they have Jesus (Matthew 5:5).[61] Christians who hunger and thirst for God's righteous standards now are filled with the blessing of God's righteousness because of Jesus (Matthew 5:6)[62] Merciful Christians in need of mercy and forgiveness now receive the blessing of God's mercy in Jesus (Matthew 5:7)[63] Christians are blessed with pure hearts (Matthew 5:8),[64] peace, and new identities as children of God (Matthew 5:9)[65] because of Jesus.

In the same way, Jesus closes the Sermon on the Mount by reminding Christians of the foundational blessings of new identity and life that are found only in Him. He is the gate and way to life (Matthew 7:13–14; John 14:6),[66] the tree of life (Matthew 7:16–20, John 15:5),[67] and the rock of life (Matthew 7:24, Acts 4:11).[68] A Christian with a new identity and transformed heart rooted in Christ is able to respond and bear fruit in practice. A Christian with an identity and heart founded on the rock and cornerstone of Christ's grace responds by putting God's Word into practice. Christianity's Gospel-centered, grace-based approach recognizes that God's grace and acceptance in Christ transforms a Christian's identity and heart, which leads to new reasoning and practice. Instead of our performance leading to Christ's blessings, Christ's blessings in the Beatitudes lead to our performance.

Notes

1 For example, Ketz (2006) notes in the summary to his 2,000-page, four-volume compilation of the 100 most influential accounting ethics manuscripts that none of these manuscripts considered the influence of religion. Recently, accounting ethics research is examining the connection between religiosity and ethics in accounting and auditing (e.g., Gul and Ng 2018), and religiosity is being explored in other business disciplines (e.g., Roberts and David 2018).

2 The Christian Bible is composed of two sections, the Old Testament (with 39 books) and the New Testament (with 27 books), and is preeminent to Christians, who hold that it is the divinely inspired Word of God.

3 Jesus means "the Lord saves."

4 See the Christian definition and discussion of God's grace at: www.allaboutgod.com/definition-of-gods-grace-faq.htm.

5 "Surely I was sinful at birth, sinful from the time my mother conceived me" (all Bible verses cited from NIV) (Psalm 51:5).

6 "While we were God's enemies, we were reconciled to him through the death of his Son" (Romans 5:10).

7 Sins are rebellions against God and immoral acts of transgression against His Word (Deuteronomy 9:7; Joshua 1:18), divine commands, and laws (1 John 3:4).

8 "As for you, you were dead in your transgressions and sins" (Ephesians 2:1). "Jesus replied, 'Very truly I tell you, everyone who sins is a slave to sin'" (John 8:34).

9 "We love because God first loved us" (1 John 4:19).

10 The International Federation of Accountants (IFAC), American Institute of Certified Public Accountants (AICPA), and Institute of Management Accountants (IMA) promulgate specific codes of conduct for professional accountants.

11 See Oxford dictionary: https://en.oxforddictionaries.com/definition/christianity.

12 The Bible states that "these words are written that you may believe that Jesus is the Christ, the Son of God, and that by believing you may have life in His name" (John 20:31). "He is the image of the invisible God, the firstborn over all creation. For by him all things were created. . . . For God was pleased to have all his fullness dwell in him" (Colossians 1:15, 16a, 19). Jesus Christ is recognized as God and Savior (e.g., Titus 2:13; 2 Peter 1:1, among other references).

13 Christians believe the Bible is God's Word: "For prophecy never had its origin in the human will, but prophets, though human, spoke from God as they were carried along by the Holy Spirit" (2 Peter 1:21).

14 John 1:1, 14 states, "In the beginning was the Word, and the Word was with God, and the Word was God." Moreover, "the Word [Jesus] became flesh and lived among us" (John 1:14).

15 John 3:16 states that "God so loved the world that he gave his one and only Son, that whoever believes in him shall not perish but have eternal life."

16 God's sovereignty and control is revealed in the Bible. For example, ""He is before all things, and in him all things hold together" (Colossians 1:17). "The earth is the Lord's, and everything in it, the world, and all who live in it" (Psalm 24:1). "I know that God can do all things; no purpose of God's can be thwarted" (Job 42:2). "The LORD does whatever pleases him, in the heavens and on the earth, in the seas and all their depths" (Psalm 135:6).

17 Hebrews 11:3 states that "By faith we understand that the universe was formed at God's command, so that what is seen was not made out of what was visible."

18 Colossians 1:16b states that "all things have been created through him and for him."

19 1 Corinthians 10:31 clarifies the purpose of the Christian life: "whatever you do, do it all for the glory of God."

20 We serve the Lord with our work: "Whatever you do, work at it with all your heart, as working for the Lord, not for human masters. . . . It is the Lord Christ you are serving" (Colossians 3:23–24).

21 The term *eudaimonia* captures the idea of well-being and flourishing and is a central concept in Aristotelian ethics to identify the highest good.

22 " 'You will not certainly die,' the serpent said to the woman. 'For God knows that when you eat from it your eyes will be opened, and you will be like God, knowing good and evil.' When the woman saw that the fruit of the tree was good for food and pleasing to the eye, and also desirable for gaining wisdom, she took some and ate it. She also gave some to her husband, who was with her, and he ate it" (Genesis 3:4–6).

23 "Sin entered the world through one man, and death through sin, and in this way death came to all people, because all sinned" (Romans 5:12). "For all have sinned and fall short of the glory of God" (Romans 3:23).

24 "While we were God's enemies, we were reconciled to him through the death of his Son" (Romans 5:10).

25 "Surely I was sinful at birth, sinful from the time my mother conceived me" (Psalm 51:5).

26 "As for you, you were dead in your transgressions and sins" (Ephesians 2:1). "Jesus replied, 'Very truly I tell you, everyone who sins is a slave to sin'" (John 8:34).

27 "God says, 'I will give them an undivided heart and put a new spirit in them'" (Ezekiel 11:19). "God says, 'I will give you a new heart and put a new spirit in you'" (Ezekiel 36:26).

28 Instead of humans making a sacrifice to appease God, God performed a loving sacrifice in Jesus for the salvation of humankind to restore community and relationship with us. "This is love: not that we loved God, but that God loved us and sent his Son as an atoning sacrifice for our sins" (1 John 4:10). A sample of other passages that communicate the sacrificial love of Jesus include: "The blood of Jesus, his Son, purifies us from all sin" (1 John 5:7). "For Christ also suffered once for sins, the righteous for the unrighteous, to bring you to God" (1 Peter 3:18). "When Jesus died, he died once to break the power of sin. But now that he lives, he lives for the glory of God" (Romans 6:10). "For if, by the trespass of Adam, death reigned through that one man, how much more will those who receive God's abundant provision of grace and of the gift of righteousness reign in life through the one man, Jesus Christ!" (Romans 5:17). "For the wages of sin is death, but the gift of God is eternal life in Christ Jesus our Lord" (Romans 6:23).

29 "'Blessed are the pure in heart, for they will see God'" (Matthew 5:8) "Create in me a pure heart . . . and renew a steadfast spirit in me" (Psalm 51:10).

30 "'Blessed are the peacemakers, for they will be called children of God'" (Matthew 5:9).

31 Our presentation and interpretation of the Sermon on the Mount are (1) consistent with the literature, (2) avoid a simplistic, literalistic reading without compromising the serious intent of the message, and (3) above all take the whole Gospel of the New Testament into consideration (Hagner 1997).

32 "When we were still powerless, Christ died for the ungodly. . . . While we were still sinners, Christ died for us" (Romans 5:6,8).

33 "While we were God's enemies, we were reconciled to God through the death of his Son" (Romans 5:10).

34 "God predestined us for adoption to sonship through Jesus Christ, in accordance with his pleasure and will" (Ephesians 1:5). "God sent his Son . . . to redeem [us] that we might receive adoption to sonship. . . . So you are no longer a slave, but God's child; and since you are his child, God has made you also an heir" (Galatians 4:4–5, 7).

35 "Jesus died for all, that those who live should no longer live for themselves but for him who died for them and was raised again" (2 Corinthians 5:15).

36 "A new command I give you: Love one another. As I have loved you, so you must love one another. By this all people will know that you are my disciples, if you love one another" (John 13:34–35). "Do nothing out of selfish ambition or vain conceit, but in humility consider others better than yourselves. Each of you should look not only to your own interests, but also to the interests of others. Your attitude should be the same as that of Christ Jesus" (Philippians 2:3–5).

37 "You are the salt of the earth. . . . You are the light of the world. . . . Let your light shine before others, that they may see your good deeds and glorify your Father in heaven" (Matthew 5:13,14,16).

38 "'Do not store up for yourselves treasures on earth. . . . But store up for yourselves treasures in heaven. . . . For where your treasure is, there your heart will be also. . . . No one can serve two masters. . . . You cannot serve both God and money'" (Matthew 7:19–21, 24).

39 A heart motivated to use the freedom of God's love and forgiveness in Jesus as license to indulge selfish and sinful pursuits is a heart still captured by the motives of sin and in need of God's transforming love. "You . . . were called to be free. But do not use your freedom to indulge the flesh; rather, serve one another humbly in love" (Galatians 5:13). "What shall we say, then? Shall we go on sinning so that grace may increase? By no means! We are those who have died to sin; how can we live in it any longer?" (Romans 6:1–2).

40 "'You have heard that it was said to the people long ago, "You shall not murder, and anyone who murders will be subject to judgment. But I tell you that anyone who is angry with a brother or sister will be subject to judgment'" (Matthew 5:21–22).

41 "'You have heard that it was said, "You shall not commit adultery." But I tell you that anyone who looks at a woman lustfully has already committed adultery with her in his heart'" (Matthew 5:27–28).

42 When asked to summarize the principles of the law, Jesus identified expressions of the principle of love by saying, "'"Love the Lord your God with all your heart." . . . And . . . "Love your neighbor as yourself."'" (Matthew 22:37).

43 "'So, in everything, do to others what you would have them do to you, for this sums up the Law'" (Matthew 7:12).

44 "'Be careful not to practice your righteousness in front of others to be seen by them. If you do, you will have no reward from your Father in heaven'" (Matthew 6:1).

45 "'So when you give to the needy, do not announce it with trumpets, as the hypocrites do in the synagogues and on the streets, to be honored by others. Truly I tell you, they have received their reward in full'" (Matthew 6:2).

46 "'And when you pray, do not be like the hypocrites, for they love to pray standing in the synagogues and on the street corners to be seen by others. Truly I tell you, they have received their reward in full'" (Matthew 6:5).

47 "'When you fast, do not look somber as the hypocrites do, for they disfigure their faces to show others they are fasting. Truly I tell you, they have received their reward in full'" (Matthew 6:16).

48 "'Do not judge, or you too will be judged. For in the same way you judge others, you will be judged, and with the measure you use, it will be measured to you'" (Matthew 7:1–2).

49 "'You have heard that it was said, "Eye for eye, and tooth for tooth." But I tell you, do not resist an evil person. If anyone slaps you on the right cheek, turn to them the other cheek also'" (Matthew 5:38–39).

50 "'You have heard that it was said, "Love your neighbor and hate your enemy." But I tell you, love your enemies and pray for those who persecute you'" (Matthew 5:43–44).

51 Motive and motion come from the Latin root "mot," meaning "to move."

52 Acceptance of life's outcomes, events, and situations is consistent with the Stoic concept of *amor fati*, or the love of fate.

53 "The crucible for silver and the furnace for gold, but the Lord tests the heart" (Proverbs 17:3). "The Lord . . . will expose the motives of the heart" (1 Corinthians 4:5).

54 "Consider it pure joy, my brothers and sisters, whenever you face trials of many kinds, because you know that the testing of your faith produces perseverance. Let perseverance finish its work so that you may be mature and complete, not lacking anything" (James 1:2–4).

55 "All the people saw this and began to mutter, 'He has gone to be the guest of a sinner'" (Luke 19:7).

56 "When Jesus reached the spot, he looked up and said to him, 'Zacchaeus, come down immediately. I must stay at your house today'" (Luke 19:5).

57 "Zacchaeus stood up and said to the Lord, 'Look, Lord! Here and now I give half of my possessions to the poor, and if I have cheated anybody out of anything, I will pay back four times the amount'" (Luke 19:8).

58 The New Testament reveals the good news of the Gospel and what Jesus has done for us. "We have been made holy through the sacrifice of the body of Jesus Christ once for all." Every Old Testament priest "day after day . . . offers the same sacrifices, which can never take away sins." "By the one sacrifice, Jesus has made perfect forever those who are being made holy" (Hebrews 10:10, 11, 14). "God made Christ who had no sin to be sin for us, so that in him we might become the righteousness of God" (2 Corinthians 5:21).

59 "'Blessed are the poor in spirit, for theirs is the kingdom of heaven'" (Matthew 5:3).

60 "'Blessed are those who mourn, for they will be comforted'" (Matthew 5:4).

61 "'Blessed are the meek, for they will inherit the earth'" (Matthew 5:5).

62 "'Blessed are those who hunger and thirst for righteousness, for they will be filled'" (Matthew 5:6).

63 "'Blessed are the merciful, for they will be shown mercy'" (Matthew 5:7).

64 "'Blessed are the pure in heart, for they will see God'" (Matthew 5:8).

65 "'Blessed are the peacemakers, for they will be called children of God'" (Matthew 5:9).

66 "'Enter through the narrow gate. For wide is the gate and broad is the road that leads to destruction, and many enter through it. But small is the gate and narrow the road that leads to life, and only a few find it'" (Matthew 7:13–14). "Jesus answered, 'I am the way and the truth and the life. No one comes to the Father except through me'" (John 14:6).

67 "'By their fruit you will recognize them . . . every good tree bears good fruit, but a bad tree bears bad fruit. A good tree cannot bear bad fruit, and a bad tree cannot bear good fruit. Every tree that does not bear good fruit is cut down and thrown into the fire. Thus, by their fruit you will recognize them'" (Matthew 7:16–20). "[Jesus said,] 'I am the vine; you are the branches. If you remain in me and I in you, you will bear much fruit; apart from me you can do nothing'" (John 15:5).

68 "'Therefore, everyone who hears these words of mine and puts them into practice is like a wise man who built his house on the rock'" (Matthew 7:24). "Jesus is the stone you builders rejected, which has become the cornerstone" (Acts 4:11).

References

Cahill, L. S. 1987. "The Ethical Implications of the Sermon on the Mount." *Interpretation: A Journal of Bible and Theology* 41 (2): 144–56. https://doi.org/10.1177/002096438704100204.

Campbell, T. 2005. "Introduction: The Ethics of Auditing." In *Ethics and Auditing*, edited by K. Houghton, xx1–xxxii. Canberra: The Australian National University E Press. http://doi.org/10.22459/EA.06.2005.

Cheffers, M., and M. Pakaluk. 2011. *Accounting Ethics – and the Near Collapse of the World's Financial System.* Sutton, MA: Allen Davis Press. www.allendavidpress.net/accountingethics-andnearcollapseoftheentirefinancialsystemoftheworld.aspx.

Cloud, H. 2006. "Forget About Playing Fair." In *9 Things a Leader Must Do: Breaking through to the Next Level*, 85–94. Nashville: Thomas Nelson. www.thomasnelson.com/9781591454847/9-things-a-leader-must-do/.

Crane, A., and D. Matten. 2007. *Business Ethics: Managing Corporate Citizenship and Sustainability in the Age of Globalization*, 2nd ed. Oxford: Oxford University Press.

Cressey, D. R. 1953. *Other People's Money; a Study of the Social Psychology of Embezzlement.* New York: Free Press.

Eisenhardt, K. M. 1989. "Agency Theory: An Assessment and Review." *Academy of Management Review* 14 (1): 57–74. https://doi.org/10.5465/amr.1989.4279003.

Espinosa-Pike, M., and I. Barrainkua-Aroztegi. 2014. "A Universal Code of Ethics for Professional Accountants: Religious Restrictions." *Procedia – Social and Behavioral Sciences* 143: 1126–32. https://doi.org/10.1016/j.sbspro.2014.07.565.

Evans, J. 2013. "Features: Stoicism and Christianity." Accessed June 10, 2019. https://modernstoicism.com/features-stoicism-and-christianity-by-jules-evans/.

Godar, S., P. O'Connor, and V. Taylor. 2005. "Evaluating the Ethics of Inversion." *Journal of Business Ethics* 61: 1–6. https://doi.org/10.1007/s10551-005-1176-2.

Gul, F. A., and A. C. Ng. 2018. "Auditee Religiosity, External Monitoring, and the Pricing of Audit Services." *Journal of Business Ethics* 152 (2): 409–36. https://doi.org/10.1007/s10551-016-3284-6.

Guthrie, V. L. 1997. "Cognitive Foundations of Ethical Development." *New Directions for Student Services* 77: 23–44. https://doi.org/10.1002/ss.7702.

Hagner, D. A. 1997. "Ethics and the Sermon on the Mount." *Studia Theologica* 51 (1): 44–59. https://doi.org/10.1080/00393389708600200.

Haidt, J. 2001. "The Emotional Dog and its Rational Tail: A Social Intuitionist Approach to Moral Judgment." *Psychological Review* 108 (4): 814–34. http://dx.doi.org/10.1037/0033-295X.108.4.814.

Haidt, J. 2013. *The Righteous Mind: Why Good People Are Divided by Politics and Religion.* London: Penguin Books. www.penguinrandomhouse.com/books/73535/the-righteous-mind-by-jonathan-haidt/.

Hengel, M. 1973. *Victory Over Violence: Jesus and the Revolutionists.* Philadelphia: Fortress Press.

Jensen, M. C., and W. H. Meckling. 1976. "Theory of the Firm: Managerial Behavior, Agency Costs and Ownership Structure." *Journal of Financial Economics* 3: 305–60. https://doi.org/10.1016/0304-405X(76)90026-X.

Ketz, J. 2006. "General Introduction, Volume 1: Foundations." In *Accounting Ethics: Critical Perspectives on Business and Management.* New York: Routledge.

Kohlberg, L. 1969. "Stage and Sequence: The Cognitive Developmental Approach to Socialization." In *Handbook of Socialization Theory*, edited by D. A. Goslin, 347–480. Chicago: Rand McNally.

Kohlberg, L., and R. H. Hersh. 2001. "Moral Development: A Review of the Theory." *Theory into Practice* 16 (2): 53–59. https://doi.org/10.1080/00405847709542675.

Lane, T. S., and P. D. Tripp. 2005. "How Christ Changes Us by His Grace." *Journal of Biblical Counseling*: 15–21. https://tavernhall.files.wordpress.com/2019/06/how_christ_changes_us_by_his_grace.pdf.

Larry, A., and M. Moore. 2008. "Deontological Ethics." In *The Stanford Encyclopedia of Philosophy*, edited by E. N. Zalta, U. Nodelman, C. Allen, and J. Perry. Stanford: Stanford University Press. https://plato.stanford.edu/archives/win2016/entries/ethics-deontological/.

Libby, T., and L. Thorne. 2004. "The Identification and Categorization of Auditors' Virtues." *Business Ethics Quarterly* 14 (3): 479–98. https://doi.org/10.5840/beq200414331.

MacIntyre, A. 2013. *After Virtue: A Study in Moral Theory.* London: Bloomsbury. www.bloomsbury.com/uk/after-virtue-9781780936253/.

May, W. F. 2001. *Beleaguered Rulers: The Public Obligation of the Professional.* Louisville, KY: Westminster John Knox Press.

Melé, D. 2009. *Business Ethics in Action: Seeking Human Excellence in Organizations*. Houndmills: Palgrave Macmillan.

Mintz, S. M. 1995. "Virtue Ethics and Accounting Education." *Issues in Accounting Education* 10 (2): 247–67. http://works.bepress.com/steven_mintz/6/.

Mintz, S. M. 1996a. "Aristotelian Virtue and Business Ethics Education." *Journal of Business Ethics* 15 (8): 827–38. https://doi.org/10.1007/BF00381851.

Mintz, S. M. 1996b. "The Role of Virtue in Accounting Education." *Accounting Education* 1 (1): 67–91.

Mintz, S. M. 2006. "Accounting Ethics Education: Integrating Reflective Learning and Virtue Ethics." *Journal of Accounting Education* 24: 97–117. https://doi.org/10.1016/j.jaccedu.2006.07.004.

Mintz, S. M. 2010. "Linking Virtue to Representational Faithfulness in Making Judgments in a Principles-Based Environment." *Research on Professional Responsibility and Ethics in Accounting* 14: 113–36. https://doi.org/10.1108/S1574-0765(2010)0000014009.

Navarez, D., and J. Rest. 1995. "The Four Components of Acting Morally." In *Moral Behavior and Moral Development: An Introduction*, edited by W. Kurtines and J. Gewirtz, 385–400. New York: McGraw-Hill.

Niebuhr, R. 1951. *Christ and Culture*. New York: Harper & Row. www.harpercollins.com/9780061300035/christ-and-culture/.

Pigliucci, M. 2017. *How to be a Stoic*. New York: Basic Books. www.basicbooks.com/titles/massimo-pigliucci/how-to-be-a-stoic/9780465097968/.

Ramsey, D. R. 2008. "Business Ethics in the Sermon on the Mount." *Leaven* 16 (4): 177–80. https://digitalcommons.pepperdine.edu/leaven/vol16/iss4/7.

Rest, J. R. 1983. "Morality." *Handbook of Child Psychology* 3: 556–629. https://doi.org/10.1002/9781118963418.

Rest, J. R. 1984. "Research on Moral Development: Implications for Training Counseling Psychologists," *The Counseling Psychologist* 12 (3): 19–29. https://doi.org/10.1177/0011000084123003

Rest, J. R. 1994. *Moral Development in the Professions: Psychology and Applied Ethics*. Hillsdale, NJ: Erlbaum.

Roberts, J. A., and M. E. David. 2018. "Holier Than Thou: Investigating the Relationship Between Religiosity and Charitable Giving." *International Journal of Nonprofit and voluntary Sector Marketing*. https://doi.org/10.1002/nvsm.1619.

Samsonova-Taddei, A., and J. Siddiqui. 2016. "Regulation and the Promotion of Audit Ethics: Analysis of the Content of the EU's Policy." *Journal of Business Ethics* 139: 183–95. https://doi.org/10.1007/s10551-015-2629-x.

Schwartz, B., and K. Sharpe. 2010. *Practical Wisdom: The Right Way to Do the Right Thing*. New York: Riverhead. www.penguinrandomhouse.com/books/307231/practical-wisdom-by-barry-schwartz/.

Siker, L. 1989. "Christ and Business: A Typology for Christian Business Ethics." *Journal of Business Ethics* 8 (11): 883–88. https://doi.org/10.1007/BF00384532.

Smith, A. (1776) 1976. *The Wealth of Nations*, reprint ed. Chicago: The University of Chicago Press. https://press.uchicago.edu/ucp/books/book/chicago/I/bo3637045.html.

Solomon, R. C. 1992. "Corporate Roles, Personal Virtues: An Aristotelean Approach to Business Ethics." *Business Ethics Quarterly* 2 (3): 317–39. https://doi.org/10.2307/3857536.

Solzhenitsyn, A. I. 1974. *The Gulag Archipelago, 1918–1956: An Experiment in Literary Investigation*. New York: Harper & Row.

Sturz, H. A. 1963. "The Sermon on the Mount and its Application to the Present Age." *Grace Journal* 4 (3): 3–15. www.galaxie.com/article/gj04-3-01.

Thorne, L. 1998. "The Role of Virtue in Auditors' Ethical Decision-Making: An Integration of Cognitive-Developmental and Virtue-Ethics Perspectives." In *Research on Accounting Ethics* (4), edited by L. Ponemon, 291–308. Greenwich, CT: JAI Press.

Watts, R. L., and J. L. Zimmerman. 1986. *Positive Accounting Theory*. Englewood Cliffs, NJ: Prentice Hall.

Zeff, S. A. 1978. "The Rise of Economic Consequences." *The Journal of Accountancy*: 56–63. www.macam.es/leandro/2007/Tema%208%20T%20Positiva/Zeff_1978.pdf.

10

HUMAN ACCOUNTABILITY AND DIVINE GRACE IN THE QUR'AN PERCEIVED THROUGH AN ACCOUNTING PERSPECTIVE

Athar Murtuza, Khalid R. Al-Adeem, and Mary B. Curtis

Introduction

This chapter seeks to elucidate the ethical and regulatory prescriptions that concern commerce and accounting, as well as the pursuit and uses of wealth, in the Qur'an. While that may seem to be a stretch, insomuch as any religion's teachings relate to this specific business discipline, there are numerous Qur'anic lessons that deal either indirectly or directly with issues very relevant to our profession. We discuss the broad, indirect lessons first and then three specific provisions of the Qur'an.[1]

In the section titled "The Basis of Accounting for Salvation in the Qur'an," the first lesson we address is the admittedly abstract, yet pragmatic, use of accounting for good and bad deeds in one's seeking to enter the Kingdom of Heaven. In the teachings of the Qur'an, one's life-time income statement may contain many of both but must have what may be referred to as a positive balance when they die. When considering the use of the earth, Islam enjoins its followers to realize that natural resources have been created and provided by God to humanity in order to facilitate human existence. We also discuss the teachings of the Qur'an to employ rationality and reasoning in our dealings in all regards. In the section titled "Qur'anic Teachings on Trade," the chapter mentions the Qur'an's many very specific teachings related directly to commerce, while surveying the concepts of *Riba*, *Zakat*, and *Hisba*, which undergird to a great extent the pursuit of wealth and economic endeavors as enjoined in the Qur'an and in the model furnished through Prophet Muhammad's[2] life and teaching. In more common usage, *Riba* is equated with usury, *Zakat* with charity, and *Hisba* as moral censor, but as we hope to show, their connotations extend to much more.

The chapter has more to say about what the Islamic scriptures ask of their Muslim readers and much less about what Muslims are in fact doing or have done in the past, and this is to be expected given the diversity of Muslims globally. Not surprisingly, not every injunction of the scriptures is practiced all the time by their adherents. However, the variance between what the Qur'an teaches and what Muslims have done or do is no different from the separation between words and deeds underscored by Luke 6:46: "And why call ye me, Lord, Lord, and do not the things which I say?" (Biblehub 2020).

An overview of the exhortations to Muslims shows that the values emphasized by Islam reflect the same ideals as the 18th-century Western Enlightenment. Among them are the importance of reason as well as the relationship between faith and reason. The Qur'an instructs its readers about the rule of law, the rights of both men and women to life and property, human equality, the respect for the rights of women, a respect for the environment, and a strong condemnation of economic exploitation and usurious conduct, in which the pursuit of wealth is a zero-sum game (Tinker 2004). Such practices were very prevalent in the broad reaches of the Muslim world, or what is called Islamdom or Islamicate, in terms coined by Marshall Hodgson (1974), considered by some as the most influential Islamic scholar in the United States.

The basis of accounting for salvation in the Qur'an

We begin with one of the most basic notions of all religions, that of how a person should act in this world in order to ensure the most propitious life after death. It is interesting to note how close the Qur'an comes to setting an antecedent for a double entry accounting system:

> Allah is in standing account with every man. Each good work is counted in man's favor, each bad deed is a debt. This reckoning is generally allowed to run during man's lifetime, but must at last be settled by full payment of all balances. This fact of the final settlement was uppermost in Mohammed's mind at the time he began his public ministry. All other facts were of minor significance, in comparison.
>
> *(Torrey 1892, 8–9)*

The closing of accounts is similar to the closing that accountants know, the periodic closing of income and expense accounts to generate the periodic income statement or profits. The "final settlement" is in fact similar to the income statement: income or profit means the excess of righteous action over one's trespasses, and this permits salvation (Torrey 1892).[3] Additionally, Qur'anic accounting follows the entity principle: That all human beings are unique and responsible only for their deeds and decisions. The accounting one finds in the Qur'an is better construed as a principles-based framework rather than rule-based accounting, which is well illustrated by a recently published text, *Principles of Islamic Accounting* (Baydoun et al. 2018).

An example of the application of this accounting system is how the expulsion from the Garden impacted the "balance sheets" of both Adam and Eve. The couple, according to the Qur'an, do not carry the prior balances in their income statement ledgers to transactions after exile. Neither they nor their progeny carry with them the ramification of their "original sin." They, in Qur'anic terms, start their earthly, post-exile income and expense ledgers without prior balances in them as befits proper accounting – somewhat like a bankruptcy clears one's debts. But the pair still retained their assets, which was that both them and their progeny are created in their Creator's likeness (Richter-Bernburg 2011). On the liability side of the balance sheet, the couple and their progeny remain saddled with major liabilities. Among their liabilities is their tendency to make errors, resulting from their own choices. Another liability is their propensity for being taken in by the temptations thrown their way by the unmitigated enmity of Satan, a presence made manifest in the Qur'anic, though the contemporary world does not seem so inclined to believe.[4],[5] Torrey describes the relationship between the Creator and His creatures as follows:

> The mutual relations between God and man are of a strictly commercial nature. Allah is the ideal merchant. He includes all the universe in his reckoning. All is counted, everything measured. The book and the balances are his institution, and he has made himself the pattern of honest dealing. Life is a business, for gain or loss. He who does a good or an evil work ("earns" good or evil), receives his pay for it, even in this life. Some debts are forgiven, for Allah is not a hard creditor. The Muslim makes a loan to Allah; pays in-advance for paradise; sells his own soul to him, a bargain that prospers. The unbeliever has sold the divine truth for a paltry price, and is bankrupt. Every soul is held as security for the debt it has contracted. At the resurrection, Allah holds a final reckoning with all men. Their actions are read from the account-book, weighed in the balances; each is paid his exact due, no one is defrauded. Believer and unbeliever receive their wages. The Muslim (who has been given manifold payment for each of his good deeds) receives moreover his special reward.
>
> *(Torrey 1892, 48)*

This idea of God keeping a running account of man's deeds is absent in both Old Testament and New Testament, according to Torrey, and yet it is an oft-recurring reminder to the readers in the Qur'an (Torrey 1892, 14). An apt illustration will be *Surah* (Chapter)[6] 83, notably titled "*al-Mutaffifin*," translated as "The Defrauders," which talks about such books of accounts being shown to human beings on Judgment Day. Such registers, *Kitabun Marqoomun*, (83:10) will cover the records of the transgressors as well as the righteous in separate journals (83:21).[7] In summary, a recompense is not what God needs or desires in return for the gifts associated with creation, but He will measure how His gifts are being used and treated by His creatures.

The Qur'an does not bifurcate the sacred and secular spheres of life. It expects human beings to be mindful of their Creator in all things they undertake or wish to do. What are usually deemed secular and worldly activities can become forms of worship for Muslims if they are undertaken as a way to encounter and to know what the Creator expects from human beings who are created in His image. All pursuits are part of a life that needs be constantly mindful of the Creator and other creatures and requires one to recognize one's place in creation. Such a mindful life does not seek to conquer nature or dominate or exploit fellow beings; instead, it cultivates the environment and treats others the way one would like to be treated, or more importantly treat others the way one has been treated by the Creator. The notion of the mindful human beings who desire for others what they want for themselves has been repeatedly enjoined by Prophet Muhammad. One of the well-known sayings reads, "None of you believes until he wishes for his brother what he wishes for himself." The Qur'an and the Prophet are saying what is known as The Golden Rule. They are repeating what is similar to what both Matthew 22:37–39 and Mark 12:28–31 document as Jesus' commandment to his followers. Further examples are included in Buddhism: "Do not hurt others in ways you yourself would find hurtful" (Udanavarga 5:18); Hinduism: "This is the sum of duty: do nothing to others that would cause you pain if done to you" (Mahabharata 5:117); and Judaism: "That which is hateful to you, do not do to your fellow. That is the whole Torah; the rest is commentary" (Talmud, Shabbat 31a).

Care for the environment in the pursuit of trade in the Qur'an

The Islamic perception concerning human trusteeship over the oceans, heavens, and earth and all that they contain is also common to the Jewish and Christian faiths. The following verses from the Qur'an shed more light on the Islamic perceptions of the economic pursuits by human beings:

> It is Allah who has subjected the sea to you that ships may sail through it by His command, that you may seek of His bounty, and that you may be grateful. And He has subjected to you, as from Him, all that is in heavens and on earth. Behold, in that are signs indeed for those who reflect.
>
> *(45:12–13)*

The emphasis is on the fact that human control over what is in the oceans, heavens, and earth is, in fact, a bounty from the Creator (12:2). It behooves human beings to use the Divine gifts with gratitude and to exercise control over the earthly resources with respect. Clearly, the Divinely bestowed control over nature requires that human beings use rather than abuse that which has been entrusted to their control. The use and development of natural resources must not be without moral restraints, nor should their use become an end in and of itself. Natural resources, furthermore, must not be monopolized in order to benefit a few while being denied to society at large. One could argue that the expropriation of coastlines and beachfronts by resort hotels or mansions for the wealthy, as is done in many of the resort towns around the world, would not be an acceptable practice according to Islam, but such uses do exist in contemporary Muslim countries.

The Islamic notions of private ownership, public domain, and wealth are grounded in the notion of human custodianship described here. The following ramifications may be extracted from it (Yusuf 1990):

- Ownership of property implies a transferable right to develop and use natural resources.
- The right of ownership requires that natural resources be put to use and developed.
- Owners are encouraged to not hoard the wealth accruing from the economic development of natural resources.
- Not all natural resources can be handed over to private individuals. There are resources such as rivers and ocean shores that must be available to everyone in the community.
- The right to own property brings with it a requirement to respect the interests of others as well as the natural resources themselves.

Islam places considerable emphasis on showing concern and care as regards the uses of the natural environment and resources. Islam enjoins human beings to refrain from destroying or wasting God-given resources. Abu Bakr, Caliph of the Islamic state,[8] exhorted his designated army commander being sent to battle "not to kill indiscriminately or to destroy vegetation or animal life, even in war and on enemy territory"; thus, there was no question of using torture or environmental abuse and degradation being "allowed in peacetime or on home territory" (Rice 1996, 7).

Significance of "rationality" in the Qur'an

By describing the Creator in language associated with commerce, the Qur'an is showing that commercial pursuits are not profane; rather, they can be an instrument for serving God, the very purpose for which humans were created. Using accounting terms and concepts for theological purposes is a manifestation of the lack of bifurcation between the sacred and the secular in the Qur'an.[9] Of special interest for this chapter is Maxime Rodinson's (1966, 78) assertion that, in the Qur'an, "rationality plays a big part." Rodinson (1966) surveys terms related to reason and discernment to show the Qur'an's appeal to human reasoning and powers to observe and deduce. Rodinson notes that "repeated about fifty times . . . is the word 'aqala,' which means 'connect ideas together, reason, understand an intellectual argument.' Thirteen times we come upon the refrain 'a fa-la ta 'qilun,' have ye then no sense?" (Rodinson 1966, 79). In the same frame, the infidels, who were not paying attention to the teaching of the Prophet, "are stigmatized as 'people of no intelligence,'" persons incapable of the intellectual effort needed to cast off routine thinking (5:63/58, 102/103; 10:43/42; 22:45/46; 59:14). In this respect "they are like cattle (2:166/171)" (Rodinson 1966, 79). In Chapter 8:22, the Qur'an says: "Verily, the vilest of all creatures in the sight of God are those deaf, those dumb ones who do not use their reason." Later, the same chapter (8:55) uses the exact phrase, and this time it describes those who persist in their disbelief despite evidence to the contrary: "Verily, the vilest creatures in the sight of God are those who are bent on denying the truth and therefore do not believe." In linking those who hear and see, but do not care to discern with those persist in their disbelief, the Qur'an is equating discernment with faith.

Even though it uses accounting terms to expound matters pertaining to theology and worship and in doing so underscores the lack of bifurcation between the Sacred and the worldly, it should still be seen as an exhortation to human beings created in His image to find Divinely bestowed grace in all things, material and spiritual. God does not expect anything in return for the grace he has bestowed on human beings. But human beings are accountable and tested for their intentions and deeds when it comes to using their assets. Those assets are not to be hoarded or to become the manifestation of self-aggrandizement but are to be shared with others. The worst of the prohibited behavior would be to take what is given by God in His infinite and boundless Grace to be something owned and created by human beings themselves. The Divinely bestowed Grace should not make human beings into god-wannabes. Grace by itself does not mean human salvation, nor should it become like a "get out of jail free" card in the board game of Monopoly. Salvation is ultimately a matter of Divine will in the Qur'an, but it is facilitated by doing good and avoiding evil. Such conduct calls on human beings to use discernment and the belief in the Divine. This is where human accountability comes in: did one use the Divine gifts for good or hoard them out of greed, cruelty, and evil proclivities, suggesting failure to reason and lack of gratitude.

In summary, this section has discussed the teachings of the Qur'an in regard to how human beings, in anticipation of the ultimate Judgment, are to act accountably. The section to come deals with the ethical framework provided in the Qur'an, comprising the forbidden, the beneficial, and the specific steps that make individuals more likely to do good and avoid bad.

Qur'anic teachings on trade

Everywhere in the Qur'an, a lively interest in matters of trade is manifested. This interest is exemplified in Chapter 106, which calls upon human beings to recognize the role of Allah in ensuring the prosperity of their trade caravans. It is also seen in references to carrying on trade using animals such as camels, donkeys, and horses in Chapter 16:7, as well as in 16:14, which refers to sailing ships that further commercial pursuits. In addition, "the practical legislation" of the Qur'an frequently deals with business transactions, as seen in the verse calling upon believers to document their transactions in the presence of witnesses and treating such behavior as tantamount to worship having been ordained by God (2:282). The Qur'an also permits pilgrims traveling to perform Hajj to engage in trade while they journey for their pilgrimage to Mecca (2:194). Such permission to mix sacred with the secular is an indication of the importance assigned to trade by the Qur'an (Torrey 1892). In addition, there are exhortations calling upon the believers to be fair while bargaining with other human beings (6:153; 17:37; 55:7–8; 57:25; 12:59; 12:83; 11:85–86; and 26:181–3). In the Qur'an, no form of sin is more fiercely attacked than that of "unfair dealing," with invectives against those who give short weight and shortchange their customers (83:1–9). Additionally, the 12th chapter in the Qur'an, discussing Prophet Joseph, has a lot to say about planning, and the 103rd chapter talks about time management – both planning and time management can be seen as management accounting topics.

The presence of the vocabulary traditionally associated with commerce especially stands out when its use pertains to describing the "theology of the Qur'an" (Torrey 1892, 3). These terms belong to some 20 different Arabic language stems occurring about 370 times in the Qur'an (Torrey 1892, 3). Of the first 50 chapters, only four (1, 43, 44, and 50) do not contain one or another of them (Torrey 1892, 3). Accounting terms dealing with lending, payment, wages, fraud, exploitation, use of security in borrowing, weights and measures, profit and loss, and buying and selling are used to describe the relationship between God and human beings. The presence of such a large number of terms associated with commercial finance is very noticeable, and it imparts a certain commercial tone to Qur'anic theology.[10]

The specific teachings of *Riba*, *Zakat*, and *Hisba*

The Qur'an enjoins accountability, but it has also created a systemic framework that could, if practiced, promote both financial accountability and social justice. Three notions in the Qur'an particularly address ethical issues related to business. They include *Riba*, *Zakat*, and *Hisba*.

RIBA: *Islamic injunction against usurious exploitation*

To encourage economic activity while seeking to keep it from being exploitive or becoming an end in itself, Islam has exhorted its adherents to refrain from *Riba*, which translates literally as unlawful or exploitive monetary gains. *Riba* should not be equated only to interest-based lending, but it should include various forms of fraud and deception as well; not just usury, but all forms of behaviors that manifest usurious exploitation are forbidden (Chapra 1983). Unjustified and exorbitant enrichment is a lot closer to what the term means, since *Riba* is really a symptom of exploitation grounded in economic injustice (Ibn al Qayyim, quoted by Vogel and Hayes 1998, 82). The prohibition against *Riba* results from the same considerations that are intended to promote ethical economic activities that do not exploit other human beings in order to create wealth for an individual, as described by Mohammad Hashim Kamali (2013):

> Fighting bribery (*rashwah*) and corruption (*fasad*) is an integral part of the teachings of the *Quran* and *Hadith* (*the sayings of the Prophet*). The *Quran* prohibits "devouring/misappropriation of the property of others" (*akl al-maal bi'l-batil* – Q 4:29 and 2:188), which is a broad concept that subsumes such other offences as fraud, hoarding, theft, and gambling. The text also condemns those in authority who spread corruption and mischief among people, bestowing favours on some and oppressing others.
>
> *(Q 28:4 and 89:10–12) (Kamali 2013)*

All too often, Muslim jurists and a large number of laity equate *Riba* only to the interest charged on loans (e.g., Rahman 1964; Saleh 1986; Haque 1995; Saeed 1997). Doing so, one could argue, limits the prohibition to symptoms of transactions such as borrowing and purchases based on interest. It would be more in keeping with the teaching of the Qur'an if the prohibition against usurious behavior is extended to what causes these transactions and brings about exploitation of the borrowers by lenders. When lenders loan money under usurious terms, they are exploiting the borrower's needs for the lender's enrichment. This renders usurious loans and transactions similar to all forms of activities where exploitation is at work. Such activities, all too common in the world we inhabit, are described in the cited excerpt of Kamali (2013). Ahmed (2005, 2020) has gone to considerable length in documenting corruption and unethical behavior, and he links economic corruption with exploitation, anarchy, chaos, extortion – conduct that fits in with usurious conduct, which underlies various forms of injustice that impede human freedom. In short, the prohibition against *Riba* should not be limited only to interest-based transactions; instead, it must be construed as meant to prohibit usurious behavior in general, to ensure the freedom of human beings from being exploited by others. Islam prohibits exploitation of all sorts and in any form. Such prohibition extends to welfare fraud, Medicare overcharges, bribery, cheating, dealing drugs, and environmental degradation, even activities covered under the Foreign Corrupt Practices Act (FPCA). The pricing of medicines being developed to treat COVID-19 in the summer of 2020, as well as insulin price increases, are examples of usurious behavior and exploitation. It should be up to the sellers not to deceive, extort, and exploit market conditions. The attitudes implied in "buyers beware" and charging prices that are clearly extortion is not Qur'anic and actually the antithesis of what Jesus enjoins: "Thou shalt love the Lord thy God . . . and thou shalt love thy neighbour as thyself" (Mark 12:28–31, KJV). Just as the prohibition of *Riba* suggests the commandment enjoined by Jesus, so does the exhortation to practice *Zakat*, discussed in the next section.

To sum up the discussion of *Riba*, one could use the Qur'anic verse, which sees it as the opposite of *Zakat* according to the Qur'an (30:39):

> And [remember:] whatever you may give out in usury so that it might increase through [other] people's possessions will bring [you] no increase in the sight of God whereas all that you give out in charity, seeking God's countenance, [will be blessed by Him:] for it is they, they [who thus seek His countenance] that shall have their recompense multiplied!

To repeat, *Riba* should not be limited to transactions involving interest but to the kind of behavior that disrupts the equilibrium needed for the society to flourish. In other words, usurious behavior is far worse than usury.

ZAKAT: *society's tax for the welfare of those less privileged*

Muslims are religiously obligated to share their wealth with the community; such sharing is known as *Zakat*. This requirement of faith has elements in common with practices documented from earlier times, as noted by Michael Hudson (2018). For practicing Muslims, it is to be equated with giving to "charity" 2.5% of their accumulated wealth, not their income, every year. Anyone who is a Muslim adult (has reached puberty) and sane is expected to give *Zakat* if they have the minimum amount of wealth (*Nisab*) (National Zakat Foundation (NZF) 2020).

We could start the discussion of *Zakat* by citing the verse 30:39 with which we concluded the previous section. In it, the pursuit of wealth is not forbidden, but the verse underscores the difference between two approaches to its acquisition by using two terms that translate as increase. Both *Riba* and *Zakat* linguistically refer to *increase* or *growth*. The verse enjoins that transactions that lead to *Riba* are forbidden by God, while transactions embodying *Zakat* are favored. Through *Riba*, the increase in wealth becomes a zero-sum game for the society-at-large, where the lenders gain at the expense of others. The total wealth remains unchanged even as it gets concentrated in fewer hands, which in turn leads to an increase in inequality and consolidation of wealth among the wealthy, prohibited specifically in the Qur'an (59:7). In contrast, the *Zakat* helps all parties involved in the transactions. In addition to an increase, the term linguistically also means purification. It is literally an act of giving away the prescribed amount of one's accumulated (what some have called "hoarded") wealth. Doing it is a way to purify wealth, a good way of *money laundering*. It thus leads to increasing the size of the economy and diminishes concentration of wealth. The levying of *Zakat* on hoarded wealth rather than on wealth that is reinvested in the economy suggests what Adam Smith called the Dead Capital (de Soto 2000). It provides an incentive for believers to not hoard their wealth but to reinvest it back in the economy.

The term "Zakat literally means growth and increase" (Aghnides 1916, 203). Verse 30:39 clearly differentiates between *Riba* and *Zakat*; while they both refer to seeking an increase in wealth, the former is disdained by the Creator, while the latter is blessed as the proper and effective means for enhancing one's wealth. Practicing *Riba* permits one to ask for interest on lending (renting) one's money, while practicing *Zakat* is to get God's blessing on one's wealth by sharing a proportion of it with segments of society prescribed in the Qur'an (9:60). That the word *Zakat* literally means "that which purifies" and "that which fosters growth" leads Hamidullah (1969, 1974) to see Muslims' payment of a part of their wealth to the community as being intended to not only purify their wealth and them from sins (Aghnides 1916, 203) but also to help the economy to grow (Islahi 2015, 54).

Kuran (2020, 1) provides interesting insights regarding this requirement of faith, in suggesting that in the founding decades of Islam, *Zakat* serves as "a predictable, fixed, and mildly progressive tax system . . . meant to finance various causes typical of a pre-modern government." In calculating *Zakat*, one determines what they own, reduced by what they owe, and checks that it is more than the *Nisab* value. If so, 2.5% of that is their *Zakat* amount, which must be given away. Implicit in this transfer system is personal property rights as well as constraints on the government's power to tax.

In addition to providing resources to meet the needs of the community, *Zakat* serves other functions. It can curb human tendencies toward acquisitiveness and greed. It may also act as a reminder to the rich to share their wealth with those who are indigent. It serves as the instrument to help the community by meeting the social and economic needs of its members. Lastly, it serves to implement the Quranic injunction to prevent the accumulation of wealth in only a few hands (59:7) and to prevent inequality (Mannan 1970).

The nature of Zakat, a pillar of belief

As should be clear, Muslims are religiously obligated to share their wealth with the community. For practicing Muslims, this is to be equated with giving away as "*Zakat*" 2.5% of their accumulated *wealth*, not their *income*, every year. *Zakat* contains elements that one associates with tax, in addition to being a requirement of faith. It is a monetary obligation that has elements in common with taxation, in addition to being a religious requirement. The scholars seem to think that the Qur'anic verses that treat *Zakat* as a tax date from a period when the Muslim community was growing beyond the city of Medina, while those that treat it as charity given out of devotion are from Islam's earlier decades in Mecca (Kuran 2020, Torrey 1892). The seventh-century growth of the Islamic state on three continents likely impacted the decision to let individual believers distribute it themselves or set up trusts that provided ongoing benefits.

In the beginning of the Islamic state, all taxes, such as those on agricultural produce, on subsoil exploitation, on commercial capital, on herds of domesticated animals grazing on public pastures, as well as on cash and personal wealth, were paid directly to the government, but later, during the time of the Caliph Uthman, it was decided that Muslims could spend directly the tax on the hoarded wealth to its beneficiaries, as prescribed by the Qur'an, without the intermediary of the government (Hamidullah 1974). The rates of *Zakat* due on various forms of property and the manner in which it is collected are not specified in the Qur'an. The rate used and what sort of wealth it should be levied on owe their origin to the Prophet and to the religious scholars. This requirement of faith, according to Kuran (2020, 2), existed for about 1,250 years as an "unenforced canonical requirement in almost every part of the Muslim world." It was left up to individuals' discretion to give: "Whether individual believers paid zakat essentially was left to their own discretion, as were the forms, amounts, and recipients of any transfers" (Kuran 2020, 2–3).

Given its religious sanction, this requirement of Islamic belief becomes an exceptional mode of public finance, a levy that individual Muslims are obliged to pay as a required part of the observance of their faith. In fact, in several verses of the Qur'an, the obligation of *Zakat* is mentioned in the same sentence as *Salat*, the formal prayers performed five times daily. Unlike the five daily prayers, the formal giving of such wealth purification is done annually, often in *Ramadan*, the month of obligatory fasting. Despite such differences in timing, the equivalence between the two of the five requirements enjoined on Muslims implies the importance believers are to accord to the required purification of their accumulated wealth. Both requirements of faith aim to ensure that believers are constantly and continuously mindful of their Creator and His Grace. The importance of this religious obligation is seen in the fact that the Caliph Abu Bakr, as the head of the Muslim state, made war upon those tribes who refused to pay it. These days, tax-avoidance is not only rampant but well documented in many Muslims countries, who often top the list of corruption-ridden nations, but how widespread the avoidance of *Zakat* is not as well documented.

Prescribed uses of Zakat

The Qur'an enjoins in (3:92) "[But as for you, O believers,] never shall you attain to true piety unless you spend on others out of what you cherish yourselves; and whatever you spend verily, God has full knowledge thereof." It exhorts the importance of sharing and donating, while implying it is the excess that remains after one's own needs are met that should be donated. Those needs are left to individuals themselves, although verse 9:34 denounces "all who lay up treasures of gold and silver and do not spend them for the sake of God's." Other than such broad principles, the Qur'an is silent as to the property and wealth objects that are subject to *Zakat* (Kuran 2020, 4).

Zakat, as enjoined by the Qur'an, should be given to one or more of eight groups:(1) the poor, (2) the needy, (3) to those who work on (administering) *Zakat*, (4) for bringing hearts together, (5) to (free) those in bondage, (6) for those in debt, (7) for the cause of God, and

(8) for the stranded traveler (9: 60). The categories have been the subject of much discourse. There is no mention in the scripture about how the distributions ought to occur, nor is much said about the relative importance of the categories. There is silence as to what constitutes a needy person and how need should be determined. Such details are left unsaid and are matters left to individual discretion, prevailing governance, and environmental circumstances.[11] Through specifying such uses of the *Zakat* funds as "bringing hearts together" and "freeing those in bondage" side by side with the needs of the needy and indigent, the Qur'an is seeking to extend the uses of *Zakat* beyond meeting the basic needs of food, clothing, and shelter of the indigents. As shown by the last three uses -– helping those heavily indebted, promoting the cause of Allah, and helping travelers – *Zakat* becomes more than an act of charity; it is an instrument for enriching a community through an eradication of the underlying causes of and for preventing conditions that make economic exploitation of human beings more likely. The injunction to use it to help those who are heavily indebted can be taken to mean helping those who have encountered hardships, natural disasters, and even those needing aid in the time of the COVID-19 pandemic. Noor and Pickup (2017) have noted "some striking commonalities between the sustainable development goals (SDGs) and *Zakat*." They provide illustrations of how this is leading to the use of *Zakat* to alleviate human suffering, not as individual charity but for programs that use management tools to have better impact. They cite examples such as a loan to a fisherman for buying a better fishing boat that are being made through *Zakat* funds for promoting sustainable development goals.

In short, the uses prescribed by this pillar of faith make it a lot more than an act of charity; instead, it turns it into a resource for eradicating conditions that potentially promote exploitation of human beings. The requirement that Muslims, as an expression of their faith, pay *Zakat* is meant to help fulfill the community responsibility to take care of its members' needs. What is important is to keep in mind that its uses not only address poverty but are also meant to eradicate conditions that foster exploitation of the kind the usurious economy brings forth. It is an instrument which helps to make the Qur'anic prohibition of usurious conduct more than just pious rhetoric.

HISBA: *guarding the public interest and regulating the marketplace*

The word *Hisba* has been derived from the root h-s-b and means "arithmetical problem," "sum," or "reward." When used as a verb, it means "to compute" and "to measure." Pragmatically, *Hisba*, which is Arabic for "verification," may refer to accountability, and the institution it led to anticipates the present-day regulators and even the certified public accountants (CPA), which we discuss later. The term has two meanings. It refers to what is believed to be the divinely imposed duty of every Muslim to perform the Quranic injunction repeated several times in the Qur'an: *Amr bi al-Maruf wa'l-Nahy an al-Munkar*, meaning promote the right and impede the wrong. It behooves all believers to be activists, which is one meaning of the term as discussed at length by Michael Cook (2000, 2001). It also refers to a specific public office within the state held by a state officer who is also called the *Muhtasib*. This second function is our focus.

A cursory awareness of managerial accounting tells us that budgets require more than plans to be optimally useful. The term "planning" is often used alongside "control" to point out that plans are empty resolutions without provisions for their implementation. The Qur'an seems aware of this relationship. As discussed earlier, not only does it urge its readers to refrain from *Riba*, but in making *Zakat* a religious requirement, it suggests eliminating conditions that lead to usurious behavior. In addition, it suggests the practice of *Hisba*, which could be equated with what cost accountants label "control," to insure plans are more likely to be implemented (Murtuza 2002). The three elements taken together help a believer be mindful of his Creator, as well as promote a just and ethical society.

The Islamic jurists trace inspection of merchants selling in the marketplace in order to prevent fraudulent exploitation of consumers to the time of the Prophet Muhammad himself (Khan 1992).[12] After its origin in Medina, *Hisba* moved along with Muslims as Islam spread. It is of interest to note that the Prophet himself and the second Caliph appointed women whose role was to inspect the marketplace to protect the public interest (Cook 2000).

Even though Muslim authors such as Khan (1992) see *Hisba* as being entirely an indigenous Islamic institution that was put in place by the Prophet himself, one must note that a similar function existed before the advent of Islam (Foster 1970; Mottahedeh and Stilt 2003; Klein 2006). The Islamic variation of regulating commerce and trade has similarities with Greek *Agoranomus*, as it also does with the American regulatory agencies such as the Securities and Exchange Commission (SEC) and the Federal Trade Commission (FTC) (Foster 1970). Before and after the Islamic Age, civilizations sought to regulate their economies and the marketplace, as well as to protect the public from exploitive, fraudulent business practices. During the long history of marketplace regulation, from Classical Greece through the Islamic Middle Ages and to contemporary times, the rationales for such regulatory oversight were by no means identical. However, the regulation of merchants and markets, despite its diversity in various locales, shares a certain amount of contextual commonalty in seeking to protect the public at large from exploitation at the hands of fraudulent merchants.

Functions performed by the Muhtasib

The administrative roles related to *Riba* were performed by the *Muhtasib*, an official appointed by the ruler whose public duties included serving as a moral censor as well as the policing of merchants and marketplaces. Functions performed by Muhtasibs belong to three main categories (Abdallah and Murtuza 2007). First, they performed various municipal services, especially hygienic conditions in the town, including street lighting, removal of garbage, architectural designs of buildings, water supply, and anti-pollution sanctions (e.g., preventing the building of a factory or dwelling place that could damage community health). Second, they oversaw the mosques and their maintenance, appointment of muezzins and imams, and the arrangements for the five daily prayers, as well as for the congregational Friday prayers. Last, they oversaw the implementation of justice in society by protecting the public interest. They were to enforce fair play among different parties to minimize possibilities of exploitation. There exists a wide variety of manuals that provide a long list of such instructions, similar to the contemporary standard operating procedures manual. These manuals prescribed the inspection of weights and measures, the metallic content of coins, and the quality of food products. In keeping with their charge to protect the public interest, they would check for manipulation of prices, supplies and production; monopolistic collisions; cheating; fraud; and any other form of unfair practices. In brief, they intervened wherever economically powerful individuals or groups manipulated economic flows for their selfish ends. In other words, we can construe it to mean they acted to prevent usurious behavior.

One can appreciate the nature of the institution of *Hisba* by looking at those designated to carry out its functions (Abdallah and Murtuza 2007). Traditionally, in contrast to the practice of the Prophet and the early Caliphs, the Muhtasib was a free Muslim male with a high degree of integrity, insight, reverence, and social status.[13] He was supposed to be a *Shari'a* scholar with a high degree of knowledge of social customs and local mores. The desirable traits of a Muhtasib were considered to be *Ilim* (knowledge), *Rifq* (kindness), and *Sabr* (patience). The Muhtasib could appoint technically qualified staff that could investigate the affairs of different crafts and trades. He received complaints from the public but could also initiate an investigation on his own. He had wide powers but was required to use them sensibly. There were a number of steps that he could take, including the provision of simple advice, a reprimand, or a rebuke or obstruction by force, threat, imprisonment, or even expulsion from the town. The Muhtasib was required to choose a stronger punishment only if a milder one was either ineffective or seemed to carry no weight with the person being admonished (Moukheiber 2017).

The code of conduct for a Muhtasib provided a system of checks and balances (Mottahedeh and Stilt 2003; Klein 2006). For example, he could not doubt a prima facie approved behavior, nor was he to engage in secret probing into a doubtful affair. The behavior of a person should be clear and obviously against the prescribed norms in order for a Muhtasib to intervene. He could only take action on which there existed a consensus of jurists. He was also to act with wisdom and foresight and not be overzealous. In addition, his actions were not to cause a greater mischief than the one being addressed. Before he took on evil practices of powerful groups, he was to make sufficient arrangements to counter their reactions effectively. On questions of social convenience, the Muhtasib should invite community participation and should not impose his personal opinion on the majority.

It would be warranted to compare the responsibilities of the certified public accountant (CPA) in the contemporary United States with those expected of a Muhtasib (Murtuza and Abdallah 2007). At first, such comparison may seem implausible, given that CPAs were formally initiated in 1937 thanks to the legislation put in place by the United State Congress, and their primary function was and remains to attest the financial reports issued by publicly owned corporations seeking to raise investment capital. Attestation as it is known now was not a part of the duties performed by a Muhtasib. Even though public auditors of the 21st century and Muhtasibs of the Islamic Middle Ages are seemingly different, the rationale for comparing the American and the Islamic institutions does not seem so far-fetched if one looks not at what the former actually does but at why he is doing it: auditing is mandated ostensibly in the public interest and to foster trust. The very label used to describe CPAs indicates its ostensible role: the "P" in CPA represents "public." Seeing the conceptual basis of public auditing in the United States as being related to protection of public interests and promoting trust provides reason to compare the two. Islamic Muhtasibs were to serve as guardians of the public interest. Throughout its early history, the Islamic world had in place institutions that allowed accountable governance, and they could indeed be adapted for the 21st century. It can in fact provide a relevant precedent for Muslim countries seeking to develop accountability and accounting procedures in the 21st century (Gambling and Karim 1991; Kamla and Haque 2019).

In addition to Muhtasib, there also existed a functionary whose job it was to review account books maintained by state officials (Zaid 1997). Such auditing (review of books) played a very important role in the Islamic state and was designated as one of the accounting specializations. The person appointed to audit the accounts needed to command a high standard of the language (Arabic), be able to recite the Qur'an, be an expert in *hadith* and *fiqh*, and be perceived as intelligent, wise, trustworthy, and objective, neither prejudiced nor inimical. When the auditor/reviewer was satisfied with the contents of the account books under review, he was to attest by signing in the book as an indication of his satisfaction with its contents (Zaid 1997). It is reasonable to assume there were individuals within each organization or business entity responsible for keeping accounts for monetary and nonmonetary resource use. Such officials were likely described as Muhasibs, whose function was similar to what bookkeepers and financial accountants perform in 2020 (Zaid 2000).

Conclusions

The most important message of this chapter is that the Qur'an does not bifurcate the sacred and secular spheres of life, and it enjoins doing *Maruf* (good) and avoiding *Munkar* (harm). It expects believers to be mindful of their Creator in all things, whether sacred or secular, they undertake or wish to do. The Qur'anic teachings incorporate ethical practices of business as well as the more spiritual considerations of all religions. The Qur'an instructs its followers in appropriate behavior for the purpose of seeking salvation, earning one's way into the afterlife they seek. Thus, in suggesting the "bookkeeping" process, the running balances employed to evaluate human beings, the Qur'an reminds them of their accountability (1:4). It also suggests specific activities that would be considered debits or credits on the balance sheet of one's life. Using the language not usually associated with theology, it reminds human beings of the Divine grace that is inherent in the creation, as well as suggesting to them their accountability as the beneficiary of the grace, which is freely given. It does so by using accounting concepts and terms and, in doing so, it is suggesting that the signs of Creator are to be found in all of His creations, in all things, sacred and profane.

Notes

1 There is a wide variety of spellings for the name of the Islamic scripture. We use "Qur'an," unless the source we cite uses a different version.
2 We use the prefix "Prophet" but leave out the customary (pbuh), and in so doing we do not intend to disrespect him. If the source we cite is using a different spelling, we employ that instead.
3 This chapter is particularly indebted to Charles Torrey's 1892 doctoral dissertation from the University of Strasburg titled *The Commercial-Theological Terms in the Koran.*
4 These human liabilities necessitate the need for the periodic guidance provided for human beings through the Divinely ordained and anointed prophets who seek to guide their people in their respective languages. For Muslims, the last of such messengers is their Prophet Muhammad, who represents the end of Divinely ordained prophets. In following the model of human conduct in the person of their Prophet, they are able to avoid making errors. Avoiding errors of judgment is also helped by following the *Sharia,* literally the way or right path, and by keeping the *Hududs,* which literally means staying within borders, boundaries, limits, being moderate in one's behavior.
5 The sometime practice of seeing *Hudud* limited only to the punishments that under Islamic law (*Sharia*) are mandated and construed as fixed by God is a misreading of what the Qur'an itself enjoins when it calls the Muslims a "middle nation" in the Qur'anic verse (2:143). The verse does not favor limiting the concept to such form of punishments.
6 Surah is the term for the chapters in the Qur'an. Similarly, a number following this term or within parentheses, such as in note 5, references a chapter and verse of the Qur'an.
7 This chapter will use Muhammad Asad's translation of the Qur'an. One digital resource is www.islam awakened.com, which provides the Arabic text as well as all the currently available translations.
8 The term "Islamic state" is used here to describe the nations whose primary religion is Islamic, derived from the seventh-century spread of Islam on three continents.
9 Another study that compares with Torrey is that of Toshihiko Izutsu, *Ethico Religious Concepts in the Qur'an,* published in (1966). It was originally published as *The Structure of Ethical Terms in the Qur'an* ([1959] 2002), and in it, Izutsu's approach is similar in that he too uses the Qur'anic terms, but he is not so bound by Orientalism, one could argue.
10 Of particular mention is the recent rendering of the Qur'anic term as follows: "It is a locked-in digital data record" (Kaskas and Hungerford 2016).
11 In May 2020, Egypt's Dar al-Iftaa issued a fatwa ruling that it is permissible for Muslims to give Zakat . . . to non-Muslims who need treatment or preventative measures to fight off coronavirus

infection and other diseases. According to the ruling it is permissible to give Zakat to non-Muslims to meet their other needs. It cited the precedent set by the behavior of 'Umar Ibn al-Khattab, who used Zakat to meet the needs of non-Muslims under his rule, in particular when a leprosy pandemic hit under Umar ibn al-Khattab (Al-Youm 2020).

12 Among those who have looked at the institutional version are Kristen Stilt, *Islamic Law in Action: Authority, Discretion, and Everyday Experiences in Mamluk Egypt* (2011) and Benjamin Foster (1970). Additionally, Michael Cook (2000, 2001) has the distinction of studying having surveyed this concept by various Islamic scholars, including al-Ghazzali and ibn-Taymiya.

13 While Muhtasib still exist today, in some countries, their functions are different than what they used to be.

References

Abdallah, W., and A. Murtuza. 2007. "Islamic Muhtasib And American CPAs: A Comparative Study of Institutions Meant to Protect Public Interest." *Journal of Accounting, Business & Management* 14 (April 1): 41–52.

Aghnides, N. P. 1916. *Mohammedan Theories of Finance (No. 166)*. New York: Columbia University Press.

Ahmed, F. B. J. 2005. *The Dilemma of Corruption in Southeast Asia*. Kuala Lumpur, Malaysia: University Malaya Press.

Ahmed, F. B. J. 2020. "Conceptualizing Islamic Ethics for Contemporary Muslim Societies." *Intellectual Discourse* 28 (1): 319–44.

Al-Youm, A. 2020. "Egypt's Dar Al-Iftaa Rules It Permissible to Give Non-Muslims Zakat Funds." *Egypt Independent*. https://egyptindependent.com/egypts-dar-al-iftaa-rules-it-permissible-to-give-non-muslims-zakat-funds.

Baydoun, N., M. Sulamain, R. Willet, and S. Ibrahim. 2018. *Principles of Islamic Accounting*. Singapore: Wiley & Sons.

Biblehub. 2020. https://biblehub.com/luke/6-46.htm.

Chapra, M. U. 1983. "Comments on CII Report on Elimination of Interest." *Money and Banking in Islam*: 212–23.

Cook, M. 2000. *Commanding Right and Forbidding Wrong in Islamic Thought*. Cambridge: Cambridge University Press.

Cook, M. 2001. *Commanding Right and Forbidding Wrong in Islamic Thought*. Cambridge: Cambridge University Press. (a shorter version of Cook (2000)).

de Soto, H. 2000. *The Mystery of Capital: Why Capitalism Triumphs in the West and Fails Everywhere Else*. New York: Basic Books.

Foster, B. R. 1970. "Agoranomos and Muhtasib." *Journal of the Economic and Social History of the Orient* 13(1): 128–44.

Gambling, T., and R. A. A. Karim. 1991. *Business and Accounting Ethics in Islam*. London, England: Mansell Publishing.

Hamidullah, M. 1969. *Introduction to Islam*, 3rd ed. Paris: Centre Culturel Islamique.

Hamidullah, M. 1974. *Muhammad [pbuh] Rasulullah*. Paris: Centre Culturel Islamique.

Haque, Zia-ul. 1995. *Islam and Feudalism: The Moral Economics of Usury, Interest and Profit*. Kuala Lumpur: S. Abdul Majeed & Co.

Hodgson, M. 1974. *The Venture of Islam: Conscience and History in a World Civilization*, vol. 1–3. Chicago: The University of Chicago Press.

Hudson, M. 2018. *And Forgive Them Their Debts: Lending, Foreclosure and Redemption From Bronze Age Finance to the Jubilee Year*. Dresden: ISLET-Verlag.

Islahi, A. A. 2015. *Muhammad Hamidullah and His Pioneering Works on Islamic Economics*. Jeddah: Islamic Economics Research Center, King Abdulaziz University.

Kamali, M. H. 2013. *Islam Prohibits All Forms of Corruption*. Malaysia: International Institute of Advanced Islamic Studies (IAIS). www.shariahlaw.com/public/ext_high_articles_preview.asp?id=12&tit=ISLAM%20PROHIBITS%20ALL%20FORMS%20OF%20CORRUPTION.

Kamla, R., and F. Haque. 2019. "Islamic Accounting, Neo-Imperialism and Identity Staging: The Accounting and Auditing Organization for Islamic Financial Institutions." *Critical Perspectives on Accounting* 63 (C): 1–20.

Kaskas, S., and D. Hungerford. 2016. *The Qur'an – with References to the Bible: A Contemporary Understanding*. New York: Bridges of Reconciliation.

Khan, M. A. 1992. "Al-Hisba and the Islamic Economy." Published as Appendix in 1997 by Ibn Taymiya, *Public Duties in Islam: The Institution of Hisba*, translated by Muhtar Holland. Leicester: Islamic Foundation.

Klein, Y. 2006. "Between Public and Private: An Examination of Hisba Literature." *Harvard Middle Eastern and Islamic Review* 7: 41–62.

Kuran, T. 2020. "Zakat: Islam's Missed Opportunity to Limit Predatory Taxation." *Public Choice* 182: 395–416.

Mannan, M. A. 1970. *Islamic Economics – Theory and Practice*. Lahore: Sh. Muhammad Ashraf.

Mottahedeh, R., and K. Stilt. 2003. "Public and Private as Viewed Through the Work of the Muhtasib." *Social Research: An International Quarterly* 70 (3): 735–48.

Moukheiber, K. 2017. "Hisba: An Ordering Principle for an Islamic Way of Life." www.academia.edu/21042510/Hisba_an_Ordering_Principle_for_an_Islamic_Way_of_Life.

Murtuza, A. 2002. "Islamic Antecedents for Financial Accountability." *International Journal of Islamic Financial Services* 4: 1–19.

Murtuza, A., and W. Abdallah. 2007. "Islamic Muhtasib and American CPAs: A Comparative Study of Institutions Meant to Protect Public Interest." *Journal of Accounting, Business & Management* 14 (April 1): 41–52.

National Zakat Foundation (NZF). 2020. https://nzf.org.uk/

Noor, Z., and F. Pickup. 2017. "Zakat Requires Muslims to Donate 2.5% of Their Wealth: Could This End Poverty?" www.theguardian.com/global-development-professionals-network/2017/jun/22/zakat-requires-muslims-to-donate-25-of-their-wealth-could-this-end-poverty.

Rahman, F. 1964. "Riba and Interest." *Islamic Studies* (March): 1–43.

Rice, G. 1996. *Philosophy and Practice of Islamic Ethics: Implications for Doing Business in Muslim Countries*. Discussion Paper #96-5. Glendale, AZ: Thunderbird Business Research Center, The American Graduate School of International Management. Reprinted in *Journal of Business Ethics* 18 (February 1999): 345–58.

Richter-Bernburg, L. 2011. "God Created Adam in His Likeness, in the Muslim Tradition." In *The Quest for a Common Humanity*, 67–82. Leiden: Brill.

Rodinson, M. 1966. *Islam and Capitalism*. Translated from French by Brian Pearce. New York: Pantheon.

Saeed, A. 1997. *Islamic Banking and Interest: A Study of the Prohibition of Riba and Its Contemporary Interpretation*. Leiden: Brill.

Saleh, N. 1986. *Unlawful Gain and Legitimate Profit in Islamic Law: Riba, Gharar and Islamic Banking*. London: Cambridge University Press.

Stilt, K. 2011. *Islamic Law in Action: Authority, Discretion, and Everyday Experiences in Mamluk Egypt*. Oxford: Oxford University Press.

Tinker, T. 2004. "The Enlightenment and Its Discontents: Antinomies of Christianity, Islam and the Calculative Sciences." *Accounting, Auditing & Accountability Journal* 17 (3): 442–75.

Torrey, C. 1892. "The Commercial-Theological Terms in the Koran." PhD diss., University of Strasburg. https://ia801903.us.archive.org/33/items/commercialtheolo00torr/commercialtheolo00torr.pdf. [Reprinted November 2, 2013], Nabu Press. Available at https://www.amazon.com/Commercial-theological-Terms-Koran-Primary-Source/dp/1294195522.

Toshihiko, I. 2002. *Ethico-religious Concepts in the Qur'ān* Montreal [originally published as *The Structure of Ethical Terms in the Qur'an* ([1959] 2002)]. Ithaca, NY: McGill-Queen's University Press.

Vogel, F., and S. Hayes. 1998. *Islamic Law and Finance: Religion, Risk, and Return*. Arab and Islamic Laws Series, vol. 16. Leiden: Brill. https://brill.com/view/title/11455.

Yusuf, S. M. 1990. *Economic Justice in Islam*. Islamabad, Pakistan: Da'wah Academy, International Islamic University.

Zaid, O. A. 1997. Could Auditing Standards Be Based on Society's Values? *Journal of Business Ethics* 16: 1185–2000.

Zaid, O. A. 2000. The Appointment Qualification of Muslim Accountants in the Middle Ages. *Accounting Education* 9 (4): 329–42.

PART IV

Topical perspectives on accounting ethics

11

ETHICS IN AUDITING

Georgios Papachristou and Michalis Bekiaris

Introduction

Auditing issues involve decisions that affect others and so, by definition, involve ethics. Auditors play a vital role in the financial reporting process, functioning as "critical gatekeepers in the area of issuer reporting and disclosure," according to Andrew Ceresney, director of the US Securities and Exchange Commission's Division of Enforcement (Ceresney 2016). Their opinions concerning financial reporting have broad impact on stakeholders, investors, and other related parties. Thus, it is crucial for auditors to consider the moral implications of their decisions.

The auditing profession involves two counterparties: the accounting firm and the auditee firm. The agency-theoretic challenge lies in the fact that the accounting firm is hired and paid to assess and issue an opinion on the auditee's financial statements. Therefore, there is no doubt that in this dependent relationship, ethics is the cornerstone of the auditing profession, an important element in the corporate reporting process, and a prerequisite for auditors to enhance public confidence in the firms preparing the financial statements.

To maintain public trust, auditors must be independent from their clients, sufficiently competent, and act professionally. During the last 20 years, we have been witnesses to numerous high profile corporate and accounting scandals worldwide; the most prominent include Enron, WorldCom, and Satyam. These failures led to firm collapse, unemployment, and damage to the reputation of the audit profession globally. Because of their role in allowing these situations to occur, the public has held auditors responsible.

To preserve trust and continuously improve the image of the profession, auditors should be encouraged to operate in accordance with an accepted code of ethics; a code of ethics reflects the ideology that a profession would like to demonstrate (Bedard 2001). Casier (1964) defines a code of ethics as a "unique, dynamic record of the movement of an occupational group toward professional status." The most widespread code is issued by the International Ethics Standard Board for Accountants (IESBA), the International Federation of Accountants (IFAC) ethics body. This code follows a principles-based approach that incorporates five fundamental ethical principles: integrity, objectivity, professional competence and due care, professional behavior, and confidentiality.

Reviewing the existing literature for ethics in auditing, we note that auditors' moral attitude is an issue attracting considerable attention, indicative of their critical role in ensuring the fair representation of firms' financial information upon which the markets rely. In this chapter, we review the literature published in leading journals related to auditing, accounting, and ethics.[1] The review is not exhaustive; it covers the papers examining auditors' ethical principles as implemented by IFAC's code of ethics and those that discuss how auditor judgment and overall audit quality may be impaired. Our goal is to provide feedback on the research done so far in the post-Sarbanes-Oxley era, following the implementation of the US (U.S. House of Representatives 2002) and EU (EC 2010) regulations regarding auditors' conduct, and provide useful avenues to academics and regulators for further research and consideration.

Overview of auditing ethics literature

Integrity and objectivity

Auditors are required to act independently by maintaining and preserving their integrity and objectivity during their audit engagements. Independence is defined as "an auditor's unbiased viewpoint when preparing and issuing an audit report" (Nouri and Lombardi 2009). Auditor independence is vital because it affects audit quality. DeAngelo (1981) notes that audit quality incorporates both the discovery of a breach in a client's accounting system and the report of this breach by the auditor. If the auditor is not independent, his judgment is impaired, and his opinion is biased; the audit quality will suffer.

The US Supreme Court in 1984 ruled, in a case involving Arthur Young & Co., that auditors serve as "public watchdogs" ensuring the reliability of firms' financial reporting. This role requires total independence from the client; however, it does not ignore the contract between the accounting firm and the auditee firm that hires it, which makes its independence doubtful. The IFAC provides two types of independence: independence of mind and independence in appearance. The former is defined as "the state of mind that permits the expression of a conclusion without being affected by influences that compromise professional judgements, allowing an individual to act with integrity, and exercise objectivity and professional skepticism" (IESBA 2006, Sec. 290.8). Independence in appearance is defined as

> the avoidance of facts and circumstances that are so significant that a reasonable and informed third party, having knowledge of all relevant information, including safeguards applied, would reasonably conclude a firm's or a member of assurance team's integrity, objectivity or professional skepticism had been compromised.
>
> *(IESBA 2006, Sec. 290.8)*

Thus, if auditors' decisions have been or seem to be impaired, financial information would be perceived of as uncertain, auditors would lose public trust, the accounting profession would suffer, and investor losses may increase.

Corporate collapses associated with accounting scandals in the 21st century have raised doubt around the value and the role of auditors (Ye, Carson, and Simnet 2011). Regulators have argued that audit failures are likely to occur due to lack of objectivity and integrity in the performance of the audit. Therefore, regulatory bodies (e.g., SEC, PCAOB, EC) have issued rules and policies to preserve the auditors' independence. In particular, the main issues leading to the erosion of auditor independence include the social and economic bonds resulting from the provision of non-audit services (NAS) by audit firms to their clients, the relationship developed between auditor and auditee due to continuous tenure, and the Public Company Accounting

Oversight Board's (PCAOB) recommendation to external auditors to rely more on the work of a firm's internal auditors, which calls independence into question.

Given the critical role of independence for the auditing profession, many studies have been performed in this area, exploring NAS, audit firm rotation, and the impact of the PCAOB's Auditing Standard No. 5 on auditors' objectivity and integrity. Table 11.1 chronologically summarizes the prior research examining these relations in the post-SOX era.

Understanding in depth: NAS and auditor independence

One of the most controversial audit independence issues has been the provision of NAS by audit firms to their audit clients. Following audit failures in the late 1990s and early 2000s, the United States passed the Sarbanes-Oxley Act (SOX) (US House of Representatives 2002). SOX restricts external auditors' ability to provide a number of NAS to audit clients[2], reducing their dual role as auditors and consultants and lessening the economic bond with their clients. Nearly 12 years later, as a response to the global financial crisis and to address the weaknesses remaining in the audit profession (Horton, Tsipouridou, and Wood 2017), the European Commission (EC) endorsed a directive (201/56/EU) and a regulation (537/2014) designating the prohibition of numerous NAS[3] and a fee cap at 70% of the audit fee on the permissible ones.

However, despite strong opinions in favor of limited NAS, studies (Robinson 2008; Brody, Haynes, and White 2014) argue that there is no significant empirical evidence relating the rendering of NAS to reduced audit quality. Additional advantages include the reduction of the relative costs for finding another competent provider and of the risk of receiving low-quality consultant services due to the lack of familiarization and experience with the firm's environment and practices. Against these opinions, equally robust arguments have been made stating that such services increase the economic and social bond between the auditor and the client, impairing auditors' independence. Examining the studies in the post-SOX period (for pre-SOX era, review Sharma 2014), we find evidence supporting both arguments, showing that the relation between the provision of NAS and auditors' independence is still a debated issue demanding further research.

Supporting the proponents of NAS provision, Robinson (2008) analyzed data from 201 US firms, examining the relationship between NAS fees and the likelihood of issuing a going-concern opinion, and found no significant correlation. In the same line, more recent studies in the United States provide additional experimental evidence supporting the view that auditors are able to provide NAS while preserving their objectivity and also that NAS fees do not lessen audit quality (Brody, Haynes, and White 2014; Lennox 2016). In the European context, studies conducted in Norway and Germany support the same argument, finding no evidence that the NAS provision impairs auditors' independence (Hope and Langli 2010; Dobler 2014). Ianniello (2012) examined 239 listed companies in Italy and found no significant relation between NAS and audit quality. This research is of notable importance, as it is the only study made in a context where specific consulting services have been prohibited since 2005.

On the other hand, David and Hollie (2008), incorporating eight experimental sessions with 48 participants in the United States, finds opposite results; the provision of NAS and the level of NAS fees reduce auditors' independence in appearance. Basioulis, Papakonstantinou, and Geiger (2008), examining 392 UK listed companies, finds a significant negative relationship between NAS fees and going-concern modified audit reports. Quick and Warming-Rasmussen (2009), examining auditor independence in appearance in Germany, reaffirm David and Hollie's (2008) results under a different cultural and regulatory environment. Ye, Carson, and Simnet (2011) find a negative association of NAS with going-concern opinions using 626 Australian

Table 11.1 Published Literature on Auditors' Independence

Study	Country	Method	Sample	Main Findings
Jennings, Pany, and Reckers (2006)	US	Survey	49 judges	Rotating audit firms and strong corporate governance structure enhance auditor independence.
Bamber and Iyer (2007)	US	Survey	257 CPAs	Audit firm tenure associates with greater auditor objectivity and improves audit quality.
Basioulis, Papakonstantinou, and Geiger (2008)	UK	Regression Analysis	392 firms	Significant negative relationship between NAS fees and going-concern modified audit opinions.
David and Hollie (2008)	US	Experimental	48 participants	NAS fees reduce independence in appearance.
Robinson (2008)	US	Regression Analysis	209 firms	No significant relation between non-tax component of NAS fees and going-concern opinion.
Quick and Warming-Rasmussen (2009)	Germany	Survey	600 participants	NAS provision reduces auditor independence in appearance.
Ruiz-Barbadillo, Gomez-Aguilar, and Carrera (2009)	Spain	Regression Analysis	3,119 firms	Mandatory rotation does not reduce the effects of economic bond.
Hope and Langli (2010)	Norway	Regression Analysis	59,686 obs	No relation between fee dependence and auditor independence.
Ye, Carson, and Simnet (2011)	Australia	Regression Analysis	626 firms	Negative relation among NAS, alumni affiliation, and going-concern opinion.
Brody (2012)	US	Experimental	96 auditors	Auditors' working style affects their decision to investigate more and/or rely on the internal auditors' work.
Stefaniak, Houston, and Cornell (2012)	US	Experimental	88 auditors	The external auditors' reliance on work of internal auditors could improve audit quality.
Ianniello (2012)	Italy	Regression Analysis	239 firm	No significant association between NAS and auditors' opinions.
Dobler (2014)	US	Regression Analysis	368 firms	Weak evidence on threats to auditors' independence of NAS provision.
Brody, Haynes, and White (2014)	US	Experimental	153 auditors	External auditors can remain objective when performing NAS.
Bauer (2015)	US	Experimental	92 auditors	Client identification leads auditors to agree more with their clients and accept smaller asset write-downs.

Study	Country	Method	Sample	Main Findings
Dhaliwal et al. (2015)	US	Regression Analysis	2,145 obs	No relation between auditor selection and auditor independence.
Hedra and Lavelle (2015)	US	Survey	102 auditors	Client identification is negatively related to auditor objectivity.
Svanberg and Ohman (2015)	Sweden	Survey	141 auditors	Client identification is negatively associated with auditor independence.
Cameran, Prencipe, and Trombetta (2016)	Italy	Regression Analysis	1,184 firms	The year prior to mandatory audit firm rotation, audit quality improves.
Campa and Donnelly (2016)	UK	Regression Analysis	207 firms	Auditor independence of mind is impaired by the NAS fees.
Lennox (2016)	US	Regression Analysis	41,435 obs	PCAOB's restrictions on auditors' tax services have no impact on audit quality.
He et al. (2017)	China	Regression Analysis	6,998 obs	Audit committee members and auditor social ties influence auditor independence and due care.
Svanberg and Ohman (2017)	Sweden	Survey	199 auditors	Negative relation between client identification and auditor objectivity. Positive relation between auditor independence and the extent to which auditors perceive client leaders as charismatic.
Williams and Wilder (2017)	US	Archival Research	15 public accounting firms	Public accounting firms opposed to mandatory audit firm rotation.
Aschauer and Quick (2017)	Austria	Experimental	140 investment consultants	Audit firm rotation does not affect objectivity. Auditor independence in appearance improves with the tax services prohibition.
Bhattacharjee and Brown (2018)	US	Experimental	91 audit seniors	Social client identification can raise auditor objectivity and skepticism.

firms. More recent research in the United Kingdom finds similar results concerning auditors' independence of mind (Campa and Donnelly 2016), finding that both independence in appearance and independence of mind may be affected by the provision of NAS.

Mandatory audit-firm rotation

Another long-standing debate is the mandatory audit firm rotation issue. Regulators have raised questions on whether mandatory audit firm rotation would enhance auditors' independence and audit quality (GAO 2003, 2008; PCAOB 2011). Recently, the EC issued a regulation

(537/2014) requiring mandatory audit firm rotation after 10 years; specific exceptions to the tenure exist. Reduced economic incentives, a "fresh" aspect to the audit, and minimization of close social ties between the auditor and the client are some of the benefits that mandatory audit firm rotation may provide (Ruiz-Barbadillo, Gomez-Aguilar, and Carrera 2009). Opponents to mandatory audit firm rotation state that this practice would compromise audit quality due to the time restriction over which auditors have to acquire client-specific knowledge; a newly appointed auditor is unlikely to immediately detect a misstatement because of lack of knowledge of specific business practices (William and Wilder 2017). Another argument against mandatory rotation is the high cost for companies to change auditors; despite the EC regulation on mandatory rotation, the EU appears not to acknowledge that many firms would have to deal with this costly change (William and Wilder 2017; Lennox 2016).

Research related to mandatory rotation does not provide unequivocal evidence in favor of or against its implementation. Jennings, Pany, and Reckers (2006), surveying 49 US judges over their perception of auditor independence related to audit rotation, find that rotating audit firms improves auditors' independence in appearance. More recent studies conducted in the US also provide evidence supporting mandatory audit firm rotation, concluding that auditors' long tenure in a firm may lead them to identify with their clients; there is a negative relation between client identification and an auditor's objectivity (Bauer 2015; Herda and Lavelle 2015; Bhattacharjee and Brown 2018). Similar evidence supporting the negative relation between client identification and objectivity are provided by Svanberg and Ohman (2015, 2017) in Sweden. Examining the issue in a different context, He et al. (2017) provides evidence in favor of mandatory audit firm rotation; they find that the social relationship developed between audit committee members and auditors as a result of long tenure impair auditors' independence and due care in the Chinese environment.

Archival research on the comment letters of 15 US public accounting firms upon the request of the PCAOB (2011) reveals that public accounting firms oppose mandatory rotation (William and Wilder 2017). Bamber and Iyer (2007) support this opinion, providing evidence that audit firm tenure is related to greater objectivity and audit quality and concluding that there is no need for mandatory rotation. Evidence against mandatory rotation is also provided by Ruiz-Barbadillo, Gomez-Aguilar, and Carrera (2009) in Spain and Aschauer and Quick (2017) in Austria. Both find that mandatory rotation does not improve auditors' independence and argue that mandatory rotation does not improve independence.

PCAOB's Auditing Standard No. 5

Limited research exists regarding the impact of the PCAOB's Auditing Standard No 5 (AS 5) "An Audit of Internal Control Over Financial Reporting that is Integrated with an Audit of Financial Statements" on auditors' independence. Issued in 2007, AS 5 encourages external auditors to rely more on internal controls and on the work of internal auditors to reduce cost and duplication of effort. According to the PCAOB, external auditors' reliance on the work of internal auditors should enhance efficiency without impairing objectivity. However, as Franzel (2015) stated, "the issue is serious when the external auditors' use of internal audit work does not meet PCAOB's standards and results in insufficient evidence to support the external audit opinion." So, does PCAOB AS 5 impair auditors' independence?

Brody (2012) experimentally examines the factors that influence external auditors' decision to rely on the work of internal auditors. According to the responses of 96 US internal and external auditors, they conclude that external auditors' working style and their perceptions about internal auditors' competence and independence influence their judgment. Stefaniak, Houston, and Cornell (2012), comparing the levels and effects of client identification on the control evaluations of internal and external auditors, conclude that the external auditors' reliance on the work of internal auditors would improve audit quality without impairing their objectivity. However, PCAOB's continuous guidance to external auditors to use the work of others and the dual role of internal auditors' impact on their independence are issues that require more research (PCAOB 2013; Roussy 2015; Ahmad and Taylor 2009).

Professional skepticism and industry specialization

In response to the great concerns regarding auditors' independence, regulators such as the PCAOB and the International Audit and Assurance Standards Board (IAASB) have also focused on auditors' competence and due professional care. Recent audit failures have raised questions about an auditors' duty to maintain knowledge and skills on a high level and to follow professional standards throughout the audit engagement, motivating researchers to study these core ethical principles.

Given the complexity of business transactions and of accounting standards, together with the continuous demand for more reliable financial reporting, a heightened academic interest in auditors' application of professional skepticism and the relation between auditor industry specialization and audit quality is perhaps not surprising. Table 11.2 chronologically summarizes the prior research examining these features since 2003.

Understanding in depth: professional skepticism

Professional skepticism, like independence, is vital for the auditing profession but is often a challenge to define and measure (Hurtt et al. 2013). The word skepticism has its origin in the Greek word "skeptikos," which means "inquiring or reflective." In other words, a person characterized as "skeptikos" is someone who seeks information by questioning, observes carefully, and looks beyond the obvious (Glover and Prawitt 2014). Thus, professional skepticism requires an auditor to exercise due care, be competent, and follow audit standards during his audit assignments.

The academic and accounting literature has defined professional skepticism inconsistently. Nelson (2009) discusses the "neutral" and "presumptive doubt" perspectives of skepticism. A "neutral" perspective indicates that an auditor should assume that management is neither honest nor dishonest. On the other hand, a "presumptive doubt" perspective of skepticism implies that an auditor should be aware of the possibility that financial statements are materially misstated; this view of professional skepticism "assumes some level of carelessness, incompetence, or dishonesty on the part of financial preparers" (Glover and Prawitt 2014). While the "presumptive doubt" view is more likely to improve audit quality (Hurtt et al. 2013; Quadackers, Groot, and Wright 2014), Cohen, Dalton, and Harp (2017) argue that "presumptive doubt" skepticism may have a negative, indirect impact on audit quality via lower levels of organizational citizenship behavior (OCB), lower levels of partner support for professional skepticism, and higher auditor turnover intentions. To solve this issue and enable auditors to use a perspective depending on a particular situation during an audit and balance audit efficiency and effectiveness, Glover and Prawitt (2014) provide a framework of a professional skepticism continuum. This continuum allows the auditor to consider the specific audit area and the related risks and choose an appropriate skepticism level; while this

Table 11.2 Published Literature on Auditors' Due Professional Care and Competence

Study	Country	Method	Sample	Main Findings
Balsam, Krishnan, and Yang (2003)	US	Regression Analysis	19,091 obs	Firms audited by industry specialists have higher earning quality than clients with no specialists.
Payne and Ramsey (2005)	US	Experimental	184 auditors	Auditors predisposed to low fraud risk assessment were less skeptical than those with no knowledge.
Hammersley (2006)	US	Experimental	65 auditors	Industry-specialist auditors are more likely to discriminate the presence of a misstatement; industry specialization improves audit quality.
Cairney and Young (2006)	US	Regression Analysis	39,059 obs	Auditors achieve high level of audit quality in homogenous industries.
Romanus, Maher, and Fleming (2008)	US	Regression Analysis	456 firms	Auditor industry expertise reduces the possibility of issuing restatements in core accounts; industry specialization improves audit quality.
Hurtt (2010)	US	Experimental	230 auditors	A 30-item scale to measure trait professional skepticism was developed.
Cahan, Jeter, and Naiker (2011)	US	Regression Analysis	9,565 obs	Audit specialists obtaining a large market share produce low-quality audits.
Popova (2012)	US	Experimental	79 students	There is a positive relation between auditor fraud judgment and previous experiences; auditors who apply more skepticism are more sensitive to fraud evidence when evaluating this evidence.
Carpenter and Reimers (2013)	US	Experimental	80 audit managers	A partner's emphasis on professional skepticism plays a crucial role on the identification of fraud risks and the selection of relevant audit procedures
Gul, Wu, and Yang (2013)	China	Regression Analysis	14,802 obs	Individual auditor past experiences, skills, and competences affect audit quality.
Grenier (2017)	US	Experimental	171 auditors	Industry specialization inhibits some aspects of due care and professional skepticism.
Robinson, Curtis, and Robertson (2018)	US	Experimental	126 auditors	A scale to measure state professional skepticism was developed.

framework identifies different levels of professional skepticism, it implies a gradation of more or less doubt within these categories concerning the relative risks and indications of material misstatement provided by audit evidence.

The professional skepticism continuum is a new step forward to understand this concept in depth. Professionals and academics should continue to work to better define, analyze, and measure professional skepticism, as "enhancing the level of professional skepticism applied in practice is one important means of improving audit quality" (Glover and Prawitt 2014).

Following the "presumptive doubt" view of professional skepticism, many studies relate fraud risk assessment to the proper application of skepticism. SAS No. 99 indicates that fraud may be present despite an auditor's opinion about the honesty of managerial assertions. The PCAOB in its recent auditor inspections (PCAOB 2011, 2013) has reported the lack of professional skepticism as a severe issue in auditor fraud investigations. James Doty (2011), PCAOB chairman, also stated that "auditor skepticism is the foundation of investor confidence in financial reporting. But it can fail in spite of both fundamental competence and high ethical standards."

Payne and Ramsey (2005) confirm these statements, finding that auditors who were predisposed to a low planning-stage fraud risk were less skeptical of management assertions than those given no information about fraud risk. Popova (2012) also examines how prior experiences with a client may influence an auditor's decisions. She concludes that there is a positive relation between auditor fraud judgments and previous experiences, indicating that auditors who apply more skepticism are more sensitive to fraud evidence when evaluating this evidence. Trying to answer PCAOB questions on lack of professional skepticism and the role of tone at the top set by audit partners, Carpenter and Reimers (2013) examine the effects of audit partners' emphasis on professional skepticism on auditors' fraud assessments. They provide evidence that a partner's emphasis on professional skepticism is vital for the identification of relative fraud risks and for the selection of appropriate audit procedures.

These studies suggest that professional skepticism is critical for the fraud risk assessment process and the related fraud audits. Given their conclusions and recommendations, future research could examine how auditors' personality traits may affect their skepticism about fraud risks and also whether fraud-related experience with one client influences the level of an auditor's professional skepticism applied to another auditee.

Another issue worth discussion is the measurement of professional skepticism; despite its considerable importance, it is still challenging for professionals and academics to measure professional skepticism. Two publications have greatly expanded our understanding about this subject. First, Nelson (2009) developed a model of professional skepticism clarifying how traits, knowledge, motives, and previous experience combined with evidential input affect an auditor's skeptical thinking and actions. Second, Hurtt (2010) developed a scale to measure trait professional skepticism, based on a set of characteristics being subject to professional skepticism; combining multidimensional characteristics of skeptics (e.g., questioning mind, self-esteem etc.), she determines an auditor's level of trait skepticism, which influences his behavior and actions. Following these studies and answering Hurtt's call for a measure of state professional skepticism, Robinson, Curtis, and Robertson (2018) developed a scale to measure state skepticism; results also support the distinction between trait and state professional skepticism as different, measurable components of professional skepticism and due care. Additional research could examine the effectiveness of this state scale or even explore how other components of the trait scale, modified to reflect the Robinson et al. scale, would affect auditors' decisions (Robinson, Curtis, and Robertson 2018).

Auditor industry specialization

Throughout the audit engagement, an auditor's industry specialization may either positively or negatively influence professional skepticism and decisions. The US Government Accountability Office (GAO 2008) states that more than 80% of firms viewed industry specialization or expertise as being a significant factor in the process of selecting an auditor. However, the results provided by many studies regarding the association between auditor industry specialization and audit quality are controversial.

Romanus, Maher, and Fleming (2008) provides empirical evidence that auditor industry specialization improves audit quality by reducing the probability of accounting restatements. Their conclusions confirm previous studies' findings (Balsam, Krishnan, and Yang 2003; Hammersley 2006; Cairney and Young 2006), indicating that auditor industry expertise plays a crucial role in enhancing audit quality. Likewise, Gul, Wu, and Yang (2013) find that past experiences in similar firms, skills, and academic background influence due care and, in turn, audit quality. On the other hand, more recent studies support an opposite view. Cahan, Jeter, and Naiker (2011) conclude that audit specialists obtaining a large market share produce low0quality audits; they do not act with proper due care and diligence over their client's controls and systems and they do not develop their competence and skills accordingly. Further, Grenier (2017) finds that industry specialization inhibits specific aspects of due care and professional skepticism because auditors rely increasingly more on their special knowledge and their pattern recognition ability developed through homogenous audits; such confidence may result in audit failures.

Given the aforementioned studies about auditors' due care and competence, further research is necessary. Future studies could examine the development of a new measure of professional skepticism involving factors affecting an auditor's behavior, such as specific skills and competences, for example, leadership, integrity, academic/professional background. Moreover, additional research is needed regarding the elements that impact professional skepticism and due care, for example, alumni effect (Hurtt et al. 2013).

Professional behavior

As mentioned before, over the last years the accounting profession has been disgraced, not unjustifiably (Zeff 2003b); once, auditors were the epitome of honesty, trust, and integrity (Zeff 2003a); now their reputation is questioned, and they have work to do to recover the public's trust. Just as greed seems to be the main force at many companies, it is also an issue in accounting firms. In turn, the culture of the accounting firms has changed from a dominant role of delivering assurance services in a professional manner to one that gives prominence to revenue growth and profitability (Wyatt 2004).

Wyatt (2004) discusses the new context and role of the accounting firms, expressing his concerns that commercial interests erode an auditor's professional behavior. Seeking to please the client and do whatever is needed to maintain a positive relationship are matters that did not exist in the past, when auditing seemed straightforward and the public could count on them to be independent, honest, and exercise professionalism (Carnegie and Napier 2010). The change in auditors from the traditional stereotypes to business professionals has created concerns regarding their behavior; this change may lead to the gradual disparagement of the accounting profession (Carnegie and Napier 2010).

Given the heightened importance of auditors' profile, limited research exists that examines the individual and situational characteristics of the auditors punished for unprofessional behavior (Fisher, Cunz, and McCutcheon 2001; Hottegindre, Loison, and Farjaudon 2017).

Research shows that gender is a critical determinant of ethical behavior (Kohlberg 1976; Gilligan 1982; Craft 2013); Hottegindre, Loison, and Farjaudon (2017) find that male auditors are more likely to behave in a way discredited for the accounting profession, while their female fellows mainly commit disciplinary offences relating to audit quality and to nonconformance to professional peer-review procedures. Specifically, male auditors' misconduct relates to alcohol, drugs, or gambling addictions, whereas female auditors are more likely to be accused of nonconformance with the audit standards.

In additional to personal characteristics, organizational context and content of professional work may be another determinant of professional behavior (Leich and Fenell 1997). Suddaby, Gendron, and Lam (2009) conclude that most Canadian accountants adapt to the changes of the context and content of their work, remaining committed to their profession and following the code of ethics. Along the same line, Lander, Koene, and Linssen (2013) find that mid-tier accounting firms embed in their principle role an emphasis on ethics and professionalism. According to their results, while the leadership of these firms understands that they have to modify their structures and content of their work – otherwise they will not be profitable in the near future – they state that offering any service not directly associated with the accounting profession would probably endanger auditors' professional attitude and core ethical values.

Given the limited literature regarding professional behavior, Table 11.3 chronologically summarizes the existing research; future research is necessary to determine the effects of individual auditor characteristics and organizational factors – for example, pressure, incentives,

Table 11.3 Published Literature on Auditors' Professional Behavior

Study	Country	Method	Sample	Main Findings
Subbady, Gendron, and Lam (2009)	Canada	Online Survey	1,324 auditors	A majority of Canadian accountants adjust to the changes of the context and content of their work, remaining committed to their profession and following the code of ethics.
Lander, Koene, and Linssen (2013)	Netherlands	Survey	13 mid-tier firms	Mid-tier accounting firms embed in their principle role, emphasizing ethics and professionalism.
Hottegindre, Loison, and Farjaudon (2017)	France	Factorial correspondence analysis	163 disciplinary reports	Male auditors are more likely to behave in a way discredited for the accounting profession, while their female fellows mainly commit disciplinary offences relating to audit quality and to nonconformance to professional peer-review procedures.

compensation – that are likely to affect an auditor's professional behavior. To better understand auditors' psychological profiles and personality traits and their impact on professionalism would add value to academic literature.

Confidentiality

As we know, auditors cannot conduct effective financial statement audits successfully in the absence of an auditor's trust in and cooperation with client management. Members of the client's management have more knowledge about their organization than do the auditors; thus, it is essential for the auditors to gain access to information provided by management, regardless of its sensitivity and importance (Rennie, Kopp, and Lemon 2010).

Given the IFAC code of ethics' fourth principle, "confidentiality," auditors should not disclose any client information without appropriate permission or use it for personal gain. However, since 2012, the IESBA, which insists that an auditor should directly report a client's illegal acts to an appropriate authority upon becoming aware of them, has given the issue of information disclosure considerable attention. Although this behavior would probably enhance the reliability of financial reporting, it would be detrimental to the auditor–client relationship (Eickemeyer and Love 2014). Moreover, disclosing a client's information may lead to an auditor being subject to a lawsuit where a client argues that it has endured damages due to an unwarranted disclosure of confidential information. Brasel and Daugherty (2017) provide a table with selected client confidentiality litigation against auditors; the most recent case involves the accusation of KPMG LLP by Cast Art Industries regarding irregularities not found in the financial statements of Papal Giftware, a firm merged with Cast Art Industries. Although the New Jersey Supreme Court judged KPMG LLP not guilty, defending a lawsuit consumes time and resources, "even if the claim is found to be without a merit" (Eickemeyer and Love 2014).

Werner (2009) discusses the matter of accountant confidentiality, presenting numerous cases where auditors' confidentiality has been tested. Apart from the directive to report "illegal acts" to the appropriate authorities, he raises questions about the cases where an auditor learns some information affecting financial statements, for example, the client has omitted a transaction, while working for another client, or when information come to an auditor's attention during an advisory engagement. Hess, Haney, and MacPhail (2017) provide an instructional case, based on a real-life experience, of an accountant who serves as tax preparer and auditor for related parties. In this case, during his NAS, the auditor discovers that the executive director of the audit client, for whom he prepares the income tax return, has a gambling addiction that led him to a loss of a large amount of money not explained by his annual income or any other source. The auditor experiences an ethical dilemma, considering how the information gained through a non-audit service would influence the audit process and if the use of this information would constitute a violation of the client's confidentiality. This study provides an example that finds although confidentiality is a core aspect of auditors' code of conduct, it can possibly lead them to difficult situations in which ethics and standards may be conflicting.

However, despite the vital significance of confidentiality, there is no evidential study examining these concerns. Future research is needed to address Werner's (2009) questions and investigate auditors' moral and ethical attitude regarding issues of disclosing confidential information of illegal acts to the appropriate authorities, especially after having notified the firm's board and having seen them take no or insufficient action to correct the issue.

Conclusion

"Auditing is as much an ethical discipline as it is a technical discipline" (Shaub and Braun 2014). The extent to which auditors' decisions are made based on professional ethics has been subject to much criticism in recent decades. Changing auditor personas from the traditional stereotypes of public watchdog to client partners in business has raised doubts about their independence and compliance with core ethical principles (Carnegie and Napier 2010).

The provision of non-audit services to clients, the gradual development of large accounting firms (Big-4), and the attention to clients and profit generation have modified the culture and original role of auditing. Regulatory bodies such as PCAOB and IESBA and academics (Quick, Turley, and Willenkens 2008; Sikka 2009) argue that the profession's growing commercialization at the expense of more traditional morally professional values has contributed to the occurrence of audit failures exposed by corporate scandals (e.g., Enron, WorldCom). To improve the image of the accounting profession and maintain trust, auditors should exercise their duties following IFAC's professional code of ethics, a code of ethics that reflects the Aristotelian view of ethics, that is, "virtue ethics," emphasizing the traits of an auditor rather than the consequences of his actions and decisions (Samsonova-Taddei and Siddiqui 2016).

Among auditors' virtues, independence has been identified as the most significant one in the accounting literature. If an auditor is not independent, his judgment may be impaired and his opinion may be biased; audit quality will suffer. Concerns have been raised about the impairment of auditors' objectivity and integrity because of the social and economic ties developed between the auditors and the auditees, as a result of the provision of non-audit services by the auditors to their clients, the continuous tenure of the same accounting firm, and the PCAOB's suggestion to external auditors to rely more on the work of others. Many studies have examined these issues and have provided controversial conclusions, making further research on the subject of auditors' independence necessary.

Apart from independence, there are also other virtues an auditor should adopt: due care and competence, professional behavior, and confidentiality. Adequate research about due professional care and competence has been conducted so far over the issues of professional skepticism and auditors' industry specialization. Although expertise and skepticism through the audit engagement are likely to improve audit quality, these traits are frequently missing or inadequate in situations such as corporate collapses, frauds, and audit failures; such events raise doubts about whether auditors possess the appropriate skills and competencies and exercise considerable due care (Sikka 2009). Research is limited regarding professional behavior focusing on how gender, context, and content of auditors' work have affected their professional behavior. Moreover, opportunities for further research by academics and professionals exist regarding issues of confidentiality.

In conclusion, while the research on ethics in auditing is so far inconclusive, providing different perspectives on this subject, many advances have been made in the literature. Access to proprietary information from accounting firms would provide researchers the opportunity to examine these issues in more depth. Moreover, interdisciplinary researchers from psychology and sociology could probably shed light on the influence of personality traits and environmental context on auditors' behavior and decisions. Finally, given the importance of confidentiality and the different expectations from clients, auditors, and the public, studies should be conducted to address the moral aspects of confidentiality matters and also to examine whether auditors' sharing of information with others through brainstorming workshops or self-assessment processes benefits audit quality or is too costly to the auditor-client relationship.

Notes

1 Review was conducted at the following leading journals: *Abacus*; *Accounting and Business Research*; *Accounting Horizons*; *Accounting, Auditing and Accountability Journal*; *Accounting, Organizations and Society*; *Advances in Accounting*; *AUDITING: A Journal of Practice and Theory*; *Behavioral Research in Accounting*; *Contemporary Accounting Research*; *Current Issues in Auditing*; *European Accounting Review*; *International Journal of Auditing*; *Journal of Accounting, Auditing and Finance*; *Journal of Business Ethics*; *Managerial Auditing Journal*; *The Accounting Review*; and *The British Accounting Review*.

2 The auditor is prohibited from providing the following non-audit services to an audit client: "book-keeping or other services related to the accounting records or financial statements of the audit client; financial information systems design and implementation; appraisal or valuation services, fairness opinions, or contribution-in-kind reports; actuarial services; internal audit outsourcing services; management functions or human resources; broker or dealer, investment adviser, or investment banking services; legal services and expert services unrelated to the audit; any other service that the Board determines, by regulation, is impermissible" (U.S. House of Representatives 2002, Section 201).

3 "A statutory auditor or an audit firm carrying out the statutory audit of a public-interest entity, or any member of the network to which the statutory auditor or the audit firm belongs, shall not directly or indirectly provide to the audited entity, to its parent undertaking or to its controlled undertakings within the Union any of the following prohibited non-audit services: tax services relating to preparation of tax forms, payroll tax, customs duties, identification of public subsidies and tax incentives unless support from the statutory auditor or the audit firm in respect of such inspections is required by law, calculation of direct and indirect tax and deferred tax, provision of tax advice; services that involve playing any part in the management or decision-making of the audited entity; bookkeeping and preparing accounting records and financial statements; payroll services; designing and implementing internal control or risk management procedures related to the preparation and/or control of financial information or designing and implementing financial information technology systems; valuation services, including valuations performed in connection with actuarial services or litigation support services; legal services, with respect to the provision of general counsel, negotiating on behalf of the audited entity and acting in an advocacy role in the resolution of litigation; services related to the audited entity's internal audit function; services linked to the financing, capital structure and allocation, and investment strategy of the audited entity, except providing assurance services in relation to the financial statements, such as the issuing of comfort letters in connection with prospectuses issued by the audited entity; promoting, dealing in, or underwriting shares in the audited entity; human resources services, with respect to management in a position to exert significant influence over the preparation of the accounting records or financial statements which are the subject of the statutory audit, where such services involve searching for or seeking out candidates for such position or undertaking reference checks of candidates for such positions, structuring the organization design and cost control" (EU 2014, Article 5).

References

Ahmad, Z., and D. Taylor. 2009. "Commitment to Independence by Internal Auditors: The Effects of Role Ambiguity and Role Conflict." *Managerial Auditing Journal* 24 (9): 899–925.

Aschauer, E., and R. Quick. 2017. "Mandatory Audit Firm Rotation and Prohibition of Audit Firm-Provided Tax Services: Evidence from Investment Consultants' Perceptions." *International Journal of Auditing* 22 (2): 131–49.

Balsam, S., J. Krishnan, and J. Yang. 2003. "Auditor Industry Specialization and Earnings Quality." *Auditing: A Journal of Practice & Theory* 22 (2): 71–97.

Bamber, E., and V. Iyer. 2007. "Auditors' Identification with Their Clients and Its Effect on Auditors' Objectivity." *Auditing: A Journal of Practice & Theory* 26 (2): 1–24.

Basioulis, I., E. Papakonstantinou, and M. Geiger. 2008. "Audit Fees, Non-Audit Fees and Auditor Going-Concern Reporting Decisions in the United Kingdom." *Abacus* 44 (3): 284–309.

Bauer, T. 2015. "The Effects of Client Identity Strength and Professional Identity Salience on Auditor Judgments." *The Accounting Review* 90 (1): 95–114.

Bedard, J. 2001. "The Disciplinary Process of the Accounting Profession: Protecting the Public or the Profession? The Quebec Experience." *Journal of Accounting and Public Policy* 20: 399–437.

Bhattacharjee, S., and J. Brown. 2018. "The Impact of Management Alumni Affiliation and Persuasion Tactics on Auditors' Internal Control Judgments." *The Accounting Review* 93 (2): 97–115.

Brasel, K., and B. Daugherty. 2017. "Cook and Thomas, LLC: Balancing Auditor Liability, Client Confidentiality, and the Public Interest." *Issues in Accounting Education* 32 (1): 17–32.

Brody, R. 2012. "External Auditors' Willingness to Rely on the Work of Internal Auditors: The Influence of Work Style and Barriers to Cooperation." *Advances in Accounting* 28 (1): 11–21.

Brody, R., C. Haynes, and C. White. 2014. "The Impact of Audit Reforms on Objectivity During the Performance of Non-Audit Services." *Managerial Auditing Journal* 29 (3): 222–36.

Cahan, S., D. Jeter, and V. Naiker. 2011. "Are All Industry Specialist Auditors the Same?" *Auditing: A Journal of Practice & Theory* 30 (4): 191–222.

Cairney, T., and G. Young. 2006. "Homogenous Industries and Auditor Specialization: An Indication of Production Economies." *Auditing: A Journal of Practice & Theory* 25 (1): 49–67.

Cameran, M., A. Prencipe, and M. Trombetta. 2016. "Mandatory Audit Firm Rotation and Audit Quality." *European Accounting Review* 25 (1): 35–58.

Campa, D., and R. Donnelly. 2016. "Non-Audit Services Provided to Audit Clients, Independence of Mind and Independence in Appearance: Latest Evidence from Large UK Listed Companies." *Accounting and Business Research* 46 (4): 422–49.

Carnegie, G., and C. Napier. 2010. "Traditional Accountants and Business Professionals: Portraying the Accounting Profession After Enron." *Accounting, Organizations and Society* 35 (3): 360–76.

Carpenter, T., and J. Reimers. 2013. "Professional Skepticism: The Effects of a Partner's Influence and the Level of Fraud Indicators on Auditors' Fraud Judgments and Actions." *Behavioral Research in Accounting* 25 (2): 45–69.

Casier, D. J. 1964. *The Evolution of CPA Ethics: A Profile of Professionalization*. East Lansing: Michigan State University.

Ceresney, A. 2016. "U.S. Securities and Exchange Commission." Accessed September 22. https://www.sec.gov/news/speech/ceresley-enforcement-focus-on-auditors-andauditing.html.

Cohen, J., D. Dalton, and N. Harp. 2017. "Neutral and Presumptive Doubt Perspectives of Professional Skepticism and Auditor Job Outcomes." *Accounting, Organizations and Society* 62: 1–20.

Craft, J. 2013. "A Review of the Empirical Ethical Decision-Making Literature: 2004–2011." *Journal of Business Ethics* 117 (2): 221–59.

David, S., and D. Hollie. 2008. "The Impact of Nonaudit Service Fee Levels on Investors' Perception of Auditor Independence." *Behavioral Research in Accounting* 20 (1): 31–44.

DeAngelo, L. 1981. "Auditor Independence, 'Lowballing', and Disclosure Regulation." *Journal of Accounting and Economics* 3: 113–27.

Dhaliwal, D., P. Lamoreaux, C. Lennox, and L. Mauler. 2015. "Management Influence on Auditor Selection and Subsequent Impairments of Auditor Independence During the Post-SOX Period." *Contemporary Accounting Research* 32 (2): 575–607.

Dobler, M. 2014. "Auditor-Provided Non-Audit Services in Listed and Private Family Firms." *Managerial Auditing Journal* 29 (5): 427–54.

Doty, J. 2011. "Looking Ahead: Auditor Oversight. Speech presented at The Council of Institutional Investors Spring meeting." https://pcaobus.org/News/Speech/Pages/04042011_DotyLookingAhead.aspx.

Eickemeyer, J., and V. Love. 2014. "Protecting Client Confidentiality When Responding to a Suspected Illegal Act." *The CPA Journal*: 68–71.

European Commission. 2010. "Commissioner Barnier Will Launch a Green Paper on Auditing in the Autumn." Accessed April 27. http://ec.europa.eu/archives/ commission_2010-2014/ barnier/headlines/news/ 2010/04/20100427_en. Html.

European Union. 2014. "Regulation No 537/2014 of the European Parliament and of the Council." https://www.legislation.gov.uk/eur/2014/537/contents.

Fisher, J., S. Cunz, and J. McCutcheon. 2001. "Private/Public Interest and the Enforcement of a Code of Professional Conduct." *Journal of Business Ethics* 31: 191–207.

Franzel, J. M. 2015. "Protecting Investors through a Coordinated System of Audit and Audit Oversight." *Speech Presented at the Institute of Internal Auditors 2015 General Audit Management Conference*. http://pcaobus.org/News/Speech/Pages/03092015_IIA.aspx.

General Accounting Office (GAO). 2003. *Public Accounting Firms: Mandated Study on Consolidation and Competition*. GAO Report 03–864. Washington, DC: Government Printing Office.

General Accounting Office (GAO). 2008. *Audits of Public Companies: Continued Concentration in Audit Market for Large Public Companies Does Not Call for Immediate Action*. GAO Report 08–163. Washington, DC: Government Printing Office.

Gilligan, C. 1982. *In a Different Voice: Psychological Theory and Women's Development*. Cambridge, MA: Harvard University Press.

Glover, S., and D. Prawitt. 2014. "Enhancing Auditor Professional Skepticism: The Professional Skepticism Continuum." *Current Issues in Auditing* 8 (2): 1–10.

Grenier, J. 2017. "Encouraging Professional Skepticism in the Industry Specialization Era." *Journal of Business Ethics* 142 (2): 241–56.

Gul, F., D. Wu, and Z. Yang. 2013. "Do Individual Auditors Affect Audit Quality? Evidence from Archival Data." *The Accounting Review* 88 (6): 1993–2023.

Hammersley, J. 2006. "Pattern Identification and Industry-Specialist Auditors." *The Accounting Review* 81 (2): 309–36.

He, X., J. Pittman, O. Rui, and D. Wu. 2017. "Do Social Ties Between External Auditors and Audit Committee Members Affect Audit Quality?" *The Accounting Review* 92 (5): 61–87.

Herda, D., and J. Lavelle. 2015. "Client Identification and Client Commitment in a Privately Held Client Setting: Unique Constructs with Opposite Effects on Auditor Objectivity." *Accounting Horizons* 29 (3): 577–601.

Hess, D., Haney, M., and MacPhail, C. 2017. "What You Do Know Can Hurt You: An Instructional Case Requiring Application of Professional Standards to an Ethical Dilemma Facing an Auditor and Tax Preparer". *Current Issues in Auditing Teaching Notes* 11 (1):1–9.

Hope, O., and J. Langli. 2010. "Auditor Independence in a Private Firm and Low Litigation Risk Setting." *The Accounting Review* 85 (2): 573–605.

Horton, J., M. Tsipouridou, and A. Wood. 2017. "European Market Reaction to Audit Reforms." *European Accounting Review*: 1–33.

Hottegindre, G., M. C. Loison, and A. L. Farjaudon. 2017. "Male and Female Auditors: An Ethical Divide? Male and Female Auditors: An Ethical Divide?" *International Journal of Auditing* 21 (2): 131–49.

Hurtt, R. 2010. "Development of a Scale to Measure Professional Skepticism." *Auditing: A Journal of Practice & Theory* 29 (1): 149–71.

Hurtt, R., H. Brown-Liburd, C. Earley, and G. Krishnamoorthy. 2013. "Research on Auditor Professional Skepticism: Literature Synthesis and Opportunities for Future Research." *Auditing: A Journal of Practice & Theory* 32 (Suppl. 1): 45–97.

Ianniello, G. 2012. "Non-Audit Services and Auditor Independence in the 2007 Italian Regulatory Environment." *International Journal of Auditing* 16: 147–64.

International Ethics Standards Board for Accountants. 2006. *Handbook of the International Code of Ethics for Professional Accountants*. New York: IFAC.

Jennings, M., K. Pany, and P. Reckers. 2006. "Strong Corporate Governance and Audit Firm Rotation: Effects on Judges' Independence Perceptions and Litigation Judgments." *Accounting Horizons* 20 (3): 253–70.

Kohlberg, L. 1976. "Moral Stages and Moralization: The Cognitive-Developmental Approach." In *Moral Development and Behavior: Theory, Research, and Social*, edited by T. Lickona, 31–53. New York: Holt.

Lander, M., B. Koene, and S. Linssen. 2013. "Committed to Professionalism: Organizational Responses of Mid-Tier Accounting Firms to Conflicting Institutional Logics." *Accounting, Organizations and Society* 38 (2): 130–48.

Leich, K., and M. Fenell. 1997. "The Changing Organizational Context of Professional Work." *Annual Review of Sociology* 23: 215–31.

Lennox, C. 2016. "Did the PCAOB's Restrictions on Auditors' Tax Services Improve Audit Quality?" *The Accounting Review* 91 (5): 1493–512.

Nelson, M. 2009. "A Model and Literature Review of Professional Skepticism in Auditing." *Auditing: A Journal of Practice & Theory* 28 (2): 1–34.

Nouri, H., and D. Lombardi. 2009. "Auditors' Independence: An Analysis of Montgomery's Auditing Textbooks in the 20th Century." *Accounting Historians Journal* 36 (1): 81–112.

Payne, E., and R. Ramsey. 2005. "Fraud Risk Assessments and Auditors' Professional Skepticism." *Managerial Auditing Journal* 20 (3): 321–30.

Popova, V. 2012. "Exploration of Skepticism, Client-Specific Experiences, and Audit Judgments." *Managerial Auditing Journal* 28 (2): 140–60.

Public Company Accounting Oversight Board (PCAOB). 2011. "Order Instituting Disciplinary Proceedings, Making Findings, and Imposing Sanctions in the Matter of Price Waterhouse, Bangalore." April 5: Release No. 105-2011-002.

Public Company Accounting Oversight Board (PCAOB). 2013. "Report from the Working Group on Audit Quality Indicators." October.

Quadackers, L., T. Groot, and A. Wright. 2014. "Auditors' Professional Skepticism: Neutrality Versus Presumptive Doubt." *Contemporary Accounting Research* 31 (3): 639–57.

Quick, R., S. Turley, and M. Willenkens. 2008. *Auditing, Trust and Governance: Developing Regulation in Europe.* New York: Routledge.

Quick, R., and B. Warming-Rasmussen. 2009. "Auditor Independence and the Provision of Non-Audit Services: Perceptions by German Investors." *International Journal of Auditing* 13 (2): 141–62.

Rennie, M., L. Kopp, and W. Lemon. 2010. "Exploring Trust and the Auditor-Client Relationship: Factors Influencing the Auditor's Trust of a Client Representative." *Auditing: A Journal of Practice & Theory* 29 (1): 279–93.

Robinson, D. 2008. "Auditor Independence and Auditor-Provided Tax Service: Evidence from Going-Concern Audit Opinions Prior to Bankruptcy Filings." *Auditing: A Journal of Practice & Theory* 27 (2): 31–54.

Robinson, S., M. Curtis, and J. Robertson. 2018. "Disentangling the Trait and State Components of Professional Skepticism: Specifying a Process for State Scale Development." *Auditing: A Journal of Practice & Theory* 37 (1): 215–35.

Romanus, R., J. Maher, and D. Fleming. 2008. "Auditor Industry Specialization, Auditor Changes, and Accounting Restatements." *Accounting Horizons* 22 (4): 389–413.

Roussy, M. 2015. "Welcome to the Day-to-Day of Internal Auditors: How Do They Cope with Conflicts?." *Auditing: A Journal of Practice & Theory* 34 (20): 237–264.

Ruiz-Barbadillo, E., N. Gomez-Aguilar, and N. Carrera. 2009. "Does Mandatory Audit Firm Rotation Enhance Auditor Independence? Evidence from Spain." *Auditing: A Journal of Practice & Theory* 28 (1): 113–35.

Samsonova-Taddei, A., and J. Siddiqui. 2016. "Regulation and the Promotion of Audit Ethics: Analysis of the Content of the EU's Policy." *Journal of Business Ethics* 139 (1): 183–95.

Sharma, D. 2014. "Non-Audit Services and Auditor Independence." In *The Routledge Companion to Auditing,* edited by D. Hay, R. Knechel, and M. Willikens, 67–88. Oxon: Routledge.

Shaub, M., and R. Braun. 2014. "Auditing Ethics." In *The Routledge Companion to Auditing,* edited by D. Hay, R. Knechel, and M. Willekens, 264–75. Oxon: Routledge.

Sikka, P. 2009. "Financial Crisis and the Silence of the Auditors." *Accounting, Organizations and Society* 34: 868–73.

Stefaniak, C., R. Houston, and R. Cornell. 2012. "The Effects of Employer and Client Identification on Internal and External Auditors' Evaluations of Internal Control Deficiencies." *Auditing: A Journal of Practice & Theory* 31 (1): 39–56.

Suddaby, R., Y. Gendron, and H. Lam. 2009. "The Organizational Context of Professionalism in Accounting." *Accounting, Organizations and Society* 34 (3–4): 409–27.

Svanberg, J., and P. Ohman. 2015. "Auditors' Identification with Their Clients: Effects on Audit Quality." *The British Accounting Review* 47 (4): 395–408.

Svanberg, J., and P. Ohman. 2017. "Does Charismatic Client Leadership Constrain Auditor Objectivity?" *Behavioral Research in Accounting* 29 (1): 103–18.

U.S. House of Representatives. 2002. *The Sarbanes-Oxley Act of 2002.* Public Law 107-204 [H. R. 3763]. Washington, DC: Government Printing Office.

Werner, C. 2009. "Accountant Confidentiality." *The CPA Journal* 79 (6).

William, L., and W. Wilder. 2017. "Audit Firm Perspective on Audit Firm Rotation and Enhancing Independence: Evidence from PCAOB Comment Letters." *Current Issues in Auditing* 11 (1): 22–44.

Wyatt, A. 2004. "Accounting Professionalism – They Just Don't Get It!" *Accounting Horizons* 18 (1): 45–53.

Ye, P., E. Carson, and R. Simnet. 2011. "Threats to Auditor Independence: The Impact of Relationship and Economic Bonds." *Auditing: A Journal of Practice & Theory* 30 (1): 121–48.

Zeff, S. 2003a. "How the U.S. Accounting Profession Got Where It Is Today: Part I." *Accounting Horizons* 17 (3): 189–205.

Zeff, S. 2003b. "How the U.S. Accounting Profession Got Where It Is Today: Part II." *Accounting Horizons* 17 (4): 267–86.

12

PROMOTING A STRONGER ETHICAL FOCUS IN MANAGEMENT ACCOUNTING RESEARCH AND PRACTICE

Wioleta Olczak and Robin W. Roberts

Introduction and background

A theory is a system of ideas, built from general philosophical principles, created to improve our understanding of the world. Theory does not merely help to explain the world; in the social realm, theories also shape the world. Once a theory is selected, the results of research studies utilizing that theory are predictable. If the theories used to investigate management accounting are too limited in scope, management accounting can be shaped so that in practice it fails to consider ethical issues that are actually very important to individuals and society. A narrow, commonly adopted theoretical focus in managerial accounting is *shareholder theory*. Implicit in any theory about firms is a statement about the desirability of ends. Ethics is not just about consideration of permissible behavior; it is also about what the proper ends to be served by our behavior are. The end served by shareholder value theory is singularly that of the economic well-being of shareholders, which can result in management accounting ignoring the ethicality of the means by which shareholder wealth maximization may be achieved. Shareholder value theory promotes accounting and management practices that aim to maximize a company's profits, with less regard for how these practices might negatively impact employees, communities, and other stakeholders in society. When management accountants and other business professionals internalize shareholder theory as their sole criterion for developing and executing management accounting practice, it is likely that the practices developed will fail to adequately consider ethical concerns for other individuals and society. For example, under this theory, management decisions that have negative consequences for non-shareholder stakeholders and broader society are viewed as *externalities* for which a company is not held accountable. Psychologists call this way of thinking the *business case mentality* (Kouchaki et al. 2013).

In this chapter we consider how our common understanding of the nature of management accounting has been shaped by this particularly narrow view of what management accounting can be. We assess the shortcomings of such a narrow focus, particularly delving more specifically into why and how current theories and research approaches ignore important ethical issues relevant to management accounting. By doing this we hope to accomplish two goals. We hope to use academic research to help explain and illustrate (1) why ethical considerations often are not explicitly incorporated into management accounting practice and (2) how ethical considerations can help build a more inclusive view of management accounting practice.

Management accounting tends to focus on a selective group of managerial topics, with the major four topics being management control, budgetary slack, employee effort, and compensation schemes. These topics are usually examined by researchers through one of three basic research methods. Examinations are performed through the use of archival methods (quantitatively analyzing large data sets through statistical techniques), qualitative field methods (going out to individual businesses to observe and inquire about their specific practices), and experimental methods (running behavioral experiments under controlled conditions) (Hesford et al. 2006). In this chapter we discuss management accounting research that has used each of these methods; however, later in the chapter we focus on behavioral, experimental management accounting research because we think it best illustrates how management accounting practice can infuse more ethical concerns into daily practice. While we find the narrow set of managerial topics and research methodologies to be a concern, we believe that a greater concern lies in the limited number of theories used to help explain and advise management accounting practice. Most often, shareholder theory is the underlying basis for the development of research and practice, and additional psychological theories are employed to bring additional understanding to how individuals make decisions in a business or accounting setting.

Contemporary management accounting research also tends to be positivist (i.e., concerned with uncovering empirical relationships between things), focusing primarily on the relationship between management decision making (Lachmann, Trapp, and Trapp 2017) and the financial success of the organization. However, very few studies in this stream of research have thoroughly examined these topics using ethical lenses. For instance, research examines the financial benefit of improving employee effort through the utilization of different compensation schemes for the primary benefit of the organization.[1] This stream of literature, however, tends to overlook the consequences of these compensation schemes on the individual, with some of these consequences producing ethical harms for the individual employee and for individuals in broader society. For example, outcome-oriented sales incentives can implicitly encourage employees to lie about product quality or about the timing of deliverables. Furthermore, the widespread adoption of these types of management practices can undermine the general integrity of social interactions in business and society. In sum, a consistent theme in prior management accounting is its focus on understanding the financial or economic impact of management accounting techniques at the organizational (i.e., company) level, generally ignoring other critical ethical impacts at the individual or societal level. This focus does not mean that there are no ethical implications of management accounting research that could help shape practice. It just means that ethical aspects of management accounting practice are neglected when the research emphasizes economics over ethics. It is important to note, however, that ethical perspectives are studied by some highly regarded management accounting researchers who examine management accounting practices from an alternative theoretical view.

The current book chapter examines three relevant behavioral management accounting topics and assesses their ethical implications. Specifically, we achieve this goal by examining a body of behavioral management accounting research in prominent accounting journals, obtaining a sense of understanding of how different researchers approach the study of management topics. By gaining this understanding, we show that there are differences in how researchers approach behavioral management topics, driven in large part by their research paradigms (i.e., beliefs about how knowledge is created and tested) and whether their level of analysis is on the individual, organization, or broader society. These viewpoints impact how researchers examine management topics (i.e., the theoretical perspective applied and methodology used). Thus, it is essential to understand how management accounting research examines these management tools, techniques, and processes to help behavioral management accounting research and practice progress toward a stronger focus on ethics. Achieving this goal can provide insight into management accounting's future direction.

General framework for analyzing behavioral management accounting research

In order to evaluate behavioral management accounting research for the purpose of encouraging ethical viewpoints in research and practice, we address six specific questions:

1   What management accounting topics are generally being examined?
2   What research paradigms guide research as it seeks to influence practice?
3   What theories are used to help us understand managerial accounting?
4   What are researchers' viewpoints and the resulting implications of their study for management accounting practice?
5   Is there an ethical perspective used?
6   How can we make progress toward a greater emphasis on ethical issues in management accounting behavioral research?

These six questions are addressed by conducting a literature review of related accounting research and relating these studies to management accounting practice. This exploration provides evidence that management accounting research – and specifically behavioral management accounting – focuses on managerial topics fundamentally from a shareholder theory perspective. Further, we explain that this fundamental starting point in the development of management accounting research and practice limits alternative research and practice perspectives that can more directly integrate ethical considerations into management accounting decision making.

Question 1: What management topical areas are generally being examined?

Management accounting research focuses on several relevant topics including workload, independence, employee effort, time constraints, budget slack, budgets, budget participation, self-, social, and organizational controls, costing, cost allocation, balanced scorecard, and management controls. Some of these topics have consistently grown in interest (i.e., employee effort and organizational controls) while others have decreased (i.e., budget slack and balanced scorecard). Other research topics include incentive compensation schemes, employee trust, employee and manager relationships, performance measurement and evaluation, and employee and manager errors. This list is by no means exhaustive. The three commonly referred to areas in all of management accounting research are management control systems, cost accounting, and a small "other" section (Hesford et al. 2006). These three areas also represent the bulk of professional activities that constitute management accounting practice.

Management control systems

Management control system (MCS) is a term that describes one of the most broadly used concepts in management accounting. About 70% of management accounting research articles deal with accounting's role in management control (Hesford et al. 2006). Defined as a decision-aiding tool that assists managers in achieving their and their organization's goals (Chenhall 2003; Chenhall, Hall, and Smith 2010), MCS refers to an integrated approach to control design, including budgeting, organizational control, and performance measurement and evaluation. The definition of MCS has significantly evolved over time, and thus the particular aspects of managing that are considered to be components of an MCS also has changed. For example, Arnold, Hannan, and Tafkov (2018) examined how the allocation of rewards enhances employees' effort and team performance. Brüggen, Feichter, and Williamson (2018) investigated whether input and output targets improve employees' creativity and performance. Regarding budgets, Cools, Stouthuysen, and Van den Abbeele (2017) examined how budgets play different roles in an organization's creative spending. In addition to budgeting and reward systems, MCS encompasses other topics such as controls. Hesford et al. 2006 considers management control as the most explored topic in management accounting research. Over the last few decades, management control topics have seen a shift from budgeting and organizational control toward a greater emphasis on performance measurement and evaluation (Hesford et al. 2006). Performance measurement and evaluation topics include incentive contracts, contract selection, employee effort and performance, and employees' relationship with their manager.

Cost accounting

A second area that is studied by management accounting researchers is known as *cost accounting*. About 20% of all managerial accounting articles focus on cost accounting topics (Hesford et al. 2006). Cost accounting is further classified into topics such as cost allocation and cost practices. For instance, Rossing and Rohde (2010) address whether overhead cost allocation system designs in organizations are affected by transfer pricing tax regulation. However, Hesford et al. (2006) suggest that articles publishing cost accounting topics continue to decline over time. Another stream of research classifies cost as cost management. Banker et al. (2018) classify *cost management* as the costs that are caused by managers' operating decisions. They find that this specific area has grown in the past few years.

Other

The last section discussed by Hesford et al. 2006 is classified as *other* because it consists of a wider range of management accounting topics. This classification includes other areas such as, but not limited to, accounting information systems (AIS), quality management, strategic management, and benchmarking. AIS examines accounting systems by specifically analyzing computer-based systems. Strategic management accounting research examines the relationship between management control systems and organizational strategy (Hesford et al. 2006). Nixon and Burns (2012) provide evidence that strategic management accounting techniques and tools are being increasingly utilized in attempts to link management accounting practice more closely to corporate strategic goals. Only 10% of all management accounting articles publish a topic that is considered *other* (Hesford et al. 2006).

Question 2: What research paradigms guide research as it seeks to influence practice?

Management accounting researchers belong to different paradigms. A paradigm is a community of scholars who share similar sets of assumptions, concepts, beliefs, and methodologies regarding how science in their discipline should be conducted (Malmi 2010). These communities work together to assimilate knowledge about their shared interests. Management accounting researchers are trained and instructed on selecting one paradigm, but focusing exclusively on one paradigm can potentially pose obstacles for the development of both management accounting research and practice. In recent years, management accounting researchers have become concerned that doing so results in a narrow focus on research questions that are less interesting to both research and practitioner audiences (Malmi 2010; Merchant 2010).

The majority of published academic works on managerial accounting provide empirical results that are based on an economic or applied psychological perspective. These results suggest that management accounting researchers with an economics-based view tend to approach research as *positivists* (Lachmann, Trapp, and Trapp 2017). Positivist researchers believe that social order and consensus exist in the management accounting profession and more generally in society. Management accounting, from their perspective, serves management as it works to meet the demands of shareholders, consistent with shareholder theory. Lachmann, Trapp, and Trapp 2017 analyzed positivist management accounting research in the last four decades. They show that even positivist management accounting researchers' focus has substantially become narrower, employing similar methods and using similar theoretical perspectives. This narrowness in positive management accounting is especially evident between 2010 and 2012 (Lachmann, Trapp, and Trapp 2017).

As expected, positivist management accounting researchers also tend to take on a corporate or organizational-level approach. Positivist behavioral management accounting researchers apply an economics-based perspective and a functionalist approach to evaluate how management control impacts and assists the organization in achieving organizational goals such as wealth maximization, efficiency, and effectiveness.

These analyses suggest that although overall management accounting research continues to converge toward a functionalist approach, functionalist researchers are further narrowing their interests and focus on similar topics, methods, and theories. This can be concerning because if this trajectory continues, management accounting research will eventually conform and lack a healthy diversity in theoretical and methodological perspectives. Without this diversity, management accounting research might not be able to holistically understand a variety of current relevant management accounting issues, particularly those issues that are decidedly ethical ones.

Although management accounting research is continuously converging toward a functionalist, positive, and organizational approach, there is still a current smaller subset of researchers who take an alternative approach. This group, also considered positivist, examine management control systems and costs from a psychological (individual level) or sociological (societal level) perspective. Further, behavioral management accounting researchers who identify and provide potential suggestions for change are considered non-positivists. These types of researchers focus on the negative impact of management controls and cost on the individual and society. Commonly known as alternative management accounting researchers, these scholars focus, for example, on conflict resolution and improving our current management accounting system to more directly consider the interests of non-shareholder stakeholders.

Question 3: What theories are used to help us understand management accounting?

The more that management accounting practices reflect a shareholder theory purpose, the more likely it is that management accounting researchers investigate these practices through the assumptions and priorities embedded in shareholder theory, which is a primary theory arising from the functionalist, positivist paradigm. This research focuses on how well management accounting practice helps meet the company's primary objective of maximizing shareholder wealth. It works the other way around as well; practice learns from the research findings and makes requisite changes to practice. Thus, research and practice are mutually reinforcing. In answering Question 3 we discuss management accounting research with a focus on the root academic disciplines that "bring" theories to accounting; they are economics, psychology, and sociology. These root disciplines provide the foundational theories most often used to study management accounting and to influence the direction of management accounting research and practice. You probably have some intuition about how these root disciplines are positioned in management accounting research and practice. Economics is wedded to ideas of economically rational decision-making and shareholder theory of the firm. Psychology focuses on individual decision making, and its theories help us understand cognitive issues that might affect a management accountant's thinking process. Sociology looks beyond the individual or the company to help us understand the societal implications of management accounting practice. As we answer some of our later questions, we will revisit these root disciplines, especially psychology, as a way to more directly include ethical considerations in management accounting research and practice.

It is important to note that, over the last two decades, the number and types of theories used in management accounting research have decreased significantly. Management accounting articles published between 1990 and 2000 generally shifted their theoretical lenses from psychology toward economics and sociology. Specifically, in 1990 to 2000, economics provided the primary theories used in 43% of all management accounting articles. Sociology was the second commonly used theoretical source, with approximately 40% of the articles utilizing sociological theories. Psychological theories were only used 15% of the time (Hesford et al. 2006). Management accounting research focusing on management *control* topics drew heavily from psychology. In recent years, however, articles studying management *control* topics have seen a shift from psychology toward economics. Comparatively, management accounting research examining *cost* topics tend to use economics to theoretically motivate their research examination (Hesford et al. 2006), which seems appropriate.

Narrowing our focus to behavioral managerial accounting research, the theoretical lenses used tend to be either economics or psychology, with the majority of behavioral management accounting research using economics-based perspectives such as agency theory or prospect theory. For example, Wiseman and Gomez-Mejia (1998) examine managerial risk taking by building on agency theory and prospect theory. Management accounting research also uses theories from psychology and sociology. The theories drawn from these two root disciplines have promise in bringing a stronger ethical dimension to management accounting practice. Psychology theories previously used in management accounting research include moral disengagement, ethical reasoning, attribution theory, and social identity. From sociology, management accounting researchers have built on work in institutional theory, as well as writings by Bourdieu (e.g., Bourdieu 1977) and Foucault (e.g., Foucault 1980). We don't expect you to know these specific theories or theorists; we just want to introduce you to ideas that might spur further study and discussion.

Mundy (2010) uses levers of control to investigate controlling and enabling uses of management control systems. Other research applies different theoretical lenses. Bebbington, Larrinaga, and Moneva (2008) apply legitimacy theory to investigate risk management in corporate social reporting while Cooper and Owen (2007) utilize critical lenses to assess corporate accountability. However, management accounting research continues to see a decrease in the utilization of these theories, especially psychology. Additionally, there is a limited number of studies that incorporate multiple theoretical perspectives. Articles that examine organizational control tend to be interdisciplinary by incorporating both economics and sociology (Berry et al. 2009), but this is not common in management accounting research.

Although management accounting researchers rarely apply multiple theoretical perspectives, Hesford et al. (2006) show that management accounting articles applying psychology will draw from other theoretical perspectives, including economics and sociology. Hannan, Krishnan, and Newman (2008) apply both economic theory and social comparison theory to examine employees' incentive schemes and relative performance feedback. Whitener et al. (1998) draw on agency and social exchange theories to examine managers' trustworthy behavior. Articles applying a sociology or economics-based lens tend not to reference other theoretical work. Given that most management accounting research, including behavioral management accounting research, is shifting toward an economics-based approach, current and future articles are less likely to use more than one theoretical lens. This observation suggests that management accounting research might be narrowing its focus on the type of theoretical lens applied.

Table 12.1 depicts a summary of Questions 1 and 2 showing how management accounting research is classified, topics considered under each classification, theoretical perspectives and methods used, and which line of research cites other work outside of their own domain. Table 12.1 also presents a narrower view on behavioral management accounting research and whether management accounting research is expected to converge.

Question 4: What are researchers' viewpoints and the resulting implications of their study for management accounting practice?

Behavioral management accounting, with a greater emphasis on economics, tends to focus on management controls. Specifically, management accounting research with an economics-based lens typically studies whether the implementation or utilization of management controls can have a positive effect on the organization, a further illustration of the practical application of shareholder theory. This focus led research to include the examination of how management controls can be used to improve employee trust, effort, and performance for the overall benefit of the organization's profitability and efficiency. For example, Arnold, Hannan, and Tafkov (2018), using both behavioral and economics-based theories, find that communication enables the manager to allocate bonuses, which then enhances employee and team performance. Employees' performance enhancement then essentially boosts the organization's profitability and efficiency. Similarly, Brüggen, Feichter, and Williamson (2018) find that providing an input and output target improves employees' creative performance and thus improves the organization's effectiveness, because employees are able to achieve their daily responsibilities. Other research employing psychology theory also observes the positive effects on the organization. For example, Kaplan, Pope, and Samuels (2015) investigate how manager likeability affects employees' willingness to report fraud, suggesting that organizations should implement strong policies and procedures to promote this behavior. This set of literature further focuses on how management controls or cost can be used to improve the organization's overall output, including profits and reputation. We are not saying that this focus is inherently immoral or amoral. The important takeaway is that the research is intended to inform management accounting practice only on the consequences of these findings for the organization. The research fails to inform practice of any negative consequences for employees or other stakeholders. For example, an alternative research question might seek to understand how these controls add undue stress or anxiety for employees and the costs this has on family life.

Table 12.1 Summary of Management Accounting Research

Classification	Topics	Primary Theoretical Perspective	Method	Behavioral Management Accounting Research	Overall Convergence
Management Control	Controls, performance measurement and evaluation, reward systems, budgeting	Psychology, sociology, and economics	Experiments and surveys dominate psychology, while archival and analytical dominate economics-based management control research	Utilizes psychology or economics to conduct experiments	To management control, archival method, and economics-based thinking
Cost	Cost allocation and cost participation	Mostly economics	Analytical and archival dominate economics while survey, field, and case studies dominate sociology	Mixture of methods and tends to use economics, sociology, and critical perspectives	
Other	AIS, strategic management	Psychology, economics, and sociology	Mixture of all methods	Mixture of methods and tends to use economics, psychology, and critical perspectives	

We find that alternative viewpoints on management accounting bring a different focus to research and practice. There also is behavioral management accounting research with a focus on psychology or sociology that searches for different implications than those drawn from a shareholder theory lens. This stream of literature examines management controls and cost by focusing on the impact of these topics on the *individual* or *societal* level rather than the *organizational*. For example, Mölders et al. (2019) examine how employees respond when managers are trustworthy, leading to more positive emotions and reduced turnover. Another study drawing on contingency theory examines how organizations can improve employee satisfaction and boost individuals' positive attitudes (Wang and Xu 2019). Other research utilizes behavioral methods to explore how to improve societal problems such as water risk management (Burritt and Christ 2017, 2018) and improve environmental management accounting (Schaltegger 2018).

These topics focus on two sets of implications. First, behavioral management accounting research with a psychology lens examines the positive and negative effects of management controls and costs at an *individual* level. Second, behavioral accounting research with a focus on sociology provides suggestions on how to resolve *societal* problems created from the implementation of management controls and costs. Articles with a sociological lens tend to provide some understanding of how management controls and costs are harming society or the environment. These articles then provide empirical evidence to show how management accounting practice can be improved to aid society in reducing or mitigating this harm.

Question 5: Is there an ethical perspective used?

Positivist management accounting researchers utilizing an economics-based, organizational level analysis focus on the implications of management control and cost on the organization rather than the individual or society (e.g., Chen, Williamson, and Zhou 2012; Kachelmeier, Reichert, and Williamson 2008; Tian, Tuttle, and Xu 2016), and thus rarely focus on ethical implications. They have a limited view of the role of an organization as one that strictly serves the economic needs of shareholders. Positivist researchers believe that management accounting controls are de facto normative and support the current social norms of the organization, suggesting that management controls are functional and deemed necessary for the longevity of the organization. Further, a large majority of positive behavioral management accounting research shows how management control and cost can assist the organization in meeting its strategy or objective (i.e., maximization of wealth). Prior literature finds that minimizing time and providing certain employee controls can assist the organization but does not reference how these controls affect the individual employee, nor does it examine any other ethical implications of those controls. To sum, one fairly consistent theme in positivist management accounting research tends to revolve around improving or maintaining current organizational procedures and employee behavior for the primary benefit of the organization. This is achieved with minimal ethical consideration of the effects on the individual.

In comparison, management accounting research that is considered non-positivist or alternative more commonly has an ethical perspective. These researchers generally believe that knowledge is derived by examining the individual or society. For example, Bouilloud, Deslandes, and Mercier (2019) apply Foucault's (Foucault 1984) study of truth-telling to assess the ethical dimension of individuals' truth-telling. This study further assesses ethical consequences that leaders confront when they omit rather than disclose relevant information. In a second example, Milne, Tregidga, and Walton (2009) analyze how organizations can implement or improve their sustainable business processes to positively impact the natural environment. Specifically, they analyze company reports and communications by applying an interpretivist approach to evaluate how companies continue to achieve economic goals while also focusing on environmental conservation. Milne, Tregidga, and Walton (2009) analyze and recommend ethical and sustainable practices to companies. Bebbington, Larrinaga, and Moneva (2008) further conduct a single case study on Shell, an oil and gas company, to assess their risk and reputation management, finding that corporate social responsibility reporting is an integral part of risk and reputation management undertaken by companies. Overall, these articles focus on a broader sociological viewpoint and tend to assess how the implementation of managerial constraints and controls induce negative consequences on the individual or society, including decreased work quality, misreporting, decreased satisfaction, and increased stress and pressure. This stream of research also extends to the societal-level by examining the impact of an organization's behavior on the environment or society, including procedures that waste or harm the environment or reducing compensation packages for employees to cut costs. Researchers applying a sociological perspective to examine ethical implications of management controls and cost are more commonly referred in a radical or critical paradigm. Researchers in this paradigm focus on these issues

Table 12.2 Behavioral Management Accounting Researchers' Approach

Paradigm	Characteristics	Focus	Practice	Approach
Functional/ Positivist	Economic, rational, functional	Practical	Maintain status quo	Organizational level
Non-Positivist	Critical and alternative	Ethical	Progress and change	Individual- or societal-level

and provide several suggestions for improvement, including processes that could improve waste management or safeguard society's interests.

Table 12.2 shows the two types of paradigms that this chapter investigates. It is important to note that there are significantly more paradigms than the two we depict here, but given that positivist researchers dominate management accounting research, this bi-categorization assists with our discussion and understanding.

We see from our review of this literature that research sometimes seeks to understand management accounting practice from the functional theoretical perspective of shareholder theory and its supplementary perspectives, and also from alternative perspectives that question the legitimacy of a shareholder-centric view of management accounting practice. As we move to Question 6, we hope to provide avenues for management accounting research and practice to bring more focus to ethical considerations regardless of whether these practice emanate from shareholder theory or an alternative theoretical viewpoint.

Question 6: How can we make progress toward a greater emphasis on ethical issues in management accounting behavioral research?

Hesford et al. (2006) suggests that one of the concerns in management accounting research is that researchers become rooted in one paradigm without consideration or evaluation of research published by other paradigms. Hesford et al. (2006) further suggest that researchers' approaches are different based on the type of journal in which they publish. Researchers establish their network through their association with other researchers and these journals, all of which often work within different paradigms. Although working across networks and undertaking research that is relevant to multiple audiences can be challenging and risky, attempts to broaden the scope of managerial accounting behavioral research can enrich our collective understanding of practice.

Potential suggestions for the improvement of ethical considerations in behavioral management accounting research include (1) referencing external work and targeting multiple audiences and (2) examining management accounting practices by including individual, organizational, and societal concerns.

Reference external work and target multiple audiences

Prior research has shown that accounting research tends to lie in its own "hub." Researchers targeting a specific journal are more likely to cite other publications within that journal. Additionally, researchers also have a tendency to cite other researchers that are associated with that specific journal. This establishes a concept known as a "hub." Researchers in a hub are less likely to cite work that is outside their hub. When this happens, research can only have a self-perpetuating influence on practice, and practice can only serve to feed research with the same types of research questions.

We believe that management accounting plays a service role in organizations. It serves to provide information to management regarding performance and strategic directions. As such, we think management accounting research and practice can benefit from the lessons learned by management researchers and practitioners. Treviño, Weaver, and Reynolds (2006) state that the current management field requires researchers to focus on new uninvestigated topics, theory development, methodological rigor, and practical significance. Two ways to accomplish this goal are by referencing external work and targeting multiple audiences. However, researchers are trained to write toward a very specific type of audience. Mainly, accounting researchers cluster to other individuals whose topical interests, methodology, or theoretical perspectives align, creating a potential problem as these clusters of researchers are only targeting each other rather than the whole accounting community. Bonner et al. (2012) note that several notable accounting researchers communicate and shift between hubs. Thus, while moving beyond the comfort of one's hub is difficult, it can be done. Bonner et al. (2012) further suggests that accounting researchers should attempt to cite other researchers' work who are not within their hub and thus target multiple audiences and reference external work.

Bromwich and Scapens (2016) observe that there is a lack of communication between management accounting researchers, especially when their research arises from two different methodologies. Specifically, they suggest that qualitative research could be useful in informing quantitative studies and vice versa. Bonner et al. (2012) find that accounting research tends to focus on their own hub's research topic. For example, positivist management accounting research (e.g., Arnold, Hannan, and Tafkov 2018; Chen, Williamson, and Zhou 2012; Kachelmeier, Reichert, and Williamson 2008) explores how organizational controls can be used to improve employee behavior while other management research examines how organizational controls can be used to improve individual's ethical decision-making, judgment, attitudes, and behavior (e.g., Hörisch, Freeman, and Schaltegger 2014; Johnson and Schaltegger 2016; Schaltegger 2018; Zapata-Sierra and Manzano 2017; Zhou et al. 2018). Referencing external work that is not within one's hub can create potential benefits for management accounting research and practice. For example, Parker (2012) states that qualitative management accounting could assist quantitative research because it provides insights into accounting processes and practices at the organizational level, which positivist quantitative research is primarily based upon. Qualitative research also provides multiple perspectives through the utilization of non-positivist theoretical perspectives (Parker 2012).

By building a research study on a broader set of underlying work, management accounting researchers could collectively provide a more cohesive and holistic view of management control and accountability (Merchant and Otley 2007). Referencing multiple journals and authors can bring researchers from different backgrounds together, bringing other skills, knowledge, and solutions than those from one hub. Behavioral management accounting research might be best helped by leveraging experimental work originating from the organizational behavior literature. Several ethics-related organizational behavior topics can be adapted to focus on accounting aspects of ethical decision making. For example, work in organizational behavior and applied psychology can and should be incorporated more directly into mainstream behavioral accounting research, as they speak directly to issues of situational moral disengagement (Kish-Gephart et al. 2014), the role of employee emotions such as fear in ethical decision making (Kish-Gephart et al. 2009), and managerial leadership influence on employee productivity (Detert et al. 2007). Management accounting practice can use the findings from this type of research to develop MCS and AIS that integrate ethical considerations. For example, prior research has shown that unexpected prompts embedded in computer interface can trigger employees to incorporate ethical considerations into their decision making.

Examination at multiple levels

Management accounting research overall is considered to be mainly positivist, organizational-level based, economics-based, and archival in method. This homogeneity leads to a narrow view of research that might not contribute to overall knowledge (Lukka 2010). Although there are benefits of a homogenous paradigm because researchers will have similar interests and knowledge, there is some concern that researchers' contribution to research and practice will be marginal (Lukka 2010).

Given that positivists use an organizational-level approach, the set of research questions that can be examined can be limited and irrelevant because management accounting issues require analysis at the individual and societal level. Additionally, these researchers use archival methods as well as behavioral methods such as experiments and surveys, but they rarely examine a topic with multiple methods. For instance, Merchant and Otley (2007) suggest that using only one level, whether methodological or theoretical, can limit the types of research questions posed and addressed. This is especially concerning when researchers continue to use the same theoretical perspective or method, as is the case for mainstream accounting (Lukka 2010). This potentially results in research that is not intellectually stimulating and fairly conservative.

By examining a research topic through multiple levels, whether theoretical, methodological, or organizational-, individual-, or societal-level, researchers can undertake innovative research that contributes to developing a more holistic understanding of managerial accounting practice. Conducting research through multiple levels can shed light on the ethical consequences and implications of management accounting research. Behavioral managerial accounting research can take cues from multilevel work on management that examines individual, group, and organizational responses to ethical dilemmas through the nesting of research questions dealing with ethical issues that permeate each level, such as the work by Spell and Arnold (2007) dealing with organizational justice and mental health. This research can help inform management accounting practice of psychological issues faced by lower-level managers and other employees, especially when budgets are overly tight or performance standards unreasonably high.

Sample research that references external work, targets multiple audiences, or examines work at multiple levels

In addition to the management research highlighted earlier, there are several management accounting works that reference external work outside of their own hub or analyze research using multiple levels, whether methodologically or theoretically. Weik (2019) references external work to advance theoretical and conceptual knowledge of organizations by advancing knowledge from rational and cognitive thinking to affective processing. Other research has embodied these suggestions to explore an ethical component. For example, Ditillo and Lisi (2016) explore mainstream management control through an ethical lens, specifically addressing how management control relates to sustainability. Ditillo and Lisi (2016) explore this topic through the utilization of a multiple case design that is further supplemented by empirical data such as archival documents, observations, and interviews. This multidimensional analysis provides researchers the ability to holistically explore sustainable management control systems.

Theoretically, Whitener et al. (1998) use economics, psychology, and sociology to examine management accounting. Specifically, they apply agency theory and social exchange theories to examine how organizational and individual factors affect manager's trustworthy behavior and judgment. Our main point is that the type of research topics and methods we advocate to help bring ethical considerations into behavioral management accounting research and practice has been done to a modest extent, and therefore is perhaps worthy of serious attention.

Exemplars of behavioral management accounting research promoting an ethics-based focus

Considering the concerns addressed in this chapter, we now outline two potential behavioral management accounting studies that embody an ethics-based focus. The purpose of these outlines is only to demonstrate the possible first step in more fully developing a research study that includes an ethical dimension. We believe that studies such as the ones outlined here speak to ethical issues in management accounting practice and, if executed, can promote a stronger ethical focus in management accounting. We hope these two outlines provide some help as you think about research projects you undertake in your program of study.

1   Research Question: Does providing employees the freedom to customize and select their compensation contract impact their overall job satisfaction and morale?

    a   Paradigm: Functionalist and interpretivist
    b   Viewpoint: Individual
    c   Potential Theoretical Perspectives: Moral Engagement, Reciprocity, Employee Morale
    d   Methodology: Multilevel

        i   Survey a population to assess the type of compensation contracts that impact their job satisfaction
        ii   Natural experiment in a service industry to understand how employees respond to the different types of compensation contracts surveyed in the previous population

    e   Ethics: Understand how management control systems can be designed to cater to each individual employee as the workforce continues to diversify in needs and wants
    f   Implication: Exploratory and confirmatory study to understand how to boost individual job satisfaction for the sole purpose of establishing employee morale

2   Research Question: Can oil and gas companies implement sustainable processes to minimize their ecological footprint, and how will society perceive this initiative?

    a   Paradigm: Critical
    b   Viewpoint: Societal and organizational
    c   Potential Theoretical Perspectives: Implicit Bias, Pro-Environmental Citizenry, Behavioral Change Model
    d   Methodology: Multilevel

        i   Assess a sample of oil and gas industry companies' current processes and evaluate the cost and benefit of implementing sustainable practices (i.e., cost to the business and benefit to society and the environment through reduction of pollution)
        ii   Interview oil and gas companies to understand their perspective on implementing more sustainable practices

iii   Supplement by running an experiment that asks the general population their opinion of an oil and gas company that implements sustainable practices, incurring a greater cost to ensure the environment and society benefit through reduced pollution

e   Ethics: Understand whether the population would still have implicit bias against oil and gas companies or whether their perception would change

i   Understand how much cost a company would incur for the sake of improving and maintaining a healthy environment

f   Implication: This study explores whether companies with a negative environmental reputation can remove societal implicit bias by implementing sustainable practices. Would committing a corporate social good improve companies' negative environmental reputation? Companies might not change because they believe that even after doing a social good, individuals are predisposed to negative perceptions of an oil and gas company.

Conclusions and closing remarks

The purpose of this chapter is to briefly review the major topics typically investigated in the management accounting research community and to encourage a stronger research emphasis on the ethical aspects of management accounting practice. In order to accomplish our stated purpose, we organize our chapter around six questions, sequentially laying out the basic status of the inclusion of ethics in management accounting research, the fundamental reasons that might be responsible for an underrepresentation of ethics focus in the area, and possible avenues for progress in management accounting. While we discuss the general state of this overall stream of research, we focus our commentary on behavioral, particularly experimental, management accounting research. This focus is adopted because we believe behavioral management accounting research dictates how management accounting is practiced and advanced.

In answering our chapter's questions, we observed two fundamental aspects of management accounting research critical in understanding how to improve the inclusion of ethics in behavioral management accounting. First, we see that researchers' choice of paradigm plays a significant role in how management accounting research in general – and behavioral work in particular – is oriented. The bulk of management accounting research assumes a positivist, functional perspective that focuses on how management practices, such as management controls, budgeting, and incentive compensation, can best work for the organization's immediate financial benefit. While this functional, shareholder theory perspective might seem obvious to some, by adopting this rather strict economic perspective that focuses on investor returns, management accounting relegates other stakeholder concerns (e.g., employee well-being, questionable business practices that negatively affect customers or the natural environment, paying a fair share of taxes that impacts government services) to the trivial shadows. We find that a research paradigm's assumptions underlying the different strands of management accounting research creates a schism within this whole body of work and denies ethics its rightful place in management accounting practice.

Both management accounting research and practice seem to perpetuate a business case mentality. Although a positivist, functionalist stance dominates the field, some prominent management accounting scholars, primarily based in Europe, anchor their research in interpretivist or critical research paradigms that challenge a functionalist focus. Often grounded in social theory, this stream of qualitative work often decenters the organization from the analysis, engaging in analyses of broader issues of social justice and the general integrity of social interactions, bringing broader social issues into prominent light. We believe this stream of qualitative behavioral research can be leveraged to propel behavioral management accounting scholars who conduct psychological experiments to develop and investigate important research questions that include a stronger ethical focus. This revised focus can then be translated into changes in management accounting practice.

Second, although we encourage behavioral management accounting researchers to conceive of their research questions more broadly by enlisting the aid of interpretivist and critical paradigms, we also believe that experimental management accounting researchers can investigate substantive ethical questions while staying within a functionalist paradigm. Although we notice early work that utilized industrial/organizational psychology theories of employee motivation and satisfaction, this use has dwindled, giving way to stricter economic-based theoretical bases. Researchers' overwhelming fixation with the strict organizational economic consequences of management accounting practices often blinds them from questioning the ethicality of the practices being studied. Management accounting practices have significant economic, social, and environmental consequences for broad sets of stakeholders. While issues of fairness, justice, and equity are deeply entrenched in the experimental organizational behavior literature, they are scarcely mentioned in experimental management accounting research. This lack of interest is puzzling given that accounting practices often ultimately govern the implementation of management practices designed to promote fairness, justice, and equity (or the lack thereof). Thus, we encourage a revitalization of experimental management accounting research that incorporates the ethical concerns studied in the organizational behavior literature. This management literature adopts a positivist, functional perspective yet deals straight on with issues of fairness, justice, and equity. In sum, management accounting practices based in shareholder theory can benefit from a more enlightened perspective on the consequences of the business case mentality and on the role that ethics can play in the long-term success of any company.

It is often repeated that integrity is the cornerstone of the accounting profession. Yet ethical issues seldom, if ever, seem to rise to the forefront of behavioral, experimental management accounting research. Through the analyses and reflections presented in this chapter, we hope to spark a renewed interest in ethics in management accounting.

Note

1 The economist Thomas Piketty (Piketty 2014) attributes the radical concentration of income and wealth in the United States that has occurred over the past three decades to the compensation schemes adopted by corporations to reward their top executives. This vividly illustrates the performative nature of the theories we adopt to shape the social world.

References

Arnold, M. C., R. L. Hannan, and I. D. Tafkov. 2018. "Team Member Subjective Communication in Homogeneous and Heterogeneous Teams." *The Accounting Review* 93 (5): 1–22. https://doi.org/10.2308/accr-52002.

Banker, R. D., D. Byzalov, S. Fang, and Y. Liang. 2018. "Cost Management Research." *Journal of Management Accounting Research* 30 (3): 187–209. https://doi.org/10.2308/jmar-51965.

Bebbington, J., C. Larrinaga, and J. M. Moneva. 2008. "Corporate Social Reporting and Reputation Risk Management." *Accounting, Auditing & Accountability Journal* 21 (3): 337–61. https://doi.org/10.1108/09513570810863932.

Berry, A. J., A. F. Coad, E. P. Harris, D. T. Otley, and C. Stringer. 2009. "Emerging Themes in Management Control: A Review of Recent Literature." *The British Accounting Review* 41 (1): 2–20. https://doi.org/10.1016/j.bar.2008.09.001.

Bonner, S. E., J. W. Hesford, W. A. Van der Stede, and S. M. Young. 2012. "The Social Structure of Communication in Major Accounting Research Journals." *Contemporary Accounting Research* 29 (3): 869–909. https://doi.org/10.1111/j.1911-3846.2011.01134.x.

Bouilloud, J. P., G. Deslandes, and G. Mercier. 2019. "The Leader as Chief Truth Officer: The Ethical Responsibility of 'Managing the Truth' in Organizations." *Journal of Business Ethics* 157 (1): 1–13. https://doi.org/10.1007/s10551-017-3678-0.

Bourdieu, P. 1977. *Outline of a Theory of Practice*. Cambridge: Cambridge University Press.

Bromwich, M., and R. W. Scapens. 2016. "Management Accounting Research: 25 Years on." *Management Accounting Research* 31: 1–9. https://doi.org/10.1016/j.mar.2016.03.002

Brüggen, A., C. Feichter, and M. G. Williamson. 2018. "The Effect of Input and Output Targets for Routine Tasks on Creative Task Performance." *The Accounting Review* 93 (1): 29–43. https://doi.org/10.2308/accr-51781

Burritt, R. L., and K. L. Christ. 2017. "The Need for Monetary Information Within Corporate Water Accounting." *Journal of Environmental Management* 201: 72–81. https://doi.org/10.1016/j.jenvman.2017.06.035

Burritt, R. L., and K. L. Christ. 2018. "Water Risk in Mining: Analysis of the Samarco Dam Failure." *Journal of Cleaner Production* 178: 196–205. https://doi.org/10.1016/j.jclepro.2018.01.042

Chen, C. X., M. G. Williamson, and F. H. Zhou. 2012. "Reward System Design and Group Creativity: An Experimental Investigation." *The Accounting Review* 87 (6): 1885–911. https://doi.org/10.2308/accr-50232.

Chenhall, R. H. 2003. "Management Control Systems Design Within Its Organizational Context: Findings from Contingency-Based Research and Directions for the Future." *Accounting, Organizations and Society* 28 (2–3): 127–68. https://doi.org/10.1016/s0361-3682(01)00027-7.

Chenhall, R. H., M. Hall, and D. Smith. 2010. "Social Capital and Management Control Systems: A Study of a Non-Government Organization." *Accounting, Organizations and Society* 35 (8): 737–56. https://doi.org/10.1016/j.aos.2010.09.006

Cools, M., K. Stouthuysen, and A. Van den Abbeele. 2017. "Management Control for Stimulating Different Types of Creativity: The Role of Budgets." *Journal of Management Accounting Research* 29 (3): 1–21. https://doi.org/10.2308/jmar-51789.

Cooper, S. M., and D. L. Owen. 2007. "Corporate Social Reporting and Stakeholder Accountability: The Missing Link." *Accounting, Organizations and Society* 32 (7–8): 649–67. https://doi.org/10.1016/j.aos.2007.02.001.

Detert, J. R., L. K. Trevino, E. R. Burris, and M. Andiappan. 2007. "Managerial Modes of Influence and Counterproductivity in Organizations: A Longitudinal Business-Unit-Level Investigation." *Journal of Applied Psychology* 92 (4): 993. https://doi.org/10.1037/0021-9010.93.2.328

Ditillo, A., and I. E. Lisi. 2016. "Exploring Sustainability Control Systems' Integration: The Relevance of Sustainability Orientation." *Journal of Management Accounting Research* 28 (2): 125–48. https://doi.org/10.2308/jmar-51469

Foucault, M. 1980. *Power Knowledge*. Brighton: Harvester Press.

Foucault, M. 1984. "L'éthique du souci de soi comme pratique de liberté." *Concordia: Revue Internationale de Philosophie Paris* 6: 99–116.

Hannan, R. L., R. Krishnan, and A. H. Newman. 2008. "The Effects of Disseminating Relative Performance Feedback in Tournament and Individual Performance Compensation Plans." *The Accounting Review* 83 (4): 893–913. https://doi.org/10.2308/accr.2008.83.4.893.

Hesford, J. W., S. H. S. Lee, W. A. Van der Stede, and S. M. Young. 2006. "Management Accounting: A Bibliographic Study." *Handbooks of Management Accounting Research* 1: 3–26. https://doi.org/10.1016/s1751-3243(06)01001-7.

Hörisch, J., R. E. Freeman, and S. Schaltegger. 2014. "Applying Stakeholder Theory in Sustainability Management: Links, Similarities, Dissimilarities, and a Conceptual Framework." *Organization & Environment* 27 (4): 328–46. https://doi.org/10.1177/1086026614535786.

Johnson, M. P., and S. Schaltegger. 2016. "Two Decades of Sustainability Management Tools for SMEs: How Far Have We Come?" *Journal of Small Business Management* 54 (2): 481–505. https://doi.org/10.1111/jsbm.12154

Kachelmeier, S. J., B. E. Reichert, and M. G. Williamson. 2008. "Measuring and Motivating Quantity, Creativity, or Both." *Journal of Accounting Research* 46 (2): 341–73. https://doi.org/10.2139/ssrn.1003414.

Kaplan, S. E., K. R. Pope, and J. A. Samuels. 2015. "An Examination of the Effects of Managerial Procedural Safeguards, Managerial Likeability, and Type of Fraudulent Act on Intentions to Report Fraud to a Manager." *Behavioral Research in Accounting* 27 (2): 77–94. https://doi.org/10.2308/bria-51126.

Kish-Gephart, J., J. Detert, L. K. Treviño, V. Baker, and S. Martin. 2014. "Situational Moral Disengagement: Can the Effects of Self-Interest Be Mitigated?" *Journal of Business Ethics* 125 (2): 267–85. https://doi.org/10.1007/s10551-013-1909-6.

Kish-Gephart, J. J., J. R. Detert, L. K. Treviño, and A. C. Edmondson. 2009. "Silenced by Fear: The Nature, Sources, and Consequences of Fear at Work." *Research in Organizational Behavior* 29: 163–93. https://doi.org/10.1016/j.riob.2009.07.002.

Kouchaki, M., K. Smith-Crowe, A. P. Brief, and C. Sousa. 2013. "Seeing Green: Mere Exposure to Money Triggers a Business Decision Frame and Unethical Outcomes." *Organizational Behavior and Human Decision Processes* 121 (1): 53–61. https://doi.org/10.1016/j.obhdp.2012.12.002.

Lachmann, M., I. Trapp, and R. Trapp. 2017. "Diversity and Validity in Positivist Management Accounting Research – A Longitudinal Perspective Over Four Decades." *Management Accounting Research* 34: 42–58. https://doi.org/10.1016/j.mar.2016.07.002.

Lukka, K. 2010. "The Roles and Effects of Paradigms in Accounting Research." *Management Accounting Research* 21 (2): 110–15. https://doi.org/10.1016/j.mar.2010.02.002.

Malmi, T. 2010. "Reflections on Paradigms in Action in Accounting Research." *Management Accounting Research* 21 (2): 121–23. https://doi.org/10.1016/j.mar.2010.02.003.

Merchant, K. A. 2010. "Paradigms in Accounting Research: A View from North America." *Management Accounting Research* 21 (2): 116–20. https://doi.org/10.1016/j.mar.2010.02.004.

Merchant, K. A., and D. T. Otley. 2007. A Review of the Literature on Control and Accountability. *Handbook of Management Accounting Research*: 785–804. https://doi.org/10.1016/s1751-3243(06)02013-x

Milne, M. J., H. Tregidga, and S. Walton. 2009. "Words Not Actions! The Ideological Role of Sustainable Development Reporting." *Accounting, Auditing & Accountability Journal* 22 (8): 1211–57. https://doi.org/10.1108/09513570910999292.

Mölders, S., P. Brosi, M. Spörrle, and I. M. Welpe.2019. "The Effect of Top Management Trustworthiness on Turnover Intentions Via Negative Emotions: The Moderating Role of Gender." *Journal of Business Ethics* 156 (4): 957–69. https://doi.org/10.1007/s10551-017-3600-9.

Mundy, J. 2010. "Creating Dynamic Tensions Through a Balanced Use of Management Control Systems." *Accounting, Organizations and Society* 35 (5): 499–523. https://doi.org/10.1016/j.aos.2009.10.005.

Nixon, B., and J. Burns. 2012. "The Paradox of Strategic Management Accounting." *Management Accounting Research* 23 (4): 229–44. https://doi.org/10.1016/j.mar.2012.09.004.

Parker, L. D. 2012. "Beyond the Ticket and the Brand: Imagining an Accounting Research Future." *Accounting & Finance* 52 (4): 1153–82. https://doi.org/10.1111/j.1467-629x.2012.00507.x.

Piketty, T. 2014. *Capital in the 21st Century*. Cambridge, MA: Harvard University Press.

Rossing, C. P., and C. Rohde. 2010. "Overhead Cost Allocation Changes in a Transfer Pricing Tax Compliant Multinational Enterprise." *Management Accounting Research* 21 (3): 199–216. https://doi.org/10.1016/j.mar.2010.01.002.

Schaltegger, S. 2018. "Linking Environmental Management Accounting: A Reflection on (Missing) Links to Sustainability and Planetary Boundaries." *Social and Environmental Accountability Journal* 38 (1): 19–29. https://doi.org/10.1080/0969160x.2017.1395351.

Spell, C. S., and T. J. Arnold. 2007. "A Multi-Level Analysis of Organizational Justice Climate, Structure, and Employee Mental Health." *Journal of Management* 33 (5): 724–51. https://doi.org/10.1177/0149206307305560.

Tian, Y., B. M. Tuttle, and Y. Xu. 2016. "Using Incentives to Overcome the Negative Effects of Faultline Conflict on Individual Effort." *Behavioral Research in Accounting* 28 (1): 67–81. https://doi.org/10.2308/bria-51147.

Treviño, L. K., G. R. Weaver, and S. J. Reynolds. 2006. "Behavioral Ethics in Organizations: A Review." *Journal of Management* 32 (6): 951–90. https://doi.org/10.1177/0149206306294258.

Wang, Z., and H. Xu. 2019. "When and for Whom Ethical Leadership Is More Effective in Eliciting Work Meaningfulness and Positive Attitudes: The Moderating Roles of Core Self-Evaluation and Perceived Organizational Support." *Journal of Business Ethics* 156 (4): 919–40. https://doi.org/10.1007/s10551-017-3563-x.

Weik, E. 2019. "Understanding Institutional Endurance: The Role of Dynamic Form, Harmony, and Rhythm in Institutions." *Academy of Management Review* 44 (2): 321–35. https://doi.org/10.5465/amr.2015.0050

Whitener, E. M., S. E. Brodt, M. A. Korsgaard, and J. M. Werner. 1998. "Managers as Initiators of Trust: An Exchange Relationship Framework for Understanding Managerial Trustworthy Behavior." *Academy of Management Review* 23 (3): 513–30. https://doi.org/10.2307/259292.

Wiseman, R. M., and L. R. Gomez-Mejia. 1998. "A Behavioral Agency Model of Managerial Risk Taking." *Academy of Management Review* 23 (1): 133–53. https://doi.org/10.5465/amr.1998.192967.

Zapata-Sierra, A. J., and F. Manzano-Agugliaro. 2017. "Controlled Deficit Irrigation for Orange Trees in Mediterranean Countries." *Journal of Cleaner Production* 162: 130–40. https://doi.org/10.1016/j.jclepro.2017.05.208.

Zhou, Z., L. Liu, H. Zeng, and X. Chen. 2018. "Does Water Disclosure Cause a Rise in Corporate Risk-Taking? – Evidence from Chinese High Water-Risk Industries." *Journal of Cleaner Production* 195: 1313–25. https://doi.org/10.1016/j.jclepro.2018.06.001.

13

DEVELOPMENT AND ANALYSIS OF THREE SUSTAINABILITY INITIATIVES

Robert Bloom

Background

Justification for sustainability reporting pertains to "stakeholder theory," which asserts that the management of corporations should consider the interests and concerns of its diverse stakeholders, including any individual or entity that affects or is affected by the corporation's actions (Corplaw 2013). The stakeholders consider employees, community, consumer groups, and government in their actions and performance. Put differently, corporations ought to be responsible to society, not just to their shareholders and investors (Carroll 1991; Freeman 1984, 1994). That mission should be pursued even if profits decline as a result. In the long run, advocates of stakeholder theory argue that the corporation will perform better by adhering to this theory, which keeps the diverse interests of its stakeholders into account. The employees will be more productive, and consumers will be more inclined to purchase the corporation's products and services. Advocates of this theory contend that corporations today cannot afford to focus on their shareholders at the expense of their other stakeholders (Laplume et al. 2008).

Stakeholder theory contrasts diametrically with "shareholder theory," which asserts that companies are primarily responsible to their shareholders while pursuing their performance in a legal and ethical manner (Friedman 1970; Lantos 2001). Endorsed by the late Chicago conservative economist Milton Friedman, this theory has also been further formulated by Rochester economists Michael Jensen and William Meckling (1976). Jensen and Meckling, in particular, view shareholders as "principals" and managers as their "agents." Managers should be engaged in maximizing shareholder wealth, and if they are not doing that, they are incurring unnecessary agency costs and lowering social welfare. However, some might attribute the accounting scandals of the early 2000s and the financial crisis in 2008–10 to an emphasis on shareholder theory. Furthermore, it might be said that there is no specific fiduciary requirement in corporate law indicating that corporate managers are required to maximize shareholder wealth (Foroohar 2016).

Savitz has chronicled the ever-changing role of American corporations in the sustainability realm (2013). In the 1950s, business was expected to be overwhelmingly profitable, if not to maximize shareholder wealth, and as far as sustainability goes, to provide at least some residual funds for charity. The role of business changed in the 1960s, when President John Kennedy in his inauguration speech said: "Ask not what your country can do for you, but what you can do for your country" (John F. Kennedy's Inaugural Address, January 20, 1961). The Peace Corps was created in his administration to send Americans to aid in construction projects and education in less-developed countries. Rachel Carson wrote an expose in *Silent Spring* (1962), which found ordinary household chemicals such as DDT harmful to humans, birds, and the environment. In 1969, the Environmental Protection Administration was created, combining several agencies in the process. Ralph Nader (1965) became the first consumer advocate, denouncing General Motors' (GM) Chevrolet Corvair as hazardous to drive (*Unsafe at Any Speed*). By the 1970s, corporate responsibility expanded to include safe products and environmental protection. What is good for GM is not necessarily good for the country – then or now (witness the planned layoffs and factory closings today). In the last 50 years, there has been a significant shift away from government to business responsibility on so many fronts. There are far greater expectations today from corporations in terms of the following: promoting diversity, fostering human rights, maintaining safe working conditions, producing safe products, ensuring privacy, protecting the public, and protecting the environment. Indeed, organizations, whether they are business or not-for-profit, are accountable today not just for their own sustainability actions or inactions, but of those pertaining to their entire supply chain of entities.

Financial reporting standards do not deal explicitly with sustainability matters, omitting a significant facet of each company's overall performance. (The AICPA's 1973 Trueblood Report, 53–55, the precursor to the FASB's objectives of financial reporting, actually stipulated a sustainability objective, but it was never acted upon in standard setting.) Additionally, existing standards present short shrift to corporate intangible assets, such as brands and reputation, research and development, and human resources, which undoubtedly account for a significant aspect of the firm's activities, growth, and valuation. Without generally accepted sustainability standards, companies are free to disclose what they desire in this realm, and they do just that, often omitting their negative actions and using the disclosures for public relations purposes. Below is an overview of the social stewardship objective in historical accounting literature, authoritative and non-authoritative, followed by a discussion of each of three models, all intended to improve such disclosures and to facilitate comparability among companies – the General Reporting Initiative (GRI) now and for 2025, the Sustainability Accounting Standards Board (SASB) industry standards, and the Feng/Gu model.

Social stewardship in historical accounting literature

A social objective of accounting has developed over the years, starting in the early 1900s, and has become more visible, if not much more specific, over time. This section of the chapter will explore this subject in official pronouncements of standard-setting bodies and the accounting literature at large. Canning clearly envisioned a social objective in his celebrated 1929 book, *The Economics of Accountancy*. DR Scott, writing in the 1940s, is widely attributed to having advanced such an objective. Paton and Littleton in their influential book on accounting theory also described the role of accounting in a social responsibility vein. Spacek at Arthur Andersen emphasized the importance of fairness to all stakeholders in financial reporting. In more recent years, social stewardship is evident in ASOBAT (1966), APB Statement No. 4 (1970), and especially in the AICPA's Trueblood Report (1973). The latter actually established a separate social objective of financial reporting. The FASB's conceptual framework followed suit, unfortunately with a vaguer objective. Early social reporting models have been advanced in the 1960s and 1970s by Linowes, who was a practitioner, and Abt Associates, a Boston consulting firm. Around the same time frame, human resource accounting models have been proposed by Lev (2015) and Schwartz and Flamholtz as well as R.G. Barry, an Ohio company. More specific observations from those writngs follow.

Scott (1941, 342–43) observes:

> Accounting rules, procedures and techniques must be continuously revised to allow for changing economic conditions in order that they may continue to embody the principles of justice, fitness, and truth.

Paton and Littleton ([1941] 1962, 3) point out that:

> The social importance of accounting . . . is clear, especially in relation to income statements, since dependable information about earnings power can be an important aid to the flow of capital into capable hands and away from unneeded industries.

Accounting Research Study 1 notes (1961, 28):

> As social and economic conditions change, the aspects that ought to be stressed in published financial statements can change without necessarily altering the kinds of underlying data that are accumulated.

ASOBAT (1966, 5) says that:

> Accounting makes possible efficiency in the acquisition, maintenance and use of the resources. . . . In addition, accounting . . . provides the major means of appraising the effectiveness with individuals and groups perform their assignment.

That represents a social role for accounting, providing information to help achieve the target objective – effectiveness – and also to be productive and cut down on waste.

Spacek may have been influenced by Scott in the following (1962, 5–6):

> I firmly felt that accounting principles should be based upon a principle of accounting that was fair to the consumer, to labor, to management, to the Investor and to the public. Now, to the public, so the public would know that no one is lying.

Rooted in Scott and Spacek, APB Statement 4 (1970, 225) asserts:

> The qualitative objectives are related to the broad ethical goals of truth, justice, and fairness that are accepted as desirable goals by society as a whole.

The Trueblood Report (AICPA 1973, 66) sets forth the social objective of financial reporting:

> An objective of financial statements is to report on those activities of the enterprise affecting society which can be determined and described or measured and which are important to the role of the enterprise in its social environment.

Yet SFAC No. 1 (1978, vii), the de facto successor to the Trueblood Report, offers a vague substitute for social accountability:

> The objectives of financial reporting are not immutable – they are affected by the economic, legal, political, and social environment in which financial reporting takes place.

Ramanathan (1976, 519), who has written on developing a theory of social accounting, defines such accounting:

> The process of selecting firm-level social performance variables, measures, and measurement procedures; systematically developing information useful for evaluating the firm's social performance; and communicating such information to concerned social groups, both within and outside the firm.

As for attempts to develop social accounting statements, Linowes (1971) proposed what he called a "socioeconomic operating statement that would contain information on the firm's costs incurred to produce improvements" for employees, the environment, and product safety. Additionally, this statement provided "detriments" based on costs that might have been incurred in each of those three areas for specific items. This statement was strictly cost-based without attempting to evaluate the benefits monetarily, which could be multiplier effects of the costs considered.

In other attempts to operationalize social accounting statements, Abt Associates, a Boston-based consulting firm, experimented with social balance sheets and income statements, including social costs and benefits to employees, the local community, and the public at large. The social assets encompassed human resource training, equipment, and buildings. The social liabilities pertained to non-socially productive contracts and environmental pollution. The social income benefits included company-paid health insurance and tuition reimbursement. The social costs were exemplified by employee overtime not paid by the company (Hedge, Bloom, and Fuglister 1997, 167–69).

On the subject of putting human resources on the balance sheet, Lev and Schwartz (1971) developed a model based on individual earnings as a proxy for economic value, using discounted cash flows and assuming the employees would remain at the same organization until retirement. Flamholtz (1985) refined that model without making that assumption, using probabilities to deal with mobility and separation of employees. R.G. Barry, a Columbus, Ohio, footwear company, experimented in the early 1970s with capitalizing human resource training and acquisition costs on a pro forma balance sheet, even to the point of showing deferred tax liabilities to reflect a timing difference between the accounting and tax treatment of those costs (Hegde, Bloom, and Fuglister 1997, 170–71).

There has been a gap in the accounting literature on corporate social responsibility from the late 1990s until the last few years. Writers and researchers have experienced difficulty trying to find publications willing to accept their pieces on this subject. One reason was the dominance in academic journals on database research using efficient market theory to a great extent, only recently superseded by agency theory. The emphasis on corporate profit maximization by Friedman and Jensen and Meckling has not helped to advance meaningful corporate social accountability as opposed to greenwashing in the corporate sector. Our American myopic cultural accent on short-run gratification – do not worry about the distant future – has not helped. After all, as the thinking goes, the free market forces à la Adam Smith will take care and direct what our economy and society really need. Congress has been as dysfunctional as a law-making body can be. It cannot get anything done, by and large, apart from the catastrophic coronavirus legislation. The Democrats and Republicans argue over everything, reflecting ideological and philosophical schisms on almost all issues, not just the key sustainability controversies underlying climate change and health care. Democrats favor regulation, Republicans laissez-faire. Individuals elected to Congress depend on large corporations for fundraising to secure reelection, so that Congress has to cater to a large degree to those interests and their ever-present lobbyists. Accordingly, major corporations in this country wield enormous influence (Lessig 2011). The Trump administration has just relaxed auto emissions standards nationwide. Automakers are uncertain about how to deal with this directive inasmuch as some states, most notably California, have enacted strict emission regulations.

GRI

The GRI, which began in 1997, is a private, nonprofit organization that provides guidelines for disclosure on sustainability issues for business and other organizations, including NGOs and trade associations. The GRI guidelines are based on the 17 sustainable development goals of the United Nations. For each goal, very much aspirational rather than readily attainable, there are targets or subgoals to pursue, and for each target there are indicators to promote concrete data collection and comparison over time. The goals tend to interrelate rather than be self-contained. Nevertheless, they serve as a foundation for all the more specific sustainability models, including the three discussed in this chapter.

These guidelines cover a wide range of issues – including economic conditions, labor management relations, climate change, pollution, human rights, and corruption – applied at the discretion of the organization. They can be time-consuming and costly to follow. The UN Research Institute for Social Action is developing criteria for assessing the progress of attaining those goals. The criteria include the following: reliability, data accuracy; complexity, in view of ever-expanding data ranges and points to consider; feasibility, considering differences pertaining to gathering information from lower ends of the supply chain; comparability, among different firms with different models and disclosures; relevance, deciding whether the data captures the environment, social, and governance dimensions of sustainability; and materiality, evaluating whether the data would make a difference in company decision making. (Utting September 11, 2018) Those criteria are also essentially used in the three sustainability models analyzed in this chapter.

In particular, capitalizing on the UN Sustainability Goals, the GRI disclosure framework is characterized by an overriding emphasis on material disclosures used in strategic decision making. Sustainability reporting in accounting today is essentially pursuing and reporting on the GRI, the most popular model used worldwide. While these standards do not call for monetary figures, they do require specific metrics on a variety of enterprise performance measurements and can be used to compare entities within and beyond particular industries. In 2000, the first set of standards was issued by this organization. A revised set of standards was furnished in 2006. Still another revision occurred in 2013 (Brundtland 1987).

Under the GRI, most enterprises report their own data in accordance with the criteria set forth in the framework. No longer does the GRI 4.0 (2013) require the best coverage be subject to independent assurance. (Nor do the other two models considered in this chapter have this requirement.) Emphasis is placed on balance, comparability, accuracy, reliability, clarity, and timeliness in reporting. There are three principal aspects to the GRI rubric – strategy and profile, management approach, and the economic, environmental, and social performance indicators. Strategy and profile deal with the goals of sustainability in the organization. Profile covers the nature of enterprise governance. The economic indicators include wages and supply costs; the environmental indicators pertain to use of natural resources and sustainability improvements; the social indicators reflect labor management relations, human rights, and product responsibility.

The GRI offers two options in complying with the GRI guidelines – a core option and a comprehensive option. The core option calls for reporting the material aspects of those sustainability factors. The comprehensive option goes beyond the core to disclose the nature of the strategy and governance of the organization and how the organization is structured to effectuate its purpose and to deal with the sustainability issues. Regardless of the option, disclosure under the latest version of the GRI should include the manner in which the organization manages its sustainability issues pertaining to material impacts of their supply chain, including suppliers and their labor practices and human rights. An improvement over 3.0, 4.0 emphasizes just those sustainability issues materially affecting a particular enterprise. See Table 13.1: "Analysis of Sustainability Accounting Models."

Project 2025

The aim of Project 2025 is to delineate the principal Sustainability trends. The emphasis is on how disclosures can improve decision making by organizations and their investors. In 2015, to solicit their views, the GRI brought together many different thought leaders representing business and other organizations along with sustainability specialists from think tanks and NGOs.

As a generalized disclosure network, the GRI is not geared to specific industries or sectors that are affected differently by different sustainability issues such as carbon footprint, corruption, and human rights. To its credit, GRI 4.0 emphasizes the following key themes: transparency, governance, stakeholders, strategy, integrated reporting, the environment, the economy, human rights, and labor practices. The SEC has not mandated the GRI or other sustainability disclosures, so they are strictly voluntary in the United States. Companies are undoubtedly reluctant to provide specific information for an array of issues in view of the uncertainty involved in measuring the costs and the litigation exposure stemming from providing misleading information, not to mention the illusory benefits. While the European Union does mandate sustainability disclosures in general for major firms, the format and framework used are the individual company's choice. In view of the lack of uniformity in reporting, whether here or abroad, there is limited comparability in reporting from company to company even for those using the same framework in the same industry. I have to wonder how realistic it will be for organizations to monetize their positive and negative externalities, let alone plan to eliminate the negatives, actions recommended in the 2025 version of GRI. Nevertheless, even before instituting the major changes envisioned in the new project, the GRI framework is likely to remain the overriding favorite sustainability disclosure framework because it is generalized, not industry specific. However, it might be asserted that the fundamental problem with the GRI model is that it is generalized. Different industries have different issues and controversies that need to be addressed.

SASB standards

Launched in 2011, the SASB is a private, nonprofit body that has developed and issued standards for investors in the broad realm of sustainability. The board currently includes Mary Schapiro, former SEC chair in the Obama Administration, and Robert Herz, former FASB chair. SASB

Table 13.1 Analysis of Sustainability Accounting Models

GRI GUIDELINES 4.0	SASB SUSTAINABILITY ISSUES	LEV/GU STRATEGIC RESOURCES AND CONSEQUENCES ANALYSIS
Strategy and Analysis Organizational Profile Report Profile Governance Ethics and Integrity Aspects: Materials Aspects: Energy Aspects: Emissions Aspects: Effluents and Waste Aspects: Products and Services Aspects: Compliance Aspects: Overall Aspects: Occupational Health and Safety Aspects: Customer Health and Safety Aspects: Product and Service Labeling	**Economic:** Air Quality Gas Emissions Fuel Management Water Management Waste Management **Social Capital:** Human Rights Accessibility Affordability Fair Marketing **Human Capital:** Labor Management Relations Fair Compensation Employee Health Diversity Recruitment Retention **Business Model and Innovation:** Enterprise Life Cycle Products and Services – Quality, Packaging, Safety **Leadership and Governance:** Risk Management Safety Management Competitive Behavior Materials Sourcing Regulatory Capture Political Influence Supply Chain Management	**Resource Development:** Research and Development Technology Acquisition Customer Acquisition Costs **Strategic Resources:** Oil and Gas Exploration Resource Stocks Patents and Trademarks Customer Additions and Departures Oil and Gas Reserves Brands Market Share **Resource Preservation:** Patent Infringement Detection Programs Resource Decay Preservation Knowledge Management Workforce Quality Management **Resource Deployment:** Patents – Development, Sale, Expiration Oil and Gas Rights – Exploration and Production Alliances and Joint Ventures **Value Creation:** Cash Flow from Operations Investment in Research and Development Cost of Equity Capital Resource Value Changes – Customers, Oil and Gas Reserves, Brands

has developed standards on an industry-by-industry basis in contrast to the generalized GRI standards, which are applicable to all industries. SASB maintains that one set of standards would not be suitable for the many different industries affected by so many different sustainability issues. The board has been critical of the vague and boilerplate nature of contemporary sustainability disclosures, questioning their usefulness for decision making by investors and companies.

SASB codified its standards in November 2018. What makes SASB industry specific standards unique is their emphasis on investors with a special focus on materiality, not in the financial reporting sense of this term but rather based on what the most relevant issues facing the particular industry are. Materiality is also a key attribute of the GRI as perceived by the organization preparing the disclosure data. The standards are the result of five years of research, from 2012–16. SASB convened industry working groups with more than 2,000 experts contacting 655 companies and 41 industry associations and met with equity analysts.

SASB, not related to the FASB or SEC, has codified standards for publicly traded companies in 77 industries. Those industries are included in ten sectors: health care, financials, technology and communication, nonrenewable resources, transportation, services, resource transformation, consumption, renewable resources and alternative energy, and infrastructure. SASB covers the broad range of sustainability issues. One set of issues is economic – such as air quality, gas emissions, fuel management, water management, and waste management. A second set is social capital – embracing human rights, accessibility, affordability, and fair marketing. Human capital is a third issue – encompassing labor–management relations, fair compensation, employee health, diversity, recruitment, and retention. Still another set of issues is the business model and innovation – pertaining to the enterprise life cycle, products and services, their quality, packaging, and safety. A fourth set of issues falls under the caption of leadership and governance – entailing risks management, safety management, competitive behavior, materials sourcing, regulatory capture, political influence, and supply chain management.

An overview of the key issues from each sector follows. In the extractive industries and minerals processing sector, the main discussion points relate to climate change scenarios that firms in the oil and gas industry perform, managing hydrocarbon reserves, and referencing external-based industry performance indicators in the SASB disclosure standards. In the health care sector, the focus is on affordability and pricing policy in the biotechnology and pharmaceutical industries, data security in managed health care, and drug-monitoring databases in dealing with the opioid crisis. The infrastructure sector is concerned about affordability of water resources, nature of water scarcity and the risk of inadequate supply, and industry-specific greenhouse gas emissions, particularly in the waste management industry. The technology and communications sector addresses the issues of assessing and auditing facilities and achieving independent certification for cybersecurity. The food and beverage sector raises the issues of metrics pertaining to advertising by the media directed specifically to children and the cost-effectiveness of collecting data from contracted suppliers in the meat, poultry, and dairy industries. The consumer goods sector emphasizes employee engagement metrics in the e-commerce industry and customer privacy metrics in that industry. The financial sector focuses on measurement of environmental, social, and governance (ESG) issues in major financial activities in its different industries and, in particular, assessment of systemic risk within the insurance industry.

While the SEC has yet to explicitly require ESG disclosures, the commission released a questionnaire to examine the interest that may exist by users, preparers, and auditors in requiring such disclosures ("Business and Financial Disclosure Required by Regulation S-K" April 2016). Investors, the focus of SASB standards, have clearly responded with interest to the SEC's overture. Other parties did not, in particular companies that are already inundated with questionnaires from many organizations on ESG. Unfortunately, there has yet to be widespread interest in the development of sustainability standards among American corporations. To them, this kind of reporting has often been pursued for public-relations' purposes on a voluntary basis, with few examples of third-party or auditor involvement providing compilation reviews. Furthermore, many would say that American financial reporting is complex enough as it stands, a theme Lev and Gu emphasize, without entering into the sustainability domain. Given that different industries would be affected differently by the various sustainability issues, it is still unclear why SASB decided to develop standards for each of the 77 industries. While different ESG issues affect different industries differently (e.g., climate change is not a top priority for the banking industry), many companies explicitly emphasize that their personnel are their most important asset. However, SASB, in contrast to the GRI, does not stress human resource management, minority compensation, and gender equality in its metrics for most of the industries considered. This is also a weak spot relative to the Lev/Gu model analyzed in the next section. Moreover, we have yet to hear from independent auditors on their reactions to the new SASB standards. One positive aspect of applying SASB standards is the transparency that SASB has exercised in disclosing its work, releasing its proposed standards for public view and criticism and soliciting and using the feedback to revise the standards. SASB is moving forward to make its standards more global rather than just US oriented and to emphasize the importance of quality reporting regardless of the geography of disclosure – such as including the information in reports to the SEC, annual reports, or separate reports. (Welsch, SASB Blog, August 22, 2018) In an international orientation, SASB is behind GRI, which has had such an outreach and acceptance since inception. Nevertheless, SASB has recently evaluated the global nature of its standards for each of the 77 industries, finding them to be generally applicable worldwide, with the notable exceptions of the financial and health care industry metrics.

Thus far, 150 companies have been using SASB standards since 2017 exclusively for their sustainability disclosures, but in varying degrees of implementation and with a wide range of disclosures. Some actually include third-party reviews. Other companies do not seem to be aware of the guidance and technical protocol that comes with these standards. In any case, it is not the board's responsibility to evaluate the quality of implementation. At this point, it is fair to assert that compliance with the specific metrics to date has yet to be successful. The board could very well reach out to companies to provide tutorials to encourage and assist in application of its standards (SASB Board Meeting, September 19, 2019).

A SASB intermediate group, its Standards Advisory Group, was surveyed in 2019 for feedback to the board. This group overall called for guidance to accompany the metrics, including greater clarity in technical protocols. Some members of this group suggested sample case situations on implementation of the industry metrics, some additional work on improving industry descriptions, and dealing with companies in several altogether different lines of business (SASB Board Meeting, September 19, 2019).

Lev and Gu model

Lev and Gu provide a model for financial reporting in their book, *The End of Accounting and the Path Forward for Investors and Managers*, published in 2016. The authors present an openly candid discussion of why financial statements no longer furnish accountability to stakeholders. The authors, who maintain that conventional financial statements provide only 5% of the information investors need, find fault with the overriding emphasis on estimates in those statements, the balance sheet approach adopted by standard setters, and fair valuation in reporting. The financial statements are geared to a dated manufacturing age rather than a 21st-century information age, Lev and Gu contend. The strategic assets of the enterprise tend to be intangibles, as pointed out in the GRI Project and the SASB framework as well, to which conventional accounting gives short shrift by expensing those costs instead of capitalizing and subsequently amortizing them over periods of benefit. In particular, research and development, along with human resource costs, which are key resource expenditures, are expensed, leaving net income mismatched between revenues and expenses as a result. These costs provide long-term expected benefits and hence should be reflected as assets. Should identifiable intangible assets with limited life spans be acquired from an independent third party, those assets are capitalized and subsequently amortized over the periods of expected benefit. Additionally, research and development costs acquired in business combinations, known as in-process R & D (INPRD), is capitalized and treated as having an indefinite life until the activities are completed or discontinued. INPRD is subject to impairment loss testing (ASC 805–50 2017) Furthermore, if undefined intangibles are acquired from an independent, third-party in a business combination from paying more than the fair value of its identifiable assets minus liabilities, the costs are reflected as "goodwill." Such a lump-sum caption may include brand quality, trademarks, and other specific intangibles not usually shown as assets. On the other hand, the so-called goodwill may not be a positive aspect at all but rather due to paying more for another company than it is worth.

This model is intended to reduce the complexity of financial reporting by disclosing facts that are useful in managing companies and valuing their worth. The authors point out that accounting income is based on "multiple subjective managerial estimates," including transitory items reflected in accordance with new FASB and IFRS standards; many of those items turn out to be misleading, if not downright wrong. As a result, the income statement, in particular, reflects a mix of expenses and investments. Furthermore, there is no required pronouncement to disclose those errors in subsequent statements. Companies also mislead users today with a host of non-GAAP earnings figures. Lev and Gu assert that cash flows are vastly superior to earnings in terms of predicting future corporate performance, a theme also observed by SASB.

The authors call for new disclosures, especially on an industry basis as in the SASB framework, to capture the innovativeness of the company. The ability of the enterprise to create unique value is the key to its success. Examples of metrics providing significant performance indicators to evaluate strategies include client retention and the new clients in the insurance industry, test results of prospective drugs in the pharmaceutical industry (including the company's ability to market new drugs), changes in proven reserves in the oil and gas industry, and order backlogs in high-tech companies.

Lev and Gu formulate an innovative Strategic Resources and Consequences Report to reflect the value added by corporations in each period, which should only amount to one or two pages for each company. This new report, in stark contrast to traditional accounting, accents the importance of disclosing factual information to include customer data and market share data as well as the following measures: cash flows from operating events, investments made, and the cost of capital incurred. The Lev/Gu report, encompassing both quantitative and qualitative information, would include sections applied to each industry on resource development, strategic resources, resource preservation, resource deployment, and value creation. The resource development section would contain research and development, technology acquisition, and customer acquisition costs. Strategic resources would include oil and gas exploration, resource stocks, patents and trademarks – their quantity and quality, customer additions and departures, proven oil and gas reserves, brand numbers and market shares. Resource preservation encompasses infringement detection programs on patents and trademarks, resource decay preservation programs, knowledge management, and work force quality management. Resource deployment entails patents developed, sold, and expired, oil and gas rights explored and produced, and alliances and joint ventures. Finally, value created includes operating cash flows, investments incurred, and the cost of equity capital involved, along with resource value changes involving customers, oil and gas reserves, and brands. This model emphasizes intangible assets in a service-oriented economy in contrast to conventional financial reporting.

If financial reports are as useless as Lev and Gu claim, then why should firms incur the significant cost of their preparation and audit? The authors apparently believe that the reports have historical significance, since society does not learn from the past and therefore tends to repeat previous mistakes. Nevertheless, the authors could have made a stronger case for retaining traditional reports in a revised form, the specific nature of which they fail to specify.

This model calls for measures not only applicable to specific industries but also to all industries, including sources and uses of cash flows as well as resources developed, used, and conserved. While the model reflects mostly factual data as opposed to the myriad of estimates in our current financial reports, it is not likely to be adopted by the SEC because it is too radically different from conventional accounting. Companies are not going to report the data Lev and Gu propose on a voluntary basis even though much of the information they recommend is publicly available – since companies do not disclose their key performance indicators to competitors. Nevertheless, this model highlights the importance of intangible assets by disclosing key performance indicators and ratios pertaining to those assets, not to mention existing "balanced scorecards" used to evaluate managers on several criteria. Furthermore, this model would appear to be the most open ended and the least costly to apply to companies in diverse industries.

Conclusion

Today, sustainability reporting is voluntary in the United States. There is a lack of generally accepted accounting principles addressing such disclosures. The upshot is a free-for-all in reporting that is not comparable, not auditable, and not helpful to investors, creditors, and other users of financial reports. Too many companies are using sustainability disclosures undoubtedly as public relations tools, accenting what they consider their positive actions and neglecting to provide full disclosure. What is missing is an attempt to reflect positive and negative externalities, from converting private costs to social benefits and from converting private benefits to social costs.

By contrast, in 2016 the European Union Directive (2014) on Disclosure of Non-Financial Reporting and Diversity Information took effect. Companies meeting specific criteria are required in the European Union countries to report on sustainability, though the framework they use is their individual choice. They can report the required information separately on their websites, whether or not it is released at the same time as the annual report. Specifically, public-interest companies having more than 500 employees are required to issue a non-financial statement reflecting annual environmental, social, and employee matters, respecting human rights and diversity, and counteracting corruption and bribery. European countries in general are more concerned with social welfare relative to the United States, and unions have far more influence and power there, often including representatives on company boards of directors than is the case in the United States. Beyond actions taken by the European Union, more than half the stock exchanges worldwide now have guidelines, if not requirements, for listed companies to disclose their sustainability transactions. Still another global development is an increased emphasis on fusing sustainability performance with financial outcomes in integrated financial reports. Each of the models analyzed in this manuscript – GRI, SASB, and Lev/Gu – could be cast into an integrated reporting framework.

The three models discussed in this chapter offer different pathways to reforming the nature of financial reports. Yet all the models are disclosure-oriented, providing inputs to a broad array of users, including investors, creditors, and governments, to apply as they see fit. Furthermore, all the models are concerned with the concept of materiality in terms of which issues the organization has selected to focus on in its sustainability reporting. The models are not mutually exclusive nor collectively exhaustive. To achieve uniformity and move to required SEC disclosures, the three models conceivably can complement one another in terms of risk analysis and assessment, fusing financial and sustainability risks together. Each framework calls for material information about an organization's activities for use in strategizing and decision making. While the conventional financial reports are currently complex, the new data proposed could capture the innovative creativity of the firm even though they would undoubtedly add to the complexity and the cost of preparation.

Sustainability data at this stage of development is crude and unreliable – often lacking adequate underlying internal controls. Furthermore, it is not clear how existing financial reports could accommodate the proposed standards in an integrative manner. The GRI and SASB, along with several other standard-setting bodies, are attempting to map their frameworks to align their work (SASB Alliance Newsletter 2018). Beyond that, many high-profile international companies are currently preparing an integrated annual report to incorporate the financial statements along with sustainability disclosures. Nevertheless, the "beauty" of each of the three models – GRI, SASB, and Lev/Gu – is that they are calling for uniformity in sustainable reporting from company to company, in general for GRI and for specific industries in the other two models.

Perhaps an independent third-party should audit corporate sustainability reporting once a common model is selected for reporting, but that may be asking too much for any one organization to manage. As we have observed, sustainability reporting is a multifaceted task with different industries affected differently by issues and controversies. Therefore, different standards and metrics should be available for different industries to apply in this process, as in the SASB framework and to a lesser extent in the Lev/Gu model.

An alternative sustainability approach might be to develop industry or sector specialists to conduct the audit function. If a major firm is in various different industries, it could call upon different specialists to perform those functions. There undoubtedly would be significant costs associated with adhering to sustainability standards, not just generalized standards like the GRI but specialized industry standards as in the SASB and Lev/Gu models. Whether the standards are generalized or industry-oriented, the standard-setting process and the audit process are expensive endeavors. The costs are bound to be passed on to the consumer in the final analysis.

In November 2016, the International Federation of Accountants (IFAC) issued a report on the accounting profession's role in effectuating the United Nations Sustainability Goals. This report asserts:

> The skillset, experience, and influence professional accountants possess gives them enormous scope to shape solutions to sustainable development challenges. IFAC's Charles Tilley observes: [I]f business ignores the goals, they do so at their own peril.
>
> *(Kennedy 2016, 10)*

Sustainability and other disclosures would appear to be more credible when the company is fully committed to the activities reported. We have seen how companies such as Volkswagen and BP have used sustainability reporting as a smokescreen for "green-washing." Once companies such as these deceive the public, it is difficult, costly, and time-consuming to regain credibility and trust. In the short run, enterprises can manage sustainability reporting to suit their own ends. In the long run, companies cannot get away with untruthful disclosures in this realm. Uniform reporting standards will be enacted and required to be used in response to disgruntled constituents. Furthermore, it should not just be quantitative information that should count in sustainability reporting ("what gets measured gets done"), but the qualitative information – the narrative – behind the firm's actions or inactions are equally important.

Today there is a potentially high cost to companies not inclined to disclose sustainability data. While most such companies do face disinvestment, they may be passed over by new investors and will be criticized for not doing so. Collective investor groups are increasingly concerned and pressuring companies to be transparent about their Sustainability issues. Coca-Cola is now disclosing its plastics footprint, Ford and Tyson Foods their effects on ecosystems, Nike listing its suppliers (Sardon 2019). Blackrock, the largest global institutional investor, decided to focus its investment decision making on sustainability issues, especially climate change (2020).

References

Accounting Principles Board. 1970. *Statement No. 4, Basic Concepts and Accounting Principles Underlying Financial Statements of Business Enterprises.* New York: AICPA.

Accounting Standards Codification (ASC) 805–50. 2017. *Acquisition of Assets Rather than a Business.* Norwalk, CT: FASB.

American Accounting Association. 1966. *A Statement of Basic Accounting Theory.* Sarasota, FL: American Accounting Association.

American Institute of Certified Public Accountants. 1973. *Objectives of Financial Statements (Trueblood Report).* New York: AICPA.

Blackrock. 2020. "World's Largest Asset Manager Puts Climate as the Center of its Investment Strategy." www.npr.org.2020/01/14.

Brundtland Commission Report. 1987. *Our Common Future.* New York: Oxford University Press, United Nations.

Canning, J. B. 1929. *The Economics of Accountancy.* New York: Ronald Press.

Carroll, A. B. 1991. The Pyramid of Corporate Social Responsibility Toward the Moral Management of Organizational Stakeholders. *Business Horizons* 34 (4): 39–48.

Carson, R. 1962. *Silent Spring.* New York: Houghton-Mifflin.

CorpLaw. 2013. "Shareholder & Stakeholder Theories of Corporate Governance." *Corplaw Blog,* July 16. Accessed October 5, 2016. www.corplaw.ie/blog/bid/317212/Shareholder-Stakeholder-Theories-Of-Corporate-Governance.

European Union. 2014. *Non-Financial Reporting Directive.* Brussels: European Union.

Financial Accounting Standards Board. 1978. *Statement of Financial Accounting Concepts No. 1, Objectives of Financial Reporting by Business Enterprises.* Stamford, CT: Financial Accounting Standards Board.

Flamholtz, E. 1985. *Human Resource Accounting.* San Francisco, CA: Jossey-Bass.

Foroohar, R. 2016, October 3. "Donald Trump's 'Fiduciary Duty' Excuse on Taxes Is Just Plain Wrong." *Time.com.* Accessed August 29, 2018. https://we2learn.wordpress.com/2016/10/03/ideas-donald-trumps-fiduciary-duty-excuse-on-taxes-is-just-plain-wrong

Freeman, R. E. 1984. *Strategic Management: A Stakeholder Approach.* Boston: Pitman.

Freeman, R. E. 1994. "The Politics of Stakeholder Theory: Some Future Directions." *Business Ethics Quarterly* 4 (4): 409–21.

Friedman, Milton. 1970. "The Social Responsibility of Business Is to Increase Its Profits." *The New York Times Magazine,* September 13. www.umich.edu/~thecore/doc/Friedman.pdf.

GRI 4.0. 2013. Standards are now in Portuguese. www.globalreporting.org/media/ukgpbiqx/linking-the-gri-standards-and-cass-csr-40-english.pdf.

Hegde, P., R. Bloom, and J. Fuglister. 1997 "Social Financial Reporting in India: A Case." *International Journal of Accounting* 32 (2).

Jensen, M. C., and W. H. Meckling. 1976. "Theory of the Firm: Managerial Behavior, Agency Costs and Ownership Structure." *Journal of Financial Economics* 3 (4): 305–60.

Kennedy, Elizabeth. 2016. "Establishing Accountancy's Role in Sustainability Goals." *Strategic Finance* 98 (6): 10. http://sfmagazine.com/post-entry/december-2016-establishing-accountancys-role-in-sustainability-goals/.

Lantos, G. P. 2001. "The Boundaries of Strategic Corporate Social Responsibility." *Journal of Consumer Marketing* 18 (7): 595–632.

Laplume, A. O., K. Sonpar, and R. A. Litz. 2008. "Stakeholder Theory: Reviewing a Theory That Moves Us." *Journal of Management* 34 (6): 1152–89.

Lessig, L. 2011. *Republic Lost.* New York: Twelve Books.

Lev, B. 2015. "Blog on the End of Accounting and the Path Forward for Investors and Managers." https://levtheendofaccountingblog.wordpress.com/.

Lev, B., and F. Gu. 2016. *The End of Accounting and the Path Forward for Investors and Managers*. Hoboken, NJ: Wiley.

Lev, B., and A. Schwartz. 1971. "On the Use of the Economic Concept of Human Capital in Financial Statements." *Accounting Review* (January): 103–22.

Linowes, D. 1971. "Accounting for Social Progress." *New York Times*, March 14.

Moonitz, M. 1961. *Accounting Research Study No. 1. The Basic Postulates of Accounting*. New York: AICPA.

Nader, R. 1965. *Unsafe at Any Speed*. New York: Grossman.

Paton, W., and A. Littleton. [1941] 1962. *An Introduction to Corporate Accounting Standards*. Evanston, IL: American Accounting Association.

Ramanathan, K. V. 1976. "Toward a Theory of Corporate Social Accounting." *Accounting Review* 51 (3): 516–28.

Sardon, M. 2019. "The Potentially High Cost of Not Disclosing ESG Data." *Wall Street Journal*, September 22.

SASB Alliance Newsletter. December 2018. San Francisco, CA.

SASB Board Meeting. September 19, 2019. San Francisco, CA.

Savitz, A. 2013. *Talent, Transformation and the Triple Bottom Line*. New York: Jossey-Bass, Wiley.

Scott, D. R. 1941. "The Basis for Accounting Principles." *Accounting Review* 16 (4): 341–49.

Spacek, L. 1962. "The Need for Unbiased Reporting." *NAA Bulletin* 44 (2).

Utting, P. September 11, 2018. Email to the author.

Welsch, M. 2018. SASB Blog, August 16. Accessed August 29, 2018. www.sasb.org/lessons-from-the-market/.

14

GOVERNMENTAL ACCOUNTING ETHICS

Providing accountability to maintain the public trust

Patrick T. Kelly

Introduction

There are a significant number of government agencies in the United States. When one considers counties, municipalities, townships, school districts, and special districts, there are over 90,000 US state and local governments (U.S. Census State Government Finances 2012). Coupled with the more than 25 federal government agencies, over $7 trillion was spent by US governmental organizations in 2012 (GASB 2017; U.S. OMB 2018). This government spending represented over 40% of the more than $16 trillion of the 2012 US gross domestic product reported by the US Department of Commerce (GASB 2017).

Tens of thousands of government accountants and financial managers work for the federal, state, and local governments. A 2017 Government Accounting Standards Board (GASB) White Paper described the differences between accounting and financial reporting for governments and for-profit businesses. While both private sector and public sector financial reporting focus on making economic choices, government financial information is also needed for social and political decision making by government officials. Furthermore, governments necessarily emphasize accountability in their accounting and financial systems to satisfy the information needs of various stakeholders, including elected and other government officials, taxpayers, and those receiving government services (GASB 2017).

Government accountants and financial managers have many and varied roles. They may work for federal and state tax departments, manage government debt, plan and budget for federal agency, state, and municipal operations, ensure proper spending in accordance with approved budgets, maintain pension and retiree health care plans, and conduct audits to maintain the level of accountability expected by stakeholders. There are also specific accounting differences associated with government accounting, such as the use of governmental budgetary systems, fund accounting, grant management, encumbrance accounting, pension and post-employment benefits accounting, and accounting for public services (GASB 2017; Bora 2018). The performance of these many and wide-ranging duties by federal, state, and local government accountants and finance officials affects every US citizen.

Underlying all of the roles and responsibilities of government accountants and financial managers are the ethical guidelines that promote both the required accountability desired by the public, as well as the effective and efficient services provided to US citizens. In general, the vast majority of government accountants and finance officials abide by these ethical principles and perform their duties honorably and professionally. When government accountants and other officials do not behave ethically, faith in the integrity of government drops and trust in government suffers.

The remainder of this chapter is organized as follows. The next section describes the various ethical standards that apply to government accountants and financial professionals. This is followed by examples of government accountants and officials who have not acted ethically, with a focus on those committing financial fraud that detracts from accountability and reduces the public's confidence in government finances. Then I examine the internal control measures that help prevent and detect fraud. I conclude with a discussion of the roles government accountants and finance professionals play in designing and maintaining the internal control systems, including fraud prevention and detection measures. These internal control systems help ensure ethical conduct and accountability, thereby maintaining the public trust in government organizations.

Ethical standards guiding government accountants

Several different organizations provide ethical guidelines for government accountants and financial professionals. Depending on the particular government accounting position, specific federal, state, and local rules guide one's ethical behavior regarding topics such as integrity, conflicts of interest, and confidentiality. There are also professional organizations that provide ethical guidance for their members. This section will provide the ethical standards for those conducting federal government audits, along with codes of conduct for certified public accountants doing government accounting work, including the American Institute of Certified Public Accountants (AICPA) and those for accountants in three of the more populous states where certified public accountants (CPAs) practice (California, New York and Texas). This section also includes the codes of conduct for two organizations that emphasize ethics for their members, the Association of Government Accountants and the Government Financial Officer Association. The significant overlap and consistency in ethical guidance from these different organizations will also be discussed.

The US Government Accountability Office (GAO) provides ethical guidelines for those engaged in auditing government organizations in accordance with generally accepted government auditing standards (GAGAS). The most recent version of GAO's *Government Auditing Standards*, commonly referred to as the Yellow Book, was promulgated in 2018 for use by a wide variety of users, including federal agency internal auditors, federal inspectors general auditing federal agencies, certified public accounting firms auditing government entities, state auditors, and municipal auditors (GAO 2018). The *Government Auditing Standards* also provides ethical principles for these auditors, which along with independence guidelines, are included in Table 14.1A (GAO 2018). These GAO ethical auditing standards are consistent with many of the principles contained in the AICPA Code of Professional Conduct (AICPA 2016) and contribute to government audits that ensure the accountability demanded by the public (GAO 2018).

The AICPA Code of Professional Conduct applies to all AICPA members when carrying out their professional responsibilities. This includes government accountants and those who audit federal, state, or local government organizations. This code of conduct provides detailed definitions and guidance on principles and rules, along with interpretations of the rules that guide professional conduct. Excerpts of the Principles of Professional Conduct are included in Table 14.1B and include brief descriptions of responsibilities, the public interest, integrity, objectivity and independence, and due care (AICPA 2016).

Table 14.1A Government Auditing Standards – Summaries of Key Ethical Principles and Independence Guidelines

	Government Auditing Standards Ethical Principles – The Public Interest
3.07–3.08	Government auditors serve the public interest and maintain the public trust by maintaining integrity, objectivity, and independence when performing their duties.
	Integrity
3.09–3.10	Government auditors perform their duties with integrity, which focuses on objective and nonpartisan information and leads to honest judgments and reports that are free from bias.
	Objectivity
3.11	Auditors maintain objectivity when performing their duties, which focuses on independence of mind and appearance, remaining impartial, and avoiding conflicts of interest.
	Proper Use of Government Information, Resources, and Positions
3.12–3.15	Government auditors use official information appropriately, safeguard government resources, and abide by applicable laws and regulations pertaining to the performance of their duties. They recognize the importance of disclosing information properly and maintaining transparency desired by the public. They do not use their position for improper personal financial gain.
	Professional Behavior
3.16	Professional behavior involves government auditors performing their duties honestly and abiding by applicable legal, regulatory, and professional standards, while not engaging in inappropriate conduct that would be perceived as problematic by the public.
	Independence
3.17–20	Generally Accepted Government Auditing Standards require that auditors and their organizations be independent from the audited entity during the professional engagement and any period covered by the financial statements. Auditors should take actions to maintain their objectivity and impartiality relating to all aspects of the engagement.

Sources: U.S Government Accountability Office (GAO). *Government Auditing Standards – 2018 Revision* (pp. 26–29).

Different state certified public accounting societies also have codes of conduct that apply to their members, including those who work in government accounting and auditing positions. Similar to the GAO auditing ethical guidelines, the state accounting codes of conduct are generally consistent with the AICPA Code of Conduct. For example, the Texas Society of Certified Public Accountants (TXCPA) has adopted the AICPA Code of Conduct and supplemented it with the Texas State Board of Public Accountancy Rules of Professional Conduct, which provides specific guidance on independence, integrity and objectivity, competence, and confidential client communications (TXCPA 2019; TSBPA 2019). The California Society of Certified Public Accountants' (CalCPA) Code of Professional Conduct has principles (moral judgment, the public interest, integrity, objectivity and independence, and due care) and rules (independence, integrity and objectivity) that also conform to the AICPA Code of Professional Conduct and the California State Board of Accountancy (CalCPA 2019). The New York State Society of Certified Public Accountants (NYSSCPA) also publishes a Code of Professional Conduct with principles related to the public interest, integrity, objectivity, due professional care, competence, confidentiality, and independence, along with rules and interpretations that specifically address integrity, independence, and objectivity (NYSSCPA 2013).

Table 14.1B American Institute of CPAs (AICPA) – Summaries of Principles of Professional Conduct

	0.300.020 Responsibilities
.01–.02	Members are professionals who have a vital duty to society. They should make professional and ethical decisions that promote public confidence in the profession.
	0.300.030 The Public Interest
.01–.05	The profession has a significant responsibility to the public including clients, credit grantors, governments, employers, investors, and the business and financial community. AICPA members should carry out their duties professionally and with integrity, which serves the public interest and honors the public trust.
	0.300.040 Integrity
.01–.05	Integrity involves carrying out professional duties honestly while maintaining high levels of objectivity, independence, and due care expected of AICPA members. These professionals should abide by both the letter and the spirit of ethical guidelines, and where standards are not clear or do not exist, strive to maintain the integrity expected of them. This will reinforce the public confidence and trust in these professionals.
	0.300.050 Objectivity and Independence
.01–.05	AICPA members are required to maintain objectivity and independence, which are related topics. Objectivity involves being impartial and avoiding conflicts of interest. Maintaining objectivity leads AICPA members to be independent in fact and appearance as they engage in public practice. This involves an ongoing independence assessment regarding clients to avoid conflicts of interest. Members not engaged in public practice should maintain objectivity as they perform professional services relating to financial statement preparation, consulting, auditing, or tax.
	0.300.060 Due Care
.01–.06	Due care involves sustaining a high level of competence and striving for excellence when carrying out professional responsibilities. Competence includes acquiring knowledge and understanding and maintaining the expertise needed to perform the requested services. This includes an ongoing commitment to learning and professional development throughout one's career.

Sources: American Institute of CPAs (AICPA). 2016. Code of Professional Conduct (pp. 5–7).

In addition to the organizations already mentioned, a professional member organization, the Association of Government Accountants (AGA), has also created a code of ethics for government accountants and financial management professionals. The AGA Code of Ethics applies to all members, as well as those who have achieved the Certified Government Financial Manager designation. The AGA Code of Ethics focuses on serving the public interest, considering the interests of both the government organizations and those who rely on them, including taxpayers, investors, and other citizens. The code identifies four objectives that help achieve professionalism and positively contribute to the public interest (credibility, professionalism, quality of service, and confidence), along with four basic principles, as described in Table 14.2A: integrity, objectivity, professional competence and due care, and confidentiality. These four principles facilitate high levels of expected performance that helps professionals serve the public interest. The AGA Code of Ethics also prescribes eight professional conduct rules that guide member behavior, including adhering to applicable laws and standards of conduct, exercising integrity and professional care when performing duties, and avoiding conflicts of interest. The AGA

Table 14.2A Association of Government Accountants (AGA) – Code of Ethics Summaries of AGA Code of Ethics Principles and Professional Conduct

Integrity	Performs duties honestly, with respect for others, and as guided by laws and professional standards.
Objectivity	When making decisions and providing services, do so without prejudice, bias, or conflict of interest.
Professional Competency and Due Care	Maintain professional knowledge and skills to accomplish tasks both effectively and efficiently, while supervising subordinates to a similar high standard of performance.
Confidentiality	Do not reveal confidential information obtained while performing professional services, unless reporting misconduct to appropriate authorities.

Source: Association of Government Accountants (AGA). 2019. Code of Ethics.

Code of Conduct also has a provision for its enforcement that describes how ethics complaints are investigated and the possible disciplinary actions that can result from ethical violations of the code (e.g., warnings, member suspension or termination) (AGA 2019).

Another member organization of public officials from the United States and Canada is the Government Financial Officers Association (GFOA). The GFOA's 20,000 members have a mission "to advance excellence in public finance" (GFOA 2019). The GFOA recognizes the important role of finance officials in serving the public and the special trust associated with their positions. Recognizing the potential ethical challenges that can face finance officials, the GFOA has developed a code of ethics that helps it members meet their public service obligations. The GFOA Code of Ethics is contained in Table 14.2B and is consistent with the other codes of ethics examined earlier, such as the AGA Code of Ethics (GFOA 2019). Both codes of ethics emphasize integrity and honesty, respecting others and treating them fairly, and professionally performing duties (AGA 2019; GFOA 2019).

In general, the existing ethical standards and guidance for government accountants, auditors, and other financial officials are quite consistent. As can be seen in Tables 14.1 and 14.2, there is a uniform focus on integrity in all of these profiled standards, and this principle forms the foundation of ethical decisions made by public officials. The characteristics associated with the principle of integrity, including honesty, transparency, and fairness, along with nonpartisanship and factual analyses, contribute to the accountability that is expected as government accountants perform their various duties. There is a similar emphasis on the concept that accompanies integrity, namely earning the trust of the public and serving the public interest. For example, both the GAO Auditing Ethical Principles and the AICPA Code of Conduct specifically discuss the responsibility "to serve the public interest and honor the public trust." The concept of responsibility associated with serving the public is a key component of the government accountant ethical standards. Coupled with the value of integrity, serving the public compels government accountants to take the morally correct action – at the right time, for the right reasons – to serve the community and other members of the public who rely on their professionalism (GAO 2018; AICPA 2016; AGA 2019; GFOA 2019).

There are other important ethical characteristics commonly described as ethical standards in Tables 14.1 and 14.2. Maintaining objectivity and minimizing conflicts of interest are also vital ethical principles that are desired in government accounting and financial professionals. The concept of technical competence is reinforced by the emphasis on due care and professionalism as government accountants strive for excellence in the performance of their duties.

Table 14.2B Government Finance Officers Association (GFOA) – Summary of the Code of Professional Ethics

Integrity and Honesty	Integrity and honesty provide the basis for trust between GFOA members and the community. Community members trust that public finance officials will perform their duties ethically and act in the interest of the community when making fiscal decisions.
Producing Results for My Community	Public finance officials use their knowledge and abilities to produce positive results for their communities. Achieving community goals results in high levels of trust for these finance officials.
Treating People Fairly	Public finance officials build trust in their communities by treating people fairly and establishing objective and impartial policies and procedures for their government organizations. This will result in greater support for government entities, leading to an improved financial position.
Diversity and Inclusion	Public finance officials frequently work in communities that are becoming more diverse. Valuing diversity and being inclusive benefits these communities and increases public trust in these officials.
Reliability and Consistency	Public finance officials frequently interact with community members. As these officials apply policies and procedures consistently and reliably meet commitments, they earn the trust of their respective stakeholders.

Sources: Government Financial Officers Association (GFOA). 2019. Code of Professional Ethics.

Finally, independence in fact and in appearance is highlighted, particularly for those government accountants serving as auditors (GAO 2018; AICPA 2016; AGA 2019; GFOA 2019).

Ethical problems and fraud that damage accountability and public trust

The codes of conduct examined here are explicit and specific in promoting the ethical actions expected of government accountants and financial professionals. In general, the vast majority of these government professionals perform their duties honorably and proficiently. While there is not an extensive amount of academic research that documents unethical actions by government accountants and financial professionals, the existing literature suggests that unethical actions and fraud do occur. This section reviews some of the prior research on state and local government financial fraud. I then describe the types of occupational frauds involving government organizations reported in the 2018 Association of Certified Fraud Examiners (ACFE) Global Study on Occupational Frauds and Abuse – Government Edition (ACFE 2018). The fraud triangle is then presented, along with some specific examples of frauds that have served to detract from accountability and shake the public trust in government organizations.

A number of studies have used government auditors to examine state and local government fraud. Ziegenfuss (1996) reported on a survey of members of the National Association of Local Government Auditors (NALGA) and the Virginia Local Government Auditors Association. Seventy-one percent of the responding auditors were aware of fraud in their own agency, and the majority of these frauds related to the misappropriation of funds (29%) and theft (28%). One noted concern highlighted in the study is when "red flags" were present (e.g., disregarding internal controls or reports, employee comments, changes in employee behavior or lifestyle), they were acted on in only 32% of the cases. The study concluded that government fraud was a major problem and was expected to increase. Furthermore, management tended not to take appropriate action when fraud was identified (Ziegenfuss 1996). A second study found that local governments with a stronger ethical environment experienced less fraud. Ethical environment considerations included whether managers demonstrated actions regarded as unethical, whether improper behavior was accepted without adverse negative consequences, and whether such negative consequences would result if the governmental organization benefited from the unethical behavior in question (Ziegenfuss 2001).

Huefner (2011) examined fraud risks in local government by analyzing 307 municipal New York Comptroller audit reports from 2003–09. He found 234 audits that discussed internal control problems, and the results suggested that weak internal controls significantly increased the potential for municipal fraud. Some of the identified control deficiencies included a lack of segregation of duties, transaction authorization problems, a lack of independent checks, such as audits and reconciliations, safeguarding assets (including cash, inventories, and fixed assets), and inadequate documentation. Furthermore, the study results indicated that fraud may have occurred in 25% of the audited towns and villages (Huefner 2011).

More recently, the 2018 Association of Certified Fraud Examiners (ACFE) Global Study on Occupational Frauds and Abuse (Government Edition) presented statistics on 364 cases of occupational frauds in government organizations worldwide. More than 50% of the frauds occurred in the United States, resulting in a median loss of $70,000. Most of the government organization frauds involved asset misappropriation (88% of the cases), with a median loss of $100,000. While the two other categories of occupational fraud, corruption (47%) and financial statement fraud (6%), were not as prevalent as misappropriation, both involved greater median losses, with corruption at $400,000 and financial statement fraud at $315,000 (ACFE 2018).

Since misappropriated assets are so prevalent, the ACFE examined these more closely, identifying the most common categories of misappropriated assets fraud schemes. Noncash asset misappropriation was the most prevalent, occurring in 20% of the cases, followed by fraud schemes related to billing (15%), cash on hand (13%), skimming (13%), cash larceny (12%), expense reimbursement (11%), and payroll (10%). As reported in the ACFE study, the largest number of government fraud cases occurred at the federal or national government level (38% of the reported cases), followed by states or provinces (26% of the cases), and local governments (31% of the cases). The federal governments also suffered the largest median losses ($200,000 per case), followed by state governments ($110,000 per case), and local organizations ($84,000 per case) (ACFE 2018).

The ACFE study also considered age, gender, tenure with their respective organizations, and whether those who committed fraud acted alone; all had an effect on the median fraud losses at government organizations. The median age for government fraudsters was 45; for those over the median age, the median loss was much greater ($200,000) than the median loss for those under the median age ($71,000). Men committed 68% of frauds, and the median loss was $200,000, while the median loss for women was $51,000. Those who had worked at their organizations for over five years embezzled $150,000, while those who had been at their organizations for less than five years stole an average of $100,000. Collusion was also an important factor in the median loss amounts. Those acting with one or more other fraudsters misappropriated $280,000, while for individuals acting alone the median loss was $40,000 (ACFE 2018).

The fraud triangle developed by criminologist Donald R. Cressey is helpful in explaining the actions of individuals who engage in unethical behavior and ultimately commit fraud, including government accountants and financial professionals. The three sides of the triangle are:

1 Perceived Pressure,
2 Perceived Opportunity,
3 Rationalization (AGA 2019; Albrecht et al. 2012).

Perceived pressure deals with the motivation to commit the fraud. Factors that might contribute to this motivation include financial pressure due to personal finances or problems (e.g., gambling or drug addictions). Perceived opportunity relates to the fraudster's ability to obtain something of value. Lack of internal controls such as poor segregation of accounting functions can contribute to the perceived opportunity to commit fraud. Rationalization relates to the fraudster's reason(s) for committing the fraud that the individual uses to justify the inappropriate behavior (AGA 2019; Albrecht et al. 2012). For example, one common rationalization for problem gamblers who commit fraud is that they are not stealing but rather borrowing the money and will pay it back with gambling winnings (Kelly and Hartley 2010).

While government accountants and financial professionals were not involved in many of the frauds identified by the 2018 ACFE Government Frauds Report, there are instances of these officials not acting in accordance with the values of integrity, objectivity, due care, and the public interest as previously discussed. When ethical failures occur, particularly those relating to fraud, accountability suffers along with the trust that the public places in the government. Provided next are examples of some individuals who did not uphold the ethical values contained in the codes of conduct identified in Tables 14.1 and 14.2. Profiled here are the unethical actions of Rita Crundwell, Henry Centrella, Michael Nguyen, and other government accountants and finance officials whose unethical actions have detracted from accountability and failed to maintain the public trust.

Rita Crundwell has gained notoriety for committing the largest municipal government fraud in United States history. In 1983 she began serving as the treasurer and comptroller of Dixon, Illinois, President Ronald Reagan's hometown. Over a 20-year period beginning in 1991, she stole over $50 million of Dixon's funds, which she mainly used for a quarter horse breeding organization, RC Quarter Horses, LLC. Her horse breeding operation became tremendously successful. At the time of her arrest in 2012, she owned 400 horses, and her organization produced 52 American Quarter Horse Association (AQHA) world champions. Prior to her arrest, Crundwell received the AQHA breeder of the year award for eight straight years. While many Dixon citizens thought that Crundwell's RC Quarter Horses organization was profitable, the town's funds were supporting her horse business, along with her lavish lifestyle, paying for horses and their care, horse farms and trailers, several residences, an expensive motor home, automobiles, and jewelry (McKenna 2013; Pope 2013; Verschoor 2012).

Inadequate segregation of duties was a primary cause of Rita Crundwell's ability to accomplish this major fraud. In 1990 Crundwell opened a City of Dixon checking account at Fifth Third Bank named "City of Dixon and RSCDA" (RSCDA stood for "Reserve Sewer Capital Development Account"). The checks were imprinted with "RSCDA c/o Rita Crundwell," and she had signature authority over this account. She then transferred Dixon funds from other accounts to the RSCDA account, supporting these transfers with fraudulent capital projects and invoices. Once the funds were deposited into the RSCDA account, she would write checks from that account to support her horse business and extravagant lifestyle (Apostolou, Apostolou, and Thibadoux 2015; McKenna 2013; Pope 2013; Verschoor 2012).

Crundwell's $53 million fraud damaged the city of Dixon significantly. Funds were not available for public safety programs (police, ambulance, and fire protection), public works programs (city buildings and road repairs), and city workers, who did not receive raises for multiple years and saw their jobs eliminated. Her fraud was particularly difficult because Crundwell, regarded uniformly as the long-term, trusted comptroller and treasurer, ultimately betraying the public trust placed in her by her fellow citizens (Apostolou, Apostolou, and Thibadoux 2015; McKenna 2013; Pope 2013; Verschoor 2012).

While other government-related frauds did not rise to the level of over $50 million, they have similarly devastated the affected communities. For example, Henry Centrella was a native of Winsted, Connecticut, and served as the first finance director of that city. Winsted exists within the Town of Winchester, and Centrella was the finance director from 1983 until 2013, when he was fired for embezzling more than $2 million during the previous five years. Similar to the case of Rita Crundwell, poor segregation of duties existed in Winsted, and Centrella would steal cash tax payments and use other town funds to conceal his theft. He used the embezzled money for gambling activities and to support a mistress who lived in Florida. He pleaded guilty in 2014 and was sentenced to 11 years in prison ("Former Winsted Finance Director Pleads Guilty to Stealing Money from Town" 2014; Lambert 2018).

Also comparable to the Rita Crundwell and Dixon, IL case, the Town of Winchester suffered financially because of Henry Centrella's fraud. While the town was able to recover Centrella's pension (worth approximately $92,000), it was challenged to fund expenses, including its schools, infrastructure, and public safety, as well as obtain credit for municipal operations. The confidence in town operations was also shaken, particularly since Centrella was one of the most trusted city officials. ("Former Winsted Finance Director Pleads Guilty to Stealing Money from Town" 2014; Lambert 2018).

Other Connecticut accounting and financial officials embezzled government funds to support gambling activities after two large casinos began operations in that state. Kelly and Hartley (2010) examined cases of problem gambler workplace fraud in that region and found that tax collectors and other government accounting/financial officials were among those embezzling in the workplace. Similar to the cases of Rita Crundwell and Henry Centrella, the lack of segregated duties and poor internal controls facilitated the frauds. And the trust placed in these officials enabled many of the frauds to take place over a long period of time (Kelly and Hartley 2010).

> Many of the problem gamblers in southeastern Connecticut had been law abiding citizens with no prior criminal history They tended to be long-term, trusted employees who were good performers in their organizations and who were so familiar with their operating and accounting systems that they could commit the frauds and conceal them for an extended period.
>
> *(Kelly and Hartley 2010, 236)*

More recently, in 2017, Michael Minh Nguyen, the former finance manager of Placentia, CA, received a 25-year prison sentence for stealing more than $5 million of city funds. His duties included making wire transfers from city accounts. When Nguyen found a lack of internal controls over these transfers, he began to wire transfers into his personal accounts and adjusted the city's accounting records to conceal the embezzlement. Similar to Henry Centrella from Connecticut, Nguyen was a problem gambler who lost a significant amount of the stolen funds while gambling (Salazar et al. 2016; Emery 2017).

In these and other cases where government accountants and finance officials acted inappropriately, they violated the ethical guidelines described in Tables 14.1 and 14.2. They did not act with the integrity and its associated characteristics of honesty and transparency demanded of them as public officials. Their actions detracted from the accountability required for government finances and caused significant financial damage to their respective communities. Perhaps even more important than the financial damage caused by government accounting and finance-related fraud was the violation of the public trust in these officials and the governments they represented. When the government fraudster is a long-term trusted representative, which is frequently the case and may have facilitated the financial crime, this betrayal is exacerbated. In the case of Rita Crundwell, her three decades of service to her hometown of Dixon, IL, resulted in the town's citizens relying on her completely. She was described "as trusted and efficient as a church tithe collector" (Smith 2012a) and was praised by a former town finance commissioner when he departed, noting that "She looks after every tax dollar as if it were her own" (Verschoor 2012, 15). After the discovery and subsequent investigation and guilty plea associated with Crundwell's crimes, the citizens of Dixon were described as "stunned, furious, and heartbroken" (Smith 2012b).

Comparable situations to Rita Crundwell's existed for the other government frauds discussed earlier. Henry Centrella also worked in his hometown of Winchester, CT, for decades and served as its finance director for about 30 years. Years after his guilty plea, Winchester's Mayor Candy Perez notes the town damage from Centrella's embezzlement.

> There are few words that can adequately express the profound violation of public trust that Mr. Centrella's actions have had on the town of Winchester. . . . The many years of theft, deceit, and corruption continue to impact our community and its citizens.
>
> *(Lambert 2018)*

A similar sentiment was expressed by Damien Arrula, Placentia City Administrator, when considering the embezzlement of Michael Nguyen. At his sentencing, Arrula noted that city leaders were trying to restore citizens' trust and stated, "Perhaps what pains me the most is that you, Mr. Nguyen, grew up here and spent most of your professional career in this area. . . . This was your home. This was our home. And you took a torch to it" (Emery 2017).

Internal control measures that help prevent and detect fraud

Fortunately, almost all government accountants and financial professionals do not engage in the misconduct of Rita Crundwell, Henry Centrella, and Michael Nguyen. Given the challenges and loss of public trust associated with unethical actions by government accounting and financial professionals, it is essential that systems and processes are in place to maintain accountability that contributes to the public trust. This trust is needed for the vitality and proper operation of democracies. If citizens are able to rely on and trust their respective governments, they are more likely to participate in government activities, such as voting, paying taxes, and otherwise volunteering support.

For government organizations, systems and processes for accountability include establishing successful fraud prevention and detection programs. Since the accounting scandals in the 1990s and early 2000s, much has been written about fraud prevention and detection. This section examines characteristics of sound prevention and detection programs of government organizations, with a focus on internal controls designed, implemented, and maintained by government accountants and finance officials.

The Committee of Sponsoring Organizations of the Treadway Commission (COSO) updated the *Internal Control – Integrated Framework* in 2013, noting that "COSO believes the Framework will enable organizations to effectively and efficiently develop and maintain systems of internal control that can enhance the likelihood of achieving the entity's objectives and adapt to changes in the business and operating environments" (COSO 2013, 1). This version updated the 1992 original framework, and one of the updated edition's considerations was the expectations concerning fraud prevention and detection. The five components of internal control identified in the original framework were retained in the 2013 *Integrated Framework*:

1   Control environment,
2   Risk assessment,
3   Control activities,
4   Information and communication, and
5   Monitoring activities (COSO 2013, 4–5).

While a primary focus of the *Internal Control – Integrated Framework* is private organizations, internal control is also emphasized in the federal government. The Federal Manager's Financial Integrity Act (FMFIA) mandated that the Comptroller General provide federal government internal control standards. The resulting *Standards for Internal Control in the Federal Government* (GAO-14–704G), commonly referred to as the Green Book, adapted for government application the COSO principles for the five components of internal control listed; these same five components are included in Table 14.3 (GAO 2014) along with 17 applicable principles of internal control. While the Green Book provides the structure for the design and operation of an internal control system for the federal government, it may also be used by state, local, and nonprofit organizations in the creation and operation of their internal control systems. "Internal controls" are a moral code in their own right because of what they communicate to people subject to those controls.

For internal control to be effective, the Green Book posits that the five components of internal control listed in Table 14.3 should be successfully designed, implemented, and operating in an integrated way. The 17 principles listed in Table 14.3 facilitate the design, implementation, and operation of the internal control system (GAO 2014).

It seems appropriate that the control environment is considered the foundation of the internal control system and the first identified principle focuses on the "commitment to integrity and ethical values" by management and the oversight body (GAO 2014, 21). This principle is supported by the attributes of tone at the top, standards of conduct, and adherence to those standards. It outlines important roles for both management and the oversight body in setting a proper tone at the top, including identifying integrity and ethical values, acting consistently with these values, and responding appropriately when actions are needed to reinforce the desired behaviors. An ethical tone at the top contributes positively to the development of principled standards of conduct, can guide behaviors of organization members, and can determine how those standards are obeyed. These expected standards and how they are implemented in the organization has an added benefit of providing confidence to those outside the organization (e.g., members of the public) that proper actions are established, monitored, and followed (GAO 2014).

Within the control environment, the oversight body and management play an important role in addressing the other ethics-related principles. The oversight body is tasked with supervising the organization's internal control system, including its design and operation by management. This requires oversight members to possess an understanding of the organization's goals, risks, and capabilities regarding internal control systems. This may require specific knowledge by an entity's oversight body members in such areas as an organization's programs, financial capabilities, technology characteristics, and applicable laws/regulations (GAO 2014).

Management plays a major role in the remaining three principles associated with the control environment. This includes establishing the organization's structure that permits accomplishing its goals and objectives, assigning internal control responsibilities to appropriate organizational

Table 14.3 The Five Components and 17 Principles of Internal Control

I Control Environment	1 The oversight body and management should demonstrate a commitment to integrity and ethical values.
	2 The oversight body should oversee the entity's internal control system.
	3 Management should establish an organizational structure, assign responsibility, and delegate authority to achieve the entity's objectives.
	4 Management should demonstrate a commitment to recruit, develop, and retain competent individuals.
	5 Management should evaluate performance and hold individuals accountable for their internal control responsibilities.
II Risk Assessment	6 Management should define objectives clearly to enable the identification of risks and define risk tolerances.
	7 Management should identify, analyze, and respond to risks related to achieving the defined objectives.
	8 Management should consider the potential for fraud when identifying, analyzing, and responding to risks.
	9 Management should identify, analyze, and respond to significant changes that could impact the internal control system.
III Control Activities	10 Management should design control activities to achieve objectives and respond to risks.
	11 Management should design the entity's information system and related control activities to achieve objectives and respond to risks.
	12 Management should implement control activities through policies.
IV Information and Communication	13 Management should use quality information to achieve the entity's objectives.
	14 Management should internally communicate the necessary quality information to achieve the entity's objectives.
	15 Management should externally communicate the necessary quality information to achieve the entity's objectives.
V Monitoring	16 Management should establish and operate monitoring activities to monitor the internal control system and evaluate the results.
	17 Management should remediate identified internal control deficiencies on a timely basis.

Source: U.S Government Accountability Office (GAO). 2014. *Standards for Internal Control in the Federal Government* (p. 9).

entities and individuals, and documenting the internal control system so that it functions successfully. Once established, management makes sure that individuals perform in accordance with their assigned duties and provides for accountability for those who do not adequately carry out their internal control functions effectively. Management is also responsible for recruiting and developing members who will be able to successfully operate within the internal control system developed for the organization (GAO 2014).

Of the remaining 12 principles identified in the Green Book, two management-oriented principles are particularly ethics-related. The first applies to the risk assessment component and directs that management should assess the potential for fraud when addressing the internal control system. This includes examining fraud factors identified in the fraud triangle (opportunity, incentive/pressure, and rationalization) and the types of fraud that are likely to occur, including asset misappropriation, fraudulent financial reporting, and corruption. Management should strive to reduce these types of fraud so the organization can achieve its goals and objectives (GAO 2014).

The second ethics-oriented principle applicable to management is a control activity component and instructs that management "should design control activities to achieve objectives and respond to risks" (GAO 2014, 44). This encompasses a variety of control activities, including segregating duties, safeguarding vulnerable assets, providing information processing controls, and monitoring performance. Segregation of duties was particularly emphasized in preventing fraud, and where this is not possible, additional controls to address fraud risk are recommended (GAO 2014).

As previously noted, the Green Book is applicable for other governments, including state and local governments. Accounting and finance officials at smaller, local municipalities particularly need to institute and maintain both effective fraud prevention and detection programs to ensure the accountability expected by the public. These include proper segregation of duties, along with preventing asset misappropriation associated with cash receipts and billing, disbursement and purchasing, and payroll (Hall 2014).

As noted, segregation of duties is considered one of the most useful measures to prevent fraud (GAO 2014; Albrecht et al. 2012; Hall 2014). In his book on local government fraud prevention, Hall (2014) noted that poor segregation of duties contributes to the opportunity to misappropriate assets and government fraud potential increases when one individual has control over more than one of the following functions:

1　Custody of assets
2　Reconciliations
3　Authorization
4　Bookkeeping (Hall 2014, 15).

A lack of segregated duties existed in all of the government-related frauds cited in the last section. For example, Rita Crundwell had control in all four areas, which facilitated her ability to engage in the fraud over many years. Hall (2014) notes that small government organizations may not be able to have segregated duties in these four areas. In those cases, compensating controls can be used, such as assigning another individual to review the function. If this is not possible, a certified public accountant or certified fraud examiner could do periodic, unexpected checks of the government accounting system (Hall 2014).

Stopping transaction level fraud is another key aspect of a fraud prevention program for government organizations. For cash receipts and billing systems, cash embezzlements can occur when there are decentralized cash collections and inadequate accounting controls. The theft of cash is facilitated when cash is being received in various places within the government organization and when a lack of consistency in the cash receipt procedures exists. Disbursements and purchasing transactions also have a high potential for fraud in government organizations, particularly concerning the misappropriation of assets. Inappropriate wire transfers, payments to fictitious vendors, duplicate payments to legitimate vendors, and fraudulent checks with altered check payees/amounts and forged signatures can all result in cash embezzlement from a government organization. Payroll fraud may involve duplicate payroll checks, payments to fictitious employees, or improper pay rates and amounts of work time recorded for payroll purposes. The effective internal controls identified in the Green Book can help address these and other ways cash can be stolen (GAO 2014; Hall 2014).

While the measures identified can prevent government fraud, government accountants and finance officials also administer the fraud detection program associated with the Green

Book Principle 5 (providing accountability for internal control) and Principle 8 (assessing fraud potential when considering risks) (GAO 2014). While fraud prevention programs are vital in ensuring governments operate effectively and efficiently, fraud still exists and needs to be detected when it occurs. In its 2018 report on government fraud, the ACFE reported that government agency fraud was initially detected by tip (45%), internal audit (15%), management review (9%), external audit (6%), or when notified by law enforcement (5%) (ACFE 2018). It is therefore prudent for government organizations to maintain a hotline to receive tips, conduct appropriate internal audits and management review, and work with external auditors to detect fraud. These measures will also help to address the perception of detection axiom: "Employees who perceive that they will be caught engaging in occupational fraud and abuse are less likely to commit it" (Wells 2008, 399).

Concluding remarks

This chapter addresses government accounting ethics, which forms the basis of trust in over 90,000 government organizations in the United States. Measures that contribute to public trust in government are particularly relevant in the United States today. A recent Gallup Poll reported that American's trust in the federal government to deal with domestic and international problems fell to the lowest point in 20 years. Only 35% of those surveyed had "a great deal" or "a fair amount" of confidence in the government's ability to handle domestic problems, while 41% expressed such confidence in the government's ability to handle international problems (Brenan 2019).

Ample ethical standards, structures, and processes exist to promote public trust in governments. These include federal, state, and professional organization principles that articulate what is appropriate and inappropriate behavior for thousands of government accountants and finance professionals. Fortunately, these public servants generally abide by the ethical guidelines in the honest and professional performance of their duties. In the relatively rare instances when government accounting or finance officials behave unethically and commit crimes, as occurred in the case of Rita Crundwell, the public trust and faith in government suffers. As stewards of government resources, it is incumbent on these individuals to promote public trust by developing and maintaining internal control systems, a central tenet of which is displaying a commitment to integrity and ethics.

This dedication to integrity and ethics is critical for government accounting and financial professionals for an ancillary reason. As these individuals establish and maintain internal control systems for federal, state, and local governments, ethical considerations are paramount in ensuring proper accountability of the organizations' resources, along with their effective and efficient use in serving the public. Not only are these public officials providing control systems to promote ethical behavior of government employees, they are establishing procedures to govern their own actions, which necessitates a high level of integrity throughout the process.

Finally, ethics will remain important to government accounting and financial officials well into the future. A politically divided nation, record deficits, and additional demands on government programs and resources will all necessitate that these public servants maintain a high level of integrity and ethics as they perform their duties. There is also to be a period of transition, as 34% of federal employees working in 2015 will be eligible to retire by 2020. This will require the hiring and training of new government accountants and financial managers for a variety of positions (Bora 2018). Inculcating these new hires with proper ethical values will help maintain accountability and the public trust in government.

References

Albrecht, W. S., C. O. Albrecht, C. C. Albrecht, and M. F. Zimbelman. 2012. *Fraud Examination*. Mason, OH: South-Western, Cengage Learning.

American Institute of CPAs (AICPA). 2016. "Code of Professional Conduct." www.aicpa.org/content/dam/aicpa/research/standards/codeofconduct/downloadabledocuments/2014december15contentasof2016august31codeofconduct.pdf.

Apostolou, B., N. Apostolou, and G. Thibadoux. 2015. "Horseplay in Dixon: Lessons Learned from the Rita Crundwell Fraud." *Journal of Forensic and Investigative Accounting* 7 (1) (January–June): 275–91. http://web.nacva.com/JFIA/Issues/JFIA-2015-1_11.pdf.

Association of Certified Fraud Examiners (ACFE). 2018. "Report to the Nations: 2018 Global Study on Occupational Fraud and Abuse – Government Edition." www.acfe.com/uploadedFiles/ACFE_Website/Content/rttn/2018/RTTN-Government-Edition.pdf.

Association of Government Accountants (AGA). 2019. "Code of Ethics." www.agacgfm.org/About/Code-of-Ethics.aspx.

Bora, I. 2018. "New Generation Needed to Fill Retirements at Federal, State, and Local Agencies." *The CPA Journal,* April. www.cpajournal.com/2018/05/23/urgent-need-for-governmental-accounting-education/.

Brenan, M. 2019. "Americans' Trust in Government to Handle Problems at a New Low." *Gallup News Politics*, January 31. https://news.gallup.com/poll/246371/americans-trust-government-handle-problems-new-low.aspx.

California Society of Certified Public Accountants (CalCPA). 2019. "Code of Professional Conduct." www.tscpa.org/advocacy/ethics.

Committee of Sponsoring Organizations of the Treadway Commission (COSO). 2013. "Internal Control – Integrated Framework." *Executive Summary*, May. www.coso.org/Documents/990025P-Executive-Summary-final-may20.pdf.

Emery, S. 2017. "Former Placentia Finance Manager Gets 25 Years in Prison for Embezzling More Than $5 Million." *Orange County Register,* March 10. www.ocregister.com/2017/03/10/former-placentia-finance-manager-gets-25-years-in-prison-for-embezzling-more-than-5-million/.

Government Accounting Standards Board (GASB). 2017. "White Paper – Why Governmental Accounting and Financial Reporting Is – And Should Be – Different." September. www.gasb.org/cs/ContentServer?c=Document_C&cid=1176169371273&d=&pagename=GASB%2FDocument_C%2FDocumentPage.

Government Financial Officers Association (GFOA). 2019. "Code of Professional Ethics." www.gfoa.org/membership/code-professional-ethics.

Hall, C. 2014. *The Little Book of Local Government Fraud Prevention – How to Prevent It, How to Detect It.* Middletown, DE: Koiner Co., LLC.

Huefner, R. 2011. "Fraud Risks in Local Government: An Analysis of Audit Findings." *Journal of Forensic and Investigative Accounting* 3 (3). http://web.nacva.com/JFIA/Issues/JFIA-2011-3_5.pdf.

Kelly, P., and C. Hartley 2010. "Casino Gambling and Workplace Fraud – A Cautionary Tale for Managers." *Management Research News* 33 (3): 224–39. https://doi.org/10.1108/02686909610150395.

Lambert, B. 2018. "Parole Application Denied for Former Winsted Finance Director." *The Register Citizen* (March 9): 3. www.registercitizen.com/news/article/Parole-application-denied-for-former-Winsted-12741365.php.

McKenna, F. 2013. "The Madoff of Munis." *Forbes,* June 5. www.forbes.com/sites/francinemckenna/2013/06/05/the-madoff-of-munis/#2549b8935ef8.

New York State Society of Certified Public Accountants (NYSSCPA). 2013. "Code of Professional Conduct." www.nysscpa.org/docs/default-source/default-document-library/nysscpa-code-of-professional-conduct.pdf?sfvrsn=0#:~:text=The%20Code%20of%20Professional%20Conduct,of%20professional%20services%20by%20members.

Pope, K. R. 2013. "The $54 Million Fraud – What CPAs Can Learn from the Fleecing of Dixon, Ill." *AICPA Store,* July 31. www.aicpastore.com/Content/media/PRODUCER_CONTENT/Newsletters/Articles_2013/ForensicValuation/54-million-dollar-fraud.jsp.

Salazar, D., K. Puente, S. Schwebke, and T. Sforza. 2016. "Placentia's No. 2 Finance Manager Faces 17 Charges in Embezzlement of $4.3 Million," *Orange County Register,* April 15. www.ocregister.com/2016/04/15/placentias-no-2-finance-manager-faces-17-charges-in-embezzlement-of-43-million-from-city/.

Smith, B. 2012a. "Rita Crundwell and the Dixon Embezzlement." *Chicago Magazine,* December. www.chicagomag.com/Chicago-Magazine/December-2012/Rita-Crundwell-and-the-Dixon-Embezzlement/index.php?cparticle=4&siarticle=3&requiressl=true#artanc.

Smith, B. 2012b. "Rita Crundwell Pleads Guilty in Dixon Embezzlement Case." *Chicago Magazine,* November 14. www.chicagomag.com/Chicago-Magazine/The-312/November-2012/Rita-Crundwell-Pleads-Guilty-in-Dixon-Embezzlement-Case/.

Texas Society of Certified Public Accountants (TXCPA). 2019. "Ethics." www.tscpa.org/advocacy/ethics.

Texas State Board of Public Accountancy (TSBPA). 2019. "Rules of Professional Conduct – Texas Administrative Code – Title 22, Part 22, Chapter 501." Accessed October 13, 2019. https://texreg.sos.state.tx.us/public/readtac$ext.ViewTAC?tac_view=4&ti=22&pt=22&ch=501.

The Register Citizen. 2014. "Former Winsted Finance Director Henry Centrella Pleads Guilty to Stealing Money from Town." *The Register Citizen,* January 24. www.registercitizen.com/news/article/Former-Winsted-finance-director-Henry-Centrella-12011361.php.

U.S Census State Government Finances. 2012. https://factfinder.census.gov/faces/tableservices/jsf/pages/productview.xhtml?pid=SGF_2012_SGF001&prodType=table.

U.S Government Accountability Office (GAO). 2014. "Standards for Internal Control in the Federal Government." www.gao.gov/assets/670/665712.pdf.

U.S Government Accountability Office (GAO). 2018. "Government Auditing Standards – 2018 Revision." www.gao.gov/assets/700/693136.pdf.

U.S. Office of Management and Budget (OMB). 2018. "Table 1.4 – Summary of Receipts, Outlays and Surpluses or Deficits (-) in Current Dollars, Constant (FY 2009) Dollars, and as Percentages of GDP: 1940–2020." www.whitehouse.gov/omb/budget/Historicals.

Verschoor, C. 2012. "Comptroller Steals $53 Million from City Funds." *Strategic Finance,* July. https://sfmagazine.com/wp-content/uploads/sfarchive/2012/07/ETHICS-Comptroller-Steals-53-Million-from-City-Funds.pdf.

Wells, J. 2008. *Principles of Fraud Examination*, 2nd ed. Hoboken, NJ: John Wiley and Sons, Inc.

Ziegenfuss, D. 1996. "State and Local Government Fraud Survey for 1995." *Managerial Auditing Journal* 11 (9). https://doi.org/10.1108/02686909610150395.

Ziegenfuss, D. 2001. "The Role of Control Environment in Reducing Local Government Fraud." *Journal of Public Budgeting, Accounting and Financial Management* 13 (3) (Fall). http://connection.ebscohost.com/c/articles/5383752/role-control-environment-reducing-local-government-fraud.

15

ETHICS AND ACCOUNTING INFORMATION SYSTEMS

Richard B. Dull and Lydia F. Schleifer

Introduction

"The world needs a huge injection of ethics."

(Luciano Floridi 2015, 165)

The most basic interest in the study of ethics is related to identifying the "right" thing to do. It is almost a universal belief that it is ethical to do right and unethical to do wrong.[1] With the ubiquitous nature of information systems, the universality of connectivity among devices, as well as the speed with which technology changes, it can sometimes be extremely difficult to determine what is the right thing to do. In addition, there is a big difference between the outlooks reflected by "it is unethical to misuse big data and harm the rights of individuals" and "it is ethical to use data to make life better for society." So how does one, given the pervasiveness of IS, ensure that an equally pervasive approach to ethics is maintained? The primary purpose of this chapter is to provide a background regarding ethics in accounting information systems, examine several current IS topics, and identify some of the corresponding ethical implications that should be considered when dealing with those topics.

What specifically about IS requires a consideration of ethical approaches? Primarily, it is the expectation for privacy and confidentiality. Is it ethical to use data to which you should not have access? In the US, even nonprofit organizations that operate with much openness and transparency may have information that gives the organization a competitive advantage related to the public services that they provide. Most for-profit organizations have operated with assurance of the privacy and security of information to protect business operations and processes, as well as trade secrets. In an e-environment, the likelihood of data misuse (internal and external, legal and illegal) increases dramatically. This is due to the increase in data that are collected and stored online, requiring that physical controls are replaced by electronic controls, thus enabling the possibility of copying and altering data without a physical presence or visible evidence that a breach occurred. We are at a point in history when most people believe that data misuse is no longer an "if" but a "when." Who is impacted by ethical and nonethical use of data? Biot-Paquerot and Hasnaoui (2009) point out several types of e-commerce stakeholders that participate in the sharing of information in a financial information system; in addition to those that visit and/or purchase from a website, there are "corporate suppliers, competitors, software developers, banks and monetary agencies, intermediaries, and legislative bodies" (Biot-Paquerot and Hasnaoui 2009, 62).

Even the most diligent ethical mindset cannot solve or protect against every ethical dilemma. This is because the underlying dilemma may include competing ethical interests among participants (e.g., the individual vs. groups vs. society) and competing ethical approaches (e.g., stakeholder vs. stockholder vs. social contract theories [Mingers and Walsham 2010]). There are various aspects of ethical decision making (e.g., ethics, moral outlook, professional duty [Sherratt, Rogerson, and Fairweather 2005]) that may enter into the decision process. There are also various ethics theories that may come into play as they are applied to business ethics (e.g., consequentialism, deontology, and virtue ethics and communitarianism [Mingers and Walsham 2010]). There are even fluid definitions of privacy and sensitive data that may complicate the situation (Wang and Jiang 2017).

Despite the difficulty of identifying how ethics and information systems (IS) relate, interact, or even collide, in some cases, there is a growing interest in the nature of ethics in the domain of IS. The development of IS is essentially "people driven," arising from the need to understand processes and make decisions. Therefore, an unavoidable aspect of IS is the fact that the underlying nature of the personal morality of people will always be a salient consideration in the functioning of IS. The study of ethics is crucial because people make decisions, for good or ill, that impact other people (Taylor and Daigle 2017). However, the research related to ethics and IS does not necessarily have clear boundaries that enable a researcher to clearly identify when that research is focused on ethics and IS. For example, Stahl (2008) illustrates/discusses the plausibility of the idea that critical research in IS (CRIS) is basically all about ethics related to IS. "Critical research in information systems is based on and inspired by ethics and morality" (Stahl 2008, 137). Therefore, ethics and morality can be seen as influencing four main aspects of CRIS: critical intentions, topics, theories, and methodologies. IS researchers who are interested in further exploring Stahl's concept of a link between CRIS and ethics can look into critical research and IS.

In the field of accounting, the research has primarily related to professional ethics, with a focus on adherence to the rules promulgated by specific professional organizations. The rules are seldom general enough to deal with changes in technology that are occurring in today's environment. The Appendix provides links to the code of ethics of several of these professional organizations. Although ethical codes may not yet reflect it, the profession of accounting appears to be embracing the idea of remaining relevant to and staying on the front lines of the evolution of IS. It is essential that the profession's ethics address technology changes and the issues that arise due to those changes. The scope of this chapter will reach into some broad technological areas that are likely to affect the way that the accounting profession functions.

This chapter is organized to help convey the evolutionary nature of the ongoing determination of what is ethical in particular domains and the challenge of identifying the ethical conflicts that present themselves as technology changes. The next section, "Ethics in Technology," addresses computing and computer ethics as what could be readily recognized as the foundation or most central component of modern-day information systems. Moving from the general to the specific, from the core of computer ethics, through information technology and information systems, the section then addresses ethics in the accounting domain via accounting information systems/enterprise systems. The following section, "Current Technology Trends," includes discussions of ethics related to big data, privacy, the Internet of Things (IoT), cloud computing, and blockchain. The chapter ends with the "Conclusion" section, summarizing and providing ideas to consider within the realm of accounting information systems.

Ethics in technology

Throughout the hierarchy of technology, from the general topic of computers, through information technology and information systems, to today's accounting systems, there have been ethical concerns and attempts to address those concerns with research and codes of professional ethics. This section explores some of those concerns and responses.

Computer ethics – the core

There is relatively little ethics research specifically related to IS, but the research related to computer ethics and information ethics is relevant to IS (Mingers and Walsham 2010). Computer ethics is the study of ethical problems that arise related to computer technology (Iqbal and Beigh 2017). They describe the history of computer ethics, which has focused on the need for ethics codes, laws, and regulations to deal with "new and challenging ethical issues generated by the application of pervasive technology" (Iqbal and Beigh 2017, 983).

The Association for Computing Machinery (ACM) is "a global scientific and educational organization representing the computing community" (ACM 2018). It is interesting to note that the ACM Code of Ethics and Professional Conduct's preamble asserts that "[c]omputing professionals' actions change the world," clearly accepting the responsibility for playing a large role in maintaining the ethics of the computing profession. A common underlying theme for the ACM ethics code is a focus on human well-being (ACM 2018). While the ACM Code of Ethics and Professional Conduct only officially applies to members of the organization, it is a solid starting point for thinking about overall ethics in information technology, information systems, and accounting information systems.

Information technology and ethics – the widening scope of ethical concern

A stream of research and writings by Luciano Floridi has developed ideas related to the ethics of information and the ethics of information technology (Floridi 1999, 2002, 2005, 2006, 2009; Floridi and Sanders 2002; Cath and Floridi 2017; Taddeo and Floridi 2016). This research has added a layer to the scope of ethical concern related to information and technology; just as we consider human ethics, bioethics, and environmental ethics – because people, animals, and nature have intrinsic rights and/or value – we should consider the ethics of information (Mingers and Walsham 2010; Floridi 2009). "We need to adopt an ethics of stewardship towards the infosphere," which is the informational environment of an organization (Floridi 2002, 300).

Another domain within information technology is information and communication technology (ICT), with the "unique features of ICT, such as its speed of transmission, globalisation, anonymity, and ability to manipulate information" that present new situations and ethical challenges without a clear-cut ethical resolution (Sherratt et al. 2005, 299). Sherratt et al. (2005, 300) suggest that ICT professionals can learn about ethical issues by studying conflicts that arise from "unethical computer use." Their framework for ethics and ICTs includes ethical issues related to "promises/contracts, personal rights/freedoms, harm, computer misuse, information use, and property ownership." They support the idea that professionals involved with ICTs should make ethical decisions being mindful of their professional and personal moral duties.[2]

Information systems and ethics

IS has evolved into "integrated systems that reach into every aspect of individual, corporate, and social life" (Pauleen, Rooney, and Intezari 2017, 400). This evolution has necessitated an examination of whether and/or how IS can effectively, beneficially, and ethically impact society. Whether the exercise by professionals of pretty good foresight can or cannot identify every potential ethical issue that may arise from development of new technologies, the ethical dilemmas resulting from a "misuse of data" can serve to alert the IS community, in hindsight, that it needs to take seriously and protect the well-being of "individuals, organizations, and societies" (Pauleen, Rooney, and Intezari 2017, 400). Pauleen, Rooney, and Intezari (2017, 401) advance the idea of an ethical approach to IS by discussing, in the context of the Global Financial Crisis of 2007–08, how a framework for wisdom (which includes ethical skill) can be used to gain insight into how to recognize and avoid the "perils of unwise use of data, information and predictive (algorithmic) knowledge in a complex context."

Mingers and Walsham (2010) also put forth an approach to determining what is ethical in the IS context. They note the fairly meager coverage of ethics and IS in the research literature. After discussing three main types of ethics (consequentialism, deontology, and virtue ethics and communitarianism),[3] they advocate for the use of a discourse approach, which aims to determine what is ethical by actually employing a discourse whereby participants come to a consensus about what action should be taken, say, to solve an ethical dilemma. Mingers and Walsham (2010, 846) provide an example of an IS topic area, open source software, "where one could argue a prima facie case for the application of discourse ethics" because it is "considered to be a relatively bottom-up and consensus approach to the development of software."

The accounting profession, as part of the IS community, endeavors to stay on the front line of how accountants' involvement with their clients' IS may impact their professional ethics, including independence. Recent efforts to update the code of conduct illustrate this desire to stay current and relevant. As of May of 2018, the AICPA was accepting comments on their proposed revision of "independence rules for information system services" in the Code of Professional Conduct; currently, the rules are "silent on what constitutes an FIS [financial information system], and therefore bans all design or development services for an FIS regardless of magnitude" (AICPA 2018a). The proposal defines FIS and provides guidance about non-attest services an AICPA member may perform with regard to FIS. In another move related to independence, the AICPA, as of October 2018, has extended the effective date for its guidance related to hosting services. "The new interpretation to the 'Independence Rule' in the AICPA *Code of Professional Conduct* explains that taking responsibility for hosting an attest client's data or records impairs a CPA's independence" (AICPA 2018b). However, the profession will have 10 additional months to prepare for the change, illustrating the challenge of providing professional guidance in a rapidly changing environment and of consistently applying the profession's ethics.

Accounting information systems/enterprise systems – connecting the dots

The connection between accounting information systems (AIS) and ethics is based on the fact that people are involved in "selecting, designing, performing, maintaining, and updating" AIS as well as in overall system use and decision making (Taylor and Daigle 2017, 1). It is important to gain insights into individuals' ethical perceptions and behaviors in order to most effectively aim for/accomplish ethical AIS impacts and outcomes. The rest of this section describes how a number of researchers have investigated how people can use AIS to affect the well-being of other people (Taylor and Daigle 2017) through theoretical (Brown, Marcum, and Stuebs 2017), survey (Burney, Radtke and Widener 2017), and experimental research (Holt, Lang and Sutton 2017; Crossler et al. 2017) that involves a focus on the human element of the ETHOs framework proposed by Guragai et al. (2017).

Guragai et al. (2017, 65) develop an ETHOs framework that examines prior research related to how "environmental, technological, human, and organizational" factors interact with the "recordkeeping, reporting, and control" functions within AIS. There are ethical implications and potential dilemmas that can arise "because people are key elements in AIS" (Guragai et al. 2017, 65). This comprehensive overview of research related to ethics and AIS also discusses areas in need of future research, with the authors noting that AIS "researchers rarely explicitly tie their research questions and motivations underlying ethical goals" (Guragai et al. 2017, 77). It also encourages researchers to more explicitly address the need to consider the human (ethical) aspects of AIS.

Brown et al. (2017) propose a theoretical framework that describes the attributes of a virtuous AIS professional. They propose that efforts to improve professional virtues will also lead to improved functioning of an AIS and increased trust in the AIS. Their Systems Trust Model is grounded in "the confidence of multiple AIS stakeholder groups that AIS professionals will voluntarily accept and fulfill their information management duties to recognize and protect the rights and interests of AIS stakeholders and the public" (Brown et al. 2017, 8).

Burney et al. (2017, 26) explored "the intersection of AIS and business ethics." They examined the performance measurement system (PMS) as a very specific component of AIS, and the specific aspect of business ethics that relates to the "ethical nature of both the individual and the work unit" (i.e., ethical climate) (Burney et al. 2017, 27). The focus was on the enabling use of the PMS to control (that is, "motivate, direct, and influence," [Burney et al 2017, 39]) employees. Their study found that an enabling PMS may be associated with less counterproductive work behavior (CWB) since employees likely value their freedom (and less ethical employees can have the freedom to engage in self-interested behaviors without having to engage in obviously counterproductive work behavior). However, a combination of self-focused employees, a perceived self-focused ethical work climate, and an enabling PMS could result in more CWB.

Crossler et al. (2017, 49) examined ethics in the context of "Bring Your Own Device (BYOD) policy compliance," important to organizations in addressing risks related to employees using their own devices "to access or store company data." Their results were consistent with the idea that if companies emphasize that compliance is ethical, then employees will be more likely to comply with company BYOD policies.

Holt, Lang, and Sutton (2017, 108) examined the "ethical implications of employee monitoring" using contractarian ethics as a framework.[4] In the context of advances in technology leading to better capability for and wide-range use of data analytics, it is necessary to consider the possibility that there are privacy issues and other ethical concerns (like perceptions of fairness in the workplace) related to active employee monitoring methods (like video surveillance). Holt, Lang, and Sutton's (2017) experimental results supported a conclusion that participants' perception of the presence of active monitoring led to perceptions of less organizational ethics, even in the face of a justification for the monitoring.

Research studies such as those discussed underscore the value of exploring the perceptions and choices made by stakeholders and participants in the context of AIS, in order to have an empirical basis for steering the evolution of technology and systems in the right, that is, ethical, direction.

Current technology trends

Each new technology introduced into accounting provides opportunities and challenges. This section discusses several technologies, including big data, which introduces speed and variety into the data collection process – as well as associated privacy issues. Also included are the topics of the Internet of Things (providing data that until recently was not feasible to collect), cloud computing, and blockchain.

Big data

According to Ahmadi, Dileepan, and Wheatley (2016), big data is so called due to its being a very large amount of data (volume) that can be accumulated very quickly (velocity) from many different sources (variety). Even without a detailed definition of "big data" it is obvious that it is all made possible by computing technology. Therefore, the underlying ethics of the world of computing is absolutely relevant in the examination of ethics and big data. New horizons in IS bring new challenges. According to Appelbaum, Kogan, and Vasarhelyi (2017, 4), the newest audit challenges relate to big data and data analytics, as the "environment of Big Data . . . is progressively interconnecting with corporate systems." This interconnectedness provides access to a wider range of people with a wider range of skills to use and manipulate the data.

Richins et al. (2017) discuss the debate over whether big data is a threat or an opportunity for the accounting profession; will big data analytics automate and replace many accounting and auditing jobs, or will it enable accountants to move into the opportunities for using skills they already have for dealing with large amounts of data? Big data will impact business activity measurement, which will of course impact accounting measurement and assurance (Vasarhelyi, Kogan and Tuttle 2015) and, furthermore, will necessitate the "creation and refinement of accounting standards" (Warren, Moffitt and Byrnes 2015, 397) and changes in auditing standards (Krahel and Titera 2015). The primary threat to accounting –as currently practiced – from big data and analytics is the replacement of many manual tasks and tasks that were developed to compensate for lack of time and data, particularly in the area of auditing. For example, why would one test a sample of transactions when one has the tools that are capable of testing the entire population of data with virtually the same effort; today the data and tools that enable analysis to search for anomalies are commonplace (Richins et al. 2017). Not using these new tools that potentially provide results that are better than sampling will at best be difficult to defend and, at worst, lead to a reduction of the importance of the role of accountants in the information assurance process.

The professional and research literature shows that the accounting profession is responding to changes in technology by creating resources needed to react to big data as an opportunity. For example, the Open Compliance and Ethics Group (OCEG), an international organization created in 2002, provides resources to help organizations deal with "governance, risk management, and compliance" (GRC) issues in the current environment of technology and big data (Anders 2016, 64). Also, the International Ethics Standards Board for Accountants (IESBA) and the International Federation of Accountants (IFAC) (which includes the AICPA and IMA) provide extensive ethics resources for the purpose of helping the profession deal with the "moving target" of ethics in the changing professional environment (Anders 2018, 72). The Association of Chartered Certified Accountants (ACCA) has also produced a report, "Ethics and Trust in a Digital Age" (2017), based upon a global survey of over 10,000 accountants about their attitudes regarding ethics. The survey revealed the expectation that ethical behavior will increase in importance as the digital age evolves. The report "offers insight and guidance to professional accountants and auditors on issues from cyber-security to crypto-currencies" (ACCA 2017).

The accounting profession needs to embrace and use big data and analytics to remain competitive as well to increase profit margins (Tschakert et al. 2016). Being proactive, rather than taking a reactionary approach, should put accountants in a strong long-term position when dealing with the onslaught of big data and analytics. According to Drew (2018) the accounting profession needs to incorporate a working partnership with data scientists and big data engineers who will be able "to help develop the audit and advisory products" and "be responsible for putting together the final communications" (Drew 2018, 48), and who will have the "technical and ethical competencies" to deal with big data in the context of the accounting profession. In addition, accounting educators will need to include in the curricula a coverage of "ethical issues related to IT" (AACSB 2014) in order to prepare students for a "data-driven and analytics-enabled future" (Gamage 2016, 602).[5]

Privacy

In addition to incorporating technological advances into their practices, accountants also need to consider some of the side effects of big data, specifically the potential loss of privacy. The issue of potential misuse of big data is probably the foremost concern. Part of the concern is that "the nature and extent of threat to privacy is not fully understood in the context of big data" (Ahmadi, Dileepan and Wheatley 2016, 290).

In a Business Ethics Briefing on Business Ethics and Big Data, the Institute of Business Ethics (IBE) (2016), suggested six questions that should be considered by accountants:

* Do we know how the company uses big data and to what extent it is integrated into strategic planning?
* Do we send a privacy notice when we collect personal data? Is it written in a clear and accessible language which allows users to give a truly informed consent?
* Does my organization assess the risks linked to big data?
* Does my organization have any safeguard mechanisms in place to mitigate these risks?
* Do we make sure that the tools to manage these risks are effective and measure outcome?
* Do we conduct appropriate due diligence when sharing or acquiring data from third parties?

While this is an example of one professional body considering ethics in one area of advanced technology, laws have not consistently kept pace with technology changes. In a study of data privacy laws in 92 countries and regions and 200 data breaches worldwide, Wang and Jiang (2017) found inconsistencies between what the laws consider to be sensitive data and what the data breaches showed to be the actual vulnerable data. Most countries include the following in a list of sensitive data: racial or ethnic origin, political opinions, religious or philosophical beliefs, trade union membership, data concerning health or sex life, genetic data, and biometric data (the "EU standard" of sensitive data). However, it is financial data that usually leads to the financial losses and economic damage resulting from data breaches. Wang and Jiang (2017, 3299) conclude that "[t]his is the practical paradox: What needs special protection in practice is not granted special protection in legislation."

An area that may have an impact on the success of organizations and their constituents, as well as on academic research, is the use of big data analytics to reveal information that has been anonymized, or de-identified. Because of the sheer volumes of data, it is becoming more likely that multiple datasets can be linked together, removing the privacy protection that was available in specific data sets. In the medical field, there have been studies on the de-identification and re-identification of private information[6], but this concept has not been addressed in accounting and financial systems. As the population of data increases in volume and variety, how accountants de-identify data will become more important.

It is clear that where the laws do not necessarily force ethical conduct, it is essential that professions fill the void with their continual monitoring of where ethics guidance is needed in order to protect people who may be harmed if their data are compromised. Examples of current internal control technologies that may impact privacy concerns include geolocation tracking of inventory on trucks. By default, this control also tracks every move of the truck driver, which may be considered a violation of privacy. Using biometrics such as fingerprints or facial recognition for access to secure areas may also have ethical implications. For example, the standard by which the face is recognized must be stored on a system. If that data were misappropriated, the parameters might be used to identify when an individual is at locations other than the work environment.

The accounting profession has always focused on financial data, internal controls, and the necessity to conduct their business under their pervasive code of conduct. Currently, the profession is in a unique position to stay at the front of this technological wave and help determine where it goes and how it affects stakeholders.

The Internet of Things

"The incipient Internet of Things will only exacerbate the privacy concerns of big data." (Ahmadi, Dileepan and Wheatley 2016, 292) Clearly, ethical issues will ensue. "[T]he IoT will allow billions of objects, such as mobile devices, and virtual environments to exchange data" (Adams 2017, 15), likely resulting in vulnerable data, inadequate data security, and potential data breaches, especially as the aggregation of data from interconnected devices leads to increased access to that data (Perera et al. 2015).

From pills, to lightbulbs, to cameras, to airplanes, any object that can be attached to and controlled over the internet becomes part of the Internet of Things (IoT) (Ranger 2018). Alarcon and Staut (2016) describe very tangible ways in which the IoT will affect the accounting profession. For example, in manufacturing, physical asset management/maintenance can be facilitated with sensor chips that allow tracking, monitoring, and data collection related to usage. Inventory flows can be monitored with sensors. The large amounts of data automatically collected by sensor devices will allow for continuous monitoring and auditing, transforming the nature of audits and assurance services (Alarcon and Staut 2016). It is plausible that the use of sensor chips and connected devices could substantially enhance internal controls, but the use of such devices may require auditor assessment of the device effectiveness.

Supply chain and logistic systems have been a natural place for IoT implementation. Products with chips can be tracked throughout the supply chain process to aid in real-time inventory management. Chips are being placed in shipping containers to monitor location and temperature of the products, providing better control over quality of products and ultimately enhancing revenues. Another application to help refine revenue models comes from the insurance industry; today one can attach a device to an automobile to monitor driving habits and adjust rates charged to drivers based upon driving habits, which can impact the cost of an insurance policy

(Alarcon and Staut 2016). By improving the pricing of policies and managing risks, companies can positively impact overall revenues.

One of the most significant impacts from IoT technologies relates to the automotive industry. IoT technologies are driving the movement toward autonomous cars. Most if not all automakers are experimenting with the concept. Soon, automobiles without drivers will be available to take passengers from point A to Point B using IoT; actually, on a very limited basis, it is happening now, but it may take decades to substantially replace the cars on the road today (Higgins 2019). Ethical implications include risk management and decision making – such as what decision to make in a situation where two negative (and no positive) alternatives exist. For example, if a collision is inevitable and two options are available, what ethical parameters are built into the system that drive the system – minimize loss of life or loss of property? Decisions made under such circumstances may impact accounting through creating liabilities based on loss of property or life related to a specific decision. Additional ethical decisions that may impact revenues could include the rates charged based on where an individual is going (medical appointment) or the purpose of a trip (emergency) or based on the perception of a customer's ability to pay. These revenue choices may also be made in light of competing demands for resources (for example, pick up a customer without the ability to pay who needs a ride to a medical appointment, versus a customer with the ability to pay who needs a ride to a medical appointment.)

In addition to new business opportunities, IoT enables businesses to automate routine tasks. Lights, coffee makers, appliances, printers, phone systems, and security systems are just a few examples of items that may use the IoT. Data may be stored in unencrypted space; devices may be used to hack into corporate networks; personal information may be accessed. As devices age, even when encryption was originally incorporated, it will likely become outdated and become a risk for an organization (Young Entrepreneur Council 2018).

Accounting risks include potential lost revenues from a variety of sources, including denial of service attacks, the cost of violation of privacy laws, and the loss of competitive advantage due to the loss of corporate secrets. Related to IoT technology is edge computing, the ability to process and analyze data on the same device that collects the data. By processing in this manner, sensitive data may not need to be transmitted, reducing privacy issues that can occur by transmitting information over the network and through the cloud (Talluri 2017), but it can increase privacy issues when IoT devices are not secure. Edge computing can produce significant cost savings to an organization through the reduction of data storage in the cloud, as well as reduced cost related to network traffic. One of the ethics issues related to edge computing relates to balancing cost savings and privacy concerns. It should be noted that the benefits of edge computing only can be realized with proper security and controls within the device.

Cloud computing

According to Drew (2012, 111) "CPAs increasingly will use mobile devices to access cloud-based applications, communications, and data. This connectivity will help CPAs work more efficiently." But of course this connectivity will present ethical challenges.

De Bruin and Floridi (2017), in what they call the first publication about the ethics of cloud computing, discuss the idea that cloud customers have "mutual informational (epistemic) obligations to provide and seek information about relevant issues such as consumer privacy, reliability of services, data mining and data ownership. The concept of interlucency is developed as an epistemic virtue governing ethically effective communication" (21).

According to de Bruin and Floridi (2017, 26), cloud computing stakeholders include "owners, investors, employers, employees, customers, suppliers, competitors, governments and the environment." The authors conclude that in order to determine what is best for all these stakeholders, it is necessary to determine what they value. For example, stakeholders in the cloud computing environment value freedom more than ownership, that is, would rather be able to do what they want to with information (use and share things) than actually own the information. This concept requires accountants to consider the users of technology to properly implement controls related to systems and data. In a cloud environment, users may consider themselves to be "custodians" of data (and using the data for the good of society) rather than "owners" of the data (using the data for the good of the organization). Organizations need to recognize and consider these differences when deciding on the types of information to be stored in the cloud.

Blockchain

At the current time, no discussion of information systems would be complete without a discussion of blockchain technology, which could substantially change how accounting systems operate (Drew 2017; Dai and Vasarhelyi 2017). Ethical considerations of blockchain should be separated between the platform (blockchain) and the primary application (Bitcoin) that has been implemented on the platform.

In theory, the blockchain platform positively addresses many of the ethical issues that arise in traditional accounting systems. First, due to the distributed nature of blockchain, nefarious changes to data are almost impossible. This makes the platform an appropriate choice for chain-of-custody applications, such as property records. All transfers for a specific property are linked together, in one place, and should reduce challenges of unfounded claims. Likewise, smart contracts, such as performance of various parties of a real-estate transaction, can be securely documented prior to a transfer. The security and structure of the platform should reduce fraud when blockchain is implemented properly.

The primary application, Bitcoin, demonstrates some of the ethical issues that can exist on the blockchain platform. Cryptocurrencies, including Bitcoin, use what may be seen as an environmentally unacceptable amount of world resources to maintain the application. Morgan Stanley (2018) estimated that in 2018, cryptocurrency mining could use more electricity than the country of Argentina or .6% of world power consumption. While much of these resources may be renewable, there will still be a cost of infrastructure to support the Bitcoin application.

Another ethical issue with cryptocurrency applications is the anonymity of users, which provides very high levels of privacy; that feature has been used for nefarious purposes, such as market manipulation and marketing of illegal goods. Historically, currency was used for such transactions, but with the IRS requirement for banks to report currency transactions over $10,000, currency transactions are not as appealing for illegal activities. Alternatives to cash transactions such as electronic funds transfer (EFT) and apps such as Venmo (a mobile payment service) create traceable transactions. This change in payment trends may be increasing the usage of Bitcoin for illegal activities. Illegal Bitcoin activities have been estimated to be executed by 25% of all users and reflect nearly one-half of all Bitcoin transactions (Foley, Karlsen, and Putnins 2018). Cryptocurrency users should be aware of the scope of illegal activities, and determine if operating in such an environment will meet their ethical standards. At the same time, developers of blockchain applications should be aware that the decisions made during implementation may produce unintended consequences. One of the consequences relates to the volatility of cryptocurrency values. Vigna (2019) reports that approximately 95% of Bitcoin's trading volume is artificially created. When a cryptocurrency is valued based upon the last transaction, false trades support false market values. False market values can introduce errors into an organization's financial statements.

Conclusion

Technology has increased the scope of ethical situations that must be considered by accountants. In the future, as these technologies continue to advance, accountants must ensure that the impact of the advancements are aligned not only with profits but also with the ethical standards of the profession. The purpose of the chapter was to discuss the roots of ethics in accounting information systems as well as consider a subset of current technologies and explore the ethical issues surrounding those technologies. While this discussion may be interesting, the authors recognize that there are not clearly delineated solutions to the issues, as one might expect. In fact, the issues are frequently cloudy, based on the perspectives of the system builder, their professional perspectives (and requirements), and the intended and unintended users/usage of the system. Unanticipated/unintended usage of a technology (such as Bitcoin/blockchain) presents the final challenge identified – the asymmetry of the intentions of system builders and the actions of system users. Even a system built using a strong base (adhering to ethical standards) may be used by an individual or individuals who do not adhere to the ethical standards on which the system was built. This brings the conversation to the individual interacting with the system. Builders of systems that store and use data that users expect to be private must not only consider the ethical requirements expected of them but must also consider and address possible actions of those who do not adhere to the same or similar ethical standards as the builder or targeted user.

When creating, adapting, installing or using an accounting information system, there is a wide range of issues to contemplate. Just as it is impossible for an accounting system to have perfect controls, it is not possible to anticipate all potential ethical issues. Although perfection is not achievable, one should ensure that the system processes are designed to adhere to current applicable professional ethic, and, whenever possible, adaptable to new technologies and the ethical considerations they bring. To do this, as a minimum one must be operationally aware of the professional ethics standard, and related laws that are applicable to the situation.

In an accounting information system setting, there are frequent changes. Those changes may relate to technologies, profitability, the legal or business environment, and a myriad of other issues. It is important to remember that in such a setting, while the accountant's ethical model may be static, that the model must be constantly re-applied as the accounting systems environment evolves. The goal of that re-application should be to ensure that the accounting information system is used to do the "right" thing.

Appendix

CODES OF ETHICS FROM SELECTED ACCOUNTING AND TECHNOLOGY-RELATED PROFESSIONAL ORGANIZATIONS

American Institute of Certified Public Accountants (AICPA)/Code of Professional Conduct: www.aicpa.org/research/standards/codeofconduct.html.

Association for Computing Machinery (ACM): Code of Ethics and Professional Conduct: www.acm.org/code-of-ethics.

Association of Certified Fraud Examiners (ACFE)/Code of Ethics: www.acfe.com/code-of-ethics.aspx.

Association of Chartered Certified Accountants (ACCA)/Code of Ethics and Conduct: www.accaglobal.com/us/en/about-us/regulation/ethics/acca-code-of-ethics-and-con duct.html.

CPA Canada: Code of Ethics of chartered professional accountants (legislated code): http://legisquebec.gouv.qc.ca/en/ShowDoc/cr/C-48.1,%20r.%206.

Institute of Management Accountants (IMA)/Statement of Ethical Professional Practice: www.imanet.org/career-resources/ethics-center?ssopc=1.

ISACA/Code of Professional Ethics: www.isaca.org/Certification/Code-of-Professional-Ethics/Pages/default.aspx.

The Institute of Internal Auditors (IIA)/Code of Ethics: https://na.theiia.org/standards-guidance/mandatory-guidance/pages/code-of-ethics.aspx.

Notes

1 While ethics have been studied and debated from philosophical and cultural perspectives for thousands of years, the authors believe there are some points of basic agreement. Rushworth Kidder (1994) studied values from around the world, and identifies seven universal "shared values" including, love, truthfulness, fairness, freedom, unity, tolerance, responsibility, and respect for life. This chapter approaches the topic from the assumption that generally shared values exist that drive ethical decisions.

2 Sherratt et al. (2005, 308) espouse such professional duties as maintaining "confidentiality, impartiality, professional relationships, efficacy, a duty of care to others, competence, and avoidance of inducements and bribes" and emphasize personal moral duties such as "trust, integrity, truthfulness, justice, beneficence/nonmaleficence, self-improvement, gratitude/ reparation."

3 Consequentialism postulates that it is ethical to do that which will "maximize the overall good"; deontology postulates that it is ethical to act in accord with one's duty to treat others as worthy individuals

rather than a means to an end; virtue ethics emphasizes the desirability of becoming a virtuous person and acting in accord with those virtues (Mingers and Walsham 2010, 834).

4 Contractarian ethics examines what outcome would be determined, or agreement reached, if neither party knew beforehand which side of a situation they would end up on (e.g., the surveillant or the surveilled). Under contractarian ethics, a party might give up certain rights if the agreement is perceived as fair overall (Holt, Lang, and Sutton 2017).

5 According to the Association to Advance Collegiate Schools of Business's (AACSB) Accounting Accreditation Standard A7: "The dynamic nature of IT developments related to data creation, data management and processing, data sharing, data analytics, data mining, data reporting, data security, and storage within and across organizations is critical for the development of emerging professional accountants. The underlying learning experiences for accounting graduates demands an interdisciplinary approach that draws input from professionals and academic scholars with expertise in information systems, statistics, computer science and engineering, ethical issues related to IT and big data." (AACSB 2014, 5).

6 An example of the medical research in this arena relates to sharing genomic data among researchers, and the potential for misuse of the data that is re-identified (Schleidgen et al. 2019).

References

AACSB (Association to Advance Collegiate Schools of Business). 2014. *Accounting Accreditation Standard A7: Information Technology Skills and Knowledge for Accounting Graduates: An Interpretation*. White Paper. Tampa, FL: AACSB.

ACCA. 2017. *Ethics and Trust in a Digital Age*. London: ACCA. Accessed June 14, 2020. www.accaglobal.com/content/dam/ACCA_Global/Technical/Future/pi-ethics-trust-digital-age.pdf.

ACM (Association of Computing Machinery). 2018. "ACM Code of Ethics and Professional Conduct." Accessed June 14, 2020. www.acm.org/code-of-ethics.

Adams, Mackenzie. 2017. "Big Data and Individual Privacy in the Age of the Internet of Things." *Technology Innovation Management Review* 7 (4): 12–24.

Ahmadi, Mohammad, Parthasarati Dileepan and Karen K. Wheatley. 2016. "A SWOT Analysis of Big Data." *Journal of Education for Business* 91 (5): 1–6.

AICPA. 2018a. "AICPA Proposes Revising Independence Rules for Information System Services." *Journal of Accountancy* 225 (5) (May). Accessed June 14, 2020. www.journalofaccountancy.com/issues/2018/may/aicpa-independence-rules-for-information-system-services.html.

AICPA. 2018b. "New Effective Date for Ethics Interpretation on Hosting Services." *Journal of Accountancy* 226 (4) (October). Accessed June 14, 2020. www.journalofaccountancy.com/issues/2018/oct/ethics-interpretation-on-hosting-services.html.

Alarcon, J. L., and Marc T. Staut. 2016. "The Internet of Things: The CPA's Role in the New World of Business." *Pennsylvania CPA Journal*. Accessed January 31, 2019. www.picpa.org/articles/picpa-news/2016/11/28/the-internet-of-things-the-cpa-s-role-in-the-new-world-of-business.

Anders, Susan B. 2016. "Governance, Risk Management, and Compliance: OCEG and the Network." *CPA Journal* 86 (3): 64–65.

Anders, Susan B. 2018. "Ethics Resources: IFAC and IESBA." *CPA Journal* 88 (3): 72–73.

Appelbaum, Deniz, Alexander Kogan, and Miklos A. Vasarhelyi. 2017. "Big Data and Analytics in the Modern Audit Engagement: Research Needs." *Auditing: A Journal of Practice & Theory* 36 (4): 1–27.

Biot-Paquerot, Guillaume, and Amir Hasnaoui. 2009. "Stakeholders Perspective and Ethics in Financial Information Systems." *Journal of Electronic Commerce in Organizations* 7 (1): 59–70. doi:10.4018/jeco.2009010105.

Brown, J. Owen., James A. Marcum, and Martin T. Stuebs, Jr. 2017. "Professional Virtue Reinforcements: A Necessary Complement to Technological and Policy Reforms." *Journal of Information Systems* 31 (2): 5–23. doi:10.2308/isys-51664.

Burney, Laurie L., R. R. Radtke, and S. K. Widener. 2017. "The Intersection of 'Bad Apples,' 'Bad Barrels,' and the Enabling Use of Performance Measurement Systems." *Journal of Information Systems* 31 (2): 25–48.

Cath, Corinne, and Luciano Floridi. 2017. "The Design of the Internet's Architecture by the Internet Engineering Task Force (IETF) and Human Rights." *Science & Engineering Ethics* 23: 449–68. doi:10.1007/s11948-016-9793-y.

Crossler, Robert E., James H. Long, Tina M. Loraas, and Brad S. Trinkle. 2017. "The Impact of Moral Intensity and Ethical Tone Consistency on Policy Compliance." *Journal of Information Systems* 31 (2): 49–64. doi:10.2308/isys-51623.

Dai, Jun, and Miklos A. Vasarhelyi. 2017. "Toward Blockchain-Based Accounting and Assurance." *Journal of Information Systems* 31 (3): 5–21.

de Bruin, Boudewijn, and Luciano Floridi. 2017. "The Ethics of Cloud Computing." *Science & Engineering Ethics* 23: 21–39. doi:10.1007/s11948-016-9759-0.

Drew, Jeff. 2012. "Technology and CPAs: Visions of the Future." *Journal of Accountancy*. Accessed January 31, 2019. www.journalofaccountancy.com/issues/2012/jun/20114844.html.

Drew, Jeff. 2017. "Real Talk About Artificial Intelligence and Blockchain." *Journal of Accountancy*. Accessed January 31, 2019. www.journalofaccountancy.com/issues/2017/jul/technology-roundtable-artificial-intelligence-blockchain.html.

Drew, Jeff. 2018. "Merging Accounting with 'Big Data' Science." *Journal of Accountancy*. Accessed January 31, 2019. www.journalofaccountancy.com/issues/2018/jul/big-data-and-accounting.html.

Floridi, Luciano. 1999. "Information Ethics: On the Philosophical Foundation of Computer Ethics." *Ethics and Information Technology* 1: 37–56.

Floridi, Luciano. 2002. "On the Intrinsic Value of Information Objects and the Infosphere," *Ethics and Information Technology* 4: 287–304.

Floridi, Luciano. 2005. "The Ontological Interpretation of Informational Privacy." *Ethics and Information Technology* 7: 185–200.

Floridi, Luciano. 2006. "Four Challenges for a Theory of Informational Privacy." *Ethics and Information Technology* 8: 109–19.

Floridi, Luciano. 2009. "Network Ethics: Information and Business Ethics in a Networked Society." *Journal of Business Ethics* 90: 649–59.

Floridi, Luciano. 2015. "The Anti-Counterfeiting Trade Agreement: The Ethical Analysis of a Failure, and Its Lessons." *Ethics and Information Technology* 17 (2): 165–73.

Floridi, Luciano, and J. W. Sanders. 2002. "Mapping the Foundational Debate in Computer Ethics." *Ethics and Information Technology* 4 (1): 1–9.

Foley, Sean, Jonathan R. Karlsen, and Talis J. Putnins. 2018. "Sex, Drugs, and Bitcoin: How Much Illegal Activity Is Financed Through Cryptocurrencies?" *Review of Financial Studies* 32 (5): 1798–853.

Gamage, Pandula. 2016. "Big Data: Are Accounting Educators Ready?" *Accounting and Management Information Systems* 15 (3): 588–604.

Guragai, Binod, Nicholas C. Hunt, Marc P. Neri, and Eileen Z. Taylor. 2017. "Accounting Information Systems and Ethics Research: Review, Synthesis, and the Future." *Journal of Information Systems* 31 (2): 65–81. doi:10.2308/isys-51265.

Higgins, Tim. 2019. "Driverless Cars Tap the Brakes After Years of Hype." *The Wall Street Journal*. Accessed June 14, 2020. www.wsj.com/articles/driverless-cars-tap-the-brakes-after-years-of-hype-11547737205?mod=article_inline.

Holt, Matthew, Bradley Lang, and Steve G. Sutton. 2017. "Potential Employees' Ethical Perceptions of Active Monitoring: The Dark Side of Data Analytics." *Journal of Information Systems* 31 (2): 107–24. doi:10.2308/isys-51580.

Institute for Business Ethics (IBE). 2016. "Business Ethics and Big Data." In *Business Ethics Briefing*. London: IBE. Accessed June 14, 2020. www.ibe.org.uk/resource/business-ethics-and-big-data.html.

Iqbal, Juneed, and Bilal Maqbool Beigh. 2017. "Computer Ethics from Obscure to Ubiquitous." *International Journal of Advanced Research in Computer Science* 8 (3): 983–90.

Kidder, Rushworth, M. 1994. *Shared Values for a Troubled World*. San Francisco, CA: Jossey-Bass.

Krahel, John Peter, and William R. Titera. 2015. "Consequences of Big Data and Formalization on Accounting and Auditing Standards." *Accounting Horizons* 29 (2): 409–22.

Mingers, J., and G. Walsham. 2010. "Toward Ethical Information Systems: The Contribution of Discourse Ethics." *MIS Quarterly* 34 (4): 833–54.

Morgan, Stanley. 2018. "Power Play: What Impact Will Cryptocurrencies Have on Global Utilities." Accessed June 14, 2020. www.morganstanley.com/ideas/cryptocurrencies-global-utilities.

Pauleen, David J., David Rooney, and Ali Intezari. 2017. "Big Data, Little Wisdom: Trouble Brewing? Ethical Implications for the Information Systems Discipline." *Social Epistemology* 31 (4): 400–16.

Perera, Charith, Rajiv Ranjan, Lizhe Wang, Samee U. Khan, and Albert Y. Zomaya. 2015. "Privacy of Big Data in the Internet of Things Era." *IEEE IT Professional Magazine* 17 (3): 32–39. doi:10.1109/MITP.2015.34.

Ranger, Steve. 2018. "What Is the IoT? Everything You Need to Know About the Internet of Things Right Now." *ZDNet*. Accessed January 21, 2019. https://www.zdnet.com/article/what-is-the-internet-of-things-everything-you-need-to-know-about-the-iot-right-now/.

Richins, Greg, Andrea Stapleton, Theophanis C. Stratopoulos, and Christopher Wong. 2017. "Big Data Analytics: Opportunity or Threat for the Accounting Profession?" *Journal of Information Systems* 31 (3): 63–79. doi:10.2308/isys-51805.

Schleidgen, Sebastian, Alma Husedzinovic, Dominik Ose, Christoph Schickhardt, Christof von Kalle, and Eva C. Winkler. 2019. "Between Minimal and Greater Than Minimal Risk: How Research Participants and Oncologists Assess Data-Sharing and the Risk of Re-Identification in Genomic Research." *Philosophy & Technology* 32 (1): 39–55.

Sherratt, Don, Simon Rogerson, and N. Ben Fairweather. 2005. "The Challenge of Raising Ethical Awareness: A Case-Based Aiding System for Use by Computing and ICT Students." *Science & Engineering Ethics* 11 (2): 299–315.

Stahl, Bernd Carsten. 2008. "The Ethical Nature of Critical Research in Information Systems." *Information Systems Journal* 18 (2): 137–63.

Taddeo, Mariarosaria, and Luciano Floridi. 2016. "The Debate on the Moral Responsibilities of Online Service Providers." *Science & Engineering Ethics* 22 (6): 1575–603.

Talluri, Raj. 2017. "Why Edge Computing Is Critical for the IoT." *NetworkWorld*. Accessed January 21, 2019. www.networkworld.com/article/3234708/internet-of-things/why-edge-computing-is-critical-for-the-iot.html.

Taylor, Eileen Z., and Ronald J. Daigle. 2017. "Special Section of JIS on AIS and Ethics (Editorial)." *Journal of Information Systems* 31 (2): 1–3.

Tschakert, Norbert, Julia Kokina, Stephen Kozlowski, and Miklos Vasarhelyi. 2016. "The Next Frontier in Data Analytics." *Journal of Accountancy*, August 1. Accessed June 14, 2020. www.journalofaccountancy.com/issues/2016/aug/data-analytics-skills.html.

Vasarhelyi, Miklos A., Alexander Kogan, and Brad M. Tuttle. 2015. "Big Data in Accounting: An Overview." *Accounting Horizons* 29 (2): 381–96. doi:10.2308/acch-51071.

Vigna, Paul. 2019. "Markets: Most Bitcoin Trading Faked by Unregulated Exchanges, Study Finds." *Wall Street Journal*, March 22. Accessed June 14, 2020. www.wsj.com/articles/most-bitcoin-trading-faked-by-unregulated-exchanges-study-finds-11553259600.

Wang, Min, and Zuosu Jiang. 2017. "The Defining Approaches and Practical Paradox of Sensitive Data: An Investigation of Data Protection Laws in 92 Countries and Regions and 200 Data Breaches in the World." *International Journal of Communication* 11: 3286–305.

Warren, J. Don, Kevin C. Moffitt, and Paul Byrnes. 2015. "How Big Data Will Change Accounting." *Accounting Horizons* 29 (2): 397–407.

Young Entrepreneur Council. 2018. "10 Big Security Concerns about IoT for Business (And How to Protect Yourself)." *Forbes*, July 31. Accessed June 14, 2020. www.forbes.com/sites/theyec/2018/07/31/10-big-security-concerns-about-iot-for-business-and-how-to-protect-yourself/#594104417416.

16

BLOCKCHAIN TECHNOLOGY IN ACCOUNTING INFORMATION SYSTEMS

Intended and unintended consequences

Robin R. Pennington

Introduction

Investments in blockchain technology are growing at a substantial rate despite the volatility of the cryptocurrency markets (del Castillo 2019). Bitcoin and the multitude of cryptocurrencies on the market today have led the way for blockchain technology to emerge as perhaps one of the most influential technologies of the future. With such potential, is this technology appropriate for accounting information systems? Accounting information systems collect, record, store and process data, while providing controls over that data, to produce accounting information (Romney et al. 2020). Accounting information provides details about accountability relationships and make explicit who is accountable to whom and for what (Williams 2002). The accountability relationship requires accurate and reliable information and a certain degree of transparency and confidentiality between participants. Blockchain technology is often promoted for its transparency and immutability features. But does that transparency feature come as a tradeoff with confidentiality and privacy?

Blockchain transaction processing systems are part of the larger accounting information system. The accounting information system affects decisions such as contracting, investing, hiring, purchasing, and selling, all of which have ethical implications (Guragai et al. 2017). The implications for accounting information systems is therefore significant with blockchain technology, as many decisions makers will rely on blockchain technology as part of that system. The billions of dollars currently invested in the technology provides evidence that blockchain is here to stay and at a minimum will be an important part of the accounting information system of the future.

The purpose of this chapter is to consider the ethical ramifications of the technology by exploring both the intended and unintended consequences of implementing blockchain technology in accounting information systems. The focus will not be on cryptocurrencies, an application of blockchain technology, but rather on the application of the technology for transaction processing needs. *Forbes* recently introduced the "Forbes Blockchain 50," which features 50 of the largest companies currently leading the way with investments in blockchain, including tech firms (e.g., SAP, Oracle, and IBM), retail giants (e.g., Amazon and Walmart), financial service firms (e.g., Citigroup, ING, and JP Morgan Chase) and various other industries, showing the broad appeal of the technology for accounting information systems (del Castillo 2019).

Blockchain technology has its share of skeptics, who contend that the technology is much too costly, unproven, and prone to fraud and chaotic competition (Smith 2019). Others argue the only real blockchains are "public" blockchains such as those used for cryptocurrencies and that implementing distributed ledger technology for operational use (i.e., "private" blockchains) is simply hype and nothing more than a distributed append-only data structure (Schneier 2019). The concept of trust is a reoccurring theme to both the arguments for and against blockchain technology. Blockchain is often described as a "trustless technology" because the need to have trust in the transaction is accomplished through the technology itself rather than a third party intermediary. However, this idea of trust is viewed differently depending on how the technology is implemented.

Blockchain technology has been implemented in a broad spectrum of use cases by many different industries and entity types. The appeal of blockchain technology from a social impact perspective has been the impetus for applications in voting, banking, public records, vital records, health records, and preventing human trafficking (Lapointe and Fishbane 2018). Examples of the variety of uses include such applications as the bonds issued by World Bank's "Bond-i" and managed by a blockchain; vehicle titles maintained on a blockchain by state authorities; individuals' medical records stored on blockchains by hospitals; and supply chain transactions that utilize "triple entry accounting" (i.e., three sets of entries, one each for the seller, purchaser, and the blockchain) (Stern and Reinstein 2019). Thus, supply chain blockchains have the potential to improve supply chain transparency from the original raw material supplier all the way to the consumer.

A good example of supply chain applications include blockchains developed for food safety that have proved valuable in tracking food products to their source. Walmart implemented IBM Food Trust along with Dole, Wegmans, and Unilever. At each stop in the Walmart produce, yogurt, and poultry supply chain, the people handling the food make entries into the blockchain. When goods are received then shipped entries are made recording all stops in the supply chain, resulting in an ability to track a food product to its source in a matter of seconds where previously it took days (Corkery and Popper 2018). The implications for blockchain as a tool for food safety are compelling and could be the standard in the future.

While the arguments for transparency in transactions are compelling from a supply chain perspective, confidentiality remains a significant concern both for businesses and individuals. The design challenges for implementing blockchain technologies as part of the accounting information system are based in the optimization of the trade-off between creating a transparent system with the appropriate degree of security for privacy and confidentiality concerns. Ethical design principles can help guide this process for companies seeking to deploy this promising technology.

The first section in the chapter is devoted to explaining the technology in basic terms. The following sections include discussions of (1) the trade-off between confidentiality and transparency, (2) ethical design considerations, (3) adoption and diffusion of the technology, and (4) concluding remarks summarizing the intended and unintended consequences surrounding blockchain technology.

Blockchain technologies – the basics

Blockchain is a type of distributed ledger technology that stores data across a network of computers. According to Deloitte (2017),

> blockchain technology consists in a decentralized ledger that operates in a transparent environment. Each block of the ledger contains data about transactions that have

been executed on the platform. In order to add a block to the ledger, every computer node of the network needs to verify and validate it. Thanks to this verification, the system does not need an intermediary to check transactions. Information stored in a blockchain can never be deleted and serves as a verifiable and accurate ledger of every transaction made within the system.

Cryptography is an important element in the blockchain. The data stored in the blocks are linked together one to another and secured using cryptography. The structure of the blocks linked together differentiates blockchain from other forms of distributed ledger technology, which may not necessarily employ a chain of blocks to provide a secure and valid distributed consensus (Ray 2018).

Consensus is the process used to verify transactions. There are various consensus mechanisms that can be used as a way to agree on the validity of a transaction. Once consensus is reached by the members of the network, the block is added to the ledger, thereby creating one version of the truth for all the nodes in the network. Furthermore, after the transaction is posted to the blockchain, it becomes tamper resistant (Dai and Vasarhelyi 2017). This immutable characteristic of blockchain technology makes it very desirable for accounting information systems and auditing.

Blockchain networks can be public or private. Public blockchains, also known as permissionless blockchains, are accessible by anyone willing to participate in the network, and therefore all the transaction history is also public. Cryptocurrencies operate on public blockchains. Public blockchains use the process of "mining" in order to reach consensus concerning a transaction. Mining involves solving algorithmic problems with computers. The "miners" are awarded bitcoin for their computational effort in support of the network (AICPA 2017). Currently, due to the inherent nature of the mining process, public blockchains, such as the Bitcoin blockchain, consume significant computing resources and thus energy (Zhao 2018). Additionally, if the initial transaction volume or size settings become outdated as technology advances, the transaction speed then slows down and becomes a limitation (AICPA 2017).

Private blockchains, also known as permissioned blockchains, are accessible only to participants that have been granted permission to the network by agreed-upon administrators (AICPA 2017). Arguably, this type of blockchain is more desirable for accounting information systems due to the limited accessibility feature, which limits who can add transactions or view the transaction history. Privacy and confidentiality of business data can be protected and consensus of validated transactions can be accomplished much quicker (Dai and Vasarhelyi 2017). However, permissioned blockchains sacrifice data transparency and public participation, thereby giving managers control over the blockchain, and with that control the potential to collude and tamper with transactions (Wang and Kogan 2018), as will be discussed later in the chapter.

Advancements in blockchain technology include the application of smart contracts. Smart contracts can be implemented on either public or private blockchain platforms. Smart contracts automate the contracting process between parties by allowing for a set of agreed-upon rules to be encoded and autonomously executed (Dai and Vasarhelyi 2017). The automation of the contract aids monitoring and enforcement and improves efficiency, as well as reduces settlement time and errors (AICPA 2017) – a real benefit given the previously mentioned concerns about speed, resources and energy use. The application of smart contracts can be useful for property trading, lease contracts, wills and testaments, derivative hedge contracts, etc. Smart contracts encoded with accounting rules can be used to control business processes and reduce the incidence of fraud (Dai, Wang, and Vasarhelyi 2017) and implement complex revenue recognition rules (Chou et al. 2019).

Blockchain technology continues to evolve as investments in the emerging technology continue to grow and expand into all industries. Often the question arises: Will blockchain technology replace traditional transaction processing systems in the accounting information system of the future? Opinions vary on that topic. Current research in accounting information systems uncovers many of the limitations and obstacles for implementing a functional blockchain transaction processing system (for example, see Coyne and McMickle 2017; O'Leary 2017) and also explores various use cases where the technology is deemed very useful in an accounting setting.

Confidentiality vs. transparency – ethical concerns

One of the major impediments to adoption of blockchain is dealing with the tradeoff between confidentiality and transparency. Transparency calls for more sharing of information; however, the more information is shared the higher the risk that business secrets and confidentiality will be compromised (Wang and Kogan 2018). Public blockchains offer transparency at the cost of confidentiality. Private blockchains offer confidentiality at the cost of transparency. The resulting dilemma is an unintended consequence of blockchain design in its current form. Transparency in business transactions and confidentiality of private information are both significant ethical concerns. Consumers are increasingly concerned about ethical business practices and therefore desire transparency in the supply chain (e.g., labor practices in the production of goods, fair trade practices, environmental stewardship and sustainable practices). Confidentiality of private information, both personal (e.g., health records, social security numbers, credit cards) and corporate (e.g., trade secrets, confidentiality agreements, pricing strategies) requires secure protection. Can blockchain technology provide both transparency and confidentiality?

Another ethical issue to consider is that immutability may also be at risk. In private blockchains where a central authority has control over the blockchain, the potential to tamper with the transactions is possible. Thus the desirable feature of tamper resistances is lost when one organization controls the blockchain. A decision has to be made between the confidentiality feature of a private blockchain that diminishes transparency and the transparency feature of the public blockchain that could potentially expose a company to a confidentiality breach (Wang and Kogan 2018). To achieve the best of both worlds, intentional design of the blockchain is paramount. One proposal is to use a cryptographic method known as zero-knowledge proof (ZKP), where one party can prove the validity of another party's transaction without revealing sensitive information (Wang and Kogan 2018). As blockchain technology continues to evolve, so does the opportunity to incorporate ethical design features in order to create a sustainable, transparent, and confidentiality-preserving blockchain for the future.

Blockchain ethical design considerations

Three main elements in ethical design of blockchains include: (1) deciding if blockchain is an appropriate technology for the desired outcome, (2) recognizing the impact of design choices on the desired outcome and on the people affected by the design, and (3) revisiting the design to reassess the root issues at transition points in a blockchain's life cycle (Lapointe and Fishbane 2018). There are many convincing arguments that blockchain *is not* the appropriate technology for a variety of reasons. A useful question to ask is: When should a business consider using a blockchain versus other types of technologies such as a traditional database? If a traditional database provides the same outcomes, then perhaps the only reason to opt for a blockchain is if additional efficiencies would be possible; if not, then a traditional database may be the best fit.

The Blockchain Decision Chart (Richardson 2018) offers guidance to help in determining *if* a blockchain is appropriate for an application and if so *what type* of blockchain would be best given certain parameters. As mentioned earlier, if a traditional database would work, then it is probably the most efficient solution. However, in cases when a traditional database will not work, then a series of questions help guide the decision of *what type* blockchain to adopt. Consider the following questions: Do all the participants trust each other or share a common goal? Is the database likely to be compromised or attacked? Should the data be private? If the answer to these three questions is yes, then a private blockchain could be the best option for the application. Conversely, if the participants do not trust each other, a third party is not required, and there is no need to control who has access to the database, then a public blockchain could be the best choice for the application (Richardson 2018). Working through the decision chart is useful, as it may save time and resources on the front end of systems development by guiding decisions toward the most optimal type of system (i.e., traditional database, private blockchain, public blockchain).

Before leaving the question of *is* blockchain the appropriate technology for the desired outcome, there is also an argument to be made that the social impact of the technology should be considered in the decision to adopt (or not to adopt) blockchain. The potential for reaching underserved populations for banking, voting, tracking health and education records, and establishing identities for individuals without identification papers are strong arguments that blockchain may be the appropriate technology (Lapointe and Fishbane 2018). In addition to these applications, blockchain provides a platform for various other government applications as well, including tax collection and property recording. Recently, 22 European countries signed a declaration to begin a European Blockchain Partnership, which will encourage member states to rethink their information systems to enhance trust, protect of personal data, and increase business opportunities to benefit citizens, public services, and companies (Maslova 2018). One promising area for governmental accounting is in the context of intragovernmental transactions. Intragovernmental transactions are business activities conducted between governmental entities that need to be reconciled and in balance for consolidated financial statements. The US Governmental Accountability Office audit report for fiscal years 2017 and 2016 reports that the federal government continues to be unable to reconcile intragovernmental activity between agencies. The lack of proper reconciliation can lead to the loss of billions of dollars, inaccurate reporting, and lack of trust (Chew et al. 2018). Taken together, the social impact arguments for adopting the technology are compelling and speak to how the public good can be served, particularly in the case of permissioned blockchains that overcome the environmental concerns associated with public blockchains.

Assuming we get past the question of *if* and decide that blockchain *is* the appropriate technology, the next step is to consider six root issues. How is governance managed? How is identity managed? Who owns the data? How is access managed? How is security managed? How are inputs verified? (Lapointe and Fishbane 2018). One could argue that the six root issues should always be considered when designing an accounting information system regardless of the technology employed. Indeed, the answers to these issues are reminiscent of the high-level abstract constructs discussed in accounting information systems theory, which recognizes that systems design alternative choices made at a high level will often limit design choices made at lower levels of development, such as implementing the technology (Mauldin and Ruchala 1999).

A key design issue is governance of the blockchain. Governance decisions, such as who is in charge of the blockchain and the set of rules that will apply, are vital to ethical design. A control environment should be established to set the proper tone. As part of the control environment, oversight is needed with respect to data security and privacy of participants and how participants will be invited, onboarded, managed and retired from the blockchain (PwC 2018). Without effective governance, the identities of those participating in the blockchain could be at risk, especially because of the immutability feature of the technology (i.e., once a transaction is recorded, it becomes a permanent record). Thus, data ownership rules should be established. Blockchain technology can be configured to enable users to exercise control over their data. An example, following ethical design principles, is the Sovrin Foundation's self-sovereign identity trust framework, which allows people to have control over their personal digital identity information (Lapointe and Fishbane 2018).

Next, the question of how access is managed should be addressed. Rules for accessibility should be determined by the roles of the participants, which is similar to that of role-based access controls implemented in database technology. Roles, in the permissioned blockchain, are set up based on tasks and nodes. For example, consider the following transaction flow for an order of goods based on a Hyperledger application where roles are set up as clients, peers, orderers, and endorsers.

> A client creates and invokes transactions. Peers maintain the ledger, receive ordered updates from orderers, upon which they commit the transaction into the ledger. A specific type of peers, called endorsers, check whether the transactions meet the necessary conditions, (for e.g. required signatures) and endorse them.
>
> *(edChain 2018)*

Notice that in this example the consensus mechanism is not dependent on anonymous miners, like in a public blockchain, but rather it is the endorsers who verify the transactions and come to consensus. Role-based access is an important design characteristic and also helps to ensure the security of the transactions.

What about security? Blockchain security is dependent on the strength of the encryption algorithms used in its design and the public/private key management. The distributed network of computers hold copies of the encrypted records, making it hard (if not impossible) for tampering to occur. The private key of a network participant serves as a personal digital signature (Miles 2017). However, if a network participant loses their key or their key is compromised, then the record could be lost or stolen. An important security design feature is the infrastructure. Three security features should be built into the infrastructure: Access prevention to sensitive information (including administrators); denying illicit attempts to change data or applications; and carefully guarding encryption keys with the highest grade security (Miles 2017).

Finally, how is independent verification achieved? Currently, blockchain auditing is evolving into a set of best practices. A continuous auditing approach is possible due to the shared ledger and hence increased auditability of the information contained in the chain. Consider smart contracts that contain an agreed-upon set of rules. Posting and encrypting the code of smart contacts on the blockchain allow managers and auditors to continuously verify the integrity of the programs (Dai and Vasarhelyi 2017). Digital continuous audit allows auditors to review a full population of data continuously with techniques that rely on machines to monitor the transactional flow and provide reports and issue opinions on processes (PwC 2018). The continuous auditing approach increases confidence and transparency in blockchain transactions. Additionally, fraud prevention can be enhanced due to the increase in information transparency and the various independent parties who perform verification, which ensures the validity and accuracy of the transactions (Dai, Wang, and Vasarhelyi 2017).

Blockchain adoption and diffusion

It is hard to predict the adoption and diffusion patterns of blockchain, given the challenges and innovations in the technology. However, according to Deloitte (2018), the momentum is shifting with blockchain technology from learning and exploring to identifying and developing a wider range of use cases all across the business value chain. The speed of blockchain adoption is likely contingent on improvements in areas such as ease of use of the applications and validating auditing techniques and will likely be more noticeable in certain industries (Appelbaum and Smith 2018).

An example of an industry currently making significant strides in employing blockchain technology is the banking industry. The cost and inefficiencies in cross-border payment transactions are driving the need to develop blockchain solutions to reduce the time, number of intermediaries, and expense of an overly complicated settlement system. Cross-border payments made business to business or person to person via vendor blockchain-based payment "rails" can reduce transaction costs by 40% to 80%; reduce time from 2–3 days to 4–6 seconds; and provide secure, data-rich, irreversible transactions (Deloitte 2016). Currently, it is estimated that almost 2 billion adults worldwide have no access to banking services and that blockchain technology could be deployed as a solution to provide remote and isolated populations with affordable customer payment services (Wiatt 2019). The social impact for the billions of people worldwide is a force for furthering the diffusion and adoption of blockchain technology in the banking industry.

Conclusions

The focus of this chapter was on blockchain technologies for transaction processing as part of an accounting information system. The good intentions of implementing blockchain technology to improve accounting information systems in areas such as transparency in the supply chain, ease of use, accessibility, and public good applications (e.g., voting, property records, health records, banking services for underserved populations, etc.) can be foiled by unintended consequences of design choices that do not line up with original objectives. Unintended consequences from poor design choices can lead to a lack of transparency and privacy, inefficiency in processing transactions, inaccessibility of supply chain partners, and inaccessibility for underserved populations – all of which have significant ethical implications. It would seem that blockchain technology is capable of providing accurate and reliable accounting information about accountability relationships (who is accountable to whom and for what – Williams [2002]). However the challenge will be balancing the needs of transparency and confidentiality. Adhering to ethical design principles can provide a solid path forward in order to avoid the unintended consequences.

References

AICPA, CPAC, and University of Waterloo. 2017. "Blockchain Technology and Its Potential Impact on the Audit and Assurance Profession." www.aicpa.org/interestareas/frc/assuranceandadvisoryservices/blockchain-impact-on-auditing.html.

Appelbaum, D., and S. S. Smith. 2018. "Blockchain Basics and Hands-On Guidance: Taking the Next Step Towards Implementation and Adoption." *The CPA Journal* (June): 28–37.

Chew, B., W. Henry, A. Lora, and H. Chae. 2018. "Assessing Blockchain Applications for the Public Sector: Blockchain Basics for Government." *Deloitte Insights.* https://documents.deloitte.com/insights/Assessingblockchainapplicationsforthepublicsector.

Chou, C. C., N. C. Hwang, T. Wang, C. W. Li, and C. S. Lee. 2019. "Using Smart Contracts to Establish Decentralized Accounting Standards: An Implementation of Revenue Recognition under USC 606." Paper presented at American Accounting Association Accounting Information Systems Midyear Meeting, San Antonio, TX, January 10–12.

Corkery, M., and N. Popper. 2018. "From Farm to Blockchain: Walmart Tracks Its Lettuce." *The New York Times.* www.nytimes.com/2018/09/24/business/walmart-blockchain-lettuce.amp.html.

Coyne, J. G., and P. L. McMickle. 2017. "Can Blockchains Serve an Accounting Purpose?" *Journal of Emerging Technologies in Accounting* 14 (2): 101–11.

Dai, J., and M. A. Vasarhelyi. 2017. "Toward Blockchain-Based Accounting and Assurance." *Journal of Information Systems* 31 (3): 5–21.

Dai, J., Y. Wang, and M. A. Vasarhelyi. 2017. "Blockchain: An Emerging Solution for Fraud Prevention." *CPA Journal* (July): 12–14.

del Castillo, M. 2019. "Blockchain 50: Billion Dollar Babies." *Forbes.* www.forbes.com/sites/michaeldelcastillo/2019/04/16/blockchain-50-billion-dollar-babies/#5402e58f57cc.

Deloitte. 2016. "Cross-border Payments on Blockchain." https://www2.deloitte.com/content/dam/Deloitte/global/Documents/grid/cross-border-payments.pdf.

Deloitte. 2017. "Distributed Ledger Technologies Services: Using the Power of Blockchain." https://www2.deloitte.com/content/dam/Deloitte/lu/Documents/technology/lu-blockchain-services-21092017.pdf.

Deloitte. 2018. "Breaking Blockchain Open: Deloitte's 2018 Global Blockchain Survey." https://www2.deloitte.com/content/dam/Deloitte/us/Documents/financial-services/us-fsi-2018-global-blockchain-survey-report.pdf.

edChain. 2018. "A Comparison Between 5 Major Blockchain Protocols." https://medium.com/edchain/a-comparison-between-5-major-blockchain-protocols-b8a6a46f8b1f.

Guragai, B., N. C. Hunt, M. P. Neri, and E. Z. Taylor. 2017. "Accounting Information Systems and Ethics Research: Review, Synthesis, and the Future." *Journal of Information Systems* 31 (2): 65–81.

Lapointe, C., and L. Fishbane. 2018. "The Blockchain Ethical Design Framework." *Innovations: Blockchain for Global Development II* 12 (3/4): 50–71.

Maslova, N. 2018. "Blockchain: Disruption and Opportunity." *Strategic Finance,* July.

Mauldin, E., and L. V. Ruchala. 1999. "Towards a Meta-Theory of Accounting Information Systems." *Accounting, Organizations and Society* 24: 317–31.

Miles, C. 2017. "Blockchain Security: What Keeps Your Transaction Data Safe?" www.ibm.com/blogs/blockchain/2017/12/blockchain-security-what-keeps-your-transaction-data-safe/.

O'Leary, D. E. 2017. "Configuring Blockchain Architectures for Transaction Information in Blockchain Consortiums: The Case of Accounting and Supply Chain Systems." *Intelligent Systems in Accounting Finance & Management* 24 (4): 138–47.

PwC. 2018. "Governance in the Age of Blockchain Distributed Ledger Technology." www.pwc.com/us/en/about-us/new-ventures/assets/pwc-governance-in-the-age-of-blockchain-distributed-ledger-technology.pdf.

Ray, S. 2018. "The Difference Between Blockchains & Distributed Ledger Technology." https://towardsdatascience.com/the-difference-between-blockchains-distributed-ledger-technology-42715a0fa92?gi=763a27851962.

Richardson, M. 2018. "Blockchain or Database Decision Chart." https://blockchaintrainingalliance.com/blogs/news/blockchain-or-database-decision-chart.

Romney, M. B., P. J. Steinbart, S. L. Summers, and D. A. Wood. 2020. *Accounting Information Systems.* Hoboken, NJ: Pearson Education.

Schneier, B. 2019. "There's No Good Reason to Trust Blockchain Technology." *Wired.* www.wired.com/story/theres-no-good-reason-to-trust-blockchain-technology/.

Smith, N. 2019. "Blockchain Hype Missed the Mark, and Not by a Little." www.bloomberg.com/opinion/articles/2019-05-03/blockchain/blockchain-hype-missed-the-mark-and-not-by-a-little.

Stern, M., and A. Reinstein. 2019. "How to Evaluate the Feasibility of Proposed Blockchain Use Cases." Working Paper, Detroit, MI: Wayne State University, 1–13.

Wang, Y., and A. Kogan. 2018. "Designing Confidentiality-Preserving Blockchain-Based Transaction Processing Systems." *International Journal of Accounting Information Systems* 30: 1–18.

Wiatt, R. 2019. "From the Mainframe to the Blockchain." *Strategic Finance*, January: 26–35.

Williams, P. F. 2002. "Accounting and the Moral Order: Justice, Accounting, and Legitimate Moral Authority." *Accounting and the Public Interest* 2: 1–21.

Zhao, H. 2018. "Bitcoin and Blockchain Consume an Exorbitant Amount of Energy. These Engineers are Trying to Change That." *CNBC*. www.cnbc.com/2018/02/23/bitcoin-blockchain-consumes-a-lot-energy-engineers-changing-that.html.

17

ETHICAL CONSIDERATIONS OF CORPORATE TAX AVOIDANCE

Diverging perspectives from different stakeholders

Nathan C. Goldman and Christina M. Lewellen

Introduction

Over the past decade, many knowledgeable observers, including academics, practitioners, the public, and politicians, have debated the ethicality of US publicly traded corporations' tax avoidance practices. This chapter theoretically explores the diverging perspectives of these activities among different groups of corporate stakeholders. We also review findings from empirical academic literature providing evidence on different stakeholders' perceptions of corporate tax avoidance and the effectiveness of reputational considerations in reducing corporations' tax avoidance behavior.

The topic of tax avoidance by corporations is important to many direct (i.e., managers, employees, shareholders, and creditors) and indirect (i.e., academics, practitioners, tax authorities, politicians, and the taxpaying public) corporate stakeholders. Corporate tax revenues constitute a material portion of the annual budget (Congressional Budget Office 2019). Despite the vast wealth in large public corporations, corporate tax revenues comprise a smaller portion of overall tax revenues in the United States compared to individual income taxes and employment taxes; thus, whether corporate taxpayers are contributing a just amount of their income for the public good is a major concern for non-corporate taxpayers.[1] Given the steep growth of the budget deficit in the United States, the perceived fairness of the relative corporate tax burdens is a growing concern.

While corporations are legal entities, they are not designed to have the capacity to consider harm to others in the way that individuals might. Rather, teams of corporate executives who make rational decisions based on their direct responsibilities and incentives are responsible for making decisions in corporations. Understanding the different perspectives on the ethicality of tax avoidance is vital so that various important corporate and non-corporate stakeholders understand the tax behavior of corporations, as well as corporate tax-related decision processes. Practitioners must also decide when to draw the line with regards to ethics when it comes to deciding whether and when to assist their clients in tax planning (Field 2017).

Income taxation textbooks teach students that it should not be regarded as unethical to organize one's affairs in a tax-efficient way (e.g., Jones, Rhoades-Catanach, and Callaghan 2019; Scholes et al. 2015). However, the media, the public, and politicians propose that it is unethical for corporations to engage in aggressive tax-avoiding strategies. Corporate managers are agents of the corporation, and they are generally incentivized in a way to persuade them to avoid taxes legally. Moreover, the courts have held that there is nothing sinister about avoiding tax and that taxpayers have no moral obligation to pay more tax than they legally owe.

We provide a theoretical examination of the ethicality of corporate tax avoidance. Our discussion does not provide clear insights that tax avoidance on the part of corporations is inherently unethical and also does not suggest that corporate tax avoidance behavior is harmful to society as a whole. While at first glance it may seem like a simple conclusion that corporations should bear a greater portion of the tax burden, this chapter highlights the complexity of this issue. While corporate (as well as noncorporate) tax avoidance may reduce aggregate tax revenues, many direct stakeholders, and even some indirect stakeholders, may be better off because of lower corporate tax burdens. Our review of the empirical literature examining different stakeholders' perspectives on tax avoidance suggests that shareholders generally positively value tax avoidance; however, especially aggressive or risky tax-planning strategies may also present risks to corporate stakeholders such as shareholders and creditors, which may erode the benefits. In addition, while the public generally views corporate tax avoidance negatively, there is limited evidence that tax "shaming" or scrutiny encourages corporations to reduce their tax avoidance. Our discussion also suggests that if indirect stakeholders such as the general public or policy makers desire that corporations bear greater tax burdens, they will likely be forced to change the tax law to close loopholes rather than attempting to coerce corporations to pay more tax voluntarily.

Theory of tax avoidance and ethics from the perspective of tax practitioners, corporate taxpayers, and the courts

Paul and Elder (2013), in their guide to ethical reasoning, propose that the role of ethics is to differentiate between acts that enhance the well-being of others and those that harm or diminish the well-being of others. While some acts in a business setting are clearly and indisputably unethical, such as fraud, other acts require an abundance of critical thinking and reasoning to determine their ethicality (Paul and Elder 2013). Some acts may, in fact, enhance the well-being of a group of people but could be perceived as inadvertently harming another group of people. Thus, acts that are in the "gray area" might be perceived as ethical by one person and as unethical by another person.[2] Corporate tax avoidance is one particular act that fits into this category of no clear distinction between ethical and unethical, about which rational and moral people can disagree over its ethicality.

Following textbooks and prior academic literature, we define tax avoidance as a legal and legitimate means of reducing explicit tax burdens (e.g., Jones, Rhoades-Catanach, and Callaghan 2019; Hanlon and Heitzman 2009). Tax avoidance ranges on a spectrum from activities that are undisputed legal preferences provided by the tax law (e.g., investments in tax-free securities or accelerated depreciation) to activities that involve a very aggressive interpretation of ambiguous tax law (e.g., transfer pricing strategies that shift income abroad).[3] Tax avoidance strategies used by large multinational corporations commonly involve setting up subsidiaries in "tax haven" countries (i.e., low tax jurisdictions) and shifting income either from the United States or from foreign sources into the tax havens to reduce overall tax burdens (e.g., Dyreng and Lindsey 2009). These practices have been shamed and deemed unethical or immoral by some spectators because they potentially reduce tax revenues that may have otherwise been received by the home country or another country (Van Heeke et al. 2014; Gravelle 2015).[4] While these transactions are not necessarily illegal, whether they have a business purpose might be called into question, and thus, it is not always clear whether they should be allowed under the economic substance doctrine.[5]

Since our focus is corporate taxes (and to what extent it is ethical to reduce them), it is of value to observe historically how corporate tax collections compared to taxes paid by other taxpayers.[6] Over the last several decades, corporate tax collections have comprised approximately 10% of overall revenues in the United States, compared to individual income tax revenues, which have comprised approximately 50% of overall tax revenues (Congressional Budget Office 2019). However, importantly, there are currently just less than 5,000 publicly traded corporations in the United States (Bloomberg 2018) as compared to more than 140 million individual taxpayers (York 2018). However, despite the relatively small number of corporations, many large publicly traded corporations in the United States hold billions of dollars of wealth (Bloomberg 2018).[7] This is likely the reason why politicians and the taxpaying public balk at the fact that corporations pay such a staggeringly lower percentage of the overall tax burden compared to individuals.

Given that the public's opinions on tax avoidance appear to be divergent with corporate incentives, we methodically evaluate whether corporate tax avoidance is unethical, using the framework from Paul and Elder (2013). We first must try to determine whether others or "society as a whole" are harmed by tax avoidance. While paying income tax does not entitle taxpayers to specific goods or service in return for the tax payments, tax revenues are used to pay for infrastructure, to assist elderly or low-income citizens, and to protect the country's citizens, among many other important objectives, and taxpayers generally receive these indirect benefits from their tax payments.[8] All taxpayers are legally and ethically responsible for bearing some portion of the tax burden. The debate about the ethicality of taxes is not *whether* citizens should pay taxes but rather *what relative portion* of the tax burden that different groups of taxpayers should bear.

While many interested parties debate the fairness of the corporate tax burden, several important points are relevant to the discussion of whether avoiding corporate taxes causes harm to "society." First, while many parties may argue that corporate tax avoidance contributes to the national deficit and harms society in that way, it is not necessarily the case that increasing corporate tax burdens would reduce budget deficits and improve economic outcomes. For example, Alesina and Ardagna (2010), in a cross-country study, find that spending cuts are more likely to reduce national debts and are less likely to result in recessions when compared to tax increases. In addition, Shevlin, Shivakumar, and Urcan (2019) find that aggregate corporate tax avoidance is associated with future macroeconomic growth. Thus, it is difficult to conclude directly that corporate tax avoidance harms economic and fiscal outcomes.

In addition, a large number of corporate stakeholders may directly benefit from lower tax burdens achieved by corporate tax avoidance. While corporations are separate legal entities, in reality, they are a collection of external and internal stakeholders, a large percentage of which are individuals (Rosenthal 2016). Although many may perceive that corporate stakeholders are primarily comprised of wealthy individuals, many non-wealthy individuals are also stakeholders in public corporations (Rosenthal 2016). For example, many individuals hold corporation's stock via their retirement accounts and mutual funds, and employees and customers have vested interest in the success of the corporation and the corporation's ability to continue to operate. Earnings are taxed at the corporate level, and then after-tax income that is distributed to shareholders as dividends are taxed again at the individual level. While shareholders may bear some of the corporate tax burden (in the form of lower after-tax returns), corporate tax burdens may also be borne by some other important stakeholders, including employees (in the form of lower wages) and customers (in the form of higher prices).[9] Because of these corporate tax dynamics, some have argued that the corporate tax should be eliminated (e.g., Reid 2017). Thus, lower tax burdens afforded by corporate tax avoidance may yield positive externalities to shareholders, employees, and customers, among many other potential stakeholders.[10]

When analyzing whether tax avoidance harms society, we must understand corporate tax-payers' responsibilities with regard to tax burdens. While many public spectators (including politicians) call for corporations to "be socially responsible" and "pay their fair share of tax," taxes are enforced contributions that are determined by tax laws rather than voluntary contributions (Jones, Rhoades-Catanach, and Callaghan 2019). Accordingly, the courts have generally concluded that taxpayers have a civic duty only to pay the legally required tax. As an example, federal Judge L. Hand stated in *Commissioner v. Newman* (1947):

> Over and over again courts have said that there is nothing sinister in so arranging one's affairs as to keep taxes as low as possible. Everybody does so, rich or poor; and all do right, for nobody owes any public duty to pay more than the law demands: taxes are enforced exactions, not voluntary contributions. To demand more in the name of morals is mere cant.

By this argument, tax textbooks (e.g., Jones, Rhoades-Catanach, and Callaghan 2019; Scholes et al. 2015) generally teach students that tax planning should not be regarded as immoral or unethical. While this argument was originally made in 1947, it is among the most common referenced tax-related court decisions even throughout the years as tax laws and dynamics of our tax system have incurred significant change.

It is also useful to understand the responsibilities of corporate managers with regard to corporate tax burdens. Corporations are collections of individuals (and other stakeholders) who hire employees to manage the company on their behalf. These employees (i.e., the managers) are most directly ethically bound to act on behalf of their shareholders. Managers are also legally and ethically bound to remit taxes *legally* owed by the corporation to the US Treasury. It is not clear that managers are ethically bound to remit *higher* amounts of taxes than the firm legally owes or that it is ethical for the manager to voluntarily forgo legal tax avoidance opportunities. Conversely, if the tax law provides opportunities for managers to reduce the corporate tax burden, it is not clear that leaving these opportunities on the table would be an ethical or unethical action on the part of the managers, since the manager's most direct obligation is to the shareholders rather than to the general public.

In sum, while the public and politicians propose that corporate tax avoidance schemes are unethical and immoral and that reducing corporate tax burdens results in avoiding social and moral obligations, our theoretical analysis does not provide clear insights that tax avoidance on the part of corporations is inherently unethical or harmful. While reducing corporate tax burdens may reduce aggregate tax revenue collections, it is not clear that it is the corporate manager's responsibility to voluntarily contribute more than the applicable tax law requires. In contrast, if regulators believe that the tax law in place leads the corporations to pay a lower portion of taxes than the Treasury's optimal level, then it is the responsibility of the politicians and regulators to change the law to better align with their political and economic objectives.[11]

Review of the literature: empirical evidence on differing perspectives on the ethicality of tax-avoidance from corporate suppliers of capital and the public

Every dollar of taxes avoided represents two items: (1) a dollar less of taxes paid to the government and (2) a dollar more of income to the firm's shareholders. This conflict between a firm's legal obligation to pay taxes owed to the government and the manager's fiduciary duty to represent the shareholder's best interest has generated significant tension as to whether and the extent to which tax avoidance is, in fact, ethical. Weisbach (2002) suggests that firms do not avoid as much taxes as the opportunities afforded to them and questions why firms are "undersheltered." Thus, as it pertains to the firm's tax avoidance decisions, it appears as though managers carefully balance the amount of taxes paid to the government with the amount of tax savings afforded to shareholders. Furthermore, once the firm avoids taxes, the firm's managers have a fiduciary duty to allocate the funds in a way that will benefit the firm's stakeholders.

Numerous interested parties have debated the ethicality of tax avoidance. Academic research provides empirical evidence on the implications of tax avoidance on different stakeholders, and these studies yield interesting conclusions. In this section, we discuss two fundamental areas where academics generate conclusions on the perceived ethicality of tax avoidance and the effectiveness of different tactics in reducing corporations' tax avoidance behavior. First, we discuss literature providing evidence on the valuation of tax avoidance by direct corporate stakeholders (i.e., providers of capital), and specifically whether and how tax avoidance affects these stakeholders' wealth. Second, we review literature examining whether reputational concerns and backlash from the public for aggressive tax practices influence corporate tax strategy.

The effects of tax avoidance on direct corporate stakeholders

The first area that we examine is whether tax planning influences direct corporate stakeholders' wealth. Tax avoidance can increase wealth on the part of capital providers by generating a stream of higher cash flows. Because tax planning represents a tradeoff between tax benefits and non-tax costs, prior literature suggests that capital providers' valuation of tax avoidance can help provide evidence on whether tax planning does, in fact, return value to external stakeholders.

Desai and Dharmapala (2009) are among the first to examine the relation between tax avoidance and firm value directly. The authors use Tobin's q, which captures the difference between how the market values the corporation versus how the accounting numbers dictate the value of the corporation as a proxy for shareholder value and document a positive relation between firm value and tax avoidance in the presence of strong corporate governance. Moreover, Inger (2014) examines the valuation of different tax avoidance methods. She finds that, on average, tax avoidance is positively associated with firm value but that more risky tax avoidance through shifting income to tax havens is negatively associated with firm value. Similarly, Drake, Lusch, and Stekelberg (2019) provide evidence that tax risk moderates the relation between firm value and tax avoidance and that tax avoidance with higher costs provides fewer benefits to the firms' equity holders.

Related studies also provide further evidence on how benefits versus risks influence shareholders' valuation of tax avoidance. For example, Goh et al. (2016) posit and provide evidence that tax avoidance increases firms' cash flows, which decreases risk to shareholders and thus lowers the cost of equity capital. However, they find that shareholders of firms with better outside monitoring and firms with stronger information environments primarily bear these benefits.

These characteristics allow equity holders to monitor managers' actions more effectively, thereby lowering the risk associated with tax planning activities. Hanlon and Slemrod (2009) examine stock price reactions to the company's tax shelter involvement being publicly disclosed. Among the spectrum from low aggressive to high aggressive tax avoidance, tax sheltering represents among the most aggressive ways to lower income taxes and thus is a risky endeavor. Consistent with high-risk tax avoidance outweighing the benefits to stakeholders of a lower effective tax rate, the study provides evidence of a stock price decline following the public disclosure of a firm's involvement in these activities.

The benefits of tax avoidance also appear to vary based on the type of capital provider. For instance, Hasan et al. (2014) examine the relation between the cost of debt and tax avoidance. Contrary to studies examining equity shareholder value and tax avoidance, they find that tax avoidance increases risk on the part of debt holders, as evidenced by a higher cost of debt. In considering the tradeoffs between benefits and risks of tax avoidance, this result highlights the inherent differences in benefits among stakeholders. While equity holders benefit from the higher stream of cash flows generated by tax avoidance, debt holders only receive a fixed income and therefore benefit from lower risk transactions and more consistent cash flow streams. In other words, the debt holders benefit significantly less from companies choosing risky tax avoidance strategies, and tax avoidance strategies may, in fact, increase the likelihood of default; therefore, debt holders increase interest rates charged for companies choosing more aggressive tax avoidance. As a result, when stakeholders do not benefit from tax avoidance, the heightened risk of these activities appears to diminish rather than increase these stakeholders' value.

In sum, this evidence from papers examining direct stakeholder valuation of tax avoidance is consistent with two key points: (1) If the expected cash flows from tax planning are higher, then stakeholders can realize significant value from tax planning activities, and (2) if the risks of tax planning are lower, then stakeholders can realize significant value from tax planning activities. These two points combine to suggest that tax avoidance yields both benefits and risks, which must be balanced carefully.

Other studies provide evidence that corporate tax avoidance can also result in tangential effects, which may deteriorate the potential benefits of tax savings. Desai and Dharmapala (2006) posit that managers can use the opacity and complexity of tax avoidance to divert corporate resources for their own private benefit when corporate governance is ineffective.[12] Blaylock (2016) finds no evidence of manager diversion of tax savings among US firms, which generally face strong country-level corporate governance. However, Atwood and Lewellen (2019) find that managers of firms with a tax haven parent entity can divert the tax savings from tax avoidance when the firm is based primarily in a weak-governance country. In addition, Desai and Dharmapala (2009) find that the positive association between tax avoidance and firm value goes away in firms facing weak governance. These studies suggest that in weak-governance settings, managers may primarily be the beneficiary of cash flows from tax avoidance, rather than shareholders or other corporate stakeholders. Another indirect negative effect of tax planning may be lower financial statement transparency. Balakrishnan, Blouin, and Guay (2019) provide evidence that corporate tax aggressiveness reduces financial-reporting related transparency, which increases information asymmetry between managers and financial statement users and may make interpreting the benefits of tax avoidance more difficult. Overall, these papers suggest that in some circumstances, the complexity and opacity of tax avoidance may erode the potential benefits to direct stakeholders.

In sum, the firm's managers have a fiduciary duty to the corporation, and thus the managers should maximize long-run shareholder value (Jensen and Meckling 1976). As it pertains to tax avoidance, the evidence appears consistent with high amounts of tax planning strategies that are not overly risky achieving that outcome. However, this decision is not made in isolation, and large amounts of tax avoidance appear to have adverse effects on interest rates on debt borrowings. Lastly, the US government, an indirect stakeholder in each firm by virtue of the 21% statutory tax rate, has obvious incentives to minimize tax avoidance. Higher amounts of tax planning can generate more IRS scrutiny (Hoopes, Mescall, and Pittman 2012; Bozanic et al. 2017), which can increase the risks of corporate tax planning and result in future tax cash outflows. As part of the manager's fiduciary duty, he or she should consider the entire effect on stakeholder value and thus balance the effects of tax avoidance on the cost of equity capital versus the cost of debt, on regulatory scrutiny, and on the effects of opacity on financial statement users. As a result, whether corporate tax avoidance appears to be unethical in terms of harming direct external corporate stakeholders depends on the specific circumstances of the firm. Managers must identify tax avoidance practices where stakeholders collectively benefit most from these activities. Thus, some extremely aggressive tax strategies (such as tax sheltering) may be unethical, since these strategies shift wealth away from the government and also may not benefit corporate stakeholders. In any circumstance, managers utilizing tax practices to divert corporate wealth is clearly unethical, and corporate stakeholders should carefully consider corporate governance mechanisms in place to mitigate this concern.

The public perception of tax avoidance and the effect of reputational concerns on corporate tax planning

Anecdotal evidence suggests that the public views tax avoidance as unethical. For example, an article in *The Guardian*, titled "Avoiding Tax May Be Legal, but Can It Ever Be Ethical?" proposes that paying tax is a social responsibility and that "avoiding tax is avoiding a social obligation" (Back 2013). Similarly, the Tax Justice Network proposes, "Tax avoidance is probably the most misunderstood and misused word in the field of tax. We rarely use the word: we prefer terms like 'tax cheating' or 'tax dodging' or 'escaping tax' instead" (Tax Justice Network 2019). Large corporations in the United States and other countries are frequently criticized and shamed for their "shady" tax avoidance tactics. For example, former President Obama proposed that a commonly used practice involving tax havens was "the biggest tax scam on record" (Peretti 2016). We review the literature on whether potential scrutiny from the public can motivate firms to back off from aggressive tax practices.

Academic researchers provide evidence on how the public perception of tax avoidance activities influences corporate tax policy. Graham et al. (2014) help spark this line of literature with their survey of 594 tax executives. In this study, 69% of executives identify that their firms may pass on a tax planning strategy due to "potential harm to firm reputation." This evidence suggests that firms engaging in tax avoidance carry the risk that the general public labels them as "poor corporate citizens," and thus avoiding too much tax can lead to firms bearing significant reputational and political costs. In finding this evidence, the authors paved the way for numerous empirical studies that could raise the question of whether reputation does, in fact, affect tax planning strategies.

As it pertains to reputation, Chen, Schuchard, and Stomberg (2019) use large sample evidence to examine the role of the media in shaping tax strategy. Specifically, the authors provide evidence that the media is more likely to cover a firm's tax planning activities when the firm's effective tax rates fall below the top US statutory tax rate and for firms with greater visibility. However, the authors do not find that firms decrease tax avoidance activities following the media exposure of this information, thereby suggesting that media attention has only a minor impact on the firm's tax planning activities. On the contrary, Austin and Wilson (2017) posit and provide evidence that firms with more valuable brands have higher effective tax rates, suggesting that these firms engage in lower levels of tax avoidance than firms with less valuable brands. However, they provide mixed evidence on whether higher reputational value deters more aggressive tax avoidance in the form of tax sheltering.

Furthermore, Gallemore, Maydew, and Thornock (2014) examine 113 firms that were subject to scrutiny for aggressive tax avoidance activities (i.e., tax shelters). These 113 firms are presumably some of the most egregious tax-avoiders, and their tax-related accusations have been brought to the public forefront. However, in this study, the authors fail to document evidence that these firms face any significant reputational harm. Specifically, the authors note that the firms' CEOs and CFOs do not face any higher turnover, there is not significantly higher external auditor turnover, there are no lost sales, and there is no decreased likelihood of the firm making the *Fortune* list. Furthermore, even after being accused of egregious tax avoidance, the firms do not appear to change their tax avoidance activities, as the firms' effective tax rates do not increase, nor do they change their tax sheltering decisions.

Consistent across the aforementioned studies is an examination of firms with high visibility and brand value. As a result, the findings can be more of a function of *perceived* reputation damages versus actual reputation damages. To more effectively examine whether *actual* reputation damages have an effect on tax planning, other studies examine changes to the regulatory disclosure environment on tax planning. First, Dyreng, Hoopes, and Wilde (2016) provide evidence that when UK firms were forced to disclose subsidiary locations, including highly scrutinized haven subsidiaries, they subsequently lowered their tax planning activities. Similarly, Henry, Massel, and Towery (2016) find that firms decrease their levels of tax avoidance following the onset of the FIN 48 disclosure requirements, which required firms to present relatively detailed disclosures of uncertain tax positions in their financial statements. A recent working paper by Dhaliwal et al. (2017) examines whether reputational damage during a period of numerous consumer protests over tax avoidance affects firms' tax practices. They find that firms experiencing the most negative media sentiment over the period have higher ETRs after the protest period, suggesting that the reputational costs may have motivated firms to decrease tax avoidance. In a related study, Hoopes, Robinson, and Slemrod (2018) examine another setting where there was a regulatory increase in the information required to be disclosed. In contrast to the other papers, the authors find that when public firms disclose more tax return information, they *lower* their effective tax rates, suggesting that the disclosure encourages *more* tax avoidance.

In sum, whether it is actual or perceived effects of tax avoidance on a firm's reputation, the evidence on whether reputational concerns affect tax planning and relatedly whether indirect corporate stakeholders (including the public) can affect firms' tax planning decisions through "tax shaming" is mixed at best. A common theme across the studies is that firms vary their reaction to increased scrutiny based on the type of *firm* and the type of *scrutiny*. As a result, the archival evidence is not able to connect back to Graham et al.'s (2014) survey evidence, and thus it remains to be seen whether and to what extent reputational costs affect tax avoidance.

Conclusion

In this chapter, we provide a theoretical framework for evaluating the ethicality of corporate tax avoidance, and we discuss the differing perspectives of different external corporate stakeholders on tax avoidance ethicality. Our review of the empirical literature suggests that tax avoidance may, in fact, be value increasing to shareholders depending on the riskiness of the tax planning scheme. In addition, relevant research finds that tax avoidance may be beneficial to employees and also can result in future macroeconomic growth, which would be beneficial to a wide range of corporate stakeholders. Thus, whether tax avoidance is unethical in terms of harming stakeholders in addition to shifting wealth away from the government is a complicated issue that may be best determined on a case-by-case basis.

Given that the taxpaying public differs in their perspective on the ethicality of tax avoidance from corporate managers, we also review the literature to try to synthesize whether indirect stakeholders (e.g., the public) can affect corporations' tax planning decisions. The evidence is mixed at best, suggesting that reputational costs and "tax shaming" have little success in motivating corporations to decrease levels of tax avoidance. Thus, if the public and tax authorities prefer for corporate taxpayers to bear a greater amount of the overall tax national burden, they may be more successful by changing the tax law rather than by attempting to pressure corporations to voluntarily leave tax savings on the table. Major tax reform in the United States (Tax Cuts and Jobs Act of 2017) was recently passed, which includes provisions to significantly limit the abilities of multinational corporations to lower tax burdens by shifting income abroad. However, the TCJA also reduced the corporate statutory tax rate from 35% to 21%. Thus, corporations may demand less aggressive tax strategies in lieu of an already low tax rate. Conversely, managers may still continue to avoid taxes aggressively while also taking advantage of the newly reduced corporate tax rates. In sum, it remains to be seen whether the TCJA indeed results in reduced tax planning by corporations.

Notes

1 According to Jones, Rhoades-Catanach, and Callaghan (2019), "a tax is equitable if it redresses inequities existing in a capitalistic system." However, Jones, Rhoades-Catanach, and Callaghan (2019) also note that while many people agree with the concept of distributive justice, "many people also oppose the notion of Uncle Sam playing Robin Hood" (Jones, Rhoades-Catanach, and Callaghan 2019, 2–17). Therefore, the amount of progressivity in the system and the equitable distribution of the tax burden are issues that many rational and moral people may disagree about and becomes a matter of socioeconomic beliefs and preferences (i.e., what are the beliefs of each individual person or entity for generating the most positive economic results on their firm and society as a whole).

2 In a review of over 300 documents, including textbooks and academic articles, Phillip Lewis concluded that finding a consensus on the meaning of business ethics was like "nailing jello to a wall" (Lewis 1985, 381). Hence, there are many judgments in business settings that require an in-depth analysis to try to determine whether or not they are ethical.

3 In contrast, tax evasion involves a clear and purposeful disregard for the tax law, such as under-reporting income that is clearly taxable or deducting expenses that are phony or should clearly not be deductible. Tax evasion falls under the category of fraud, which should be clearly perceived as unethical behavior by any rational person.

4 While the focus of this chapter is on corporate taxpayers, the literature also documents that individual taxpayers can engage in similarly aggressive tax avoidance activities using tax havens to reduce tax liabilities (Hanlon, Maydew, and Thornock 2015), although individual tax-avoiding strategies involving tax havens usually involve tax evasion.

5 See §7701(o)(1) of the Internal Revenue Code for specific details on the economic substance doctrine. While all transactions have varying levels of economic substance, the IRS uses the economic substance doctrine to identify and combat taxpayers that do not have a substantial purpose for entering into specific transactions.

6 Another way that corporations can affect the tax burden is by affecting the political process. However, Barrick and Brown (2019) note in their review of the tax-related corporate political activity research that there is limited empirical evidence that corporations have specific effects on the tax-law writing process, as well as whether or not corporations benefit from investing in tax-related political activity.

Specifically, while many studies document relations between political activities and tax outcomes, these studies generally suffer from empirical challenges such as not being able to examine firm-level effects, not knowing what other activities firms use to influence taxation, self-selection, and construct validity. See page 71 of their study.

7 For example, as of February 2019, the market capitalization of Amazon, Inc., is approximately $800 billion.

8 While all taxpayers indirectly receive societal benefits from tax payments, individuals may benefit more directly compared to corporations, such as through free public education, government entitlements, etc.

9 For example, if the corporation is subject to a tax increase, by default, the tax increase reduces after-tax income, and the tax increase is therefore fully borne by the shareholders. Conversely, managers could cut jobs or wages to maintain the pre-tax-increase level of after-tax income available to shareholders, shifting the tax burden to the workers. In fact, academic literature supports this supposition by finding that workers bear approximately one-half of business's tax burden (Fuest, Peichl, and Siegloch 2018), and nonacademic work by the Tax Foundation (2018) states "that corporate income taxes are the most harmful type of tax and that workers bear a portion of the burden" (page 1).

10 For example, following the Tax Cuts and Jobs Act of 2017, numerous corporations increased salaries and paid out one-time bonuses to employees (Balakrishnan and Levi 2017; Mishel 2018). Other tax cuts have also positively affected these activities (e.g., Dyreng and Hills 2018).

11 While corporate managers may increasingly view contributing to society as an important objective, they may not view this role as being achieved through higher tax payments. For example, during a recent CEO roundtable, some CEOs noted that contributing to society is an essential part of running their corporation, even though it does not necessarily provide a direct benefit to its shareholders (Gelles and Yaffe-Bellany 2019). However, the CEO roundtable made no reference to increasing the amount of taxes paid and rather made references to objectives such as treating employees fairly, fostering diversity and inclusion, and preserving the environment.

12 Corporate governance is the set of controls at the country level or firm level that assure corporate suppliers of finance of getting a return on their investment (Shleifer and Vishny 1997).

References

Alesina, Alberto, and Silvia Ardagna. 2010. "Large Changes in Fiscal Policy: Taxes Versus Spending." *Tax Policy and the Economy* 24 (1): 35–68. https://doi.org/10.1086/649828.

Atwood, T. J., and Christina Lewellen. 2019. "The Complementarity between Tax Avoidance and Manager Diversion: Evidence from Tax Haven Firms." *Contemporary Accounting Research* 36 (1): 259–94. https://doi.org/10.1111/1911-3846.12421.

Austin, Chelsea Rae, and Ryan J. Wilson. 2017. "An Examination of Reputational Costs and Tax Avoidance: Evidence from Firms with Valuable Consumer Brands." *The Journal of the American Taxation Association* 39 (1): 67–93. https://doi.org/10.2308/atax-51634.

Back, Philippa. 2013. "Avoiding Tax May Be Legal, but Can It Ever Be Ethical?" *The Guardian*, April 24, 2013. Sec. Social Impact: Guardian Sustainable Business.

Balakrishnan, Anita, and Ari Levi. 2017. "AT&T, Comcast Giving $1,000 Bonuses to Hundreds of Thousands of Workers after Tax Bill." *CSNBC*, December 20, 2017. Sec. Tech. www.cnbc.com/2017/12/20/tax-reform-reaction-att-is-giving-bonuses-to-200000-employees.html.

Balakrishnan, Karthik, Jennifer L. Blouin, and Wayne R. Guay. 2019. "Tax Aggressiveness and Corporate Transparency." *The Accounting Review* 94 (1): 45–69. https://doi.org/10.2308/accr-52130.

Barrick, John A., and Jennifer L. Brown. 2019. "Tax-Related Corporate Political Activity Research: A Literature Review." *The Journal of the American Taxation Association* 41 (1): 59–89. https://doi.org/10.2308/atax-52026.

Blaylock, Bradley S. 2016. "Is Tax Avoidance Associated with Economically Significant Rent Extraction among U.S. Firms?" *Contemporary Accounting Research* 33 (3): 1013–43.

Bloomberg. 2018. "Where Have All the Public Companies Gone?" *Bloomberg Opinion*, April 9, 2018. www.bloomberg.com/opinion/articles/2018-04-09/where-have-all-the-u-s-public-companies-gone.

Bozanic, Zahn, Jeffrey L. Hoopes, Jacob R. Thornock, and Braden M. Williams. 2017. "IRS Attention." *Journal of Accounting Research* 55 (1): 79–114. https://doi.org/10.1111/1475-679X.12154.

Chen, Shannon, Kathleen Schuchard, and Bridget Stomberg. 2019. "Media Coverage of Corporate Taxes." *The Accounting Review* 94 (5): 83–116. https://doi.org/10.2308/atax-52026.

Commissioner of Internal Revenue v. Newman. 1947, 35 AFTR 857. U.S. Court of Appeals, Second Circuit.

Congressional Budget Office, Erika. 2019. "Historical Budget Data." www.cbo.gov/about/products/budget-economic-data#2.

Desai, Mihir A., and Dhammika Dharmapala. 2006. "Corporate Tax Avoidance and High-Powered Incentives." *Journal of Financial Economics* 79 (1): 145–79.

Desai, Mihir A., and Dhammika Dharmapala. 2009. "Corporate Tax Avoidance and Firm Value." *Review of Economics and Statistics* 91 (3): 537–46.

Dhaliwal, Dan S., Theodore H. Goodman, P. J. Hoffman, and Casey M. Schwab. 2017. *The Incidence, Valuation and Management of Tax-Related Reputational Costs: Evidence from a Period of Protest*. Working Paper, University of Arizona, Perdue University, Indiana University, University of North Texas.

Drake, Katharine D., Stephen J. Lusch, and James Stekelberg. 2019. "Does Tax Risk Affect Investor Valuation of Tax Avoidance?" *Journal of Accounting, Auditing & Finance* 34 (1): 151–76. https://doi.org/10.1177/0148558X17692674.

Dyreng, Scott D., and Robert Hills. 2018. *Foreign Earnings Repatriations and Domestic Employment*. Working Paper, Duke University, Penn State University.

Dyreng, Scott D., Jeffrey L. Hoopes, and Jaron H. Wilde. 2016. "Public Pressure and Corporate Tax Behavior." *Journal of Accounting Research* 54 (1): 147–86.

Dyreng, Scott D., and Bradley P. Lindsey. 2009. "Using Financial Accounting Data to Examine the Effect of Foreign Operations Located in Tax Havens and Other Countries on U.S. Multinational Firms' Tax Rates." *Journal of Accounting Research* 47 (5): 1283–316.

Field, Heather M. 2017. "Aggressive Tax Planning & the Ethical Tax Lawyer." *Virginia Tax Review* 36: 261–321.

Fuest, Clemens, Andreas Peichl, and Sebastian Siegloch. 2018. "Do Higher Corporate Taxes Reduce Wages? Micro Evidence from Germany." *American Economic Review* 108 (2): 393–418. https://doi.org/10.1257/aer.20130570.

Gallemore, John, Edward L. Maydew, and Jacob R. Thornock. 2014. "The Reputational Costs of Tax Avoidance." *Contemporary Accounting Research* 31 (4): 1103–33. https://doi.org/10.1111/1911-3846.12055.

Gelles, David, and David Yaffe-Bellany. 2019. "Feeling Heat, C.E.O.s Pledge New Priorities." *New York Times*, August 20.

Goh, Beng Wee, Jimmy Lee, Chee Yeow Lim, and Terry Shevlin. 2016. "The Effect of Corporate Tax Avoidance on the Cost of Equity." *The Accounting Review* 91 (6): 1647–70.

Graham, John R., Michelle Hanlon, Terry Shevlin, and Nemit Shroff. 2014. "Incentives for Tax Planning and Avoidance: Evidence from the Field." *The Accounting Review* 89 (3): 991–1023. https://doi.org/10.2308/accr-50678.

Gravelle, Jane G. 2015. "Tax Havens: International Tax Avoidance and Evasion." *Congressional Research Service Report for Congress*: 7–5700. www.crs.gov, R40623.

Hanlon, Michelle, Edward L. Maydew, and Jacob R. Thornock. 2015. "Taking the Long Way Home: U.S. Tax Evasion and Offshore Investments in U.S. Equity and Debt Markets." *The Journal of Finance* 70 (1): 257–87. https://doi.org/10.1111/jofi.12120.

Hanlon, Michelle, and Joel Slemrod. 2009. "What Does Tax Aggressiveness Signal? Evidence from Stock Price Reactions to News about Tax Shelter Involvement." *Journal of Public Economics* 93 (1–2): 126–41.

Hasan, Iftekhar, Chun Keung (Stan) Hoi, Qiang Wu, and Hao Zhang. 2014. "Beauty Is in the Eye of the Beholder: The Effect of Corporate Tax Avoidance on the Cost of Bank Loans." *Journal of Financial Economics* 113 (1): 109–30. https://doi.org/10.1016/j.jfineco.2014.03.004.

Henry, Erin, Norman Massel, and Erin Towery. 2016. "Increased Tax Disclosures and Corporate Tax Avoidance." *National Tax Journal* 69 (4): 809–30.

Hoopes, Jeffrey L., Devan Mescall, and Jeffrey A. Pittman. 2012. "Do IRS Audits Deter Corporate Tax Avoidance?" *The Accounting Review* 87 (5): 1603–39.

Hoopes, Jeffrey L., Leslie Robinson, and Joel Slemrod. 2018. "Public Tax-Return Disclosure." *Journal of Accounting and Economics* 66 (1): 142–62. https://doi.org/10.1016/j.jacceco.2018.04.001.

Inger, Kerry K. 2014. "Relative Valuation of Alternative Methods of Tax Avoidance." *The Journal of the American Taxation Association* 36 (1): 27–55. https://doi.org/10.2308/atax-50606.

Jensen, Michael C., and William H. Meckling. 1976. "Theory of the Firm: Managerial Behavior, Agency Costs and Ownership Structure." *Journal of Financial Economics* 3 (4): 305–60.

Jones, Sally, Shelley Rhoades-Catanach, and Sandra Callaghan. 2019. *Principles of Taxation for Business and Investment Planning*. 22nd ed. New York: McGraw Hill Education. www.mheducation.com/highered/product/principles-taxation-business-investment-planning-2019-edition-jones-rhoades-catanach/M9781259917097.html.

Lewis, Phillip V. 1985. "Defining 'Business Ethics': Like Nailing Jello to a Wall." *Journal of Business Ethics* 4 (5): 377–83. https://doi.org/10.1007/BF02388590.

Mishel, Lawrence. 2018. "Bonuses Are up $0.02 since the GOP Tax Cuts Passed." Economic Policy Institute. *Working Economics Blog* (blog), December 14, 2018. www.epi.org/blog/bonuses-are-up-0-02-since-the-gop-tax-cuts-passed/.

Paul, Richard, and Linda Elder. 2013. *The Thinker's Guide to Ethical Reasoning*. Tomales, CA: Foundation for Critical Thinking Press.

Peretti, Jacques. 2016. "The Cayman Islands – Home to 100,000 Companies and the £8.50 Packet of Fish Fingers." *The Guardian*, January 18, 2016.

Reid, T. R. 2017. "Don't Just Cut the Corporate Tax Rate. Eliminate It." *Washington Post*, November 15, 2017. www.washingtonpost.com/opinions/republicans-want-to-cut-the-corporate-tax-rate-how-about-we-eliminate-it/2017/11/15/758331fe-c956–11e7-aa96–54417592cf72_story.html.

Rosenthal, Steven. 2016. "Only About One-Quarter of Corporate Stock Is Owned by Taxable Share-holders." *Tax Policy Center*, May 16, 2016. www.taxpolicycenter.org/taxvox/only-about-one-quarter-corporate-stock-owned-taxable-shareholders.

Scholes, Myron S., Mark A. Wolfson, Merle M. Erickson, Michelle Hanlon, Edward L. Maydew, and Terrence J. Shevlin. 2015. *Taxes & Business Strategy*. 5th ed. Upper Saddle River, NJ: Pearson Prentice Hall.

Shevlin, Terry, Lakshmanan Shivakumar, and Oktay Urcan. 2019. "Macroeconomic Effects of Corporate Tax Policy." *Journal of Accounting and Economics* 68 (1): 101–233. https://doi.org/10.1016/j.jacceco.2019.03.004.

Shleifer, Andrei, and Robert W. Vishny. 1997. "A Survey of Corporate Governance." *The Journal of Finance* 52 (2): 737–83. https://doi.org/10.2307/2329497.

Tax Foundation. 2018. "The Benefits of Cutting the Corporate Income Tax Rate." https://taxfoundation.org/benefits-of-a-corporate-tax-cut/.

Tax Justice Network. 2019. "Tax Avoidance." www.taxjustice.net/faq/tax-avoidance/.

Van Heeke, Tom, Benjamin Davis, Phineas Baxandall, and Dan Smith. 2014. *Picking Up the Tab 2014: Average Citizens and Small Businesses Pay the Price for Offshore Tax Havens*. Denver, CO: U.S. PIRG.

Weisbach, David A. 2002. "Ten Truths About Tax Shelters." *Tax Law Review* 55 (2): 215–53.

York, Erika. 2018. "Summary of the Latest Federal Income Tax Data, 2017 Update." *Tax Foundation*, January 17, 2018. https://taxfoundation.org/summary-federal-income-tax-data-2017/.

18

PERSONAL TAX COMPLIANCE

Ethical decision making in the tax context

Jonathan Farrar, Dawn W. Massey, and Linda Thorne

Introduction

According to Pulitzer Prize-winning author Herman Wouk, income tax returns are the most imaginative fiction being written today. If there is even the slightest bit of truth to this statement, tax authorities should be concerned. A tax return is a reporting document filed with a tax authority, and is the primary mechanism by which a tax authority learns the amounts, nature, and sources of taxpayers' income.

Tax authorities can deter taxpayers from being noncompliant by levying interest and penalties on unpaid tax amounts. Research on taxpayers' compliance tends to be behavioral, as it tends to be rooted in the social psychology literature and investigate factors that influence taxpayers' decisions to be tax compliant. Nevertheless, there is a large economics literature investigating tax compliance that establishes the importance of deterrence approaches to taxpayers' compliance (for an overview, see Slemrod 2007). However, tax authorities have neither the time nor the resources to verify every amount on each tax return taxpayers submit and can do little in the way of enforcing compliance and deterring noncompliance. Enforcement activities consist primarily of audits. In 2016, for example, the Internal Revenue Service audited 1.06 million individual tax returns, which represented just 0.5% of all individual tax returns it processed.[1]

Consequently, tax reporting used throughout the Western world is essentially based upon the "honor system" of self-reporting (rather than taxes being collected by force). In a self-reporting system, the fairness of the tax system is critical, although what makes it "fair" or just is subjective. For instance, philosophers such as Nozick (1974), Rawls (1971) and Sen (2009) have opined about what makes a society just or fair. Nozick (1974) suggests that a fair society is one in which a government does not attempt to enforce a pattern of distribution, including redistribution of taxes, for the good of society, as enforcing patterns of distribution violates individuals' rights and will eventually result in coercion. In contrast, Rawls (1971) contends that in a just society, everyone should share in the wealth of a society and receive benefits from the distribution of that wealth. Thus, Rawls' (1971) conception of a just society involves the redistribution of taxes for the good of members of a society. Sen (2009) believes that a just society is a product of putting the right institutions in place, which would include a tax authority. Although there is not agreement among philosophers about the role of fairness in society, they do agree that fairness is important, as do economists (Basu 2011). Tax researchers also agree that fairness is important and have made some inroads into understanding what constitutes tax fairness. Later in this chapter we summarize tax literature about the construct of fairness and how it influences voluntary tax compliance.

A tax reporting system relying upon the self-reporting honesty of taxpayers is based on voluntary compliance. Taxpayers are "compliant" when they report all their income and claim only expenses or deductions to which they are legally entitled, i.e., permitted by tax laws. Otherwise, they are "noncompliant." Tax compliance tends to refer to "reporting compliance." There are other forms of compliance, such as paying an interim tax payment before a deadline (e.g., Wenzel 2006), but the bulk of tax compliance research focuses on reporting compliance, as does this chapter.

Tax noncompliance can be intentional or unintentional. Intentional noncompliance is unethical behavior and synonymous with tax evasion and tax fraud, as there is a deliberate attempt to deceive the government (scienter). In addition to civil penalties (interest and/or penalties on unpaid taxes) imposed by tax laws, intentional noncompliance can result in criminal penalties. On the other hand, unintentional noncompliance (by mistake) is neither unethical nor the result of an unethical intention. Unintentional noncompliance can still result in financial penalties but is generally treated less severely than intentional noncompliance; however, the tax authority must be convinced that the lack of compliance occurred as a result of ignorance or without intent to deceive before less severe penalties are imposed. Regardless of intentionality, noncompliance imposes a cost to society and places an unfair burden on compliant taxpayers (Holmes and Sunstein 1999).

Tax avoidance is different from noncompliance. Tax avoidance is using every legal means available – such as tax planning over time and over different jurisdictions – to minimize legitimate taxes owed to the tax authority. Tax avoidance is not considered to be illegal and usually is not considered to be unethical. An example of tax avoidance that generally is considered ethical is to claim deductions that are allowed by the tax authority, which would include tax deductions for dependents or for mortgage interest paid. However, not all tax avoidance is perceived to be ethical. For example, the use of offshore tax havens, while legally permitted, may be perceived as unethical, for at least two reasons. One is that only wealthy individuals have the means to hire tax professionals with expert knowledge to navigate something as complex as tax havens. The other is that the use of offshore tax havens runs afoul of the principle of paying one's fair share. Thus, while tax avoidance is not illegal, it is not always ethical.

Tax compliance is also associated with the detectability of noncompliance. In cases where a third party is responsible for providing tax information to the tax authority, a detection of noncompliant tax reporting is heightened. For example, income or deductions that are subject to third-party verification, such as a salary from an employer or an employee's pension contribution, tend not to result in noncompliance, since tax authorities easily can match what the employee reported on their tax return to the amount on the tax records the employer provided to the employee and the tax authority. By contrast, income and deductions not directly associated with third-party reporting procedures have more latitude for tax noncompliance. For instance, employment or business activities where cash is exchanged and other transactions that are difficult to trace or verify are more likely to result in noncompliance.

The literature about tax compliance is considerable. Relatively recent literature reviews include Devos (2014), Kirchler and Hoelzl (2018), James and Edwards (2010), Kirchler et al. (2010), and Kornhauser (2007).[2] Olsen, Kang, and Kirchler (2018) provide a recent review of the tax psychology–tax compliance literature. These reviews suggest that tax ethics scholarship investigating tax compliance behavior has shifted from demographic factors (such as age and income) and economic variables (such as tax rates and audit probability) to socio-psychological constructs including perceptions of fairness, tax morale, trust in tax authorities, perceived legitimacy of tax authorities, social norms, and motivational posturing (describing how taxpayers engage with the tax authority). The findings in these literature reviews suggest these socio-psychological constructs are positively associated with tax compliance behavior.

A large emphasis in the investigation of the factors that influence tax compliance is research into the tax fairness–tax compliance association (Murphy 2004, 2005). A large stream of tax fairness shows that taxpayers perceptions of tax fairness encourages taxpayers' compliance in tax reporting (Hartner et al. 2010; Kirchler, Niemirowski, and Wearing 2006; Murphy 2004, 2005, 2009; Verboon and Goslinga 2009; Van Dijke and Verboon 2010; Wenzel 2002). Tax fairness scholarship has identified multiple factors that influence taxpayers' perceptions of fairness, each of which influences tax compliance in different ways (Farrar et al. 2020). For example, taxpayers' perceptions of how taxes are allocated among taxpayers is associated with compliance (Gerbing 1988; Christensen, Weihrich, and Newman 1994), as are the fairness of tax procedures (Eichfelder and Kegels 2014) and the perceived fairness of an encounter between a taxpayer and a tax agent (Farrar, Kaplan, and Thorne 2019). If taxpayers perceive different facets of the tax system to be fair, they are more willing to be cooperative and therefore compliant.

More recently, there is research straddling economics and social psychology investigating factors that influence taxpayers' compliance (see Alm, Kirchler, and Muehlbacher 2012, Kirchler 2007; Kirchler and Hoelzl 2018 for a review). Moreover, several studies find taxpayers are more likely to be compliant if they perceive the tax authority as powerful (Kogler et al. 2013; Kogler, Muehlbacher, and Kirchler 2015; Muehlbacher, Kirchler, and Schwarzenberger 2011; Wahl, Kastlunger, and Kirchler 2010). Tax decision making is an economic decision, but is not purely economic, as there are social psychological issues that apply simultaneously, such as perceptions of fairness (cf., Nagel 1970). If the tax fairness literature is any indication, perhaps future researchers could explore the nuances of these other constructs to determine their factor structure and explore the extent to which each sub-factor differentially impacts compliance. As well, economic and psychological aspects appear to jointly influence compliance, which could provide practical insights for tax authorities on how best to motivate compliance.

Another direction for future tax fairness research is to explore antecedents of factors that are known to influence tax fairness. That is, what influences taxpayers' perspectives of tax fairness, which, in turn, influences tax compliance behavior? Recent research by Farrar, Hausserman, and Pinto (2020) investigated antecedents to trust in the tax authority and found evidence that accountability dimensions of tax authority blameworthiness and tax authority responsiveness impacted trust and subsequent compliance following identity theft. As well, tax researchers could consider the role of professional accountants and corporations in supporting or undermining perceptions of tax fairness.

The tax literature investigating personal taxpayers' compliance also includes research into the impact on tax amnesties and tax whistleblowing. These other research domains have historically developed independently of tax compliance research, with little cross-pollination in terms of methodology, results, or researchers. Nevertheless, we hope, through understanding the similarities and differences between these research domains, we can forge a bridge with the goal of developing a more comprehensive understanding of the ethics of personal taxation.

Tax amnesties

A tax amnesty program provides taxpayers who have incorrectly reported amounts on past tax returns to "come clean" and correct past mistakes without criminal penalties. These programs tend to target individuals who have committed tax evasion or whose tax avoidance activities may be subject to litigation. Taxpayers who participate in a tax amnesty still have to pay unpaid taxes. Interest and penalties are often assessed but may be reduced or waived, sometimes contingent upon a taxpayer repatriating capital to their home country and investing it there so that the income can be taxed there.

Tax amnesties are usually one-time programs and generally are a rarity. Indonesia, for instance, has only ever offered one tax amnesty (in 2016). An exception to this norm is Italy, which has offered 58 amnesties since 1900 (Malherbe 2011). Tax amnesties that are ongoing are known as voluntary disclosure programs. Canada, the Netherlands, and Spain offer voluntary disclosure programs (Malherbe 2011).

A tax amnesty is a low-cost and reasonably effective method to detect tax evasion, since the taxpayer, who has incentives to self-report, has the onus to self-report a transgression and the tax authority only has administrative costs. Tax amnesties can be offered for all taxpayers or can be targeted only to those with certain characteristics. Belgium, for example, had a tax amnesty in 2004 just for foreign bank accounts (Malherbe 2011). Tax amnesties can also be offered by non-national levels of government. In the United States, for instance, 42 of 50 states have offered income tax amnesties (Baer and Le Borgne 2008), and 26 states have offered sales tax amnesties (Luna et al. 2006).

Hasseldine (1989) suggests that tax amnesties not only increase the revenues paid to the tax authority but also encourage subsequent voluntary compliance by taxpayers. Therefore, tax amnesties have both a fiscal and an ethical aspect. From a fiscal perspective, tax amnesties exist because it is easier and less costly for a tax authority to incentivize a taxpayer to report their mistakes than detect those mistakes through audits and other enforcement activities. The fiscal objective of a tax amnesty program is captured by the slogan of the state of Michigan's 1986 tax amnesty: "Get to us before we get to you." By incentivizing taxpayers with immunity from criminal prosecution and possible reduced interest and/or penalties, taxpayers avoid more severe repercussions that would have occurred had the tax authority discovered the tax evasion. Nevertheless, drawbacks to tax amnesties are that they reward miscreant taxpayers at the expense of law-abiding taxpayers, and they may discourage timely compliance if taxpayers can wait for the next amnesty to make a correct reporting of their tax situation.

Tax ethics research about tax amnesties is sparse, with a small stream of research that analyzes the net economic cost/benefit associated with tax amnesties (e.g., Das-Gupta and Mookherjee 1996) and with just three behavioral studies we know of: Rechberger et al. (2010), Farrar and Hausserman (2016), and Dunn, Farrar, and Hausserman (2018).

Rechberger et al. (2010) used an experimental economics approach in which a tax amnesty was offered midway through the experiment, which consisted of ten rounds of a tax "game." Participants were significantly more likely to report all their income after the amnesty than before the amnesty. There was also evidence of an indirect effect of perceived fairness of the amnesty on compliance through retribution and value restoration.

Farrar and Hausserman (2016) conducted a quasi-experiment in which they investigated intrinsic and extrinsic motivations for taxpayer participation in a tax amnesty following an unintentional taxpayer error. They found that desire to avoid a penalty is the most influential extrinsic motive and responsibility to pay one's taxes is the most influential intrinsic motive. Extrinsic influences accounted for approximately two-thirds of the amnesty decision. Their results were consistent across three magnitudes of taxpayer error ($500, $5,000, and $50,000).

Dunn, Farrar, and Hausserman (2018) studied the role of guilt cognitions – interrelated beliefs about an individual's role in a negative event – in influencing taxpayers' amnesty decisions following tax evasion. They investigated three guilt cognitions – responsibility for a decision, justification for a decision, and foreseeability of consequences – and found that taxpayers are likely to make voluntary disclosures when the consequences are foreseeable, unless they can diffuse responsibility and justify their evasion.

The paucity of research into the decision-making processes of taxpayers in situations where they have made intentional or unintentional errors suggests that more research can and should be done. The number of taxpayers who have made intentional or unintentional errors is difficult to estimate, but given the size of the personal tax gap (the difference between the amount of tax that should be paid versus what is actually paid) in countries such as the United States ($458 billion),[3] Canada ($12 billion),[4] and the UK (£33 billion),[5] there appears to be a substantial number of taxpayers.

Future research could investigate the likelihood of taxpayers making a disclosure in an ongoing amnesty program (a voluntary disclosure program) versus an occasional amnesty program, and whether taxpayer motivations are similar for each. This issue has practical implications for tax authorities, as tax authorities worldwide differ in how they structure tax amnesties and their willingness to offer them (Malherbe 2011). Future research could also try to reconcile the findings of Rechberger et al. (2010), who found that compliance persisted after an amnesty, with the findings of Mittone (2006) and Mittone, Panebianco, and Santoro (2017), who, using an experimental economics approach, found that there was a strong decrease in taxpayers' compliance after an audit, a finding they termed the "bomb crater effect." That is, tax ethics researchers could investigate why taxpayers are more compliant after an amnesty but not after an audit.

Tax whistleblowing

Whistleblowing is the reporting of suspected or observed misconduct to someone in authority. In a tax context, whistleblowing refers to the act of reporting another's tax fraud to a tax authority. A tax whistleblower has not personally engaged in tax noncompliance; rather, the whistleblower is holding another taxpayer accountable for potential tax noncompliance by reporting the suspected wrongdoing. Tax whistleblowing is carried out by phoning a tax authority, making an online submission through a dedicated portal on the tax authority's website, or by filing a paper form.

Whistleblowing creates a moral dilemma because there is a tradeoff between loyalty to one's organization and the liberty to speak out against wrongdoing (Paeth 2013). In organizational contexts, employees have a legal and moral obligation to be loyal to their employer but also have the freedom to stop immoral behavior. In the income tax context, this dilemma is not as acute, as taxpayers who are aware of another taxpayer's fraud are not always going to belong to an organization, and therefore loyalty considerations may not be relevant. Thus, the moral dilemma for a taxpayer is likely to be whether tax fraud is immoral behavior and whether the behavior should be stopped. If there is a social norm against tax fraud, it would be easier for a whistleblower to blow the whistle.

Tax whistleblower programs exist because not all taxpayers are fully reporting compliant at the time a tax return is due to be filed, and it is easier and less costly for a tax authority to incentivize taxpayers to report other taxpayers' mistakes than detect these mistakes through audits and other enforcement activities. Detection risk is often low, particularly for amounts not subject to third-party verification, as tax authorities do not have the resources to do a thorough inspection of all tax returns each year. Since detection risk is low, whistleblowing becomes an important way for tax authorities to learn about tax fraud.

Some tax whistleblower programs offer financial rewards, which tend to be a percentage of the additional taxes collected as a result of the whistleblower tip. In the United States, for example, Congress enacted a tax whistleblower program in 2006. In cases where the amount recovered exceeds $2 million or an individual taxpayer's income exceeds $200,000, the reward is 15–30% of the taxes collected. In other situations, the reward is at the discretion of the Internal Revenue Service and is up to 15% of taxes collected. In the decade following enactment of the whistleblower program, the IRS paid out $499 million in rewards to whistleblowers while collecting $3.6 billion in taxes.[6]

In the broader whistleblowing literature, a whistleblower tends to be an organization member or former organization member (Near and Miceli 1985); however, in the tax context, a whistleblower does not have to be a member or former member of an organization, and tax whistleblowing does not have to occur within an organization. Whistleblowing can be internal or external to an organization. The organizational whistleblowing research tends to focus on internal whistleblowing and examine what factors encourage whistleblowing in organizations (e.g., Mesmer-Magnus and Viswesvaran 2005; Miceli, Near, and Dworkin 2009). Organizational whistleblowing research tends to neither examine how impediments to whistleblowing can be overcome (MacGregor and Stuebs 2014) nor focus on whistleblowing external to organizations. This distinction is important, as internal and external whistleblowing involve different processes (Dworkin and Baucus 1998).

Tax whistleblowing is an example of external whistleblowing, as it is carried out by taxpayers who are not employees or otherwise affiliated with an organization (i.e., a tax authority). The tax context provides whistleblowing researchers an opportunity to examine external whistleblowing, as it involves taxpayers reporting to an external organization (a tax authority). The tax context is unique in that it involves a universal phenomenon (paying taxes) and has two external stakeholders with a vested interest in tax compliance. One stakeholder is the tax authority that administers the tax system; the other is the national government responsible for funding and administering the tax authority. This context could allow whistleblowing researchers unique insights into whistleblowing behavior, as tax whistleblowing has national implications rather than highly localized implications within an organization. Research in tax whistleblowing is limited to Farrar, Hausserman, and Rennie (2019), who investigated the interplay between revenge and financial incentives in influencing taxpayers' whistleblowing intentions.

There are significant additional opportunities to pursue whistleblowing in the tax context. For instance, tax whistleblowing researchers can investigate circumstances in which financial incentives do and do not work (Gneezy, Meier, and Rey-Biel 2011), since tax authorities with whistleblower programs can and do offer monetary rewards.

Discussion

Our understanding of the ethics of personal taxation tends to be situated in literature focused on understanding the decision process taxpayers use to engage in tax compliance, engaging in an amnesty program, and whistleblowing. Nevertheless, only relatively recently has research been conducted that straddles economics and psychology (Kirchler and Hoelzl 2018). Future research on the ethics of personal taxation must incorporate both underlying research domains, as tax decisions are neither purely economic nor solely moral but are economic and ethical simultaneously.

One methodological gap in understanding the ethics of personal taxation is that qualitative approaches to studying this research domain have been overlooked. We know of no research that uses interview data of taxpayers or tax authority employees to shed light on the tax compliance phenomena. Interviewing taxpayers convicted of tax fraud, as well as tax auditors, would doubtless provide additional insight into the ethics of personal taxation and lead us to understand how and to what extent taxpayers consider ethical and economic aspects of their decisions.

While most of the existing literature on the ethics of personal taxation has focused on compliance and the fairness–compliance association, more research remains to be conducted into tax amnesty disclosures and tax whistleblowing. There are opportunities for tax ethics researchers to examine the antecedents of constructs known to influence compliance, and there are opportunities for tax ethics researchers to examine the persistence of compliance following a tax amnesty and a tax whistleblowing report. For tax amnesty and tax whistleblowing decisions, much remains to be learned about the motivation for these decisions and how to overcome impediments for each.

Notes

1 2017 Internal Revenue Service Data Book, p. 23. Online: www.irs.gov/pub/irs-soi/17databk.pdf
2 James and Edwards (2010) summarize tax compliance literature reviews from Ahmed et al. (2003); Evans (2003), Fischer, Wartick, and Mark (1992), Jackson and Milliron (1986), Kirchler (2007), and Richardson and Sawyer (2001).
3 www.irs.gov/newsroom/the-tax-gap
4 www.canada.ca/en/revenue-agency/news/2018/06/tax-gap-estimates-in-canada.html
5 https://assets.publishing.service.gov.uk/government/uploads/system/uploads/attachment_data/file/715742/HMRC-measuring-tax-gaps-2018.pdf
6 IRS Whistleblower Program Fiscal Year 2017 Annual Report to Congress, p. 3. Online: www.irs.gov/pub/whistleblower/fy17_wo_annual_report_final.pdf

References

Ahmed, Eliza, Jason McCrae, Valerie Braithwaite, and Yuka Sakurai. 2003. *Bringing it Together BIT). Vol.1: An Annotated Bibliography Relating to Voluntary Tax Compliance.* Canberra: Centre for Tax System Integrity, Australian National University.

Alm, James, Erich Kirchler, and Stephan Muehlbacher. 2012. "Combining Psychology and Economics in the Analysis of Compliance: From Enforcement to Cooperation." *Economic Analysis & Policy* 42 (2): 133–51.

Baer, Katherine, and Eric Le Borgne. 2008. *Tax Amnesties: Theory, Trends, and Some Alternatives.* Washington, DC: International Monetary Fund.

Basu, Kaushik. 2011. *Beyond the Invisible Hand: Groundwork for a New Economics.* Princeton: Princeton University Press.

Christensen, Anne, Susan Weihrich, and Monica D. G. Newman. 1994. "The Impact of Education on Perceptions of Tax Fairness." *Advances in Taxation* 6: 63–94.

Das-Gupta, Arindam, and Dilip Mookherjee. 1996. "Tax Amnesties as Asset-Laundering Devices." *Journal of Law, Economics and Organization* 12 (2): 408–31.

Devos, Ken. 2014. *Factors Influencing Individual Taxpayer Compliance Behaviour.* Dordrecht: Springer.

Dunn, Paul, Farrar Jonathan, and Cass Hausserman. 2018. "The Influence of Guilt Cognitions on Taxpayers' Voluntary Disclosures." *Journal of Business Ethics* 148 (3): 689–701.

Dworkin, Terry, and Melissa Baucus. 1998. "Internal vs. External Whistleblowers: A Comparison of Whistleblowing Processes." *Journal of Business Ethics* 17 (12): 1281–98.

Eichfelder, Sebastian, and Chantal Kegels. 2014. "Compliance Costs Caused by Agency Action? Empirical Evidence and Implications for Tax Compliance." *Journal of Economic Psychology* 40: 200–19.

Evans, Chris. 2003. "Studying the Studies: An Overview of Recent Research into Taxation Operating Costs." *eJournal of Tax Research* 1 (1): 64–92.

Farrar, Jonathan, and Cass Hausserman. 2016. "An Exploratory Investigation of Extrinsic and Intrinsic Motivations in Tax Amnesty Decision-Making." *Journal of Tax Administration* 2 (2): 47–66.

Farrar, Jonathan, Cass Hausserman, and Morina Rennie. 2019. "The Influence of Revenge and Financial Incentives on Tax Fraud Reporting Intentions." *Journal of Economic Psychology* 71: 102–116.

Farrar, Jonathan, Cass Hausserman, and Odette Pinto. 2020. "Trust and Compliance Effects of Taxpayer Identity Theft: A Moderated Mediation Analysis." *Journal of the American Taxation Association* 42 (1): 57–77.

Farrar, Jonathan, Steven Kaplan, and Linda Thorne. 2019. "The Effect of Interactional Fairness and Detection Expectations on Taxpayers' Compliance Intentions." *Journal of Business Ethics* 154 (1): 167–80.

Farrar, Jonathan, Dawn Massey, Errol Osecki, and Linda Thorne. 2020. "Tax Fairness: Conceptual Foundations and Empirical Measurement." *Journal of Business Ethics* 162 (3): 487–503.

Fischer, Carol, Martha Wartick, and Melvin Mark. 1992. "Detection Probability and Taxpayer Compliance: A Literature Review." *Journal of Accounting Literature* 11 (1): 1–46.

Gerbing, Monica. 1988. "An Empirical Study of Taxpayer Perceptions of Fairness." Ph.D. thesis, Austin, TX: The University of Texas at Austin.

Gneezy, Uri., Stephan Meier, Pedro Rey-Biel. 2011. "When and Why Incentives (don't) Work to Modify Behavior." *Journal of Economic Perspectives* 25 (4): 191–210.

Hartner, Martina, Erich Kirchler, Andrea Poschalko, and Silvia Rechberger. 2010. "Taxpayers' Compliance by Procedural and Interactional Fairness Perceptions and Social Identity." *Journal of Psychology & Economics* 3 (1): 12–31.

Hasseldine, John. 1989. "Increasing Voluntary Compliance: The Case of Tax Amnesties." *Australian Tax Forum* 6 (4): 509–24.

Holmes, Stephen, and Cass Sunstein. 1999. *The Cost of Rights: Why Liberty Depends on Taxes.* New York: W.W. Norton & Company.

Jackson, Betty, and Valerie Milliron. 1986. "Taxpayers' Compliance Research: Findings, Problems, and Prospects." *Journal of Accounting Literature* 5: 125–66.

James, S., and A. Edwards. 2010. *An Annotated Bibliography of Tax Compliance and Compliance Costs.* MPRA Paper 26106, University Library of Munich, Germany.

Kirchler, Erich. 2007. *The Economic Psychology of Tax Behaviour.* New York: Cambridge University Press.

Kirchler, Erich, and Erik Hoelzl. 2018. *Economic Psychology: An Introduction.* Cambridge: Cambridge University Press.

Kirchler, Erich, Stephan Muehlbacher, Barbara Kastlunger, and Ingrid Wahl. 2010. "Why Pay Taxes? A Review of Tax Compliance Decisions." In *Developing Alternative Frameworks for Explaining Tax Compliance,* edited by James Alm, Jorge Martinez-Vazques, and Benno Torgler, 15–31. London: Routledge.

Kirchler, Erich, Apolonia Niemirowski, and Alexander Wearing. 2006. "Shared Subjective Views, Intent to Cooperate and Tax Compliance: Similarities between Australian Taxpayers and Tax Officers." *Journal of Economic Psychology* 27 (4): 502–17.

Kogler, Christoph, Larissa Batrancea, Anca Nichita, Jozsef Pantya, Alexis Belianin, and Erich Kirchler. 2013. "Trust and Power as Determinants of Tax Compliance: Testing the Assumptions of the Slippery Slope Framework in Austria, Hungary, Romania and Russia." *Journal of Economic Psychology* 34 (1): 169–80.

Kogler, Christoph, Stephan Muehlbacher, and Erich Kirchler. 2015. "Testing the 'Slippery Slope Framework' among Self-Employed Taxpayers." *Economics of Governance* 16 (2): 125–42.

Kornhauser, Marjorie. 2007. "Normative and Cognitive Aspects of Tax Compliance: Literature Review and Recommendations for the IRS Regarding Individual Taxpayers." In *National Taxpayer Advocate's 2007 Annual Report to Congress,* 138–80. Washington, DC: Internal Revenue Service.

Luna, Le Ann, Michael Brown, Katrina Mantzke, Ralph Tower, and Lorraine Wright. 2006. "State Tax Amnesties: Forgiveness is Divine – And Possibly Profitable." *State Tax Notes,* August 21: 497–511.

MacGregor, Jason, and Martin Stuebs. 2014. "The Silent Samaritan Syndrome: Why the Whistle Remains Unblown." *Journal of Business Ethics* 120 (2): 149–64.

Malherbe, Jacques. 2011. *Tax Amnesties.* Amsterdam: Kluwer Law International BV.

Mesmer-Magnus, Jessica, and Chockalingam Viswesvaran. 2005. "Whistleblowing in Organizations: An Examination of Correlates of Whistleblowing Intentions, Actions, and Retaliation." *Journal of Business Ethics* 62 (3): 277–97.

Miceli, Marcia, Janet Near, and Terry Dworkin. 2009. "A Word to the Wise: How Managers and Policy-Makers Can Encourage Employees to Report Wrongdoing." *Journal of Business Ethics* 86 (3): 379–96.

Mittone, Luigi. 2006. "Dynamic Behavior in Tax Evasion: An Experimental Approach." *The Journal of Socio-Economics* 35 (5): 813–35.

Mittone, Luigi, Fabrizio Panebianco, and Alessandro Santoro. 2017. "The Bomb-Crater Effect of Tax Audits: Beyond the Misperception of Chance." *Journal of Economic Psychology* 61: 225–43.

Muehlbacher, Stephan, Erich Kirchler, and Herbert Schwarzenberger. 2011. "Voluntary Versus Enforced Tax Compliance: Empirical Evidence for the 'Slippery Slope' Framework." *European Journal of Law & Economics* 32 (1): 89–97.

Murphy, Katrina. 2004. "The Role of Trust in Nurturing Compliance: A Study of Accused Tax Avoiders." *Law and Human Behavior* 28 (2): 187–209.

Murphy, Katrina. 2005. "Regulating More Effectively: The Relationship between Procedural Justice, Legitimacy and Tax Non-Compliance." *Journal of Law and Society* 32 (4): 562–89.

Murphy, Katrina. 2009. "Procedural Justice and Affect Intensity: Understanding Reactions to Regulatory Authorities." *Social Justice Research* 22 (1): 1–30.

Nagel, Thomas. 1970. *The Possibility of Altruism*. Princeton: Princeton University Press.

Near, Janet, and Marcia Miceli. 1985. "Organizational Dissidence: The Case of Whistle-Blowing." *Journal of Business Ethics* 4 (1): 1–16.

Nozick, Robert. 1974. *Anarchy, State, and Utopia*. New York: Basic Books.

Olsen, Jerome, Minjo Kang, and Erich Kirchler. 2018. "Tax Psychology". In *The Cambridge Handbook of Psychology and Economic Behaviour*, edited by Alan Lewis, 405–29 (2nd ed.). Cambridge: Cambridge University Press.

Paeth, Scott. 2013. "The Responsibility to lie and the Obligation to Report: Bonhoeffer's 'What Does it Mean to Tell the Truth?' and the Ethics of Whistleblowing." *Journal of Business Ethics* 112 (4): 559–66.

Rawls, John. 1971. *A Theory of Justice*. Cambridge: The Belknap Press of Harvard University Press.

Rechberger, Silvia, Martina Hartner, Erich Kirchler, and Franziska Hämmerle. 2010. "Tax Amnesties, Justice Perceptions, and Filing Behavior: A Simulation Study." *Law & Policy* 32 (2): 214–25.

Richardson, Maryann, and Adrian Sawyer. 2001. "A Taxonomy of Tax Compliance Literature: Further Findings, Problems and Prospects." *Australian Tax Forum* 16 (2): 137–284.

Sen, Amartya. 2009. *The Idea of Justice*. New York: The Belknap Press of Harvard University Press.

Slemrod, Joel. 2007. "Cheating Ourselves: The Economics of Tax Evasion." *The Journal of Economic Perspectives* 21 (1): 25–48.

Van Dijke, Marius, and Peter Verboon. 2010. "Trust in Authorities as a Boundary Condition to Procedural Fairness: Effects on Tax Compliance." *Journal of Economic Psychology* 31 (1): 80–91.

Verboon, Peter, and Sjoerd Goslinga. 2009. "The Role of Fairness in Tax Compliance." *Netherlands Journal of Psychology* 65: 136–45.

Wahl, Ingrid, Barbara Kastlunger, and Erich Kirchler. 2010. "Trust in Authorities and Power to Enforce Tax Compliance: An Empirical Analysis of the 'Slippery Slope Framework.'" *Law & Policy* 32 (4): 383–406.

Wenzel, M. 2002. "The Impact of Outcome Orientation and Justice Concerns on Tax Compliance: The Role of Taxpayers' Identity." *Journal of Applied Psychology* 87 (4): 629–45.

Wenzel, M. 2006. "A Letter from the Tax Office: Compliance Effects of Informational and Interpersonal Justice." *Social Justice Research* 19 (3): 345–64.

PART V

Education and accounting ethics

19

THE ROLE OF PRACTICAL WISDOM IN ACCOUNTING ETHICS EDUCATION

Steven M. Mintz and William F. Miller

Introduction

What is practical wisdom, and what role should it play in the ethics education of accounting students? This is an important question because wisdom gained informs professional judgment in accounting. The objectives of this chapter are to explain how practical wisdom comes about through developing moral skill and moral will, its relationship to Rest's Model of Moral Development (moral sensitivity, moral judgment, moral motivation, and moral action) and its usefulness in making professional accounting judgments. We also discuss the link between practical wisdom and ethical decision making in accounting in the context of the public interest obligation that defines the purpose of the accounting profession. Finally, we address pedagogical issues and an approach for integrating practical wisdom into the accounting curriculum.

The application of Rest's Model of Moral Development in teaching ethics is well documented (Melé 2005; Morales-Sanchez and Cabello-Medina 2013). Accounting researchers have extended the discussion to incorporate accounting values into the model (Thorne 1998; Melé 2005; Chang, Davis, and Kauffman 2012; Mintz and Morris 2017). What's missing is a thorough explanation of how practical wisdom fits in and enhances professional decision making in accounting and how it can be taught as part of the ethics education of accounting students.

Accounting is a social practice with the end goal of serving the public interest. Accounting professionals accomplish this goal by adhering to the profession's core values embodied in the AICPA Code of Professional Conduct, as revised on December 15, 2014. These core values define the character of an accounting professional, underlie ethical decision making, and include independence, integrity, objectivity, competence, due care, and professional skepticism. The behavior of professional accountants must be consistent with detailed rules of conduct in the AICPA Code that guide professionals on what to do and how to meet their ethical obligations to clients, credit grantors, governments, employers, investors, the business and financial community, and others who rely on the objectivity and integrity of members (CPAs) to maintain the orderly functioning of commerce (AICPA 2014).

MacIntyre (1984) defines a practice as any coherent and complex form of socially established cooperative human activity through which goods internal to that form of activity (i.e., serving the public interest) are realized in the course of trying to achieve those standards of excellence that define the practice. He says that every practice requires a certain kind of relationship among those who participate in it. Virtues are those standards of excellence that define a practitioner's relationship to others who share the same kind of purposes. A practice cannot be sustained without those standards of excellence that characterize relationships within a practice. To enter into a practice is to accept the authority of those standards, obedience to rules, and the achievement of goods.

Accountants meet their obligation to serve the public interest by acting in accordance with specific standards of excellence (i.e., objectivity and integrity) and other virtues that support ethical decision making. Morales-Sanchez and Cabello-Medina (2013) suggest that universal moral virtues such as prudence (knowledge and practical wisdom), justice (giving people what they deserve), and temperance (moderation as self-control) can influence various stages of the ethical decision-making process.

Francis (1990) believes that accounting has the capacity to be a virtuous practice if we realize that it is both a moral practice and a discursive practice. By *moral* he means that "Accounting is a practice involving human agency that has the capacity to change things in the world." By *discursive* he means that accounting not only reports the facts but, importantly, the accountant says "something (what the accounting report is about) to someone (who the accounting report is prepared for)." The discursive nature of accounting practice establishes a moral agency role for accountants. Virtuous practitioners are concerned about the moral consequences of what they do as accountants.

In various forms, accounting researchers argue that accounting educators should integrate professional rules of conduct, moral values, and moral virtues into their curriculum (Mintz 1995; Thorne 1998; Armstrong, Ketz, and Owsen 2003; Melé 2005; Libby and Thorne 2007; Mintz and Morris 2017). According to Melé (2005), moral virtues provide the inner strength for moral behavior. As such they rely on practical wisdom to develop the moral skill and moral will that can lead to ethical decision making.

Schwartz (2011) suggests that institutions rely too heavily on rules and incentives that encourage good performance. He believes that excessive reliance on external rules deprives people of the opportunity to develop moral skill, and excessive reliance on incentives undermines moral will. What's missing is what the classical philosopher Aristotle (1962) called *practical wisdom*.

The chapter proceeds as follows. The next section describes the link between moral will and moral skill and practical wisdom. This is followed by a discussion of moral and intellectual virtues. A comprehensive analysis of practical wisdom follows, drawing largely on research in the management discipline. Next, the role of practical wisdom in Rest's model and how the various components influence moral behavior and ethical decision making are discussed. Pedagogical issues are addressed, including how to teach students about practical wisdom and suggestions for curriculum development. The chapter concludes with suggestions for future research and researchers.

Moral will, moral skill, and practical wisdom

Moral will is the desire to achieve the proper aims of an activity, such as to serve the public interest in accounting. Moral skill enables people to determine how to treat others in everyday life and make decisions that are right, not wrong; good, not bad. Practical wisdom combines will with skill. Skill without will can lead to the manipulation of others to serve one's own interests, not theirs. Will without skill makes it more difficult to assess how one's actions affect others.

Aristotle considered *phronesis*, or practical wisdom, to be an intellectual virtue that directs moral virtues. As a practical, intellectual virtue, *phronesis* is both cognitive and action-guiding.

Functionally, it enables the moral agent to deliberate about choices of action that reflect the rationality of the agent's course of action (Marshall and Thorburn 2014).

In his classical book, *Nicomachean Ethics* (*NE*), Aristotle developed a systematic understanding of what constitutes a practically wise person. *Practical wisdom* tells us what we ought to do and what we ought not to do. It depends on being able to deliberate well about what is good and avoid what is bad in accomplishing one's end goals. It relies on understanding what someone else says and making judgments about how to deal with others to achieve end goals. Virtue or excellence is not only a characteristic that is guided by right reason but also a characteristic that is united with right reason; and right reason in moral matters is practical wisdom (Aristotle 1962). Thus, correct moral reasoning or judgment should be guided by practical wisdom.

There is a scarcity of research on the role of practical wisdom in accounting ethics and ethics education. Researchers who have addressed these issues generally discuss practical wisdom in the context of making good judgments as an accounting professional. Melé (2005) states that accountants have to make practical judgments about concrete situations and, above all, to behave correctly. Armstrong (2002) suggests that accountants have to determine the significance of each situation while acting in accordance with professional values, such as due care, professional competence, objectivity, integrity, independence, and so on. Accountants have to judge each situation and what each value means in that situation and then act according to this judgment. Mintz (2006) situates practical wisdom as an intellectual virtue along with understanding and good sense and claims it can be taught through reflective learning. Chang, Davis, and Kauffman (2012) call for accounting ethics education to pay more attention to providing accounting students a broad view that facilitates the development of moral sentiment, practical wisdom, and transitive virtues – virtues related to dealing with others – and self-mastering virtues – those that give self-command over one's actions.

Moral and intellectual virtues

A quote attributed to Aristotle is, "We are what we repeatedly do. Virtues become excellences of character with practice and repetition in different situations. Therefore, excellence is not an act. It is a habit" (Aristotle 1962). Following this line of reasoning, it can be said that the character of a professional accountant includes both moral and intellectual virtues that rely on practical wisdom (good judgment and reasoning abilities) to meet the profession's obligation to serve the public interest.

Moral virtues govern one's feelings, attitudes, and moral sentiments and include, for example, friendliness or courtesy, temperance or self-control, truthfulness, and courage. For Aristotle (1962), moral virtues are complex states represented situationally that rely on one's motives for acting in the right way, at the right time, for the right reasons. The exercise of moral virtues depends on *intellectual virtues* (i.e., thought process, broadly stated) including the ability to deliberate about the proper course of action and apply knowledge to each situation encountered.

Practical wisdom is the intellectual virtue uniquely responsible for guiding a person's ability to be virtuous in particular circumstances. The acquisition and practice of virtue depends on four preconditions: wish or desire (informed by moral virtues), deliberation, decision, and action (informed by intellectual virtues). Practical wisdom is the master virtue that links practice and virtue together. Knowledge, reasoning, and the exercise of practical wisdom are integral parts of the professional judgments made by accounting professionals in meeting their ethical obligations. Table 19.1 describes the relationship between practical wisdom and purpose in accounting.

Table 19.1 Practical Wisdom and the Public Interest in Accounting

Greek Virtues	Virtue in Accounting	Elements of Practical Wisdom	Purpose of Accounting
Moral Virtue	Motivation in acting	Moral Will	Meet public interest obligation
Intellectual Virtue	Deliberating on how best to serve the public interest	Moral Skill	Build trust through ethical decision making

Moral education has increasingly addressed elements of teaching practical wisdom (Melé 2005; Roca 2008; Morales-Sanchez and Cabello-Medina 2013; Marshall and Thorburn 2014; Bachmann, Habisch, and Dierksmeier 2017; Gentile 2017). Three perspectives have been explored in particular: the deliberative or rational, the perceptual or situational insight, and the collaborative or moral character (Noel 1999). These perspectives are represented in Rest's model as moral awareness, moral judgment, moral motivation, and moral action. Once a decision maker becomes aware of the moral issues and reasons through alternative courses of action (moral skill), the process turns to understanding one's moral motivation and willingness to carry through ethical intent with ethical action (moral will). Practical wisdom is the glue that binds together moral skill, moral will, and ethical decision making.

Research on the many facets of practical wisdom

In discussing the unifying aspect of practical wisdom, Bachmann, Habisch, and Dierksmeier (2017) suggest that practical wisdom is fundamentally linked to the circumstances of a particular situation and includes the integrative ability to perceive and understand the true complexity of reality in its multilayered facets and interdependent parts. Practical wisdom is never geared only toward intellectual recognition, but it always targets realization in practice; therefore, it requires the ability to transform every manifestation of knowledge, beliefs, experiences, and decisions into action.

An individual's ability to deliberate well and make appropriate judgments in specific situations occurs when practical wisdom integrates right thinking, right desire, and right action and creates harmony among reason, emotions, and behavior (Sison and Ferrero 2015). Morales-Sanchez and Cabello-Medina (2013) suggest that practical wisdom positively affects the moral sensitivity, moral judgment, and moral motivation in ethical decision making; consequently, it has an important role to play in Rest's model.

While there does not seem to exist a prescribed process by which practical wisdom is gained, there does appear to be a consensus of sorts among scholars that practical wisdom can be developed/learned through practice/experience (Noel 1999; Roca 2008; Kassam 2010; Melé 2010; Schwartz 2011; Swartwood 2013; Marshall and Thorburn 2014; Hacker-Wright 2015). Marshall and Thorburn (2014, 1544) state that "experiences help practical wisdom to develop as they provide the opportunity to review choices, practice moral action and develop habits" and further note that "group experiences and deliberation help the awareness and discernment characteristic of practical wisdom." Roca (2008) suggests that to develop practical wisdom, business students should be provided with discipline-specific exercises for resolving ethical issues, such as through the analysis of case studies.

Sison, Hartman, and Fontrodona (2012) posit that ethical decision making has to start with practical wisdom. Hartman (2013) and Sison and Ferrero (2015) tie practical wisdom to being a virtuous leader as it is an integration of ethical thinking, ethical desire, and ethical action. People can acquire practical wisdom by repetition of virtuous acts, since practical wisdom is developed by practicing moral virtues. Even though there has been a recent resurgence of interest in practical wisdom among researchers, a framework for how best to develop or teach it has yet to be put forward.

Bachmann, Habisch, and Dierksmeier (2017) provide an integrative detailed review of 143 articles/studies from philosophical, theological, psychological, and managerial perspectives. They synthesize the recent work in this area with a managerial focus that is of particular interest and relevance to our study because of its link to ethical decision making. Of particular note are the following themes that emphasize the intersection of the individual and the organization.

- All virtuous decisions require practical wisdom because it considers, in the first place, which goals and ends are worth pursuing rather than just maximizing the good consequences over the bad ones.
- Practical wisdom is an important feature to solving complex problems, rejecting "one-size-fits-all" solutions of other ethical reasoning methods.
- The complex nature of decisions requires practical wisdom to deliberate and make appropriate judgments on each particular situation and the capacity to choose the right means.
- Decision makers can deal with the challenge of conflicting stakeholder interests through the application of practical wisdom.
- Through moral leadership, practical wisdom facilitates ethical decision making and the solving of complex problems, and finally requires the involvement of others in the decision-making process.
- Practical wisdom improves judgment and decision-making processes when faced with complex decisions, and good ethical decision making requires critical self-reflection.

The role of practical wisdom in Rest's model and ethical decision making

Aristotle (1962) links proper action with right reason, and right reason always involves prudence, either implicitly or explicitly. Making good decisions requires practical wisdom: deliberating well is a characteristic of prudent men and women. Prudence requires us to distinguish between what is right and what is wrong. In the context of virtue ethics, wisdom and prudence refer to *phronesis* in the sense that it relates to practical action, requiring both good judgment and excellence of character and habits. It is often translated as "practical wisdom" (Aristotle 1962).

Ethical decision making is a systemized process of deciding what is right or wrong based on certain moral features, such as the awareness of a moral issue, and a moral judgment about its implications through to moral action, once moral intent has been established. Practical wisdom is an integral part of the thought process.

Employing practical wisdom and moral virtues in evaluating the morality of a decision focuses on intrinsic states of goodness – virtuous character and right action – and differs from how conventional ethical theories, such as deontological or utilitarian theories, evaluate such decisions, because these are extrinsic to the action. Practical wisdom introduces ethics in decision making by considering both the end or goal pursued and the means to achieve such an end from the perspective of the human good. Conventional theories focus on the ends, such as the universality of an action from the perspective of Kantian categorical imperative or consequences of action in utilitarianism (Melé 2010). Practical wisdom as a unifying concept in virtue ethics focuses on both the character of decision making and the act taken. It links action (moral character) with the thought process (moral decision making) through moral will and moral skill.

Rest's Four-Component Model of Moral Behavior is a well-established process of ethical decision making that establishes four different stages for resolving a moral problem (Rest 1986): moral awareness, moral judgment, moral motivation, and moral character. The following briefly summarizes each component of the model as described by Morales-Sanchez and Cabello-Medina (2013).

Moral sensitivity. Awareness of the moral problem is needed for ethical behavior to occur. The decision maker should be aware of two aspects: (1) the behavior will impact stakeholders by harming or helping them, and (2) alternatives exist to be considered in making the decision (Jones 1991; Hannah, Avolio, and May 2011).

Moral judgment. Ability to assess the "good" or "bad" of each action and decide which is morally right (Rest 1986).

Moral motivation. Willingness to take the moral course of action or moral intention, placing moral values above others, including personal values, and taking personal responsibility for moral outcomes (Melé 2005).

Moral action. Executing and implementing the chosen behavior; directing one's character to rightful action (Rest 1986).

The ability to spot the moral dimension of a problem creates an awareness that ethical issues exist. Practical wisdom helps to identify alternative courses of action and to assess the goodness of each in deliberating on how each action might affect others. In this sense, practical wisdom is a moral skill.

Prudence enables individuals to govern themselves by regulating behavior through the use of reason. A prudent act is one that occurs through thoughtful deliberation on what is good and holding in check that which is bad. In deliberation, practical wisdom plays a key role in that the accumulation of wisdom throughout time can help individuals make sound judgments. These experiences help to strengthen moral intent. In this sense, practical wisdom is moral will.

Through experience and practice, practical wisdom plays an important role in developing the willingness to take the moral course of action: placing moral values above others, including self-interest, and taking responsibility for moral actions. Moral motivation is the driving force for making good moral judgments and plays a crucial role in selecting the right course of action and executing it. Moral will attends to carrying out moral intent with moral action.

Practical wisdom and transitive moral virtues promote moral motivation for acting well. It also drives self-mastering virtues that enable practical choices to be made (Melé 2005). For example, an accounting professional should be objective and exercise professional skepticism (transitive virtue) in evaluating audit evidence and have the courage (self-mastering virtue) to reason through what should be the proper course of action. Practical wisdom connects both types of virtues and enables them to be understood as motivating forces for ethical decision making. In this sense, practical wisdom enables moral action.

Figure 19.1 depicts the relationship between the elements of practical wisdom and components of moral behavior in Rest's (1986) model that lead to ethical decision making. Practical wisdom informs the elements of moral behavior by enabling decision makers to reason rightly about the proper course of action and by directing behavior toward the end goal of ethical decision making.

The four components of Rest's model must exist for ethical decision making to occur. Rest does not offer the framework as a linear decision-making model, suggesting instead that the components interact through a complicated sequence of "feed-back" and "feed-forward" loops.

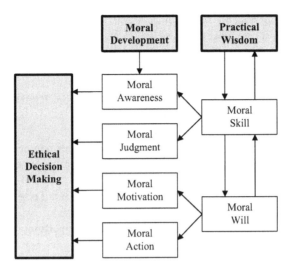

Figure 19.1 Integrative Model of Ethical Decision Making

An individual who demonstrates adequacy in one component may not necessarily be adequate in another, and moral failure can occur when there is a deficiency in any one component (Dellaportas et al. 2011). For example, an individual who intends to act morally (has the moral will) may not have the capacity to apply good moral reasoning (lacks moral skill). Thus, practical wisdom depends on both moral will and moral skill, and deficiency in either may influence ethical decision making.

Teaching students about practical wisdom

Hacker-Wright (2015) posits that in order to solve complex problems, individuals must know how to conduct themselves (know how to analyze the issue) and must possess the following five cognitive skills: intuitive, deliberative, meta-cognitive, self-regulative, and self-cultivation. These can be taught in ethics courses or ethics modules integrated into existing courses.

In discussing why practical wisdom should be taught in management classes, Roca (2008) analyzes three intrinsic characteristics: usefulness to analyze complex, particular, and changeable issues (moral skill); ability to detect the moral content and implications of a specific situation; and relevance to the moral person configuration (moral will).

> Through the exercise of practical wisdom, one must be able to discern the significant aspects of a particular situation and to apply one's knowledge, experience and values to make a "good decision." This deliberation is enabled by prudence which inspires and illuminates the exercise of practical wisdom.
>
> *(615)*

By thinking critically about their decisions, students will be better prepared to make decisions consistent with their values, virtues, and principles. Roca notes that the exercise of practical wisdom can guide students to an awareness of the moral and social implications of their decisions and develop a capacity for self-reflection, which is particularly appropriate for ethics education of accounting students. Roca concludes that "management programs should prepare students to critically evaluate what they hear and to make decisions coherent with their values and virtues" and points out that "an integrated model of ethics and practical wisdom promotes education of cognition and education of affect as well" (2008, 607–14). The processes illustrated in Figure 19.1 can help to address these issues.

The following are objectives and strategies identified by Roca (2008) in teaching practical wisdom in management courses.

- Stimulate moral imagination, recognize critical ethical issues, and develop analytical skills.
- Provide students with specific exercises for resolving ethical issues using their wisdom in relevant discipline domains.
- Increase the students' awareness and attitudes on the one hand (i.e., ethical sensitivity), and their reasoning ability on the other (i.e., ethical judgment).
- Use stories that convey practical wisdom and provide an opportunity for students to reflect on their role in the narrative.
- Use case studies that might not directly address practical wisdom but invite students to experience the story personally and consider their choices and dilemmas depending on their own virtues, knowledge, and experiences.

Experiential learning

Marshall and Thorburn (2014) recommend that education in practical wisdom should be based on experiential learning. Experiences offer particular, situated opportunities to practice good deliberation and virtue. Thoughtful attention to experience and the practice of deliberation tend to lead to good decisions. Virtue-forming practices – reflection and deliberation – can help to develop cognitive skills and affective qualities characteristic of practical wisdom.

Kassam (2010) describes the context for a senior-level course in development studies in which critical reflection was combined with practice. His pedagogical framework facilitates reflection-in-action in the form of practical wisdom. The practice of knowing about an activity is explained as *knowing that* and *knowing how*. Knowing that inquiries into whether something is the case. Knowing how considers how to achieve something and is embedded in experience. He gives the example of learning by doing as an example of knowledge generation through knowing how to get something done. Thought is not separated from action, and doing is not simply habitual practice; it is intelligent practice, because each practice is modified by its predecessor. It is reflection-in-action (Schon 1983). Concluding on his experience, Kassam says that by giving voice to student reflection, we can begin to understand the experience of learning how.

Swartwood (2013) argues for the expert skill model of practical wisdom. He likens wisdom to an expert decision-making skill in domains requiring complex choices and challenging performance. Wisdom also provides guidance on how to overcome internal obstacles of doing so, as would be the case if an internal accountant was being pressured by higher-ups to manipulate the financial results. In this sense, wisdom is an integral component of moral will, as sensitivity to complex interrelationships and one's obligations to others provides the moral motivation for moral behavior.

The expert skill model has particular relevance to the practice of professional accounting. Bachmann, Habisch, and Dierksmeier (2017) point out that practical wisdom goes beyond intellectual recognition in a thought process and always targets realization in practice. Accountants and auditors gain wisdom through a variety of experiences that involve complex relationships with various stakeholders. Practical wisdom gained through these activities enables professionals to overcome obstacles to virtuous behavior. The expert skill model can be discussed in the context of Figure 19.1 by incorporating professional accounting experiences into the moral skill dimension and virtues/behavioral characteristics into discussions about moral will. The incorporation of professional accounting experiences into the accounting curriculum can be accomplished through the use of the Giving Voice to Values curricular offering.

Giving Voice to Values (GVV)

GVV is a form of experiential learning that develops skills to voice and act on one's values in situations where the decision maker knows what to do but needs guidance to figure out how best to get it done in light of reasons and rationalizations that are typically provided by one's superior to do otherwise. As Kassam said (2010), giving voice to student reflection helps them to understand how to get things done. In a GVV case analysis, the protagonist looks for levers (tools) to influence others (typically starting with their superior) to support their point of view. The values dimension of GVV fits nicely with teaching students about practical wisdom because of the deliberative nature of the process and action orientation that are provided through moral skill and moral will. It also provides a process to guide students to effectively deal with complex situations that may arise in accounting practice.

GVV was created by Mary Gentile in 2010. GVV is a post-decision-making skill that requires students to step into the shoes of those experiencing ethical dilemmas, prepare scripts, and role-play to resolve dilemmas through voicing their values. In ethical dilemmas, the protagonist very often does not follow through and report or resolve the issue/ethical conflict because they may lack the confidence to do so, may not be comfortable reporting it, may not think reporting it will do any good, and may not know who to report it to or how best to go about reporting it (Gentile 2010). In other words, most people already know what is right but lack both the will and skill to take the morally correct action. GVV provides the tools to deal with these situations by considering the typical "reasons and rationalizations" a moral agent will hear when they voice their concerns over a given situation and help in developing responses to these arguments. Table 19.2 describes the typical reasons and rationalizations encountered within ethical dilemmas.

In resolving the conflict, the protagonist should be prepared to respond to expected reasons and rationalizations by considering: How can they most effectively express their point of view?

Table 19.2 Common Reasons and Rationalizations

Type	Justification
Expected or standard practice	Everyone does it; we have to do it to remain competitive; it's a cost of doing business.
Materiality	It's immaterial; it does not harm anyone.
Locus of responsibility	It's not your job so don't worry about it; you're just following orders; just go with the flow.
Locus of loyalty	You're expected to support the company's position; your supervisor expects you to support him/her.
It is a one-time request	Just do it this one time; we won't ask you to do it again; no one will find out.

What should they say? To whom? In what sequence? And what data do they need to gather? How would they frame this situation so as to make it easier to move the relevant parties to a different position? Plump (2018, 13) suggests that acting on one's values might include "identifying and gathering allies, researching past precedents, negotiating, sharing new data or filling in missing information, finding alternative solutions, asking well-framed questions, and leading by example." The GVV offering focuses on providing students with the knowledge and confidence necessary through the exercise of practical wisdom in a variety of situations to effectively deal with conflict.

A few accounting researchers have used GVV and find it useful in some respect. Mintz (2016), created an ethical decision-making model by integrating the concepts of Rest's model with GVV. He suggests that the integration of the GVV methodology and decision-making model into accounting coursework will increase students' actual intent to behave ethically and then act on their values (moral motivation and moral action). Shawver and Miller (2016) find that accounting students who have gone through GVV training gain confidence in voicing their values, are more likely to involve others to resolve moral dilemmas, more likely to report their concerns to internal management, perhaps through company hotlines, and more likely to inform external agencies, in each case more than those without the GVV training. Cote, Goodstein, and Latham (2011) find that students with GVV instruction are better able to incorporate more people into their case analyses thereby enhancing the value of role-play exercises. The key point is GVV provides the deliberative skills that enhance ethical decision-making in the context of a model such as in Figure 19.1.

Suggestions for curriculum development

Synthesizing the suggestions from researchers about the role of practical wisdom in management education and the unique aspects of being an accounting professional, we develop the following case scenario to discuss the role of moral skill and moral will in accounting decision making, and we incorporate GVV to strengthen the behavioral and action-oriented aspects of conflict resolution. The discussion centers on the options available to the protagonist, Sharon Hart, and her thought process in applying practical wisdom, in this case reasoned deliberation, in deciding what to do. Three questions follow to address the salient ethical issues, and suggested responses are provided.

Case scenario

Sharon Hart works for a CPA firm and has been charged with deciding which of three software packages to select for a client's information system. One of the three is her firm's software. She conducted a thorough analysis based on relevance to the need, operational efficiency, cost, servicing, and ability to enhance the package over time and decided to recommend one of the other packages. Sharon's supervisor comes to her office and suggests that she may have dismissed the firm's package too quickly, and the firm is looking for opportunities to enhance sales of its software. She is asked to reconsider her decision and meet with her supervisor the next day.

Questions

Q1. What role should practical wisdom play in Sharon's deliberative process?

Moral skill heightens one's sensibilities and creates an awareness of the ethical issues, helps to assess the relevance of alternative points of view, reason through these alternatives, and decide what should be done. Moral will is the intention to choose the behavior that provides the most good and the courage to follow through ethical intent with ethical action. Moral skill and moral will are best represented by the public interest principle in the AICPA Code, which provides that conflicts between stakeholder groups should be resolved by acting with integrity, "guided by the precept that when members [CPAs] fulfill their responsibility to the public, clients' and employers' interests are best served."

Sharon should carefully deliberate about how her intended actions might affect the stakeholders in preparation for her meeting with the supervisor. The firm's interest is to select its software for the client, whereas the client expects the software selection to be the best for its needs. This creates conflict that can be resolved through the exercise of practical wisdom in the decision-making process.

Conflict resolution can be addressed by identifying the alternatives, selecting the best one through a process of reasoned action, and then deciding how best to act to make the morally correct choice. Practical wisdom guides the process by ensuring that moral values (i.e., objectivity and integrity) inform the public interest and come ahead of the interests of the firm. By acting with integrity, Sharon exercises moral will and does what is best for the client.

Q2. What reasons and rationalizations is Sharon likely to hear when she meets with her supervisor, and what responses could she have?

The first step is for Sharon to think about what the potential consequences are to her, her boss, the firm, and the profession if she changes her recommendation (both whether it is discovered later or not). First, if Sharon goes along with this request, she is subordinating her judgment to her boss. This violates the objectivity and integrity standards in the AICPA Code. It is something she will have to live with for the rest of her life. She needs to consider what toll that will take on her. Second, she needs to consider that if she does it this once, she will not have any real way of saying no to a future request, which could be more egregious then this one. If it is later discovered that the firm recommended their product over what they considered to be a better choice for their client, they could be subject to litigation from this client. That could lead to loss of reputation, loss of clients, or individual sanctions to Sharon, her boss and/or the firm. Based on this analysis, Sharon's responses to reasons and rationalizations she might hear are presented in Table 19.3. These reflect the moral skill process of good reasoning and thoughtful deliberation.

Table 19.3 Reasons and Rationalizations Sharon Might Hear

Type	Justification/Response
Expected or standard practice	Sharon can research and be ready to discuss examples of firms that have gotten into trouble for this type of breach of duty to act objectively and avoid conflicts of interest. She can discuss the ramifications to company reputation and potential loss of clients.
Locus of loyalty	Sharon can state that it is out of loyalty to the firm that she cannot go along with the supervisor's request. She needs to be prepared to discuss the risks to the firm for violating their ethical obligations to the client.
It is a one-time request	Sharon can discuss the potential risks that doing this once has in setting precedent and the message it would send to everyone in the firm if found out; it could lead to similar unethical decisions being made throughout the firm

Q3. Using the GVV methodology, explain what Sharon should do if she fails to change her supervisor's mind on the software selection issue.

To live up to the integrity standard in the AICPA Code, Sharon should not simply give in to her supervisor. In order to avoid subordinating her judgment, she needs to go up the chain of command and seek support within the firm for her position. The goal should be to avoid going outside the organization and blowing the whistle externally. To help her along the way, Sharon might consider using the levers described in Table 19.4. These reflect the moral will Sharon, if necessary, would have to carry through from ethical intent to ethical action.

Table 19.4 Examples of Levers

Lever	Description/Example
Build a coalition	Consider involving others in the organization who might support your point of view. Sharon might approach others in the consulting division of the firm for advice. She should discuss the matter with a mentor if one is provided by the CPA firm.
Reframe the issue	Sharon might respond to the reasons and rationalizations by reframing the issue. Her supervisor sees it as a revenue generation issue. Reframing it as an issue of firm integrity and building a reputation for trust with the client might help the boss view the issue differently.
Identify authoritative support	By researching company policies, procedures, and other authoritative support, Sharon will be prepared to make the best case possible to support her point of view. The company probably has a code of ethics that addresses conflicts of interest, which is the critical ethical issue. The AICPA Code also prohibits conflicts of interest. Sharon should emphasize that her ethical obligation is to act in accordance with the code, maintain her integrity, and promote the client's best interest.
Propose a solution	When bringing the problem to light, providing a solution at the same time can help Sharon mitigate defensive or negative responses. This is challenging in the software case because the boss may be unyielding. Still, with proper reframing and reference to authoritative material, it may be possible to effectuate a change in position. She should develop a nonconfrontational approach to resolving the matter to avoid further conflict.
Identify risk/consequences	Sharon should identify the consequences for the stakeholders, both long- and short-term, of not resolving the issue. She might point out to her supervisor that the vendor with the best software package may somehow figure out that its package was set aside to promote the firm's software. This would violate their trust in the process and may affect future business relationships.
Identify the impact of change	Thinking forward, Sharon may be able to win over the supervisor by explaining what may happen if the selected software provider finds out about the decision or the firm's software doesn't work as expected, leading to a negative response from the client.
Identify the benefits of the solution	Sharon should discuss the benefits of her solution to all the stakeholders. This can help convince the supervisor to go along with her proposal. The bottom line of client service is the client is best served by adopting the software that best suits its needs based on an objective analysis. Sharon should stand firm in her position.

GVV supports instruction in practical wisdom because it provides an action-oriented tool that can be implemented through moral deliberation about how best to respond to the arguments usually made to accept a questionable decision and the moral intention to voice one's values in a way that will influence the outcome. As a decision-making method, GVV looks for levers that can be used through authoritative support and influencers within the company that can help voice values in a positive way.

Concluding comments

GVV instruction is an extension of other techniques, such as role-playing and scripting responses, that support developing practical wisdom because it goes beyond just looking at the alternatives and focuses on deliberating about how to implement the best option when roadblocks exist. Students gain confidence in acting on their values by developing a game plan to positively influence others to support their position. Through practice and the experience gained in using GVV, students sharpen their moral skills, learn how to develop moral will, and can become more capable of resolving ethical issues they may encounter as accounting professionals.

GVV offers a framework to help students prepare to make difficult ethical choices by practicing responses to ethical decisions and the give and take that is a natural part of ethical decision making. The methodology is useful in teaching ethics to accounting students because it focuses on finding those within the organization who might help to positively respond to pressures to deviate from ethical norms, such as exists in the software selection case.

One final thought: Practical wisdom is not easily assessed because it involves the give and take of actual deliberations, not written responses. This is why experiential learning techniques are useful. Yet practical wisdom is essential in professional accounting to give voice to the values of the profession and best serve the public interest.

References

American Institute of CPAs (AICPA). 2014. "Code of Professional Conduct." AICPA. www.aicpa.org/content/dam/aicpa/research/standards/codeofconduct/downloadabledocuments/2014december15contentsof2015october26codeofconduct.pdf.

Aristotle. 1962. *Nicomachean Ethics*. Translated by Martin Ostwald. New York: Macmillan Publishing Co.

Armstrong, M. B. 2002. "Ethics Issues in Accounting." In *The Blackwell Guide to Business Ethics*, edited by N. E. Bowie. Oxford, England: Blackwell Publishing.

Armstrong, M. B., J. E. Ketz, and D. Owsen. 2003. "Ethics Education in Accounting: Moving Toward Ethical Motivation and Ethical Behavior." *Journal of Accounting Education* 21 (1): 1–16. doi:10.1016/S0748-5751(02)00017-9.

Bachmann, C., A. Habisch, and C. Dierksmeier. 2017. "Practical Wisdom: Management's No Longer Forgotten Virtue." *Journal of Business Ethics* 153 (1): 1–19. doi:10.1007/s10551-016-3417-y.

Chang, O. H., S. W. Davis, and K. D. Kauffman. 2012. "Accounting Ethics Education: A Comparison with Buddhist Ethics Education Framework." *Journal of Religion and Business Ethics* 3 (1): 1–22.

Cote J., J. Goodstein, and C. K. Latham. 2011. "Giving Voice to Values: A Framework to Bridge Teaching and Research Efforts." *Journal of Business Ethics Education* 8 (1): 370–75. doi:10.5840/jbee20118132.

Dellaportas, S., B. Jackling, and B. J. Cooper. 2011. "Developing an Ethics Education Framework for Accounting." *Journal of Business Ethics Education* 8 (1): 63–82.

Francis, J. R. 1990. After Virtue? "Accounting as a Moral and Discursive Practice." *Accounting, Auditing and Accountability Journal* 3 (3): 5–17. doi:10.1108/09513579010142436.

Gentile, M. 2010. *Giving Voice to Values: How to Speak Your Mind When You Know What Is Right*. New Haven, CT: Yale University Press.

Gentile, M. 2017. "Giving Voice to Values: A Pedagogy for Behavioral Ethics." *Journal of Management Education* 41 (4): 469–79. doi:10.1177%2F1052562917700188.

Hacker-Wright, J. 2015. "Skill, Practical Wisdom, and Ethical Naturalism." *Ethical Theory and Moral Practice* 18: 983–93. doi:10.1007/s10677-015-9566-8.

Hannah, S. T., B. J Avolio, and D. May. 2011. "Moral Maturation and Moral Conation: A Capacity Approach to Explaining Moral Thought and Moral Action." *Academy of Management Review* 6 (4): 663–85. doi:10.5465/amr.2010.0128.

Hartman, E. M. 2013. *Virtue in Business. Conversations with Aristotle.* Cambridge, England: Cambridge University Press.

Jones, T. M. 1991. "Ethical Decision Making by Individuals in Organizations: An Issue-Contingent Model." *Academy of Management Review* 16 (2): 366–95. doi:10.2307/258867.

Kassam, K. 2010. "Practical Wisdom and Ethical Awareness through Student Experiences of Development." *Development in Practice* 20 (2): 204–18. doi:10.1080/09614520903564207.

Libby, T., and L. Thorne. 2007. "The Development of a Measure of Auditors' Virtue." *Journal of Business Ethics* 71: 89–99. doi:10.1007/s10551-006-9127-0.

MacIntyre, A. 1984. *After Virtue.* 2nd ed. Notre Dame, IN: University of Notre Dame Press.

Marshall, A., and M. Thorburn. 2014. "Cultivating Practical Wisdom as Education." *Educational Philosophy and Theory* 46 (14): 1541–53. doi:10.1080/00131857.2013.856280.

Melé, D. 2005. "Ethical Education in Accounting: Integrating Rules, Values and Virtues." *Journal of Business Ethics* 57 (1): 97–109. doi:10.1007/s10551-004-3829-y.

Melé, D. 2010. "Practical Wisdom in Managerial Decision Making." *Journal of Management Development* 29 (7): 637–45. doi:10.1108/02621711011059068.

Mintz, S. M. 1995. "Virtue Ethics and Accounting Education." *Issues in Accounting Education,* 10 (2): 247–67.

Mintz, S. M. 2006. "Accounting Ethics Education: Integrating Reflective Learning and Virtue Ethics." *Journal of Accounting Education* 24: 97–117. doi:10.1016/j.jaccedu.2006.07.004.

Mintz, S. M. 2016. "GVV: A New Approach to Accounting Ethics Education." *Global Perspectives on Accounting Education* 13: 37–50.

Mintz, S. M., and R. E. Morris. 2017. *Ethical Obligations and Decision Making in Accounting: Text and Cases.* New York: McGraw Hill Education.

Morales-Sanchez, R., and C. Cabello-Medina. 2013. "The Role of Four Universal Moral Competencies in Ethical Decision-Making." *Journal of Business Ethics* 116 (4): 717–34. doi:10.1007/s10551-013-1817-9.

Noel, J. 1999. "On the Varieties of Phronesis." *Educational Philosophy and Theory* 31: 273–89. doi:10. 1111/j.1469-5812.1999.tb00466.x.

Plump, C. 2018. *Giving Voice to Values in the Legal Profession: Effective Advocacy with Integrity.* New York: Routledge.

Rest, J. R. 1986. *Moral Development: Advances in Research and Theory.* New York: Praeger.

Roca, E. 2008. "Introducing Practical Wisdom in Business Schools." *Journal of Business Ethics* 82 (3): 607–20. doi:10.1007/s10551-007-9580-4.

Schon, D. A. 1983. *The Reflective Practitioner: How Professionals Think in Action.* New York: Basic Books.

Schwartz. B. 2011. "Practical Wisdom and Organizations." *Research in Organizational Behavior* 31: 3–23. doi:10.1016/j.riob.2011.09.001.

Shawver, T. J., and W. Miller. 2016. "Assessing the Impact of the Giving Voice to Values Program in Accounting Ethics." Paper presented at the American Accounting Association Annual Meeting, New York, August 2016.

Sison, A. J. G., and I. Ferrero. 2015. "How Different is Neo-Aristotelian Virtue from Positive Organizational Virtuousness?" *Business ethics: A European Review* 24 (S2): S78–S98. doi:10.1111/beer.12099.

Sison, A. J. G., E. M. Hartman, and J. Fontrodona. 2012. "Reviving Traditional Virtue and the Common Good in Business in Management." *Business Ethics Quarterly* 22 (2): 211–46. doi:10.5840/beq201222217.

Swartwood, J. 2013. "Wisdom as an Expert Skill." *Ethical Theory Moral Practice* 16: 511–28. doi:10.1007/s10677-012-9367-2.

Thorne, L. 1998. "The Role of Virtue in Auditors' Ethical Decision-Making: An Integration of Cognitive-Developmental and Virtue-Ethics Perspectives." *Research on Accounting Ethics* 4: 12–33.

20

ETHICS IN HIGHER EDUCATION

Christine Cheng, Kristy Schenck, and Renee Flasher

Introduction

In this chapter, we begin the discussion with two key drivers of ethics education and complete the discussion with a foray into the literature for insights into ethics within higher education. Although accounting ethics education originated within the profession, its more recent growth has been in formal academic settings. We examine the rise of the multiple groups of stakeholders as users of financial statements and key ethical failures within the profession as contributing factors to the development of ethics education in the classroom. We follow with a review of teaching and researching ethics within the post-secondary environment. Ultimately, we conclude that the importance of ethics for the profession has not dissipated over time but that we need more training and education about ethics for instructors and students.

As ethics within the accounting classroom began with a professional need and, in the past, was sponsored by the profession, we start with the earliest accounting users to demonstrate the need for ethics within the profession. Accounting has been around for thousands of years (Robson 1992); the double-entry bookkeeping system was first described in print over 500 years ago in Luca Pacioli's *Summa de arithmetica, geometria, proportioni et proportionalita*. The change to the method of accounting was not the only major change that accounting underwent during these formative periods. Thus, we begin with the initial preparers and users of financial records to highlight how ethics has grown in importance within the profession.

Users of the financial statements

Originally, accounting was used by monarchs and leaders in early civilizations, including Mesopotamia, Israel, Egypt, China, Greece, and Rome, to keep track of the affairs of their kingdom and levy taxes (Soll 2014). Early merchants used accounting to keep track of their business dealings (Soll 2014). According to Paris (2016), as trade developed in Europe, historical records indicate that sophisticated accounting systems developed within banking houses in the early 1300s.

As trade continued to expand, the role of the accountant continued to expand. By the 1500s there were several additional books published that described how bookkeeping and the practice of accounting expanded across Europe, entering Scotland by the late 1600s (Paris 2016). The development of a practice in investing in stocks in the mid-1600s to early 1700s required the accounting profession to take on additional responsibilities, including those related to ensuring that assets and profits were properly stated not just for owners, creditors, and business partners but now for investors (Paris 2016). With the expansion of the role of the accounting profession, accountants were able to move out of a direct association with business persons and form their own, independent accounting firms, such as Tribe, Clarke, and Company, which was formed by Josiah Wade in Bristol England in 1780 (Paris 2016).

The influence that users of financial statements have on ethical practices in accounting cannot be understated. When a single individual develops and uses the accounting information, there is no ethical conflict between the creator of accounting information and the main user. The owners could lie to themselves, but the major harm is more limited than later, when these roles are separated. However, any time separation exists between the users and the creators of financial statements, the creators of financial statements have an informational advantage, which in turn provides an opportunity for ethical compromises. As an early example of this, Pacioli's (1494) writing indicates that accountants should not keep two separate sets of books for the purpose of deceiving buyers and sellers of the merchant's goods. Pacioli's (1494) admonition against this practice suggests that, even 500 years ago, business individuals were willing to use accounting information to deceive others and that accounting educators were warning future accountants against engaging in unethical practices.[1] By the mid-1600s, accountants were already serving many of the same users of financial information that they serve today, including owners, business partners, creditors, and investors. However, there was much less regulation and uniformity regarding financial statements. Thus, accountants who did not ensure a system of credible financial reporting could manipulate the statements to fool the users of financial information.

As such, it is perhaps not surprising that the rapidly growing profession soon sought to form professional associations, such as the Institute of Accountants established in Scotland in 1853, the bodies of accountants formed in London, Liverpool, Manchester, and Sheffield in the 1870s, and the Institute of Accountants and Bookkeepers established in 1882 in New York (Paris 2016). These professional organizations eventually grew, merged, and were recognized by governing bodies as capable of influencing the standards by which accounting practitioners should abide. Although they had different names and different scopes, the organizations developed during these formative periods are predecessors to the organizations we know today, including the American Institute of Certified Public Accountants (AICPA) and the Institute of Chartered Accountants in England and Wales (ICAEW).

Most importantly, these professional organizations sought to establish accountants as professionals, not tradespeople with bookkeeping skills, by funding higher education endeavors in accounting, albeit not all the ventures went smoothly. In the United States, the American Association of Public Accountant (AAPA), now part of the AICPA, started a night school under the supervision of New York University in 1892; however, the school subsequently failed (Abs et al. 1954). Van Wyhe (2007a) describes that the university forays into elevating accounting education, such as the establishment of the first formal accounting courses at the University of Pennsylvania in 1881, did not exclude them from offering lower-level courses teaching the fundamentals of bookkeeping. Practitioners continued to fund higher education initiatives in an attempted to establish accounting as a formal profession; for example, New York University taught cost accounting in 1904 (Abs et al. 1954).

The history of practitioner-funded accounting higher education is under-explored, from the beginning to the current day initiatives among accounting firms, professional societies, and educational institutions. The degree of influence that the profession had over the accounting professors and the ties the professors had to the profession are mostly unknown. Additional research could focus on the ideas and conventions of the time that were transmitted during the earliest years of these relationships. Future research could examine who was involved with the initiatives, factors for success and failure of these programs, and the textbooks used during these early time periods for ethical discussions, as these would be the predecessors to the formalization of accounting credentialing and ethical standards discussed next.

In addition to providing educational opportunities and recognized credentials for members, the larger professional organizations also set out to control membership to create prestige for the profession and elevate it from a trade. Control was exerted with barriers to entry such as oral exams given by the Council of the Institute of Accountants in 1871. In other cases, rules initially prevented, and then accepted, women and persons of color from earning professional designations.[2] Although Christine Ross became the first female certified public accountant (CPA) in 1899[3], she was not the first female applicant to earn a professional designation. In 1888, Mary Harris Smith was denied membership to the ICAEW (Paris 2016). Mary Harris Smith eventually became the first female chartered accountant in the world in 1919.[4] John Cromwell became the first black CPA just a few years later, in 1921.[5] Mary T. Washington Wylie became the first female African-American CPA in 1943, just over 20 years before Congress passed the Civil Rights Act in 1964.[6]

As membership continued to expand in these larger professional organizations, specialized organizations also began to develop to further transition accounting from a trade into a profession. The first state society of CPAs was founded in New York in 1897,[7] as it was also the first state to legally recognize CPAs. Coupling the educational requirements with credentialing requirements, New York also became the first state to institute an examination requirement (Van Wyhe 2007a). Once the exam requirement was in place, the debate about how closely higher education curricula should be modeled after the exam began in higher education within the United States. The current version of the CPA exam includes ethics in the auditing and regulation sections with references to United States Department of the Treasury publications and the AICPA's code of professional conduct (AICPA 2019).

Although practitioners have funded and started these higher education initiatives, there was tension between the academics and the practitioners as to what should be taught in the college curriculum, even in the early years of the 20th century (Van Wyhe 2007a). By the 1920s, 335 schools taught accounting; 18% awarded a bachelor degree, and almost 10% offered a master's degree (Van Wyhe 2007a, 167). What later became the American Accounting Association (AAA) in 1936[8] started out as the American Association of University Instructors in Accounting in 1916.[9] As the AAA became the premier academic organization representing higher education accounting instructors, various commissions involved partnerships between the AAA and practitioners that included an ethical dimension. Most recently, the Pathways Commission, comprised of the AAA and industry representatives, discussed ethics as important to accounting education (Black 2012). However, this was far from the only commission that resulted in a report calling for an improvement of accounting ethics education. Black (2012) discussed the Beamer Committee's work in issuing the 1967 Horizons for a Profession Report that included ethics for a newly minted CPA. The Treadway Commission in 1987 specifically stated that "Limiting students' exposure to the problem of fraudulent financial reporting to a single course on ethics is simply not enough" (Treadway Commission 1987, 80). Although ethics is often mentioned in each of these commission reports between practitioners and the AAA, future research could examine these reports using qualitative methods to identify common themes and develop theory. Research could also consider whether and why the instillation of ethical values and eliciting ethical behaviors from the profession has (or has not) been effective.

During the same period as the founding of the AAA, student organizations with their own codes of conduct and ethical behavior expectations appeared on campuses. The first chapter of Beta Alpha Psi, an international honor organization that today serves students in accounting, finance, and information systems, was formed at the University of Illinois in 1919.[10] The National Association of Black Accountants was founded in 1969, and just five years later, the Association of Latino Professionals for America (ALPFA) was founded as the American Association of Hispanic Certified Public Accountants.[11]

Each of these organizations remains active on campuses today providing multiple ethics research opportunities. Areas for research surrounding student organization membership include consideration of whether students who are members of these organizations have different ethical perceptions than students who choose not to become members; whether changes in ethical attitudes are different for students who choose to become members of these organizations than for other nonmember students in the same accounting programs; or whether these organizations seem to attract students with different ethical perceptions. Research could also examine whether the ethical attitudes of students within these organizations differ by geographical region or by the longevity of the program at that institution. Finally, research could see if the ethical attitudes of students who are members of award-winning chapters are different from those chapters without awards, exploring whether the local chapter activities, national organization exposure, or community interactions influence the ethical attitudes or the development of students.

Professional, academic, and industry groups also undertook several initiatives to develop best practices, both procedural and ethical. *The Accountant*, a well-respected trade magazine still in print today, was first published in 1876.[12] The *Journal of Accountancy*, which is still published by the AICPA, began in 1905[13] and *The Accounting Review* was first published in 1926.[14] These periodicals and journals shaped the profession by providing a forum where practitioners could debate and learn about financial reporting and accounting measurement issues.[15] Eventually these debates led to procedural standard practices. For example, in 1936, the American Institute of Accountants first used the terms "Generally Accepted Accounting Principles" in their report on "Examination of Financial Statements."[16] Many governing bodies, such as the International Accounting Standards Board, the ICAEW, and the Federal Standards Advisory Board, continue the work of developing procedural standard practices and guidance for the work of today's practitioners.

Several of the organizations also sought to develop ethical standards of practice. To this end, the AAPA created a committee to develop ethics standards for their members in 1906, and the American Institute of Accountants (AIA) put forth eight rules of professional conduct in 1917, two of which focused specifically on the accountants duties to the users of financial information: (1) requiring that professionals not certify financial statements that contained false or misleading statements or omissions; and (2) requiring that professionals avoid issuing opinions on financial statements that they have not properly examined (Chatfield and Vangermeersch 1996). In addition, other professional standards focused on ensuring that professional accountants involved in assurance maintained their independence from those whose reports they opined on. For example, the AIA first banned contingency fees in 1922, presumably concerned with the compromises that professional accountants might make if faced with a compensation model that depended on outcomes.[17] These ethical requirements remain basic tenets of professional standards in place today. These developments highlight the nature of the formalization of codes of conduct and ethics' frameworks in accounting practice.

While these codes of conduct are valuable resources for accounting instructors to incorporate ethics into various classes, there have been multiple calls for ethics material that goes beyond the code of ethics (Loeb and Rockness 1992). A partial motivation for these calls is that, while the codes of conduct offer exposure to ethical standards, these frameworks deal with more black and white issues – not the gray areas that students will often face in their professional careers. For example, the AICPA code of professional conduct section 102.05 102–4 suggests that CPAs must not misrepresent facts or subordinate their judgment when performing professional services for a client, for an employer, or on a volunteer basis.[18] While well intended and important, the requirement that CPAs not subordinate their judgment even to their supervisor or any other person within the member's organization does not help lower-level CPAs within an organization determine how, when, or if the application of this standard should supersede normal employment practices of deferring to superiors who have more experience when issues are discovered or people are asked to participate in questionable behaviors to keep their jobs/positions (Smith 2013). One example is the lower-level employees who made journal entries at the direction of their bosses in the MCI/Worldcom fraud (Jennings 2004). Future ethics research could follow up on Loeb and Rockness's (1992) work to examine which courses discuss and utilize frameworks as the basis of the ethics courses and identify best practices for extending the discussion beyond topics directly covered in these frameworks.

While there are many additional developments that impact the ethical development of the accounting profession that could be highlighted, many of the developments that came after 1925 are not largely attributable to the role that expanding users of financial statements had in shaping ethical practices and education within the profession. Indeed, by the early part of the 1900s the major users of financial information created by or certified by accountants had been set. At this point, financial statement users included owners, business partners (including suppliers and ultimate consumers), creditors, investors, regulators, and governments. Today, financial statements continue to serve these groups, as well as employees, security analysts/rating agencies, and other associations, including FINRA.[19] Beyond advances attributable to the growth in financial statement users, advancements in the development of ethical attitudes came from discussions on how to educate members regarding appropriate ethical attitudes.

Early articles on ethics in the accounting review

After the development of standards of conduct for professional members, early educational efforts were conducted through trade publications. However, the growth of the accounting profession required the profession to identify new avenues to incorporate ethics education into the profession. A natural place to start was to look to the newly developing program of accounting instruction appearing at institutions of higher learning across the United States. By 1883, the Wharton School of Finance and Commerce was offering an accounting course (Chatfield 1975). Most of these early courses, similar to the early development of the profession, focused predominantly on the technical accounting skills. There was some initial discussion on course curricula, as well as a growing distinction between the profession of accounting and bookkeepers. However, it is unclear whether ethics was an integral part of the educational process during this formative period.

To examine the formal integration of ethics into the professional discourse, we searched for articles that dealt with ethics and ethics education published in *The Accounting Review* from its first publication date in 1926 until 1978. To assist us in this review, we used "An Index to the Accounting Review 1926–1978" prepared by Gary John Previts and Bruce Committe in 1980. We focused on *The Accounting Review* during this period because it was the only American Accounting Association journal in existence until 1974, when the first issue of *The Accounting Historians Journal* was published.

Previts and Committe (1980) categorize 13 articles whose subject is ethics from 1929 until 1973. Of these 13 articles, five address ethics education as part of the accounting curricula, all

Table 20.1 Statements by Authors Regarding Incorporation of Ethics into Accounting Education

Article (ordered by date)	Statements by authors regarding incorporation of ethics into accounting education
Myer, J. C. (1931).	p. 49 "The study of ethics has been sadly neglected in the teaching of accounting."
Peloubet, M.E. (1934).	p. 170 "Any instructor should be able to furnish numbers of cases from his own experience or reading. The broader part of the subject of ethics has hardly been touched on, largely because this is not very suitable material for treatment in an examination."
Graham, W. J. (1939).	This article focuses on promoting a framework for accounting curricula, part of which he advocates for embedding ethics education. Specifically, he notes on p. 262 "What constitutes unethical accounting practices is very largely a matter of thorough education and training in accounting and related business subjects."
Carey, J. L. (1947).	p. 119 "Many accounting teachers have recognized the desirability of including professional ethics as part of the subject matter of instruction of students who are preparing for the professional practice of public accounting. So far as I know, however, not much has been done about it. It is good form to talk about the importance of ethics but subconsciously many practitioners, and some teachers too, are disposed to consider the subject of little practical significance."
LaSalle, B. (1954).	p. 687 "The discussion of ethical problems involved in accountancy is often confined to a discussion of the American Institute of Accountancy's Rules of Professional Conduct in a single lecture period and then only if time permits at the end of a semester. A professional ethical attitude cannot be taught in such a manner."

of which were published from 1931 until 1954. Given the limited number of articles, Table 20.1 lists them all.

While these articles seem to suggest that there is general agreement that ethics is an important component of both the profession and education, the articles also seem to portray an attitude that the incorporation of ethics into accounting curricula is generally neglected and left up to the teacher of the course. Unfortunately, the persistence of the teacher discretion in including ethics appears to have held until at least the early 1970s, as Loeb and Bedingfield (1972) and Bedingfield and Loeb's (1973) surveys indicate that ethics is predominantly taught as a portion of audit, when the professor covered the AICPA's guidelines for professional practice. Loeb and Bedingfield (1972) and Bedingfield and Loeb's (1973) articles seem to suggest that there was some movement toward professors wanting ethics education to go beyond the presentation of the AICPA professional guidelines, to focus more on why it is important that future accounting professionals and current accounting professionals adhere to high ethical standards. This objective was partially met with another major impetus in ethical practices and ethics education, accounting scandals.

Accounting scandals' influence on ethical practices and ethical education

Investors and students today are often taught about some of the more egregious ethical failures that happened with financial reporting in relatively recent history, including Enron, WorldCom,

HealthSouth, and more. While these recent failures might be more prominent to accounting instructors today, significant accounting failures happen each decade going back to the 1920s in the United States. The regular presence of these failures is not to say that accounting, or business by itself, is immoral. Indeed, Pacioli (1494) is clear that there is nothing morally problematic about business or the pursuit of profits (Fischer 2000). Thus, the perpetual presence of accounting failures seems at odds with the notion that there is nothing immoral about business or the pursuit of profits, until one factors in human elements such as greed, lack of oversight, and cultural and legal differences that can contribute to, at a minimum, differences in opinion regarding what constitutes ethical behavior and, at a maximum, ethical lapses. Fortunately, while these human elements lead to ethical dilemmas, the human elements are also the solution to ethical dilemmas.

Major accounting frauds often negatively impact the users of financial statements and result in significant changes in accounting regulation, professional ethical standards, and ethical education. For example, the discovery that the Hatry Group in the United Kingdom was found to be insolvent after they used fraudulent bearer certificates to obtain large loans is cited as a contributing factor to the 1929 stock market crash, which immediately preceded the Great Depression. One common response to such egregious events is increased regulation. In 1932, fearing that investors were being severely misled, the New York Stock Exchange required companies to have audits. The New Deal of 1933 improved banking regulations and required accounting oversight and independent audits. The 1933 Securities Act obligated companies to disclose pertinent information concerning securities that are publicly offered and sold. Fewer than 10 years later, in 1938, the McKesson & Robbins scandal was revealed, whereby four brothers had managed to fictitiously create approximately a quarter of the company's total assets. The SEC's investigation revealed that the auditors had failed to confirm accounts receivable and did not verify the existence of inventory. Following this scandal, the accounting profession sought to improve self-regulation, when, in 1939, the American Institute of Accountants (AIA) set up a standing committee to develop generally accepted auditing standards.

All these acts significantly contributed to the integral role that accountants play in today's financial markets and helped shape the accounting profession. However, as is evidenced by the articles referenced in the last section, there was little in the way of ethics education that dealt directly with these early accounting scandals. A major change took place in 1982, when the *Journal of Business Ethics* was first published. Just one year later, in 1983, both *Issues in Accounting Education* and *Journal of Accounting Education* published their first issues. However, the advent of these new outlets did not automatically result in the publication of accounting ethics cases such as students and professors are more familiar with today. Indeed, a review of a new textbook by Edwards and Hermanson (1991), *Essentials of Accounting with Ethics Cases*, that was published in *Issues in Accounting Education* in 1992 indicates just how recent the use of ethical case studies is in accounting. In his review of *Essentials of Accounting with Ethics Cases*, Horrigan (1992) describes the availability of cases at the end of each chapter as a distinguishing feature of the book.

More recent history indicates that accounting ethics education also reacts to scandals by increasing the focus on ethics through the emphasis of professional codes and the development of cases. The scandals of the 1970s followed by savings and loan crisis in the 1980s helped to formalize a need for more specific accounting ethics education (Van Wyhe 2007b). Indeed, most students today are familiar with WorldCom, Tyco, Enron, Health South, Parmalat, and One Tel, not because of their business operations per se, but instead because of the case studies written about the large accounting scandals that occurred at each of these organizations. These scandals greatly shaped accounting ethics education for the next two decades.

On an international level, the International Accounting Education Standards Board issued specific accounting ethics education standards, effective in 2008, that remain in effect today (McPeak, Pincus, and Sundem 2012). Dellaportas et al. (2006) highlight the reality that accounting professors could introduce educational activities to assist with developing critical thinking and sensitivity to ethical issues, irrespective of the nation of origin. However, they also call for additional research with accounting and ethics to counteract the lack of relevant course materials explicitly dealing with accounting-related ethical issues in nonmanufacturing environments typically encountered by low- or mid-level employees.

In early 2004, a special issue of *Issues in Accounting Education* was published that was dedicated to professionalism and ethics in accounting education. One need only read the introduction, written by Gaa and Thorne (2004), to see that educators were making new commitments to ensure quality advancements in ethics education following the major corporate scandals of the late 1990s and early 2000s. This special issue contained an index compiled by Thomas (2004) of materials that instructors could use for "Teaching Ethics in the Post-Enron Era." In this same special issue, Earley and Kelly (2004) call for more research into how educators can "effectively incorporate ethics into accounting courses, and increase the moral reasoning abilities of their students" (53, abstract). As stated clearly in the abstract, the goal set forth in Earley and Kelly's (2004) article for ethics education is to "[p]rovide students with the ability to reason effectively with respect to moral dilemmas" that "may help to minimize future judgmental errors in accounting and auditing settings."

The work that was started in this special issue of *Issues in Accounting Education* of developing cases that help students learn from the ethical dilemmas present during accounting scandals and evaluating the efficacy of accounting ethics educational methods continues today. While this is a great step forward, a review of the history of accounting ethics and an understanding of the current state of ethics education in accounting leads one to wonder, what is next?

Future directions of ethics education and the profession

None of this discussion is meant to take away from the great educational opportunities that arise when students have the opportunity to learn from large accounting scandals. Instead, this discussion is meant to identify a way that ethics education might supplement these cases, in the hopeful instance that accounting scandals occur less frequently, an outcome that would be consistent with ethics education that changes future behavior. The importance of such a direction in ethics education is twofold. First, both ethics education and the profession's commitment to ethical practices requires perpetual commitment. Second, ethics tied to major accounting scandals may actually make it more difficult for students to grasp the ethical context of the initial decisions. For example, it would be easy for students to identify egregious actions as unethical. However, research clearly documents that ethical failures frequently start with small infractions (Schrand and Zechman 2012; Reckers and Samuelson 2016). Fortunately, there are several advances being made on this front in ethical education.

The objective of focusing on more nuanced ethical decisions is to remove a student's ability to differentiate themselves from the individuals who committed the acts that ultimately lead to these large accounting failures. When they can distance themselves, students often believe that it will be easy to identify and therefore easy to avoid the circumstances that would result in their commission of acts that could lead to accounting failures. However, the perpetual persistence of accounting failures suggests that these views are naïve.

Instead, the astute student of ethics who carefully reviews the details of the cases will come to understand that the individuals who committed the acts that lead to these accounting failures were, in many cases, regular people who, under the circumstances that surrounded them, succumbed to the ethically questionable decisions that ultimately led to accounting failures. In short, as coined in the title of Bazerman, Loewenstein, and Moore's (2002) article in the *Harvard Business Review*, astute students of ethics will seek to understand why "Good Accountants Do Bad Audits." In this article, Bazerman, Loewenstein, and Moore's (2002) note that unethical decisions are not the result of a conscious choice to engage in unethical behavior but instead the result of subconscious choices that lead to unethical decision making.

Bazerman and Tenbrunsel (2011) help identify a potential reason for the influence of unconscious choices in ethical decision making: motivated blindness. In short, motivated blindness occurs when a person has an objective in mind, and because of this objective, the person's ethics subconsciously fade into the background of the decision making. For example, assume that a CEO has looked at the actual earnings for the 20X1, and to her surprise, the actual earnings of $0.03 per share exceed her expectations. Unfortunately, this good news also comes at a cost. The CEO's maximum bonus payout was achieved when the earnings are $0.02, and she is concerned that reporting the actual earnings of $0.03 per share could make it harder for her to hit earnings targets for 20X2. The CEO would have preferred that the actual earnings for 20X1 were $0.02. Motivated blindness may cause the CEO to manage earnings down to $0.02 as she focuses on her goal of reporting lower earnings instead of seeing the ethical dilemma inherent in this situation, whether to accurately report actual earnings or ease future expectations for herself. While this example could be extreme, most individuals succumb to the influence of motivated blindness in their daily decision making. For example, students might differ in their stance on whether sharing a streaming channel's (such as Hulu, Netflix, etc.) password is ethical.

The previous examples of how motivated blindness influences ethical decision making mark new ground for ethics education. A case by Cheng and Flasher (2018) seeks to help students understand how motivated blindness may affect their actions as students as well as their actions as new accounting professionals. Hopefully, both research on the efficacy of this form of ethics education and additional cases will be developed as the state of ethics education in accounting continues to move forward.

Current practices for teaching ethics within accounting curricula

Universities tend to follow one of two routes for the integration of ethics into their accounting curriculum based on their location – a stand-alone ethics course or integration across the curriculum (Jonson, McGuire, and O'Neill 2015; Klimek and Wenell 2011). These approaches are partly due to the state-specific accounting ethics licensure requirements. In Texas, a student must take a separate ethics course to sit for the CPA examination. Other states, like Ohio, require an ethics test based on the AICPA framework for licensure. In addition, AACSB standards require ethics be taught within an accredited program. Specifically, Standard 9 for general business accreditation requires the inclusion of ethics within the curriculum for a bachelor's degree as "Ethical understanding and reasoning (able to identify ethical issues and address the issues in a socially responsible manner)" (AACSB 2013, 35). The same requirement is explicitly included by reference in the separate accounting accreditation requirements. These outside forces contribute to the inclusion of ethics within higher education. Future research could examine which of these forces or other forces, for example, pressure from practicing alumni, appears to be more influential to the structure of accounting curriculum.

The natural research question of which method of incorporating ethics into the accounting curriculum is more effective – separate or integrated throughout the program – has been examined by researchers without a clear conclusion. More studies focus on teaching ethics as a stand-alone course (e.g. Dellaportas 2006; Chan and Leung 2006; Cloninger and Selvarajan 2010; Mintchik and Farmer 2009) than on the integrated approach (e.g. Felton and Sims 2005; McDonald 2004). In one integrated study, Hiltebeitel and Jones (1992) compares students at different stages (freshman and senior) of an accounting program and documents an increase in students' reliance on ethical principles as they move through the program. Swanson (2005) details an optimal approach for having both the separate course and integration across the curriculum, emphasizing that more is probably better when it comes to ethics exposure. To reflect the extensive literature around this topic of how best to include ethics within the curriculum, Table 20.2 summarizes select papers within the literature to reflect the variety of research methodologies and settings used to contribute to this debate.

Several studies report survey results related to outcomes associated with various degrees of integration of ethics across the curriculum. Loeb and Bedingfield (1972) survey accounting departments in the early 1970s. They find that ethics content was incorporated into specific classes but not as a stand-alone course. More recently, Anzeh and Abed (2015) survey public and private Jordanian universities and document that ethics was covered more often in auditing courses than in accounting theory or IFRS courses in 2013. Ghaffari, Kyriacou, and Brennan (2008) detail the state of ethics in the United Kingdom higher education domain and find that ethics is largely integrated into auditing and upper division financial accounting courses. Caliyurt (2007) compiles evidence of ethics teaching within Turkey and concludes that developing countries need to further integrate ethics into their accounting programs to be comparable to developed nations. At Northern Illinois University, the business school successfully implemented a program to increase ethical awareness of all students – not only accounting majors (Dzuranin, Shortridge, and Smith 2013). The degree of integration varies, as faculty often protest that teaching ethics is not what they were trained to do, nor do they know how to tackle this area (Loeb 1994; Dellaportas et al. 2006; Rebele and Pierre 2019). As a result, it is often an individual instructor's decision whether to include ethics within their specific courses.

Future research could explore why accounting faculty include ethics within their technical accounting courses and if this inclusion varies by type of educational institution (public, private, liberal arts, highly ranked, etc.). The underlying force behind this commitment might come from a faculty member obtaining and maintaining his/her own certifications, such as the CPA. Jackling et al. (2007) survey results suggest that practicing accountants support the inclusion of undergraduate ethics education in accounting programs. Thus, professors might feel a duty to the profession to include ethics in their class. Other sources of pressure for including ethics in the classroom might be accreditation requirements, assessment committees, alumni, or department chairs.

Teaching ethics in the classroom

Research on teaching ethics, specifically to accounting students, does highlight a variety of methods that appear to tackle various elements of ethics education for university students globally (e.g., O'Leary and Mohamad 2008; Kelly 2017). O'Leary (2009) examines the impact of several types of ethical exercises embedded within an auditing class in Australia. He finds that senior students appear to make positive improvements with their ethical positioning after this combination of ethical instruction. Martinov-Bennie and Mladenovic (2015) compare the impact of presenting a framework to students in contrast to ethical coursework and a combination of both for first-year students (i.e., framework only, coursework only, framework and coursework). They find that there is an ethical judgment impact from presenting a framework alone, but a larger impact on ethical sensitivity is made when students are exposed to the ethical

Table 20.2 The Variety of Research Methodologies and Settings used to this Debate

Study	Approach	Findings
Blanthorne, Kovar, and Fisher (2007)	Integrated	This study presents the results of a survey of accounting faculties' opinions regarding ethics education. The survey showed that educators support integration over a stand-alone course and believe that teaching cases dealing with ethical dilemmas offer the most effective method for ethics instruction.
Dellaportas (2006)	Separate	The results of this paper indicate that a separate course specifically focused on accounting ethics that emphasizes dilemma discussion has a positive and significant effect on students' moral reasoning and development.
Dellaportas et al. (2014)	Integrated	The authors survey department heads of accounting programs across Australia. Although they use a small sample, they collect data at two points in time to measure the change in ethics offerings within accounting programs. The survey results reflect the reality that most institutions have integrated ethics within their programs. But the authors advocate to have both the separate course and integration within the curriculum.
Felton and Sims (2005)	Integrated	The authors reflect on educator experiences with ethics education and the research to date. The authors recommend that the appropriate approach to incorporating ethics into the curriculum is conditional based on the situation. The approach should be formed based on institutional goals, student needs, the business and social environment, and other factors.
Green and Weber (1997)	Integrated	The results of this study finds that an auditing course that emphasizes the "spirit" of the AICPA Code of Professional Conduct can have a positive impact on ethical behavior.
Hiltebeitel and Jones (1992)	Integrated	The results indicated that integrating ethics into accounting courses after the topic was introduced in a separate course, such as business ethics and business and society, affected the principles on which the students relied on when making moral decisions. They found that after ethics integration that the students relied more heavily on "the disclosure rule," "the golden rule," and the "professional ethic."
Klimek and Wenell (2011)	Separate	The authors compare students who have integrated exposure to ethics to those that have a separate three-hour class on ethics using the Defining Issues Test-2. Based on their sample of 52 students, the results suggested that the separate ethics course appears to be consistent with a higher ethical reasoning ability at the end of their senior year.
McDonald (2004)	Integrated	This paper discusses how ethics can be incorporated into a curriculum as well as discusses a model for integrating ethics into the undergraduate business curriculum. This paper does not test whether the model is effective in raising ethical awareness or equipping students with ethical decision-making skills.

(Continued)

Table 20.2 (Continued)

Study	Approach	Findings
Miller and Becker (2011)	Integrated	The study presents the results of a survey of US accounting faculty and finds that ethics integration efforts on a per-course basis are minimal and perhaps inadequate. The authors suggest that programs that use the integrated approach develop a formal ethics integration plan to ensure that essential topics are covered and the impact on students' ethics maximized.
Mintchik and Farmer (2009)	Separate	The results of this study indicate that reflective thinking and moral reasoning represent separate dimensions of cognitive process that develop at a different pace. Therefore, the authors suggest that a stand-alone course of ethics in accounting education is necessary since a higher moral reasoning does not automatically follow from advanced technical education.
Shawver and Miller (2017)	Integrated	The authors examine whether there is a change in perceptions of moral intensity as a result of ethics intervention, using a curricular content recommendation of the AACSB task force in an advanced accounting course. The results indicate that the ethics intervention positively influences students' moral awareness, moral judgment, and moral intentions.

coursework, especially in the absence of an initial framework presentation. Jennings (2004) specifically lists six readings that can be used within an accounting curriculum to promote discussion about ethics that can be linked to serious corporate failures, including Enron. Frank, Ofobike, and Gradisher (2009) discuss how the Ohio Accountancy Board disciplinary actions can highlight moral development stages to students. They admit that their goal is to increase awareness of real-life consequences for unethical behavior more than to fundamentally change any student's moral orientation. Apostolou, Dull, and Schleifer (2013) summarize a variety of teaching resources for faculty in their pedagogy framework for accounting ethics. The classroom ideas for implementation range from minute papers, to using the United States Securities and Exchange Commission Accounting and Auditing Enforcement Releases (AAERS), to role-playing with various references. Also, they list cases and the related accounting course where their presentation may be beneficial.

Most frequently, accounting educators incorporate ethical elements within cases used in class. Langenderfer and Rockness (1989) detail a specific way to analyze ethical cases that allows for a teacher to guide the discussion through the class. They emphasize the importance of shorter cases. Cheng and Flasher (2018) provide examples of cases that could be covered in a single class period and appear to be effective in highlighting ethical issues to students. Andersen and Klamm (2018) provide a new model for leveraging the earliest stages of ethical thinking, the initial intuition, as an area to help students learn more about ethics. They discuss the applicability of their scenario in five different accounting courses. Liu, Yao, and Hu (2012) emphasize the combination of increased case usage along with more guest speakers discussing ethics as beneficial to accounting students. Producing ethics cases alone is not a sufficient response to the call for ethics education. The AAA created and distributed an ethics casebook in the mid-1990s (Gunz and McCutcheon 1998). Gunz and McCutcheon (1998) examined the adoption of this casebook and determined that it was not widely used even though it had a wide distribution across accounting programs.

However, while much work has been done on ethics in the classroom, additional work is needed. O'Leary and Stewart (2013) examine auditing students' performance on ethical vignettes after passive and active learning techniques for ethics occur. They find that when the congruence between students' self-assessed learning style and method of instruction is high, the best learning outcomes occur. Tweedie et al. (2013) detail the reality of ethics coverage in accounting-related textbooks and highlight the necessity of a broader approach to ethics education as cultural values vary across the globe and even within a classroom. These broader values are derived from different ethical frameworks that may impact student responses to ethical situations. Future research is needed to determine how long positive interventions' effects last (i.e., how long the improved ethical reasoning or awareness persists beyond the class) and which teaching techniques are most appropriate for what types of accounting classes and students. With the rise in online accounting courses, how should instructors refine the delivery of accounting related ethics? Does separate tailoring for graduate master's of accounting students need to be done as compared to undergraduates, since students usually sequentially complete these degrees? With accounting electives such as internal auditing, forensic accounting, and government and nonprofit accounting being offered, are there ethics scenarios and teaching that should be tailored to these environments?

Student perceptions of ethics education

Students appear to believe that ethics awareness and behavior are necessities for a successful accounting career. Students recognize the importance of ethics and acknowledge student honor code violations among students (e.g., Kerr and Smith 1995). Students are aware of the ethics violations but do not necessarily report them. Future research could examine the reasons for the resistance to reporting violations. Koumbiadis and Okpara (2008) survey students within an accounting program and find the fifth-year students more aware of the necessity of this than the four-year degree students (i.e., 120-hour majors). Graham (2012) details that second-year accounting students recognize the need for ethics education. Students appear to grow in their ethical sensitivity as they transition through an undergraduate program (Jeffrey 1993). Accounting majors do appear to recognize significant ethical dilemmas particular to the major but with limitations on understanding the situations where more subtle manipulations are being performed (Fischer and Rosenzweig 1995).

Adkins and Radtke (2004) survey accounting students and faculty and provide evidence that students may be relying more on faculty members for guidance than faculty realize. Thus, even a lower-level goal by educators of more awareness of ethical dilemmas may impact student's future lives. More concrete awareness-type goals for ethics education allow an alumnus from an institution to identify ethical issues when confronted with situations in the professional world postgraduation (e.g., Hiltebeitel and Jones 1992).

Criticisms and protest against teaching ethics in accounting have generated a debate within the literature where the naysayers' arguments are rebutted (Bampton and Cowton 2002). Bampton and Maclagan (2005) rebut the skeptics' arguments of "relevance, necessity, and effectiveness of teaching ethics" (290) to accounting students. They summarize extant reasons to not provide ethics education. These include: a lack of time in class, an assumption that auditing courses adequately cover the material, a lack of faculty confidence in teaching the subject, a lack of support materials, an assumption that practitioners will cover these items in more real world settings later, an assumption that students are not interested, and a lack of a documented long-term impact on students. Specifically, they counter these reasons with the arguments that ethics are indeed relevant (reflected by faculty with more industry experience being more likely than faculty without such experience to include ethics in their classes), necessary (the code of ethics/conduct for the professionals and organizations do not address the gray areas that arise in real life), and effective (as long as the goals are more modestly set than long-term changing behaviors of students). The reality is that *"training in systematic thinking and reasoning about ethics"* (296, emphasis in original) is what academics are capable of doing. At the other end of the spectrum, the reality of whether ethics should even be taught to students has been discussed as futile, as some believe that all ethical values have been instilled in students prior to their arrival at university (McDonald and Donleavy 1995; McDonald 2004; West, Ravenscroft, and Shrader 2004). Milam and McNair (1992) surveyed accounting faculty who expressed positive opinions for teaching ethics and who expressed a desire to see more ethics within the accounting curriculum. However, they did not explore why the faculty felt this way. Waddock (2005) outlines the moral imperative for ethics education by emphasizing that the profit maximization mantra for shareholders in management has resulted in auditors and other accountants ignoring consequences to other stakeholder when making ethical decisions. She calls on business schools to focus on how business operates within societal boundaries – not solely the world of business and the economy.

Determinants of ethical orientations of students within accounting programs provide some insight into the varied backgrounds of accounting students. Conroy and Emerson (2004) examine the impact of religiosity on the ethical awareness of students and find that self-identification as religious appeared to have more impact than a separate religion/ethics course did on students' responses. Consistent with prior literature, Tormo-Carbo, Segui-Mas, and Oltra (2016) find that Spanish accounting students who are female or older and those who have taken a prior ethics course value business ethics exposure in the curriculum. O'Leary and Cotter (2000) provide accountancy student evidence from Australia and Ireland that it is not the underlying infraction that stops students from making an unethical choice but the detection realities that seem to change the student's willingness to commit an ethical violation. Cheng and Crumbley (2018) find that students are willing to use publisher test bank questions to help improve their academic performance. Future research could examine why students believe ethics to be important but still perform academic violations.

Publishing ethics research

From a research perspective, accounting ethics researchers have generated a broad list of publications in accounting and more broad-based business journals (see Uysal 2010; Apostolou et al. 2010; Apostolou, Dull, and Schleifer 2013; Apostolou, Dorminey, and Hassell 2013, 2020 for overviews of ethics publications). Bampton and Cowton (2013) specifically provide an overview of 520 accounting ethics-related articles, in a broad list of over 35 journals, from 1987–2008, noting an increasing trend in frequency, with a slight majority for empirical papers as opposed to other research methodologies. Over a 20-year period, this averages to 26 articles a year. Apostoulou, Dorminey, and Hassell (2019) examine 101 accounting education articles from 2018, a single year. This reflects that ethics-related publications occur at a slower rate than accounting education articles, which is not the predominate research channel for tenure-track accounting faculty. Thus, researching in accounting ethics has a reputation of being undervalued by institutions within the faculty tenure process, as these numbers reveal.

Research with accounting ethics does have its issues. Bampton and Cowton (2013) highlight criticism of empirical papers, such as failure to control for social desirability. They also highlight issues with behavioral research suggesting that "more qualitative work should be undertaken . . . focused on examining issues and research questions that are not amenable to investigation by questionnaire surveys using close-ended question" (p 561). The lack of a robust selection of accounting-based ethical scenarios in the published literature seems antithetical to the profession's call for more training. The academic community could do better to capture those real-life situations that are the source of ethical stress for practitioners. Thus, there remains a need for more diverse research methodologies and topics to be published relating to accounting ethics education. Also, the general academic community should consider this research area to be as valued as financial or auditing-related research, as the application of ethics research can directly impact the next generation of accounting professionals. Arguably, ethics research contributes as much to the vibrancy of our capital markets as any other research area.

Conclusion

More can and should be done to promote ethics educations for instructors and students as the importance of ethics in the accounting field continues to increase during this time of change. While headlines with data analytics and technological innovation take center stage in business publications, the reality is that understanding ethics is critically important to the application of these tools and technological innovations like cloud computing. Data privacy is critical, because data may be shared with or could be accessed by third parties as companies outsource information technology to the cloud. Privacy is treated differently around the globe, as reflected by the European implementation of the General Data Protection Regulation, known more commonly as GDPR. Thus, even discussing GDPR and how/if it should apply to businesses with the United States or how it might impact the accounting industry shows how ethics continues to be intertwined with business today.

The classroom instructor is the primary delivery mechanism for accounting ethics within the curriculum, especially within the United States. More research can enhance an instructors' ability to make ethics education more salient to today's students. From our review of the literature, additional cases and teaching instructions on ethics will help to make instructors more comfortable in delivering this material that is so critical to the education of future accountants. The importance of teaching and applied research, along with more traditional discovery research, cannot be understated in ethics education.

Since the profession has struggled with the ethics of accounting since the first separation of the accounting function from the users of the information, there is no obvious, easy solution. It is imperative that instructors reach out to the profession and invite professionals into the classroom to discuss real world examples of ethical dilemmas. We can all play a role in valuing and promoting ethics education in all its forms within the classroom of today to ensure that future accounting graduates are better prepared to take on the challenges of business today.

Notes

1 Luca Pacioli, often called the father of accounting, was a Franciscan friar who taught mathematics and accounting in Venice, Perugia, and Milan.
2 Id. John Cromwell became the first black CPA in 1921, and in 1943, Mary T. Washington Wylie was the first African-American woman to become a CPA (http: http://maaw.info/AccountingHistory Dates and Events.htm).
3 http://maaw.info/AccountingHistoryDates and Events.htm
4 Id.
5 http://maaw.info/AccountingHistoryDates and Events.htm

6 Id.

7 www.nysscpa.org/about/about-nysscpa#sthash.26g7Mkyz.dpbs

8 Id.

9 http://aaahq.org/

10 http://maaw.info/AccountingHistoryDates and Events.htm

11 Id.

12 www.theaccountant-online.com/aboutus

13 www.journalofaccountancy.com/issues/2005/oct/accountingforthejournalsfirst100yearsatimeline
from1905to2005.html

14 http://maaw.info/AccountingHistoryDatesAndEvents.htm

15 Id.

16 Id.

17 http://maaw.info/AccountingHistoryDatesAndEvents.htm

18 www.aicpa.org/content/dam/aicpa/research/standards/codeofconduct/downloadabledocuments/201
3june1codeofprofessionalconduct.pdf

19 Financial Industry Regulatory Authority (FINRA) is a self-regulatory organization that oversees broker dealer firms and their brokers under the oversight of the federal government (FINRA 2019).

References

Abs, G., C. Grimstad, R. Hay, W. A. Howe, W. La Place, F. J. McGurr, and W. Serraino. 1954. "Historical
Dates in Accounting." *The Accounting Review* 29 (3): 486–93.

Adkins, Nell, and Robin R. Radtke. 2004. "Students' and Faculty Members' Perceptions of the Importance of Business Ethics and Accounting Ethics Education: Is There an Expectations Gap?" *Journal of
Business Ethics* 51 (3): 279–300.

American Institute of CPAs (AICPA). 2019. "Uniform CPA Examination Blueprints." www.aicpa.org/
content/dam/aicpa/becomeacpa/cpaexam/examinationcontent/downloadabledocuments/cpa-exam-
blueprints-effective-july-2019.pdf.

Andersen, Margaret L., and Bonnie K. Klamm. 2018. "Haidt's Social Intuitionist Model: What Are the
Implications for Accounting Ethics Education?" *Journal of Accounting Education* 44: 35–46.

Anzeh, Belal Abu, and Suzan Abed. 2015. "The Extent of Accounting Ethics Education for Bachelor
Students in Jordanian Universities." *Journal of Management Research* 7 (2): 121.

Apostolou, Barbara, Jack W. Dorminey, and John M. Hassell. 2020. "Accounting Education Literature
Review." *Journal of Accounting Education*: 100670.

Apostolou, Barbara, Jack W. Dorminey, John M. Hassell, and Stephanie F. Watson. 2013. "Accounting
Education Literature Review (2010–2012)." *Journal of Accounting Education* 31 (2): 107–61.

Apostolou, Barbara, Richard B. Dull, and Lydia L. F Schleifer. 2013. "A Framework for the Pedagogy of
Accounting Ethics." *Accounting Education* 22 (1): 1–17.

Apostolou, Barbara, John M. Hassell, James E. Rebele, and Stephanie F. Watson. 2010. "Accounting Education Literature Review (2006–2009)." *Journal of Accounting Education* 28 (3–4): 145–97.

Association to Advance Collegiate Schools of Business (AACSB). 2013. "2013 Eligibility Procedures
and Accreditation Standards for Business Accreditation." https://www.aacsb.edu/-/media/aacsb/docs/
accreditation/business/standards-and-tables/2018-business-standards.ashx?la=en&hash=B9AF18F3FA
0DF19B352B605CBCE17959E32445D9.

Bampton, Roberta, and Christopher J. Cowton. 2002. "The Teaching of Ethics in Management Accounting: Progress and Prospects." *Business Ethics: A European Review* 11 (1): 52–61.

Bampton, Roberta, and Christopher J. Cowton. 13. "Taking Stock of Accounting Ethics Scholarship:
A Review of the Journal Literature." *Journal of Business Ethics* 114 (3): 549–63.

Bampton, Roberta, and Patrick Maclagan. 2005. "Why Teach Ethics to Accounting Students? A Response
to the Sceptics." *Business ethics: A European review* 14 (3): 290–300.

Bazerman, Max H., George Loewenstein, and Don A. Moore. 2002. "Why Good Accountants do Bad
Audits." *Harvard Business Review* 80 (11): 96–103.

Bazerman, Max H., and Ann E. Tenbrunsel. 2011. "Ethical Breakdowns." *Harvard Business Review* 89 (4):
58–65.

Bedingfield, James P., and Stephen E. Loeb. 1973. "Attitudes of Professors Toward Accounting Ethics." *The Accounting Review* 48 (3): 603–5.

Black, William H. 2012. "The Activities of the Pathways Commission and the Historical Context For Changes in Accounting Education." *Issues in Accounting Education* 27 (3): 601–25.

Blanthorne, Cindy, Stacy E. Kovar, and Dann G. Fisher. 2007. "Accounting Educators' Opinions About Ethics in the Curriculum: An Extensive View." *Issues in Accounting Education* 22 (3): 355–90.

Caliyurt, Kiymet Tunca. 2007. "Accounting Ethics Education in Turkish Public Universities." *Social Responsibility Journal* 3 (4): 74.

Carey, John L. 1947. "The Realities of Professional Ethics." *The Accounting Review* 22 (2): 119–23.

Chan, Samuel Y. S., and Philomena Leung. 2006. "The Effects of Accounting Students' Ethical Reasoning and Personal Factors on Their Ethical Sensitivity." Managerial *Auditing Journal* 21 (4): 436–57.

Chatfield, Michael. 1975. "The Accounting Review's First Fifty Years." *Accounting Review*: 1–6.

Chatfield, M., and R. Vangermeersch. 1996. *The History of Accounting: An International Encyclopedia*. *Rout-ledge Library Editions: Accounting*. New York: Garland Publishing, Inc.

Cheng, Christine, and D. Larry Crumbley. 2018. "Student and Professor Use of Publisher Test Banks and Implications for Fair Play." *Journal of Accounting Education* 42: 1–16.

Cheng, Christine, and Renee Flasher. 2018. "Two Short Case Studies in Staff Auditor and Student Ethical Decision Making." *Issues in Accounting Education Teaching Notes* 33 (1): 28–37.

Cloninger, Peggy A., and T. T. Selvarajan. 2010. "Can Ethics Education Improve Ethical Judgment? An Empirical Study." *SAM Advanced Management Journal* 75 (4): 4.

Conroy, Stephen J., and Tisha L. N Emerson. 2004. "Business Ethics and Religion: Religiosity as a Predic-tor of Ethical Awareness Among Students." *Journal of Business Ethics* 50 (4): 383–96.

Dellaportas, Steven. 2006. "Making a Difference with a Discrete Course on Accounting Ethics." *Journal of Business Ethics* 65 (4): 391–404.

Dellaportas, Steven, Sutharson Kanapathippillai, Arifur Khan, and Philomena Leung. 2014. "Ethics Edu-cation in the Australian Accounting Curriculum: A Longitudinal Study Examining Barriers and Ena-blers." *Accounting Education* 23 (4): 362–82.

Dellaportas, Steven, Philomena Leung, Barry J. Cooper, and Beverley Jackling. 2006. "IES 4 – Ethics Education Revisited." *Australian Accounting Review* 16 (38): 4–12.

Dzuranin, Ann C., Rebecca Toppe Shortridge, and Pamela A. Smith. 2013. "Building Ethical Leaders: A Way to Integrate and Assess Ethics Education." *Journal of Business Ethics* 115 (1): 101–14.

Earley, Christine E., and Patrick T. Kelly. 2004. "A Note on Ethics Educational Interventions in an Under-graduate Auditing Course: Is There An "Enron Effect"?" *Issues in Accounting Education* 19 (1): 53–71.

Edwards, J., and R. Hermanson. 1991. *Essentials of Accounting with Ethics Cases*. Homewood, IL: Richard D. Irwin Publisher, 320.

Felton, Edward L., and Ronald R. Sims. 2005. "Teaching Business Ethics: Targeted Outputs." *Journal of Business Ethics* 60 (4): 377–91.

Financial Industry Regulatory Authority, Inc. (FINRA). 2019. *FINRA 2018 Annual Financial Report*. Washington, DC: FINRA.

Fischer, Marilyn, and Kenneth Rosenzweig. 1995. "Attitudes of Students and Accounting Practition-ers Concerning the Ethical Acceptability of Earnings Management." *Journal of Business Ethics* 14 (6): 433–44.

Fischer, Michael J. 2000. "Luca Pacioli on Business Profits." *Journal of Business Ethics* 25 (4): 299–312.

Frank, Gary, Emeka Ofobike, and Suzanne Gradisher. 2009. "Teaching Business Ethics: A Quandary for Accounting Educators." *Journal of Education for Business* 85 (3): 132–38.

Gaa, James C., and Linda Thorne. 2004. "An Introduction to the Special Issue on Professionalism and Ethics in Accounting Education." *Issues in Accounting Education* 19 (1): 1–7.

Ghaffari, Firoozeh, Orthodoxia Kyriacou, and Ross Brennan. 2008. "Exploring the Implementation of Ethics in UK Accounting Programs." *Issues in Accounting Education* 23 (2): 183–98.

Graham, Alan. 2012. "The Teaching of Ethics in Undergraduate Accounting Programmes: The Students' Perspective." *Accounting Education* 21 (6): 599–613.

Graham, Willard J. 1939. "Accounting Education, Ethics and Training." *The Accounting Review* 14 (3): 258–62.

Green, Sharon, and James Weber. 1997. "Influencing Ethical Development: Exposing Students to the AICPA Code of Conduct." *Journal of Business Ethics* 16 (8): 777–90.

Gunz, Sally, and John McCutcheon. 1998. "Are Academics Committed to Accounting Ethics Educa-tion?" *Journal of Business Ethics* 17 (11): 1145–54.

Hiltebeitel, Kenneth M., and Scott K. Jones. 1992. "An Assessment of Ethics Instruction in Accounting Education." *Journal of Business Ethics* 11 (1): 37–46.

Horrigan, James. 1992. "Book Reviews." *Issues in Accounting Education* 7 (2): 257.

Jackling, Beverley, Barry J. Cooper, Philomena Leung, and Steven Dellaportas. 2007. "Professional Accounting Bodies' Perceptions of Ethical Issues, Causes of Ethical Failure and Ethics Education." *Managerial Auditing Journal* 22 (9): 928–44.

Jeffrey, Cynthia. 1993. "Ethical Development of Accounting Students, Non-Accounting Business Students, and Liberal Arts Students." *Issues in Accounting Education* 8 (1): 86–96.

Jennings, Marianne M. 2004. "Incorporating Ethics and Professionalism into Accounting Education and Research: A Discussion of the Voids and Advocacy for Training in Seminal Works in Business Ethics." *Issues in Accounting Education* 19 (1): 7–26.

Jonson, Elizabeth Prior, Linda Mary McGuire, and Deirdre O'Neill. 2015. "Teaching Ethics to Undergraduate Business Students in Australia: Comparison of Integrated and Stand-Alone Approaches." *Journal of Business Ethics* 132 (2): 477–91.

Kelly, Patrick T. 2017. "Integrating Leadership Topics into an Accounting Ethics Course – Preparing Students for a Challenging Profession." *Advances in Accounting Education: Teaching and Curriculum Innovations* 20: 141–80.

Kerr, David S., and L. Murphy Smith. 1995. "Importance of and Approaches to Incorporating Ethics into the Accounting Classroom." *Journal of Business Ethics* 14 (12): 987–95.

Klimek, Janice, and Kelly Wenell. 2011. "Ethics in Accounting: An Indispensable Course?" *Academy of Educational Leadership Journal* 15 (4): 107.

Koumbiadis, Nicholas, and John O. Okpara. 2008. "Ethics and Accounting Profession: An Exploratory Study of Accounting Students in Post-Secondary Institutions." *International Review of Business Research Papers* 4 (5): 147–56.

Langenderfer, Harold Q., and Joanne W. Rockness. 1989. "Integrating Ethics into the Accounting Curriculum: Issues, Problems, and Solutions." *Issues in Accounting Education* 4 (1): 58–69.

LaSalle, Brother. 1954. "An Approach to Ethics." *The Accounting Review* 29 (4): 687–89.

Liu, Chunhui, Lee J. Yao, and Nan Hu. 2012. "Improving Ethics Education in Accounting: Lessons from Medicine and Law." *Issues in Accounting Education* 27 (3): 671–90.

Loeb, Stephen E. 1994. "Ethics and Accounting Doctoral Education." *Journal of Business Ethics* 13 (10): 817–28.

Loeb, Stephen E., and James P. Bedingfield. 1972. "Teaching Accounting Ethics." *The Accounting Review* 47 (4): 811–13.

Loeb, Stephen E., and Joanne Rockness. 1992. "Accounting Ethics and Education: A Response." *Journal of Business Ethics* 11 (7): 485–90.

Martinov-Bennie, Nonna, and Rosina Mladenovic. 2015. "Investigation of the Impact of an Ethical Framework and an Integrated Ethics Education on Accounting Students' Ethical Sensitivity and Judgment." *Journal of Business Ethics* 127 (1): 189–203.

McDonald, Gael M. 2004. "A Case Example: Integrating Ethics into the Academic Business Curriculum." *Journal of Business Ethics* 54 (4): 371–84.

McDonald, Gael M., and Gabriel D. Donleavy. 1995. "Objections to the Teaching of Business Ethics." *Journal of Business Ethics* 14 (10): 839–53.

McPeak, David, Karen V. Pincus, and Gary L. Sundem. 2012. "The International Accounting Education Standards Board: Influencing Global Accounting Education." *Issues in Accounting Education* 27 (3): 743–50.

Milam, Edward, and Frances McNair. 1992. "An Examination of Accounting Faculty Perceptions of the Importance of Ethics Coverage in Accounting Courses." *Business & Professional Ethics Journal*: 57–71.

Miller, William F., and D'Arcy A. Becker. 2011. "Ethics in the Accounting Curriculum: What Is Really Being Covered?" *American Journal of Business Education* 4 (10): 1–10.

Mintchik, Natalia M., and Timothy A. Farmer. 2009. "Associations between Epistemological Beliefs and Moral Reasoning: Evidence from Accounting." *Journal of Business Ethics* 84 (2): 259–75.

Myer, Joseph C. 1931. "Teaching the Accountant the History and Ethics of his Profession." *Accounting Review*: 47–50.

O'Leary, Conor. 2009. "An Empirical Analysis of the Positive Impact of Ethics Teaching on Accounting Students." *Accounting Education: An International Journal* 18 (4–5): 505–20.

O'Leary, Conor, and Derry Cotter. 2000. "The Ethics of Final Year Accountancy Students: An International Comparison." *Managerial Auditing Journal* 15 (3): 108–15.

O'Leary, Conor, and Shafi Mohamad. 2008. "The Successful Influence of Teaching Ethics on Malaysian Accounting Students." *Malaysian Accounting Review* 7 (2): 1–16.

O'Leary, Conor, and Jenny Stewart. 2013. "The Interaction of Learning Styles and Teaching Methodologies in Accounting Ethical Instruction." *Journal of Business Ethics* 113 (2): 225–41.

Pacioli, Luca. 1494. *Summa de Arithmetica geometria proportioni: et proportionalita . . .* Venice: Paganino de paganini.

Paris, Dubravka. 2016. "History of Accounting and Accountancy Profession in Great Britain." *Journal of Accounting and Management* 6 (1): 33–44.

Peloubet, Maurice E. 1934. "Professional Ethics and the Student." *Accounting Review.* 164–70.

Previts, G. J., and B. Committe. 1980. "An Index to the Accounting Review 1926–1978 and Proceedings of the AAUIA 1917–1925." American Accounting Association, Sarasota, FL.

Rebele, James E., and E. Kent St Pierre. 2019. "A Commentary on Learning Objectives for Accounting Education Programs: The Importance of Soft Skills and Technical Knowledge." *Journal of Accounting Education* 48: 71–79.

Reckers, Philip, and Melissa Samuelson. 2016. "Toward Resolving the Debate Surrounding Slippery Slope Versus Licensing Behavior: The Importance of Individual Differences in Accounting Ethical Decision Making." *Advances in Accounting* 34: 1–16.

Robson, Keith. 1992. "Accounting Numbers as "Inscription": Action at a Distance and the Development of Accounting." *Accounting, Organizations and Society* 17 (7): 685–708.

Schrand, Catherine M., and Sarah L. C. Zechman. 2012. "Executive Overconfidence and the Slippery Slope to Financial Misreporting." *Journal of Accounting and Economics* 53 (1–2): 311–29.

Shawver, Tara J., and William F. Miller. 2017. "Moral Intensity Revisited: Measuring the Benefit of Accounting Ethics Interventions." *Journal of Business Ethics* 141 (3): 587–603.

Smith, Weston L. 2013. "Lessons of the HealthSouth Fraud: An Insider's View." *Issues in Accounting Education* 28 (4): 901–12.

Soll, Jacob. 2014. *The Reckoning: Financial Accountability and the Rise and Fall of Nations.* New York: Basic Books (AZ).

Swanson, Diane L. 2005. "Business Ethics Education at Bay: Addressing a Crisis of Legitimacy." *Issues in Accounting Education* 20 (3): 247–53.

Thomas, C. William. 2004. "An Inventory of Support Materials for Teaching Ethics in the Post-Enron Era." *Issues in Accounting Education* 19 (1): 27–52.

Tormo-Carbó, Guillermina, Elies Seguí-Mas, and Victor Oltra. 2016. "Accounting Ethics in Unfriendly Environments: The Educational Challenge." *Journal of Business Ethics* 135 (1): 161–75.

Treadway Commission., James C., Greenspon Thompson, F. W. Woolworth, Stanley Works, Eli Lilly, Delmarva Power, Virginia Power et al. 1987. "Comment Letters to the National Commission on Commission on Fraudulent Financial Reporting, 1987 (Treadway Commission) Vol. 2." *Statements of Position.* 663. https://egrove.olemiss.edu/aicpa_sop/663.

Tweedie, Dale, Maria Cadiz Dyball, James Hazelton, and Sue Wright. 2013. "Teaching Global Ethical Standards: A Case and Strategy for Broadening the Accounting Ethics Curriculum." *Journal of Business Ethics* 115 (1): 1–15.

Uysal, Özgür Özmen. 2010. "Business Ethics Research with an Accounting Focus: A Bibliometric Analysis from 1988 to 2007." *Journal of Business Ethics* 93 (1): 137–60.

Waddock, Sandra. 2005. "Hollow Men and Women at the Helm . . . Hollow Accounting Ethics?" *Issues in Accounting Education* 20 (2): 145–50.

West, Tim, Sue Ravenscroft, and Charles Shrader. 2004. "Cheating and Moral Judgment in the College Classroom: A Natural Experiment." *Journal of Business Ethics* 54 (2): 173–83.

Wyhe, Glenn Van. 2007a. "A History of US Higher Education in Accounting, Part I: Situating Accounting within the Academy." *Issues in Accounting Education* 22 (2): 163–81.

Wyhe, Glenn Van. 2007b. "A History of US Higher Education in Accounting, part II: Reforming Accounting within the Academy." *Issues in Accounting Education* 22 (3): 481–501.

21

HAVE ADVANCED DEGREES INCREASED ETHICAL PROFESSIONALISM FOR AUDITORS?

Francine McKenna

The master's of accounting degree for auditors and the illusion of more ethical professionals

Introduction

In July 2008, at the beginning of the last major financial crisis, the Pre-Certification Education Executive Committee of the Association of International Certified Professional Accountants, or AICPA, told authors of a paper promoting increased educational requirements for accountants that it was time to put in place even higher hurdles to joining the profession.

In its comment on the draft paper prepared by the National Association of State Boards of Accountancy, "Education and Licensure Requirements for Certified Public Accountants: A Discussion Regarding Degreed Candidates Sitting for the Uniform CPA Examination with a Minimum of 120 Credit Hours (120-Hour Candidate) and becoming eligible for Licensure with a Minimum of 150 Credit Hours (150-Hour Candidate)," the AICPA's PcEEC wrote, "The accounting profession needs strong not weak requirements for licensure and high quality accounting education and auditing standards" (NASBA 2008).

The paper expressed support for a 120/150 model, but the PcEEC advocated the 150/150 model that required an equal number of credit hours of education a prerequisite for licensure. The PcEEC commenters wrote that, "although certain thoughtful accounting practitioners and educators favor the 120/150 model, continued reliance on the 150/150 model offers greater promise for protecting the public interest."

Specific licensing requirements of state boards still vary, but now all of the 55 states and territories that regulate CPA licensing, except Washington, DC, and the US Virgin Islands, require 150-hours of college credit to take the qualifying licensure exam (DCOPLA n.d.).

The drive to increase educational requirements for licensure has effectively made the graduate degree in accounting the minimum requirement for entry into the profession in the United States and licensure as a public accountant.

The dream of graduate schools of auditing described by the draft paper's authors, including now the retired director of research for the Corporate Governance Center at the University of Tennessee, Joseph V. Carcello, has been realized via the nationwide implementation of the

150-hour requirement. This is accomplished most often at this point by an additional year of graduate study, culminating in a master's of accounting degree.

A traditional four-year undergraduate program, the AICPA says, is no longer "adequate" for obtaining the "requisite knowledge and skills to become a CPA," given that so many new official accounting and auditing pronouncements and tax laws expand the knowledge that "professional practice in accounting" requires.

This chapter argues that this requirement to become a professional accountant in the United States, a graduate degree, has not improved the ethical culture of its public accounting profession, nor has it increased the focus on the professional obligations of public accounting – a public duty to capital markets and service to shareholders.

Rather, the additional educational requirement is emblematic of the industry's focus on the economic growth of the largest firms and their clients rather than, as Professor Carcello and those who originally supported the proposals may have hoped, an educational experience that imbues the profession with the spirit of ethical public service and increases its prestige in the eyes of the public.

What is a professional?

A "professional" is defined as someone who acquires and maintains a specialized body of knowledge that will give him or her a distinct advantage over clients. Professional associations such as the AICPA[1] and licensing bodies – in this case the states – ensure members live up to required standards and codes of conduct of the profession, including always placing the client's interest before self-interest.

The AICPA uses the word "professional" several times in the rationale for the increased educational requirement that now appears on its website (AICPA n.d. "150 Hour Requirement"). Licensed certified public accountants in the United States meet the legal and practical requirements to qualify, by definition, as a profession and therefore to be considered by the public as professionals.

In public testimony in December of 2007 for the Treasury Department Advisory Committee on the Auditing Profession, or ACAP, Carcello suggested that the US Securities and Exchange Commission (SEC) or Congress should expand the responsibilities of the Public Company Accounting Oversight Board (PCAOB) to include accounting education and licensure of public accountants (ACAP 2007).

In a cooperative partnership with the American Accounting Association, Carcello said the PCAOB could also develop the standards to accredit "professional schools of auditing." He believed that a "prime benefit" of professional schools of auditing would be that the "accreditation process could include developing a student culture of professional responsibility."

AICPA members had been discussing how to add prestige to the profession through higher education for more than 100 years (Van Wyhe 1994). In 1937, the governing council of the American Institute of Accountants, now superseded by the AICPA, publicly stated that the "highest practicable standards of preliminary education similar to those effective in other professions, such as law or medicine" should be required for the accounting profession (Allen and Woodland 2006).

The savings and loan scandal of the 1990s, after 1980s-era failures such as Penn Square Bank in Oklahoma and Continental Illinois National Bank, led the AICPA to implement reforms in the mid-1980s to beef up the industry's self-regulatory regime and fend off further congressional scrutiny (Madison and Meonske 1991).

One of those reforms was to recommend that AICPA members and CPA candidates have 150-semester hours of college education prior to becoming eligible for membership (NASBA 2008) rather than the 120 hours that had been common until then and attainable via an undergraduate degree. The AICPA said that the requirement was intended to "improve the overall quality of work performed by CPAs" and "ensure the quality of future audits" by improving the quality of audit staff and those entering the profession (AICPA 2003).

At its annual meeting in New York City in 1988, 84% of the AICPA's voting members backed the proposal, to be effective in the year 2000. The new rule required 150 semester hours rather than a master's degree, maintaining flexibility for colleges and universities to continue to design programs that could meet the requirement with an undergraduate degree if desired (Jacob and Murray 2006).

However, beginning in 2000, the dot-com bust and the Enron scandal that resulted in the demise of Arthur Andersen (along with accounting scandals at WorldCom, HealthSouth, Tyco, and many others) led to further scrutiny of the profession and increased instability in the markets. The NASDAQ Composite index, for example, dropped 78% from spring 2000 to fall 2002.

There was a subsequent close call in 2005 when KPMG was nearly indicted by the US Department of Justice for tax fraud (Baugh et al. 2019). These events, along with a substantial increase in corporate accounting restatements, disrupted financial markets and shook investor confidence in the integrity of the audit and auditors.

Consequently, ACAP was established in October 2007 to "examine the sustainability of a strong and vibrant auditing profession," according to its charter. The committee, consisting of a cross-section of former regulators, industry professionals, academics, and investor representatives, sought to review the role of auditors in the capital markets and the latest risks to the viability of the profession and major firms, highlighted during the scandals.

ACAP's final report (ACAP 2008), issued in October 2008, recommended that the AICPA and the American Accounting Association, founded in 1916 as the American Association of University Instructors in Accounting, form a joint commission to study the possible future structure of higher education for the accounting profession. The recommendation was prompted in part by Carcello's testimony that suggested the possibility of establishing a free-standing, postgraduate professional educational structure for auditing.

The audit industry trade association addressed the increased scrutiny of auditors and CPAs as a result of the Enron and WorldCom scandals and the legislative response – the Sarbanes-Oxley Act of 2002. The Sarbanes-Oxley legislation, focused on instilling renewed confidence in the auditing profession, had passed overwhelmingly 99–0 in the US Senate and 423–3 in the House of Representatives.[2] Sarbanes-Oxley also replaced the industry's self-regulatory model with the PCAOB.

Central to the identity of a professional is managing the conflict between personal (or firm) interests and client interests. The scope and scale of a professional service firm such as a public accounting firm is determined by how strictly that firm's professionals define their conflicts.

The definition of potential conflicts also determines the level of exclusivity of the membership of the profession and the level of competition for the industry, both of which determine pricing and profitability of services. That's because professional service providers sell intangibles – knowledge, experience, reputation. By their nature, professional services can only be delivered by individuals or firms that are licensed, have completed additional education, have met other qualifications such as on-the-job experience or an apprenticeship, and have passed a qualifying exam.

Clients trust professionals such as CPAs or lawyers to put their interests first, before individual or firm interests, because the expert professional is performing a service that the client is unable to perform itself or does not have sufficient knowledge to fully monitor.

A doctor performs his or her public duty by providing medical services to individual patients or "clients." The doctor's act of reducing disease in one person, for each member of society, is a service to the public interest. Lawyers represent the interests of their respective clients in adversarial proceedings, either in opposition to the government or in representing the client in an adversarial process that in law is expected to provide for justice to be served.

By comparison, the 1984 Supreme Court case *United States v. Arthur Young & Co.* explained the role of a public accountant thusly:

> The Hickman work-product doctrine was founded upon the private attorney's role as the client's confidential adviser and advocate, a loyal representative whose duty it is to present the client's case in the most favorable possible light. An independent certified public accountant performs a different role. By certifying the public reports that collectively depict a corporation's financial status, the independent auditor assumes a public responsibility transcending any employment relationship with the client. The independent public accountant performing this special function owes ultimate allegiance to the corporation's creditors and stockholders, as well as to the investing public. This "public watchdog" function demands that the accountant maintain total independence from the client at all times and requires complete fidelity to the public trust.

Compared to physicians and attorneys, audit professionals have competing affiliations and ethical obligations. External auditors serve the specific interests of a specific public company under a contractual obligation wherein the company pays the auditor. However, the audit function for public companies is mandated by federal law to be provided only by licensed accountants who serve a quasi-regulatory function to protect shareholder interests and the capital markets as a whole.

CPAs juggle ethical responsibilities to clients and shareholders, to their own firms as owners or employees, to the public and capital markets, and to the profession. Professional accountants that provide services to companies in order to maintain the companies' ability to remain publicly traded, and which lend credibility to financial information that the companies disclose to the public, are not always serving the public interest. In fact, the service could be actually detrimental to the public interest.

A professional services provider is expected to manage client relationships in the spirit of *noblesse oblige* – with honorable, generous, and responsible behavior – not in the spirit of *caveat emptor* or "let the buyer beware" (Nanda 2003). Conflicts are supposed to be managed proactively under the oversight of regulators. Professional associations such as the AICPA also have an interest in monitoring these conflicts, since failure to do so can damage the profession's reputation.

The economic rationale for the 150-hour requirement

Regulators, academic researchers, and the public can scrutinize whether increased educational requirements improve ethical culture in the firms and audit quality or, instead, simply raised barriers to entry to employment at the largest global audit firms simply to extract additional economic rents.

In economics, licensing schemes are driven by a desire to increase regulatory capture and the private-interest motive. That would suggest that changes in licensing requirements, especially those making them more stringent, are introduced by current members of the profession to limit the supply of new entrants and extract monopoly rents (Friedman 1962; Stigler 1971; Maurizi 1974).[3]

The introduction of the additional 30-credit hour requirement – the 150-hour rule – increases the marginal cost of becoming a CPA and may reduce the number of new CPAs, according to this theory. The average quality of candidates in the market will remain unchanged or even be reduced, however, according to one study.[4] That's because there still are a number of ways to meet the 30-credit-hour requirement that may render it ineffective in filtering out low-quality candidates. In addition, the higher opportunity cost of one more year of study may dissuade high-quality candidates from pursuing the more demanding certification (Akerlof 1970; Barrios 2019).

That's exactly what happened. Despite record numbers of students studying accounting in recent years, the number of students taking the CPA exam declined significantly between 2010 and 2011 and then stayed flat until 2016. Between 2015 and 2016 the number of new CPA examination candidates did increase again, rising to 13% (AICPA 2017). Projected accounting bachelor's graduates did trend upward in the 2015–16 academic year after a dip in 2013–14, but a decrease in projected accounting master's graduates has led recently to a slight decline in overall degrees awarded.

It's not easy to balance the desire to increase the profession's prestige and promote competitive pay by raising standards while also making sure there is a sufficient supply of labor for the largest firms that is maintained at an economically feasible price. Concerns over fewer CPA exam candidates led to an AICPA initiative to revise the CPA exam. A substantially updated version of the CPA exam was introduced on April 1, 2017, that strives to be less knowledge-based and more practice-based, modeling it after the legal profession's bar exam.

The updated version places greater emphasis on an assessment of a candidate's analytical, problem-solving, and critical thinking skills. This is what the AICPA says stakeholders want from newly licensed CPAs. However, according to the AICPA, even though the number of exam candidates rose again between 2015 and 2016, hiring of new graduates slowed 19% that year after reaching historic highs in the previous four years.

The role of the AICPA and the Center for Audit Quality in promoting ethical professionalism

After passage of the Sarbanes-Oxley Act, AICPA leaders created the Public Company Auditors' Forum in 2005 for the AICPA, large audit firms, and public members as an autonomous public policy entity focused exclusively on public company audits. The forum was renamed the Center for Audit Quality, or CAQ, in January 2007.

Professional associations protect the reputation of their members by making sure client interests are protected (Nanda 1999). Since its founding, the CAQ team has kept an "unwavering focus" on primarily serving its members – public company auditing firms registered with the PCAOB. The CAQ only secondarily says it is also focused on the true clients of public company auditors – investors – and on "building investor confidence in capital markets."

The CAQ and AICPA are no longer responsible for establishing and enforcing standards for public company auditors. That rests with the PCAOB. However, the AICPA and state boards of accountancy use certification and licensure powers to restrict entry to the profession and reduce the impact of competition on the industry.

Public trust in the profession will diminish and de-professionalization will begin if, over time, investors and the capital markets believe auditors and their professional associations prioritize activities that benefit members of the industry rather than activities that monitor and enforce ethical conduct and professionalism that mitigates self-interest and conflicts of interest.

Ethical professionalism since 2008

As the Supreme Court noted in *Arthur Young* more than 30 years ago, auditors play a crucial role in the financial reporting process by serving a "public watchdog function" that demands "total independence from the client at all times and requires complete fidelity to the public trust."

The consequences of de-professionalization – reducing emphasis on monitoring and enforcing ethical conduct within the firms – go beyond creeping loss of public trust in individual professionals and audit firms as a result of chronic reputational damage. They also include legal and regulatory actions and significant financial penalties.

The SEC brings enforcement actions against accountants and auditors for two primary reasons – audit failures and auditor independence violations. An audit failure occurs when an auditor does not comply with the applicable professional standards to the extent that its audit report opinion is materially non-supported by audit evidence or is even false.

Independence violations occur when an auditor is not independent or wholly separate of material relationships with its SEC audit clients, either in fact or appearance, according to SEC and PCAOB rules.

Rule 102(e) of the SEC's Rules of Practice is the remedial tool that ensures accountability for audit quality and auditor independence. The SEC has the authority under federal law (17 C.F.R. § 201.102(e)(1)(ii)) to censure or temporarily or permanently deny accountants and auditors the privilege of appearing or practicing before the SEC if said professionals are engaged in improper professional conduct.

The SEC can also charge auditors with direct violations of the securities laws, including charging them with primary violations of the anti-fraud provisions of the securities laws in those somewhat rare situations where auditors commit fraud, or secondary violations where they aided and abetted or caused primary violations by others.

Section 10A of the Exchange Act (15 U.S.C. § 78j-1(b)(1)(B)) requires the auditor of a public company to investigate and report upwards to the SEC when they determine it is likely that an illegal act has occurred.

The Sarbanes-Oxley Act of 2002 established external, independent oversight for auditors of US public companies for the first time in history. The profession was previously self-regulated by its professional association, the AICPA. The PCAOB "enforce[s] compliance with [Sarbanes-Oxley], the rules of the [PCAOB], professional standards, and the securities laws relating to the preparation and issuance of audit reports."

The Sarbanes-Oxley Act gave the PCAOB four primary responsibilities: registration of accounting firms that audit public companies or SEC-registered brokers or dealers; inspection of registered public accounting firms; establishment of auditing, quality control, ethics, independence, and other standards for registered public accounting firms; and investigation and discipline of registered public accounting firms and their associated persons for violations of specified laws or professional standards (PCAOB 2017).

In April 2003, the PCAOB adopted preexisting standards established by the AICPA as its Interim Independence Standards and Interim Ethics Standards (PCAOB 2003), consisting of the independence standards described in the AICPA's Code of Professional Conduct Rules 101 and 102 and interpretations and rulings related to these standards in existence on April 16,

2003. The PCAOB Interim Independence Standards do not supersede the SEC's auditor independence rules, such as Rule 2–01 of Reg. S-X, 17 C.F.R.§ 210.2–01, so to the extent that a provision of the SEC's rule is more restrictive – or less restrictive – than the PCAOB's Interim Independence Standards, a registered public accounting firm must comply with the more restrictive rule.

In spite of the increased educational requirements, recent enforcement actions against certified public accountants at the largest global firms demonstrate the extent to which the accounting and audit industry has lost focus on ethical professionalism since 2000.

Examples of recent major ethical lapses by the audit profession

Insider trading

There have been several cases of insider trading by leadership-level, high-ranking partners in the largest global audit firms since the Sarbanes-Oxley Act of 2002. These cases should have shown that not only was such behavior illegal and unethical but that violators would be caught and punished.

However, the cases persist, including an increasing number of cases against lower-level CPAs, pressing even the most supportive of the profession to accept that CPAs – whether audit, tax, or consulting professionals – were never capitalist eunuchs, immune from market forces that tempt humans to choose self-interest over public duty and clients' interests.

On August 7, 2019, the SEC permanently barred Thomas W. Avent, Jr., an attorney and former partner at KPMG from 1999 and 2016, from appearing or practicing before the SEC as an attorney or accountant. The action is the result of a 2016 civil enforcement action against Avent, a CPA and attorney who led KPMG's mergers and acquisitions due diligence group and tipped his stockbroker, who in turn tipped his friend and other associates about three merger and acquisition transactions at Radiant Systems, Inc., Midas, Inc., and BrightPoint, Inc. Avent settled the charges by agreeing to pay a civil penalty of $125,000 but did not admit or deny the allegations. On August 14, 2019, jurors in Atlanta federal court found Avent's broker guilty of insider trading in advance of the three transactions based on the information he obtained from Avent (SEC 2019a).

On August 8, 2018, Lauren Zarsky and her mother, Dorothy Zarsky, settled in federal court (SEC 2018a) with the SEC for allegedly selling shares of a pharmaceutical company based on tips they received from Cameron Collins, the son of US Congressman Christopher Collins and Lauren Zarsky's fiancé. Representative Collins was himself a board member of the company. Lauren graduated from Villanova University in 2015 and invested in the company for the first time on June 20, 2017, buying 40,464 shares in a brokerage account she opened the previous day. Congressman Collins then tipped his son with material nonpublic information about the company's negative drug trial results, and Cameron divulged the information to Lauren at the home they shared. A few moments later, according to the SEC complaint in the case, Lauren sold the shares she had bought just two days before.

Lauren Zarsky did not admit or deny the charges but agreed to cough up her gains of $19,440, plus prejudgment interest of $839, and pay a civil penalty equal to her gains of $19,440 (SEC 2018a). Lauren, a CPA who worked until May 2018 at PricewaterhouseCoopers (PwC) as an assurance associate, is barred from appearing or practicing before the SEC as an accountant for five years, at which point she can apply for reinstatement.

In another case, Joseph Jennings (SEC 2018b), a 35-year-old CPA licensed since 2007 in Illinois and since 2013 in the state of New York, worked until March 2018 as a director at a "major accounting and auditing firm," according to the SEC's complaint. Jennings, formerly a director with PwC's transaction services practice, was charged with insider trading after he purchased 100 Kraft Foods Group, Inc. call options via a relative's brokerage account in March 2015 while in possession of material nonpublic information about a merger between Kraft and H.J. Heinz Company. After the merger was announced, Jennings's Kraft options increased in value by around $150,500.

In early June 2015, both Jennings and his relative who owned the account contacted the brokerage firm to instruct it to allow the Kraft options to expire without being exercised, but Jennings did not inform PwC that he controlled the account or that he had traded in Kraft securities in that account. This was ahead of July 2015, when the Financial Industry Regulatory Authority requested that PwC have employees identify individuals and entities with advance knowledge of the merger, a list which would have included Jennings' relative.

On August 20, 2018, the SEC settled an administrative charge with Jennings, who did not admit or deny the allegations but did agree to pay a $150,500 penalty on an installment basis over the next three years. He is barred from appearing before the SEC as an accountant for two years and thereafter can apply for reinstatement.

In April 2013, Scott London, a senior partner from KPMG who led its audit practice for the Pacific Southwest, was criminally charged with one count of conspiracy to commit securities fraud through insider trading. London pled guilty to providing confidential information about KPMG clients to a close friend of his, a crime that took place over a period of several years. That friend used this information to make highly profitable securities trades that generated more than $1 million in illegal proceeds (McKenna 2013).

London was sentenced to serve 14 months in prison but only served about eight months in prison, with the rest in home detention. In an interview with Francine McKenna in June 2018, London confirmed he "retired" from KPMG with his accrued benefits after he was indicted.

Deloitte was alerted by the Financial Industry Regulatory Authority (FINRA), the securities self-regulatory organization, about profitable trading activity by an audit firm partner that aligned with M&A activity at Deloitte audit and consulting clients. Tom Flanagan, a firm vice chairman and Chicago charity circuit regular, was trading on the inside information of several Fortune 500 companies, including Berkshire Hathaway (McKenna 2008).

Deloitte tax partner Arnold McClellan's wife lied to the FBI (McKenna 2010c) about her own involvement in insider trading on the confidential information about her husband's client's M&A targets by her sister and brother-in-law, James and Miranda Sanders of London. The in-laws made approximately $20 million by trading on information Annabel McClellan had allegedly heard by eavesdropping on her husband's phone calls when he discussed acquisition targets of clients Hellman & Friedman, McKesson, and Microsoft. McKesson and Microsoft are also Deloitte audit clients.

The SEC charged Arnold McClellan and his wife with providing advance notice of at least seven confidential acquisitions to Annabel's sister and brother-in-law. Annabel McClellan was sentenced to 11 months in federal prison after pleading guilty and paid a $1 million civil penalty to the SEC. The SEC dismissed the charges against her husband, who she said was innocent. Arnold McClellan currently works as a partner in the M&A Transaction Services practice at a mid-size firm in San Francisco.

Ernst & Young (EY) didn't discover that tax partner James Gansman was passing M&A tips to his lover, who, in turn, passed them to hers (Berkman 2009). It was Gansman's "swinging" partner who ended up on an SEC watch list because of her trading activity, and Gansman went to jail based on her testimony against him (McKenna 2011a). Gansman did not financially profit from his breach of client confidentiality.[5]

KPMG did have to resign as auditor from two of Scott London's clients, Herbalife and Skechers. In the Flanagan case, Deloitte paid for the necessary independent investigations to support the firm's claim to clients that it was still independent as an auditor (McKenna 2010b). None of the affected clients, including Berkshire Hathaway, Walgreens, and Sears Holdings, fired the firm.

The SEC and PCAOB have never fined or sanctioned the firms – PwC, KPMG, Deloitte, or EY – in any of these insider trading cases.

Auditor independence

Auditor independence is not a thing of the past, solved by the prohibited services provisions of the Sarbanes-Oxley Act of 2002.

The Big Four global audit firms have been publicly lobbying to repeal the auditor independence rules and additional prohibitions implemented by the Sarbanes-Oxley Act of 2002 for the last several years (McKenna 2017).

Jay Clayton's SEC proposed loosening auditor independence rules in December 2019, while in the United Kingdom, the Financial Reporting Council (FRC) has been issuing revised auditing standards aimed at strengthening auditor independence.

That is despite three significant SEC auditor independence enforcement actions in 2019, against PwC (SEC 2019d), RSM (SEC 2019b), and Deloitte in Japan (SEC 2019c), which suggests that the violations occurred because the largest global audit firms have insufficient governance and internal controls, policies, and procedures to prevent yearslong blatant violations of the post-Enron, post-Sarbanes-Oxley auditor independence rules.

The PwC case is particularly egregious. In September 2019, the SEC charged PwC with improper professional conduct that occurred between 2013 and 2016 in connection with 19 engagements on behalf of 15 SEC-registered issuers. The SEC alleged PwC had also violated auditor independence rules in connection with engagements for one issuer where the firm performed prohibited non-audit services. PwC was censured, agreed to several remedial activities, and was fined nearly $8,000,000.

The SEC also charged one PwC partner, Brandon Sprankle (SEC 2019e), with causing the firm's independence violations. Sprankle was barred for four years for appearing before the commission as an accountant and was fined $25,000.

The SEC sought to "modernize" auditor independence rules back in 2000, long before the Enron failure, Arthur Andersen's demise, and the passage of the Sarbanes-Oxley Act in 2002. The regulator's actions were a reaction to the growing concern that the global audit firms' increasing focus on consulting was distracting them from their core purpose: auditing.

In February 2000, Ernst & Young Consulting was sold to Cap Gemini. In February 2001, KPMG Consulting, later renamed BearingPoint, Inc., was floated with an IPO that had been delayed and repriced several times in order to wait for more favorable market conditions after the millennium change. In July 2001, Accenture, known as Andersen Consulting before its split from Arthur Andersen, also conducted a public share offering.

In June 2002, PwC's consulting arm announced it would change its name to "Monday" once it was spun off from parent firm PricewaterhouseCoopers LLP, a move that was expected later that summer. However, it instead attempted to sell the practice to HP, which ultimately failed, and then completed a transaction with IBM in October 2002.

Only Deloitte Consulting did not, in the end, separate from Deloitte & Touche. However, in July 2002, Deloitte Consulting of New York announced it would change its name to "Braxton" after a consulting firm Deloitte had purchased in 1984 called Braxton Associates.

"While our competitors are distancing themselves from their consulting roots, we are reaffirming our commitment to the profession," said Doug McCracken, chief executive officer of Deloitte Consulting at the time (McKenna 2006). Deloitte Consulting has grown significantly ever since.[6]

In approving significant updates to its auditor independence rules on February 5, 2001, the SEC said it was reacting to what it said was a "dramatic transformation" (SEC 2001). The mergers of several of the firms, resulting in much bigger firms domestically and internationally, had expanded international networks, creating even larger and more complex affiliations and marketing schemes under common names. The accounting firms had become "multi-disciplinary service organizations and are entering into new types of business relationships with their audit clients," the SEC commissioners wrote.

The increase in dual-career families and the trend toward audit clients hiring firm partners, professional staff, and their spouses for high-level management positions had necessitated new rules and an update of old ones. Accounting firms had expanded the services they offered to audit clients, and the list would continue to grow. Companies were turning to the auditors to perform their internal audit and their pension, financial, administrative, sales, data processing, and marketing functions, among many others.[7]

The SEC wrote,

> We remind registrants and accountants that auditor independence is not just a legal requirement. It is also a professional and ethical duty. That duty requires auditors to remain independent of audit clients,[8] and includes an obligation to "avoid situations that may lead outsiders to doubt [the auditors'] independence."[9]

Between 2002 and 2014, regulators demonstrated a laissez-faire attitude toward the conflicts presented by the firms' consulting practices, even after they started rebuilding them in 2007 (McKenna 2012b). There was no increase in regulatory scrutiny of auditor independence after the Sarbanes-Oxley Act was passed in 2002. The SEC and PCAOB rarely enforced any of the pre- or post-SOX auditor independence rules, making only a handful of minor enforcement actions primarily related to infractions that had occurred before the 2002 SOX service prohibitions were enacted.

Beginning in 2014, however, under the leadership of Chairwoman Mary Jo White, the SEC played catch-up on auditor independence issues.

In 2014, KPMG paid $8.2 million to settle SEC charges related to KPMG providing various non-audit services – including restructuring, corporate finance, and expert services – to an affiliate of one company that was an audit client. KPMG provided such prohibited non-audit services as bookkeeping and payroll to affiliates of another audit client. In a separate instance, KPMG hired an individual who had recently retired from a senior position at an affiliate of an audit client. KPMG then loaned him back to that affiliate to do the same work he had done as an employee of that affiliate, which resulted in the professional acting as a manager, employee, and advocate for the audit client. These services were prohibited by Rule 2–01 of Regulation S-X of the Securities Exchange Act of 1934.

In another violation, KPMG had hired an individual who had recently retired from a senior position at an affiliate of an audit client and then KPMG loaned him back to that affiliate to do the same work he had done as an employee. That is prohibited by Rule 2–01 of Regulation S-X of the Securities Exchange Act of 1934, a pre-Sarbanes-Oxley rule, because it resulted in the professional acting as a manager, employee, and advocate for the audit client.

The 2014 investigation also separately considered whether KPMG's independence was impaired by its practice of loaning non-manager tax professionals to assist audit clients on-site with tax compliance work performed under the direction and supervision of the clients' management, reportedly at its longstanding audit client GE (Weil 2014). The SEC did not bring an enforcement action against KPMG for the GE activities, which it did not name in its report on the investigation. It did note that, by their very nature, so-called "loaned staff arrangements" between auditors and audit clients appear inconsistent with pre-SOX Rule 2–01 of Regulation S-X, which prohibits auditors from acting as employees of their audit clients.[10]

The SEC brought an independence-related case against EY in 2014 for lobbying on behalf of audit clients (SEC 2014). Then, in 2015, the SEC brought cases against Grant Thornton and Deloitte for service by audit firm employees or affiliates on boards of their audit clients (SEC 2015a, 2015b).

In late 2014, the SEC sanctioned eight smaller public accounting firms for preparation of financial statements of brokerage firms who also were audit clients, another smaller firm for circumvention of the Sarbanes-Oxley Act lead audit partner rotation requirements and for indemnification provisions included in engagement letters, and another small firm for including indemnification provisions in its engagement letters (Ceresney 2016).

In 2016, the SEC brought more than one enforcement action against EY and several of its partners for close personal relationships between senior management at audit clients and senior engagement personnel. Sixteen years after the adoption of increased educational requirements intended to enhance ethical professionalism for auditors, the SEC brought its first-ever independence-related actions based on too-close personal relationships between auditors and audit clients.

In one case, according to the SEC's order, the EY audit partner maintained a close personal and romantic relationship with the chief accounting officer of the issuer (SEC 2016b). The coordinating partner on the engagement team was also aware of the possibility there was a romantic relationship but failed to follow up on the red flags.

In the second case, according the SEC's order, the EY audit partner had been asked to repair the firm's troubled relationship with the issuer, and so he developed a close personal friendship with the client's CFO that included spending extensive leisure time, including regular overnight, out-of-town trips and attendance at sporting events, both with the CFO and with the CFO's family, over three audit periods (SEC 2016a). These activities resulted in incurring more than $100,000 in entertainment expenses in connection with the client. EY was notified of the audit partner's excessive expenses but failed to take appropriate steps to determine whether these expenses were red flags signaling that the audit partner's independence was impaired.

The SEC concluded there was a systemic independence issue at EY and fined the firm over $9.3 million in combined disgorgement, interest, and penalties. The three firm partners collectively agreed to pay $95,000 in penalties and to be suspended from appearing or practicing before the SEC as accountants, with rights to apply for reinstatement after three years. The SEC also fined the client personnel.

The SEC and PCAOB do not address all allegations of violating longstanding auditor independence rules. These rules have been in force since pre-Sarbanes-Oxley. But violations continue long after their passage in spite of measures taken. The PCAOB has been on the job inspecting audit engagements and firms, and the professionals involved have been exposed to higher educational standards and more ethics education and compliance-monitoring activities, but these have done little to stymie independence issues.

Despite the number of auditor independence enforcement actions from the SEC and PCAOB since 2008, the violations continue, since the benefits of breaking the rules via the revolving door and the expansion of the firms' non-audit services practices outweigh the *de minimis* "cost of doing business" fines and sanctions regulators have so far imposed.

On August 26, 2016, PwC reached a confidential settlement mid-trial in the $5.5 billion negligence case brought against the firm by the Taylor, Bean & Whitaker Plan Trust in 2012 (Raymond 2016). Taylor, Bean & Whitaker and Colonial Bank, its partner in fraud, both went bankrupt in 2009, and executives from both companies were jailed.

During the trial, Lynn Turner, a former chief accountant for the SEC and a witness for the plaintiffs, testified that PwC had violated auditor independence standards after one of the PwC senior managers, T. Brent Hicks, was hired by Colonial in a top financial oversight position. Turner testified that, as a result, PwC was not independent in 2005 and 2006. PwC tried to suppress Turner's testimony, but the court denied the motion to suppress the testimony.

That was not the only potential independence violation mentioned during the trial. The court also determined pretrial that PwC was not independent, "as a matter of law," for audit year 2004 because a contract between PwC and a Colonial subsidiary included prohibited indemnification language, a violation of SEC rules.

Finally, after PwC objected, the judge prevented testimony about a third potential independence violation for the 2008 audit. Hicks, the former Colonial accounting chief and PwC audit team member, is currently the senior vice president at BB&T Bank, another PwC audit client.

A federal judge decided on July 2, 2018, that PricewaterhouseCoopers LLP must pay $625 million to the Federal Deposit Insurance Corporation in the case of *Colonial BancGroup Inc. and the FDIC v. PwC*, in the largest-ever judgment against an audit firm in the United States. The award was intended to compensate the FDIC for its losses as the receiver of Colonial, a crisis-era bankruptcy.

On March 15, 2019, the FDIC said it had agreed to settle the professional negligence claims it brought related to the audits of Colonial Bank with PwC for $335 million, dropping its remaining claim against the firms and preempting PwC's potential appeal.

The SEC and PCAOB have never publicly acknowledged an investigation of these alleged independence violations, and no disciplinary action ever occurred, for the firm or for any of the individuals.

The war against the PCAOB and KPMG's theft of regulatory data

Partners from the largest global audit firms backdate and fabricate workpaper documents, lie to regulators, and, now, allegedly conspire to steal regulatory inspection data to "cheat the exam."

The audit firms have resisted the authority of the new regulator, the PCAOB, since its establishment. They have publicly embarrassed the PCAOB and have openly disagreed with it (McKenna 2007, 2010a). The animosity of the largest global audit firms toward the PCAOB by partners all over the world, but in particular in the United States, has been palpable. Outside of the United States, the PCAOB recently notched enforcement orders for a rash of subversive actions against it by Big Four member firms (McKenna 2016).

In December 2015, *Reuters* reported that the Big Four used the Center for Audit Quality to meet to undermine then-PCAOB Chairman James Doty. Representatives of several big firms criticized Doty by utilizing a meeting of a PCAOB advisory group at the CAQ. "He's beating up on our profession, this has to stop," *Reuters* reported one firm leader complaining (Levinson 2015).

But no one anticipated that resentment against the PCAOB's regulatory activities would result in civil enforcement actions and criminal indictments for the theft of regulator data allegedly used in subverting the audit inspection process.

In April 2017, KPMG announced that it had fired five senior partners, including the head of its audit practice and members of its national office, after it determined that the firm had improperly obtained information about which audits its regulator planned to inspect. The PCAOB also fired one employee who media reports at the time alleged was a leaker.

KPMG's statement said that it had learned in late February 2017, from an internal source, "that an individual who had joined KPMG from the PCAOB subsequently received confidential information from a then-employee of the PCAOB, and shared that information with other KPMG personnel. That information potentially undermined the integrity of the regulatory process" (KPMG 2017).

KPMG said it immediately reported the situation to the PCAOB and the SEC, and that it retained outside counsel to investigate. It learned through its investigation that the six KPMG individuals either had improper advance warnings of engagements to be inspected by the PCAOB, or else were aware that others had received such advance warnings and had failed to properly report the situation in a timely manner.

On January 22, 2018, the SEC and the US Department of Justice announced civil and criminal charges against five former KPMG executives – two of whom had previously been working for the PCAOB – and one more former PCAOB professional who was still employed at the regulator when the KPMG whistleblower came forward.

SEC Chairman Jay Clayton immediately put out an optimistic statement intended to calm markets about potential tainted or late audits and prevent the panicked dropping of KPMG by clients.

> Based on discussions with the SEC staff, I do not believe that today's actions against these six individuals will adversely affect the ability of SEC registrants to continue to use audit reports issued by KPMG in filings with the Commission or for investors to rely upon those required reports. I do not expect that these actions will adversely affect the orderly flow of financial information to investors and the US capital markets, including the filing of audited financial statements with the Commission.
>
> *(McKenna 2007)*

In the statement in January 2017 announcing it had terminated the partners (KPMG 2017), KPMG said they had violated the firm's code of conduct, titled "Our Promise of Professionalism" (KPMG 2018).

The US Department of Justice's criminal indictments say that the three former PCAOB personnel, all CPAs, had violated Sarbanes-Oxley rules about sharing confidential regulatory information.

> SOX commands that the rules of the PCAOB (the "PCAOB Rules"), among other things, establish ethics rules and standards of conduct for Board members and staff. The PCAOB Rules are subject to the approval of the SEC. SOX also provides that a violation of a PCAOB rule shall be treated as a violation of the Securities Exchange Act of 1934 (the "Exchange Act") or rules issued pursuant to the Exchange Act, and that any person violating PCAOB Rules will be subject to the same penalties applied to a violation of the Exchange Act. One rule promulgated by the PCAOB as part of its ethics code and approved by the SEC, is Ethics Code 9 ("EC 9"), which is entitled "Nonpublic Information." EC 9 states: Unless authorized by the Board, no Board member or staff shall disseminate or otherwise disclose any information obtained in

the course and scope of his or her employment, and which has not been released, announced, or otherwise made available publicly.

(United States v. Middendorf 2018)

Brian Sweet, who moved from the PCAOB to a direct-entry partner role with KPMG, settled charges with the SEC and pleaded guilty to the criminal allegations and cooperated with the government in bringing the original civil and criminal charges. On October 30, 2018, former KPMG partner Thomas Whittle changed his plea to guilty from not guilty on all five criminal counts in the case of the alleged use of stolen confidential regulator information to subvert KPMG's regulatory inspection process. Whittle also agreed to cooperate with the government.

Also in October 2018, Cynthia Holder, who also was hired from the PCAOB to KPMG, pleaded guilty to conspiracy to defraud the United States as well as to wire fraud.

On March 11, 2019, David Middendorf, KPMG's former national managing partner for audit quality and professional practice, was convicted by a federal court in Manhattan of four of five criminal charges in the case, including conspiracy and wire fraud, after a trial. Jeffrey Wada, a former employee of the PCAOB, was also convicted on three of four charges, including conspiracy and wire fraud.

David Britt, former co-leader of KPMG's Banking and Capital Markets Group, pleaded guilty in late 2019. He is awaiting sentencing.

In June of 2019 the SEC fined KPMG $50 million for violating securities laws related to the actions of the four partners and one executive who faced civil and criminal charges for stealing the PCAOB inspection data (SEC 2019f).

But in a surprise development no one anticipated, the SEC's enforcement order said that during the investigation of the PCAOB data theft, it had uncovered an even more widespread ethics and standards test-cheating scandal that went on longer than even the PCAOB-related scheme and pervaded the firm's entire US audit practice. KPMG professionals, including senior partners in leadership positions, were caught sharing answers to SEC-mandated tests involving ethics, integrity, and compliance over a number of years.

No one at KPMG had ever reported the test cheating to the firm's ethics hotline, unlike the PCAOB scheme, which was halted by a female partner who blew the whistle to the firm's lawyers.

Three more partners have now been sanctioned for the test-cheating scandal (SEC 2020).

There has been no news of any investigation into whether the same type of activity could have occurred at another firm (McKenna 2018).

The KPMG/PCAOB scandal is the latest in a long line of breaches of ethical conduct by KPMG, including violating auditor independence rules after the passage of the Sarbanes-Oxley law in 2002 and in the last 18 years since the 150-hour proposal became effective in 2000.

In 2005, in the largest criminal tax case ever filed at the time, KPMG admitted that it had engaged in tax fraud, one that generated at least $11 billion dollars in fake tax losses that, according to court filings, cost the United States at least $2.5 billion dollars in taxes that were evaded. KPMG's former deputy chairman and two former heads of KPMG's tax practice were indicted.

A jury convicted two of the former KPMG executives – former KPMG tax partner Robert Pfaff and former KPMG senior tax manager John Larson – on multiple counts of tax evasion and acquitted former KPMG tax partner David Greenberg on the five counts of tax evasion he had faced. US District Judge Lewis A. Kaplan in Manhattan dismissed 13 more former KPMG executives from the case after finding prosecutors had violated their rights to counsel by putting undue pressure on KPMG not to pay their legal defense costs.

The prosecution of the criminal charge against KPMG was deferred until December 31, 2006, after KPMG agreed to pay $456 million in fines, restitution, and penalties. The penalty included $100 million in civil fines for failure to register the tax shelters with the IRS; $128 million in criminal fines representing disgorgement of fees earned by KPMG on the four shelters; and $228 million in criminal restitution "representing lost taxes to the IRS as a result of KPMG's intransigence in turning over documents and information to the IRS that caused the statute of limitations to run," according to the IRS press release announcing the settlement (IRS 2005).

After KPMG's deferred prosecution agreement expired on December 31, 2006, a US district judge approved a request by the US Attorney for the Southern District of New York to drop the criminal case against KPMG relating to the alleged tax fraud, since according to prosecutors, KPMG had complied with terms of its agreement with the government.

Researchers found that the deferred prosecution had no impact on KPMG's audit practice (Baugh et al. 2019). Specifically, their results suggest that the audit quality for KPMG clients did not change between the pre-probation and probation periods. KPMG was able to effectively insulate the firm's audit practice from its tax practice, according to the researchers.

Prior to the tax fraud prosecution, KMPG had not been alone in marketing illegal tax shelters. All of the Big Four firms had been aggressively hiring tax lawyers to expand their tax services by developing and marketing tax shelters as investment strategies to their clients since the late 1990s (Bryan-Low 2003; Kahn 2003; Rostain 2006). If there had been no inside whistleblower at KPMG to provide sufficient details to the US government for a prosecution, KPMG would likely not have been singled out among the Big Four firms (Baugh et al. 2019).

Additional issues at KPMG have also come to light in the wake of the SEC's investigation of the PCAOB data theft. The SEC fined KPMG $50 million in June of 2019 for violating securities laws related to the actions of the four partners and one executive who faced civil and criminal charges for stealing the inspection data.

But the SEC's investigation uncovered an even more widespread ethics and standards test-cheating scandal that went on longer than the PCAOB-related scheme and pervaded the firm's entire US audit practice. KPMG professionals, including senior partners in leadership positions, were caught sharing answers to SEC-mandated tests involving ethics, integrity, and compliance over a number of years.

The SEC made a point to say that, unlike the PCAOB scheme, which was halted by a partner who blew the whistle to the firm's lawyers, no one at KPMG had ever reported the test cheating to the firm's ethics hotline.

In combination with the PCAOB scandal, this new scandal further mars the reputation of KPMG, a firm already under fire for audit failures all over the world, but also jeopardizes the Big Four's overall professional credibility as a competent judge of financial statement integrity on behalf of capital markets.

The Big Four contradicted itself on professionalism when defending overtime lawsuits

Even unlicensed CPAs now hold jobs that require a graduate degree, similar to an extended course of specialized study like law or medicine. Accounting is now eligible to be considered a "learned" profession, allowing judges in the future to interpret that as allowing an exemption to overtime for unlicensed associates under state and federal law (McKenna 2011b).

Jason Campbell; Sarah Sobek; et al., v. PricewaterhouseCoopers, LLP (Campbell et al. 2011) was the first overtime case to reach the class certification stage against one of the Big Four accounting firms. Kershaw, Cutter & Ratinoff's Bill Kershaw, who represented the plaintiffs, was quoted by CFO.com at the time regarding the rationale for bringing the case:

> For years, the Big Four accounting firms have ignored Federal and State laws mandating the payment of overtime to unlicensed accountants. This is in stark contrast to smaller accounting firms, many of whom comply with California's overtime law and pay overtime to their unlicensed associates as non-exempt employees.
>
> *(Taub 2007)*

California's 2001 Wage Order, the prevailing statute in this case, has professional exemption for overtime. The professional exemption is provided to a person employed in a professional capacity, which means any employee who is licensed or certified by the state of California and is primarily engaged in the practice of one of the following recognized professions: law, medicine, dentistry, optometry, architecture, engineering, teaching, or accounting, or who is primarily engaged in an occupation commonly recognized as a learned or artistic profession.

The audit firms defended themselves against the overtime lawsuits by testifying that unlicensed auditors are not eligible for overtime because they meet an "administrative" exemption. This exemption, in California (n.d.) for example, is defined as any employee:

> California, §11040. Order Regulating Wages, Hours, and Working Conditions in Professional, Technical, Clerical, Mechanical, and Similar Occupations

(a) Whose duties and responsibilities involve either:

  (i) The performance of office or non-manual work directly related to management policies or general business operations of his/her employer or his/her employer's customers; or

  (ii) The performance of functions in the administration of a school system, or educational establishment or institution, or of a department or subdivision thereof, in work directly related to the academic instruction or training carried on therein; and

(b) Who customarily and regularly exercises discretion and independent judgment; and

(c) Who regularly and directly assists a proprietor, or an employee employed in a bona fide executive or administrative capacity (as such terms are defined for purposes of this section); or

(d) Who performs under only general supervision work along specialized or technical lines requiring special training, experience, or knowledge; or

(e) Who executes under only general supervision special assignments and tasks; and

(f) Who is primarily engaged in duties that meet the test of the exemption.

In April 2011, KPMG asserted this same administrative exemption as a defense to the overtime case filed against it in the federal district court in New York in *Pippins v. KPMG*. Orrick, Herrington & Sutcliffe, the law firm defending KPMG in the Litchfield case, an overtime case in Washington State, is the same firm that defended PwC at the district court stage in *Campbell v. PwC*.

The Code of Federal Regulations explains an important component of the administrative exemption – the exercise of discretion and independent judgment – more fully:

> § 541.202 Discretion and independent judgment
>
>   To qualify for the administrative exemption, an employee's primary duty must include the exercise of discretion and independent judgment with respect to matters of

significance. In general, the exercise of discretion and independent judgment involves the comparison and the evaluation of possible courses of conduct, and acting or making a decision after the various possibilities have been considered. The term "matters of significance" refers to the level of importance or consequence of the work performed.

There are two reasons that arguing the administrative exemption for audit associates is contrary to public policy.

First, more than one judge has cited the California code to the audit firms to explain that expecting audit associates to perform "office or non-manual work directly related to management policies or general business operations of . . . his/her employer's customers" is contrary to auditor independence rules (Campbell 2009).

In the overtime case against KPMG in Washington State court, *Litchfield v. KPMG*, the judge concluded the following:

> The independence rules of the accounting profession as a matter of law preclude accountants performing work on audit engagements from qualifying for the administrative exemption.
>
> *(Litchfield 2010)*

The second is that when audit firms say they expect entry-level professionals to "exercise discretion and independent judgment with respect to matters of significance," they perpetuate a performance requirement that contradicts PCAOB Auditing Standards.

The PCAOB's Auditing Standards say that as the risk of material misstatement increases, the supervision of engagement team members by partners should increase. When "matters" become "material," the entry-level audit associates are not supposed to be going it alone.

Firms must create policies and procedures that provide it

> with reasonable assurance that, among other things, (1) those hired possess the appropriate characteristics to enable them to perform competently, and (2) work is assigned to personnel having the degree of technical training and proficiency required in the circumstances. PCAOB standards further provide that the more able and experienced the personnel assigned to an engagement are, the less direct supervision is needed.
>
> *(PCAOB 2011)*

In February 2015, after several years of litigation, the Campbell case was settled before trial, and PwC's defenses that contradicted PCAOB standards were never aired in open court.

In May 2018, a US Supreme Court decision eliminated much of the risk of class action overtime lawsuits when, in *Ernst & Young v. Morris*, the court reversed the Ninth Circuit, holding that under the Arbitration Act, agreements to arbitrate must be enforced. The Big Four has been requiring for a while that new hires sign arbitration agreements that waive the right to bring class action litigation against the firms. The agreements also have a waiver against any concerted action, preventing employees from initiating or joining any class action or collective action proceedings against the company in any forum.

Orrick,[11] the law firm that represented PwC in the Campbell overtime class action case in California, is ironically one of the large national law firms that have been pressured by law schools, on behalf of their students, to abandon mandatory arbitration clauses for its new law firm hires. Master's of accounting students do not get the same support from their universities when the firms come to recruit.

The growth of MAcc programs and the ethics of the 150-hour rule

The nationwide implementation of the 150-hour rule emboldened the Big Four firms to begin to insist that university accounting programs develop and implement graduate degree programs as a condition of recruitment of the students. Requiring all entry-level auditors to take a "course of specialized study" made public accounting more like law or medicine, "learned" professions that are often automatically considered exempt from overtime (McKenna 2011b). Requiring a master's of accounting (MAcc) graduate degree for entry-level positions gives the Big Four a much better chance of meeting the legal requirement for overtime exemption for unlicensed associates.

The AICPA's website says students do not necessarily have to get a master's degree to meet the 150-hour requirements. "They can meet the requirement at the undergraduate level or get a bachelor's degree and take some courses at the graduate level," the website says. However, "in most cases, the additional academic work needed to acquire the technical competence and develop the skills required by today's CPA is best obtained at the graduate level" (AICPA n.d.a "150 Hour Requirement").

In May 2018, when US Supreme Court decision eliminated much of the risk of class action overtime lawsuits in the *Ernst & Young v. Morris* decision, the MAcc programs were well established.[12] Until 1993, MAcc degrees awarded were approximately 10% of the total bachelor's and master's degrees awarded in accounting. MAccs grew to account for approximately 25% of the total degrees awarded by 2017, according to the AICPA's Trends Report (AICPA 2017).

However, projected master's enrollments declined in the 2015–2016 period, returning to pre-2014 levels after an influx of master's enrollments and graduates in the last several years.

No state requires a master's degree for CPA licensure. Most states also allow the CPA exam to be taken after 120 units (and usually at least at least a bachelor's degree), but 150 hours must be completed for licensure. Both California and New York, for example, were relatively late adopters of the 150-hour rule. Compared to Texas, where a tradition had developed for students to automatically stay for five years at the same school where they received their undergraduate degree and proceed directly into the master's degree program, the global public accounting firms in New York and California, for example, allowed students to finish the remaining 30 hours somehow before starting full-time.

Universities that educate prospective CPAs generally prefer the 150-hour requirement because it drives expansion of accounting programs, adding another year of tuition revenue for a now-mandatory program for nearly anyone who wants to work in public accounting.

In many cases, the programs draw primarily from the same school's undergraduate accounting or business program.

Accounting faculty generally also enjoy MAcc programs, as they can add graduate teaching experience to CVs, too. The 150-hour campaign was a long but successful one and was always supported strongly by academics, who believed the accounting profession deserved more prestige. Experienced faculty are also now in demand. Accounting student enrollments have risen almost every year since 1999, but enrollments in accounting PhD programs have not, leading to a shortage of full-time faculty, according to the *Journal of Accountancy* (Bishop et al. 2016).

A new CPA exam, launched in April 2017, is modeled after the bar exam for lawyers – it is intended to encompass everything you need to know to start practicing once you pass it. Technology enhancements announced in January 2018 are intended to "make the Exam more closely resemble the professional tools and business environment a CPA would experience in their everyday work life" (AICPA 2018).

The exam covers "ethics, professional responsibilities and general principles" in the audit and attestation section; these topics take up about 15–25% of the questions in that section. Ethics requirements for licensure vary by state and are not universal. Alabama, Georgia, Louisiana, North and South Dakota, and Wisconsin, for example, have no ethics requirements for licensure (JN CPE Courses n.d.).

Many students now attempt to pass the CPA exam before even starting full-time at a firm after graduation. That goal is aided by the longer time they spend in school, given the 150-hour requirement and the increasing number of internships they can do – up to four if they start interning after their first undergraduate year. Internships are relatively well paid and eligible for overtime, unlike the eventual full-time job.

Master's degree holders peaked in 2014–15 and are still not a majority of accounting degrees awarded. The supply of graduates and demand from US CPA firms were both going down as of 2018 (AICPA 2019). The absolute number and percentage of master's degree holders hired by the CPA firms peaked in 2014 at about 42% of total hires, dropping to about 36% in 2018.

Given the economic impact on all businesses of the 2019-–20 coronavirus pandemic, the downward trend for 2019 is expected to continue.

The last frontier – the firm-sponsored MAcc

The connection between the firms and graduate education programs has now taken its ultimate step – firm-sponsored programs and students.

The KPMG Master of Accounting with Data and Analytics Program was a first-of-its-kind collaboration with The Ohio State University Max M. Fisher College of Business and the Villanova University School of Business. Fifty-one students sponsored by KPMG (who paid tuition, room and board, and some other expenses) were accepted to the program and began their studies at those two schools in the fall of 2017.

In return for allowing a branded program at their school, KPMG says it "provides each school with access to proprietary KPMG technologies that integrate easily into its academic programs" (KPMG 2020). The program has since expanded and, as of June 2020, is in operation at nine more universities.

The students work as interns on KPMG audit or tax teams and will join KPMG's audit or tax practices through an advanced entry program upon graduation. Applicants must first apply one year before their undergraduate degree is completed and then be accepted by KPMG. Following this, they can apply to the schools partnered with KPMG.

Program participants must remain employed at KPMG for three years after graduation to avoid a requirement for full reimbursement of all costs. Only time will tell if these golden handcuffs have a chilling effect on audit professionals reporting firm or client wrongdoing, potentially risking retaliatory terminations, or leaving an untenable situation in the first three years, since in either case they would be required to pay back what they were granted for MAcc program tuition and expenses.

If not more education, then what can ensure ethical conduct?

In an interview with the New York State CPA Association (Gaetano 2014), KPMG's inside trader Scott London said:

> I took the ethics and compliance training for about 20 some odd years and I knew it – it was ingrained my head. I understood the independence rules, ethics and so forth. I was also in a position of having had to deal with noncompliance in my own firm, with people who had inadvertent independence issues, like taking out a loan from a bank that's a client – that's a serious independence violation.
>
> I guess it was more perception over substance, though. I understood the rules, but there was just a complete lack of consideration of those rules when I did what I did. I knew those rules, I understood them, but I still allowed my professional standards to be lowered to do what I did, and almost every day I think, "What the hell was I thinking – I know better!"

Will more credit hours, especially if the additional requirements include more ethics training, make auditors more professional and therefore more ethical? The discussion and evidence in this chapter says not necessarily.

So how can we ensure present and future auditors fulfill the "Promise of Professionalism" to the public, the capital markets, investors, their firms, and their fellow professionals, including ethical professionalism?

The largest global audit firms operate with impunity because of the implied "too few to fail" doctrine established when the US Attorney General decided not to indict KPMG for the 2005 tax shelter frauds. The implosion of Arthur Andersen in 2001 did not scare the firms and professionals into honorable behavior; instead, it created a general fear in prosecutorial circles of guilty pleas and severe punishment, lest that prosecutor be responsible for ruining a man's reputation or putting a firm out of business, with the attendant loss of jobs and potential systemic impact on the economy and markets.[13]

No regulator is willing to sue or sanction a global audit firm if the enforcement means the firm will legally, or practically, become unable to continue to perform its mandated primary business – audit. The US Department of Justice guaranteed that moral hazard going forward with its choice to not criminally prosecute KPMG.

The KPMG tax shelter scandal also brought regulators to the uncomfortable realization that there is no contingency plan for the failure of a global audit firm, either. There is then no strategy, and there is a paralyzing fear of economic damage if a regulator anywhere in the world determines a particular member firm is corrupt beyond repair or a private plaintiff sends a member firm into collapse by imposing a catastrophic legal judgment.

The audit firms and their professionals will continue to push the envelope on legality, ethics, and self-interest with impunity. There is no longer sufficient "professional" disdain for reputation risk to act as a restraint on conflicts of interest by the firms and by the accounting profession. Only more significant civil and criminal penalties to deter self-interested behavior – including jail terms for firm executives – will fully deter more unprofessional acts.

The Roman satirist Juvenal asked, "Sed, quis custodiet ipsos custodes?"

But who guards the guardians?

Certainly not their own professional standards anymore.

Notes

1 In 2017, members of the Chartered Institute of Management Accountants, CIMA, and the American Institute of Certified Public Accountants formed the Association of International Certified Professional Accountants "to unite and strengthen the accounting profession globally. Representing an influential network of more than 667,000 members . . ." (AICPA n.d. "Quick Facts").

2 Not much, unfortunately, changed. Sarbanes-Oxley, enacted by Congress "to enhance corporate responsibility, enhance financial disclosures and combat corporate and accounting fraud," was a failure. Sarbanes-Oxley has not restored investor confidence in audit companies (McKenna 2012a).

3 Licensing raises entry costs into a profession by imposing a fee as well as training requirements. That shifts the short-run and long-run supply curves upward and left (Maurizi 1974).

4 Several other studies about other occupations have provided empirical evidence on how occupational licensure reduces supply (Shepard 1984; Carroll and Gaston 1981).

5 Recently Gansman won a court case against his ex-wife, who sought a bigger share of the value of a $4.75 million Manhattan apartment where they used to live. The court reduced her share from 75% to 60%, saying that "the husband's adulterous conduct is not sufficiently egregious and shocking to the conscience to justify making an unequal distribution of the marital home" (Marsh 2017).

6 "Since 2012, the firms' combined global revenue from consulting and other advisory work has risen 44%, compared with just 3% growth from auditing. The result is that the bulk of the firms' revenue now comes from consulting and advisory, $56 billion last year, compared to only $47 billion from auditing. Five years earlier, auditing pulled in roughly the same amount – $46 billion – while consulting and advisory's haul was only $39 billion" (Rapoport 2018).

7 In its footnote to the final rule in February 2001, the SEC cited Beverly Gordon, "KPMG Spies Rapid Growth in 'Shared Services,'" *Accounting Today*, at 12 (June 3, 1996); "KPMG Restructures to Reposition Outsourcing," *Public Accounting Report*, at 1 (May 15, 1996); websites of Deloitte & Touche (www.deloitte.com) and KPMG (www.us.kpmg.com). [Need Reference items for Accounting Today, Public Accounting Report]

8 In 2001, the SEC cited AICPA SAS No. 1, AU § 220.03; AICPA Code of Professional Conduct, ET § 101. Of course, accountants also have to comply with applicable state law on independence.

9 In 2001, the SEC cited AICPA SAS No. 1, AU § 220.03

10 PwC eventually took over the tax co-sourcing arrangement for GE. In a twist, PwC bought the employees and is loaning them back to GE (Rapoport 2017).

11 Orrick is among a few firms that have since made arbitration optional for non-partners (Tribe 2018).

12 "Congress has instructed in the Arbitration Act that arbitration agreements providing for individualized proceedings must be enforced, and neither the Arbitration Act's saving clause nor the NLRA suggests otherwise" (*Ernst & Young v. Morris* 2018).

13 "Andersen was already collapsing because it had shredded its own reputation, but the business community and the corporate defense bar played up the idea that an overzealous prosecution had put thousands of people out of work. Bigwig defense lawyers like Mary Jo White (future chair of the SEC) claimed that Andersen proved that the Justice Department should go easier on companies" (Kwak 2017).

References

ACAP (Advisory Committee on the Auditing Profession to the US Department of the Treasury). 2007 (Posted). "Prepared Testimony by Dr. Joseph V. Carcello, Ph.D., CPA, CIA, CMA)." Washington, DC: US Department of the Treasury. Accessed March 7, 2012. https://www.treasury.gov/about/organizational-structure/offices/Documents/Carcello%20Oral%20Statement%2012-03-07.pdf.

ACAP (Advisory Committee on the Auditing Profession to the US Department of the Treasury). 2008. "Final Report." www.treasury.gov/about/organizational-structure/offices/Documents/final-report.pdf.

AICPA (Association of International Certified Public Accountants). 2003. "Background Information on the 150-hour Education Requirement for CPA Certification and Licensure."

AICPA. 2017. "2017 Trends in the Supply of Accounting Graduates and the Demand for Public Accounting Recruits." www.aicpa.org/InterestAreas/AccountingEducation/NewsAndPublications/DownloadableDocuments/2017-trends-report.pdf.

AICPA (Association of International Certified Public Accountants). 2018. "AICPA Announces New CPA Exam User Experience is Coming." Durham, NC: AICPA. https://www.aicpa.org/press/pressreleases/2018/aicpa-announces-new-cpa-exam-user-experience-is-coming.html.

AICPA. 2019. "2019 Trends in the Supply of Accounting Graduates and the Demand for Public Accounting Recruits." www.aicpa.org/content/dam/aicpa/interestareas/accountingeducation/newsandpublications/downloadabledocuments/2019-trends-report.pdf.

AICPA. n.d. a. "150 Hour Requirement for Obtaining a CPA License." Accessed June 16, 2020. www.aicpa.org/becomeacpa/licensure/requirements.html.

AICPA. n.d. "Quick Facts." Accessed June 16, 2020. www.aicpa-cima.com/about-us/quick-facts.html.

Akerlof, George A. 1970. "The Market for 'Lemons': Quality Uncertainty and the Market Mechanism." *The Quarterly Journal of Economics* 84 (3) (August): 488–500. www.jstor.org/stable/1879431.

Allen, Arthur, and Angela M. Woodland. 2006. "The 150-Hour Requirement and the Number of CPA Exam Candidates, Pass Rates, and the Number Passing." *Issues in Accounting Education* 21 (3): 173–93. doi:10.2308/iace.2006.21.3.173.

Appearance and Practice Before the Commission, 17 CFR § 201.102 (2000).

Audit Requirements, 15 U.S.C. § 78j – 1 (2011).

Barrios, John Manuel. 2019. "Occupational Licensing and Accountant Quality: Evidence from the 150-Hour Rule." Becker Friedman Institute for Research in Economics Working Paper No. 2018–32.

Baugh, Matthew, Jeff P. Boone, Inder K. Khurana, and K. K. Raman. 2019. "Did the 2005 Deferred Prosecution Agreement Adversely Impact KPMG's Audit Practice?" *AUDITING: A Journal of Practice & Theory* 38 (1): 77–102. doi:10.2308/ajpt-52015.

Berkman, Dennis K. 2009. "Insider Affair: An SEC Trial of the Heart." *The Wall Street Journal*, July 28, 2009. www.wsj.com/articles/SB124873671770285097.

Bishop, Carol C., Douglas M. Boyle, Brian W. Carpenter, and Dana R. Hermanson. 2016. "Transitioning into Academia: A New Pathway for Practitioners." *Journal of Accountancy*, March 1, 2016. www.journalofaccountancy.com/issues/2016/mar/accounting-professor-pathways.html.

Bryan-Low, C. 2003. "Accounting Firms Aim to Dispel Cloud of Corporate Fraud." *Wall Street Journal* 27.

Campbell v. Price Waterhouse Coopers, LLP, 602 F. Supp. 2d 1163 – Dist. Court, ED California 2009. See also Cal.Code Regs. tit. 8, § 11040(1)(A)(2)(a)(I).

Campbell, Jason, Sarah Sobek, et al. 2011. Plaintiffs – Appellees, v. PricewaterhouseCoopers, LLP, Defendant – Appellant, United States Court of Appeals, Ninth Circuit, No. 09–16370. June 15, 2011.Carroll, Sidney L., and Robert J. Gaston. 1981. "Occupational Restrictions and the Quality of Service Received: Some Evidence." *Southern Economic Journal* 47 (4): 959–76. doi:10.2307/1058155.

Ceresney, Andrew. 2016. "The SEC Enforcement Division's Focus on Auditors and Auditing." American Law Institute Conference on Accountants' Liability 2016: Confronting Enforcement and Litigation Risks, September 22, 2016. www.sec.gov/news/speech/ceresney-enforcement-focus-on-auditors-and-auditing.html#_ftn62.

DCOPLA (District of Columbia Board of Accountancy). n.d. "Educational Requirements – CPA Examination." Accessed June 16, 2020. www.dcopla.com/accountancy/wp-content/uploads/sites/5/2018/03/Educational-Requirements-CPA-Examination-1.pdf.

Ernst & Young v. Morris, 584 U.S. __ (2018).

Friedman, Milton. 1962. *Price Theory*. Chicago, IL: Aldine.

Gaetano, Chris. 2014. "Former KPMG Partner Scott London Talks Insider Trading Conviction." *The New York State Society of CPAs*, July 7, 2014. www.nysscpa.org/news/publications/the-trusted-professional/article/former-kpmg-partner-scott-london-talks-insider-trading-conviction.

IRS (Internal Revenue Service). 2005. "KPMG to Pay $456 Million for Criminal Violations." News Release IR-2005–83, August 29, 2005. www.irs.gov/newsroom/kpmg-to-pay-456-million-for-criminal-violations.

Jacob, John, and Dennis Murray. 2006. "Supply-side Effects of the 150-hour Educational Requirement for CPA Licensure." *Journal of Regulatory Economics* 30 (2): 159–78.

JN CPE Courses. n.d. "State Ethics CPE Requirements." Accessed June 16, 2020. https://jncpe.com/state-ethics-cpe-requirements/.

Kahn, Jeffrey H. 2003. "Tax Reality Bites." *Tax Notes* 100: 1196. https://ssrn.com/abstract=694825.

KPMG (KPMG LLP). 2017. "KPMG Removes Audit Personnel, Including Head of Audit Practice." Press Release, April 11, 2017. https://home.kpmg/us/en/home/insights/2017/04/kpmg-removes-audit-personnel-including-head-of-audit-practice.html.

KPMG (KPMG LLP). 2018. "KPMG Code of Conduct: Our Promise of Professionalism." https://home.kpmg/content/dam/kpmg/us/pdf/2018/02/kpmg-code-of-conduct-latest.pdf.

KPMG (KPMG LLP). 2020. "Frequently Asked Questions – KPMG Master of Accounting with Data and Analytics Program." https://kpmgcampus.com/portal/32/assets/files/MADA_FAQ_External_WEB_FINAL.pdf.

Kwak, James. 2017. "America's Top Prosecutors Used to Go After Top Executives. What Changed?" Review of *The Chickenshit Club*, by Jesse Eisinger. *The New York Times*, July 5, 2017. www.nytimes.com/2017/07/05/books/review/the-chickenshit-club-jesse-eisinger-.html.

Levinson, Charles. 2015. "Accounting Industry and SEC Hobble America's Audit Watchdog." *Reuters*, December 16, 2015. www.reuters.com/investigates/special-report/usa-accounting-PCAOB/.

Litchfield v. KPMG LLP, No. 2:2007cv00722 (W.D. Wash. 2007).

Litchfield v. KPMG LLP, No. 07-2-11179-4 SEA (Wash. Super. Ct., 2010).

Madison, R. L., and N. R. Meonske. 1991. "150 Semester Hours: The Train Has Not Left the Station." *Woman CPA* 53: 53–56.

Marsh, Julia. 2017. "Hubby Whose Cheating wasn't 'Shocking' Wins Bigger Cut of Park Ave. Pad." *New York Post*, November 14, 2017. https://nypost.com/2017/11/14/hubby-whose-cheating-wasnt-shocking-wins-bigger-cut-of-park-ave-pad/.

Maurizi, Alex. 1974. "Occupational Licensing and the Public Interest." *Journal of Political Economy* 82 (2, Part 1): 399–413. doi:10.1086/260199.

McKenna, Francine. 2006. "Auditor Independence and Management Consulting – Deja Vu All Over Again." *re: The Auditors*, October 21, 2006. http://retheauditors.com/2006/10/21/auditor-independence-and-management-consulting-deja-vu-all-over-again/.

McKenna, Francine. 2007. "PCAOB Criticizes PwC – PwC Respectfully Disagrees." *re: The Auditors*, October 19, 2007. http://retheauditors.com/2007/10/19/pcaob-criticizes-pwc-pwc-respectfully-disagrees/.

McKenna, Francine. 2008. "Deloitte and Flanagan – A Culture of Non-Compliance?" *re: The Auditors*, November 7, 2008. http://retheauditors.com/2008/11/07/deloitte-a-culture-of-non-compliance-2/.

McKenna, Francine. 2010a. "Send Lawyers, Guns And Money . . . The Big 4 And Their Litigation." *re: The Auditors*, March 2, 2010. http://retheauditors.com/2010/03/02/send-lawyers-guns-and-money-the-big-4-and-their-litigation/.

McKenna, Francine. 2010b. "HP, Hurd, Deloitte and Tone at the Top." *re: The Auditors*, August 9, 2010. http://retheauditors.com/2010/08/09/hp-hurd-deloitte-and-tone-at-the-top/.

McKenna, Francine. 2010c. "@Forbes: Did Deloitte Compromise Independence in the McClellan Insider Trading Scandal?" *re: The Auditors*, December 8, 2010. http://retheauditors.com/2010/12/08/forbes-did-deloitte-compromise-independence-in-the-mcclellan-insider-trading-scandal/.

McKenna, Francine. 2011a. "Inside The Mind of An Inside Trader." *re: The Auditors*, March 5, 2011. http://retheauditors.com/2011/03/05/inside-the-mind-of-an-inside-trader/.

McKenna, Francine. 2011b. "Say Anything: The Big Four Defense Of Overtime Exemptions." *re: The Auditors*, June 20, 2011. http://retheauditors.com/2011/06/20/say-anything-the-big-4-defense-of-overtime-exemptions/.

McKenna, Francine. 2012a. "Ten Years after Sarbox, Time for an Audit of the Auditors." *Financial Times*, July 29, 2012. www.ft.com/content/fd8b1a10-d7e1-11e1-9980-00144feabdc0.

McKenna, Francine. 2012b. "McKenna Panelist At NYU On Auditor Independence And Consulting." *re: The Auditors*, November 28, 2012. http://retheauditors.com/2012/11/28/mckenna-to-speak-at-nyu-on-auditor-independence-and-consulting/.

McKenna, Francine. 2013. "Another 'Rogue' Audit Partner; Another 'Duped' Audit Firm." *Forbes*, April 10, 2013. www.forbes.com/sites/francinemckenna/2013/04/10/another-rogue-audit-partner-another-duped-audit-firm/#692055f4865d.

McKenna, Francine. 2016. "At Deloitte, the Problems with Audit Quality and Professionalism Start at the Top." *MarketWatch*, December 10, 2016. www.marketwatch.com/story/at-deloitte-the-problems-with-audit-quality-and-professionalism-start-at-the-top-2016-12-09.

McKenna, Francine. 2017. "How the Global Audit Firms, Led by Deloitte, Are Using Their Lobbying Clout to Dilute Sarbanes-Oxley Reforms." *ProMarket*, May 12, 2017. https://promarket.org/global-audit-firms-led-deloitte-using-lobbying-clout-dilute-sarbanes-oxley-reforms/.

McKenna, Francine. 2018. "KPMG Turned to Palantir to Help Predict Which Audits Would Be Inspected." *MarketWatch*, June 26, 2018. www.marketwatch.com/story/kpmg-turned-to-palantir-to-help-predict-which-audits-would-be-inspected-2018-06-26.

Nanda, Ashish. 1999. "The Professional Pledge and Conflict of Interest." Harvard Business School, January 25, 1999.

Nanda, Ashish. 2003. "Managing Professional Services Firms." Harvard Business School. Executive Education course.

NASBA (National Association of State Boards Of Accountancy). 2008. "120/150 Discussion." www.nasba.org/app/uploads/2011/03/120_150_Hour_Education_Paper-Jul08.pdf.

PCAOB (Public Company Accounting Oversight Board). 2003. "Establishment of Interim Professional Auditing Standards." https://pcaobus.org/Rulemaking/Interim_Standards/Release2003-006.pdf.

PCAOB. 2011. "Order Instituting Disciplinary Proceedings, Making Findings, and Imposing Sanctions." https://pcaobus.org//Enforcement/Decisions/Documents/Chisholm.pdf.

PCAOB. 2018. "2017 Annual Report." https://pcaobus.org/About/Administration/Documents/Annual%20Reports/2017-PCAOB-Annual-Report.pdf.

Pippins v. KPMG LLP, No. 13–889. (2d Cir. 2014).

Rapoport, Michael. 2017. "GE Tax Trade: Sending Hundreds of Accountants to PwC." *The Wall Street Journal*, January 12, 2017. www.wsj.com/articles/ge-tax-trade-sending-hundreds-of-accountants-to-pwc-1484233382.

Rapoport, Michael. 2018. "How Did the Big Four Auditors Get $17 Billion in Revenue Growth? Not From Auditing." *The Wall Street Journal*, April 7, 2018. www.wsj.com/articles/how-did-the-big-four-auditors-get-17-billion-in-revenue-growth-not-from-auditing-1523098800.

Raymond, Nate. 2016. "PwC reaches mid-trial deal in lawsuit by Taylor Bean trustee." *Reuters*, August 26, 2016. www.reuters.com/article/pricewaterhouse-trial-idUSL1N1B70WY.

Rostain, Tanina. 2006. "Sheltering Lawyers: The Organized Tax Bar and the Tax Shelter Industry." *Yale Journal on Regulation* 23: 77. doi:10.2139/ssrn.696704.

Sarbanes-Oxley Act of 2002, Public Law 107–204, July 30, 2002.

SEC (US Securities and Exchange Commission). 2001. "Final Rule: Revision of the Commission's Auditor Independence Requirements." 17 CFR Parts 210 and 240. www.sec.gov/rules/final/33-7919.htm#P531_206695.

SEC. 2014. "SEC Charges Ernst & Young With Violating Auditor Independence Rules in Lobbying Activities." Press Release 2014–136, July 14, 2014. www.sec.gov/news/press-release/2014-136.

SEC. 2015a. "SEC Charges Deloitte & Touche With Violating Auditor Independence Rules." Press Release 2015–137, July 1, 2015. www.sec.gov/news/pressrelease/2015-137.html.

SEC. 2015b. "SEC Charges Two Grant Thornton Firms With Violating Auditor Independence Rules." Press Release 2015–225, October 1, 2015. www.sec.gov/news/pressrelease/2015-225.html.

SEC. 2016a. Release No. 78872. September 19, 2016. www.sec.gov/litigation/admin/2016/34-78872.pdf.

SEC. 2016b. Release No. 78873. September 19, 2016. www.sec.gov/litigation/admin/2016/34-78873.pdf.

SEC. 2018a. Release No. 83854. August 15, 2018. www.sec.gov/litigation/admin/2018/34-83854.pdf.

SEC. 2018b. Release No. 83889. August 20, 2018. www.sec.gov/litigation/admin/2018/34-83889.pdf.

SEC. 2019a. Release No. 24554. August 7, 2019. www.sec.gov/litigation/complaints/2019/comp24554.pdf

SEC. 2019b. Release No. 86770 / August 27, 2019. www.sec.gov/litigation/admin/2019/34-86770.pdf

SEC. 2019c. Release No. 4020 / February 13, 2019. www.sec.gov/news/press-release/2019-9

SEC. 2019d. Release No. 87052 / September 23, 2019. www.sec.gov/litigation/admin/2019/34-87052.pdf

SEC. 2019e. Release No. 87053 / September 23, 2019. www.sec.gov/litigation/admin/2019/34-87053.pdf

SEC. 2019f. "KPMG Paying $50 Million Penalty for Illicit Use of PCAOB Data and Cheating on Training Exams." Press Release 2019–95, June 17, 2019. www.sec.gov/news/press-release/2019-95

SEC. 2020. "SEC Charges Three Former KPMG Audit Partners for Exam Sharing Misconduct." Press Release 2020–115, May 18, 2020. www.sec.gov/news/press-release/2020-115

Shepard, Lawrence. 1984. "Personal Failures and the Bankruptcy Reform Act of 1978." *The Journal of Law and Economics* 27 (2): 419–37. doi:10.1086/467072.

Stigler, George J. 1971. "The Theory of Economic Regulation." *The Bell Journal of Economics and Management Science* 2 (1) (Spring): 3–21. www.jstor.org/stable/3003160.

Taub, Stephen. 2007. "Accountants Suing PwC for Overtime." *CFO.com*, October 24, 2007. www.cfo.com/human-capital-careers/2007/10/accountants-suing-pwc-for-overtime/.

Tribe, Meghan. 2018. "Will Law Firms Bow to Pressure to End Mandatory Arbitration?" *The American Lawyer*, May 24, 2018. www.law.com/americanlawyer/2018/05/24/will-law-firms-bow-to-pressure-to-end-mandatory-arbitration/.

United States v. Arthur Young & Co., 465 U.S. 805 (1984).

United States v. Middendorf, 18-CR-36 (JPO) (S.D.N.Y. 2018).

United States Securities and Exchange Commission v. Lauren Zarsky, No. 18-cv-7129 (S.D.N.Y. 2018).

United States Securities and Exchange Commission v. Thomas W. Avent, Jr., et al., 1:16-cv-02459-WMR (N.D. Ga., 2019).

Van Wyhe, Glenn. 1994. *The Struggle for Status: A History of Accounting Education*. New York: Garland.

Weil, Jonathan. 2014. "Is the SEC Going Easy on General Electric?" *Bloomberg*, January 24, 2014. www. bloomberg.com/opinion/articles/2014-01-24/is-the-sec-going-easy-on-general-electric-.

22

A BUSINESS PRACTITIONER'S GUIDE TO RESOLVING MORAL DILEMMAS

Employing a Location Map[1] to define boundaries of permissible behavior

Michael Alles and Michael Kraten

Introduction and purpose

What are moral dilemmas? How do business practitioners confront them? And how often do they do so? In the article *Morality and Ethics* that appeared in the July 1942 issue of the *Journal of Philosophy*, Paul Weiss declared that "A man is moral if he conforms to the standard practices and customs of the group in which he is. He is ethical if he voluntarily obligates himself to live in the light of an ideal."[2]

Three decades later, in 1975, James Rest developed a test of moral development known as the Defining Issues Test (DIT). It incorporated Rest's Four Component Model of Moral Development, which states that an individual's sense of morality progresses from sensitivity to judgment to motivation to character (see Table 22.1). In other words, Weiss (1942) defines morality in rules-based terms and ethics in principles-based terms. But Rest (1975) notes that the concept of morality encompasses far more than conformity to rules.

James Rest's Model of Moral Functioning has been adapted numerous times and in various formats. In most cases, though, the model has featured a sequence of four components that begins with sensitivity and concludes with character.

Table 22.1 defines the four components in accordance with the goals of this chapter. Each box of Table 22.1 represents a question that a business manager should ask when confronted with a moral decision.

Weiss (1942) and Rest (1975) each make a valid contribution to our understanding of moral behavior. Morality is an important consideration in accounting and business contexts because morality provides guidance on what is permissible behavior in any particular context. Humans are continually confronted with situations where some action must be taken, so decisions must be made about what behavior is "permissible." Social norms, laws and regulations, natural laws, and moral convictions are all constraints that limit what are permissible behaviors in any particular situation. The idea of a "moral dilemma" is a situation where morally guided permissible behavior is in conflict somehow with the other sources of limitations on permissible behavior. However, neither Weiss (1942) nor Rests' (1975) definitions provide business practitioners with

Table 22.1 Rest (1975) Model of Moral Functioning

Do I possess: **SENSITIVITY** to the perspectives of others?	Do I possess: **JUDGMENT** that is informed by standards of right and wrong?	Do I possess: **MOTIVATION** to want to "do the right thing"?	Do I possess: **CHARACTER** to act morally, even when there is a price to pay for it?

clear methodology for resolving moral dilemmas. Given the frequent need in practical situations to resolve moral dilemmas, how should practitioners grapple with them in order to engage in permissible behavior as described by these authors?[3]

The purpose of this chapter is to assist practitioners by describing a methodology for assessing moral dilemmas. It describes an instrument known as a "Location Map" and illustrates how mapping practices can be employed to identify boundaries of acceptable behavior.

In our complex civilization, the "rule of law" establishes boundaries of behavior on the basis of legislation and regulation. Organizational "codes of conduct" also establish boundaries of behavior on the basis of business control systems. And religious, cultural, and social mores establish boundaries of behavior on the basis of group morality. By preparing Location Maps of the zones of acceptable behavior that fall within each of these boundaries, business practitioners can develop their own guides for analyzing dilemmas that challenge their abilities to make moral choices. With the use of these maps, practitioners can determine how close (or how far) each situational decision resides in relation to the boundaries of the zones.

The next section of this chapter discusses the need to model moral dilemmas. The third section introduces the Location Map as an instrument for visualizing moral dilemmas. The fourth section presents a pair of examples of moral dilemmas in accounting and illustrates the application of Location Maps to resolve the dilemmas. The fifth section contains a discussion of whistleblowing, an act with significant ethical and moral implications that is essential to accounting and other professions. The sixth section concludes this chapter with a summary of its key principles.

Modeling moral dilemmas

Practitioners face an initial challenge when confronting moral dilemmas: Will they be able to recognize that they are confronting moral situations? After all, if it were always obvious when circumstances call for the use of a Weiss (1942) definition, a Rest (1975) model, or some other moral framework, practitioners would be more likely to make moral decisions.

Furthermore, moral dilemmas often occur at the social and organizational levels, generating confusion about the parties that are responsible for making final decisions. For instance, governments, churches, and the medical and legal professions all bear some responsibility for making decisions about abortion and euthanasia while simultaneously placing significant responsibilities in the hands of individuals.[4]

In certain situations, it may not even occur to one individual to consider moral factors, while another individual may sincerely believe that such inconsideration is itself immoral in nature. "Culture wars," for instance, have been waged over historical figures who made decisions that were acceptable to a majority of citizens of the United States in their time but that are unacceptable today. Such figures are now posthumously condemned for acts such as performing in blackface, objecting to homosexuality, and promoting colonialism.[5]

In our contemporary business environment, moral disagreements often occur when one party demands that another acknowledge the "self-evident fact" that a behavior is both objectively incorrect and morally repugnant. Passionate public disputes frequently explode over issues like corporate social responsibility, the existence of climate change, the use of fossil fuels, the purchase of conflict minerals, the manufacture of products made by children and other exploited workers, trade with South Africa, Israel, and other controversial nations, actions perceived as pro- or anti-LGBTQ, etc. Such matters genuinely engage the moral sensibilities of the parties. Nevertheless, the normative imposition of one individual's moral standards on another individual's behavior is subjective and is thus unlikely to result in reconciliation and consensus.

To prevent the degeneration of moral decision-making into a subjective debate about "right" and "wrong," all decision makers must become skilled at: (a) recognizing the moral implications of the circumstances that confront them, and (b) assessing the moral outcomes of different decisions on their own individual belief systems. In the absence of this individual dimension, a moral debate devolves into an argument *between* individuals rather than a personal dilemma that rages *within* an individual. When business practitioners ask themselves "What does morality mean to me in the context of this decision?" they appropriately place the agency of the individual at the center of their dilemmas.

Interestingly, of all the decisions that individuals make in the course of daily living, very few trigger such individual feelings of uncertainty. Why is most of human behavior so mundane and non-problematic? When individuals simply do what tradition, accepted morality, laws, and employers expect of them, they may not believe that their decisions involve any moral dilemmas.

Nevertheless, as Weiss (1942) implied, dilemmas periodically arise when contextual "established practices and customs" conflict with an individual's personal "light of an ideal good." The Rest (1975) Model identifies a different source of moral dilemmas, one that arises when moral sensitivity fails to result in an action of moral character. Action is an application of morality, triggered (or not triggered) by a judgment about the relative importance of a moral situation.

Thus, the critical generator of moral dilemmas is the natural tension between the exogenous, external drivers of social expectations and the endogenous, internal codes of private behavior. If there is no conflict between these external and internal factors, an individual will not be aware of a moral dilemma.

Furthermore, as Weiss (1942) implied, moral behavior is itself a voluntary decision. In other words, an individual must make a conscious choice to assess a moral dilemma. If they choose to ignore the dilemma, it vanishes from their perspective, and others may suffer the consequences. The individual, of course, may suffer consequences as well.

An individual may thus define a moral dilemma as follows:

> When there is a conflict between a potential decision that is consistent with an individual's internal sense of "what is right" and "what is wrong," based on conscience, religious beliefs, or other personal criteria, and a potential decision that is recommended by external sources of guidance, an individual faces a moral dilemma.
>
> A moral action requires a moral character to reconcile this conflict. And in professions like accounting, such actions may be required frequently.

In certain cases, individuals may attempt to avoid making conscious choices in order to incur the least personal cost (or risk) to themselves. The field of business control systems focuses on the development of organizational policies and procedures that address this behavioral bias.

The design, development, and implementation of control systems distinguish the field of business ethics from the fields of ethics of other professions, such as bioethics and legal ethics. Internal control systems are essential factors in the design of models of moral behavior in the accounting profession.

Nevertheless, the purpose of this chapter is to assist individuals in identifying and resolving moral dilemmas. It is not to assist organizations by recommending specific internal controls, and it is not to define moral or ethical codes of behavior for application in various situations. Management consultants can help design internal controls, and religious and spiritual leaders can help define moral codes.

The remainder of this chapter describes a process for visualizing the conflict that lies at the heart of all moral dilemmas. Though it does not prescribe the moral acts that can resolve these conflicts, it does identify the source of the conflict, and thus it prepares an individual to diagnose the conflict as a predecessor activity to choosing an appropriate solution.

Throughout this chapter, we present six figures, with two focused on tax avoidance/evasion, two on earnings management/profit smoothing, and two on employee fraud/whistleblowing. Each pair of figures cites a well-known case for illustrative purposes, and each figure illustrates an important procedural element of Location Mapping.

Visualizing ethical dilemmas with location maps

A Location Map provides a visual depiction of a moral dilemma by illustrating the boundaries of legitimate behavior that are prescribed by the sources of guidance in a particular decision context. A sense of conflict must exist between an individual's sense of morality and one (or more) other sources of guidance in order to create the dilemma.

Furthermore, for any individual, a moral dilemma can exist only when a situation lies outside of the boundary of an individual's morality domain but inside the boundary of one or more of the other sources of guidance. These boundaries and sources will vary from individual to individual and from context to context. In an accounting setting, the sources may include the criminal justice code (e.g., prison sentences for theft of funds), business regulation (e.g., prohibitions against insider trading or misleading public disclosures), and employer control systems (e.g., documentation requirements for employee expense reimbursements).

Location Maps represent an application of set theory. An individual who must weigh three different sources of moral guidance, for instance, would define each source as a set. The Location Map would thus contain three circles, with the perimeter of each circle representing the boundary of the set of moral behavior as defined by its applicable source of moral guidance.

The entire interior area of each circle is moral; thus, any choice that falls within an area is defined as moral by at least one source of moral guidance. The entire area that is not included in any circle is not moral; thus, any choice that falls within an exterior area is defined as immoral by every source of moral guidance.

Each of the illustrative figures in this chapter provides an example of a Location Map that addresses an individual's sense of morality, legislative and regulatory codes, business control systems, or other sources of ethical codes.[6]

In an ideal situation, all of the decision criteria would overlap and act in concert, thereby preventing the existence of any sense of conflict and, thus, any moral dilemma. Under such circumstances, the individual may not even consider moral factors before making a decision. Conversely, as the overlap between the boundaries of permissible behavior lessens, the probability that a behavior will fall outside of the domain of one or more acceptable zone(s) increases. In addition, as the level of emphasis that an individual places on the importance of moral behavior increases, the likelihood of moral conflict increases as well.[7]

Furthermore, as the surface area of a zone of permissibility increases, an organization's acceptable level of behavior increases commensurately. In other words, a relatively large circle connotes a code of conduct that permits a broad range of permissible behaviors.

For an illustrative example, consider the simple purchase of a cup of coffee. For certain individuals, a cup of coffee is simply a cup of coffee. For a supporter of environmental groups, though, the coffee must be "rain forest friendly." The latter organization's domain of morality encompasses the choice of coffee that group members purchase, a decision that is based on an awareness of the relationship between coffee plantation farming and tropical deforestation.

The first individual is only interacting with the coffee seller. His purchase of a cup falls within the circle of that coffee seller. However, the second considers the zones of acceptable behavior of two organizations, that is, of the environmental group and the coffee seller. Thus, the coffee purchase falls outside of the circle of the first organization and within the circle of the second organization.

For another illustrative example, consider controversies regarding bakers who refuse to sell cakes for gay weddings or pharmacists who decline to fill prescriptions for "morning after" birth control pills. Such individuals assert that their personal moral codes of conduct do not permit such behavior, even though the legal system may require them to do so.

Interestingly, Location Maps can prove helpful when an individual asserts that a law is immoral. Such assertions were made when the colonial Continental Congress rebelled against the British Crown during the American War of Independence, when Mahatma Gandhi engaged in acts of passive resistance to British colonial rule in India, and when American civil rights protesters encouraged acts of civil disobedience to overturn Jim Crow laws. A Location Map could be utilized for each of these conflict situations.

Such conflicts are exacerbated when the entities that determine the boundaries of behavior possess different levels of power. In their work "Ethics Research in AIS" that appeared in the 2002 text *Researching Accounting as an Information Systems Discipline*, J. Dillard and K. Yuthas explained that "Ideally, free discussions of values, interests, and goals take place in an environment of equal participation of all affected stakeholder groups, and are ensured through the suspension or negation of power differentials." But until this ideal state of affairs is achieved, power differentials will continue to influence outcomes. And on a Location Map, they can be illustrated through differential region shapes and shades.

Finally, Location Maps can be utilized to explain historical empirical shifts in public opinion. For instance, American society now considers child labor to be immoral. Nevertheless, the practice was commonplace a century ago, and it is still prevalent in many non-Western countries. In 2015, for instance, the Bolivian nation actually legalized child labor, defining it as an essential element of Andean culture.

Dynamic forces continually impact personal definitions of moral behavior, social standards regarding the imposition of business control systems, and levels of cultural willingness to support the enforcement of laws. All of these factors are suitable for mapping; they can be tracked via the utilization of Location Maps.

These examples provide illustrations of social, economic, and political applications of Location Maps. The following section presents a number of illustrations of Location Maps in the field of accounting.

Ethical dilemmas in accounting

Most accountants, of course, do not face the types of ethical dilemmas that compel them to engage in acts of civil disobedience as Mahatma Gandhi or Rosa Parks did. Nevertheless, many do observe gaps and other inadequacies in the internal control frameworks of their employer and client firms. Accordingly, promulgators of professional standards may be expected to issue guidance about the ethical and moral dilemmas that occur in such circumstances.

Rule 201 of the AICPA (2018) Code of Professional Conduct addresses ethical dilemmas. However, the code only mentions the word "morality" once, in a note stating that "in carrying out their responsibilities as professionals, members should exercise sensitive professional and moral judgments in all their activities." The AICPA does not, however, specify what "moral judgments" should actually be exercised.

Nevertheless, the AICPA (2018) code of conduct does represent a comprehensive set of rules-based guidance that lists specific situations that feature ethical concerns, such as the need to maintain independence, the need to respect client confidentiality, etc.

The IMA promulgates a brief set of principles as well. In its Statement of Ethical Professional Practice, the IMA notes that its "overarching ethical principles include: Honesty, Fairness, Objectivity, and Responsibility. Members shall act in accordance with these principles and shall encourage others within their organizations to adhere to them." Oddly, though, the IMA's Statement does not explicitly mention the word "morality."

Are these professional guidelines insufficient? Not necessarily; after all, most CPAs are employed by organizations that also maintain codes of ethical behavior. Thus, the boundaries of behavior that are established by professional bodies serve to complement those of employers.

Through continuing professional education, the professional bodies also support the development and employment of individual codes of moral behavior. Furthermore, principles-based standards like the IMA's can be helpful, because no rules-based system can anticipate every possible ethical dilemma.

Tax avoidance, evasion

Tax avoidance may or may not be considered immoral, depending on an individual's scruples and the nature of the tax. Nevertheless, tax avoidance is a legal activity. Conversely, tax evasion is an illegal and widely regarded as an immoral activity, as well.

Our first pair of figures introduces the format of a Location Map and the purpose of the circle(s) within it. It demonstrates how changes in a code of conduct can affect a decision.

The two figures illustrate "Double Irish with A Dutch Sandwich (DIwDS)," an aggressive tax reduction strategy that utilized foreign entities to shift taxable income to low-tax jurisdictions. Government tax authorities eventually outlawed the strategy.

Figure 22.1 presents a single circle entitled Tax Law. The inner area is labeled Avoidance, and the outer area is labeled Evasion. A dot labeled DIwDS is within the circle, and a dot labeled Unreported Income is outside the circle.

When accountants define permissible behavior more stringently, they reduce the diameters of their boundaries of behavior on their Location Maps, thus constraining what behaviors are acceptable and excluding what is unacceptable. Figure 22.2, for instance, presents a second circle within the first circle. The diameter of the circle has contracted because of government action. Both dots now fall outside of the smaller circle.

The mapping process can be used as a dynamic learning activity for ethics education because the outlining of behavioral criteria and the plotting of ethical dilemmas require individuals to

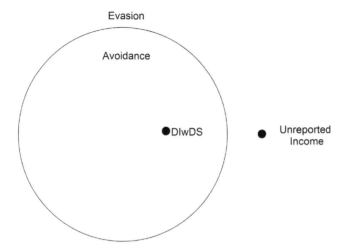

Figure 22.1   Tax Law

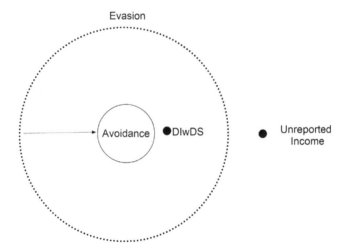

Figure 22.2   Tightening Tax Law to Outlaw DIwDS

consider the moral bases for decision making and the holistic consequences of their actions. Indeed, the very act of drawing compels individuals to consider the moral issues that are raised by their choices.

Earnings management, profit smoothing

Our second pair of figures introduces the concept of multiple circles that reflect partially (but not fully) overlapping codes of conduct. Like the first pair of figures, this Location Map includes two dots. However, unlike the first pair of figures, this pair illustrates how the degree of convergence (or divergence) of different codes impacts the decision process.

The two figures illustrate "Earnings Management," a process that General Electric and other firms utilized to engage in "Profit Smoothing" across periods. GE benefited from the practice for years, but it later harmed the firm when accruals had to be reversed.

Figure 22.3 presents a pair of partially overlapping circles entitled Regulatory Law and GAAP. A dot titled Transparent Accounting is within both circles.

Figure 22.4 adds a dot entitled Managing (Smoothing) Earnings to the Location Map in Figure 22.3. It falls inside the Regulatory Law circle but slightly outside of the GAAP circle. The "slightness" of its distance from the GAAP circle explains why GE was able to engage in the practice for years, and yet its location on the "wrong side" of the circle's diameter serves as a red flag that foreshadows the eventual harm to the firm.[8]

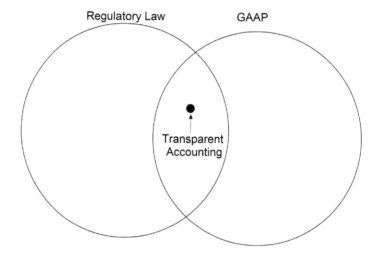

Figure 22.3   Transparent Accounting

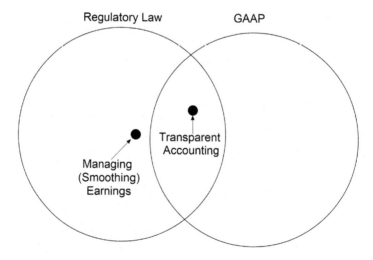

Figure 22.4   Managing (Smoothing) Earnings

What is missing from these figures? The illustrations do not present any boundary of behavior that is established by the organization's business control systems. Such governance measures constrain overly aggressive accounting practices through internal and external audit procedures, an assertive board of directors, an inquisitive audit committee, a stringent and clearly written handbook of accounting policies and procedures, and other practices.

The preceding figures presume that moral boundaries of behavior are relatively fixed in nature. Bonuses and other incentive programs, however, may compel individuals to adopt more permissive moral standards.

Does this mean that every individual has his price? In other words, if an individual's moral boundaries can be shifted by incentives, does this mean that the boundaries carry no weight? In certain organizations, and in certain situations, this worrisome state of affairs may be true.

Nevertheless, in such situations, a Location Map may still prove helpful. It can help managers assess the extent to which employees are at risk of making immoral decisions in order to earn incentives.

Employee fraud and whistleblowing

Whistleblowing is not exclusively related to the accounting profession, though it is often the only way in which fraud and earnings management come to light. Lawyers, physicians, architects, and other professionals can engage in whistleblowing activities.

In all of these disciplines, firms promulgate best practices and sponsor training sessions to provide guidance to their professionals regarding appropriate moral behavior. Of course, no rule-based regimen can foresee and address every potential situation; thus, "credos" and other principles provide supplemental guidance as well.

The Johnson & Johnson Credo, for instance, is a well-known exemplar of a statement of moral values in a business context. Russell C. Deyo, General Counsel at Johnson & Johnson, was interviewed by the *Corporate Counsel Business Journal* (*CCBJ*) on January 1, 2007. He said (Deyo 2007):

> Our Credo . . . creates a framework for decision-making. When making decisions, people will think about the quality of their decisions and their impacts. This encourages decision makers to focus on ethical considerations and long-term impact rather than merely short-term business results. This is important for a company like ours where so much accountability rests with the management boards of far-flung business units.

The credo served Johnson & Johnson well during the infamous Tylenol tampering scandal. In the same interview, Mr. Deyo explained,

> The Tylenol story is told frequently to new employees including new senior managers. . . . When management made the decision to recall every bottle of Tylenol capsules from every home and store in the United States, it was a clear demonstration of putting the safety of customers first. . . . When discussing difficult business decisions, our people still like to refer to this incident as an example of how being true to our heritage and Credo results in decisions that pay dividends many times over.

The Tylenol scandal did not involve a whistleblowing situation. Nevertheless, Deyo's depiction of the Johnson & Johnson Credo as emphasizing quality, impact, ethical considerations, and customer interest also applies to whistleblowing situations. Employees consider "blowing a whistle" when they perceive a conflict between an organizational practice and a law or regulation that serves the public interest.

The Sarbanes-Oxley Act, for instance, protects the interests of whistleblowers. Internal control systems do so as well. Sherron Watkins of Enron, Cynthia Cooper of WorldCom, and others are celebrated as role models because they are perceived as moral exemplars who placed their careers at risk by utilizing internal control systems to engage in whistleblowing activities.

But why isn't whistleblowing a universal choice? One reason is that the boundaries of behavior may be less clear in reality than on a Location Map. Lawyers, judges, and theologians must often dispense guidance because individuals cannot always be certain about the location of a boundary of behavior.

Furthermore, individuals may persuade themselves that there is "no harm, no foul" in a potential whistleblowing situation.[9] Others may convince themselves that "the buck stops" with someone in a more authoritative position than their own.

In other words, Weiss' (1942) abstract concept of an "ideal good" may not necessarily reflect an individual's personal moral beliefs. Accordingly, a Location Map can illustrate the moral dilemma that occurs when a potential whistleblowing act does not fall within the zone of acceptable behavior. Under such circumstances, an individual may modify his personal moral beliefs to allow for an expedient choice, even though his "ideal good" would dictate otherwise.

Indeed, when an individual considers a potential whistleblowing decision, they must address a number of pertinent questions:

- Have I observed an organizational act that is inconsistent with applicable laws and regulations?
- Is whistleblowing, in this circumstance, an act of organizational disloyalty?
- Is it ethical to sacrifice my own future and the security of my family by whistleblowing?
- If many organizations engage in this act without penalty, is it wrong?
- Am I misinterpreting the organizational act?

Our third pair of figures introduces the perfectionist concept of the full convergence of codes of conduct. By comparing a fully converged (i.e., identical) pair of circles to a partially converged pair of circles, this pair of figures demonstrates the difference between a theoretical, rarely experienced "perfect state" and a practical, often-experienced "imperfect state."

The two figures illustrate the diesel emissions scandal, a fraud in which employees at VW and other firms created computer programs that reported false data on government regulatory tests. The employees felt emboldened by a belief that regulators would not prosecute violations of the criminal code, perhaps because VW is such a large and influential company in Germany.

Figure 22.5 presents two fully overlapping (i.e., identical) circles entitled Criminal Code and Consumer Expectations. Diesel "cheating" lies outside of both circles, as fraud is both criminally irresponsible and contrary to consumer beliefs.

Figure 22.6 superimposes a third circle entitled Prosecutorial Judgment. It only partially overlaps the two identical circles; diesel "cheating" lies inside of this third circle. Public policy should strive to bring this third circle into alignment with the first two circles.

Conclusion

Business practitioners are often challenged to define the moral boundaries of their behavior. Although the editors of this book have noted that accounting is rife with moral judgments,

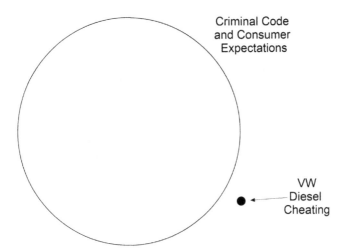

Figure 22.5   VW Diesel Cheating

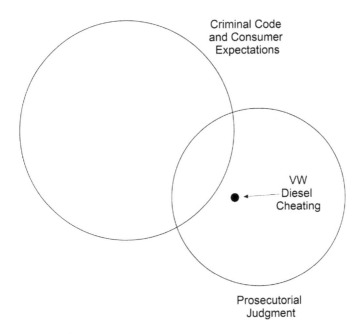

Figure 22.6   Prosecutorial Judgment

individuals like Paul Weiss and James Rest have not provided accounting practitioners with methodologies to assist in moral decision making.

The purpose of Location Maps is to define zones of acceptable behavior so that practitioners can identify and assess situations and potential choices that fall outside of the zones. Although Location Maps cannot offer constructive suggestions about *how* to shift unacceptable choices into the zones, they can help practitioners identify the *distance* and *direction* in which choices must be shifted in order to achieve this purpose.[10]

This chapter presents nonbusiness examples, non-accounting business examples, and accounting examples. It concludes with a complex example involving the act of whistleblowing.

Location Maps will be rendered unnecessary if legal, corporate, social, religious, and personal standards of morality ever become perfectly consistent with each other. Because such a scenario is extremely unlikely, practitioners may wish to become comfortable with this helpful methodology.

Notes

1 To the best of our knowledge, no prior publication has described the use of Location Maps to assess ethical situations. However, the process of drawing circles on maps to represent permissible or desirable (or, conversely, non-permissible or undesirable) outcome regions has long been utilized in different fields. Epidemiologists, for instance, are using this process to draw zones of coronavirus outbreaks; see, for instance, the World Map and the U.S. Map on the COVID-19 Dashboard by the Center for Systems Science and Engineering (CSSE) at Johns Hopkins University (2020).

2 There are no universal definitions of ethics and morality, and thus no universally accepted distinctions between the two concepts. For instance, Weiss (1942) defines morality as a group-based construct, and of ethics as a personal construct. Others make the opposite distinction while still others make no distinction between the terms. This chapter adopts Weiss's definitions, but other definitions are equally valid.

3 This chapter focuses on moral dilemmas, as defined by Weiss (1942), because organizations are primarily concerned with behaviors that impact other individuals within a group. Although an individual's morality is often impacted by one's sense of ethics (i.e. of Weiss' 'light of an ideal'), this chapter does not focus on it. In other words, this chapter assumes that most organizations would not be concerned if an individual privately used the Lord's name in vain, if that behavior had no impact on other individuals.

Nevertheless, priorities inevitably vary from organization to organization, and from society to society. A Christian organization in a libertarian democratic nation, for instance, may define the refusal to bake a wedding cake for a gay couple as moral and yet unethical. Conversely, a gay rights organization in a conservative religious theocracy may reverse these terms.

4 A society is an entire set of organizations (and individuals) that (who) occupy an interactive space and that (who) engage in behaviors that impact each other. An organization, or individual, may occupy many societies simultaneously. For instance, the primary employer in a "company town" in the American Midwest may define its local municipality as a society, its network of stakeholders as a second society, and the United States as a third society.

According to these definitions, the state "societies" of certified public accountants in the United States would define themselves as organizations and not as societies. The state "associations" of certified public accountants and the national AICPA, would do likewise.

5 Although majorities of Americans have modified their views of certain behaviors over time, minority views have always existed. Performing in blackface, for instance, was always offensive to many African Americans. Homophobic behavior was never acceptable to gay people. Slavery and colonialism was always resented by the enslaved and the colonized. As relative power shifted over time, attitudes among a majority of Americans shifted in a corresponding manner, and thus majority definitions of certain behaviors shifted from "moral" to "immoral."

6 The interior and exterior spaces of a Location Map represent every imaginable choice or act that a person could perform. The areas within each circle represent the set of moral choices or acts as defined by one or more source(s) of guidance. For instance, an African American citizen in the 1960s American South who is arrested for sitting at a "whites only" lunch counter would be making a permissible choice from the perspective of his protest group but would be making an impermissible choice from the perspectives of the lunch counter business owner and the local governmental police force.

Furthermore, consider an owner of a small agricultural business who hires undocumented foreign workers. If citizens of the region believe that this business practice "takes jobs away" from American citizens and if national laws prohibit the business practice, the hiring activity would be considered a moral choice from the perspective of the business control system and yet immoral from the perspectives of the local community and the local government.

An organization that routinely hires undocumented foreign workers would necessarily draw its circle of business controls in a manner that does not overlap its circle of government law and regulation. Its hiring practices, in other words, would be simultaneously acceptable to the business and yet illegal to the government.

7 For instance, individuals who believe that moral behavior is extremely important may be very concerned by choices that fall slightly outside of circles. However, individuals who place less emphasis on the importance of moral behavior may only be very concerned by choices that fall far outside of circles.

8 Although some circles are prescribed by organizational codes of conduct, other circles may vary from individual to individual within an organization. A very devout individual who follows the teachings of his conservative church, for instance, may draw a different circle than a less devout individual who is a member of a reformed church. Likewise, as an individual progresses from a staff position to a senior executive position, his circle(s) may change because he is assuming a different role within the organization.

9 Consider, for instance, two employees who work for a fast food restaurant. Both face the need to feed their hungry families, but only one believes that the theft of food is justified because "the restaurant can afford to lose a little food, and will never even notice the loss." That employee would likely draw a larger "Restaurant Employee Code of Conduct" circle.

10 It would be wrong to conclude that the goal of Location Mapping is to legitimize immoral choices. Instead, it would be correct to state that the goal of Location Mapping is to help managers and other employees understand the extent to which potential choices either: (a) fall within the circles of all relevant organizations, (b) fall within certain circles, but not others, or (c) fail to fall within the circle of any organization.

References

AICPA.org. 2018. "Professional Responsibilities." Last accessed October 24, 2018. https://www.aicpa.org/research/standards/codeofconduct.html.

Deyo, R. 2007. "Johnson & Johnson – True To Its Credo." *Corporate Counsel Business Journal*. Last accessed October 24, 2018. https://ccbjournal.com/articles/johnson-johnson-true-its-credo.

Dillard, J., and K. Yuthas. 2002. *Researching Accounting as an Information Systems Discipline*. Tampa: American Accounting Association Information Systems Section.

IMA. 2018. "IMA Statement of Ethical Professional Practice." Last accessed October 24, 2018. https://www.imanet.org/-/media/b6fbeeb74d964e6c9fe654c48456e61f.ashx?la=en.

Johns Hopkins University. 2020. "World Map and the U.S. Map on the COVID-19 Dashboard by the Center for Systems Science and Engineering (CSSE)." Last accessed October 24, 2020. https://coronavirus.jhu.edu/map.html.

Rest, J. 1975. "Longitudinal Study of the Defining Issues Test of moral judgment: A Strategy for Analyzing Developmental Change." *Developmental Psychology* 11 (6): 738–48.

Weiss, P. 1942. "Morality and Ethics." *Journal of Philosophy* 39 (14): 381–85.

PART VI

Ethical accountants and ethical accounting

23

AN EXAMINATION OF THE VIRTUES OF ACCOUNTING EXEMPLARS

Patrick T. Kelly, Timothy J. Louwers, and John M. Thornton

Introduction

What makes a good accountant? Extant accounting research has identified a number of qualities or virtues important to an accountant's success.[1] Mintz (1995, 247) lists the following virtues necessary for accountants:

> to resist client and commercial pressures that may result from conflicts between an accountants' obligation to a client or employer and public interest considerations: benevolence and altruism; honesty and integrity; impartiality and open-mindedness; reliability and dependability; and faithfulness and trustworthiness.

Libby and Thorne (2004) similarly list "independent," "objective," and "principled," but also add "going beyond the minimum" and "putting the public interest foremost."

Professional accounting ethics differs from general business ethics in that members of a profession agree to hold themselves to a higher standard of conduct for the purpose of serving the public interest. Members of accounting professional organizations such as the International Federation of Accountants, the American Institute of Certified Public Accountants, and the Institute of Chartered Accountants of England and Wales all have professional codes of conduct to which members promise to adhere. Mintz (1995) summarized Pincoffs's (1986, 75–79) beliefs "that virtues (and vices) are dispositional properties that provide grounds for preference (or avoidance) of persons and, therefore, they can help us decide with whom we want to enter into a relationship of trust." While the list of virtues is long, we argue that these qualities can be synthesized into two complementary categories – character and competence. Character is anchored by integrity, with honesty and candor doing what is right and just to serve the public interest. Competence requires the exercise of due care in the continual quest for excellence through education and experience.

In this chapter, we identify a number of accounting professionals who exemplified these virtues in the performance of their professional responsibilities. Armstrong et al. (2003, 1) stress the importance of identifying and promoting moral exemplars "to increase ethical motivation among accounting students, faculty, and practitioners." By identifying these individuals and highlighting their actions, we hope to extend the research in this area to further strengthen professionalism and ethics in the accounting discipline.

Frank Wilson

What would you do if you were informed that the CEO of the engagement you were working on has put out a contract on your life? In Frank Wilson's case, he shipped his family off to his in-laws and kept working. The CEO? Al Capone of the Chicago Syndicate.

Alphonse "Scarface" Capone is arguably the most notorious criminal in US history. Bootlegging, gambling, gun smuggling, prostitution – Capone had his hand in all of these illegal businesses in the 1920s. His reputation for brutality was well known. He reportedly beat two of his capos to death with a baseball bat when he suspected them of collaborating with law enforcement authorities. He was also allegedly responsible for the St. Valentine's Day Massacre in which seven members of the rival Bugs Moran gang were lined up against a wall and brutally machine-gunned on February 14, 1929.

Because of his reputation for violence to those who opposed him, none of Capone's underlings were willing to cooperate with the government to bring the mafia boss to justice. Failing to find witnesses to testify against Capone for murder, extortion, bootlegging, or any of the other crimes he had allegedly committed, the relatively new US Treasury Department Bureau of Internal Revenue (now the Internal Revenue Service) Intelligence Unit was tasked with trying to find Capone guilty of tax evasion.[2] Wilson was assigned to bring down the Chicago mobster because of his experience in bringing tax evaders to justice (including Capone's brother Ralph) and his dedication to his profession. In fact, Wilson was handpicked for the Capone case because he was seen as incorruptible. One colleague stated that he was intimidated by Wilson and that, "If assigned to do so, Wilson would investigate his own grandmother" (Spiering 1976). His courage was also evident. Elmer Irey, his boss at the Treasury Department, noted that "He fears nothing that walks; he will sit quietly looking at books eighteen hours a day, seven days a week, forever, if he wants to find something in those books. He is soft-spoken and unemotional. Only the endless stream of nickel cigars he massacres keeps him from being a paragon of virtue" (Troy 2017, 1).

Although trained as a trial lawyer, Wilson's talents lay in forensic accounting: "He relished going back again and again over the same documents, receipts, records – perhaps for the thousandth time – to indict someone, or to compel him to testify" (Spiering 1976). His effectiveness in deciphering Capone's money laundering schemes was the reason that the mob boss ordered the "hit" on Wilson and his family.

While working late one night, Wilson stumbled upon a small black ledger in an old filing cabinet seized in a Federal Bureau of Investigation raid of one of Capone's notable gambling operations. This was the "needle in the haystack" that ended up breaking open the investigation. In Wilson's own words (Wilson and Whitman 1947, 15),

> Way in the back of the cabinet was a package tied in brown paper, pretty heavy. Just out of curiosity I snipped the string and found myself holding three ledgers, black ones with red corners. The first one didn't mean much. The second I spotted as a "special column cashbook." My eye leaped over the column headings: "Bird cage," "21," "Craps," "Faro," "Roulette," "Horse bets." I took the books into my cubbyhole. Here was the diary of a big operation, with a take of from $20,000 to $30,000 a day. Net profits for eighteen months (the books were dated 1925–26) were upward of half a million.[3]

If Wilson was able to connect this income to Capone, he would have damning evidence against the Chicago mob boss in his tax fraud case. Using the relatively new science of handwriting analysis, he was able to identify the ledger's author, the casino's bookkeeper, Leslie Shumway. By promising Shumway and his family protection (and simultaneously threatening to release him on the streets after several days in custody), Wilson secured Shumway's cooperation and agreement to testify (Wilson and Day 1965).

With this amount of money rolling into the operation, Wilson realized that banks would need to be used in Capone's operation, as only so much could be kept safely on Capone's properties. After targeting daily deposits of over $10,000, Wilson was able to identify Fred Reis as Capone's courier. Knowing of Reis' taste for good living and his aversion to bugs, Wilson had Reis locked up in solitary confinement in a roach-infested jail until he agreed to cooperate (Wilson and Day 1965).

With the testimony of Shumway and Reis (supported by incriminating documents Wilson and his investigators were able to locate), the Department of Justice was able to secure Capone's conviction for tax evasion. On October 17, 1931, Capone was found guilty on five counts of tax evasion and sentenced to 11 years in prison (Spiering 1976).

Wilson's work on the Capone case led directly to his involvement in a second "Trial of the Century." In March, 1932, just months after the Capone conviction, Charles Lindbergh's 20-month-old son was kidnapped from the Lindbergh estate in Hopewell, New Jersey. Lindbergh, known as "Lucky Lindy" and the "Lone Eagle," was a national hero following his solo flight across the Atlantic in 1927. From prison, Capone contacted the Lindbergh family and stated that it was a mob operation and that he could help negotiate the "Eaglet's" return. Knowing that Capone had had no contact with the outside world (and was secretly being monitored by a Treasury Department investigator posing as an inmate), Wilson reached out to the Lindbergh kidnapping investigators to let them know that Capone's offer had no value. At the same time, he offered his assistance to the investigation (Wilson and Day 1965).

At Wilson's urging, the Lindbergh family paid a ransom of $50,000 to the kidnapper in gold certificates. Use of these gold certificates would facilitate the identification of those individuals still using gold certificates.[4] Additionally, at his urging, law enforcement officers recorded the serial numbers of the gold certificates (Wilson and Day 1965). These innovative forensic accounting methods directly led to the identification and capture of the Lindbergh baby-murderer[5] when German carpenter Bruno Hauptmann used one of the ransom gold certificates to purchase gas for his new car. While $14,600 of the ransom money was found in the wall of Hauptmann's garage, Wilson and his investigators conducted net worth analysis and expenditure analysis to account for another $35,000 of the ransom money (including a new car, stock market losses, and trips to Europe) (Wilson and Day 1965). It didn't help Hauptmann that he quit his job the day after the ransom was paid or that he kept meticulous records of every cent he spent until the day after the ransom was paid. Using handwriting analysis similar to that used in the Capone case, Wilson illustrated compelling evidence that Hauptmann had also authored the ransom notes (Wilson and Day 1965). Bruno Hauptmann was convicted of murder and executed in 1935.

Wilson's career of dedicated service after his role in these two cases did not end. Because of his money laundering investigation experience, he was named Chief of the US Secret Service (the Secret Service's mission is to protect the president and prevent counterfeiting). He served in that role from 1934–1946, including providing security for President Franklin Delano Roosevelt during World War II. Wilson later served as security consultant for the US Atomic Energy Commission. After a long career of public service in which he exhibited a great deal of courage and professional competence, Frank Wilson passed away in 1970 at age 83.

Joseph St. Denis

The subprime lending crisis saw quite a few bad actors and very few heroes. Joseph St. Denis was one of the "good guys" (American Accounting Association (AAA) 2012). Similar to the other exemplars examined in this chapter, St. Denis demonstrated competence and character and gained notoriety as someone who would do the right thing under challenging circumstances.

St. Denis began his career in public accounting as an auditor with the accounting firm Coopers and Lybrand (now PwC). He then moved to the Securities and Exchange Commission (SEC) from 1998–2004, where his positions included assistant chief accountant in the division of enforcement. His SEC enforcement actions included such notable cases as Enron and Peregrine Systems and his technical competence was demonstrated in published articles on International Financial Reporting Standards, accounting risk, accounting for stock options, and accounting fraud. He also published a 2004 study on derivatives disclosure that was considered in development of FASB Statement No. 161, Disclosures about Derivative Instruments and Hedging Activities. Upon leaving the SEC in 2004, St. Denis joined the Public Company Accounting Oversight Board (PCAOB) as a staff member in the office that developed into the Office of Research and Analysis (ORA). St. Denis clearly demonstrated his professional competence and knowledge of accounting principles through his work in public accounting and at the SEC and PCAOB (AAA 2012; PCAOB 2009; St. Denis 2008).

In fact, his accounting knowledge and expertise landed him what he called his "dream job." St. Denis left the PCAOB in 2006 to become the vice president of accounting policy at American International Group (AIG) in the company's financial products group (AIGFP). St. Denis noted that this position was created in response to material weaknesses identified by AIG's auditor and to provide more control over AIGFP's accounting policy while serving as an accounting policy resource for AIGFP's staff for accounting transactions. His duties included working with other AIG components, including the financial services division and the office of accounting policy, on AIGFP's accounting policies, including complex policies relating to unusual transactions (AAA 2012; St. Denis 2008).

Unfortunately, St. Denis' dream job soon became a nightmare. During 2007, St. Denis became aware of margin calls on AIG's Super Senior Credit Default Swaps portfolio, for which he had been intentionally excluded from the discussions of the valuation of those products. When he asked his boss, Joseph Cassano, why he had not been included, he was told that they were afraid his principles "would pollute the process" (St. Denis 2008). After reflecting on these developments and believing that he was not able to do his job in a professional manner, St. Denis resigned his position and, by doing so, he forwent his year-end bonus, which would have been in the hundreds of thousands of dollars (St. Denis 2008).

St. Denis' demonstration of character in resigning from AIG under challenging circumstances brought him congressional attention as one of the few in the financial industry who acted with integrity, rather than furthering his own self-interest. His congressional testimony highlighted the fact that during 2007, AIG executives knew about potential issues with valuing credit default swaps, resulting in the $123 billion federal bailout of AIG (Jonas 2008).

After departing AIG, St. Denis returned to the PCAOB as an associate director in the Division of Enforcement and Investigations. In June, 2009, he was named director of the PCAOB's Office of Research and Analysis. ORA staff members "identify and evaluate emerging audit and accounting matters that may present elevated risk of audit failure" and work with the PCAOB Division of Registration and Inspections on audit areas for inspection (PCAOB 2009, 2012). St. Denis remained in this position until May 2012 and, upon his departure, was praised by PCAOB Chairman James Doty: "Joe's insight, innovations, and assembly of a highly professional team of experienced auditors, data analysts, and quantitative experts have placed ORA on a firm foundation to support the PCAOB and its oversight activities" (PCAOB 2012). During his tenure, the ORA created and managed the PCAOB Academic Scholarship Program, in which civil penalties collected by the PCAOB are used to support accounting students. This program has awarded millions of dollars in scholarships since its inception (PCAOB 2012).

Albert Meyer

Everyone wants to believe there are good people out there who want to make the world a better place. This belief may be even more prevalent among those who work in the nonprofit arena, themselves serving organizations with noble causes, helping people get a meal, a roof over their heads, a place to belong, a leg up, or an education. In this environment, it is especially encouraging to know that some altruistic donors believe in a cause enough to give anonymously, helping out without drawing attention to themselves. This context fueled the rapid growth of the Foundation for New Era Philanthropy, the Radnor, Pennsylvania, nonprofit corporation founded in 1989 by John Bennett, a passionate individual with a long history of serving nonprofit organizations.

Originally created to "engage in providing, free of charge, managerial and consulting services to nonprofit organizations" (Joint State Government Commission 1995, 12), New Era Philanthropy quickly morphed into a new kind of nonprofit, matching funds from established charitable organizations, from churches to colleges, with anonymous donors who believed in their causes. Their credentials were impeccable, with oversight from board of directors members like William Simon, former US Secretary of the Treasury, to rumored donors as influential as billionaire philanthropist Sir John Templeton. As word of New Era's good work spread across the nonprofit world, leaders of these organizations hoped they might receive an invitation to participate. Organizations as prestigious as the Carnegie Foundation and Harvard University as well as relatively unknown schools and churches accepted invitations to have their endowments and building funds doubled by New Era providing matching funds from likeminded anonymous donors.

New Era grew rapidly. "The foundation relied upon its favorable reputation and demonstrated legitimacy by ostensibly performing as promised" (Joint State Government Commission 1995, 2). In the fall of 1993, Glen Thornton was looking to build a new church. In his role as chairman of the board for the independent evangelical Minnehaha Community Church near Portland, Oregon, he oversaw the building fund of the small, but growing, congregation of a few hundred members that had outgrown their existing home. Having raised about a quarter of a million dollars, he was contacted by the Pacific Northwest Conservative Baptist Association, who wanted to help. They were working with New Era Philanthropy, who in turn had six to eight anonymous donors who wanted to see new churches planted in the region (Thornton 2018a).

In order to receive a matching donation to fund the new church's construction, Thornton was to put the church building funds in the hands of New Era Philanthropy. Not only was this a sign of good faith, but it also provided proof that the church had indeed raised their own funds and was serious about completing their project. After six months, the anonymous donors would double whatever amount Minnehaha was able to raise. Minnehaha's board contacted several references to confirm that New Era was legitimate. In addition, the pastor also contacted a personal friend who attended New Era Philanthropy President John Bennett's church, who gave a glowing recommendation of Bennett's character.

That fall, Minnehaha sent their building fund to New Era. A few weeks before the six months had expired, New Era sent them a letter stating additional funds were available to double their money again, should they choose to leave it with them for six more months. After some deliberation, they accepted Bennet's offer. Six months later, in January, 1995, Minnehaha received a check for nearly a million dollars. With the matching money in hand, Minnehaha built their new church, another satisfied beneficiary of New Era Philanthropy.

Earlier that year, Albert Meyer took a job teaching accounting at Spring Arbor College in the small Michigan town by the same name (Carton 1995). He and his family had immigrated to the United States from South Africa a couple of years earlier, and he was working part-time in the college's business office to make ends meet. While doing some low-level bookkeeping, he found a troubling $294,000 bank transfer. Why was the college sending their library fund to the Foundation for New Era Philanthropy?

Unsatisfied with the administration's explanation, he went on to contact Era's President John Bennett. Bennett's explanation made perfect sense. The interest earned from these holdings was used to cover New Era's operating costs, allowing 100% of the anonymous donors' contributions to go straight to the charities they supported.

Still, Meyer wondered. Bennett's explanation made sense, but was it true? His answer was good enough for hundreds of others. Why wasn't Meyer satisfied? His response was a blend of character and competence.

Meyer exhibited an unusual combination of persistence, professional skepticism, and courage in his character, buoyed by the competencies he had gained through his years as a professional accountant. He would later quip, "I have a character flaw. I'm stubborn" (Thornton 2018c). While, in hindsight, it might look to the casual observer like Meyer had 20/20 vision, in real time, Meyer's quest to determine whether fraud existed at New Era was anything but clear.

To start with, Meyer knew his suspicions might be wrong. On the one hand, New Era's operations smelled like a Ponzi scheme. Meyer had just recently read Charles Ponzi's book about his infamous fraud scheme, so "I had a good grasp of how Ponzi schemes operated" (paying early investors back with later investors' money). Still, if one assumed the existence of an extremely wealthy donor or donors (such as Sir John Templeton who was known to have had prior associations with Bennett), then New Era's story made complete sense.

But, Meyer wondered, why did recipient organizations have to put their funds with New Era? When Meyer contacted Bennett for an answer, his explanation made sense. The interest earned by New Era from the funds held in escrow provided the resources needed to run their own operations. Even ignoring his suspicion that this could be a Ponzi scheme, Meyer wondered what might happen if New Era filed for bankruptcy? Spring Arbor College's funds were unsecured, and they had no collateral. This didn't seem prudent to Meyer. Why didn't New Era just charge them a participation fee? Bennett claimed that the anonymous donors wanted to make sure the organizations they supported had skin in the game. Indeed, this was confirmed by the fact that the size of the donation was directly proportionate to the funds provided by each nonprofit organization.

It didn't help Meyer's quest for the truth when the last thing his employer wanted was for him to rock the boat. This was especially true while their library fund was still sitting in New Era's bank account. Meyer received a significant amount of pressure from the college's president to leave the matter alone. When Meyer continued to ask questions, the pressure mounted. An accountant working for the CPA firm that audited New Era warned him that his college was in danger of being excluded from future opportunities. Bennett also intimated to the university president that Meyer should back off. When New Era's check eventually came in, the administration took the opportunity to rub Meyer's nose in their success. New Era had come through, so Meyer was wrong.

Still, Meyer wasn't satisfied. Even with his own organization out of the woods, he felt that, as a professional accountant, he had an obligation to serve the public interest. If this was a Ponzi scheme, there was much more at stake than his own college. It was this duty that motivated him to continue his investigation.

In May, 1995, after a two-year dogged pursuit, Meyer found the evidence he had been looking for (Allen and Romney 1998). Using New Era Philanthropy's tax return obtained from the Internal Revenue Service, he found that they had reported just $34,000 of interest earned on nearly $20 million dollars of funds they held for hundreds of nonprofits across the country. Based on Meyer's calculation, New Era should have earned closer to $500,000 interest. At that, Meyer said, "I knew I had him" (Thornton 2018c).

Having obtained his "smoking gun," he was able to get the attention of a reporter for *The Wall Street Journal* and a lawyer from the Securities and Exchange Commission. Overnight, the Foundation for New Era Philanthropy collapsed. At that time, it was the largest Ponzi scheme in history, with assets of only $85 million to offset $551 million of liabilities. Over $506 million of their liabilities were unsecured (Joint State Government Commission 1995).

Upon revelation of the massive fraud scheme, Minnehaha Community Church returned 100% of the matching funds they received (Thornton 2018a). Other early beneficiaries acted similarly, and groups affected by the collapse of the Foundation for New Era Philanthropy eventually received about 65% of their investments back ("Defrauded Charities Will Get 65% in U.S. Settlement of Case" 1996). Without Albert Meyer's courage, persistence, and competence, things might have been much, much worse.

Cynthia Cooper

Regardless of how you feel about those you work with, it's hard to imagine that your colleagues might be fraudsters. It is even more unimaginable that the fraud would become the biggest in corporate history, especially when your colleagues are your friends, you attend each other's baby showers, maybe even belong to the same church. Yet fraud, simply defined, is theft by deception. So who would be more likely to deceive you than those you trust the most?

This is the unlikely situation that Cynthia Cooper, as the lone female VP at WorldCom, head of internal audit, found herself. She documents WorldCom's fall from grace in her illuminating autobiographical book, *Extraordinary Circumstances: The Journey of a Corporate Whistleblower* (Cooper 2009).

WorldCom was one of the fastest growing companies in the world at a time when the world was full of fast-growing companies. It was the darling of Wall Street, and as the lone Fortune 500 Company headquartered in Cooper's home state of Mississippi, beloved by the people who lived there. Even the president of the United States praised its success. Attending WorldCom's opening of their new facility in Virginia on March 1, 2000, President Clinton gushed, "I came here today because you [WorldCom] are a symbol of 21st century America. You are the embodiment of what I want for the future" (Cooper 2009, 180).

For Cooper to land such a distinguished position while only in her 30s became even sweeter when WorldCom chose her hometown of Clinton, Mississippi, population 23,000, as their headquarters. Her own well-paying job was only one among many that the company brought to town, and the resulting economic boom made WorldCom a source of pride to Cooper and her community.

Led by maverick CEO Bernie Ebbers, WorldCom had exploded into the booming telecom market like none other of its time. In the wake of the break-up of AT&T in 1983, Long Distance Delivery Service (LDDS) started out as a small reseller of long-distance phone services. On the verge of collapse, LDDS hired Ebbers as CEO in 1986, the only investor in the company at the time who seemed to have the business savvy needed to turn the fledgling company around. By parlaying his early business experience in purchasing and turning around small hotels, he adapted his same aggressive strategic approach into buying long-distance resellers. Betting everything he owned, he became LDDS' biggest stockholder, a stake that would eventually catapult him into the top 200 richest people in the United States.

His first five years as CEO, from 1986 to 1991, Ebbers grew LDDS's revenues 80-fold, to $700 million. Taking the company public in 1987, Ebbers made acquisition after acquisition, eventually surpassing even the long-standing industry giant AT&T. Ebbers was dubbed the "telecom cowboy" for his wild, Wild West persona, cowboy boots and blue jeans. Under his lead, LDDS was renamed WorldCom in 1995. By June 1999, the company's market capitalization had reached $115 billion, the fifth widest held stock in the country.

But WorldCom's rapid expansion, driven by acquiring companies not only in America but across Europe and Asia as well, left it with a "quagmire of duplicate systems and processes" (Cooper 2009, 191). This made Cooper's role as head of internal audit very challenging, especially in an environment in which the CEO lacked the understanding of the importance of the internal audit function. With him unconvinced of its importance, her internal audit team was perennially underfunded and understaffed.

In late March 2000, the record economic expansion driven by a dot.com bubble imploded in a matter of days. This was especially true of tech companies, including the 16 telecom companies in the Fortune 500. Though by this time Ebbers had amassed a fortune, with properties ranging from over a million acres of forest and ranch lands to a trucking company, his acquisitions were almost all through debt, collateralized by his WorldCom stock. He was known to frequently chastise colleagues who sold company stock or exercised their stock options, chiding them about how much better off they would have been to retain their shares.

The plunge in the market, however, led to a series of margin calls on Ebbers' debt. WorldCom's board of directors was concerned about how investors would respond if Ebbers dumped a large block of stock at a time when the industry and WorldCom's stock price was in decline, so they agreed to loan him $50 million to cover the call. But as WorldCom's stock price continued to fall, this turned out to be only the first of many such loans over the next two years. Buoying WorldCom's stock price became Ebbers' primary concern. He encouraged his CFO, Scott Sullivan, to make sure the company met analysts' earnings forecasts.

In January 2002, Ebbers called on Cooper's internal audit division to investigate an alleged commissions fraud scheme. The investigation uncovered over $10 million in commissions to salespeople that they hadn't earned; several employees were dismissed from the company as a result. But this fraud turned out to be only the beginning.

Shortly thereafter, the disgruntled head of the wireless division questioned a reduction in the allowance of uncollectible accounts without his authorization. This fact, coupled with news of Arthur Andersen's poor performance on the Enron audit, convinced Cooper to turn the internal audit team's focus to external financial reporting. Further investigations over the next couple of months revealed that allowances for uncollectible accounts in WorldCom's wireless division were understated by $300 million. Sullivan argued that other divisions more than made up for the shortfall, but Cooper wasn't convinced. She demanded Sullivan report the drop in earnings.

In late May, 2002, Cooper read a newspaper article in a local Texas paper that recounted the story of a former WorldCom analyst who was laid off in March 2001 after calling out potential abuses related to capital spending at MCI, WorldCom's subsidiary. Despite an already strained relationship with Sullivan, Cooper determined to look into potential abuses in capital spending and instructed her team to see if there was anything to the former employee's claims.

Stonewalled by Sullivan and blocked by the accounting and finance staff, which denied her direct access to accounting records, Cooper persisted in her quest to determine if assets reported in the financial statements were accurate. Unfortunately, KPMG had just replaced Arthur Andersen as WorldCom's external auditor. Cooper was unable to obtain Arthur Andersen's working papers related to capital assets, which were tied up with legal complications stemming from unpaid fees by WorldCom. Undeterred, Cooper engaged an IT staff member who had recently developed a new software for searching their complex accounting system. It took so much computing capacity, however, that it temporarily crashed the IT system. Not wanting to draw Sullivan's attention, Cooper and her team began to work at night. This gave them the opportunity they needed to search for more accounting fraud.

The work was slow in yielding results, but despite concerns for her job and those of her team, along with concerns for her personal safety, Cooper continued the hunt. Eventually, they came across an asset account titled "prepaid capacity." No one on her team understood the account. Upon further investigation, they found that no one else understood the accounting either. By carefully analyzing a maze of transactions designed to cover the accounting tracks, they traced the account approval to Betty Vinson. She reported to David Myers, a director of accounting, who reported directly to Sullivan.

Cooper's team had uncovered a fraudulent scheme, masterminded by Sullivan, to capitalize operating leases related to line costs. By adding these costs to prepaid assets rather than properly expensing them as period costs, WorldCom was able to increase both net income and assets. Starting with financial analysts' forecasted earnings expectations, Sullivan had worked backwards, backing into the capitalized lease amounts. When totally unwound, Cooper found $3.8 billion of inappropriate journal entries, all directly increasing the bottom line. It was the largest fraud in US corporate history at the time.

Sullivan would later testify that he was able to keep the fraud hidden from external audit, the board, internal audit, analysts, and investors, until Cooper and the internal audit team discovered it in June 2002. He also testified that he lied to Cooper and her team and instructed the accounting team (David Myers, Betty Vinson, and Troy Normand) to do the same. Myers testified that he limited the internal audit team's access to the accounting system and instructed others to do the same. When forensic accountants completed their investigation, they uncovered a fraud of nearly $11 billion.

Bernie Ebbers was sentenced to 25 years in prison, with Sullivan, Myers, and Vinson all receiving prison sentences. Arthur Andersen, effectively destroyed by their failed Enron audit, settled the lawsuits against them for $65 million. Twelve board members also settled for $55 million, including $25 million from directors, an amount set at one fifth of each of their net worth.

In an interview with Thornton (2018b), Cooper reflected back,

> At times I came under tremendous pressure and hostility. Some executives testified that they tried various ways to obfuscate and head me off in a different direction. I was asked to delay an audit, instructed not to request support for certain accounting entries, and told that I was wasting company time and resources and should be reviewing other areas of the company. There were times when my hands

were shaking and my heart was pounding, and I had to find a way to push forward in the face of that fear. I can remember my mother telling me as a young girl, "Don't ever allow yourself to be intimidated." I think, as much as anything, her words ingrained from childhood have helped me find my courage at times when I needed it the most.

In exposing the massive fraud at WorldCom, Cooper exhibited courage, a quiet confidence and persistence, and ultimately the competence needed to unravel a fraud that no one else had the courage or will to face.

Abraham Briloff

Abraham "Abe" Briloff is the accounting educator who may best exemplify the characteristics of competence and character. Dr. Briloff served as an accounting professor at City University of New York's Baruch College for over 60 years and for 45 years wrote books and articles for *Barron's* that were focused on accurate financial reporting. His attempts to raise accounting standards and improve accounting professionalism led to his being considered by many to be the conscience of the profession.

Briloff was not above criticizing a corporation's financial reporting or the accounting profession in attempting to advocate for increased accuracy and transparency. He did this in a variety of ways. He frequently highlighted instances in which CRAP (cleverly rigged accounting ploys) substituted for GAAP (generally accepted accounting principles) (Criscione 2009). For example, his many *Barron's* articles pointed out accounting problems with companies such as Leasco Corp., Lockheed, Gulf and Western, General Motors, Waste Management, Metromedia, IBM, and Disney (Briloff 1980; Criscione 2009; Weiss 2012). Some of these cases were elaborated on in his book *Unaccountable Accounting: Games Accountants Play* (1972), in which he noted that while the expanding role of corporations and the executives who control them required independent auditors to ensure transparency and accountability, the auditors were falling short in this role (Briloff 1972). Briloff recommended measures to different groups (financial analysts, investors, government officials, corporate management, and the accounting profession) that would improve the state of affairs. He also advocated for a "Corporate Accountability Commission" with representation from accounting practitioners, academics, banking, labor, investment, consumers, and government that would focus on proper financial disclosures for corporations (Briloff 1972). Two decades later, Briloff revisited the topics in *Unaccountable Accounting*, noting the absence of progress; he attributed this to the oligopolistic nature of the large accounting firms, which had decreased from eight to six and maintained significant power over the accounting profession and its regulators (Briloff 1993).

Throughout his long career, Professor Briloff continually demonstrated competence and character. His competence was frequently displayed through his analyses for *Barron's* and his books. His *Barron's* articles resulted in lawsuits against both *Barron's* and Briloff by some of the companies he examined. None of these proved to be successful. Furthermore, markets paid attention to his analyses. Foster (1979) studied the market reaction to companies negatively profiled by Briloff and found approximately an 8% drop in stock price on the day Briloff's article appeared. Foster also found that this price decline persisted after 30 days. Desai and Jain (2004) examined the long-run negative market reaction to companies criticized by Briloff in his *Barron's* articles between 1968 and 1998. They found decreased stock prices of 15.51% and 22.88%

for one year and two years, respectively. Their follow-up discussions (Desai and Jain 2004, 54) with Briloff highlighted his competence:

> Our results indicate that Briloff was better able to foresee the coming decline in performance than the market, on average. Does Briloff identify some red flags that the market has overlooked? When we met with Briloff and asked him several questions to understand his thought process as well as to discern any theme to the articles he writes, he told us that he does not follow any checklist. He mentioned that many years of hard work have given him a sixth sense in analyzing financial statements. His articles indeed cover a wide range of topics, such as pooling accounting, lease accounting, and accounting for in-process R&D costs. In some sense, the topics he covers are discussed in most accounting textbooks. The only theme that we can see is an interest in finding out if the company is making an effort to overstate its financial results through aggressive accounting. His skill, it appears, lies in combining several aspects of financial statements into a coherent analysis.

Professor Briloff's superior technical competence is arguably only exceeded by his exceptional character. As already noted, he advocated for accuracy, transparency, and accountability in financial reporting and did so for decades. Even though he retired from Baruch College in 1987, he continued to recommend improvements to financial reporting and the accounting profession. He appeared before Congress 15 times between 1970 and 2002, providing testimony on different financial and accounting problems during that period. His 2002 congressional testimony, after the well-publicized accounting failures that led to the passage of the Sarbanes-Oxley Act of 2002, addressed such issues as accounting firms providing consulting services and the need for better internal controls. These were topics that Briloff had identified as problems many years earlier. His perseverance was also notable, as he worked into his 90s despite suffering from glaucoma-related blindness for the last 10 years of his life. In these later years he was assisted by his daughter Leonore, a CPA, who would help Briloff with research that while challenging, provided meaning to his life (Weiss 2012). A reporter (Weiss 2012, 38) who interviewed Professor Briloff as he approached his 95th birthday provided commentary on his positive character traits:

> Despite the years of struggle, sometimes futile, Briloff isn't cynical or defeated. Conversations with him reveal a man who certainly isn't the narrowly-focused, technically-oriented, green-eyeshaded bean counter of popular stereotype, but rather a crusader with a fervent passion for justice and equity, laced with a stern but gentle Old World sense of morality. He views himself not as whistleblower or gadfly, but as a defender of his profession, inspired by his mentor and former professor in the 1930s, Emanuel Saxe.

Upon Professor Briloff's passing in 2013 at the age of 96, one of his colleagues at *Barron's* noted "In describing Abe, especially in eulogy, it's tempting to call him a combination of an Old Testament prophet, John Milton, Sherlock Holmes, and the blind superhero Daredevil. But none of those guys did the math" (Alpert 2013). This unique combination of talents, along with his demonstration of competence and character, help explain why we will not see the likes of Abe Briloff again. He remains a shining example for other accounting educators and researchers interested in improved financial reporting transparency and accountability.

Arthur Levitt

Arthur Levitt was the longest-serving Securities and Exchange (SEC) Commissioner in history, holding that position from 1992–2001. As SEC chair, Levitt was focused on protecting individual investors and noted for his efforts to promote integrity in financial reporting, address the management of corporate earnings, and improve accounting transparency and accuracy. These topics were addressed by Levitt in "The Numbers Game" speech (Levitt 1998) given on September 28, 1998, at the New York University Center for Law and Business. This high-profile speech focused on earnings management as firms attempted to meet Wall Street corporate earnings projections. Levitt outlined five "accounting gimmicks" that were detracting from the integrity of financial statements: (1) "Big Bath" restructuring charges; (2) creative acquisition; (3) "Cookie Jar Reserves"; (4) misuse of the materiality concept when recording errors; and (5) manipulating revenue recognition. Levitt called for a number of measures to address these issues, including accounting rule changes to increase transparency, improved revenue recognition guidance by the SEC, and additional SEC oversight and enforcement for firms that appear to be managing earnings.

Chairman Levitt also focused on the role of audit committees and the accounting profession in The Numbers Game speech. He noted the important role of audit committees in protecting the interests of investors and recommended that audit committee members have a financial background, meet frequently, and ask difficult questions to both management and the firm's auditors. He also called for improved audit performance amid the recent high-profile accounting failures. He highlighted the role of auditors as the "public's watchdog" and emphasized the need for proper auditor objectivity, integrity, and judgment (Levitt 1998).

Levitt was well-prepared for the SEC chair position, having spent 28 years on Wall Street (16 years at a brokerage firm and 12 years at the American Stock Exchange, including 11 as chair of the AMEX), and four years as the publisher of *Roll Call*, which reported on Congress and permitted him to work with many congressmen and their staff members. Levitt's focus on individual investors was influenced by his father, Arthur Levitt, Sr., who served as New York state comptroller for 24 years, during which he protected the New York public employee pension fund from state and local officials who wanted to use the fund to support state and municipal finances, such as a potential bailout of New York City (Levitt and Dwyer 2002).

Chairman Levitt made various proposals to improve financial reporting transparency and accuracy, thereby providing better information for investors. These included his support of a Financial Accounting Standards Board (FASB) proposed rule calling for the expensing of stock options, his advocacy for Regulation Fair Disclosure, or Reg FD, and his support for limiting the consulting that accounting firms could do for their clients (which would promote the desired independence required of auditors) (Levitt and Dwyer 2002). Levitt was particularly concerned about auditors providing consulting services to their clients due to the significant growth of the practice and the possible independence problems. In 1976, audit fees comprised 70% of audit firm revenues; this decreased to 31% in 1998 (Levitt and Dwyer 2002). As Levitt noted in his book *Take on the Street* (Levitt and Dwyer 2002, 118):

> Independence means that auditors should not be in bed with the corporate managers whose numbers they audit. They cannot review their own work or that of their partners. If an accountant keeps the books for a client, he can't turn around and vouch for the accuracy and completeness of those books. After all, what accountants would want to draw attention to their own mistakes?

Levitt experienced mixed success in enacting these proposed changes. On a positive note, even though Reg FD received opposition from certain business leaders and even one of the SEC commissioners, it was enacted in October 2000. Reg FD led to more company disclosures to shareholders and the press. Levitt regards Reg FD as the most significant rule to increase investor confidence that took place during his tenure as SEC chair (Levitt and Dwyer 2002). However, he was not able to achieve similar success with the expensing of stock options, which amid significant political pressure was watered down to simply require that stock option grants be disclosed in the notes to the financial statements. Similarly, limiting the consulting activities of accounting firms received a political backlash as the accounting profession lobbied Congress, providing over $14 million in contributions during the 2000 election cycle. The proposal was ultimately weakened to only curtail certain types of consulting (e.g., maintaining accounting records for a client), while essentially permitting almost unlimited information systems consulting and up to 40% of internal audit work for audit clients (Levitt and Dwyer 2002).

Levitt's tenure as SEC chair was characterized by his many displays of competence and character. The measures he proposed to increase the quality of financial reporting and limit auditing consulting opportunities were sound and consistent with helping individual investors. He was not above admitting when he was wrong, as he suggested was the case with his ultimately withdrawing support for the FASB proposed rule on expensing stock options. In cases when he did back down, he tried to balance progress on the proposals discussed earlier with preserving the FASB role as standard setter and maintaining the SEC budget so it could remain an effective regulating agency. Similar to the case of Professor Briloff discussed previously, Levitt's outspoken positions appear to have been vindicated when a variety of his concerns (e.g., auditor independence issues, the role of audit committees) were addressed in the Sarbanes-Oxley Act passed in 2002.

After stepping down as SEC chair in 2002, Levitt remained an active voice for honest financial reporting and investor protection. In an address to KPMG Partners in 2003, he stressed that accounting profession measures enacted in the aftermath of the Enron and other failures would restore investor confidence and earn back the public's trust. These included putting investors (instead of management) first, cooperating with regulators and standard setters, and proactively maintaining independence (Levitt 2004). Also, in 2003, Levitt spoke to finance executives at a CFO conference. He emphasized the important roles that they play, particularly after the demise of Enron and WorldCom:

> You are in the front tier in the battle for more transparency, more accountability, and more ethical behavior on the part of Corporate America. In many ways, you hold the most important positions in your companies. You are the investors' guarantor of good information, and through that a crucial gatekeeper ensuring that our markets allocate capital efficiently and fairly. Perhaps most of all, you are the person who says no. . . . You can and should be the conscience of your companies, providing the moral, ethical, and professional grounding that our executives need.
>
> *(Levitt 2003, 1)*

In addition to stressing the need for improved performance from the accounting profession and finance executives, Levitt was proactive in his support for the Sarbanes-Oxley Act. In a 2004 *Wall Street Journal* editorial with former Chairman of the Federal Reserve Paul Volcker (Volcker and Levitt 2004), the two financial regulators defended the reforms that led to increased auditor independence, stronger audit committees, better internal controls, and improved financial reports. They argued that the Sarbanes-Oxley Act's benefits exceeded its costs and led to higher investor confidence and an improved market system that resulted from superior regulation.

Like the other accounting exemplars presented in this chapter, Arthur Levitt is known for both his competence and character as he tried to improve the accounting profession and restore investors' faith in the financial markets. His credibility in these areas was on display when Levitt spoke at the American Institute of Certified Public Accountants 2000 Fall Council Meeting. During his address, he focused on the vital roles of both large and small accounting practitioners and their need to promote trust and confidence in the financial markets. He also emphasized the auditing profession as a noble one and the importance of a CPA's integrity and independence (Levitt 2000). Levitt's dedication to these principles was recognized by Warren Buffett, who observed: "During my lifetime, the small investor has never had a better friend than former SEC chairman Arthur Levitt. His goal was unwavering: To have markets that served the interests of investors, both large and small" (Levitt 2002, cover).

Concluding remarks

In this chapter, we profiled six accounting exemplars who displayed competency, courage, and integrity in the performance of their responsibilities. Despite death threats to his family, Frank Wilson brought down Chicago mafia don Al Capone through his diligent investigation of Capone's money laundering operations; Wilson also is credited with bringing Bruno Hauptmann, the murderer of Charles Lindbergh's young son, to justice through his innovative forensic accounting methods. Although told not to continue her investigation by WorldCom CFO Scott Sullivan, Cynthia Cooper and her team worked late at night to uncover Sullivan's accounting fraud at the telecom giant. AIG's Joseph St. Denis resigned, forfeiting his massive bonus, rather than participate in the company's risky investments that led to the financial crisis in 2008–10; he also served the public through his work with the SEC and PCAOB, including, but certainly not limited to, creating a PCAOB student scholarship from penalties resulting from corporate wrongdoing. In the accounting education profession, Albert Meyer exposed a massive fraud at the Foundation for New Era Philanthropy that targeted nonprofit educational institutions and museums, and Abraham Briloff was an outspoken critic of the accounting profession while advocating for increased transparency in corporate financial statements. Lastly, we include Arthur Levitt, Jr., the longest-serving Securities and Exchange Commission (SEC) Chairman, who made positive contributions to accounting regulation that led to the increase of transparency and the reduction of fraud in corporate financial statements. It is not surprising that five of the six individuals profiled in this chapter have received the American Accounting Association's Accounting Exemplar Award. This award is presented to an accounting educator or practitioner who has made notable contributions to professionalism and ethics in accounting education and/or practice (AAA 2018).

There are many others who also certainly deserve recognition that, for space reasons, we are not able to include in this chapter. For example, Jaruvan Maintaka, the "Iron Lady" of Thailand, exposed fraud in the Thai government despite threats to her life. Marta Andreasson, a European Union (EU) whistleblower who fought corruption in the EU bureaucracy, was elected to the EU Parliament. Sylvester Hentschel, an examiner for Ohio's State Commerce Department's Division of Savings and Loans, called Home State Savings Bank "a veritable time bomb" because of its overreliance on investments with ESM Government Securities Inc.; his prescient warnings were ignored by superiors, and the bank collapsed in 1982 when federal investigators shut down the fraudulent investment fund ("Home State Warning in'82," *New York Times* 1985). US Army Corps of Engineers chief contracting officer Bunnatine "Bunny" Greenhouse's warnings about procurement fraud in the organization's dealings with defense contractor Halliburton were similarly ignored; Greenhouse's actions to bring the illegal contracts to light earned her the Association of Certified Fraud Examiner's prestigious Cliff Robertson Sentinel Award. We recognize that this list of accounting exemplars is not exhaustive.[6] There are many others who have also fought fraud and corruption whose names we don't yet know, but hopefully by sharing the stories of those we do know, those in the accounting profession will be encouraged to exhibit similar virtues of competency and character in the performance of their professional responsibilities.

Notes

1 The discussion of virtues is not new. Aristotle believed that the exercise of virtue requires "a capacity to judge and to do the right thing in the right place at the right time in the right way" (MacIntyre 1984, 149–50).
2 Tax evasion was a relatively new crime, with a permanent Federal Income Tax being implemented in 1913.
3 In today's terms, this amount would equate to a net annual profit of almost $6,000,000 in unreported revenues.
4 "In 1932, it was expected that all the gold certificates in circulation would be recalled within a year. Although legal tender, gold certificates were distinctive from the silver certificates and Federal Reserve notes that were to remain in circulation" (Irey 1948).
5 Charles Lindbergh, Jr.'s body was found in a shallow grave on May 12, 1932.
6 Although outside the scope of this chapter, we wanted to mention EY accountant Dave Karnes, who left work on September 12, 2001, to assist in the Twin Towers rescue effort and is credited with saving the last two survivors of the 9/11 terrorist attack.

References

Allen, R., and B. Romney. 1998. "Lessons from New Era." *Internal Auditors* 55 (5) (October): 40–48.
Alpert, B. 2013. "Remembering Abe Briloff." *Barron's* (December 21).
American Accounting Association (AAA). 2012. "Press Release – 2012 Public Interest Accounting Exemplar Award."
American Accounting Association (AAA). 2018. "Accounting Exemplar Award." http://aaahq.org/Education/Awards/Accounting-Exemplar-Award
Armstrong, M. B., J. E. Ketz, and D. Owsen. 2003. "Ethics Education in Accounting: Moving Toward Ethical Motivation and Ethical Behavior." *Journal of Accounting Education* 21 (1st Quarter): 1–16. doi:10.1016/S0748-5751(02)00017-9
Briloff, A. J. 1972. *Unaccountable Accounting – Games Accountants Play.* New York: Harper & Row.
Briloff, A. J. 1980. "Leveraged Leasco." *Barron's National Business and Financial Weekly*, October 20.
Briloff, A. J. 1993. "Unaccountable Accounting Revisited." *Critical Perspectives on Accounting* 4: 301–35. doi:10.1006/cpac.1993.1018
Carton, B. 1995. "Who's News: Unlikely Hero: A Persistent Accountant Brought New Era's Problems to Light." *The Wall Street Journal*, Eastern edition; New York (May 19): B1.
Cooper, C. 2009. *Extraordinary Circumstances: The Journey of a Corporate Whistleblower.* Hoboken, NJ: Wiley.
Criscione, E. R. 2009. *Abraham J. (Abe) Briloff – A Biography.* Bingley, UK: JAI Press.
"Defrauded Charities Will Get 65% in U.S. Settlement of Case." 1996. *New York Times*, August 24: 39.
Desai H., and P. C. Jain. 2004. "Long-Run Stock Returns Following Briloff's Analyses." *Financial Analysts Journal* 60 (2): 47–56. doi:10.2469/faj.v60.n2.2609
Foster, G. 1979. "Briloff and the Capital Market." *Journal of Accounting Research*, 17 (1): 262–74. doi:10.2307/2490317
Gentile, M. C. 2009. *Giving Voice to Values: How to Speak Your Mind When You Know What is Right.* New Haven: Yale University Press.
"Home State Warning in'82." 1985. *New York Times*, July 31: 8.
Irey, E. L. 1948. *The Tax Dodgers.* New York: Greenburg.

Joint State Government Commission. 1995. "The Collapse of the Foundation for New Era Philanthropy. Staff Report to the General Assembly Including a Narrative of the Foundation's Operations and an Analysis of the Relevant Regulatory Statutes, General Assembly of the Commonwealth of Pennsylvania." November 1995, 1–64. http://jsg.legis.state.pa.us/resources/documents/ftp/publications/1995-11-01%201995%20The%20Collapse%20of%20the%20Foundation%20for%20New%20Era%20Philanthropy.pdf

Jonas, I. 2008. "AIG Knew of Potential Problems in Valuing Swaps: Report." *Reuters*, October 12. www.reuters.com/article/us-aig-swaps-wsj/aig-knew-of-potential-problems-in-valuing-swaps-report-idUSTRE49B2WW20081012

Levitt, A., Jr. 1998. "The 'Numbers Game' – Remarks by Chairman Arthur Levitt, Securities and Exchange Commission." September 28, 1998. www.sec.gov/news/speech/speecharchive/1998/spch220.txt.

Levitt, A., Jr. 2000. "The Public's Profession – Remarks by Chairman Arthur Levitt, Securities and Exchange Commission." October 24, 2000. www.sec.gov/news/speech/spch410.htm.

Levitt, A., Jr. 2003. "Former SEC Chairman Arthur Levitt Offers Some Pointed Advice on How to Restore Confidence in Corporate Accounting." *CFO* (May): 1.

Levitt, A., Jr. 2004. "Reclaiming the Profession's Heritage: Remarks by Arthur Levitt, Jr." *The CPA Journal* (February): 22–27.

Levitt, A and P. Dwyer. 2002. *Take on the Street – What Wall Street and Corporate America Don't Want You to Know.* New York: Pantheon Books.

Libby, T., and L. Thorne. 2004. "The Identification and Categorization of Auditors' Virtues." *Business Ethics Quarterly* 14 (3): 479–98. doi:10.5840/beq200414331

MacIntyre, A. 1984. *After Virtue.* 2nd ed. Notre Dame, IN: University of Notre Dame Press.

Mintz, S. M. 1995. "Virtue Ethics and Accounting Education." *Issues in Accounting Educatio* 10 (Fall): 247–68.

Pincoffs, E. L. 1986. *Quandaries and Virtues.* Lawrence, KS: University Press of Kansas.

Public Company Accounting Oversight Board (PCAOB). 2009. "Joseph St. Denis Named PCAOB Director of Research and Analysis." https://pcaobus.org/News/Releases/Pages/06162009_RADirector.aspx

Public Company Accounting Oversight Board (PCAOB). 2012. "Research and Analysis Director Joseph St. Denis to Leave the PCAOB." https://pcaobus.org/News/Releases/Pages/05152012_JosephStDenisResignation.aspx

Spiering, F. 1976. *The Man Who Got Capone.* Indianapolis: Bobbs-Merrill Company, Inc.

St. Denis, J. 2008. "Letter to Henry Waxman, Chairman, House of Representatives Committee on Oversight and Government Reform." October 4. https://democrats-oversight.house.gov/sites/democrats.oversight.house.gov/files/migrated/20081007102452.pdf

Thornton, J. 2018a. Personal communication with Glen Thornton, September 4.

Thornton, J. 2018b. Personal communication with Cynthia Cooper, September 9.

Thornton, J. 2018c. Personal communication with Albert Meyer, September 12.

Troy, G. 2017. "The Bean Counter Who Put Al Capone in the Slammer." *The Daily Beast,* August 26, 2017. Accessed March 5, 2018.

Volcker, P., and A. Levitt Jr. 2004. "In Defense of Sarbanes-Oxley." *The Wall Street Journal* (June 14): A16.

Weiss, G. 2012. "Champion of Accounting and Accountability." *Barron's* 92 (21) (May 21): 38–39.

Wilson, Frank J., and Beth Day. 1965. *Special Agent; A Quarter Century with the Treasury Department and the Secret Service.* New York: Holt, Rinehart and Winston.

Wilson, Frank J., and H. Whitman. 1947. "Undercover Man: He Trapped Capone." *Collier's Weekly* (April 26): 14–15.

24

INVESTIGATING THE ETHICAL IMPLICATIONS OF WHISTLEBLOWING WITHIN ACCOUNTING

Phebian Davis, Amy M. Donnelly, and Robin R. Radtke

Introduction

Near and Miceli (1985, 4) define whistleblowing as "the disclosure by organization members (former or current) of illegal, immoral, or illegitimate practices under the control of their employers, to persons or organizations that may be able to effect action." The decision to blow the whistle often presents an ethical dilemma for the whistleblower and depends on many factors that include differing perceptions of duties, loyalties, and obligations. Employees within an organization often feel a moral obligation to report wrongdoing and are more likely to do so when the work environment supports and encourages ethical behavior and whistleblowing (Alleyne, Hudaib, and Haniffa 2018). They must also consider the possible negative consequences of blowing the whistle, specifically retaliation and personal costs, as well as costs to the company involved.

Whistleblowing research is diverse and has expanded rapidly over the last decade. While multiple studies have investigated topics such as characteristics of the whistleblower, the wrongdoing, and the organization (see Gao and Brink [2017] for a review of this literature), we focus on the ethical considerations of the whistleblowing process. It is undeniable that accountants are in a unique position to both observe as well as take part in financial wrongdoing, as accountants within organizations provide crucial bookkeeping, auditing, taxation, and overall financial analysis services, while external auditors provide attestation services. The importance of whistleblowing is exemplified by multiple famous cases including Enron and WorldCom.

Analysis of the ethical aspects of whistleblowing is important, as accountants operate under the American Institute of Certified Public Accountants' (hereafter AICPA) Code of Professional Conduct, which requires AICPA members to "discharge their responsibilities with integrity, objectivity, due professional care, and a genuine interest in serving the public" (AICPA 2018, 5). The code also states that "The accounting profession's public consists of clients, credit grantors, governments, employers, investors, the business and financial community" and "members may encounter conflicting pressures from each of those groups" (AICPA 2018, 5). Paeth (2013) suggests that conditions that warrant whistleblowing exist when the multiple loyalties an individual faces come into conflict with each other. In such circumstances, at least one loyalty may have to be sacrificed. Professional responsibilities are not unique to accountants, as many other professions also have a public interest emphasis, and within engineering, Bouville (2008) suggests that whistleblowing is mandatory for engineers whose code of the National Society of Professional Engineering has as its first canon duty to the public. Extending this logic suggests that accountants should also have a duty to report any observed misconduct given the emphasis on the public interest in the AICPA Code and similar codes of conduct for accountants (e.g., Institute of Management Accountants (hereafter IMA), Institute of Internal Auditors (hereafter IIA), Chartered Accountants Australia and New Zealand (hereafter CA ANZ), Institute of Chartered Accountants in England and Wales (hereafter ICAEW), etc.).

The remainder of the chapter is organized as follows: In the first section, we examine whistleblowing and its importance in accounting. Second, we explore the various reporting channels available for whistleblowers and under what conditions the various channels may be used. Third, we highlight ways that companies can encourage whistleblowing behavior in terms of both organizational and individual characteristics. Finally, we look at the ethical implications of the whistleblowing process by analyzing the impact of whistleblowing on the two primary parties affected: the whistleblower and the company involved.

Why is whistleblowing important for accounting?

Whistleblowing has been addressed in many different disciplines and contexts. This chapter addresses whistleblowing in the accounting context. Shareholders and other stakeholders make financial decisions based on financial statements, and thus it is imperative that the financial statements are not materially misstated. Understanding whistleblowing in the accounting context is therefore critical. Accountants and auditors effectively serve as corporate monitors and are often in a position to observe financial wrongdoing early in the process, when they can help minimize costs related to such frauds by blowing the whistle in a timely fashion (Seifert et al. 2010). According to its 2018 Global Study on Occupational Fraud and Abuse, the Association of Certified Fraud Examiners (hereafter ACFE) (2018), finds a direct and consistent relationship between fraud duration and median loss (associated with the fraud); frauds lasting over five years cost 20 times as much as frauds detected within the first six months.

Types of accounting-related misconduct that may warrant whistleblowing include many different egregious acts beyond fraud. Lee and Xiao (2018) identify 59 studies investigating accounting-related whistleblowing during their sample period of 1991 to 2017. Of these 59 studies, 40 included investigation of some sort of fraudulent act including misappropriation of assets, embezzlement, bribery, and corruption. However, the second most common type of whistleblowing investigated is violation of auditor independence and/or the Code of Professional Conduct (with ten studies included in their sample period), thus highlighting the importance of whistleblowing for accounting misconduct beyond fraud (Lee and Xiao 2018). One of the broadest studies on types of accounting misconduct and whistleblowing is Bowen, Call, and Rajgopal (2010). They investigate whistleblowing allegations against firms from 1989 through 2004 and identify overbilling, earnings management, price fixing, insider trading, tax fraud, and improper disclosure as specific types of accounting activities that necessitated whistleblowing. It is important to note that although fraud is often thought of as the most prominent type of accounting-related whistleblowing, accountants may certainly encounter other types of illegal, immoral, or illegitimate practices that may warrant blowing the whistle.

Whistleblowing and Fraud

The importance of identifying fraud is highlighted by the ACFE (2018, 6) who states "Fraud in general poses a tremendous threat to organizations of all types and sizes, in all parts of the world." In the AFCE's 2018 Global Survey on Occupational Fraud and Abuse, participating certified fraud examiners (CFEs) report a median estimated fraud loss of approximately 5% of annual firm revenues. Because we cannot possibly know of all global cases of occupational fraud, it is impossible to calculate an accurate total global fraud loss. However, when the reported estimated annual revenue loss of 5% is applied to a 2017 estimate for gross world product of $79.6 trillion, an estimated global loss to fraud would be approximately $4 trillion. In the same report, the ACFE estimates total fraud losses of over $7.1 billion in the 2,690 fraud cases investigated between January 2016 and October 2017 (ACFE 2018). While 48% of the reported fraud cases occurred within the United States, other global regions are certainly not immune to fraud, as 13% of the cases occurred in Sub-Saharan Africa and another 11% of the cases were in the Asia-Pacific region. Interestingly, while the vast majority of reported frauds occurred in the United States, the reported median loss of $108,000 in the United States was among the smallest reported, while the median loss of $236,000 in the Asia-Pacific region was the largest reported.

The accounting profession plays a vital role in the whistleblowing process, and whistleblowing has become "an effective mechanism to detect fraud" (Lee and Xiao 2018, 22). The US Securities and Exchange Commission (hereafter SEC) (2014, 1) even acknowledges that whistleblowers "perform a great service to investors and help us combat fraud." As a result, the SEC has awarded millions of dollars to whistleblowers for assisting in resolving complicated fraud schemes through the SEC's whistleblower program authorized by the Dodd-Frank Act (SEC 2017). Awards can range from 10% to 30% of the money collected in a fraud case. While the Foreign Corrupt Practices Act affords whistleblowers from outside of the US protection against retaliation (Global Whistleblower 2018), recently the European Commission published a proposed directive for whistleblower protection across the European Union (European Commission 2018). Recent improvements in whistleblower protection have also been enacted in both China in 2016 (vandePol, Wu, and Hui 2016) and Korea in 2018 (Anti-Corruption and Civil Rights Commission, Republic of Korea 2018).

Though numerous studies have highlighted the importance of whistleblowing, there remains a reluctance to blow the whistle on misconduct (Lee and Xiao 2018; Miceli, Near, and Dworkin 2008). The Ethics Resource Center (2012) reported that of the 41% of surveyed employees who observed wrongdoing in their workplace, 33% did not report it. This silence is typically a result of the organizational environment in which the employees work. Near and Miceli (1985) note that organizational structure and ethical climate can encourage or discourage whistleblowing. Whistleblowing intentions are also influenced by the potential whistleblower's perception of organizational support and whether the company will change the wrongdoing (Gao and Brink 2017).

Accountants who are in a position to stop wrongdoing and decline to do so shirk their moral duty to act by turning a blind eye. Nearly all practicing accountants are governed by some sort of code of conduct. Certified public accountants (CPAs) are governed by the AICPA Code of Professional Conduct, which includes a "Responsibilities" principle that states: "In carrying out their responsibilities as professionals, members should exercise sensitive professional and moral judgments in all their activities" (AICPA 2018, 5). Similarly, certified management accountants (CMAs) are guided by the standards of ethical practice of the Institute of Management Accountants (IMA), while the Institute of Internal Auditors (IIA) and both the Chartered Accountants Australia & New Zealand (CA ANZ) and the Institute of Chartered Accountants in England and Wales (ICAEW) have similar codes of conduct for ethical guidance of internal auditors and chartered accountants, respectively. More broadly, just recently the International Federation of Accountants (IFAC) rewrote its Code of Ethics to make the code easier to use, navigate, and enforce for the approximate 2.8 million accountants in public practice, industry, government, commerce, and education in over 130 countries and jurisdictions that constitute the IFAC (IFAC 2018).

Whistleblowing and auditors

Since corporate accountants are most likely to be the first to observe financial misconduct, many of the financial frauds over the last 20 years were not discovered by external auditors but rather were discovered and reported by employees who had access to accounting information. In fact, it was determined that external auditors were directly involved with or complicit in covering up some of the largest financial frauds, with Arthur Andersen first being fined $7 million by the SEC for its involvement in the Waste Management fraud and then later being indicted in the Enron fraud (Corporate Finance Institute 2018). Beyond a perceived responsibility to act, auditors have a greater professional duty to report known instances of fraud. With the public and other external stakeholders relying on auditors to certify that the financial statements are free of material misstatement, whether caused by error or fraud (PCAOB 2015), auditors inherently face a higher standard of duty (to the public and greater society) than the internal accountant when it comes to blowing the whistle. As such, it is imperative to understand the role of auditors in the whistleblowing process and the related implications from such a role.

Accounting research has looked at auditing and whistleblowing from several different perspectives. Some of the prior research related to whistleblowing and auditors focuses on the likelihood of auditors reporting wrongdoing within a public accounting firm (Kaplan 1995; Curtis and Taylor 2009; Taylor and Curtis 2013). Kaplan (1995) suggests that when a necessary audit step has been omitted and when the wrongdoer has a poor work history, auditors are more likely to blow the whistle. Curtis and Taylor (2009) find auditors with high moral intensity, an internal locus of control, and those who trust the firm to remedy the wrongdoing are more likely to internally report wrongdoing. Taylor and Curtis (2013) note that an auditor is more likely to report wrongdoing of a colleague over a supervisor, particularly when the organization has failed to act on wrongdoing in the past, suggesting that the whistleblower can get credit for reporting the wrongdoing while not actually causing problems for their colleague. Additionally, Robertson, Stefaniak, and Curtis (2011) look at an auditor's propensity to blow the whistle on another auditor when it involves professional responsibility. They find that experienced auditors are more likely to blow the whistle, and they prefer to do so internally, preferably on a wrongdoer who is not very likeable. However, Robertson, Stefaniak, and Curtis (2011) also find that auditors are more likely to blow the whistle externally when there are greater professional repercussions for failing to do so.

Accounting research also explores whistleblowing as it relates to the audit client and the auditor (Kaplan, Pope, and Samuels 2011; Curtis and Taylor 2009; Dyck, Morse, and Zingales 2010). Kaplan, Pope, and Samuels (2011) observed auditors as recipients of financial misconduct disclosures. They find that when an auditor makes a direct fraud-related inquiry of the client, client personnel are more likely to disclose knowledge of wrongdoing to the inquiring auditor. They also find that employees are more likely to disclose suspected wrongdoing to internal auditors over external auditors.

Unfortunately, the auditor is often poorly incentivized to act as a whistleblower (see discussion of monetary incentives within the "Environmental Characteristics" section), and the whistleblowing act is not without consequences to the auditor. Dyck, Morse, and Zingales (2010) note that auditors who blow the whistle are more likely to lose the account of the company involved in the fraud. Additionally, they find that after a fraud is revealed, the client is more likely to replace the auditor, and even more so if the auditor reveals the fraud. While auditors may incur reputational damage from blowing the whistle and being replaced, other research suggests that auditors don't always lose from whistleblowing. Fuerman (2006) finds that even though the market knew that Arthur Anderson's auditing had deteriorated before the Enron scandal, the firm's market share did not decline. In addition, Chen and Zhou (2007) find that poorly governed firms look for low-quality auditors, and Dyck, Morse, and Zingales (2010) find that there are minor positive reputation effects that increase the probability of auditors who have blown the whistle gaining new clients. Overall, incentives for auditors to blow the whistle are relatively weak. The more negative impacts on reputation, loss of clients, and not being able to attract new clients outweigh the small benefits of blowing the whistle for an auditor.

Auditors are undisputedly an integral part of the whistleblowing process. Though some research suggests that auditors hesitate to report wrongdoing by colleagues, other research notes that auditors will not hesitate to blow the whistle on other auditors under certain conditions. Auditors also tend to be recipients of potential whistleblowing information. Along with their perceived moral responsibility to act, auditors have an incentive to uphold their professional duties. The AICPA (2002) statement of auditing standards (SAS 99) section 316 requires the auditor, once there is evidence that a fraud may exist, to bring the matter to the attention of the proper level of management; at least one level above those involved.

Whistleblowing channels

Importance of multiple whistleblowing channels

The importance of providing multiple possible means of whistleblowing to employees cannot be understated, as logic dictates that an employee who does not feel comfortable blowing the whistle will hesitate to do so. Best practices advise implementing multiple reporting channels within an organization (Kaplan et al. 2012) to maximize the likelihood of reporting, since employees use a variety of channels to report fraudulent behavior. The most common way in which occupational frauds are detected is through employee tips, which are received through a variety of reporting channels, including telephone hotlines, email, fax, or direct reporting to a supervisor, executive, or internal and external auditors (ACFE 2018). Organizations that track reports from reporting channels beyond just hotlines and web submissions have higher reporting volumes, with 7.3 reports per 100 employees when tracking only web and hotline reports, compared to 14.8 reports per 100 employees when tracking all reporting channels (Navex Global 2018). These organizations have incident management systems that capture reports from other reporting channels including letters, direct emails, and open-door reports. Furthermore, the reports made through these "other" reporting channels had the highest rate of substantiation (i.e., merit) (Navex Global 2018).

Academic research provides insight into *why* employees may utilize various whistleblowing channels to report fraudulent or unethical behavior. Deciding whom to report to is an important decision for whistleblowers, as it may influence how the organization responds to the whistleblower, any retaliation that may occur, and the effectiveness of the whistleblowing process (Dworkin and Baucus 1998). For example, employees face more retaliation when they use external whistleblowing channels (Miceli, Near, and Dworkin 2008). Research shows that an employee's decision to report unethical or fraudulent behaviors is driven by a variety of personal and contextual factors (Gao and Brink 2017) that influence their use of certain reporting mechanisms.

Importance of both internal and external channels

Reporting channels are commonly classified into two groups in the academic literature: internal and external channels. Internal reporting involves reporting to someone within the organization who has the ability to address the reported issue (Dworkin and Baucus 1998). Examples of internal reporting channels include internal hotlines, reporting to the internal audit group, or reporting to a supervisor uninvolved in the wrongdoing. External reporting, on the other hand, involves reporting wrongdoing to parties outside the organization, such as a federal agency or the media (Dworkin and Baucus 1998; Kaptein 2011), where the reporting channel is not under the organization's control (Kaplan et al. 2012; Culiberg and Mihelič 2017). Research suggests that in the majority of whistleblowing cases, employees first utilize internal channels to report wrongdoing (e.g., Miceli, Near, and Dworkin 2008; Lee and Xiao 2018). It is when they feel their concern is not properly addressed that they may resort to external channels (Near and Miceli 2016).

Whistleblowers consider a variety of factors in determining which type of channel to use and weigh the costs and benefits of reporting to aid in this determination (Kaptein 2011; Culiberg and Mihelič 2017). This is an important consideration, as external whistleblowers are more effective at generating organizational change but also experience greater retaliation within the organization (Dworkin and Baucus 1998). Research shows Barbadian accounting employees' intentions to blow the whistle internally and externally are negatively related to employees' perceived personal cost of reporting and positively related to employees' perceived personal responsibility for reporting. Interestingly, the seriousness of the wrongdoing is only related to external whistleblowing intentions (Alleyne et al. 2017).

Factors outside of a whistleblower's formal decision-making process are also associated with the use of internal or external reporting channels. Research finds various organizational and personal characteristics are related to a whistleblower's preference for internal and external reporting. Nayir, Rehg, and Asa (2018) provide evidence that individual ethical value orientation (idealistic versus relativistic) and a company's business sector (private versus public) influence reporting channel preferences. They find that idealistic individuals prefer internal channels and are less likely to prefer anonymous channels. Relativistic employees, on the other hand, prefer external reporting channels compared to idealistic employees, with *private sector* relativistic employees showing the greatest preference for reporting via external channels. Relativism is also positively associated with preferences for anonymity in the reporting process. Nayir and Herzig (2012) also find that both individualistic cultural value orientations and, unexpectedly, collectivistic cultural value orientations are both positively associated with a preference for external channels and anonymity in reporting.

Beyond an individual's personal ethical values and cultural values, an organization's ethical culture also influences employees' responses to ethical wrongdoing and the use of internal and external whistleblowing channels. Based on a survey of the US working population, use of external channels is associated with a weak ethical culture (Kaptein 2011). As expected, increased transparency of the wrongdoing within an organization (where multiple individuals are aware of the unethical behavior) is positively associated with external whistleblowing. The belief that the perpetrator will be punished (sanctionability), the extent to which ethical issues can be discussed within the organization (discussability), and the extent to which local and senior managers apply organizational standards to their own behavior (congruency) are all negatively associated with external reporting (Kaptein 2011).

Perceived organizational support (POS) is found to moderate the relationship between multiple individual factors and whistleblowing intentions, further highlighting the importance of organizational culture (Alleyne, Hudaib, and Haniffa 2018). High levels of POS magnify the positive relationships between internal whistleblowing intentions and attitude to report, perceived behavioral controls, commitment to auditor independence, and perceived responsibility for reporting. High levels of POS also strengthen the negative relationship between perceived cost of reporting and the intention to blow the whistle internally. Perceived organizational support can also influence an employee's decision to blow the whistle externally. When the level of POS is low, the positive relationship between intention to blow the whistle externally and attitude to report and the positive relationship between intention to blow the whistle externally and perceived behavioral controls both are strengthened. Lastly, the positive relationship between POS and intention to blow the whistle externally is strengthened when POS is high (Alleyne, Hudaib, and Haniffa 2018).

Additional individual characteristics positively associated with the use of external reporting channels are shorter organizational tenure (< 4.5 years) and employees with strong evidence of wrongdoing, as employees with longer tenure and those with limited evidence of wrongdoing tend to use internal channels (Dworkin and Baucus 1998). The outcome of the ethical situation, whether it involves physical harm, economic harm, or psychological harm, is not associated with reporting channel (Dworkin and Baucus 1998); similarly, the type of unethical activity – misappropriation of assets or fraudulent financial reporting – is not associated with reporting intentions or reporting recipient (Kaplan, Pope, and Samuels 2010).

A relatively limited amount of research has directly assessed the use of internal and external reporting channels. Much of the research related to whistleblowing channels has focused heavily on intentions to use anonymous versus non-anonymous channels, largely motivated by the Sarbanes-Oxley Act (SOX). SOX enhanced whistleblower protections and required all public organizations to implement an anonymous reporting channel allowing employees to report suspected unethical or fraudulent behavior without providing identification (Johansson and Carey 2016). The research in this area exclusively considers internal whistleblowing channels. It manipulates various characteristics associated with internal reporting channels, including whistleblower anonymity, to better understand the effect these factors have on an individual's whistleblowing intentions.

Intention to report using anonymous reporting channels is associated with gender, as females are more likely than men to report fraud when anonymity is provided (due to women's perceptions of reduced personal costs when using such channels [Kaplan et al. 2009a]). Prior whistleblower retaliation also influences intentions to report under anonymous and non-anonymous channels. The presence of prior whistleblower retaliation is associated with decreased intentions to report wrongdoing using a non-anonymous channel (Kaplan et al. 2012). However, the absence of prior whistleblower retaliation does not influence intentions to report using anonymous channels. Additionally, when there were no negative consequences for a prior perpetrator and when an anonymous reporting channel is available compared to a non-anonymous channel, individuals have higher intentions to report (Kaplan et al. 2012).

Kaplan and Schultz (2007) and Curtis and Taylor (2009) both consider the effect of having multiple reporting channels, which we discuss as being very important for organizations to implement. Kaplan and Schultz (2007) investigate how the presence of an anonymous reporting channel impacts the use of two non-anonymous channels that are also available. The results suggest that when an anonymous channel is present, intentions to report using the non-anonymous channels decrease. In a public accounting setting, Curtis and Taylor (2009) find that an anonymous hotline and one where the whistleblower's identity is protected do not result in significantly different reporting likelihoods. However, auditors are less likely to report wrongdoing when their identity is not protected. Type of wrongdoing has not been found to be associated with the use of anonymous or non-anonymous reporting channels (Kaplan and Schultz 2007; Near et al. 2004).

How to encourage whistleblowing

Individual characteristics associated with whistleblowing

While the decision to blow the whistle is seldom an easy one, within this portion of the chapter we seek to identify both individual and environmental characteristics that can promote whistleblowing. Miceli, Near, and Dworkin (2008) identify both personality characteristics and demographic characteristics as two types of individual whistleblower characteristics that may affect whistleblowing intentions. Personality characteristics or traits have been investigated in multiple studies where whistleblowing intentions have been associated with an internal locus of control and a judging ethical style (Curtis and Taylor 2009), professional identity and organizational commitment (Taylor and Curtis 2010), lower levels of Machiavellianism (Dalton and Radtke 2013), and higher levels of conscientiousness and extroversion, as well as idealistic ethical positions (Brink, Cereola, and Menk 2015).

Demographic characteristics associated with whistleblowing intentions include female MBA students (Kaplan et al. 2009b), early career male accountants and female accountants age 45 years and older (Liyanarachchi and Adler 2011), and female older accounting professionals (Erkmen, Caliskan, and Esen 2014). In the broader population of organizational employees, Mesmer-Magnus and Viswesvaran (2005) conduct a meta-analysis of 26 samples from 21 articles and find that while older employees have a greater intent to blow the whistle, females and employees with a longer tenure with the company have a slightly greater likelihood of actually blowing the whistle. These studies are certainly not exhaustive of all potential personality and demographic characteristics, and thus, at this stage, it is difficult to paint a picture of the ideal whistleblower. The call for future research in this area is echoed by Gao and Brink (2017).

Environmental characteristics associated with whistleblowing (including incentives)

Environmental characteristics associated with whistleblowing intentions consist of a wide variety of factors. Near and Miceli (1995) suggest characteristics of the organization including appropriateness of the whistleblowing, a climate supportive of whistleblowing, a less bureaucratic structure, and an environment with low organizational power are favorable conditions for blowing the whistle. Additionally, Miceli, Near, and Dworkin (2008) identify three types of "situational" variables, including (1) characteristics of the perceived wrongdoing (such as seriousness or magnitude of the wrongdoing, type of wrongdoing, wrongdoer power or status, and supervisor support and quality of evidence), (2) characteristics of the organization (such as organizational climate or culture of supportiveness for whistleblowing, and industry type – public versus private), and (3) characteristics of the country or culture (such as level of individualism, uncertainty avoidance, and other social tendencies). In this study, we focus on organizational characteristics, as well as both internal and external incentives, since we seek to identify characteristics that can promote whistleblowing. Organizational climate (including ethical climate) and organizational structures associated with promoting whistleblowing intentions include formal structures and training (associated with reporting confidence) (Brennan and Kelly 2007), procedural justice, distributive justice, and interactional justice (Seifert et al. 2010), a strong ethical environment (Dalton and Radtke 2013), and a vivid anti-retaliation policy (Wainberg and Perreault 2016).

Additionally, some sort of internal incentive is often offered by the organization as a means to promote whistleblowing, in addition to the incentives offered by the SEC's Office of the

Whistleblower's bounty program. Feldman and Lobel (2010, 1160) present a legal analysis and experiment investigating the four most common strategies available to promote whistleblowing, which are "providing employees with antiretaliation protections, creating a duty to report, imposing liability for failure to report, and incentivizing reporting with money." They design an experimental survey with eight different combinations of the four strategies and find respondents faced with both "Duty" and "High Reward" are the most likely to *self-report* the personally discovered wrongdoing. Respondents in both the "Duty and High Reward" condition, and the "High Reward" (alone) condition had the highest scores for the likelihood that *others* would report the corporate misconduct. While these results suggest that the magnitude of the available reward is a critical factor for potential whistleblowers, the authors also point out that a crowding-out effect may occur, wherein monetary incentives take the place of other types of motivations and unintentionally lead to a lower likelihood of whistleblowing.

Xu and Ziegenfuss (2008) suggest that cash or employment contract rewards can be effective in promoting internal auditors to blow the whistle, and Rose, Brink, and Norman (2018) find that compensation with restricted stock along with large financial rewards can promote managers' whistleblowing. Brink, Lowe, and Victoravich (2013) find that employees' SEC reporting intentions are the greatest when there is a combination of strong evidence along with an internal incentive in the form of a cash reward, and Pope and Lee (2013) find that individuals are more likely to report and even disclose their identity when a financial incentive is provided. Guthrie and Taylor (2017) investigate a setting with both monetary incentives and retaliation threat and find that monetary incentives increase organizational trust, which leads to higher whistleblowing intent, but only when the threat of retaliation is low.

Berger, Perreault, and Wainberg (2017) find financial incentives are positively associated with internal whistleblowing, but only when the fraud is large enough for the whistleblower to qualify for a reward. They also suggest (2017, 10) a crowding-out effect, as when the size of the fraud does not meet the minimum threshold and financial incentives are available for a qualifying fraud, potential whistleblowers will both

> (1) assess a lower likelihood that fraud will be reported than had the whistleblower program mentioned no financial incentives at all, and (2) assess a higher likelihood that reporting will be strategically delayed in order to allow the fraud to grow in size, both of which are troubling findings.

Of the four common strategies available to promote whistleblowing (Feldman and Lobel 2010), most studies have investigated the monetary incentives option. Two recent studies, however, investigate both rewards and penalties in an attempt to assess which may be more effective. Boo, Ng, and Shankar (2016) employ an audit setting and both a reward-based (carrot) and penalty-based (stick) career-related incentive scheme to investigate auditors' likelihood of reporting an audit partner's wrongdoing that impairs financial reporting quality. The presence or absence of a close working relationship with the wrongdoer is also manipulated in their experiment. Results show a reward-based incentive scheme is associated with a lower likelihood of whistleblowing when a close working relationship is present than when it is absent. A penalty-based incentive scheme increases the likelihood of whistleblowing regardless of the presence of a close working relationship. These results suggest that in industries where most working relationships are close (such as the accounting profession), a penalty-based (instead of a reward-based) incentive structure may be more successful in promoting whistleblowing behavior.

Chen, Nichol, and Zhou (2017) also investigate both rewards and penalties, along with a company's descriptive norms supporting internal whistleblowing. In an experimental study, subjects report a greater likelihood of internal whistleblowing under both the threat of penalty for non-reporting and the presence of strong descriptive norms supporting whistleblowing. Thus, both Chen, Nichol, and Zhou (2017) and Boo, Ng, and Shankar (2016) support the premise of a penalty-based incentive being more effective than a reward-based incentive under certain working conditions.

Ethical implications of the whistleblowing process

Effective whistleblowing depends on many different factors. This chapter focuses on the importance of whistleblowing for accounting while examining characteristics of a whistleblower (both individual and environmental), incentives to blow the whistle, and the available channels to do so. The prior discussions help frame the ethical implications of whistleblowing in accounting.

Implications for whistleblowers

Whistleblowing presents an ethical dilemma, and potential whistleblowers must consider both costs and benefits of reporting wrongdoing. Research has linked whistleblowing to situations high in perceived moral intensity and individuals who perceive a responsibility to report wrongdoing (Latan, Ringle, and Jabbour 2018). Though an individual may be driven by his/her conscience to report wrongdoing, acting on moral responsibility does not always earn an employee a favorable result. While the moral courage of a whistleblower is often viewed as heroic, no good deed goes unpunished. Since whistleblowing involves one person reporting another person's suspected wrongdoings, one potential implication of whistleblowing is that an individual can become the target of retaliation by the accused wrongdoer and even by the employing company.

Internally, the accused perpetrator may find out who the whistleblower is and retaliate in some way. While some research suggests that retaliation is not inevitable (Soeken and Soeken 1987), the 2011 National Business Ethics Survey finds that 22% of employees who blew the whistle reported experiencing retaliation of some kind (Ethics Resource Center 2012). Additionally, and potentially even more worrisome, 39% of employees who blew the whistle believed that, as far as they knew, their complaint was ignored and not investigated (Ethics Resource Center 2012). When employees perceive the threat of retribution or retaliation to be low, they are more likely to utilize internal whistleblowing channels (Ethics Resource Center 2012), which are certainly the preferred channels from the point of view of companies (Near and Miceli 2016). Companies have also been known to punish whistleblowers when wrongdoing is reported to an external agency (Mesmer-Magnus and Viswesvaran 2005; Miceli, Near, and Dworkin 2008). Rather than outright salient retaliation, employees are more likely to experience micro-aggressive acts as well as subtle harassment and physical threats such as exclusion from decision-making or other workplace activities, a cold shoulder from coworkers, and verbal abuse from a supervisor or other manager (Soeken and Soeken 1987; Malek 2010; Ethics Resource Center 2012). Companies may be less likely to openly retaliate against a whistleblower due to protections afforded whistleblowers through whistleblower legislation. As previously discussed, improved whistleblower protection is a topic of international importance (e.g., Global Whistleblower 2018; European Commission 2018; vandePol, Wu, and Hui 2016; Anti-Corruption and Civil Rights Commission, Republic of Korea 2018).

There are also some potential benefits from whistleblowing. Taylor and Curtis (2010) find that greater moral intensity associated with the wrongdoing increases the likelihood of an employee reporting, suggesting that an employee often just wants to do the right thing. Relatedly, "peace of mind" may accrue from acting conscientiously, as was the case for nuclear power plant quality control inspector Charles Atchinson, who stated with respect to his whistleblowing, "I know I did right. And I know I'll always sleep right. I'll sleep just like a baby" (Kleinfield 1986). In this case and no doubt many others, the whistleblower benefits from the personal satisfaction that whistleblowing was the morally correct course of action for him/her in the situation at hand. Ultimately, potential whistleblowers must weigh the costs (trouble of reporting, risk of retaliation, and discomfort) and benefits (clear conscience and monetary reward) of reporting or not reporting wrongdoing, along with the dilemma between the duty of loyalty to the organization and duty of protection of others (the public interest) (Paeth 2013).

Implications for companies

Public companies are required by SOX to implement anonymous reporting channels for unethical accounting issues (US House of Representatives 2002), as available organizational structure and support directly influence the decision to blow the whistle. Effective whistleblowing requires both an ethical culture that supports whistleblowing and a company that is willing to attempt to change any discovered/reported wrongdoing.

Several studies find that formal structures, ethical environments, and organizational support are positively associated with employees' whistleblowing intentions (Brennan and Kelly 2007; Curtis and Taylor 2009; Dalton and Radtke 2013; Taylor and Curtis 2013; Zhang, Pany, and Reckers 2013). Curtis and Taylor (2009) suggest that the auditor is most likely to report wrongdoing if the auditor trusts that the company will investigate reports of wrongdoing, while Brennan and Kelly (2007) find that larger companies are more likely to provide formal reporting structures. However, Bowen, Call, and Rajgopal (2010) and Lee and Xiao (2018) note that larger companies are also more likely to experience external reporting rather than internal reporting for whistleblowing.

External whistleblowing is more detrimental to a company than internal whistleblowing. Internal reporting of wrongdoing allows a company to correct the wrongdoing before outside regulators and/or monitors get involved. External whistleblowing leads to higher regulatory penalties, lower subsequent stock market performance, and a greater likelihood of a subsequent lawsuit for the company involved (Bowen, Call, and Rajgopal 2010; Call et al. 2017). Although companies may initially suffer negative economic consequences from external whistleblowing, as evidenced by the negative five-day stock price reaction found by Bowen, Call, and Rajgopal (2010), as well as additional negative consequences such as earnings restatements, these companies are subsequently less likely to engage in future wrongdoing and are more likely to improve their reporting and corporate governance after the whistleblowing event. These efforts often include potentially replacing their CEO, reducing both the size of their board of directors and the number of insider members on the board, and identifying board members who are less busy and more likely to have meaningful time to spend contemplating corporate governance issues (Bowen, Call, and Rajgopal 2010).

Extant accounting research has examined characteristics of both whistleblowers and organizational environment. In trying to encourage whistleblowing in cases of wrongdoing, companies can diversify hiring to bring on employees who are not afraid to challenge the status quo or authority when appropriate, or employees with diverse opinions and worldviews who welcome and champion those willing to have their voice heard. Miceli and Near (1992) suggest that companies can use demographic characteristics and other traits to help identify potential whistleblowers, including a higher level of moral judgment, high self-confidence, and values supporting whistleblowing. However, the ACFE (2018) indicates that background checks are not effective at identifying perpetrators, as over half of the companies that reported fraud had conducted a background check on the fraud perpetrator. Additionally, hiring practices that strive to identify potential whistleblowers or fraud perpetrators may have unintended consequences by resulting in discrimination against potential employees. Companies should proceed with caution in developing such practices to avoid the reputational and legal ramifications related to discrimination.

In terms of organizational environment, both Dalton and Radtke (2013) and the 2011 National Business Ethics Survey (Ethics Resource Center 2012) observe that reporting intentions are influenced by a company's ethical environment in that a strong ethical environment (consisting of a strong ethics program and culture, ethical leadership, and employee buy-in) both reduces the risk of misconduct and also increases the likelihood of reporting if/when misconduct occurs. The implications from these studies strongly support companies creating an ethical work environment supportive of a formal whistleblowing process consisting of employees who are willing and able to act as whistleblowers. While companies cannot eliminate all possible risk of wrongdoing, a strong ethical environment can go far in minimizing the need for whistleblowers.

Conclusion

In this chapter, we explore many facets of whistleblowing within accounting. We can conclude that an employee's desire to blow the whistle is often outweighed by consideration of the implications to both the individual and the company involved in the wrongdoing. The whistleblowing decision is also affected by the available reporting channels, along with characteristics of the organization including the incentive structure (if any) and the organization's ethical climate. Thus, while whistleblowers are often viewed as brave and morally correct, the negative consequences often negate the desire to blow the whistle.

As previously discussed, accountants have an obligation to serve the public interest, and indeed, the public may generally believe that auditors have a responsibility to expose financial wrongdoing. PCAOB board member Jeanette Franzel recently discussed sources of the continuing expectations gap between what the public believes auditors are responsible for and what auditors believe their responsibilities to be (PCAOB 2016). This general misconception by the public that an audit is designed to expose fraud is consistent with the fact that the vast majority of frauds are not identified by externals audits (only 4% in the 2018 Global Study on Occupational Fraud and Abuse (ACFE 2018)). Thus, the importance of whistleblowing is heightened within this setting, as whistleblowers ultimately take on a public duty to strive to maintain trust between the company and the public.

References

Alleyne, P. M., W. Charles-Soverall, T. Broome, and A. Pierce. 2017. "Perceptions, Predictors and Consequences of Whistleblowing among Accounting Employees in Barbados." *Meditari Accountancy Research* 25 (2): 241–67.

Alleyne, P. M., M. Hudaib, and R. Haniffa. 2018. "The Moderating Role of Perceived Organizational Support in Breaking the Silence of Public Accountants." *Journal of Business Ethics* 147 (3): 509–27.

American Institute of Certified Public Accountants (AICPA). 2018. *Code of Professional Conduct*. New York: AICPA.

American Institute of Public Accountants (AICPA). 2002. *Consideration of Fraud in a Financial Statement.* New York: AIPCA.

Anti-Corruption and Civil Rights Commission, Republic of Korea. 2018. "ACRC strengthens its function of protecting corruption and public interest violation reporters." Accessed September 27, 2018. http://acrc.go.kr/en/board.do?command=searchDetail&method=searchDetailViewInc&menuId=02 0501&boardNum=70373

Association of Certified Fraud Examiners (ACFE). 2018. *Report to the Nations: 2018 Global Study on Occupational Fraud and Abuse.* Austin, TX: ACFE.

Berger, L., S. Perreault, and J. Wainberg. 2017. "Hijacking the Moral Imperative: How Financial Incentives Can Discourage Whistleblower Reporting." *Auditing: A Journal of Practice & Theory* 36 (3): 1–14.

Boo, E., T. B. Ng, and P. G. Shankar. 2016. "Effects of Incentive Scheme and Working Relationship on Whistle-blowing in an Audit Setting." *Auditing: A Journal of Practice & Theory* 35 (4): 23–38.

Bouville, M. 2008. "Whistle-blowing and Morality." *Journal of Business Ethics* 81: 579–85.

Bowen, R. M., A. C. Call, and S. Rajgopal. 2010. "Whistle-blowing: Target Firm Characteristics and Economic Consequences." *The Accounting Review* 85 (4): 1239–71.

Brennan, N., and J. Kelly. 2007. "A Study of Whistleblowing among Trainee Auditors." *The British Accounting Review* 39 (1): 61–87.

Brink, A. G., S. Cereola, and K. B. Menk. 2015. "The Effects of Fraudulent Reporting, Materiality Level, Personality Traits, and Ethical Position on Entry-level Employee Whistleblowing Decisions." *Journal of Forensic and Investigative Reporting* 7 (1): 180–211.

Brink, A. G., D. J. Lowe, and L. M. Victoravich. 2013. "The Effect of Evidence Strength and Internal Rewards on Intentions to Report Fraud in the Dodd-Frank Regulatory Environment." *Auditing: A Journal of Practice & Theory* 32 (3): 87–104.

Call, A. C., G. S. Martin, N. Y. Sharp, and J. H. Wilde. 2017. "Whistleblowers and Outcomes of Financial Misrepresentation Enforcement Actions." *Journal of Accounting Research* 56 (1): 123–71.

Chen, C. X., J. E. Nichol, and F. H. Zhou. 2017. "The Effect of Incentive Framing and Descriptive Norms on Internal Whistleblowing." *Contemporary Accounting Research* 34 (4): 1757–78.

Chen, K. Y., and J. Zhou. 2007. "Audit Committee, Board Characteristics and Auditor Switch Decisions by Andersen's Clients." *Contemporary Accounting Research* 24: 1085–117.

Corporate Finance Institute. 2018. "Top Accounting Scandals." Accessed July 30, 2018. https://corporate financeinstitute.com/resources/knowledge/other/top-accounting-scandals/

Culiberg, B., and K. K. Mihelič. 2017. "The Evolution of Whistleblowing Studies: A Critical Review and Research Agenda." *Journal of Business Ethics* 146 (4): 787–803.

Curtis, M. B., and E. Z. Taylor. 2009. "Whistleblowing in Public Accounting: Influence of Identity Disclosure, Situational Context, and Personal Characteristics." *Accounting and the Public Interest* 9 (1): 191–220.

Dalton, D., and R. R. Radtke. 2013. "The Joint Effects Of Machiavellianism and Ethical Environment on Whistle-blowing." *Journal of Business Ethics* 117 (1): 153–72.

Dworkin, T. M., and M. S. Baucus. 1998. "Internal vs. External Whistleblowers: A Comparison of Whistleblowing Processes." *Journal of Business Ethics* 17 (12): 1281–98.

Dyck, A., A. Morse, and L. Zingales. 2010. "Who Blows the Whistle on Corporate Fraud?" *The Journal of Finance* 65(6): 2213–53.

Erkmen, T., A. O. Caliskan, and E. Esen. 2014. "An Empirical Research about Whistleblowing Behavior in Accounting Context." *Journal of Accounting & Organizational Change* 10(2): 229–43.

Ethics Resource Center. 2012. *2011 National Business Ethics Survey: Workplace Ethics in Transition.* Arlington, VA: Ethics Resource Center.

European Commission. 2018. *Proposal for a Directive of the European Parliament and of the Council on the Protection of Persons Reporting on Breaches of Union Law.* Brussels, Belgium: European Commission. Accessed 27 September 2018. https://ec.europa.eu/info/law/better-regulation/initiatives/com-2018-218_en

Feldman, Y., and O. Lobel. 2010. "The Incentives Matrix: The Comparative Effectiveness of Rewards, Liabilities, Duties, and Protections for Reporting Illegality." *Texas Law Review* 88 (6): 1151–211.

Fuerman, R. D. 2006. "Comparing the Auditor Quality of Arthur Andersen to that of the 'Big 4'." *Accounting and the Public Interest* 6: 135–61.

Gao, L., and A. G. Brink. 2017. "Whistleblowing Studies in Accounting Research: A Review of Experimental Studies on the Determinants of Whistleblowing." *Journal of Accounting Literature* 38: 1–13.

Global Whistleblower. 2018. "Breakthrough in Protecting International Whistleblowers: Non-United States Citizens Now Entitled to Monetary Rewards." Accessed September 27, 2018. www.global whistleblower.org/english

Guthrie, C. P., and E. Z. Taylor. 2017. "Whistleblowing on Fraud for Pay: Can I Trust You?" *Journal of Forensic Accounting Research* 2 (1): A1–A19.

International Federation of Accountants (IFAC). 2018. "Global Ethics Board Releases Revamped Code of Ethics for Professional Accountants." Accessed October 3, 2018. www.ifac.org/news-events/2018-04/global-ethics-board-releases-revamped-code-ethics-professional-accountants

Johansson, E., and P. Carey. 2016. "Detecting Fraud: The Role of the Anonymous Reporting Channel." *Journal of Business Ethics* 139 (2): 391–409.

Kaplan, S. E. 1995. "An Examination of Auditors' Reporting Intentions Upon Discovery of Procedures Prematurely Signed-off." *Auditing: A Journal of Practice & Theory* 14 (2): 90–104.

Kaplan, S. E., K. Pany, J. A. Samuels, and J. Zhang. 2009a. "An Examination of the Association between Gender and Reporting Intentions for Fraudulent Financial Reporting." *Journal of Business Ethics* 87 (1): 15–30.

Kaplan, S. E., K. Pany, J. A. Samuels, and J. Zhang. 2009b. "An Examination of the Effects of Procedural Safeguards on Intentions to Anonymously Report Fraud." *Auditing: A Journal of Practice & Theory* 28 (2): 273–88.

Kaplan, S. E., K. Pany, J. A. Samuels, and J. Zhang. 2012. "An Examination of Anonymous and Non-anonymous Fraud Reporting Channels." *Advances in Accounting* 28 (1): 88–95.

Kaplan, S. E., K. R. Pope, and J. A. Samuels. 2010. "The Effect of Social Confrontation on Individuals' Intentions to Internally Report Fraud." *Behavioral Research in Accounting* 22 (2): 51–67

Kaplan, S. E., K. R. Pope, and J. A. Samuels. 2011. "An Examination of the Effect of Inquire and Auditor Type on Reporting Intentions for Fraud." *Auditing: A Journal of Practice & Theory* 30 (4): 29–49.

Kaplan, S. E., and J. J. Schultz. 2007. "Intentions to Report Questionable Acts: An Examination of the Influence of Anonymous Reporting Channel, Internal Audit Quality, and Setting." *Journal of Business Ethics* 71 (2): 109–24.

Kaptein, M. 2011. "From Inaction to External Whistleblowing: The Influence of the Ethical Culture of Organizations on Employee Responses to Observed Wrongdoing." *Journal of Business Ethics* 98 (3): 513–30.

Kleinfield, N. R. 1986. "The Whistleblowers' Morning after." *The New York Times.* Accessed October 1, 2018. www.nytimes.com/1986/11/09/business/the-whistle-blowers-morning-after.html

Latan, H., C. M. Ringle, and C. J. C. Jabbour. 2018. "Whistleblowing Intentions among Public Accountants in Indonesia: Testing for the Moderation Effects." *Journal of Business Ethics* 152: 573–88.

Lee, G., and X. Xiao. 2018. "Whistleblowing on Accounting-related Misconduct: A Synthesis of the Literature." *Journal of Accounting Literature* 41: 22–46.

Liyanarachchi, G. A., and R. Adler. 2011. "Accountants' Whistle-blowing Intentions: The Impact of Retaliation, Age, and Gender." *Australian Accounting Review* 21 (2): 167–82.

Malek, J. 2010. "To Tell or Not to Tell? The Ethical Dilemma of the Would-Be Whistleblower." *Accountability in Research* 17 (3): 115–29.

Mesmer-Magnus, J. R., and C. Viswesvaran. 2005. "Whistleblowing in Organizations: An Examination of Correlates of Whistleblowing Intentions, Actions, and Retaliation." *Journal of Business Ethics* 62: 277–97.

Miceli, M. P., and J. P. Near. 1992. *Blowing the Whistle.* New York: Lexington Books.

Miceli, M. P., J. P. Near, and T. M. Dworkin. 2008. *Whistle-blowing in Organizations.* New York: Routledge.

Navex Global. 2018. *2018 Ethics and Compliance Hotline and Incident Management Benchmark Report.* Lake Oswego, OR: Navex Global Americas.

Nayir, D. Z., and C. Herzig. 2012. "Value Orientations as Determinants of Preference for External and Anonymous Whistleblowing." *Journal of Business Ethics* 107 (2): 197–213.

Nayır, D. Z., M. T. Rehg, and Y. Asa. 2018. "Influence of Ethical Position on Whistleblowing Behaviour: Do Preferred Channels in Private and Public Sectors Differ?" *Journal of Business Ethics* 149 (1): 147–67.

Near, J. P., and M. P. Miceli. 1985. "Organizational Dissidence: The Case of Whistle-blowing." *Journal of Business Ethics* 4 (1): 1–16.

Near, J. P., and M. P. Miceli. 1995. "Effective Whistle-blowing." *Academy of Management Review* 20 (3): 679–708.

Near, J. P., and M. P. Miceli. 2016. "After the Wrongdoing: What Managers Should Know About Whistle-blowing." *Business Horizons* 59 (1): 105–14.

Near, J. P., M. T. Rehg, J. R. Van Scotter, and M. P. Miceli. 2004. "Does Type of Wrongdoing Affect the Whistle-blowing Process?" *Business Ethics Quarterly* 14 (2): 219–42.

Paeth, S. R. 2013. "The Responsibility to Lie and the Obligation to Report: Bonhoeffer's 'What Does it Mean to Tell the Truth?' and the Ethics of Whistleblowing." *Journal of Business Ethics* 112: 559–66.

Pope, K., and C. C. Lee. 2013. "Could the Dodd-Frank Wall Street Reform and Consumer Protection Act of 2010 be Helpful in Reforming Corporate America? An Investigation on Financial Bounties and Whistle-blowing Behaviors in the Private Sector." *Journal of Business Ethics* 112 (4): 597–607.

Public Company Accounting Oversight Board (PCAOB). 2015. *Audit Risk*. AS 1101. Washington, DC: PCAOB.

Public ComAOB. 2016. "Audit Expectations Gap: A Framework for Regulatory Analysis." Accessed October 1, 2018. https://pcaobus.org/News/Speech/Pages/Franzel-speech-Institute-12-13-16.aspx

Robertson, J. C., C. M. Stefaniak, and M. B. Curtis. 2011. "Does Wrongdoer Reputation Matter? Impact of Auditor-wrong Doer Performance and Likeability Reputations on Fellow Auditors' Intention to Take Action and Choice of Reporting Outlet." *Behavioral Research in Accounting* 23 (2): 207–34.

Rose, J. M., A. G. Brink, and C. S. Norman. 2018. "The Effects of Compensation Structures and Monetary Rewards on Managers' Decisions to Blow the Whistle." *Journal of Business Ethics* 150: 853–62.

Securities and Exchange Commission. 2014. "SEC Awards $875,000 to Two Whistleblowers Who Aided Agency Investigation." Accessed July 30, 2018. www.sec.gov/news/press-release/2014-113

Securities Exchange Commission. 2017. "SEC Announces $7 Million Whistleblower Award." Accessed July 30, 2018. www.sec.gov/news/pressrelease/2017-27.html

Seifert, D. L., J. T. Sweeney, J. Joireman, and J. M. Thornton. 2010. "The Influence of Organizational Justice on Accountant Whistleblowing." *Accounting, Organizations and Society* 35 (7): 707–17.

Soeken, K. L., and D. R. Soeken. 1987. "A Survey of Whistleblowers: Their Stressors and Coping Strategies." *Proceedings of the Hearing on H. R. 25*: 156–66. Washington, DC: U.S. Government Printing Office.

Taylor, E. Z., and M. B. Curtis. 2010. "An Examination of the Layers of Workplace Influences in Ethical Judgments: Whistleblowing Likelihood and Perseverance in Public Accounting." *Journal of Business Ethics* 93 (1): 21–27.

Taylor, E. Z., and M. B. Curtis. 2013. "Whistleblowing in audit Firms: Organizational Response and Power Distance." *Behavioral Research in Accounting* 25 (2): 21–43.

US House of Representatives. 2002. Sarbanes-Oxley Act of 2002. Public Law 107–204 [H.R. 3763]. Washington, DC: Government Printing Office.

vandePol, M., V. Wu, and S. Hui. 2016. "New Rules Offer Greater Protection and Incentives to Whistleblowers in China." Accessed September 27, 2018. https://globalcompliancenews.com/new-rules-offer-greater-protection-and-incentives-to-whistleblowers-in-china-20160504/

Wainberg, J., and S. Perreault. 2016. "Whistleblowing in Audit Firms: Do Explicit Protections from Retaliation Activate Implicit Threats of Reprisal?" *Behavioral Research in Accounting* 28 (1): 83–93.

Xu, Y., and D. E. Ziegenfuss. 2008. "Reward Systems, Moral Reasoning, and Internal Auditors' Reporting Wrongdoing." *Journal of Business and Psychology* 22 (4): 323–31.

Zhang, J., K. Pany, and P. M. Reckers. 2013. "Under Which Conditions are Whistleblowing Best Practices Best?" *Auditing: A Journal of Practice and Theory* 32 (3): 171–81.

25

THE BOUNDARY PROBLEM IN A SURVEILLANCE SOCIETY

Moving beyond individual ethics and compliance

Louella Moore

Introduction

The distinction between financial and managerial accounting has traditionally been based on a simple line of demarcation between external and internal stakeholders. "Financial" reporting processes assemble and categorize information that is verified by auditors before delivery to stakeholders *external* to the corporate boundaries. "Managerial" accountants plan, coordinate, and motivate the achievement of monetary and other objectives associated with an organization's *internal* operations. Recent scholarship suggests that there is often no bright line separating the internal and external stakeholders. This chapter will argue that unrealistic assumptions about the nature of boundaries in business and society prevents the accounting profession from addressing significant ethical issues associated with the modern surveillance society.

Mainstream accounting research is built on economic principles that assume individuals and firms function as separate, readily identifiable entities utilizing objective information to make rational decisions. Studies by Ferguson et al. (2005, 2006, 2007, 2010) argue that the decision models in commercial accounting textbooks are presented as if they were neutral and rational even as they implicitly prioritize management and shareholder goals over environmental and social goals. Economic models emphasize the competition between individual interests while downplaying collective social processes that inform and underlie the ideals and objectives of individual actors. The connection between persons and the broader society is not merely a question of "which comes first, the chicken or the egg?" Orthodox financial and economic theory is based on the assumption that individuals act independently and have wide freedom of choice. Outside the economics, accounting, and finance disciplinary boundaries, alternative perspectives suggest that it is not at all clear how much latitude individual managers have in their decision choices (Barker 1993; Souitaris, Zerbinati, and Liu 2012; Bailey 2013; Claeyé and Jackson 2012; Prasad and Prasad 2000; Ryner 2015; Dobbin, Schrage and Kalev 2015; Garner 2016). These scholars characterize managers as operating within the confines of an "iron cage" where actions are severely constrained by institutional, social, and cultural forces.

Accounting ethics education is sometimes taken to mean instruction aimed at helping professionals develop an appropriate depth of insight concerning how their actions will impact other stakeholders (Armstrong, Ketz and Owsen 2003, 3). The questions raised often assume that the focus of attention is on a single decision maker faced with choices at a point in time within a specific socio-technical cultural system. Modern digital technologies allow unprecedented levels of surveillance, influence, and control of social interactions even as digitally connected markets and personal spaces pose significant boundary problems in a system where it is not always clear who is watching whom. The accounting entity concept that informs market-based models underlying mainstream accounting practice and research treats the boundary between private and public interests as self-evident. Similarly, major accounting conceptual frameworks largely ignore the interdependence and overlap between conceptual units of classification. Financial regulators write rules that must be followed by those within their national and regional jurisdiction, but the effects of missteps in regulation are not constrained by geographic boundaries. Aftershocks associated with the 2008 subprime mortgage crisis continue to impact the global economy more than a decade after the Lehman Brothers bankruptcy (Amaro 2018). For this reason, it is important to closely examine the accounting profession's assumptions and concepts about the boundaries between private and public or even business and government domains.

This chapter will first explore assumptions about decision-usefulness, accuracy, and entities that are embedded in accounting professional literature. The body of the chapter then considers the social engineering efforts of Robert Owen (1771–1858) and Henry Ford (1863–1947). Echoing the sentiments of Foucault ([1975] 1977, 31), the intent of the history section is not merely to stare at the past but to lay a foundation for understanding the present. The biographical sketches are used to illustrate the complex intersection between managerial agency, institutional power, and sociocultural forces in periods of significant change. The final section of the chapter will argue that modern technologies have extended societies' efforts at behavioral control from systems of pan-optic surveillance, a concept popularized by Jeremy Bentham (1843), to a more complex system of mutual surveillance that Brivot and Gendron (2011) refer to as a super-opticon. The chapter concludes that modern technologies make the accounting profession's traditional individualistic view of reporting entities untenable. In a digital environment where business, government, and personal boundaries are inherently intertwined, treating ethics as merely a question of individual decision makers complying with rules and codes of behavior is counterproductive to any aspirations the accounting profession might have of providing genuine ethical leadership in service to the public at large.

Empty rhetoric of decision-usefulness and accurate accounting

Solomons (1991) observed that the accounting profession understands itself primarily as providing a neutral technology that models an objective economic reality that is separate and distinct from the observer. Horvat and Korosec (2015) argue that this perspective masks and makes it virtually impossible for accountants to address the ethical, social, and political problems inherent in their representations. The conceptual frameworks of the FASB (Financial Accounting Standards Board) and IASB (International Accounting Standards Board) depict financial reports as providing neutral, transparent information useful for investor and creditor decision-making. Zeff (2017) claims the decision-usefulness approach in these conceptual frameworks arose out of Clark's (1923) idea of "different costs for different purposes" and his subsequent influence on William Vatter, George Staubus, and George Sorter at the University of Chicago. The decision-usefulness criterion was originally intended to emphasize that neither historical cost nor market value representations could satisfy all users. Therefore, because no single measurement approach will suffice, standardized information is useful only to the degree that users recognize the limitations and qualities of the information provided. Whatever form of standardized data is provided, users will need to make appropriate adaptations to the specific decision context.

Despite the "different costs for different purposes" foundations of the decision-usefulness criterion, the business press today commonly treats accounting "accuracy" as if accounting numbers are capable of providing a singular objective and correct representation of economic stocks, flows, and claims. This misrepresentation of accounting numbers as exact and neutral carries over into documents authored by regulators and academics. Sarbanes-Oxley regulations passed after the 2001 Enron problems require financial officers to affirm financial statement "accuracy," and popular cost/managerial textbooks make declarative statements that activity-based costing is "more accurate" than traditional allocation methods (Moore 2017b). In the short term, marginal costs may be the most relevant for some decisions. In the long run, variable and fixed costs of production, selling costs, and administrative outlays all must be covered, whether these costs are allocated to inventory accounts or not. The accuracy rhetoric in regulatory and pedagogical discourse downplays the degree to which accounting information is context sensitive and consequently incapable of being standardized in such a way as to be equally appropriate for all decision or evaluative purposes. Some scholars view the vacuous, falsely neutral FASB/IASB decision-usefulness criterion as diverting attention away from substantive issues like distributional justice, fairness, and stewardship (Williams1987; Bayou, Reinstein, and Williams 2011; Williams and Ravenscroft 2015).

Searle (1995), Rudkin (2007), Ferguson et al. (2005, 2006, 2007, 2010) and Moore (2017b) all note that professional, pedagogical, and regulatory literatures downplay the degree to which accounting is impacted by subjective choices. Accounting representations model future events that are inherently unknowable in the present, e.g., default rates on receivables, liabilities for post-employment health care costs, and the useful lives of assets subject to physical and technological obsolescence. Determining where to draw the lines between related entities or among departments and/or how to classify hybrid instruments like credit default swaps or convertible bonds are examples of problems in traditional accounting that are incapable of a definitive answer. And yet the double entry accounting systems that predominate in financial reporting practices are built on an Aristotelian taxonomic logic that pretends every business transaction can be uniquely mapped to disjoint categories. When users are encouraged to view data as unrealistically objective, manipulated perceptions can eventually lead to market sabotage and even an implosion of financial market infrastructure on the order of the subprime market crisis of 2008 (Moore 2017c).

Not-so self-evident boundaries

The FASB and IASB conceptual frameworks not only downplay the degree to which elements within the financial statements do not fit neatly into rigid categories, they also describe the boundaries of the overall reporting entity as self-evident and objectively determinable. This approach inherently affirms the appropriateness of the parameters of property rights set in place by current juridical systems, leaving no space for critical assessment of the ethical status of existing power structures. Interestingly, the legal profession does not take entity or property boundaries as a given. Heller (1999) holds that the common perception of a simple dichotomy between private and public interests simply does not hold in legal theory and practice. Private property rights are often overridden by legal restrictions imposed for a public purpose. Iacobucci and Triantis (2007) demonstrate that legal scholars sometimes treat firms as integrated persons and at other times as bundles of rights; moreover, these different approaches yield different legal and business decisions. In contrast, the treatment of firm boundaries as *self-evident* in accounting and neoliberal economic theory inherently discourages discourse about the sociopolitical problems associated with boundaries that demarcate access to tangible and intangible resources.

Questionable boundaries were associated with the special purpose entities used to hide Enron losses before its implosion in 2001. Other boundary problems were implicit in the interlocking financial guarantees between entities associated with the Orange County bankruptcy of 1994 and the global subprime crisis of 2008 (Moore 2017b). When firms share the risks and rewards associated with leased equipment, there are difficult theoretical and practical problems associated with determining which party controls the residual interest. Rather than being self-evident, boundary lines are in fact the source of many problems in accountability (Moore 2017a). The drawing of boundaries is inherent in the responsibility reporting systems used by firms to match and attach costs to departmental and other cost objects. Drawing the boundaries between firms, departments, and the parameters of private and public activities is implicitly associated with the ethical administration of property rights. Indeterminate boundaries between firms and society at large, coupled with fuzzy departmental lines within a firm, can create practical problems in assigning responsibilities and in determining the dividing lines between private and public life.

Given that accounting practitioners function as taxonomists who divide up and classify the results of economic transactions, why is it that so little attention has been paid to boundary problems in accounting professional literature? Porter (1999, 96) argues that professions that are vulnerable to criticism from outsiders avoid the exercise of judgment, choosing to hide behind seemingly objective rules and standards. Professional groups with weak status adopt public relations programs that divert attention away from controversial issues. Allegiance to the popular neoclassical economic view that *laissez-faire* markets can spontaneously enhance market transparency and efficiency seems to be at the heart of recent campaigns to emphasize the accounting profession's role in promoting a "prosperous society" (Pathways 2015; Chartered Accountants 2017; Barth 2018). These efforts implicitly assume that if businesses are given virtually unlimited freedom to use all legally available information, then that data will help maximize shareholder and societal returns. The implied political stance is that governments should only restrict business freedom when there is a clear and present danger to the social order. On the other hand, Western societies also seem to value individual privacy rights. Balancing the freedom needed to enhance productive efficiency and protection of privacy is a significant normative issue. Treating boundaries as self-evident would arguably seem to privilege businesses' desire for freedom over individuals' concern for privacy.

The entity problem in codes of ethics

Boundary problems may be downplayed not only in the financial accounting literature but by management accounting professional organizations as well. Cost and managerial accounting textbooks targeted to the US market often include in their first chapter a discussion of ethics that includes the Institute of Management Accountants' (IMA 2017) Statement of Ethical Professional Practice (Garrison, Noreen, and Brewer 2015; Datar and Rajan 2018; Hansen and Mowen 2018). The IMA code emphasizes professional competence, confidentiality, integrity, and credibility. The code requires that information be kept confidential except when disclosure is authorized or legally required. The code concludes with a process for resolving ethical conflicts. The code states that information should be communicated fairly, but its guidelines arguably emphasize management over public interests. For example, the IMA code notes that communications must be "in conformance with organization policy and/or applicable law." When accountants find that company policies or actions conflict with personal sensibilities about public interest parameters of ethical behavior and the divergence cannot be resolved by discussion within the organizational chain of command, the code directs the accountant to talk to an impartial advisor in order to determine a course of action. The code adds a caveat that one would be well advised to consult their own attorney, as opposed to the company attorney, to discuss their obligations and rights.

The IMA's code of conduct is presented as a factual artifact with no critique of its problematic assumptions about the separation of private and public duties. One could easily read this procedure for resolving ethical conflicts as prioritizing company rights *vis-à-vis* those of a management accountant contemplating whistleblowing in a situation where a corporation is operating in a manner contrary to the public interest. As the membership dues to the IMA are often paid by the employing firm, perhaps it is not surprising that the code would not explicitly encourage whistleblowing. On the other hand, college textbooks serve as a tool to introduce aspiring accountants to the profession's stance on public interest responsibilities in society. By treating organizational policies as largely beyond reproach, the code seems to assume that there is a strict dividing line between internal and external rules and obligations. While consulting an attorney may indeed be prudent advice, textbooks miss an important opportunity to address issues associated with the indeterminate boundary between private and public interests.

Boundaries and the theory of the firm

In contrast to the FASB, IASB, and IMA literature, a 2010 study by the Institute of Chartered Accountants of England and Wales (ICAEW 2010) concludes that the traditional assumption that the boundaries of the firm are readily determinable has a serious conceptual flaw. The agency theory definition of "the firm" as a "nexus of contracts" derives from a 1937 study by the economist Ronald Coase. Coase argued that firms exist as an institution because they offer a more efficient means of production than relying on formal contracts negotiated in a market setting. According to Coase, informal internal relationships allow "the firm" to operate with lower transaction costs. The ICAEW (2010) study points out that the conventional Coasian logic makes it impossible to distinguish between firms and markets. If a firm is merely a nexus of contracts, then the organization is enmeshed in the larger market and the two cannot be separated.

Modern businesses routinely offer financial bonuses based on accounting measures of departmental performance. These accounting metrics utilize joint cost allocations and boundary lines that Thomas (1969) and Devine (1985) have demonstrated to be incorrigibly arbitrary. Because department boundaries and allocation of costs across department lines always include an element of subjectivity, rewards systems are inextricably entwined with problems of distributional equity whether those being rated recognize it or not. Ross Watts, Jerold Zimmerman, and Michael Jensen are among the researchers who helped revive the Coasian (Coase 1937) definition of a firm, giving impetus to a voluminous stream of positivist and agency theory-based accounting research from the 1970s to the present. And yet even Zimmerman's (2017) MBA management accounting text is built around the use of mini-cases that illustrate problems that arise when bonus schemes are tied to accounting numbers. The cases demonstrate that accounting-based bonus schemes cause managers to act like market competitors, completely overriding the Coasian theoretical rationale that cooperative rather than competitive relationships are the *raison d'être* for firms to even exist as an institution.

So how is it that firms continue to be perceived as units of cooperative activity that minimize transaction costs, when bonus schemes encourage employees to act like competing independent contractors? The French philosopher Rousseau (1754, 64) claims that

> The first man who, having fenced in a piece of land, said "This is mine", and found people naïve enough to believe him, that man was the true founder of civil society.

From how many crimes, wars, and murders, from how many horrors and misfortunes might not any one have saved mankind, by pulling up the stakes, or filling up the ditch, and crying to his fellows: Beware of listening to this impostor; you are undone if you once forget that the fruits of the earth belong to us all, and the earth itself to nobody.

Rousseau's take on the boundaries of private property contrasts starkly with the conventional view of firm boundaries as self-evident lines of demarcation put in place to act as a boon for societal prosperity through more efficient production of goods and services.

Rousseau's characterization of the foundations of private property suggests an alternative rationale for the existence of the institution of business firms. The legally protected boundaries of firms and private property serve as a mechanism that sanctions roping off what might otherwise be "common" resources in a manner that is publicly accepted while allowing managers and stockholders to override the slim profit margins that would prevail under perfect competition. Hardin (1968) argues that while privatization can serve as a mechanism necessary to prevent the irresponsible overuse of resources held in common, privatization increases accessible benefits for some parties while inherently limiting rights and freedoms for others. In short, continuous reassessment of the effects of boundaries is an essential foundation for maintaining a fair and equitable social order.

Orthodox economic thought is built on an assumption that individuals seek to maximize personal self-interest. Adam Smith (1776) and Frederick Hayek (1976) argue that when individuals seek to maximize their personal utility, they create a spontaneous order that benefits the overall society by rewarding efficient production of goods and services. In contrast, Veblen (1904, 1921) sees recurring financial depressions and market crises as evidence that financial managers use boundary lines as tools to sabotage and throw orderly markets into disarray. In the modern digital business environment, the characterization of firms and accounting reporting entities as distinct entities with self-evident boundaries is untenable (Moore 2017a,c). The voluntary nexus of contracts undertaken by what we refer to as a "firm" does not produce a static boundary line. Firms exist as fluid, dynamically managed sets of relationships. The accounting profession's dominant rhetoric that boundaries are self-evident reinforces extant power structures, upholding the ability of governments and corporate units to utilize traditional boundaries as a tool to maintain current power structures that delimit the impact of competitive forces.

Hayek (1976) and Rand (1989) strongly oppose business regulations guided by normative ideals. Classical and neoclassical economists argue that when left to their own devices, individuals will make rational decisions resulting in outcomes far superior to those imposed by regulatory interventions. As a critic of orthodox economics, Veblen argues that "[t]he institutional basis of business enterprise – the system of natural rights – appears to be a peculiarly unstable affair" (1904, 375). Whereas Rand paints altruism as an immoral restraint on individual freedom to choose, Durkheim ([1893] 1947) argues that individual actors have an implicit moral obligation to society at large. Danley (1994) suggests that both the micro-managerial (individualist) and the macro-managerial (collectivist) approach to economic theory contain inherent logical inconsistencies. Hodgson (1998, 172) claims "just as structures cannot be adequately explained in terms of individuals, individuals cannot be adequately explained in terms of structures." It is not an either/or dichotomy. Both individual decision making and macro-level institutional forces are needed to explain how businesses interact with their sociocultural environment. The next section of the chapter considers two historic cases that illustrate the dynamic nature of social, business, and government boundaries.

Owenism and Fordism as mechanisms of control

Robert Owen (1771–1858) and Henry Ford (1863–1947) both recognized that the interdependencies between firms and the surrounding society could be harnessed to engineer a new social order. Both individuals began their career at a critical junction where new technologies were transforming how businesses operated. Managing a textile mill in Scotland, Owen witnessed firsthand society's turn from a system of agrarian manual-labor production to the use of large-scale machine manufacturing in the early 19th century. In early 20th-century America, Ford not only utilized complex machinery in a standardized assembly process, he was also instrumental in actively promoting a shift toward a consumer model where businesses actively create consumer demand through manipulation of desires to acquire the products of industry. Both Owen and Ford understood the overlapping boundaries between production processes, workers, and consumers, as evidenced by their programs to influence employees' behaviors away from the work site and their engagement in politics.

Robert Owen

Robert Owen is a prominent personality in studies of the socialist and labor movements in Scotland, England, and Europe. In contrast, the American accounting/business academy treats Owen as a fringe figure at best. Owen's management ideas are highlighted because they arose out of the societal disruptions arising out of the mechanization of production. Owen's scant influence in the United States may stem in part from his failed attempt at creating a Utopian socialist society at New Harmony, Indiana. In the United Kingdom, Owen is remembered as instrumental in the political movement to outlaw child labor, regulate working hours, provide health care services for employees, encourage trade unions, and provide for free schools. Owen was also instrumental in cooperative ventures and labor exchange movements (Podmore 1924, 374–422). The labor cooperatives that developed as an offshoot of Owen's social ideology created an alternative currency based on labor time equivalencies that has some notable parallels to the modern Bitcoin movement. The American business academy affirms *laissez-faire* liberalism and decries socialist ideology, with little attention paid to how post-World War I Red Scare tactics (Nelles 1920) were instrumental in squelching honest academic debate about the pros and cons of both positions, treating liberal *laissez-faire* ideology as the only acceptable stance. Rarely given credit in the American academy, Owen's ideas were nevertheless prescient of what are now mainstream practices in labor law, human resource policy, and educational practice throughout the United States and other developed economies.

Robert Owen was born in Newton, Wales, in 1771. He infrequently revisited his birth village during his lifetime, though he moved back there prior to his death in 1858. Having received only a rudimentary formal education, he left his home at the age of 10 to become an apprentice for a seller of cloth and other household goods in Stamford, then in London (Podmore, 16–22). He tried his hand at entrepreneurial activities producing and selling "spinning mules," a type of machine used in the manufacture of cloth. He learned about business through trial and error and careful attention to financial recordkeeping. By the time he was 21 years old he was managing a state of the art textile mill in Manchester, England. He later took over management of a large mill at New Lanark in Scotland, married the owner's daughter, and became a major stockholder.[1] Getting in on the ground floor with more mechanized spinning and weaving of cloth, Owen's father-in-law had established the New Lanark mills in a rural setting on the River Clyde in 1783 (Podmore, 49). The mill owners utilized some child apprentices supplied by poor houses for work in the mills (Harrison 1969, 161) but also built living quarters to attract families to the rural site. Owen attributed the alcoholism and deviant behaviors of lower class members of society to the influence of environment on character formation. Having been active in the intellectual circles in the Manchester Philosophical and Literary society, when Owen took over the New Lanark mill, he was determined to use the residential and business site to test out his hypotheses about the relationship between behavior and environmental conditioning.

Some of his work site experiments in social engineering presage the modern focus on child-centered education. Owen referred to the factory school as an Institution for the Formation of Character. Pupils were taught about geography and morals prior to, rather than after, learning to read. Now preserved as a UNESCO world heritage site, the New Lanark schools used colorful maps, pictures of animals, music, and dance as elements of pedagogy.[2] The classrooms operated on a tutorial system with a high student-to-teacher ratio that minimized cost. Owen's philosophy was that corporal punishment, praise, and blame were all to be eschewed in favor of stimulating natural curiosity through competitive educational games. Dressed in simple uniforms, the children attended school from infancy through age 10, when they started work in the mill. Initially, parents were concerned that keeping children in school up to the age of 10 would hurt the family earnings. The objectives were overcome by providing a nursery and public cafeteria so that mothers could work in the factory, replacing the younger children's earnings.

The New Lanark mills soon became an important site for industrial tourism (Harrison 1969, 152). Businessmen, social reformers, and monarchs came to New Lanark not only to witness Owen's educational innovations but also to see the results of his behavioral experiments on the adult laborers. Owen was a teetotaler who saw alcoholism as a threat to both workplace productivity and family stability. Caretakers patrolled the streets at night identifying and fining workers for public drunkenness. Those offending more than three times could be fired. Outside vendors were prohibited from selling alcoholic beverages on the company grounds. Alcohol was sold only through the company canteen, with cumulative purchases of alcohol recorded by clerks so that excessive consumption would be a matter of public record. With up to 2,000 employees working at the mills, the work and living environment fostered the spread of contagious disease. The cotton lint and the warm, moist environment in the mills were conducive to the spread of tuberculosis and other respiratory diseases. Under these conditions, Owen saw the need to promote bathing and household cleanliness. Inspectors visited residences and made reports on insect infestation or violations of the prohibition on allowing animals within the personal space. Deductions from workers' wages were used to fund health services. Food and clothing was provided at fair prices at company canteens, with profits set aside to pay for school expenses (Podmore, 85–87).

Owen's philosophy of avoiding praise and blame among the young children did not carry over into factory operations. A comprehensive inventory of worker behavior was conducted weekly with the results put on display by a "silent monitor" hung at the assigned work station. The color-coded monitor consisted of a four-sided block of wood suspended on a string or wire. The impact of the devices was not unlike modern electronic badges or certificates that reward desired workplace behaviors. Silent monitor colors ranged from black (for bad behavior) to blue (indifferent), yellow (good), and white (excellent) (Podmore, 90). The block face was arranged to give all other workers a visual assessment of their fellow worker's rating; it was as if the results of a modern 360-degree performance assessment were made public. The modern day Society for Human Resource Management warns that peer ratings can cause employee morale problems and worker attrition (Taylor 2011). For Owen that was exactly the point – to use peer pressure to encourage workers to shape up or ship out.

Attention gained from visitors touring the mill encouraged Owen to become a regular speaker, author, and social activist. He was invited to speak to the Scottish Legislature in 1816 on the issues of cotton tariffs, work hours, and child labor in the mills. Owen demonstrated a keen awareness of the role of public relations in business and social reform. He purchased over 30,000 copies of newspapers that published his editorial opinions or covered his addresses in support of the Factory Act, receiving help with mailing costs through a franking agreement with Lord Lascelles in the Legislature (Podmore, 238). Still, his proposals for limiting work hours to ten and a half per day and increasing the age at which children could be employed to 10 met with considerable resistance from other mill owners. Fellow industrialists argued that shorter work hours would put them at a disadvantaged in competitive global markets (Podmore, 198), an argument often used by modern businesses in response to proposed environmental regulations.

Though he himself experienced considerable financial success, Owen was keenly aware of how industry's technical innovations were disrupting the social order and creating conditions of widespread unemployment among the uneducated classes. This fear of unemployment by his workers no doubt discouraged complaints about managerial encroachments on their personal freedom. By middle age, Owen turned routine mill operations over to others as he increasingly emphasized projects aimed at instituting what he called a "new moral order." He was especially interested in promoting the use of cooperative work arrangements to alleviate the plight of the unemployed. Owen spent, or squandered some might say, much of his accumulated capital on the purchase and operations of the short-lived US-based Utopian community in New Harmony, Indiana.

Owen was invited to speak on his vision of a new social order to the American president and members of Congress twice in 1825 (Johnson 1970). While Owen's ideas gained some traction with the intellectual set in the United States, he abandoned the US cooperative living sites after 1828 except for brief visits. Owen's lack of acceptance in America was in part due to the lack of economic success, but perhaps even more importantly due to a backlash against his religious ideas. Even though Owen's cooperative living centers provided for access to religious services of the members' choice, Owen was targeted by a noted Christian spokesman for a highly publicized debate aimed at demonstrating that Owen was out of step with mainstream religious orthodoxy. Reverend Campbell set out to expose Owen's disavowal of Calvinist principles of determinism and blame. Owen argued that if a God figure predetermined the course of one's life, it would be illogical to think of either improving society or casting blame (Madden and Madden 1982). Campbell used Owen's position on the arguments of determinism vs. free will to paint Owen as either a deist or atheist, and therefore not to be trusted.

Back in the British Isles, Owen found more receptive audiences for his socialist experiments, even though many of these arrangements also faced financial difficulties. Nevertheless, his English and Scottish experiments established an organizational pattern that survives in modern retirement and condominium associations, trade cooperatives, and systems of mandatory education for children. Owen's ideas inspired the creation of cooperative buyers' clubs that were started in London and other locations. These cooperative Labour Exchanges created an alternative to government-sponsored currency that foreshadowed facets of modern cryptocurrencies. Labour Notes were issued based on the time spent in creating products; these notes, rather than direct barter, could then be used to receive equivalent time and materials from other producers. The Labour Notes were intended to allow producers to have full access to the value of their time without an intermediary capitalist taking a share of the profits (Harrison 1969, 197–207). A secondary purpose of the Labour Notes is that they could serve as a hedge against volatility in sovereign currency values. This arrangement demonstrates that business and government powers are not necessarily separate and distinct but may overlap.

Owen's long-term disavowal of organized revealed religions and his advocacy for cooperative arrangements to replace the traditional ownership model of production were at odds with the aims of the landed gentry of his day. His cooperative, socialist models contrast sharply with modern neoliberal individualism and may explain his lack of influence in the American academy. Owen's experiments in social engineering illustrate that managers of influential firms have significant power to control worker behavior and to effect social reforms beyond the bounds of the traditional work day. On the other hand, the religious backlash demonstrates that even highly influential business leaders are constrained by normative social forces that push back against corporate control. Most sovereign nations today employ contributory schemes to finance health and retirement plans; these have significant parallels to the methods pioneered in Owen's educational and communal living experiments. Still, these arrangements exist within a sociopolitical setting where some business pundits (Roberts 2010) vehemently argue for fewer government regulations. These arguments are typically bolstered by reference to Smith's (1776) "invisible hand" or Hayek's (1944) *Road to Serfdom* thesis that government-coordinated social interventions will eventually create more problems than they solve.

Henry Ford

Henry Ford invented neither the automobile nor the assembly line production system. The Ford genius was partially exemplified by his production methods but even more so by his ability to get in tune with the motivations of potential consumers. Ford excelled in creating both the desire for automobiles and mechanisms to finance prospective owners' dreams. Born in 1863 to a farm family in Michigan, Ford was interested in clockworks and other machines from a young age. He apprenticed as a machinist in Detroit in 1879. He subsequently had various jobs in the Dearborn and Detroit area, taking bookkeeping classes at a Detroit business school. In 1891, he became an engineer for Edison Illuminating Company while working to develop a gas-powered vehicle. He resigned from Edison in 1899 to form the marginally successful Detroit Automobile Company (Watts 2005).

Like Owen, Ford recognized the need for publicity to drive consumer demand. To that end, he used his notoriety from successful automobile races in 1901 and 1902 to attract the capital to operate on an adequate scale. Ford mastered the use of newspaper stories, advertising, dealer word of mouth, radio shows, and ghost-written articles to drive sales of automobiles and farm machinery as well as to push his views of morality. Ford even seemed to court negative press if it would keep his name in the public eye. Nye (1979) suggests that Ford may have chosen to file a libel suit against a major newspaper as a publicity stunt. During the trial, Ford seem to go out of his way to flaunt his ignorance of common facts of American history in order to solidify his image as a friend to uneducated customers of modest means.

Ford's strategy for attracting and retaining highly productive employees was to pay an above-average wage. Even as the economy was faltering in 1914, Ford offered a $5 dollar a day wage. Roughly double the wage level of his direct competitors, the strategy got the attention of workers and newspapers alike. Along with the Ford strategy of paying higher wages was an implicit assumption that with higher wages the workers would be willing to work at a more rapid pace and not unionize. In addition to a higher base pay, workers who wanted to be considered for the profit-sharing plan had to submit to inspections by the social work department on criteria that included passing a household cleanliness inspection, avoidance of heavy drinking or gambling, and a commitment to forgo renting out sleeping quarters to "boarders" as Ford felt sharing quarters with persons outside the family unit was bad for the moral development of children

(Watts 2005, 200–24). Nash (1970, 162) points out that Ford undertook a campaign to promote traditional folk dances because he felt jazz was associated with a loosening of sexual mores. On the other hand, Watts (2005, 331–40) and Dahlinger (1978) provide credible evidence that Ford had a son that was never legally recognized stemming from a long-term affair with a woman who served as a company administrative assistant and social secretary for his wife.

Even wealthier than Owen, Ford used corporate resources to influence political processes through newsletters and sponsored radio shows. Moreover, he used his name recognition and personal funds to run for public office and to charter a ship used to head a largely unproductive peace mission to Europe in 1915 (Kraft 1978). Historians are highly critical of how Ford used his notoriety to actively incite anti-Semitic sentiment prior to the US entry into World War I. Ford's anti-Semitic newspaper articles from 1920–1927 were reprinted in Germany as a four-volume set, while Hitler was quoted as saying he kept a picture of Ford next to his desk (Woeste 2012). Ford accepted the Grand Cross of the Supreme Order of the German Eagle in 1938, the highest honor bestowed by the Hitler government on a foreigner.[3] Though initially opposed to American involvement in World War I, Ford Motor Company benefited from profits on military contracts once the war was declared.

Similar to Owen's experience, Ford's success in business gave him the confidence and financial resources to promote his personal ideals of how society should be reshaped. Ford frowned on the use of debt to purchase products like furniture or musical instruments even as he helped promote the use of automobile financing arrangements to enhance consumer demand for his own products. Vestiges of the techniques pioneered by both Owen and Ford to control the personal behaviors of their employees beyond the parameters of the manufacturing site can be seen in modern business use of smoking cessation, weight loss, and exercise programs to motivate behaviors that will decrease the cost of health care and absenteeism. These employee health initiatives and the use of advertising and publicity to generate brand recognition have come to be accepted merely as how business is done. The next section argues that in the digital environment, the boundaries between the business and personal sphere are even more blurred than in the eras of Owen's social industrial experiments or Ford's early efforts to control production, consumer demand, and the political environment.

Ethical issues in a data-driven economy

Big Data and the modern Internet of Things make it imperative to revisit the traditional assumptions that persons, businesses, and government are separate and distinct entities. What does it even mean to be a "separate" person in a technological environment where every movement and interaction is susceptible to being recorded by cellphones and smart appliances transmit data that can be analyzed and used by businesses to promote sales or by governments and their associated political parties to influence political outcomes? Political actors, accounting standard setters, and accounting professional groups seem to take it as a given that more data will lead to better decision making in support of a more prosperous society. Still, some critics warn that the ubiquity of data currently accessible by data miners, when coupled with a public naiveté about privacy issues and a *laissez-faire* business ideology, poses new ethical challenges.

O'Neil (2016) argues that "black box" data algorithms increase inequality and threaten traditional democratic ideals. As an insider in the Big Data revolution, O'Neil (2016) provides numerous examples of how data can be misused. She argues that good teachers can be fired and have no recourse when falsification of prior year data causes the new hire's performance measures to register a decrease in student learning (5–6). She sees online rankings based on dubious criteria as playing too big a role in the college recruitment process (50–67). Algorithms that track recidivism and loan default rates by neighborhood redouble the obstacles faced by responsible mortgage applicants who want to finance a home in a low-income community. If mortgages are not approved for those who want to stay and improve the old neighborhood, there is no way to overcome inner city blight.

Probabilistic data on one's genetic background can increase the cost of insurance, possibly influencing hiring processes. An arrest record, even one that was later proven to be based on false premises, can enter into the databases employers consult for preemployment background screening and decrease the chances for employment. If a prehire has ever spent time in prison or carried a high balance on a credit card, this can stigmatize them and cause seemingly neutral algorithms to implicitly rule out the individual's chances of getting a chance to work on turning around their legal or financial history. Prison sentences in theory have a specific time frame, but background checks mean even allegations of wrongdoing or growing up in the wrong neighborhood can have a lifelong negative impact.

Even when registrants on social media sites think they have opted out of having their data shared with advertisers, it is not always clear what major digital media platforms know about users or how personal data is being used (Weinberg 2018). The ability to track users' location through automobile and phone GPS systems poses a tradeoff between privacy and protection of other members of the public. Some court decisions suggest that law enforcement officers need search warrants to access location information; it is not clear that this is always the case in practice (Welty 2018). Efforts to limit purchases of Huawei security equipment in the United States and Australia suggest that government administrators recognize the potential for abuse of connective technologies (Woo and O'Keefe 2018; Selyukh and Palmer 2013). Even Tim Cook, the CEO of Apple, warns that there is a need for data privacy laws similar to those put in place in Europe to rein in what he refers to as the "data industrial complex" (Snider 2018). Presumably, his concerns extend not only to issues in how businesses use consumer data but the power that sovereign governments have to demand the release of personal data or to restrict access for political purposes.

Lohr (2015, 213) argues that

> All successful technologies raise alarms and involve trade-offs and risks. . . . The outlook for the technology we call big data is not fundamentally different. . . . The ever-smarter algorithms of big data can be seen as the new power brokers of society, determining what information we see, products we're offered, and life opportunities we're presented.

Both O'Neil (2016) and Lohr (2015) are concerned about the lack of transparency for data algorithms and the impact on vulnerable populations. Potential hires or credit applicants may have no choice but to submit to parameters used for screening purposes. When an unfavorable employee performance evaluation is received, the individual may disagree with the interpretation of the results of the data but have no reasonable, cost-effective mechanism for challenging the results. It is not uncommon for persons to be unaware that they have been subjected to data screening techniques. Terms of employment typically allow employers to use silent but highly invasive techniques to screen emails and phone conversations. Modern employees, like the Lanark mills employees or Depression-era Ford employees, have little choice but to submit to surveillance regimes because of the fear of not being able to find another job where conditions would be any different.

Chessel (2014) points out that there is a wide gap between what companies can do with data and what they should do with it. Chalcraft (2018) notes that while information professionals have articulated numerous codes of ethical practice, many of these are not mandatory. The major challenge in dealing with the datafication of modern society may be in fostering a broad recognition that information algorithms may appear neutral in structure even as they reinforce problematic power structures. Another problem is that the potential for surveillance may work to discourage employees from raising concerns about the loss of personal autonomy and freedom in the workplace and society at large.

Owen-ism and Ford-ism utilized Bentham's (1843) concept of the pan-opticon, where management holds the power to track, measure, and influence human behavior through calculative mechanisms. Staples (2014, 11) argues that modern forms of "everyday surveillance" have evolved in directions that are particularly concerning. Features of "everyday surveillance" include (1) the anonymous but permanent collection of data through methodical automatic processes, (2) the targeting of biological bodies for assessment and regulation, (3) the ubiquitous use of tracing devices, and (4) the tracking of the population at large, not merely those who have been administratively adjudicated as criminals or deviants.

In an "everyday surveillance" environment, it is unconscionable that members of a profession associated with the concept of "accountability" should not have a normative position on the ethical uses and applications of invasive digital technologies beyond minimalist compliance with the letter of existing laws. And yet one might also concur with Staples (2014, 206) that listing definitive "prescriptions for what is to be done would . . . only be a stunning display of hubris" as long as members of the profession and society at large do not even recognize that there is a problem associated with the overlapping boundaries between the private, business, and governmental arenas of action. According to Foucault (1988, 1), the source of human freedom rests on a willingness to "never accept [anything] as definitive, untouchable, obvious, or immobile." Treating boundaries as self-evident prevents recognition of the very structures that threaten personal freedom. The concluding section will focus on issues that management accounting educators need to consider as they guide accounting and business students in a critical exploration of significant ethical issues associated with the changing boundaries of society.

Moving beyond individual ethics and compliance

Business and accounting programs commonly treat finance, economics, and accounting as subjects that can be abstracted and kept distinct from their sociohistorical context. But the boundary transformations that have occurred in the process of shifting from an agrarian society subject to the whims of nature to a digital society where businesses and consumers interact in a web of mutual influence and surveillance are highly relevant to the practices and ethical concepts associated with management accounting. Many of the responsibility accounting techniques that appear in cost and managerial textbooks were created in the industrial era where management was clearly the driving force in determining the goals of the firm and in putting in place the boundaries for units under their command.

Figure 25.1 summarizes the differences and similarities in boundary problems for agrarian, industrial, consumer, and digital societies. In agrarian societies, businesses and individuals were at the mercy of weather and health epidemics. Beginning with the industrial revolution, governments and businesses alike began to exert some measure of control over the forces of nature. As a consumer society took hold, medicine, agriculture, and professional services were converted into financial products. In the interconnected digital era, data has come to be seen as the key to controlling consumption, politics, and social behavior. In a surveillance society, managers not only measure and reward employee behaviors but are themselves increasingly held

Agrarian Feudal Society	Land rights impact access to resources for cultivation; separation of aristocracy from craft and agricultural workers takes place.
	Weather impacts crop output.
	Family and religious norms control behavior.
	Medicine has limited ability to contain the spread of disease.
Owen-ist Industrial Society	Rights to equipment and other financial resources become even more important than land. Social separation of capitalists and workers takes place.
	Weather issues are less impactful as production shifts indoors.
	Industrial norms effect a stronger influence over worker behavior.
	Industrialists take an interest in education and medical issues to enhance worker productivity.
Ford-ist Consumer Society	Access to financing becomes as important as wages and other factors of production.
	Weather issues create new opportunities for development of instruments to control or protect consumers from the forces of nature.
	Mass media becomes an increasingly important influence over behavior.
	Not only manufactured products, but education, medicine, and services are converted into financial resources.
Digital Society	Access to information is used to effect control over productive processes, weather, financing, education, and consumption.
	Point-of-use data from material and digital interfaces are used by government and corporate entities to track and influence social behaviors.
	The line between formal and informal communications media becomes blurred.
	Social advocacy groups begin to amass and utilize data to push back against perceived abuses by government and corporate players.

Figure 25.1 The Evolution of Boundaries in Society

to account by what would seem to be "outside" groups that have their own ideas about managerial objectives. Media coverage of George Soros's 2018 calls for regulation of Facebook and the media giant's counter-investigation of the prominent financier demonstrate the use of surveillance and countersurveillance in business (Seetharaman 2018). In the modern digital environment, the Internet of Things has caused personal, work, and political/public spheres to become increasingly intertwined with boundaries that are rarely simple and objectively determinable.

Textbooks for management accounting and business ethics are primarily geared toward decision making by individual persons within an accounting or business firm under a given set of laws. Given that societies are not static but continuously evolving, a focus on ethics as mere compliance with existing laws is an insufficient foundation for ethical practice. While accounting institutions are often slow to adopt new concepts, university business and accounting programs are currently feeling significant pressure from business leaders and accrediting bodies alike to include more treatment of data analytics in academic programs. In response to these calls for action, it is important to be mindful of the boundary problems associated with tools that capture data for the implicit purpose of tracking and manipulating subjects.

Though social and environmental concerns are sometimes included as case material in business ethics texts, one is hard pressed to name a single college-level textbook in management accounting that provides a basis for critiquing current laws and institutional structures. Boyce et al. (2012) provide a rare example of an accounting course designed to examine the calculative practices embedded in sociocultural systems. It is not clear that accounting educators on the whole are even aware of the critical role played by grading, attendance, and learning management systems in policing unstated but implicit societal values (Walker 2010). Boundaries are central areas of contention whether the dividing line concerns the assignment of costs and responsibilities to specific departments within a firm or the delimitation of (1) geopolitical parameters that impact the market for workers, (2) sexual categories, (3) environmental responsibilities, (4) personal privacy, (5) tax domicile, (6) regulated financial taxonomies, or (6) those allowed to engage in a specific profession. Even discussions about how intangible financial assets should be measured and reported in financial statements are normative issues about boundaries.

It is perhaps not surprising that Western societies and their academic institutions alike uphold a loyalty to the rule of law to effect and maintain order. However, that does not imply that boundaries and borders should be viewed as self-evident. Durkheim ([1893] 1947) noted that the sources of solidarity and cohesion in society change as the workforce splinters into more finely grained divisions of labor. It may be that digital media are supplanting church, family, community, and government regulatory structures that have traditionally served as sources of social cohesion. On the other hand, these technologies can also work to disrupt social cohesion. Mezzadra and Neilson (2013) see global mass migration movements and the increasing politicization of geopolitical borders as an attempt to revisit traditional assumptions about boundaries and borders. Boundary issues associated with technologies that put businesses, governments, and even citizen groups under the lens of a super-opticon of digital scrutiny can gradually be dealt with through changes in laws and regulations, but only if society recognizes there is a problem. In a digital surveillance society, it is problematic for textbooks and academic programs in ethics, business, and accounting practice to continue the traditional code of silence about the purposes and side effects of administrative boundaries.

Large public accounting firms are regulated by state governments and federal agencies. Partners of these firms typically avoid political issues and rarely challenge existing regulatory structures, seeking instead to help their clients remain as unhampered as possible in their pursuit of personal gains. State boards of accountancy often impose an ethics requirement before licensure and continuing education afterwards. Unfortunately, most of these ethics programs focus on parameters of behavior that sidestep many substantive normative value issues. Professional literature such as the 2018 revision to Government Auditing Standards (GAO 2018, 26) defines the public interest as "the collective well-being of the community of people and entities that the auditors serve." Professional pronouncements evoke the public interest concept yet provide very limited guidance on the norms that should guide the collection and use of personal data by businesses, governments, and advocacy groups.

The academy could be a force for developing critical thinking among new recruits to the profession. That seems not to be happening in academic environments where "normative" research is considered a pejorative term and institutionally sanctioned ethics training does not address social justice issues that are inherent in existing laws, institutions, and professional boundaries. This chapter has argued that in today's environment, it is illogical to think of individual rights as separate and distinct from the institutions and forces that shape the social norms. If accounting practitioners and academics do not pay more attention to normative concerns associated with boundaries, the accounting profession will forfeit an opportunity to have a voice in significant conversations about the potential for the use and abuse of data in a setting where private, public, and business interests have become intimately intertwined.

Notes

1 See time line from Robert Owen Museum http://robert-owen-museum.org.uk/time_line and/or Robert Owen and New Lanark OpenLearn course from Open University www.open.edu/openlearn/history-the-arts/history/history-art/robert-owen-and-new-lanark/content-section-0?active-tab=description-tab
2 See www.newlanark.org/ with picture of a classroom at www.newlanark.org/visitorcentre/tour-classroom.shtml
3 See https://rarehistoricalphotos.com/henry-ford-grand-cross-1938/

References

Amaro, S. 2018. "Ten Years after Lehman Brothers Collapsed, this is Where European Banks Stand Now." *CNCB.Com*, September 13, 2018. www.cnbc.com/2018/09/13/10-years-since-lehman-collapse – this-is-where-european-banks-stand.html

Armstrong, B., J. E. Ketz, and D. Owsen. 2003. "Ethics Education in Accounting: Moving toward Ethical Motivation and Ethical Behavior." *Journal of Accounting Education* 21 (1): 1–16. doi:10.1016/S0748-5751(02)00017-9

Bailey, J. 2013. "The Iron Cage and the Monkey's Paw: Isomorphism, Legitimacy, and the Perils of a Rising Journal." *Academy of Management Learning & Education* 12 (1): 108–14. doi:10.5465/amle.2012.0248

Barker, J. 1993. "Tightening the Iron Cage: Concertive Control in Self-managing Work Teams." *Administrative Science Quarterly* 38: 408–37.

Barth, M. 2018. "The Future of Financial Reporting: Insights from Research." *Abacus* 54 (1): 66–78. doi:10.111/abac.12124

Bayou, M., A. Reinstein, and P. Williams. 2011. "To Tell the Truth: A Discussion of Issues Concerning Truth and Ethics in Accounting." *Accounting, Organizations and Society* 36: 109–24. doi:10.1016/j.aos.2011.02.001

Bentham, J. 1843. *Works*. Edited by Bowring. Vol. IV. http://oll.libertyfund.org/titles/bentham-the-works-of-jeremy-bentham-vol-4

Boyce, G., S. Greer, B. Blair, and C. Davids, C. 2012. "Expanding the Horizons of Accounting Education: Incorporating Social and Critical Perspectives." *Accounting Education: An International Journal* 21 (1): 47–74. doi:10.1080/09639284.2011.586771

Brivot, M, and Y. Gendron. 2011. "Beyond Panopticism: On the Ramifications of Surveillance in a Contemporary Professional Setting." *Accounting, Organizations and Society* 36: 135–55.

Chalcraft, J. 2018. "Drawing Ethical Boundaries for Data Analytics." *Information Management Journal* 52 (1): 18–22.

Chartered Accountants Australia and New Zealand. 2017. "The Quest for Prosperity: How Can New Zealand Keep Accounting Standards Rising for All?" www.charteredaccountantsanz.com/news-and-analysis/insights/future-inc/the-quest-for-prosperity

Chessel, M. 2014. "Ethics for Big Data and Analytics." www.ibmbigdatahub.com/sites/default/files/whitepapers_reports_file/TCG%20Study%20Report%20-%20Ethics%20for%20BD%26A.pdf

Claeyé, F., and T. Jackson. 2012. "The Iron Cage Re-revisited: Institutional Isomorphism in Non-profit Organisations in South Africa." *Journal of International Development* 24 (5): 602–22. doi:10.1002/jid.2852

Clark, J. 1923. *Studies in the Economics of Overhead Costs*. Chicago, IL: University of Chicago Press.

Coase, R. 1937. "The Nature of the Firm." *Economica* 4 (16): 386–405. doi:10.1111/j.1468-0335.1937.tb00002.x

Dahlinger, J. 1978. *The Secret Life of Henry Ford*. Indianapolis: Bobbs-Merrill Company, Inc.

Danley, J. 1994. *The Role of the Modern Corporation in a Free Society*. Notre Dame, IN: University of Notre Dame Press.

Datar, S., and M. Rajan. 2018. *Horngren's Cost Accounting: A Managerial Emphasis*. 16th ed. Essex, England: Pearson Education Limited.

Devine, C., ed. 1985. "Some Impossibilities – Including Allocations." *Essays in Accounting Theory* 5: 79–91. Sarasota, FL: American Accounting Association.

Dobbin, F., D. Schrage, and A. Kalev. 2015. "Rage against the Iron Cage: The Varied Effects of Bureaucratic Personnel Reforms on Diversity." *American Sociological Review* 80 (5): 1014–44. doi:10.1177/0003122415596416

Durkheim, E. 1893 (original in French, 1947 trans.). *The Division of Labor in Society*. Glencoe, IL: Free Press.

Ferguson, J., D. Collison, D. Power, and L. Stevenson. 2005. "What are Recommended Accounting Textbooks Teaching Students about Corporate Stakeholders?" *British Accounting Review* 37 (1): 23–46. doi:10.1016/j.bar.2004.08.002

Ferguson, J., D. Collison, D. Power, and L. Stevenson. 2006. "Accounting Textbooks: Exploring the Production of a Cultural and Political Artifact." *Accounting Education: An International Journal* 15 (3): 243–60. doi:10.1080/09639280600850679

Ferguson, J., D. Collison, D. Power, and L. Stevenson. 2007. "Exploring Lecturers' Perceptions of the Emphasis Given to Different Stakeholders in Introductory Accounting Textbooks." *Accounting Forum* 31 (2): 113–27. doi:10.1016/j.accfor.2006.11.003

Ferguson, J., D. Collison, D. Power, and L. Stevenson. 2010. "The Views of 'Knowledge Gatekeepers' about the Use and Content of Accounting Textbooks." *Accounting Education: An International Journal* 19 (5): 501–25. doi:10.1080/09639281003594294

Foucault, M. 1975. *Surveiller et Punit: Naissance de la prison*. Translated by Sheridan, A. 1977. *Discipline and Punishment*, released as Second Vintage Books edition, May 1995.

Foucault, M. 1988. "Power, Moral Values, and the Intellectual: An Interview with Michel Foucault by Michael Bess." *History of the Present* (4).

Garner, J. T. 2016. "Open Doors and Iron Cages: Supervisors' Responses to Employee Dissent." *International Journal of Business Communication* 53 (1): 27–54. doi:10.1177/2329488414525466

Garrison, R., E. Noreen, and P. Brewer. 2015. *Managerial Accounting*. 15th ed. New York: McGraw-Hill Irwin.

Government Accountability Office (GAO). 2018. *Government Auditing Standards*. July 2018 Revision. Comptroller General of the United States.

Hansen, D., and M. Mowen. 2018. *Cornerstones of Cost Management*. 4th ed. Boston, MA: Cengage Learning.

Hardin, G. 1968. "The Tragedy of the Commons." *Science* 162 (3859): 1243–48.

Harrison, J. 1969. *Quest for the New Moral Order: Robert Owen and the Owenites in Britain and America*. New York: Charles Scribner's Sons.

Hayek, F. 1944. *The Road to Serfdom*. Chicago, IL: University of Chicago Press.

Hayek, F. 1976. *Law, Legislation and Liberty: Vol. 2 The Mirage of Social Justice*. Chicago, IL: University of Chicago Press.

Heller, M. 1999. "The Boundaries of Private Property." *The Yale Law Journal* 108 (6): 1163–223.

Hodgson, G. 1998. "The Approach of Institutional Economics." *Journal of Economic Literature* 36 (1): 166–92.

Horvat, R., and B. Korosec. 2015. "The Role of Accounting in a Society: Only a Techn(olog)ical Solution of a Problem of Economic Measurement or also a Tool of Social Ideology?" *Nase Gospodarstov/ Our Economy* 61 (4): 32–40. doi:10.1515/ngoe-2015-0016

Iacobucci, E., and G. Triantis. 2007. "The Economic and Legal Boundaries of Firms." *The Virginia Law Review* 93: 515–70.

Institute of Chartered Accountants of England and Wales (ICAEW). 2010. *Business Models in Accounting: The Theory of the Firm and Financial Reporting*. London: ICAEW.

Institute of Management Accountants (IMA). 2017. *Statement of Ethical Professional Practice*. Montvale, NJ: IMA. www.imanet.org/insights-and-trends/business-leadership-and-ethics/ima-statement-of-ethical-professional-practice?ssopc=1.

Johnson, O. 1970. *Robert Owen in the United States*. New York: Humanities Press.

Kraft, B. 1978. *The Peace Ship: Henry Ford's Pacifist Adventure in the First World War*. New York: Macmillan.

Lohr, S. 2015. *Data-ism*. New York: Harper Business.

Madden, E., and D. Madden. 1982. "The GREAT DEBATE: Alexander Campbell vs. Robert Owen." *Transactions of the Charles S. Peirce Society* 18 (3): 207–26.

Mezzadra, S., and B. Neilson. 2013. *Border as Method*. Durham, NC: Duke University Press.

Moore, L. 2017a. "Carving Nature at its Joints: The Entity Concept in an Entangled Society." *Accounting Historians Journal* 44 (2): 125–38. doi.org:10.2308/aahj-10556

Moore, L. 2017b. "Discourse Analysis of Accounting 'Accuracy' across Regulatory, Academic, and Pedagogical Arenas." *Journal of Theoretical Accounting Research* 12 (2): 50–77.

Moore, L. 2017c. "Revisiting the Firm, Reporting Entity, and Going Concern Concepts in Light of Financial Crisis." *Accounting and the Public Interest* 17 (1): 130–43. doi:10.2308/apin-51919

Nash, R. 1970. *The Nervous Generation: American Thought, 1917–1930*. Chicago, IL: Rand McNally College Publishing Company.

Nelles, Walter. 1920. *Seeing Red: Civil liberty and the Law in the Period Following the War*. New York: American Civil Liberties Union. https://web.archive.org/web/20060923152636/http://marx.org/history/usa/groups/aclu/1920/0800-nelles-civilliberty.pdf

Nye, D. 1979. *Henry Ford, Ignorant Idealist*. Fort Washington, NY: Kennikat Press.

O'Neil, C. 2016. *Weapons of Math Destruction*. New York: Crown.

Pathways Commission. 2015. "In Pursuit of Accounting's Curricula for the Future." file:///C:/Users/LJM/Downloads/Pathways_Report_4_For_Print%20(2).pdf

Podmore, F. 1924. *Robert Owen: A Biography*. New York: D. Appleton and Company.

Porter, T. 1999. *Trust in Numbers: The Pursuit of Objectivity in Science and Public Life*. Princeton, NJ: Princeton University Press.

Prasad, P., and A. Prasad. 2000. "Stretching the Iron Cage: The Constitution and Implications of Routine Workplace Resistance." *Organization Science* 11 (4): 387–403.

Rand, A. 1989. *The Voice of Reason: Essays in Objectivist Thought*. Edited by L. Peikoff. The Ayn Rand Library, Vol. 5. New York: Meridian.

Roberts, R. 2010. "Why Friedrich Hayek is Making a Comeback." *The Wall Street Journal*, June 28, 2010.

Rousseau, J. 1754. "Discourse on the Origin of Inequality, Part Two." In *The Basic Political Writings*, translated by D. Cress, 1992. Indianapolis: Hackett Publishing Company.

Rudkin, K. 2007. "Accounting as Myth Maker." *Australasian Accounting, Business and Finance Journal* 1 (2): 13–24. doi:10.1515/ngoe-2015-0016

Ryner, M. 2015. "Europe's Ordoliberal Iron Cage: Critical Political Economy, the Euro Area Crisis and its Management." *Journal of European Public Policy* 22 (2):1–20. doi:10.1080/135-1763.2014.995119

Searle, J. 1995. *The Construction of Social Reality*. New York: The Free Press.

Seetharaman, D. 2018. "Soros Aide Urges Facebook Review." *The Wall Street Journal* 272 (122) (November 23): B4.

Selyukh, A., and D. Palmer. 2013. "U.S. Law to Restrict Government Purchases of Chinese IT Equipment." *Technology News: Reuters*, March 27, 2013. www.reuters.com/article/us-usa-cybersecurity-espionage/u-s-law-to-restrict-government-purchases-of-chinese-it-equipment-idUSBRE92Q18O20130327

Smith, A. 1776. *An Inquiry into the Nature and Causes of the Wealth of Nations*. London: W. Strahan.

Snider, M. 2018. "Apple CEO Tim Cook Supporters Stricter Data Privacy Laws, Warns of 'Data Industrial Complex'." *USA Today*, October 24, 2018. www.usatoday.com/story/tech/nation-now/2018/10/24/apple-ceo-tim-cook-calls-stricter-data-privacy-protections/1750919002/

Solomons, D. 1991. "Accounting and Social Change: A Neutralist View." *Accounting, Organizations and Society* 16 (3): 287–95.

Souitaris, V., S. Zerbinati, and G. Liu. 2012. "Which Iron Cage? Endo- and Exo-isomorphism in Corporate Venture Capital Programs." *Academy of Management Journal* 55 (2): 477–505. doi:10.5465/amj.2009.0709

Staples, W. 2014. *Everyday Surveillance: Vigilance and Visibility in Postmodern Life*. Lanham, MD: Rowman & Littlefield.

Taylor, S. 2011. "Assess Pros and Cons of 360-degree Performance Appraisal." Society for Human Resource Managers. www.shrm.org/resourcesandtools/hr-topics/employee-relations/pages/360degreeperformance.aspx

Thomas, A. 1969. *Studies in Accounting Research #3: The Allocation Problem in Financial Accounting Theory*. Sarasota, FL: American Accounting Association.

Veblen, T. 1904. *The Theory of Business Enterprise*. New York: C. Scribner's Sons. Reprinted in 1978 by Transaction Books, New Brunswick, NJ.

Veblen, T. 1921. *The Engineer and the Price System*. New York: B. W. Huebsch. Reprinted in 2001 by Augustus M. Kelley, Clifton, NY.

Walker, S. 2010. "Child Accounting and 'the Handling of Human Souls'." *Accounting, Organizations and Society* 35: 628–57. doi:10.1016/j.aos.2010.07.001

Watts, S. 2005. *The People's Tycoon*. New York: Alfred A. Knopf.

Weinberg, G. 2018. "Google and Facebook are Watching Our Every Move Online." *CNCB*, January 31, 2018. www.cnbc.com/2018/01/31/google-facebook-data-privacy-concerns-out-of-control-commentary.html

Welty, J. 2018. "Search Warrants Authorizing Law Enforcement Computer Hacking and Malware." UNC School of Government blog, July 23, 2018. https://nccriminallaw.sog.unc.edu/search-warrants-authorizing-law-enforcement-computer-hacking-and-malware/

Williams, P. 1987. "The Legitimate Concern with Fairness." *Accounting, Organizations & Society* 12 (2): 169. doi:10.1016/0361-3682(87)90005-5

Williams, P., and S. Ravenscroft. 2015. "Rethinking Decision Usefulness." *Contemporary Accounting Research* 32 (2): 763–88. doi:10.1111/1911-3846.12083

Woeste, V. 2012. *Henry Ford's War on Jews and the Legal Battle against Hate Speech.* Stanford: Stanford University Press.

Woo, S., and K. O'Keefe. 2018. "U.S. Asks its Allies to Shun Chinese Supplier." *The Wall Street Journal* 273 (122) (November 23): A1, A4.

Zeff, S. 2017. "Contemplating the Origin of Decision-usefulness." *Accounting Historians Journal* 44 (2): 189. doi:10.2308/aahj-10558

Zimmerman, J. 2017. *Accounting for Decision Making and Control,* 9th ed. New York: McGraw-Hill Education.

26

A SURVEY OF DIVERSITY ETHICS IN THE ACCOUNTING PROFESSION

Margarita Maria Lenk

Introduction

Multiple research studies have documented the positive association between diverse professional teams and integrated global professional services supply chains with increased creativity, innovation, productivity, and performance as well as increases to accounting professional impacts in society (Deloitte 2018; E&Y 2020; KPMG 2018). This chapter reviews publicly available data from the accounting profession in order to develop a deeper understanding of diversity ethics within the US accounting profession. Diversity is both the amount and the variance of differing human characteristics within the entire professional workforce or within any one organization or office. Diversity is different from "inclusion." Inclusion is how diverse employees consistently experience being treated as valued and integrated members of an organizational culture. Inclusive culture characteristics are the vehicles that embrace an organization's diversity ethics and are the required determinants of diversity's incremental and sustainable value within the profession or organization.

Influenced by professional association leadership guidance and ethical code standards, the ethics, moral principles and values within the individual accounting firms and other organizations are what drive their diversity choices. Collectively, these choices form the overall public perceptions of the accounting profession's ethics toward diversity. Professional and organizational ethics standards can only set a minimum standard and an aspirational vision for group membership behavior. They imply a freedom of discretionary choices within or above the approved set of objectives and rules and include an understanding that related choices affect their internal and external stakeholders.

Observable diversity ethics and strategies within the accounting profession span a wide variety of options in public accounting firms, private or public organizations, or government agencies alike. Signals of organizational commitments to diversity can range from a focus on regulatory and legislated compliance for equitable treatment of diverse employees (at the lowest levels) to deeply progressive participative leadership and cultural choices for both diversity and inclusion to thrive optimally. Publicly observable diversity choices can be viewed as the profession's "talk" designed to influence the public's perceptions and opinions regarding the profession's sincerity, empathy, authenticity, transparency, and commitment to diversity and inclusion values. McKinsey's (2020) research documents that companies with gender and ethnic cultural diversity experience above-average profitability significantly more often than their competitors when increased diversity was accompanied by increased inclusion of diverse professionals. This chapter summarizes the accounting profession's diversity talk, discusses a few of the continuing challenges and invites further research regarding the "walk" of building inclusive cultures in the profession.

This chapter utilizes an ecosystem approach to study the accounting profession's diversity strategies and investments. An ecosystem lens considers both how the individual stakeholder's self-interest as well as the professional financial services market environment affect and interact with each other to influence the demand for and supply of diverse accounting professionals. The FAO (2020, 1) acknowledges that ethics regarding human "welfare, freedom, and justice" are relevant to management. A systems approach, therefore, is most useful to inform whether the "intent" of professional diversity choices have resulted in the desired social and economic sustainability "impact" on the welfare, freedoms, and justice experienced by diverse professionals, their organizations, and the collective perceptions of and experience with the profession.

An underlying assumption of this research is that the accounting profession's ethics regarding diversity can be at least partially derived from observable and measurable professional leadership and individual firm choices. Alternative explanations for the profession's diversity choices should be considered as competing explanations for diversity choices. For example, diversity strategies may be a part of a larger constellation of integrated organizational and professional sustainability or growth objectives, consistent with what we would expect to witness in a wider ecological context of social and fiscal coexistence. In a capitalistic system, a commitment to diversity and inclusion may be driven by a desire to improve business performance and wealth, both of which would fortify the accounting profession's role in society. For example, professional members may intend to better match their workforce demographics to the increasingly diverse client profiles in the market for accounting services, thereby attracting more business. Alternatively, the observed increase in diversity strategies in the accounting profession may simply be due to changing labor supply demographics, a movement fueled by increasing retirements of the nondiverse baby boomer generation professionals and increasing enrollments of diverse university students in accounting degree programs. A final possible explanation for diversifying the profession may be the desire to increase the profession's political visibility, capital, and power by attracting new diversity-tagged media and capital, especially after a devastating era of fraudulent cases that have decreased public trust in the profession. For example, Tandé (2017) provides evidence of this view of diversity policies as "altruistically disguised" strategies designed to access resources from authorities rather than gain respect and benefits from respecting differences between people. This chapter chooses the assumption that regardless of original causality, diversity investments are influenced or are influencing the accounting profession's underlying ethics and values.

Regardless of the true driver(s) of diversity initiatives, the accounting profession's ethics are and continue to be the most common attribution of professional diversity choices. Therefore, a review of the observable mix of diversity choices at individual, firm or organization, and collective profession levels of analysis will illuminate new insights regarding the strength of the "social fabric" or the "social sustainability contract" that the professional services offer to society. The next two sections of this chapter summarize the diversity attitudes and initiatives provided by the profession and a few of the continuing challenges. The final section provides overall conclusions of this research.

Observable diversity ethics

Progress on improving diversity attitudes and strategies can be assessed at the collective professional regulatory and associations level as well as viewed from the perspective of individual organizations. While diversity values are not (yet) specifically mentioned in the professional codes of conduct of the leading professional accounting associations, their commitment to diversity ethics, leadership, and the dissemination of best practices are prioritized and are well articulated within their statements of vision, commitments to diversity and inclusion, professional practice guidelines, toolkits, and development programs provided for their members. Professional associations recognize the importance of overt top management diversity attitude leadership toward developing diversity value buy-in from all levels of employees. The effectiveness of the professional association diversity strategies is dependent on their transparent communication regarding how much of the professional association's diversity-related funds are pivoted and allocated each year to categories highly demanded by the professional members. Both the supply of diverse professionals and the range of diversity characteristics are rapidly changing from historic diversity categories and numbers in the profession. Such transparency helps to form the public perception of the profession's ethics as well as the accessibility of the profession to each group included in what is currently defined as a diverse accountant.

The influence of the professional association's leadership in developing and advancing diversity perspectives within the professional firms and industry organizations is clear. Diversity not only includes the legally protected categories but is now seen to also include cognitive, perspective, cultural, experience, and communication differences across team members. For example, Deloitte (2018) research reports that top-performing teams require mental frameworks that vary their focus between evidence, options, outcomes, people, process, and risks. The Institute of Managerial Accountants (2020) provides guidance for its members through a diversity commitment statement and provides a continuum of diversity commitment to help their members understand where their organization falls within the continuum. This continuum ranges from low engagement, compliance-focused conventional attitudes to high engagement strategies that are purposeful, advanced, inclusion-focused cultural attitudes. The IMA provides multiple resources in its guidance to support members' moving their organizations to a more engaged position on the diversity continuum. Professional associations also provide explanations of the more common challenges to diversity attitudes and offer useful suggestions and diversity training programs that most effectively overcome those challenges.

The American Institute of Certified Public Accountants (AICPA) has formed diversity and inclusion commissions to increase professional diversity by prioritizing access, preparation, and success on professional certifications and licensing and increasing the recruitment, retention, and promotional paths of diverse professionals. By first researching the access and inclusion challenges faced by diverse individuals, the AICPA has coordinated with its network of state chapters and integrated the efforts of educators, professionals, firms, industry and government leaders, and minority affinity groups such as ALPFA (Association of Latino Professionals in Finance and Accounting), NAFOA (Native American Finance Officers Association), and NABA (National Association of Black Accountants). In addition, the AICPA (2020) has developed ten successful diversity business cases from leading professional firms that support the McKinsey (2018) research findings that link diversity investments and increased competitive advantage and financial performance. McKinsey (2018) found that diverse organizations experience more collective and individual intelligence, more value-driving insights, and more innovation, creativity, and accurate problem solving. These benefits drive higher operational success, profitability, market share, and more success in entering new markets.

The diversity-related ethics of the public accounting firms are evidenced in their very aggressive work for the past two decades to increase the diversity of their organizations. Professional accounting firms have successfully institutionalized these objectives by first developing codes of professional conduct that support equity and diversity values. Indirect codes of conduct approaches focus on variables that create public trust in the accountants' expertise and judgment processes, with a focus on expected character traits (e.g., competence, objectivity, integrity, accountability, and trustworthiness), work habits, communication styles, due diligence, independence in form and substance, and a commitment to transparency to stakeholders who rely upon accountants' communications and information.[1] Direct approaches specifically mention respect and support for diversity and inclusion in their codes of conduct. Professional accounting firms initially focused their diversity initiatives at the entry level of recruiting, trusting that over time, the diversity would reach higher levels of management. Recently, they have expanded the scope of their diversity initiatives to higher levels of professionals within their firms.

While not alone in pioneering diversity in the accounting profession, KPMG has often been noted as the accounting profession's first firm to authentically and successfully increase diversity beyond the first wave of gender diversity initiatives. Their initial success has since been matched by tremendously successful initiatives from the other leading professional firms. KPMG's approach was to first create strong internal branding and commitment to diversity before beginning their initial diversity public press releases and recruiting efforts. They listened to and supported their new diverse hires by supporting their offices with significant diversity funding and nurturing an openness to adjusting their processes for authentic inclusion. KPMG has transparently reported their progress toward diversity goals to their clients and young people alike, frequently recognized internal diversity leaders, and aggressively partnered with external national leaders of diversity. More recently, KPMG has again led the profession by embracing human resource and cultural investments that optimize the incremental value from employees with disabilities, including autism, which has been recognized by the Disability Matters Workplace Award (KPMG, 2020).[2]

Ernst & Young (EY), for example, has since been a leader of directly and publicly owning its broadly defined diversity values. EY (2017) explicitly respects the incremental organizational learning value, innovation, relationships, and client satisfaction that is provided by diversity in their professional teams. EY explicitly states their valuation and support for employees' differences in cognitive abilities and styles, differing teamwork and leadership styles and different education, experience, and responsibility levels in addition to the traditional expressions of respect for differences in gender, race, ethnicity, ability, culture, religion, sexual orientation, age, and socioeconomic backgrounds (among other dimensions).

The Deloitte and the Billie Jean King Leadership Initiative (BJKLI) partnership has discovered that millennials do not notice the physical differences between people and rather define diversity as the differences in knowledge and experience, as that is what drives the different perspectives that are brought to the work team (Deloitte 2020). Grant Thornton (2020) ethics support a culture of authentic expression of diversity values by its nondiverse leaders and employees. When a work culture values diversity as more than just an HR issue, then more successful outcomes will be experienced for the organization's diversity initiatives, its diverse professionals, its organizational market, and its economic performance. PwC (2019) reported significant increases of women on every level of their global leadership team, their global board, and in both their partners and senior managers ranks since 2013. There are many more professional firms who have effectively implemented similar advances in the diversity within their firms or at least their diverse community offices.

A wide variety of successes have been experienced in diversity leadership and strategic diversity initiatives in mid-sized and smaller accounting firms, and while they are more numerous in number of offices than the large firms, insufficient resources oftentimes reduce their publication of their diversity success stories. The first trend to note is their competitive advantage at attracting diverse candidates as a result of their small office size and office culture. Many diverse professional candidates feel safer and more comfortable with a caring, more intimate "family" culture in smaller offices. This may be because in smaller offices every individual is more accountable for their behavior (as there is no place to hide), or that the diverse hires do not feel as outnumbered or "different" from so many others. Smaller firms can offer a wider variety of professional experiences both within and across service lines to diverse entry-level staff, which is attractive to diverse hires who have not yet decided upon which area of professional services' they want to focus their knowledge and expertise.

Finally, smaller firms have smaller, more diverse clients who serve more diverse communities and populations, both of which are often closely held values of diverse professionals who want to experience their job helping to make a difference in their communities. Larger firms have made advances in creating more consistent small teams within their large offices so that diverse new hires experience the intimate "work family," which is associated with higher retention of diverse accountants.

Higher education institutions play an important role in the diverse professional labor pipeline. Minority-serving institutions and the community colleges were the first to encourage minorities to become accountants, with the majority-serving universities joining in this work as the diversity in high schools increased. Colleges and universities oftentimes partner with professional associations, affinity groups, accounting firms, and high school partners to increase the public perceptions that accounting education and the accounting profession is accessible, inclusive, and rewarding to diverse populations. The benefits of increasing the number of diverse faculty is a critical component of successful diverse student recruitment, enrollment, retention, and graduation. Significant gaps still exist between the percentage of diverse faculty and diverse students, and the percentage of diverse students compared to the percentage size of their local and regional population segments. Mosiri and Wilson Cardon (2016) state that if diversity does not increase in colleges of business, they will be denying access to the accounting profession to one-third of the national population.

The PhD Project deserves a special highlight for the professional diversity advancements it has created in the accounting profession by working with higher education. The PhD Project, originally funded by the KPMG Foundation, now a separate nonprofit organization, has the objective to increase the number of underrepresented African American, Hispanic American, and Native American business faculty in higher education institutions (Asian Americans are not underrepresented in the accounting profession). Diverse faculty are an important driver for attracting minority students to business majors in colleges and universities.

Over the last two decades, the PhD project has partnered with the AACSB International universities (Association to Advance Colleges and Schools of Business), professional minority affinity groups, and sponsoring corporations to develop, place, coach and mentor over 1,500 new minority faculty members into tenure track faculty positions. This program has increased faculty diversity in accredited colleges of business by over 500% in a very short time. Many PhD Project faculty advisors generously mentor new diverse faculty through navigating their entrance into higher education cultures that may not yet be inclusive. They do this by developing teaching excellence in their courses and producing sufficient academic research published in high-level journals. These performance outcomes increase the diverse faculty members' likelihood of tenure and promotion, which provides them the sustainable presence on accounting faculties and provides them the platform to make inclusivity improvements. Due to the successful development and performance of these PhD Project faculty, many have been promoted to administrative positions of department chairs, assistant and associate deans, deans, provosts, and even university presidents, breaking through prior glass ceilings and creating new promotional paths for more diverse faculty.

The AICPA foundation funds the AICPA Fellowship for Minority Doctoral Students, which supports a few minority professionals through PhD programs so that there are more minority accounting faculty in higher education. Howard University spearheads the Pipeline Project, designed to attract more minority students to the profession of accounting. There are many such programs across a wide variety of affinity group professional associations and foundations that are also increasing diversity of individuals seeking accounting profession entry (e.g., Latin American Education Fund, ALPFA, NABA, Daniels fund, Hispanic and Black Chambers of Commerce, state societies of CPAs, CMAs, and IIAs, etc.)

Because most PhD Project faculty possess high levels of "give back" service ethics, they take on many service roles that are focused on increasing diversity. This service includes

- participating with their admissions personnel to attract more diverse students to their universities;
- visiting diverse K–12 schools as guest speakers, mentors, and tutors, thereby providing diverse youth with knowledge that they can become accountants;
- serving in their local CPA society's diversity initiatives;
- participating in the Pipeline Project and the CHE (Committee for Hispanic Excellence) to develop stronger minority workforce pipelines;
- serving as university student affinity group faculty advisors; and
- mentoring university students through course completion success, retention, and graduation and success in professional entry.

In many aspects, the diverse faculty at universities are the best and most visible professional service role models for all accounting students, as they transparently role model the accounting profession as focused on objectives bigger than their own self-interests. To date, 500,000 business students would be a conservative estimation of how many business students were influenced by diverse PhD Project faculty, a fact that illustrates that the reach and accomplishments of the PhD Project are a collaborative diversity pipeline success story making a material difference (PhD Project, 2020). For their diversity goals, any organization or profession can adapt and leverage the PhD Project's partnership structure and processes.

Finally, changes in the attitudes and practices in the role-modeling of the accounting profession by K–12 teachers and counselors are also helping to increase the diversity in the accounting profession. The NAF (National Academy Foundation) has been instrumental with their minority-targeted high school curriculum programs designed to attract minority students to accounting and finance careers. Professional community volunteering in programs such as Junior Achievement, Math Counts, Beta Alpha Psi chapters' financial education programs, professional guest speakers in diverse K–12 schools, and campus summer programs for diverse middle school and high school students are also contributing to increases in diversity in the accounting profession.

Whether in partnership with selected higher education institutions or acting on their own, each of the leading accounting firms are very aggressive in their recruiting of under-represented professionals, often identifying target schools and supporting these students in K–12 schools and community colleges before they take their first upper-level accounting classes at university. Research has shown that exposure to careers at or before the middle school ages significantly increases youths' ability to envision themselves as successfully achieving a career in those industries. A common feedback is that the minority youth tell these professional accounting volunteers that they have never had any prior exposure to a professional accountant or the career of professional accounting before these outreach efforts.

Continuing challenges to diversity initiatives in the accounting profession

While significant advances have been made to diversify the accounting profession, significant challenges still exist. Tandé (2017) warns that presenting diversity as an economic resource rather than an inclusivity issue of valuable and respectful collegiality can be viewed as similar to putting "old wine in new wineskins," because forced behaviors rarely result in the desired cultural dimensions of diversity's incremental value.

The first challenge is the wide range of diversity ethics and practices in the accounting profession. In spite of the widely published and applauded diversity initiatives by professional and academic organizations alike in the professional pipeline, there are still professional offices within large, medium, and small firms (as well as higher education) that have not embraced diversity or do not have more than a minimal diversity ethic. Minimal diversity approaches focus on compliance dimensions as defined and protected by federal laws, as well as any applicable state laws. Compliance approaches typically limit diversity definitions to race, creed, color, sex, sexual orientation, ability, age, religion, and national origin or ancestry differences. Applicable diversity-related federal laws include the Equal Pay Act, Title VII of the Civil Rights Act of 1964, Title I and V of the Americans with Disabilities Act, Sections 501 and 505 of the Rehabilitation Act, and the Civil Rights Act of 1991. For governmental accounting careers, diversity standards have been developed for the office of the Comptroller of the Currency (OCC), the Board of Governors of the Federal Reserve System, the Federal Deposit Insurance Corporation (FDIC), the National Credit Union Administration (NCUA), the Consumer Financial Protection Bureau (CFPB), the Securities and Exchange Commission (SEC), and the Dodd-Frank Act, which charges the Office of Minority and Women Inclusion (OMWI) to develop diversity standards, policies, and practices for the organizations regulated by the agency (Credit Union national Association, 2020).

This challenge is most visible and felt by diverse professionals, whether entering or working in the accounting profession. Diverse professional entrants evaluate the authenticity of diversity initiatives based on the level of authentic engagement with the actual diverse individuals. Less internally engaged diversity strategy choices such as "hands-off" donations to diversity-related nonprofits, events, conferences, and scholarship establishments are often perceived as "outsourced" strategies rather than authentic internal diversity values and ethics. Minimum engagement perspectives, however, can still include a wider set of workforce diversity characteristics, such as identity, culture, discipline knowledge, and learning, personality and communication styles. Often, diverse job applicants are frustrated by minimum engagement recruiting practices. They may feel used for a diversity-hiring quota rather than equitably considered as the best hires for the organization for their talents and merits. Quota-driven diversity recruiting practices can backfire and become ineffective in these organizations if their diversity commitment also includes diverse employee professional development, mentoring, and promotional path-focused coaching programs.

Diversity initiatives are perceived as having more authentic engagement when firm-wide or organization-wide support for diversity can be directly observed and experienced by the diverse populations being invited to consider the accounting profession. Diversity-related community K–12 volunteering, outreach, and mentoring efforts toward diverse university students (such as diverse business case competition coaching) are examples of more engaged diversity strategies that are perceived as better proxies for internal diversity ethics and values when they are followed by recruitment interest in the diverse individuals served. Finally, the diversity approaches considered to be most authentic have the highest levels of diverse population engagement. Coaching, tutoring, and mentoring programs as well as support for affinity group participation, activities, and feedback through the first few years of employment are often considered to be the most effective strategies to convince minorities to seriously consider the accounting profession for their lifetime career. Professional entrants, diverse and nondiverse alike, are often researching organizational culture feedback on websites such as Glassdoor, Indeed, Vault, and CareerBliss to determine how consistent the messages are from employees with what the recruiting process emphasizes.

The commitment to diversity ethics can also be inferred from published firm-specific diversity efforts such as diverse hiring success metrics and the percentages of diverse employees at each level of the professional staff. Diverse employment candidates often want to speak to current diverse professional employees directly to inquire about

- how they would describe and feel about working at that company;
- the percentage of diverse professional hires and promotions at each professional staff and management level;
- if reported employee diversity numbers have combined professional and support staff numbers; and
- what diversity (as well as how much diversity and what dimension of diversity) exists at the partner level and on the board of directors.

Unfortunately, diverse employee retention data and comparison metrics are rarely shared or published.

Diversity ethics challenges can also be observed from the difficulties in diversifying the faculty at colleges and schools of business. Unsuccessful diversity recruiting efforts often result from the low position diversity held within the incentives and perspectives of the leadership teams in colleges of business, the lack of diverse faculty on search committees, and the lack of incentives or accountability for administrators or majority faculty to hire more diverse faculty. The search committee decision makers often "outsource" their ethical responsibilities to the ex-officio equal opportunity officer and have limited access to training in authentic relationship building or innovative approaches that increase the success of recruiting diverse faculty. Oftentimes the belief cited is that their lack of diverse faculty is due to uncontrollable factors, and all that they can do is to let time pass, as more diverse faculty will enter the pipeline given the demographic changes that are occurring in the population in general.

Several initiatives have focused on increasing the diversity of accounting faculty, and leading the way are the PhD Project, the AICPA's fellowship program for tenure track faculty, and the profession's initiatives for incentivizing retiring partners to consider transition into becoming "professional practice instructors" in higher education (PhD Project, 2020). Higher education could also easily expand its premier and high-quality journal lists to include outlets that publish the highest quality diversity-related research, community outreach, and engagement programs, so that diverse faculty would be incentivized to feel valued and included in the prioritized purposes of higher education in society. Accreditation organizations such as the AACSB and the ACE have new initiatives for colleges of business to become more relevant to society and are recommending mission changes that show how colleges of business are "making a difference" (AACSB, 2020; ACE, 2012). Diverse faculty promotion and tenure will increase by adding journals that "make a diversity difference" to the preferred journal lists as well as when diverse faculty are correctly attributed for their important role in developing diversity pipeline partnerships and increasing diverse student enrollment, retention, and graduation.

The biggest challenge to diversity involves the difficulty of developing inclusive cultures within the accounting profession and higher education institutions. Inclusion ethics and strategies need to be prioritized objectives accepted by the leadership and the majority members of the accounting profession organizations and labor pipeline partners. Inclusivity involves changing beliefs and culture, which are significantly more difficult and time consuming than diversity to lead, initiate, and sustain as well as to accurately measure, fairly interpret, and communicate. While all of the major professional accounting associations and public accounting firms publicly tout their investments in inclusion culture building, Deloitte's (2017b) organizational culture survey responses indicate that diverse professionals rarely rate their inclusivity experiences higher than a very low "C" grade, a result that indicates there is still much improvement needed. Inclusion experts would argue that organizations with healthy inclusion should receive close to equal numbers of "A" and "B" level professional inclusivity experience responses from both diverse and nondiverse professionals. Other studies explain this growing disconnect and disillusionment between the diversity and inclusion "talk" and "walk" by the lack of alignment between leaders who are not committed or inspiring with regards to diversity and inclusion and the disconnect between announced diversity and inclusion policies and actual diversity hiring practices. Continual marginalization by means of exclusions and microaggressions are often cited as consequences for a lack of accountability for anti-diversity behaviors. Poorly implemented structures of affinity groups and directors of diversity have also been suggested as causes of these culture failures (Levsen et al. 2001; Roy 2013; Turner et al. 2008).

Conclusion

This chapter has summarized the status of diversity ethics in the accounting profession and the profession's future labor pipeline. The changes to organizational culture, as well as their subsequent economic repercussions that have occurred from the global pandemic of 2020 and after poorly executed recent mergers or acquisitions, have resulted in very rapid organizational cultural degradation, even after much progress and success with diversity initiatives. The sad truth at hand is that the building of a diversity ethic takes decades, while the destruction can occur very quickly. Diversity support has now been called out as "at risk" in these crises, while at the same time widely viewed as "critical for business recovery, resilience, and reimagination" (McKinsey 2020, 2). The ramifications of such degradation in diversity initiative progress will be felt disproportionally by the diverse professionals individually and felt collectively by the accounting profession's decline in public image and possible market performance.

Institutions of higher education may be perfectly poised to become catalysts in keeping diversity a professional priority. Universities are under greater pressure from a wide range of external forces and incentivized to grow their partnerships with a wide variety of parties to create sufficient critical mass regarding diversity ethics. First, more diverse students are attending universities for accounting degrees. They and their parents will soon be demanding information about and considering both the number and the inclusivity of diverse faculty in their decisions about where to go to university. Second, the demand for more diverse accounting graduates is increasing by professional firms, industry, nonprofits, and government agencies alike. These recruiting partners could easily make diverse faculty inclusion, promotion, and recognition a requirement for their organizations to choose to recruit at any university. Third, the AACSB is currently touting the importance that business colleges document how their missions, strategies, and operations are making a difference in society. Leading university ranking organizations can add measures of the effectiveness of a university accounting department's diversity and inclusion initiatives as a factor in university rankings. Finally, the existing "premier" and "high quality" journal editors and editorial boards can begin to own their bias toward topics only interesting to majority faculty and stop excluding research topics that have greater interest to diverse faculty and have greater societal justice impacts. For example, all premier and high-quality academic journals could choose to pick one high quality article from a diverse faculty member for each issue as part of the supply chain improvements needed to help more diverse faculty get tenured and promoted.

The final recommendation is to encourage more research on the inclusion aspects of the profession. More research is needed to fully document how the current state of diversity ethics in the accounting profession and in accounting departments of higher education will better illuminate the future of the profession. This research should focus on the level of congruence between the profession's intent and impact so that strategies can be created and innovated to continue to generate more social sustainability and economic value for all stakeholders in the accounting profession.

Notes

1 Combined from codes of conduct listed on the aicpa.org, imanet.org, gfoa.org and acm.org websites.
2 2017 KPMG https://home.kpmg/xx/en/home/about/what-we-stand-for/inclusion-and-diversity/global-awards.html#:~:text=2016%20Disability%20Equality%20Index%20Best,2016%20Disability%20Matters%20Workplace%20Award.

References

AICPA. 2020. "Diversity and Inclusion." www.aicpa.org/career/diversityinitiatives.html

Alexandre, Tandé. 2017. "Implementing a Diversity Policy through Public Incentives: Diversity Plans in Companies of the Brussels-Capital Region." *Journal of Ethnic and Migration Studies* 43 (10): 1731–47. doi:10.1080/1369183X.2017.1293594

Credit Union National Association. 2020. "Joint Standards for Assessing Diversity policies and Practices." www.research.net/r/DiversityStandards

Deloitte. 2017a. "Diversity and Inclusion: The Reality Gap." https://www2.deloitte.com/us/en/insights/focus/human-capital-trends/2017/diversity-and-inclusion-at-the-workplace.html

Deloitte. 2017b. "Inclusion Remains a Top Priority for Today's Evolving Workforce." https://www2.deloitte.com/us/en/pages/about-deloitte/articles/press-releases/unleashing-inclusion.html

Deloitte. 2018. "The Diversity and Inclusion Revolution: Eight Powerful Truths" (complimentary reprint from Deloitte Review, Issue 22, January 2018). https://www2.deloitte.com/content/dam/insights/us/articles/4209_Diversity-and-inclusion-revolution/DI_Diversity-and-inclusion-revolution.pdf

Deloitte. 2020. "Unleashing the Power of Inclusion." https://www2.deloitte.com/content/dam/Deloitte/us/Documents/about-deloitte/us-about-deloitte-unleashing-power-of-inclusion.pdf

E&Y. 2017. "E&Y Global Executive Diversity Inclusion Statement." https://www.ey.com/en_gl/diversity-inclusiveness/global-executive-diversity-inclusion-statement

E&Y. 2020. "E&Y Report D&I Means Growth." www.ey.com/en_us/diversity-inclusiveness/diversity-and-inclusiveness-means-growth

FAO (Food and Agriculture Organization of the United Nations). 2020. "The Role of Ethics." www.fao. org/3/y6634e/y6634e03.htm

GFOA (Government Financial Officers of America). 2020. "code of Ethics." www.gfoa.org/detail/ethics

Grant Thornton. 2020. "Diversity and Inclusion: Unlock the Power of Difference." www.grantthornton. com/library/csr/diversity-and-inclusion.aspx

IMA (Institute of Management Accountants). 2020. "D&I Jump-Start Kit." www.imanet.org/-/media/1c b71380a29540f2af5aad35e04f2930.ashx?la=en

KPMG. 2018. "The Future is Inclusive. The 2018 KPMG Global Inclusion & Diversity Report." https:// www2.deloitte.com/content/dam/insights/us/articles/4209_Diversity-and-inclusion-revolution/DI_ Diversity-and-inclusion-revolution.pdf

Levsen, Virginia, Nancy Goettel, Frank Chong, and Roy Farris. 2001, "Do we practice diversity in business schools?", *International Journal of Educational Management*, 15(4): 167-71. https://doi.org/10. 1108/09513540110394401

McKinsey. 2018. "Delivering Through Diversity." www.mckinsey.com/business-functions/organization/ our-insights/delivering-through-diversity

McKinsey. 2020. "Diversity still Matters." www.mckinsey.com/featured-insights/diversity-and-inclusion/ diversity-still-matters

Mosiri, Farrokh, and Peter Wilson Cardon. 2016. "JA Study of Faculty Racial Diversity in Business Schools: Perceptions of Business Deans." *Routledge Taylor & Francis Group, Journal of Education for Business* 91 (5): 243–50. doi:10.1080/08832323.2016.1175410

PhD Project. 2020. www.phdproject.org/our-success/milestones-achievements/

PwC. 2019. "Perspectives from our Diversity and Inclusion Journey." https://static1.squarespace.com/ static/5be20ac5cef37210432a6ebb/t/5c7864e6a4222f3e47eac81f/1551394023479/Expanding+From +Diversity+to+True+Inclusion_Camila+Negret_VFinal.pdf

Roy, Lucinda. 2013. "Faculty Diversity: We Still Have a Lot to Learn." *Chronicle of Higher Education*, November 18, 2013. http://chronicle.com/article/Faculty-Diversity-Still-a-Lot/143095/

Turner, Caroline, Juan Carlos González, and Luke Wood. 2008. "Faculty of color in academe: What 20 years of literature tells us." *Journal of Diversity in Higher Education, 1*(3): 139–68. https://doi.org/ 10.1037/a0012837

Wentling, Rose Mary. 2004. "Factors that Assist and Barriers that Hinder the Success of Diversity Initia-tives in Multinational Corporations." *HRDI* 7 (2): 165–80. London: Routledge.

INDEX

Note: Page numbers in *italic* indicate a figure and page numbers in **bold** indicate a table on the corresponding page.

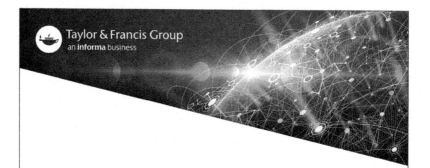